The Word Made Flesh

MW00335481

To my father,
Kenneth L. Miles (1911–2002)
whose delight in learning was contagious

"Delight orders the soul . . . where the soul's delight is, there is its treasure."

Augustine, *De musica* VI. 11. 29

The Word Made Flesh

A History of Christian Thought

Margaret R. Miles

Blackwell
Publishing

© 2005 by Margaret R. Miles

BLACKWELL PUBLISHING
350 Main Street, Malden, MA 02148-5020, USA
9600 Garsington Road, Oxford OX4 2DQ, UK
550 Swanston Street, Carlton, Victoria 3053, Australia

The right of Margaret R. Miles to be identified as the Author of this Work has been asserted in accordance with the UK Copyright, Designs, and Patents Act 1988.

All rights reserved. No part of this publication may be reproduced, stored in a retrieval system, or transmitted, in any form or by any means, electronic, mechanical, photocopying, recording or otherwise, except as permitted by the UK Copyright, Designs, and Patents Act 1988, without the prior permission of the publisher.

First published 2005 by Blackwell Publishing Ltd

8   2012

Library of Congress Cataloging-in-Publication Data

Miles, Margaret Ruth.
The Word made flesh : a history of Christian thought / Margaret R. Miles.
p. cm.
Includes bibliographical references and index.
ISBN 978-1-4051-0845-4 (hardcover : alk. paper) — ISBN 978-1-4051-0846-1 (pbk. : alk. paper)
1. Theology, Doctrinal—History.   2. Incarnation—History of doctrines.   I. Title.
BT21.3.M55 2004
230′.09—dc22

2004003090

A catalogue record for this title is available from the British Library.

Set in 10 on 12.5 pt Minion
by SNP Best-set Typesetter Ltd, Hong Kong
Printed and bound in Singapore
by Markono Print Media Pte Ltd

The publisher's policy is to use permanent paper from mills that operate a sustainable forestry policy, and which has been manufactured from pulp processed using acid-free and elementary chlorine-free practices. Furthermore, the publisher ensures that the text paper and cover board used have met acceptable environmental accreditation standards.

For further information on
Blackwell Publishing, visit our website:
www.blackwellpublishing.com

Contents

Read min of 1 from readings at end of each ~~chapter~~ section in ch 1+2
27, 34, 38 (B 3 or 4) 43 B-1 or 2 47, 54, 64. 76 83, 89, 93, 105, 114
Forum each day
1 hour chat

List of Illustrations

Book

CD Rom

List of Maps

Acknowledgments

Inardescimus et imus.

Augustine, *Confessions* 13. 9

Although written by one person, this book represents teamwork. It is utterly dependent on the students who responded to lectures, and colleagues who alerted me to what was new and important in their historical fields, and international colleagues in the Study of Religion whose research has informed and offered new approaches that examine and often overturn received ideas about historical Christians. These critical friends created the energy and information necessary for writing the book. It is exciting to gather and *think with* others' scholarship. Bibliographies at the end of each chapter acknowledge my debt to the many scholars who are presently proposing fresh perspectives on old texts.

I am grateful to have the good fortune of working with an editor, Rebecca Harkin, who shares my conviction that unless a History of Christian Thought is lively, it is not accurate. Three expert readers, my husband, Owen C. Thomas, and two anonymous readers, provided valuable questions, suggestions, and corrections. Thanks to Blackwell's expertise, a CD Rom makes possible the use of music and images as primary evidence, a more colorful palette than "words, words, as if all worlds were there" (e. e. cummings). My thanks also to Lee Gilmore for her expert computer technology, and to Mervyn Thomas for perceptive editing.

Preface

Students become teachers because we love to learn. But frequently, under the pressures of an academic career, teachers isolate themselves in a relatively narrow field where they can be confident of "mastery," forgetting the excitement of fundamentally new learning. This book began as a course taught across 18 years at Harvard Divinity School and once at the Graduate Theological Union, Berkeley. The course, with its infinite potential for learning, kept alive my love of learning. New scholarly work constantly challenged interpretations of old texts, and students' interests and questions prompted new research every single time the course was offered. Lacking confident mastery of so broad a swath of history, the considerable rewards lay in limitless learning. Teaching and learning became indistinguishable.

Each time the course was offered I showed slides, and, in later years, added music to the course's repertoire of primary historical evidence, making the point that "Christian thought" does not consist solely of language and endeavoring to reconstruct the sensory ambiance of Christian worship and devotion. It was not until 2001 that I could imagine a textbook that would preserve the richness of verbal, visual, and musical Christian thought. By then it was possible to accompany the text with a CD Rom that reproduced a representative sample of the images, architecture, and music of the Christian traditions.

The high cost of permissions to reproduce musical selections made it impossible to include them on the CD Rom. However, representative selections have been indicated in the text, and full information on recordings is given on the CD Rom so that they can be used in the classroom or privately. The difficulty of placing performances on a CD Rom for easy access can, however, serve to remind us that historical people did not listen to recorded music alone; they listened to live music with others. Music was a communal, and usually liturgical, experience.

A history of Christian thought must narrate the triumphal story in which a small local cult within Judaism became a world religion and empire. But it must also include the failures, abuses, and violence of the Christian past. In short, it must be both sympathetic and critical. It must be sympathetic in order to present the vivid beauty of Christian resources of ideas, artworks, and practices. And it must be critical because it is not only a history of the past, but also a history for the present. Present sensitivities require that issues surrounding power, social location, and the institutional affiliations that authorized some voices and ignored and persecuted others, as well as race, gender, class, and other variables, must be described. A more accurate history is simultaneously a more ambiguous history, a history of the gains *and* losses of the Christian past.

A rich, inclusive, and diverse history permits critical acknowledgment of the losses of the Christian past without leaving the impression that the Christian past is unambiguously deplorable. Noticing the rich beauty of Christian resources does not excuse or rationalize the terrible abuses of the past. Rather it disallows easy judgment. In short, *The Word Made Flesh* seeks to reveal the multiple historical expressions of Christianity, the beauty *and* the tragic harms done in its name. It endeavors to communicate a sense of the *life* of people who lived and died as Christians.

These goals make evident the importance of the CD Rom that accompanies the text. The images and music included on the CD Rom should not be regarded as "illustrations" of the text's arguments and claims; rather, along with the primary source readings listed at the end of each section, they demonstrate these claims. They are, in themselves, arguments. Interlinear notations indicate when a particular band of the CD Rom should be consulted. Recognizing that the author's interpretations of the primary evidence is *an* interpretation, not the only possible interpretation, the primary source readings, together with the CD Rom's images and music, acknowledge the sources of the section's discussion and invite readers to practice their own interpretation of historical texts. Bibliographies for each chapter appear at the end of the volume.

Across the centuries of the Common Era, Christians, participating in the religion of the "Word made flesh," have understood the necessity of engaging the senses in the worship of God incarnate. Twenty-first-century technology cannot reproduce the sensory experience of historical Christians, but it can stimulate our ability to imagine that experience. The Christian past, "boiling with life," is the subject of this book.

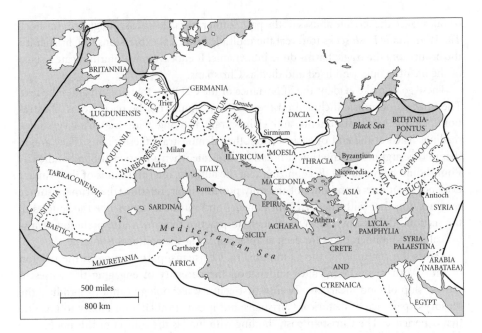

Map 1 "The Roman Empire at its height in the second century CE," from Arthur Ferrill, *The Fall of the Roman Empire.* London: Thames & Hudson, 1986, p. 11. Reprinted by permission of Thames & Hudson Ltd.

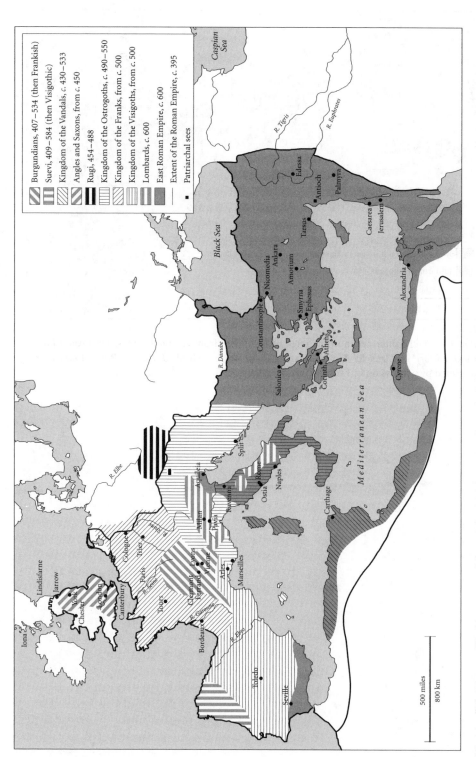

Map 2 "The Roman World to 600 CE," from John McManners, *The Oxford Illustrated History of Christianity*. Oxford, New York: Oxford University Press, 1990, pp. 86–7. Reprinted by permission of Oxford University Press.

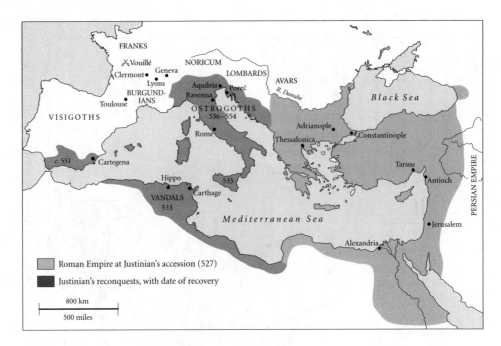

FRANKS

✗ Vouillé
Clermont ● Geneva   NORICUM
        Lyons   LOMBARDS
BURGUND-   Aquileia ●   AVARS
    IANS   Ravenna ● Poreč   *R. Danube*   *Black Sea*
Toulouse ●   OSTROGOTHS
VISIGOTHS   536–554
                Rome ●   Adrianople ●
                                Thessalonica ● ● Constantinople
c. 551   ● Cartegena
                                                    Tarsus ●
        Hippo ●   535   ● Antioch
            ● Carthage
    VANDALS   PERSIAN EMPIRE
    533   *Mediterranean Sea*
                                                    ● Jerusalem
                            Alexandria ●

▨ Roman Empire at Justinian's accession (527)

▉ Justinian's reconquests, with date of recovery

├────────────┤ 800 km

├────────────┤ 500 miles

Map 3   "The Mediterranean in the reign of Justinian," from George Holmes, *The Oxford Illustrated History of Medieval Europe*. Oxford, New York: Oxford University Press, 1988, p. 9. Reprinted by permission of Oxford University Press.

FINLAND

St. Petersburg

ESTONIA

LATVIA

Baltic
Sea

LITHUANIA

Volga

SIBERIA

• Moscow

RUSSIA

BELORUSSIA

POLAND

Kiev •

Dnieper

MORAVIA

Vienna • *Danube*

UKRAINE

MOLDAVIA

Caspian
Sea

TRANSYL-
VANIA

GEORGIA

WALLACHIA

CROATIA

Black Sea

BOSNIA

SERBIA

ARMENIA

• Rome

BULGARIA

Constantinople •

Thessalonike •

GREECE   • Mt Athos

Athens • Smyrna

CILICIA   • Antioch

Mediterranean Sea   CRETE

CYPRUS

Jerusalem •

N

Alexandria •

———— Eastern border of the Byzantine Empire *c.* 1025 CE
- - - - - - Furthest western border of the Ottoman Empire *c.* 1650

Map 4 "Eastern Orthodoxy," from Adrian Hastings, *A World History of Christianity*. Grand Rapids, MI: W. B. Eerdmans, 1999, p. 573. Reprinted by permission of Mobray, an imprint of Continuum International Publishing Group.

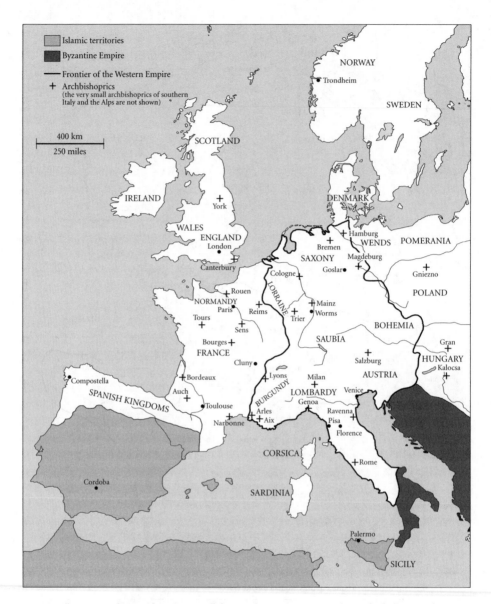

Map 5 "Western Christendom in 1050," from John McManners, *The Oxford Illustrated History of Christianity.* Oxford, New York: Oxford University Press, 1990, p. 198. Reprinted by permission of Oxford University Press.

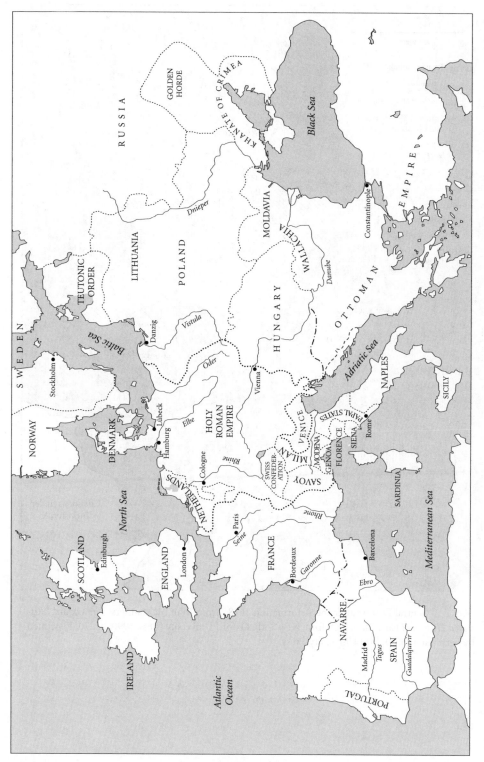

Map 6 "Europe in 1500," from Williston Walker, *History of the Christian Church*, New York: Scribner, 1970, p. 418.

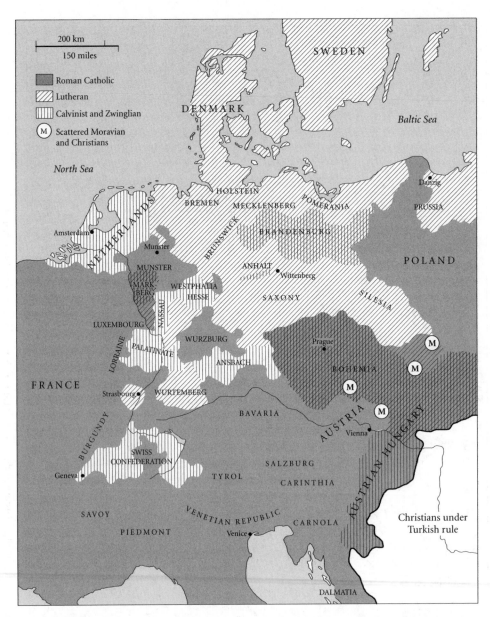

Map 7 "Central Europe after the Reformation 1618," from John McManners, *The Oxford Illustrated History of Christianity*. Oxford, New York: Oxford University Press, 1990, p. 270. Reprinted by permission of Oxford University Press.

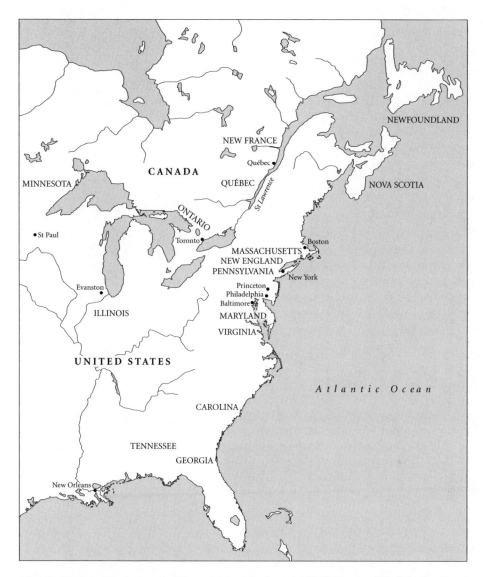

Map 8   "Eastern North America," from Adrian Hastings, *A World History of Christianity*. Grand Rapids, MI: W. B. Eerdmans, 1999, p. 580. Reprinted by permission of Mobray, an imprint of Continuum International Publishing Group.

Prelude: Flesh and Word

The subject matter of history is not the past as such, but the past for which we possess historical evidence.

R. G. Collingwood

1   An Inclusive History

His earliest followers called Jesus of Nazareth, founder of the Christian movement, "the Word made flesh." Through more than two thousand years, Christians have sought to articulate the meaning of their belief that in the human person of Jesus, God became human. In doing so, they have sought to make the flesh word. They have also fleshed out the words of teaching, doctrine, and theology in liturgies, music, images, and architecture. Histories of Christianity based solely on Christian literature do not convey the multiple ways in which Christians insisted that the religion of the Incarnation, the Word made flesh, must be experienced by the senses. Attention to making Christian bodies, not just Christian minds or souls – in their training of new members, by liturgies, and by devotional exercises – was central to the practice of Christianity.

Similarly, a history of Christianity cannot be based solely on Christians' social history, geographical movements, and institutions. We need to understand and imagine the power of Christian ideas *in the life*, that is, in the contexts of conversations, controversies, and concrete circumstances. Only then do we begin to understand why Christians, in many different times and places, have been willing to die and – even more mysteriously – to kill for their beliefs. This book features the vivid, passionate, and fertile ideas that funded the history of the Christian movement in its first 17 centuries. It presents particular authors and artists *on location*, describing their experience in words, images, music, and architecture.

Christianity is the religion of the Incarnation. Christians' core belief is that God entered the human world of bodies and senses in the person of Jesus of Nazareth, whose historical life is normative in its claim about the nature of God and the possibilities for human existence. Christianity begins with the startling statement that the center of human reality is love. In order to understand the effects of this claim, it is necessary to provide from one's own experience examples of the power of a new idea. Ideas can orient the intellect in ways that are experienced as more accurate and, therefore, more fruitful. New ideas also make possible new experiences; they can change the quality of one's life. As the religion of the Incarnation, Christianity is about the construction of Christian bodies and, according to Christian belief, the perfection of Christian bodies in the resurrection of the flesh.

The study of Christianity in particular times and places must encompass the images and architecture of the Christian traditions, the liturgical and devotional practices, women, and religious "others" – Christian dissidents, Jews, and occasionally Muslims, and Zoroastrians. It must include liturgical music, and the rhetoric and devotional practices by which Christian communities created Christian bodies.

Noticing these facets of Christianity, we also discover that "the" history of Christianity is in fact many histories. To speak of a single Christian "movement" is to obscure the multiple Christian *movements*, distinguishable not only by geographical location but also by different cultural contexts, interpretations of beliefs, emphases, and practices. Christian leaders so frequently and forcefully urged Christian "unity" that we tend to forget that in doing so they did not refer to a reality, but advocated an ideal. Diversity has been a central feature of Christianity, even if one looks only at Christians who were considered orthodox – or right thinking – in their own time. Debates between people who identified themselves as Christians, but were rejected and labeled heretics by those who claimed orthodoxy, reveal further layers of diversity. We will explore the religious sensibilities and values that led earnest Christians to painful and sometimes fatal dissent. Recovery of the rich pluralism *within* Christianity is one of the agendas of this book.

Religious "others" were essential to the self-definition of Christian communities. Christians *continuously* – not just initially – defined themselves over against their closest siblings, Jews. Christians appropriated Jewish scriptures, ritual practices, and biblical scholarship, but their animosity toward Jews increased steadily as Christianity became the dominant religion of the West. Christians' relations with people of other religions is a crucial aspect of Christianity. At different times and places, Muslims, Zoroastrians, and others interacted and debated with Christians, proposing alternative beliefs that stimulated Christians to articulate more precisely their own beliefs.

Gender assumptions and arrangements, at all times an organizing feature of Western societies, is an essential part of the study of the Christian movement. For several decades, scholars have studied women's activities and restrictions within Christian communities. Formerly unknown or little-known writings of historical women have been published in translation. Women's history can now be placed within mainstream Christianity. The mainstream is no longer what Elisabeth Schüssler Fiorenza called the "malestream." *Both* women's distinctive voices *and* the prohibitions that limited and often failed to preserve their expressions must be recognized. The study of gender is not, however, exclusively the study of women. Gender roles, assumptions, and expectations affected whole communities, as "male" and "female" were designed in contrast to one another and women and men were socialized to gender roles.

Christian literature usually uses "man" generically. Quotations in this book will usually retain historical usage. If the author, employing the literary and social conventions of his time, recognized the male as the normative human being, or if it is clear that the author thinks of his audience as male, it is dishonest to translate inclusively. Most often "man" should not be translated inclusively because "man" (the male) is what the author intended to designate. The sexism embedded in texts should not be concealed when Christian authors are quoted.

2   The Flesh Made Word

Language is the primary vehicle of ideas, although language is not the only way to communicate ideas. New ideas require new language, and the construction of a new language is a massive project. In addition to attempting to forge new language to express vivid new ideas, Christians also endeavored to create a *common* language. Church councils endeavored to specify Christian beliefs, values, and practices in a way that drew broad consensus while protecting core commitments.

Christian ideas were expressed verbally as 1) doctrine, 2) theology, and 3) tradition. Vincent of Lerins (c.450) defined doctrine as "what the Christian churches believe, teach, and confess." The main instrument for definitions of doctrine were the creeds of the Christian churches. Theology is the examination and exposition of doctrine, the ongoing interpretation and refining of what churches "believe, teach, and confess." Theology consists of attempts to describe an essentially mysterious reality that cannot finally be expressed in words. It is socially and institutionally located. It was, and is, done by human beings with perspectives informed – simultaneously enabled and constrained – by their social experience. It is important to notice what a theologian works on in addition to theology. For approximately the first 600 years of the common era, theologians were working bishops; men who were directly involved in the full range of pastoral duties. Between about 600 and 1500, theology was done by monks, women, and men whose religious experience and metaphors were largely drawn from monastic discipline. From about 1500 to the present, theology has been done primarily by university and seminary professors. These different social and institutional frameworks intimately affected theological work.

Christian ideas were also expressed as "tradition," a process of transmitting, or passing on from one generation to another, the wealth of Christian ideas, beliefs, and practices. Tradition refers both to this process, and to the content of what is passed on.

3   The Word Made Flesh

Christians are perennially unsure of what could/should be integrated from surrounding culture, and what is incompatible, contradictory, or dangerous to Christian beliefs and life-styles. This confusion was especially poignant in the early centuries when Christians lived in a persecuting state. Should secular philosophies be used to expound Christian beliefs? Should Christians wear distinctive dress? How should they manage sexuality? Should they attend gladiatorial shows in the colosseum? Should women and men have equal access to leadership roles in Christian communities? Was it possible at the same time to be a Christian and be rich? These and many other urgent issues were debated in the early Christian centuries.

Those who recorded their responses to these questions were usually educated, philosophically inclined, and almost invariably male Christian leaders. Christian *people* are often difficult, but not impossible, to find. Scholars are presently seeking the history of illiterate Christians, dissenters, women, children, and slaves. Sometimes marginalized or excluded voices can be found only in prescriptive comments that tell us a great deal about communal attitudes and assumptions, but nothing of the experience of people who did not themselves write. For example, slaves' experience can be sketched from Christian leaders' admonitions to and about them. But slaves' writings are not extant, so their own perspectives can only be imagined. Similarly, we can learn a great deal about how male church leaders expected women to dress and act; it is rare to find women articulating their own choices.

Beyond creeds, practices, and life-styles, Christians also communicated their experience artistically. The twentieth-century philosopher Michel Foucault defined "strong power" as the power to attract; by contrast, "weak power" coerces. Relatively few Christians read theological treatises, but all participated in the community's artistic repertoire. Images and architecture interpreted Christian beliefs and practices, communicating theological, religious, and social messages. Music was used in a variety of ways: to unify liturgy and practice across wide geographical distances, shape religious sensibilities, create community, communicate theology, and inspire gratitude and praise. The arts of Christian movements show how the religion of the "Word made flesh" was expressed in the world of bodies and senses, revealing what it meant to Christians to worship an incarnate God.

Christian art does not simply "illustrate" theological ideas; it is a primary resource for the study of Christianity. The CD-Rom accompanying this book displays music and images, allowing the integration of richer resources than texts alone could supply. The CD-Rom enables us to achieve deeper levels of understanding than "words, words, as if all worlds were there," as the twentieth-century poet e. e. cummings wrote. Referring to these as the text directs gives the reader access to the "media" that informed the lives of historical Christians. It also helps us to glimpse the sensory ambiance of those distant lives.

Understanding Christianity as the religion of the "Word made flesh" provides a vantage point from which to interpret historical evidence. In the religion of the Incarnation, the status of human bodies altered when God entered the sensible world in a human body. The first theological disputes were between second- and third-century Christians, who believed in the real human flesh of the incarnate God, and Gnostic Christians, who claimed that the Incarnation was in appearance only. Christians who believed in Christ's real humanity taught that the goal of Christian life was bodily resurrection in a life after death. They believed that the bodies of those executed for Christian beliefs would appear in heaven at the exact moment of their martyrdom. Clearly, Christians who believed in the Incarnation of God in human flesh did not think of human bodies as meaningless and ultimately biodegradable, but as integral to a religious commitment that transcended death.

4   Method

In addition to the complex and intriguing content of historical Christianity, the practice of history is itself a fascinating and much-debated topic. Undeniably, the past was boiling with life, chaotic, and contradictory. Should "history" reproduce the past's chaos? Or should historians attempt to "make sense" of the past, to narrate it as comprehensively and cohesively as possible, ignoring details that do not fit the narrative? If history should deliver a "story," *whose* story should be told, *whose* perspective represented? Which events should be included? How do historians' own interests and loyalties inevitably direct their selections? Since the rich "thickness" of the past cannot be fully replicated in language, how can the *life* of historical communities be adequately represented?

"New historicists" have proposed that anecdotes that do not fit or support the "great story" challenge the illusion that the past can be packaged as a coherent narrative. Anecdotes can undermine the impression that the history of Christianity can be told simply as the triumphal story of its expansion from a small local cult to a world religion and empire. Anecdotes keep the losses in view, for example, bringing back into the picture the people who went away, shaking their heads, after each new decision about the definition of a doctrine. They disrupt the constructed "story" of the past, reminding readers/hearers that the past can never be fully described.

Anecdotes have usually been used to illustrate or to make a point vivid, but they have been considered trivial asides. However, new historicists like Catherine Gallagher and Stephen Greenblatt argue that anecdotes are the real "stuff" of history in that they puncture historical narrative, insisting that there is "something – the real" outside cohesive renditions of the past. The anecdote "divulges a different reality . . . that the historian cannot assimilate." Anecdotes "open history, or place it askew . . . with flashes of the always inaccessible real" (Gallagher and Greenblatt, 2000: 50).

Applying new historicism to Christian history produces simultaneously a more honest and a less cohesive story. An example will illustrate: Fourth-century evidence of the Christian movement includes a multitude of contradictory incidents: the Diocletian persecution, the legitimation of Christianity under Constantine, rancorous debates over doctrine, magnificent and highly decorated church buildings and, at the end of the century, the Christian Empire persecuting dissidents, and marginalizing Jews from public life. No one questions that a *strain* of Christianity emerged from the fourth century stronger, more precise, richer in buildings and imperial support, and attractive to a broad range of people. The gains are evident. Yet there were also losses, clearly seen and articulated by contemporaries – ascetics, who left the institutional church in droves, and bishops with new and pressing problems around how to Christianize the crowds of converts who flocked to Christian churches. In the fourth century, women's ministries were excluded and women's voices forbidden in church choirs. The triumphal story of fourth-century Christianity ignores the costs of its establishment as the religion of empire.

Constantine (emperor 312–37) is the hero of the triumphal story. His contemporary and admirer, Eusebius, is the source for this version of fourth-century Christianity. Eusebius, who has been called the "father of Church history," gave weight to his account of Constantine's conversion by saying that he had heard it from Constantine's lips:

> Constantine said that about noon (October 27, 312), when the day was already beginning to decline, he saw with his own eyes the trophy of a cross of light in the heavens, above the sun, bearing the inscription, "By this conquer." At this sight he himself was struck with

amazement, and his whole army also, which followed him on this expedition and witnessed this miracle.

Eusebius reported this story 20 years after it happened. At the time of the battle, a Roman orator said that Constantine had seen a vision of the sun-god. Constantine, like other Roman emperors, was (and remained to the end of his life), a high priest of the sun-god.

Further complications surround the official story: in 326 Constantine, the champion of Christianity, had his eldest son, Crispus, murdered. In the same year Constantine, who was married to his rival Maxentius's sister, Fausta, had her locked into a steam room and, to quote historian Hal Drake, "poached to death." These acts, according to a contemporary chronicler (Eutropius), were followed by the murder of "innumerable friends." Constantine's nephew Julian (emperor 361–3) claimed that Constantine had turned to Christianity because pagan priests, horrified by these deeds, refused to grant him expiation for his sins.

Why tell this tasteless historical story? Because it precludes the easy assumption that fourth-century Christians – beginning with the Roman emperor – adopted twenty-first century standards of "Christian" behavior. If the "great story" is to be honestly told, it must include bishops who kidnapped or killed their rivals, martyrs and ascetics whose feats seem to us more sick than saintly, and emperors who killed family members. The anecdote reveals the distance between ourselves and historical people, destroying the illusion of seamless Christian continuities.

Scripture provides a precedent for "anti-heroic heroes," deeply flawed human beings who *nevertheless* achieved great tasks. Tasteless historical stories originate in biblical descriptions of such leaders as David (in the Old Testament), whose lust prompted him to murder, and Peter (in the New Testament), who betrayed Christ at one of Christ's darkest moments, but was nevertheless called by Christ to be the founder of the Church. Histories of Christianity, told from the perspectives of insiders, have usually rejected the scriptural pattern that acknowledged the fallibility and evil done by the heroes of Christian culture and institutions, whitewashing them and rendering them blandly righteous. But to do this is to undermine precisely what the believer most desires to communicate, namely, God's ability to bring good from the most flawed of human beings. The purpose of the "tasteless historical stories" recounted in this book is neither to titillate nor to horrify, but accountability to historical evidence. Christian believers can, in addition, interpret the ambiguity of Christian heroes as both evidence of God's power to use sinful people and encouragement to present-day Christians who know themselves to be less than perfect.

Historian Robert Darnton has raised another consideration. He urges that historians pay special attention to historical jokes, incidents that people of the time say they found hysterically funny, but which to us don't seem funny at all. Historical jokes that fall flat on modern ears, he said, provide a measure of distance between modern and historical sensibilities, stimulating historians to greater efforts to reconstruct the culture of historical humor. His own example was an eighteenth-century "great cat massacre," which those who recorded the event found enormously comical. Darnton (1984) reconstructed the social conditions, individual resentments, and class antagonisms that together made the slaughter of cats that were doted on by a hated employer funny.

Darnton's argument can also be reversed; modern sensibilities often find humor in incidents that historical people took very seriously.

Again, an example will help. The first recorded modern streakers were seventeenth-century English Quakers who adopted this practice for serious religious and political purposes. Quaker historian Kenneth Carroll (1978) reports that in 1654 William Simpson passed through the city of Oxford "naked and bare, as a sign to that generation then in being, signifying to you that the day was neare at hand, even at the dore, in which the Lord would strip you naked and bare, both from the rule and authority they were then under in this nation, and also from that covering of religion with which they seemed to be covered with." Many others did the same – women and men. In 1655 Thomas Holme went naked as a "sign to this city," reporting afterwards to a friend that "I went to the highway naked and great dread fell upon many harts." Far from a joke to its practitioners, streakers like Holme based their practice on Isaiah 20. They intended to shock, alert, and bring to repentance those who saw them.

Many anecdotes about "sacred pain," that is, pain used for religious purposes, will be told in the chapters that follow. They too indicate the fundamental distance between modern and historical attitudes toward pain. In modern Western society the suggestion that pain can have "uses" tends to horrify people. Yet numerous historical authors – like Catherine of Siena, Henry Suso, and Francis of Assisi, to name only a few – intentionally used involuntary and voluntary pain to produce religious insight and/or mystical experience. The implications of this for our study of historical people, whether mystics, inquisitors, or helpless sufferers of involuntary pain, are enormous.

But it is not only "tasteless historical stories" that provide a more honest history. Historical accounts can also diminish and bleach instances of the great, good, and beautiful by reductive explanation. The nineteenth-century German philosopher Friedrich Scheler identified two habits of thought that must be overcome if historical study is to be both accurate and insightful: 1) what he called the "postulate of the commonplace, that is, that everything that is great, good, and beautiful is improbable, for it is extraordinary, or at least peculiar;" and 2) the "axiom of familiarity," that is, "that things must always have been just as they are with us, for things are naturally like this." These two postulates will be overturned continuously as we notice not only anecdotes that interrupt the "story," but also the rich and vivid beauty of Christian lives, ideas, and artistic expressions.

5   Conclusion

The book's subtitle, "A History of Christian Thought," accurately describes the book's content. This book is not a "History of Christianity," although the growth, dispersion, and institutionalization of Christian movements is part of our story. Neither is it "Church History," understood as referring primarily to changes and developments in "the organized church." But liturgical and institutional changes, disruptions, and continuities are also part of the picture. The book aims to be, rather, a "History of Christian Thought." However, my earlier remarks have already made it clear that Christian "thought" is not limited to the verbal articulation of beliefs, doctrines, and ideas. Artistic expressions – music, architecture, painting, and sculpture – also *conceptualize* and communicate Christianity, and are accurately called "Christian thought."

Christian ideas and practices across the centuries of the common era had little uniformity. Thus, historical Christianity should not be studied with the goal of identifying the historical antecedents of present values, ideas, beliefs, and practices, though this has frequently been done. Going beyond the extant evidence, theologians and historians have projected the practices and beliefs of later centuries onto the earliest Christians. Nor can the history of Christian thought be viewed as the cumulative development of an orthodox mainstream. Rather, Christian movements consisted of clusters of volatile excitement, different in different times and places, involving ideas (visual, verbal, architectural, and musical), conversations, experiences, and practices. Indeed, the lively questions of one historical moment were seldom resolved; rather, changed circumstances yielded new questions, concerns, and excitements. Accountability to historical evidence requires that tidiness and cohesiveness be sacrificed; in return, a vivid sense of the liveliness, conflicts, and excitement of Christian movements emerges. Christian excitements and burning questions were not, however, completely chaotic. A broad question, variously articulated and diversely interpreted, occurred throughout the centuries of our exploration, namely, what did it mean to participate in the religion of the Word made flesh? That question provides the theme, or framework, for the many topics discussed in this book.

Finally, a question raised, but not addressed in the above section on method, should be given at least a preliminary response here. Namely, how do the author's – my – interests and values direct the historical choices – the inclusions and exclusions, the "tone" and style – of my narrative? I can best begin to address this question in the following way: Augustine of Hippo (356–430), one of the most influential theologians of over two thousand years of Christian history, has been a focus of my attention for more than 40 years. Augustine proposed two short definitions of God. First, quoting I John 4. 16, he said that God is love, and "that is all you need to know about God" (*Homilies on I John* 9. 10). Second, he said that the only way to think of God without absurdity is to think of God as "life itself" (*On Christian Doctrine* I. 8). For Augustine, God, the ultimate value, is life and love. Augustine was not alone in identifying life and love as God's primary characteristics. Earlier Christian authors were unanimous in claiming that Christ's gifts to Christians are life and love. These definitions and the values they entail, underlie both my choices of which features of Christianity to highlight by discussion, and the evaluations inevitably embedded in narrative description. I seek to track Christian communities' and individuals' attempts to understand and enhance life and enact love, as evidenced in their literature and material remains.

But the abstractions "life" and "love" are notoriously dependent on interpretation in particular and concrete circumstances. Each can be – and has been – invoked to rationalize abuse. Thus, it is not sufficient to focus exclusively on what we may consider the historical circulation of these gifts. For one of the most profound – and painful – lessons of historical study is the discrepancy between the *intentions* of authors and actors, and the *effects*, often writ too large to be documented with precision, of their ideas and actions. Insofar as historical evidence permits, our exploration will need to keep both in focus.

The quotation that serves as an epigram for this introduction reminds us that historians' reconstructions of the past must rely on surviving evidence; we do not have access to the past "as such." Moreover, the historian inevitably shapes historical evidence into a story *about* the past, so that it might be accurate to say that every history is primarily a history for the present. Ultimately, however, every history must *both* be grounded on historical evidence *and* it must address present concerns. No historical narration can – or should seek to – avoid present interests. Indeed, the authority of every historical account must rest both on 1) its faithfulness to evidence from the past, and 2) explicit acknowledgement of the interests of the historian, her colleagues, and her community.

For example, I have acknowledged my strong interest in the circulation of life and love in Christian communities. But these abstract values can be further specified. I value tolerance of religious diversity, gender equality, and social justice. However, these interpretations of what is meant by "life and love" have only achieved a fragile social consensus in recent times and in certain geographical areas. They are seldom exemplified in historical societies. People who firmly believed themselves en route to a Last Judgment resulting in eternal reward or punishment had vastly different values than many contemporary Christians who recite a creed that affirms the resurrection of bodies and the Last Judgment but who live in an intellectual universe that denies such "supernatural" events. Does this mean, then, that a history of the present can only deplore the past? Not at all. The fact that many twenty-first century people are not "naturally" attracted to the values adhered to by most historical people means that a reconstruction of the past that helps us to recognize why people thought and acted as they did will be both challenging and rewarding – challenging the illusion that our own perspectives are "natural," and rewarding in stretching us toward recognition of the ancient Greek axiom, "nothing human is alien to me."

The study of Christianity is a profoundly exciting adventure. We begin with second-century martyrdom accounts (*actae*), letters, "apologies" that explained and defended Christian faith, and manuals on church order. We conclude near the end of the eighteenth century as modernity begins.

1   *The Christian Movement in the Second and Third Centuries*

1   **Christians in the Roman Empire**
2   **The First Theologians**
3   **Constructing Christian Churches**

1   Christians in the Roman Empire

We begin at the beginning of the second century, a time of great stress as Christians struggled to explain their religious beliefs to their Roman neighbors, to create liturgies that expressed their beliefs and values, and to face persecution and martyrdom courageously. It may seem odd to omit discussion of the life and times of Christianity's founder, but scholarly exploration of the first century of the common era is itself a field requiring a specific expertise. Rather than focus on Christian beginnings directly, we will refer to them as necessitated by later interpretations of scripture, liturgy, and practice.

Second-century Christians were diverse, unorganized, and geographically scattered. Paul's frequent advocacy of unity among Christian communities gives the impression of a unity that was in fact largely rhetorical. Before we examine Christian movements, however, it is important to remind ourselves that Christians largely shared the world-view and social world of their neighbors. Polarizations of "Christians" and "pagans" obscure the fact that Christians were Romans. They participated fully in Roman culture and economic life; they were susceptible, like their neighbors, to epidemic disease and the anxieties and excitements of city life. As such, they were repeatedly shocked to be singled out by the Roman state for persecution and execution on the basis of their faith.

The physical world of late antiquity

The Mediterranean world was a single political and cultural unit. Twenty days sailing connected one end of the Mediterranean to the other, and ideas traveled rapidly along trade routes. The dream of one world, originated in the Greek polis, was still a powerful dream that Romans had militarized, creating a political reality. Jewish monotheism and philosophers' construction of a uni-verse also formulated the ideal of one world.

Ideas of the physical universe and human life were intimately related. The earth was thought of as a globe suspended in space in the center of concentric moving planets.

Earth was surrounded by an envelope of thick, murky, terrestrial atmosphere that reached as far as the moon. Beyond the moon were the sun and five planets. Fiery ether, the purest material element, supported the planets and the stars. The universe was pictured as a body, alive and divinely ordered, in which each part was connected by an internal *sympatheia*, or community of life. The parts of this universe were not of equal value. Earth was formed from the dregs or sediment of the universe – cold, heavy, impure stuff, whose weight had caused it to sink to the center. At the other end of the universe, the ether, atmosphere of the stars, was clear, weightless, and pure. The most influential thinker of the second century, the Platonist Numenius, said that God and the material world exist independently and in opposition to one another. Soul enters body by falling from its heavenly home, through the planetary spheres, accumulating evil as it comes into contact with the material world.

Since ether was considered the most desirable atmosphere of the universe, it was believed that contemplation of the stars could remove the strain of daily cares and occupations. A second-century man, Vettius Valens, wrote:

> I was not excited by the various courses of horses and the swift rush of the whip, or by the rhythms of dancers and the idle delight of flutes and the Muse and languorous strains, no, nor did I have any part in harmful or beneficial occupations, but having chanced upon divine and reverent contemplation of things celestial, I wished to cleanse my character of all vice and pollution, and to leave my soul immortal. Those who busy themselves with foreknowledge of the future and with the truth acquire a soul that is free from slavery, and despise fortune, and do not persist in vain hope, do not fear death, and live without perturbation, having schooled their souls to be brave, and they are not puffed up by prosperity or depressed by adversity, but are content with what they have. As they are not hankering after the impossible, they bear with equanimity what is ordained, and being freed from bondage to pleasure and flattery, they are soldiers of fate. For it is impossible for anyone by prayers or sacrifices to overcome what was fixed from the beginning and alter it to his taste; what has been assigned to us will happen to us without our praying for it; what is not fated will not happen for our prayers.

For many people, however, it was difficult to accept fate; they looked for religions that offered freedom from – or at least leverage against – the merciless tyranny of fate.

Christianity grew primarily in urban settings in which food was the most precious commodity. Roman people had constant anxiety about the availability of food as 10 percent of the population lived on the labor of the rural 90 percent. Emperors tried to appease the urban poor with the infamous "bread and circuses," distributing free bread when it was available and, when bread supplies failed, distracting the poor from their growling stomachs with shows in the public coliseum. Roman roads existed, and were maintained, because of their importance as food routes.

Rome had no internal police force. Each household was responsible for its own protection against burglary, rape, and murder. Toward the end of the third century urban life had become so hazardous that most people went to bed each night wondering if they would wake up in the morning. Individuals could disappear without a trace. The Roman historian Socrates described job recruitment for the all-important baking industry in third-century Rome:

Now the houses where bread was baked were built below ground level, and they constructed taverns at the side of each. The bakers entrapped many of those who went there by the following means: They used a certain mechanical contrivance to precipitate people from the tavern to the bakery below. This was done primarily to strangers and those who were caught in this way were forced to work in the bakery, where they were imprisoned until old age. Their friends, meanwhile, concluded that they were dead.

(*Historia ecclesiastica* 5.18)

Until the middle of the second century CE, infectious disease in the Roman Republic and Empire was relatively stable. This changed dramatically when a plague, probably smallpox (lethal in previously unexposed populations) began in 165 and lasted until about 180 in Italy and the western part of the Empire. The physician Galen estimated that between a quarter and a third of Italy's population died. Despite the untrustworthiness of ancient estimates, the numbers estimated can be taken to indicate that contemporaries experienced the plague as devastating. In 251 another new disease appeared. Called the "Antonine plague," it was probably measles. According to contemporary chroniclers, it killed 5,000 people a day in Rome alone for several months.

The person and the world

Politically, the Roman Empire was threatened and shrinking, besieged at its borders by Northern European tribes. It was a frightened society suffering from chronic malnutrition and epidemic disease. How did people experience *themselves* in these circumstances? The Stoic philosopher-emperor Marcus Aurelius (d. 180) wrote especially vividly of the human condition. Human beings, he said, are "a pinpoint in infinite time; a knife-edge between two eternities;" human activity is "smoke and nothingness;" human achievement was a "bird flying past, vanished before we can grasp it." Most startling of all, this Roman emperor described war as "puppies quarreling over a bone." He saw the world as a stage, with human beings, like puppets or marionettes "jerking on a string." Similarly, Stoic popular preachers often used images of terminal illness. In an imaginary dialogue of a patient with a doctor, Seneca has the doctor say: "You are much worse off than you will let yourself realize. Let philosophy diagnose your case." The Stoic philosopher Epictetus said, "The lecture room of a philosopher is a hospital."

The Roman world at the turn of the second century was one in which religions and philosophical schools alike were preoccupied with providing people with orientation to a world in which they could feel at least somewhat at home. One Stoic teacher mixed philosophy and practicality:

O poor wretches, learn and come to know the causes of things, what we are, for what life we are born, what the assigned order is, where the turning point of the course is to be rounded gently, what limit to set to spending money, for what it is right to pray, what is the use of hard cash, how much you ought to spend on your country and on those near and dear to you, what kind of a person God ordered you to be, and where, as a person, you are placed.

Painfully conscious of the suffering and insignificance of human existence, people were attracted by religious power. How best could one align oneself with the benevolent forces of the universe? Could one manipulate these forces at all? Philosophy, religion, and magic were often indistinguishable as spells, formulae, incantations, and amulets formed the repertoire of educated and uneducated people alike. Romans were religiously tolerant, frequently integrating several philosophies and religions in order to construct effective protection for individuals and households. They put together a religious *package*. Tolerant of everything but intolerance, Romans found Christians' insistence on "one way" puzzling and repugnant.

It has often been thought that by the second century, neither Roman civic religion nor the worship of the old Roman gods was religiously persuasive. This impression may have been based on the scarcity of literary expositions on the Roman pantheon. Yet the rhetoric of a sacred empire sanctioned Rome's civic and military goals. "Romans were meticulous in their efforts to secure divine support at every step" (Futrell, 1997: 78). Roman civic religion provided the formal bond of the empire, centered on the ritual worship of the legally deified emperor. The old Roman gods were conspicuously pictured on coins, statues, and pottery that was frequently stamped "*providentia deorum*" (the gods are looking after us). Moreover, the "mass media" of Roman society, coliseum performances, were saturated with religious ritual and clothing. Roman religion permeated Roman society. We can understand non-Christian Romans' resentment of Christianity's exclusive claims only when we recognize the centrality of Roman religion to Roman life.

In the midst of pessimistic evaluations of human life and a bewildering number of religious options, second-century sources testify over and over again to a sense of something valuable *inside* the person, the community, or the human race – something unrelated to the physical world. Philosophies and religions sought to identify and cultivate this precious entity.

The religious climate of early Christianity

The Christian movement grew in a world that was complex – religiously, socially, philosophically, and politically. Roman philosophies and religions articulated and embodied different values from those of the Christian movement, but the women and men who shaped Christian beginnings learned from them, appropriating and adapting what they had learned in the formation of Christian ethics, theology, and liturgy. In the case of their Jewish neighbors, not merely "borrowings," but deep roots and dependency must be acknowledged, although the details are difficult to document. We will look briefly at the philosophies and religions that were Christianity's primary competitors.

Philosophies: getting the mind right

Philosophical schools of the second century apparently felt little rivalry with other philosophies. Addressed to the uneducated, they were more like religions than like modern philosophies in that they were primarily concerned with alleviating anxiety. Philosophical conversions often resulted in dramatic changes of life-style, sometimes accompanied by withdrawal from society. The most popular philosophies diagnosed the problem of human existence as disorientation in the universe and prescribed a method for overcoming that painful condition.

Stoicism aimed at understanding the world in order to live in accord with it, to live "according to nature." Stoics believed that the universe was amenable to rational explanation because it is itself a rationally structured organism. Reason in human beings is the same as the reason embedded in the universe. Thus, according to Stoics, humans can be perfectly at ease in the universe if they develop their rational capacity. Rationality is, in fact, the *sole* source of human happiness. A complete indifference to external conditions must be cultivated, a disposition called "*apatheia*." *Apatheia* was not apathy, however. The model Stoic felt both pleasure and pain; what he did *not* feel were pleasures and pains resulting from mistaken judgments, or irrationality. Because of his perfect alignment with the rationality of the universe, the ideal Stoic's disposition was one of constant quiet pleasure.

Epicureans, the most misunderstood and vilified philosophers of the Roman Empire, identified human happiness as a life of pleasure. But Epicurus described the highest pleasure as *absence of pain*. None of the "pleasures" that eventuate in pain qualify:

> When we say that pleasure is the goal, we do not mean the pleasures of the dissipated, but freedom from pain in the body and from disturbance in the soul. For it is not drinking and continuous parties nor sexual pleasures, nor the enjoyment of fish and other delicacies of a wealthy table which produce the pleasant life, but sober reasoning that searches out the causes of every act of choice and refusal and which banishes the opinions which give rise to the greatest mental confusion.

Neither Stoics nor Epicureans valued knowledge for its own sake. In fact, Stoics regularly criticized learning as a source of confusion and unhappiness. Seneca wrote: "To desire to know more than is necessary is a form of intemperance. The pursuit of liberal studies makes one wearisome, wordy, tactless, and complacent; they do not learn what they need because they have already learned things which are superfluous." For Epicurus, "getting the mind right" meant rejection of *reliance* on reason. Epicurus diagnosed the cause of human unhappiness as mistaken belief in the gods, the soul, and an afterlife of reward or punishment. The gods exist, Epicurus said, but they do not interfere with human life in any way; to do so would be incompatible with the perfect happiness they enjoy. Soul and body are born, grow, and dissolve together, and there is complete and permanent loss of consciousness at death.

Although the philosophies of the Roman Empire did not value knowledge for its own sake, they did think it was crucial to understand the universe and the human place in it accurately.

Religions in the Roman Empire: direct sensuous experience

But not all Romans were attracted to philosophy in order to address nagging "dissatisfaction with oneself." Initiates in Roman religions did not seek conceptual orientation, but particular consciousness-altering experiences. There was great popular interest in mystery religions of three kinds: healing cults (such as Asclepius), oracle cults, and oriental mystery religions. In healing cults, medical attention was secondary to the interpretation of dreams and identification of destructive thoughts and self-images. The complex psychological and physical factors that made the individual sick were the focus of attention.

Oracle cults (such as Delphi) were consulted frequently. By the second century advance notice was given of questions to be asked, and the questions were increasingly practical and personal, such as: Whom will I marry? Or, will I succeed in a particular business venture? The oracle claimed, "When we serve our god, he hides nothing from us."

Robin Lane Fox has reconstructed the visit of a second-century man to an oracle shrine near Boetia in Greece. After arriving at the spot, the client

> lived for several days in the shrine, abstaining from hot baths and waiting until the priests proclaimed a favorable night from their studies of the entrails of a ram. Then he was washed and anointed. The priests took him to drink from the two springs, Memory and Forgetfulness. He then gazed on a secret image, prayed, worshipped, and dressed in a linen tunic. He was taken to the oracle's entrance, a chasm in the ground, down which he climbed on a thin ladder and then passed, feet first, into the lower darkness, holding cakes of honey. Underground, he was taught about the future, "not always in the same way," (Pausanius wrote), "for one person sees, another hears." He returned through the same narrow hole and was revived by the attendant priests, who asked him to report all that he had seen and heard. He emerged "gripped with terror and quite unaware of himself of those around him," but later his wits returned to him and also, added Pausanius, "the power to laugh."
>
> (Fox, 1987: 206)

The third kind of popular Roman religions were oriental mystery religions. Originally tribal religions from Asia Minor, Phrygia, and Egypt, the mystery religions were brought to the Roman Empire by merchants, slaves, and returning soldiers. Mystery religions featured secret rites that included an experience of the deity and the conferral of a spiritual self. According to participant reports, mystery religions knew how to *prepare* and *pace* the desired experience, and thus to produce and guarantee it.

Immortality was a consistent theme of mystery religions. Initiates rehearsed the soul's ascent after death back through the planetary spheres through which they had fallen into human life. The *Corpus hermeticum* describes the soul's ascent at death as a process in which the gross material of the physical world and the body is progressively eliminated until the soul is naked, the "true self," free to enter the divine realm and again become one with God. The right passwords to recite as one's soul travels, after death, to reunion with its source were essential. Initiations combined this knowledge with sensory experiences.

Initiations involved a series of exercises in which the initiate was weaned from habitual behavior, food, and sleep by fasting, lengthy periods of waiting, prayers, burning of incense (perhaps of intoxicating substances), and rituals of bathing and purification. Initiation in the Mithra cult included a ceremony called the *taurobolium*, first practiced in the West in 137 CE. After preparatory exercises, the initiate lay under a platform with loose slats on which a bull was slaughtered. Drenched with hot blood and gore, the initiate was instructed to make sure that he was completely covered by the blood; he was also to swallow some of the blood. Initiates who could not afford a bull could substitute a sheep, in which case the ritual became a *criobolium*.

Mystery religions promised not only immortality, but also more immediate and practical benefits, like protection from shipwreck, illness, and misfortune. They used a word that became important in the Christian movement: *soteria* – salvation. They also used metaphors of death and rebirth, speaking of initiates as reborn, changed, or deified.

No one feared being in a religious minority. Truth was not thought of as democratic; on the contrary, it was considered *necessarily* esoteric and difficult to achieve. Like those who followed the various philosophical schools, initiates in mystery religions felt they had something of ultimate value from which the rest of the world was excluded – by inability to travel to Delphi, by poverty, inability to understand, or by lack of the necessary preliminary disciplines.

Jews and Christians

Judaism was the most influential of the religious and philosophical neighbors of Christianity. The first Christians were Jews, and they continued to be influenced by Judaism throughout the common era, but Christians and Jews were also intense rivals. On the one hand, Christians, as a "new religious movement" in a society that did not value innovation, wanted to identify with the ancient and respected religion of the Jews; on the other hand, they sought to establish their difference from Judaism. Christians' strong ambivalence about Judaism appears in the earliest Christian literature. The Christian author of the *Epistle of Barnabas* (c.70–100) was shrilly angry at Jews, calling them "wretched men." Yet he called himself "one of yourselves and especially loving you all above my own life." In the early centuries, Christian ambivalence can be seen as sibling rivalry, but by the end of the fourth century the imbalance of public power between Christians and Jews in the Christian Empire changed that relationship.

Christians attempted to explain why Jewish tradition and scriptures now belonged to, or had been "inherited" by Christianity. "Supersessionist" theology claimed that Christ's birth fulfilled and completed God's promises to the Jews, rendering Judaism no longer a living religion. At the end of the fourth century, this theology led to destruction of synagogues and the marginalization of Jews from public life. Later, at the end of the eleventh century, the first pogroms occurred. Christian treatment of the ancient religion within which it originated is not an attractive aspect of the history of Christianity, but it should not be ignored.

The translation of Hebrew scripture into Greek was begun in the middle of the third century BCE in Alexandria. According to legend, 72 translators, working independently, arrived at an identical translation of the Pentateuch; other parts of the Hebrew scriptures were translated later. The so-called *Septuagint*, became Christians' "Old Testament." By the second and third centuries, some rabbis expressed their regret that the Hebrew scriptures had become accessible to non-Jews by being translated into Greek. They denounced the compilation of the *Septuagint* as a sin comparable to the worship of the golden calf.

Christians

The earliest Christians were Jews. W. H. C. Frend writes: "They used the Hebrew scriptures and they took the messianism, the eschatology, and the ethics of Judaism for granted. Like the Jews they claimed to be 'saints,' or 'people of God,' a 'royal priesthood' and a 'holy nation'" (122). Like Jews, Christians prayed three times a day and fasted twice a week. Christians also professed monotheism as did Jews. It is likely that Christians were indebted to Jews for liturgical practices like naked baptism, and the eucharistic celebration echoes the Jewish blessing of the cup after a meal. However, exactly what Christians "borrowed" from Judaism is not known. Liturgical scholar Paul F. Bradshaw concludes his detailed inspection of the evidence for the earliest Christian worship, "We must be content to remain agnostic about many of the roots of Christian worship practices which we observe clearly for the first time in the following centuries" (Bradshaw, 2002: 45). Practices associated with baptism and preparation for membership were diverse and local.

Scholars of the New Testament and Christian beginnings are presently questioning assumptions about the "early Church," rather than "filling in the blanks" of a picture that is in fact partial, local, and heavily informed by particular perspectives – the historical author's and the historian's. Moreover, "Christian" and "pagan" should not be thought of as polar contrasts. Christians participated in the everyday life of the Roman Empire, sharing a social and cultural world with non-Christian neighbors. They also had common questions concerning the place of women, the roles of slaveholders and slaves, the legitimacy of itinerant preachers, and sexuality. In short, Roman religions and Judaism were not "background" for, but interactive, *with* Christianity.

For example, Christians received from Roman culture ideas of the ideal body that informed their notion of "the Christian body." The ideal body of late classical culture was controlled through regimes of diet and the limitation of sexual activity, a body whose practices and habits were carefully chosen. The ideal body was everything that slave bodies were not and could not be, for slaves were reduced to bodies; *to soma* (body) was used synonymously with *ho doulos* (slave). Slaves were gendered female – available for any duty, without kinship relations, and sexually accessible. By law, sexual coercion on a slave could not be considered rape. Slaves could also be tortured in ways that citizens could not. Christians were slaveholders, like their neighbors. Slave collars adorned with crosses have been discovered.

Cultural historian Jennifer Glancy has shown that Christian writings, both canonical and extra-canonical, are permeated with slaveholders' perspectives. Slaves were consistently admonished to obey their masters in everything, and especially not to run away. Christians were instructed not to shelter runaway slaves, no matter what the circumstances. The lack of any writing *by* slaves means that slaves' perspectives cannot be recovered.

Two results of great importance emerge from the social reality of slavery. First, in the literature of Christian movements slavery was used as a metaphor. Numerous Christian authors claim that it is far better to be an actual slave than to be a slave of sin. The spiritualization of slavery trivialized the significance of actual slavery and its effects on the bodies of slaves. Second, like their classical ancestors and secular neighbors, Christians constructed "the Christian body" as opposite to the perpetual vulnerability and permeability of slave bodies. From the earliest extant Christian document, I Thessalonians 4.3-8, sexual purity was considered a requirement for becoming Christian. Yet slaves had no control over their sexual use by slaveholders. Under these circumstances, *could* a slave choose to be a Christian? There is evidence that some slaves were

Christians, but this may have been by their masters' choice of religion for the household rather than their own.

The Roman understanding of "body" is evident in Christians' theology of the "Word made flesh." Philosophers' ideal of a controlled body that represented a controlled self was embedded in the first Christian writings. As Christianity expanded, Christian "overachievers" went beyond the minimal demand that they forego *pornea* to practice the "pleasure of no pleasure," as one Christian author said. By the fourth century, catechesis, or instruction leading to membership in Christian communities, aimed not only at converting the mind to Christian beliefs, but also at christianizing by specific practices bodies hitherto understood as owned by the devil. The culmination of training for membership was baptism, naked, in the full congregation. Moreover, the Christian body was gendered male; women martyrs and ascetics were thought of as "becoming male" because, in Roman society, defining the self by ascetic practices was a male prerogative. Yet, ironically, the Christian body was also seen as a spiritualized slave body, a body perfectly obedient to Christ.

Both their belief in the "Word made flesh," and urgent social reality pressed Christians to examine and reconstruct their attitude toward bodies. The threat and reality of state-initiated martyrdom shaped Christians' experience and thought until well into the fourth century. Christian literature of the early centuries of the common era reflected preoccupation with martyrdom and the conflicts internal to Christian communities that were generated by persecution. This literature included manuals of church order, like the Syrian *Didache*, or "Teaching," that addressed practical problems and described a simple theology consisting of "the way of life," and "the way of death." Letters were also preserved, like those of Clement of Rome (c.100) and Ignatius of Antioch (d. c.117). *Actae*, or accounts of Christians' trials and martyrdoms, were read during liturgy on a martyr's "birthday" (the anniversary of her/his death).

Actae cannot be taken as literal accounts of martyrs' gestures and words, except to the extent that earlier *actae* might have prompted a later confessor's responses. They do, however, reveal Christians' thinking about martyrdom. A young Roman woman confessor's prison journal from the early third century, discussed in the next section, is especially revealing.

Martyrdom

Romans were usually tolerant, but they despised Christian intolerance. We can reconstruct, largely from trial transcripts and other Christian literature, some of the reasons Christians were hated and persecuted. Christians were considered subversive to the Roman state. Large-scale persecution did not occur until there were large enough numbers of Christians to make their presence threatening. In the eyes of their neighbors, Christians were "atheists" in that they refused to worship the deified emperor and the Roman gods that protected the Roman state. Christians were secretive in their worship; most people only heard rumors about them. Christians were also sometimes belligerent or supercilious. During the persecution in Lyons, when the governor questioned the bishop about the Christian God, he replied, "If you are worthy you will know."

Christians claimed repeatedly that conversion to Christian faith felt to them like transformation from death to life. Yet "stubborn" adherence to Christian faith sometimes resulted in premature and violent death. Until the so-called "Peace of the Church" under Constantine in 313 (later in the Eastern Empire), the threat of martyrdom was constant, but the reality was sporadic. Until the middle of the third century, persecutions were local and episodic. A persecution occurred in Rome in 64, in Smyrna in 117, and in Lyons in 177, but they were neither widespread nor systematic. In the early fourth century, however, scholars estimate that in the Eastern Empire between 303 and 312, 2,500 to 3,000 Christians were martyred. In the West during the same period, there were approximately 3,000 to 3,500 martyrs.

Sometimes persecution was initiated by provincial governors acting on the emperor's orders, but more frequently outbreaks of popular hatred against Christians prompted persecution. In about 197 the North African author Tertullian wrote: "If the Tiber reaches the walls, if the Nile does not rise to the fields, if the sky doesn't move or the earth does, if there is a famine, if there is plague, the cry is at once, 'The Christians to the lion.' What [he remarked sarcastically], all of them to one lion?" (*Apology* 40.2).

Martyrs appeared to gain nothing. Their God did not rescue them from death, and the Roman government seemed to have triumphed in putting them to death. The fourth-century historian, Eusebius, imagined pagans saying among themselves, "Where is their god, and what good was their religion to them which they preferred even to their own lives?" (*Ecclesiastical History* 5.1.60).

Christian martyrdom occurred in the context of public entertainment in Roman arenas. A brief description of coliseum culture will help to contextualize Christians' experience of martyrdom. Coliseum "games" originated in the Roman Republic as funeral celebrations; in the Empire, they developed into popular entertainment. The Roman coliseum, built in the first century under the Emperor Vesapian, seated about 50,000. Seating was by social order, with women and slaves at the top of the arena, farthest from the sights, sounds, and smells of the combats.

Roman religion was inseparable from the games. No clear distinction existed between capital punishment and sacrifice to the state gods. Victims were often dressed in cult garments according to the religious calendar. Christians objected to being clothed in such garments. The third-century *Actae of Perpetua and Felicity* described the two women's unwillingness to meet martyrdom in the robes of priests of Saturn. Appealing to the Roman sense of justice, Perpetua said, "We came to this of our own free will, that our freedom should not be violated. We agreed to pledge our lives provided that we would do no such thing. You agreed with us to do this." The tribunal relented, and the women were allowed to proceed to martyrdom in their own garments.

A typical day at the coliseum began with wild beast hunts (*venationes*). Exotic wild animals were brought from the ends of the Empire at tremendous expense to be tortured and killed in the coliseum. Elephants – as many as 140 were used in a single celebration – bulls, foxes, bears, and lions were favorites. At noon most spectators took a lunch break while criminals and prisoners were summarily executed. In the afternoon, gladiators with elaborate costumes and stage sets fought, often to the death. Due to the expense, gladiatorial combats (*munera*) were usually sponsored by emperors. Most of the men who died in the coliseum were political prisoners or criminals. Punishment was *intended* to be "cruel and unusual," both entertainment and a public statement about imperial power. Since punishment was considered a deterrent, it was made a spectacle.

The point of the gladiatorial combats was not their violence, however; rather, they were regarded as sport. Trained gladiators exhibited skill, self-control, and style. The crowd acted as umpire, deciding the fate of the defeated. If a gladiator had exhibited courage and skill, the crowd would be likely to yell, "Back off from the wounded man!" ("*Retro a saucio.*") If not, he received the death blow.

Did no one object to these displays? Moralists like Seneca objected, not to the cruelty to victims, but to the damage to spectators of viewing this violence. He wrote, "Nothing is so damaging to good character than the habit of wasting time at the games; for then it is that vice steals secretly upon you through the avenue of pleasure. . . . I come home more greedy, more ambitious, more voluptuous, and more cruel and more inhumane because I have been among other human beings." There is also evidence of sympathy for the slaughtered animals, but none is recorded for the human beings who suffered and died in the arena.

For Christians, however, martyrdom in Roman arenas came to be seen as nothing less than *proof* of the power of Christian faith. After the early fourth century Diocletian persecution, Athanasius wrote:

> Is martyrdom, then, a light proof of the weakness of death or is it a slight demonstration of the victory won over death by the Savior, when the young men and women that are in Christ are unafraid to die? For people are naturally afraid of death and of the dissolution of the body; but there is this most startling fact, that one who has put on the faith of the cross disregards even what is naturally fearful, and for Christ's sake is not afraid of death. . . . This is no small proof, but is rather an obvious guarantee of the power of the Savior.
>
> (*On the Incarnation* 28)

Although Christians revered martyrs, *volunteering* for martyrdom by acts that instigated one's own arrest and execution, was repeatedly forbidden by Christian leaders. Clement of Alexandria wrote, "We ourselves blame those who leap on death; for there are some who are eager to deliver themselves over in hatred of the creator, passionate for death. We say that these people commit suicide and are not martyred, even if they are officially executed."

Actae reveal that Christians did not blame their persecutors. The devil was their enemy; their tortures and pain were the result of the devil's activities, only indirectly attributable to the state's condemnation. It was the devil that influenced the judges who condemned them and the crowds who demanded their execution. Even judges' admonitions in the interest of saving them from death were seen as part of the devil's strategies. Christians also repeatedly blamed Jews for inciting persecution.

Why were Christians willing to suffer and die for their faith, when a simple civic act of throwing a few grains of incense on a fire in front of the emperor's portrait could save them? What reasons did *they* give? Three rationales occur repeatedly in letters and accounts of martyrdom. The most frequent explanation was that martyrdom imitated and participated in Christ's sufferings. The letters of Ignatius, bishop of Antioch, a chained prisoner on his way to execution in Rome, described martyrdom as participation in the sufferings of Christ. The martyr accepts and shares Christ's suffering, but

Christ also suffers in, and instead of, the martyr. During a difficult childbirth in prison one of the guards asked the African confessor Felicity, "'You who so suffer now, what will you do when you are flung to the beasts?' And she answered, 'Now I suffer what I suffer; but then another will be in me who will suffer for me, because I too am to suffer for him.'"

In the *Martyrdom of Polycarp*, martyrdom as participation in Christ's passion is especially vivid. The anonymous author presents both the reported events and Polycarp's responses as revealing a "martyrdom conformable to the gospel." Numerous details link Polycarp's martyrdom to that of Christ: Polycarp "waited to be betrayed just as the Lord did;" the name of the chief of police who arrested him was Herod; he was betrayed by members of his household at the instigation of Jews. Moreover, Polycarp's reported response to his arrest was not a pious formula, but an intentional repetition of Christ's words in the garden of Gethsemane, "God's will be done." Even the stab wound from which he died imitated Christ's pierced side. Miracles surrounding his death emphasized further Polycarp's access to Christ's power through sharing his death.

The second rationale referred to in Christian literature is that martyrdom constituted "release from a wicked and lawless society." Death apparently seemed to many confessors a welcome relief from a society that sneered at and rejected them, a society they saw as violent and corrupt. Anger and rage is evident in the taunts with which martyrs greeted coliseum crowds, in the scorn with which they wrote about their contemporaries, and in the belligerent words and acts with which they sometimes responded to judges and bystanders. Historians have often ignored both martyrs' anger, and their expectation of immediate heavenly reward, preferring to see acceptance of martyrdom as solely the result of Christians' love for Christ. Anger and rejection of a society that rejected and killed them, expectation of reward, *and* love for Christ must, however, be seen as aspects of their complex motivation.

The third motivation for accepting martyrdom was the repeated suggestion that the martyr's sufferings occurred "no longer in the flesh." Even in prison, awaiting execution, confessors experienced a heightened consciousness unlike ordinary consciousness. The noble young Carthaginian woman, Perpetua, left a prison journal in which she described the *privileges* associated with martyrdom. As a confessor, Perpetua felt empowered to perform acts that ranged from settling local church disputes to improving the other-world status of a long-dead brother.

Christians did not regard martyrdom as "heroic" in the ordinary sense. Martyrdom accounts assumed that a person *cannot* approach shameful death with peace and joy *except* by a special grace. If a confessor was not given this grace, s/he was unable to maintain her/his confession. Because of this belief, confessors were remarkably generous to other Christians who renounced their faith in persecution. They were seen as simply "unready," "feeble," or "unable to bear the strain of a great contest." They were simply not *there*. Confessors felt "sorrow and grief immeasurable" for those who lapsed, but they did not seem to resent or judge them. Those who denied their faith were thought of as helpless victims of the devil, who dragged them, one *acta* says, into "unconsciousness."

Martyrdom accounts never hinted that bodies should be despised. Rather, martyrs died in the faith that they would be resurrected bodily in heaven at the instant of their death. While it was believed that Christians who died ordinary deaths would sleep until the general resurrection, martyrs were believed to be in paradise "today, this very day." Just before his death, Polycarp is reported to have said:

> I bless thee because thou hast thought me worthy of this day and hour, to take my part in the number of the martyrs, in the cup of thy Christ, for resurrection to eternal life of soul and body in the immortality of the Holy Spirit, among whom may I be received into thy presence this day as a rich and acceptable sacrifice.

Polycarp's apparent "denial of death" was the result of his self-identification, body and soul, with Christ's life. A letter from the church of Lyon during persecution expresses this common theme of martyrdom literature. "They [the martyrs] asked for life and God gave it to them, which they shared with their neighbors, and departed to God, in all ways victorious." The Greek Christian, Justin the Martyr (d. c.165) wrote in his *Apology*, "You can kill us, but you cannot do us any real harm." Christians thought of the new life they experienced in Christ as stronger than death, as capable of reaching across death to bring body and soul intact to paradise.

Second-century apology

Romans, Jews, and Christians all believed that the survival and fortune of individuals and the state depended on divine favor. Romans believed that if the gods who protected Rome and made her great did not receive the worship to which they were accustomed, they would withdraw their favor and protection. "We acknowledge that we are atheists with regard to such gods," Justin wrote, "but not with regard to the most true God." At the beginning of the fifth century, Augustine wrote the *City of God* to answer similar charges, namely, that Christians' defection caused the Sack of Rome in 410.

Christians tried to explain and defend beliefs and practices that seemed strange or threatening to their non-Christian neighbors. "Apology," although formally addressed to an emperor or an opponent, was more likely to be read by Christian communities for their support and reassurance. There is no evidence that emperors received and read any of the Christian apologies addressed to them. The primary themes of Christian apology were the unique truth of Christianity, the harmlessness and innocence of Christians, the folly of pagans, and animosity toward Jews. Apologetic literature also responded to accusations that Christianity was a threat to the state; they presented an ethical defense to charges of immorality; and they undertook philosophical explanation.

At the beginning of the second century, Pliny the Younger, governor of Bithnia in northern Asia Minor, wrote to the Emperor Trajan asking what to do about Christians. He inquired "whether the name itself should be punished, or only crimes attaching to that name."

> Meanwhile [he said] this is the course that I have adopted in the case of those brought before me as Christians. I ask them if they are Christians; if they admit it I repeat the question a second and a third time, threatening capital punishment; if they persist I sentence them to death. For I do not doubt that, whatever kind of crime it may be to which they have confessed, their pertinacity and inflexible obstinacy should certainly be punished.

But Christians only admitted to the most innocent activities. Puzzled by their denial of any crimes, Pliny said that he ordered the torture of two servants "who were called deaconesses [*ministrae*]."

> They revealed, however, only that they had been accustomed to assemble on a fixed day before daylight and sing a hymn to Christ as to a god; and that they bound themselves with an oath not for any crime, but to commit neither theft, nor robbery, nor adultery, not to break their word, and not to deny a deposit when demanded; after these things were done it was their custom to depart and meet together again to take food, but ordinary and harmless food; and they said that even this had ceased after my edict was issued, by which, according to your commands I had forbidden the existence of clubs.

Trajan agreed with Pliny's casualness in his dealings with Christians, not seeking them out for persecution, but condemning them to death if they were discovered and persisted in their stubborn error.

In North Africa, Tertullian's *Apology* (d. c.225) protested the unfairness of such treatment:

> If it is certain that we are the most wicked of men, why do you treat us so differently from all fellows, that is, from other criminals, it being only fair that the same crime should get the same treatment? When the charges made against us are made against others, they are permitted to make use of both their own lips and of hired pleaders to show their innocence. They have full opportunity of answer and debate; in fact, it is against the law to condemn anyone undefended and unheard. Christians alone are forbidden to say anything in exculpation of themselves, in defense of the truth, to help the judge to a righteous decision; all that is cared about is having what the public hatred demands – the confession of the name, not examination of the charge.
>
> (*Apology* II)

Christians were not accused of subversive or treasonous activities aimed at the overthrow of the Roman state after the late first century. Yet Christians maintained detachment from an Empire that required the full investment of its citizens' hopes and energies in political society. Christians claimed to be in the world but not *of* it. "We do not place our hopes in the present," Justin wrote. Second-century Christian apologists' demythologizing of the Roman state initiated a long process of secularization of the state that was formalized by Constantine in the fourth century. By legitimizing Christianity, along with other sects, cults, and religions, the so-called Edict of Milan (313) implicitly declared the state indifferent to religion. But in the second century, this was far in the future.

In all practical matters, Christian authors consistently advised the gospel injunction to "pay to Caesar what belongs to Caesar." Justin wrote, "We worship God alone, but in all other things we gladly obey you." Apologists emphasized repeatedly that Christians are good citizens, but they acknowledged that they did not support the idea that the state was a sacred entity and the supreme good of human life.

> When you hear that we look for a kingdom, you rashly suppose that we mean something merely human. But we speak of a kingdom with God, as is clear from our confessing Christ when you bring us to trial, though we know that death is the penalty for this confession.

For if we looked for a human kingdom, we would deny it in order to save our lives, and would try to remain in hiding in order to obtain the things we look for. But since we do not place our hopes in the present order, we are not troubled by being put to death, since we will have to die somehow in any case.

(Justin, *First Apology* 11)

Christian apologists were also called upon to defend other aspects of their faith and practice.

Ethical defense

Charges of moral depravity were often brought against Christians. Incest and cannibalism were the most frequent accusations. Tertullian in North Africa, and Athenagoras (fl. c.177), a Greek philosopher from the other end of the Mediterranean, responded to these charges. Tertullian's strategy was to take the offensive, accusing Romans of projecting their own crimes onto Christians. His *Apology* is flamboyant and vitriolic, the stuff of television courtroom drama. Tertullian thought that Romans' bloodthirstiness was responsible for their misunderstanding of Christians. He cited the time-honored Roman practice of exposing unwanted children (usually girls) to refute accusations that Christians eat babies. Murder is forbidden to Christians, Tertullian said; Christians are not even permitted to destroy the fetus in the womb (*Apology* 9). Moreover, Christians do not eat bloody meat. At their trials Christians were often offered sausages filled with blood – a Roman delicacy – as a test, since it was known that they would not eat them.

Perhaps the many accusations of cannibalism brought against Christians came from overhearing Christians speak of the bread and wine of the Christian eucharistic ritual as the body and blood of Christ. On the other hand, the charge of cannibalism was common to late antique mud slinging. The Roman Senate prohibited human sacrifice in 97 BCE, but both archeological and textual evidence reveals that human sacrifice continued into the common era in some places. The entrails of sacrificial victims were used to predict the future, and human sacrifices were thought to appease angry gods in times of disaster, famine, or plague. In the cult of Saturn, practiced primarily in the vicinity of Carthage in North Africa, children were sacrificed to appease the god or to seek an advantage. Numerous urns containing children's bones have been found, together with altars and sacrifice paraphernalia. Tertullian claimed that infant sacrifices were still performed in his own day, but there is no archeological evidence that such practices continued past the middle of the second century CE. Nevertheless, the recent reality of human sacrifice apparently provided a context in which accusations of cannibalism were credible to Christians' contemporaries.

A different kind of context is needed for assessing charges of incest and, more broadly, sexual immorality. Responding to these charges by going on the offensive, Tertullian, Justin, and Clement of Alexandria all cited infant exposure to claim that Romans frequently committed incest with their own unrecognized daughters. In the Roman world, the second largest source of slaves, next to children born of slave mothers, was exposed infants who, if they were rescued and raised, were almost always raised as slave prostitutes.

After considering evidence for Gnostic sects in Asia Minor, the Carpocratians and the Phibionites, historian Stephen Benko concluded that they practiced what he calls "liturgical sex." Benko argued that libertinism was a strain in early Christianity, but that it was limited to a few sects who were vigorously ostracized from the mainstream by St Paul's purity injunctions. According to opponents' accounts, these acts were rationalized as actualizing the unity of Christ urged in Ephesians 1.3. Christian authors complained that their critics did not bother to differentiate among groups that called themselves Christian; activities that may have been done by one group were quickly assumed to be true of all Christians.

Remnants of libertinism may have persisted in the "holy kiss," a ritual greeting in Christian liturgies that symbolized the love of the brethren in Christian communities. Several second-century Christian authors acknowledged that the holy kiss was sometimes abused. Clement of Alexandria wrote:

> And if we are called to the kingdom of God, let us walk worthy of the kingdom, loving God and our neighbor. But love is not proved by a kiss, but by kindly feelings. But there are those that do nothing but make the churches resound with a kiss, not having love itself within. For this very thing, the shameless use of a kiss, which ought to be mystic, occasions foul suspicions and evil reports. The apostle calls the kiss holy. When the kingdom is worthily tested, we dispense the affection of the soul with a chaste and closed mouth, by which chiefly gentle manners are expressed. But there is another – unholy – kiss, full of poison, counterfeiting sanctity. Often kisses inject the poison of licentiousness.
>
> (*Paedegogus* 3.11)

Christians insisted on integrating body and senses in their worship. They believed strongly that the religion of the Incarnation should not be expressed in a bland, intellectual worship that excluded the life and energy that Christians experienced. Did Christians' neighbors misunderstand Christians' attempt to include the senses in their worship? We will continue to discuss the inclusion of bodies and senses in fourth-century liturgies, when more evidence exists.

Against general charges of immorality, Tertullian appealed to the Platonic maxim that virtue is a precondition of knowledge. One's behavior, he said, either enables or prevents accurate knowledge. Athenagoras' *Apology* agreed both that knowledge requires virtue, and that evidence of virtue is the best test of accurate and adequate knowledge.

> Who of those who analyze syllogisms, resolve ambiguities, explain etymologies, or teach homonyms, synonyms, predicates, axioms, and what the subject is and what the predicate – who of them have so purified their own hearts as to love their enemies instead of hating them; instead of upbraiding those who first insult them, to bless them; and to pray for those who plot against them? . . . With us, on the contrary, you will find unlettered people, tradesmen and old women who, though unable to express in words the advantages of our teachings, demonstrate by acts the value of their principles. For they do not rehearse speeches, but evidence good deeds. When struck, they do not strike back; when robbed, they do not sue; to those who ask, they give, and they love their neighbors as themselves.
>
> (Athenagoras, *A Plea for the Christians* 11)

According to Athenagoras, Christians who acted with integrity, even if they were unable precisely to articulate their beliefs, possessed real knowledge.

Christian morality must also be considered in relation to slavery in late antiquity. Slaves had no independent access to courts of law, they were not permitted social bonds of kinship and, as has been mentioned, slaveholders had unlimited sexual access to their slaves. In the earliest extant Christian document, I Thessalonians 4. 3–8, Paul instructed his readers that sexual morality is essential to Christianity, but it is striking that he did not explicitly forbid slaveholders sexual access to their slaves. Sex between slaveholders and slaves was so conventional that it may not have been thought of as immoral, even in Christian communities.

Philosophical apologetic

The first Christian apologists to enter philosophical dialogue were Justin Martyr (d. c.165) and Athenagoras (d. after 177). For them, the question was not whether or not Christians should accept or reject philosophy, but whether the inevitable philosophical framework of Christian theology is acknowledged and self-critical, or implicit and unexamined. Tertullian famously asked, "What has Athens to do with Jerusalem?" and he answered, "Nothing!" But he nevertheless used a Stoic framework to explain central theological ideas. Justin and Athenagoras, on the other hand, examined their philosophical assumptions both in order to clarify Christian self-understanding and to defend Christian faith to outsiders.

As Christian apologists began to engage in debate with philosophers and defenders of Roman religions, they realized that Christianity had no monopoly either on moral teachings or on doctrinal teachings like monotheism and creation. How did they account for this without surrendering ground to their opponents?

Justin posited a connection and continuity between Christian and non-Christian philosophers based on a "seed of reason" (*logos spermaticos*) within all human beings. He said that the seed of reason, dimly seen by philosophers, and clearly revealed in Jesus Christ, explains why Christians and non-Christian philosophers often understand the same truth. The rationality (*logos*) pre-existent in God was, Justin said, incarnated in Jesus Christ. He described the *logos* as intermediate between God and the world, a description that would prompt a heated debate in the fourth century. The *logos*, God's agent in creation, continues to be the means by which the human mind can know God. Justin wrote: "We adore and love *next to God* the *logos* derived from the increate and ineffable God, seeing that for our sakes he became human" (*Second Apology* 13.4). Justin believed that both the promises of the Hebrew Bible and the truths of the philosophers were fulfilled and completed in Christ.

Irenaeus and Tertullian had a different explanation for the awkward fact that there were good and wise people before there were Christians. Tertullian posited a natural law that provides all human beings with fundamental knowledge of the existence, goodness, and justice of God and with moral precepts. This primordial natural law, he said, is now "reformed for the better" in Christianity.

Once these affinities with philosophy had been identified, acknowledged, and placed in a Christian context, some serious intellectual objections to Christianity had to be met. For example, pagans accused Christians of teaching absurd myths. In Greek and Roman myths, the gods walk on earth among humans, but these myths had long since been allegorized and emancipated from anthropomorphic interpretations. Secular Romans found Christians' stories of Jesus of Nazareth, who was called the "son of God," very similar to their own ancient myths, but hopelessly naive in their literalism. Christians' belief that Jesus was born of a virgin also appeared to lack sophistication, if not basic medical information. And belief in the resurrection of body seemed at best misguided, at worst an ignorant superstition, a confusion of two very different beliefs, immortality of the soul and the resurrection of body.

This objection, so intimately connected to fundamental differences between secular Romans and Christians over the meaning and value of bodies, was not adequately answered for centuries. Against the Platonic teaching that the soul is naturally immortal, Christians insisted that immortality of the soul was a gift from God, and that it was insufficient without the resurrection of body. "The soul participates in life because God wills it to live; thus it will not even have such participation when God no longer wills it to live." Athenagoras linked the bodily resurrection with creation. "Without the resurrection of body," he said, "the person would not be permanent as a person" (*The Resurrection of the Dead* XXV).

Apologists also emphasized the "reasonableness" of belief in bodily resurrection. Justin found a satisfying analogy in the massive physical changes human bodies undergo in conception and birth; why not, then, another massive change in a physical resurrection? As a Stoic, Tertullian believed the soul to be material, like body, although of a very fine substance. Since soul and body are essentially of the same substance, he said, they are bonded together in life and death; thus, resurrection of body is necessary if bodies are to participate in reward or punishment. Moreover, Tertullian wrote, absolute, final death is completely outside human experience and observation; we observe a world in which a rhythm of seasons, life and death, continually produces the death of the living and the birth of new forms of life. Most apologists, however, were content to simply invoke the power of God as full explanation for the resurrection of body.

Finally, pagans were critical of Christian teachings on grace, forgiveness, and salvation. Celsus, an early third century Platonist philosopher, summarized these objections: "Those who summon people to the other mysteries make this preliminary proclamation: 'Whoever has pure hands and a wise tongue, let him come.' But let us hear what folk these Christians call: 'Whoever is a sinner,' they say, 'whoever is unwise, whoever is a child, and, in a word, whoever is a wretch, the kingdom of God will receive him'" (*On the True Doctrine* IV). Non-Christian Romans found the lack of moral qualifications for Christian conversion unintelligible and irresponsible.

Along with adherents of other Roman religions, second-century Christians assumed the necessity of salvation, but they did not have a fully articulated *doctrine* of salvation. They believed and affirmed that, as Arnobius (d. c.330) later wrote, "Christ gave assistance in equal measure to the good and to the evil." The distinctive character of the Christian invitation was based on *need* rather than worth. Many eucharistic prayers and hymns also identified need and the response of gratitude as the essential ingredients of salvation.

Christian apology encouraged Christians in their beliefs and practices, but they relied on intellectual argument to do so. Images played a more intimate role in comforting and sustaining Christians in personal and communal crises. Later in this chapter we turn to the material evidence of Christian worship and devotion.

READINGS

The *Letters* of Ignatius, Bishop of Antioch
The Martyrdom of Polycarp

The Martyrdom of SS Perpetua and Felicity
First Apology of Justin, the Martyr
Athenagoras, *A Plea Regarding Christians*
Tertullian, *Apology*

2   The First Theologians

Theology – the clarifying, defining, and organizing of ideas – occurs when people find ideas imprecise or when there is conflict over practices or liturgy. It then becomes necessary for the poetic language of scripture, liturgy, or devotion to be examined and explicated. The first efforts to examine and articulate beliefs took the form of polemic against rival Gnostic Christians. The tools employed in theological work will be discussed first, after which we will consider how the first theologians used these tools.

Theological tools: scripture

Second- and third-century Christians believed that scripture was not only exempt from error, but also that it contained nothing superfluous. They did not, however, agree on which writings should be included in scripture. Marcion (d. c.160), was the first Christian to work on a canon, or list of authoritative Christian scriptures. He was prompted to criticize Christian scriptures' account of Christ's birth as occurring in the normal human way by his repugnance for birth. Yet he acknowledged that human birth was essential to true humanity; thus he could not think of Christ as fully human. Against Marcion, Tertullian insisted in graphic detail on the reality of Christ's birth: "In loving humans," he said, God "loved the process of birth also, and human flesh." Marcion also wanted to exclude the Old Testament from the Christian canon. He believed that the God of the Old Testament created evil while the God of the Christian scriptures was the loving "Father of our Lord Jesus Christ." Marcion was excommunicated in 144. He started his own church, which spread rapidly and lasted for over a hundred years. Marcion's attacks on the Old Testament provoked Christian authors to identify a list of authorized Christian scriptures, but a consensus was still about a century and a half distant.

Justin Martyr was familiar with all four of the gospels, which he called "the memoirs of the apostles." Irenaeus (d. c.200) was the first to speak of a "New Testament" that paralleled the "Old Testament." Although the broad outline was settled by the beginning of the third century, the first official document listing the twenty-seven books of the New Testament (alone) as canonical was Athanasius's Easter Letter of 367. II Peter, II and III John, and Jude were absent from most lists of canonical books until the late third century. Hebrews was still under suspicion in the West; Revelation was excluded in Syria until the end of the fourth century; and the Western churches were silent about the book of James until the end of the fourth century. The main criterion for inclusion in the Christian canon was apostolicity; apostolicity and canon became almost synonymous terms. It was argued, for example, that II Peter, since written by an apostle, must be canonical. On the other hand, Hebrews, since it seemed clearly to deserve canonical status, must have been written by an apostle.

Descriptions of the inspiration of scripture varied widely. Some believed that the authors of scripture wrote in ecstatic states in which their own intellectual powers were suspended. Others, like Origen (d. 254) taught that the Holy Spirit enabled the authors of scripture to understand divine truth without suspending their own wills.

Tradition

For Irenaeus, the Christian scriptures were tradition, but tradition was not confined to scripture. Tradition was also handing on what Irenaeus simply called "life." In order to safeguard scripture against dissident interpretations, Irenaeus insisted that scripture belonged to the tradition originated by the apostles and that it could be accurately interpreted only within the Church. In the third century, however, it became important to define how the churches were connected to the apostles. This was done in three ways. First, Tertullian defined apostolicity as the continuity of doctrine:

> All doctrine that accords with those apostolic churches, the sources and originals of the faith, must be reckoned as the truth, since it preserves without doubt what the churches received from the apostles, the apostles from Christ, and Christ from God. . . . We are in communion with the apostolic churches; there is no difference of doctrine; this is the testimony of the truth.
>
> *(De praescriptione haereticorum* 21)

Second, Irenaeus claimed that the connection between apostolic times and the third century existed in a chain of personal acquaintance:

> Polycarp, who not only was taught by the apostles, and associated with many who had seen Christ, was also installed by apostles for Asia as bishop in the church in Smyrna – I saw him myself in my early youth – [he] survived for a long time and departed this life in a ripe old age by a glorious and magnificent martyrdom. He always taught what he learned from the apostles, which the Church continues to hand on . . .
>
> *(Adversus haereses.* III.iii.4.)

Third, Cyprian (d. 258) said that the continuity between apostles and the third century churches was guaranteed by a succession of bishops: "This unity we ought to hold and preserve, especially we who preside in the Church as bishops, that we may prove the episcopate to be one and undivided. . . .The episcopate is one; the individual members have each a part, and the parts make up the whole: *(De unitate ecclesiae* 5).

These descriptions of the continuity of Christian churches from the apostles to the third century arose in the context of conflict over the incarnation of Jesus Christ.

Christian Gnosticism

Gnosticism was a broad and diverse movement. It had philosophical, Jewish, and Christian strains. Gnostics were considered heretical by their opponents, Christians who believed in the physical Incarnation of Jesus Christ. Until recently, historians have largely accepted this verdict. But the relatively recent (1945) discovery of the Nag Hammadi

Gnostic texts provides evidence on which to understand the teachings, religious sensibilities, and values of Christian Gnostics on their own terms.

Gnostic groups differed greatly from one another, but they held in common the belief that the human soul is a fragment of the divine imprisoned in an alien medium, bodies and the sensible world. They believed that the soul can be redeemed by realizing its greatness, a greatness resulting from its origin in the spiritual world. The redemption of the soul, for Gnostics, was *from* body and excluded body. When the soul is redeemed, the biodegradable body continues on its way to death and corruption, but without dragging the soul in its wake. The *Treatise on the Resurrection* states: "The visible members [of body] . . . shall not be saved; only the living members which exist within them will arise." Irenaeus reported that for the Gnostic Valentinus:

> The knowledge of the ineffable greatness is itself perfect redemption. . . . Knowledge is the redemption of the inner person. This, however, is not corporeal, since the body is corruptible; nor is it animal, since the soul is the result of a defect, and is, as it were, the habitation of the spirit. The redemption must therefore be spiritual; for they claim that the inner, spiritual person is redeemed through knowledge, that they possess the knowledge of the entire cosmos, and that this is true redemption.
>
> (*Adversus haereses.* I.xxi.4)

Gnostics believed that the world is the evil creation of an inferior god. Creation occurred when souls fell away from the spiritual world into mixture with matter. They held docetic beliefs about Christ's appearance on earth (from the Greek word *dokeo*, "I seem," or *doka*, vision, illusion, or fancy). According to Irenaeus, the Gnostic Basilides described Christ's Incarnation in the following way:

> Then the unborn and unnamed Father. . . . sent his first-begotten mind (and this is he they call Christ), for the freeing of them that believe in him from those who made the world. And he appeared to the nations of them as a man on the earth, and performed deeds of virtue. Wherefore he suffered not, but a certain Simon, a Cyrenian, was impressed to bear his cross for him; and Simon was crucified in ignorance and error, having been transfigured by him so that men would suppose him to be Jesus, while Jesus himself took on the appearance of Simon and stood by and mocked them. . . . If any therefore acknowledge the crucified, he is still a slave and subject to the power of them that made our bodies; but he that denies him is freed from them, and recognizes the ordering of the Unborn Father.
>
> (*Adversus haereses.* I.xxiii.4)

Gnostic teachings had two common characteristics. They claimed to have secret teachings beyond the recorded teachings of Christ and, according to their opponents, they taught that bodies held no religious or moral importance. Irenaeus, Clement, and Tertullian were eager to show that Gnostics' view of human bodies could equally dictate hedonism or asceticism. Body seen as mere obstacle to the spiritual life, and body as instrument of pleasure have fundamentally the same conception of body; both refuse to integrate and give religious meaning to body. In fact, most of the Gnostic groups were ascetic.

Gnostics had a pessimistic view of the sensible world, but an exhilarating view of the human soul. They posited a fundamental opposition between necessity, associated with body and the material world, and the freedom enjoyed by soul. Since liberation is always experienced as liberation *from* an oppressor, Gnostics' claim to transcend body by identifying with spirit comprises the first "liberation theology." Emphasizing the pain of temporality and body's irreversible "progress" toward death, Gnostics sought to energize identification with the "true self," the soul. They extended St Paul's *experiential* dualism to a metaphysical dualism. Many Gnostic hymns have been preserved; they express Gnostics' passionate yearning to be reunited with their home in the spiritual world.

Gnostic Christians believed that bodies and the sensible world are evil. Christians who believed in Christ's real incarnation rejected this explanation of evil, finding it incompatible with belief in creation by God, the Incarnation, and the doctrine of a bodily resurrection. Nevertheless, incarnationist Christians had to account for the existence of evil. The philosophical answer sometimes used, namely, that evil exists to provide a contrast or foil for good so that good can be recognized was, however, less than existentially satisfying.

In the third century, incarnationist Christians' extensive treatment of the role of the devil and demons answered the need to identify and localize the forces of evil. For them, the devil and his demonic hosts were not quaint mythology but existing and active entities, the source of evil and harm. While contemporary secular authors and Jews referred to demons casually, Christian authors, by contrast, found demons essential as an explanation of evil. In contrast to the classical Roman hypothesis that illness was caused by an imbalance of humors within the body, Christians found the cause of illness in the devil and demons, forces external to the person.

An alternative to Gnostic's necessary and permanent evil, demons and the devil were understood as temporary and contingent. They were real enough to cause effects, but they were also ultimately manageable since Christ had already overcome the devil. Thus Christians could cope, for now, and await a final promised victory over the devil and evil. Irenaeus's *Adversus haereses* (*Against the Heresies*) concludes with a lengthy and detailed description of demons' activities.

Irenaeus (d. c.200)

Irenaeus was the first Christian author to articulate a comprehensive picture of human life in its cosmic setting. His concerns were not primarily philosophical, but pastoral; he considered an accurate orientation to history and the cosmos essential for living as a Christian. *Against the Heresies*, in which "each one preaches himself," Irenaeus set Christianity within a narrative that made its basic principles accessible.

Irenaeus described the theologian's task:

> Having more understanding does not mean that people can change the basic idea [of Christian faith]. . . . but it consists in *working out* the things that have been said in parables and building them into the foundation of the faith; in *expounding* the activity of God for the sake of humankind . . . in *showing clearly how* . . . in *declaring* . . . in *showing why* . . . in *teaching* . . . in *unfolding* . . . in *not being silent* . . .
>
> (*De haer.* I.10.2)

Irenaeus can be called a systematic theologian in that he sought to demonstrate the cohesiveness and comprehensiveness of Christian faith. But he was also aware of another, equally important, theological task, that is, to provide an evocative theology that provokes response, focuses energy, and organizes life.

Irenaeus distrusted "skillful language." Because Gnostic leaders attracted "simple hearers" through their flowery rhetoric, Irenaeus claimed, by contrast, to be unable and unwilling to use "power in writing," and "beauties of language and style." Rather, he said, "I write to you out of love, plainly and simply and truly." His claim was, of course, also a rhetorical strategy, for Irenaeus was adept in the use of rich and subtle imagery, strong and moving language, and powerful constructions of ideas.

His theology revolved around a powerful insight, namely, that human life can only *go on* from the place at which it was arrested. Late in the nineteenth century, Freud rediscovered this insight, applying it to individuals. In clinical psychoanalytic and psychotherapeutic practice, the individual remembers and re-experiences the trauma that has paralyzed intellect and deadened feeling. In this process, the repetitiously reinforced pattern of painful and destructive behavior can be dislodged so that psychic life can resume.

Irenaeus described the human race as a whole in this predicament. The disobedience of Adam had traumatized the human race, arresting development, freezing response, and deadening feeling. Christ, the new Adam, reenacted the original crisis situation, the temptation to be one's own god. Adam's response had been to succumb to this temptation, to use his freedom for disobedience; Christ's response was obedience. Because of his solidarity with human beings, by returning to the primal situation and reversing the human response, Christ effectively overcame the human race's deadness, making it possible for human beings to be, in the words of a fourth-century eucharistic prayer, "truly alive."

Recapitulation

Irenaeus used Paul's theory of recapitualation to develop this insight. He began with God, who is "rich, complete, and in need of nothing," containing all things in Godself. Adam, though created in the image and likeness of God, was still, in Paradise, an undeveloped child.

> God made man lord of the earth. . . . but he was small, being but a child. He has to grow and reach full maturity. . . . God prepared a place for him better than this world, a paradise of such beauty and goodness that the Word of God constantly visited it, and walked and talked with man. . . . But man was a child, and his mind was not yet fully mature; and thus he was easily led astray by the deceiver.
>
> (*Apostolic Preaching* 12)

Intended to use his freedom to advance toward closer resemblance to God, Adam, through weakness and immaturity instead disobeyed and lost his likeness to God, although he retained the image of God consisting of reason and free will.

Irenaeus was the first theologian to sketch an idea of what would later be called "original sin." "Through the disobedience of that one man who was first formed out of the untilled earth, the many were made sinners and *lost life*." Just as human beings fell through their solidarity with Adam, they are restored through solidarity with Christ, the second Adam. Christ recapitulates or "sums up" all things in himself: "Our Lord Jesus Christ, the Word of God, in his boundless love, *became what we are that he might make us what he himself is.*"

Irenaeus emphasized the continuity between creation and redemption. He described redemption as a process of growth. Adam's sin disturbed the growth of the human race at a formative stage in the childhood of the race; Christ made growth possible. Irenaeus identified three stages of growth: infancy, maturity, and deification. He emphasized Christ's incarnation and *life* as salvific, not his death.

> He was thirty years old when he came to be baptized. Then, having reached the required age for a teacher, he came to Jerusalem, that all should have a fair opportunity to hear his teaching. He did not appear to be other than what he really was, as they say who hold that his appearance was illusory. No, he appeared as he really was. Thus, as a teacher, he was of a teacher's age; he did not reject humanity nor go beyond its limitations; he did not abrogate the laws for humanity in his own case. Rather he sanctified each stage of life by making possible a likeness to himself. He came to save all through his own person, all, that is, that through him are reborn to God; infants, children, adolescents, young people and old. Therefore he passed through every stage of life. He was made an infant for infants, sanctifying infancy; a child among children, sanctifying childhood, . . . a young man among young men. . . . So also he was a grown man among older men, that he might be a perfect teacher for all, not merely in respect of revelation of the truth, but also in respect of this stage of life. . . . And thus he came even to death, that he might be the first-born from the dead . . . the author of life, who goes before all and shows the way.
>
> (*Adv. haer.* II.22)

[handwritten margin notes: A perfect teacher for all]

Irenaeus used many verbs of process: increase; gain; endure; obey; discipline; grow; progress; persevere, mount: all these occur in a single paragraph (*Adv. haer.* IV.38).

For Irenaeus, the whole process of sin and salvation is necessary. Even evil is necessary and has a positive function within the process: "When God showed his kindness, we learned the good of obedience and the evil of disobedience; our minds perceived *by experience* the distinction between good and evil. . . . How could they be trained in the good without knowledge of its contrary?" (*Adv. haer.* IV.19).

Irenaeus rejected Gnostics' claim that knowledge itself is essential and efficacious. In place of their intricate metaphysical knowledge, Irenaeus insisted on participation and growth in Christ as a practical, daily form of salvation. Human beings "cannot know God in his greatness, for the Father cannot be measured, but by participating in God's love, we ever learn in obeying God." In short, Irenaeus accused Gnostics of knowing too much about God.

> [They] call God indescribable and unnamable and then, as if they had assisted at God's birth, they talk largely about the production and generation of his first begetting. . . . It is not our duty to indulge in conjecture and make guesses about infinite things . . . the knowledge of such matters is to be left to God.
>
> (*Adv. haer.* III.24)

The struggle between Christian Gnostics and incarnationist Christians was a debate among self-identified Christians. The duration, intensity, and acrimony of the struggle demonstrates that Christ's actual body was central to the solidarity incarnationist

Christians experienced with Christ. For incarnationists, a purely spiritual savior could not save. Against the "spirituality" movement of the second century, incarnationist Christians like Irenaeus and Tertullian insisted on the human birth and life of Jesus Christ. Pressured on the one hand by persecution and martyrdom and, on the other hand, by Gnosticism, Christians were forced to decide what they thought about the body's role in redemption. This question prompted the first theological work.

READINGS

Irenaeus, *Against the Heresies*, Book V
Tertullian, *The Prescription against Heretics*
Nag Hammadi, *The Gospel of Truth*

Clement of Alexandria (c.150–c.215)

Clement, bishop of Alexandria at the beginning of the third century, was distressed by the "popularization" of Christian ideas that had led to a bewildering plurality and variety of interpretations. His own writings reflected Christianity's complexity and sophistication: "There are some things which my work will speak in riddles; to some it will display its meaning clearly; some things it will only suggest; it will try to say things secretly, to display in a hidden fashion, to show while keeping silence." According to Clement, Christianity contained precious esoteric knowledge, difficult to access and understand. He tried to shelter this knowledge from interpretations by people who either lacked education or were unprepared by their moral lives to understand it in depth.

Clement's theology occurred in a different location, mood, and social setting from that of the *Actae of Perpetua and Felicitas*, the letters of Ignatius of Antioch, and even Justin's *Apology*. In Clement's theology, preoccupation with an immanent return of Christ to the earth or with the personal apocalypse of martyrdom changed to interest in the *process* of Christian life. The earliest Christians believed that they would not need to carry on for long. Their writings described Jesus, not as the rational *logos* of the apologists, but as breaking the power of the demons and ushering in a new age, last days. But by the third century, if Christians were not to lose hope when Christ did not appear as expected, a change of orientation was needed. The first Christian literature that focused on practicing Christianity over a lifetime came from Alexandria.

In fact, settling down to practicing Christianity with the expectation of a normal lifespan was premature. Empire-wide fierce persecution was yet to come, as the Decian persecution in the middle of the third century and the Diocletian persecution early in the fourth century brought unprecedented terror and suffering. Premature or not, however, attention to daily Christian living represented a significant change of perspective in Christian literature. Clement's writings examined in detail what could be integrated in a Christian life and what needed to be excluded.

Christians in Alexandria
By the end of the second century a wealthy and flourishing Christian community existed in Alexandria. It had seldom been persecuted and had already moved from house

churches to buildings built especially for worship. Under these conditions of relative stability the Egyptian church committed itself to the instruction of catechumens, polemics against Gnostic rivals, and theological construction.

This work was carried on at the famous catechetical school of Alexandria. The school, open to both sexes and all ages, trained converts according to their intellects and abilities. There was a short course and a long course. The short course consisted of memorizing and reciting the facts of the creed. The long course included philosophical and theological instruction.

Third-century theological education was divided into three parts. The first part aimed at strengthening the student's ability to observe and reason by the study of geometry, physiology, and astronomy. The second stage consisted of philosophy; the classical poets and philosophers were studied, especially Plato. The second stage culminated in ethics, which was taught as discussions of definitions of good and evil, justice, and virtue. In the third stage, theology was the subject. The first two stages were preparation for studying theology.

Clement was the second principal of the catechetical school. His emphasis on living the Christian *life* came from his belief that Christ's promised return had already taken place with the coming of Jesus, the *logos* made flesh. He was the first Christian author to describe Christian life, faithfully lived, as equal in value to martyrdom.

Clement's theology

Clement's theology had two mutually dependent foci, the establishment of Christian theology as the apex and goal of classical philosophy, and moral and ascetic teachings. In the context of the catechetical school, Clement wanted to correct *both* what he saw as the stubbornly unreflecting faith of simple "Jesus believers," and sophisticated intellectuals' attraction of to Gnostics' secret knowledge. He also wanted to modify what he considered Christians' exaggerated respect for Greek philosophy. He taught that all Greek wisdom was learned from the so-called "barbarians," non Greek-speaking northern European tribes that were little known and consistently feared and vilified by Mediterranean people. But Clement himself was learned in Platonic philosophy. Thus, rather than renouncing it, he positioned philosophy as a "preparatory discipline" to the study of Christian theology; Greek philosophy was to be the "handmaiden" of theology.

Clement taught that faith and knowledge are mutually interdependent. Faith is sufficient for salvation, but the mature Christian, whom Clement (confusingly) called the "true gnostic," must seek a higher understanding. His doctrine of redemption highlights the intellect: "It was to us who had strayed *in our minds* that the Savior came." A "true gnostic's" knowledge differed from that of Gnostics in that Clement did not picture a series of cosmic emanations and falls from the world of pure spirit. His doctrine of God, his understanding of Christ (Christology), and his anthropology all rest on the doctrine of creation.

Clement's treatise "On Spiritual Perfection" (*Stromateis* VII) described a cosmic order in which the universe, created by the power of the *logos*, depends on "one original principle." It is a graded, rank-ordered series, reaching from the original principle to "the first and second and third gradations and so, even down to ourselves, ranks below ranks are appointed, all saving and being saved by the instrumentality of the One." All things come from the One. There is no second source. In his theology, cosmic hierarchy replaced Gnostic dualism. Clement used Plato's metaphor of a magnet attracting iron rings to describe the Holy Spirit's power of attraction.

Those who choose virtue and contemplation are irresistibly drawn to "the highest mansion." Progress toward God consists of beginning where one is – in the lower ranks of creation – to discipline the mind by knowledge and the body by virtue, and thus to move up the ranks to "that which is lovely." But not everyone chooses to undertake the ascent. The two causes of inertia are ignorance and weakness. To overcome ignorance, Christ revealed true philosophy: "That which the chief of philosophy (Plato) merely guessed at, the disciples of Christ have both apprehended and proclaimed." Weakness can be overcome by ascetic disciplines.

Clement's use of Platonic philosophy is evident in his anthropology. He pictured humans as dual, made up of body and soul, and ill at ease in composite form. The life-long task of the "true gnostic" is to cultivate the soul's liberation from the body's necessities. This definition of humanity led Clement dangerously close to docetism, the belief that Jesus Christ came to earth in appearance only. Clement affirmed the real flesh of Christ, but it played little part in his theology of redemption:

> In the case of the Savior it would be absurd to suppose that his body demanded [food, drink, sleep, etc.] for his stay [on earth]. For he ate, not because of bodily needs, since his body was supported by holy power, but so that his companions might not entertain a false notion about him, as in fact certain men did later, namely that he had been manifested only in appearance. He himself was, and remained "untroubled by passion;" no movement of the passions, either pleasure or pain, found its way into him.
>
> (*Stromateis* VI.9)

Clement said that sin was not transmitted from Adam and Eve through reproduction. That interpretation, he said, assumes a Gnostic principle of substantial evil. There is no inherited pollution, and it would be incompatible with the Incarnation to consider the body evil. Nevertheless, embodiment is distracting, due to its vulnerability and finitude that obscure soul's clarity of vision. Body is, however, a perfect *tool* for soul's learning.

> Without the body how could the divine plan for us achieve its end? Surely the Lord himself ... came in the flesh. . . . [And] does not the Savior who heals the soul also heal the body of its passions? But if the flesh were hostile to the soul, Christ would not have raised an obstacle to the soul by strengthening with good health the hostile flesh.
>
> (*Stromateis* III.17)

Commenting on Plato's famous phrase, *soma/sema* ("body is the tomb of soul)," Clement says that body has the potential for being *either* tomb or temple. If the passions that humans have "because of the body" are not to capture the soul's energy and "bind it with the fetters of the flesh," one's mind must be disciplined by knowledge and one's body by ascetic practices.

What did Clement mean by "asceticism"? Later ascetics who sometimes engaged in body-damaging practices are not typical of most Christian asceticism. For Clement, as for classical authors, the primary areas of human life in which asceticism should be practiced were diet and sex. His objection to sex was Aristotle's objection, namely that while engaged in sexual activity, one simply doesn't *think* well! Yet it was not sex itself that Clement found problematic, but being "under the *control of the passions*."

Clement reasoned that Christ gave Christians "free and sovereign power and has allowed us to live *as we choose*." He shared with philosophers and Gnostics a horror of automatic, socialized behavior. But humans' freedom does not imply that behavior is morally indifferent; "how is it possible to become like the Lord and have knowledge of God if one is *subject* to physical pleasure?" The key word is "subject." The best contemporary translation is "compulsive." He quoted Plato: "I escaped from sexuality as if I had escaped from a wild and raging tyrant," adding, "let us not call *bondage* to pleasure freedom, as if bitterness were sweet."

Thus far, Clement's and Aristotle's ideas of sex are indistinguishable. The specifically Christian element in Clement's teaching came from his insistence that Christian asceticism is God-given; it is not a matter of teeth-gritting will power: "the soul that has to concentrate upon endurance is lost." Recourse to will power defeats the purpose of freeing a person from compulsive behavior for one must still focus on (avoiding) the compulsive action. Like the courage to suffer martyrdom for the faith, celibacy is God's gift. "Our aim is not that when a person feels desire, he should get the better of it." Rather, the aim of asceticism, whether celibacy or marriage, is *integration*: "In us it is not only the spirit that ought to be sanctified, but also our behavior, manner of life, and our body" (*Stromateis* III.7). Far from rejecting sex, Clement favored marriage as an optimum condition for learning.

> True manhood is shown not in the choice of a celibate life; on the contrary, the prize in the contest of men is won by him who has trained himself in the discharge of the duties of husband and father and by the supervision of a household, regardless of pleasure and pain – by him, I say, who in the midst of his solicitude for his family shows himself inseparable from the love of God and rises superior to every temptation which assails him through children and wife and slaves and possessions. . . . *He who has no family is in most respects untried.*
>
> (*Stromateis* III.70; emphasis added)

Clement's *Paedagogus* (Instructor, or Teacher) painstakingly discussed many aspects of Christian comportment, finding little that is indifferent to Christian life. Clement was the only Christian author of his time who gave advice on men's, as well as women's, dress. He advised on the Christian way to eat, drink, walk, sit, and behave at banquets. His advice on the Christian way of sitting for men is: "Let them not have their feet crossed, nor place one thigh on another, nor apply the hand to the chin. For it is vulgar not to bear oneself without support . . . and perpetually moving and changing one's position is a sign of frivolousness." Even sneezing should be done in the Christian way:

> If anyone is attacked with sneezing, just as in the case of hiccup, he must not startle those near him with the explosion, and so give proof of his bad breeding; but the hiccup is to be quietly transmitted with the expiration of the breath, the mouth being composed becomingly, and not gaping and yawning like the tragic masks. . . . In a word, the Christian is characterized by composure, tranquility, calmness, and peace.
>
> (*Paedagogus* II.7)

Although such instructions may strike us as humorous, Clement's attention to behavior was similar to classical philosophers' fascination with the practices that create a carefully chosen and cultivated self. Like his contemporaries, Clement believed that a chosen self was a male prerogative. As in the catechetical school, women were not excluded, but if they participated they were thought of as "becoming male," and there is no evidence that any women undertook the long course of instruction. His project was nothing less than the construction of "the Christian body," part of his theology of integration – cosmic, intellectual, and practical.

Christian life included self-discipline, but only for the sake of *more life*. Clement advocated asceticism for freeing one from *attachment* to pleasures. But he criticized Gnostics for setting "too ascetic a tone;" they proclaim, he wrote, "the necessity of continence on the ground of opinions which . . . arise from hatred of what God has created." For Clement, hatred of creation does not provide an adequate stimulus for learning. Quite the opposite: "Starting with admiration for creation which he brings with him as evidence for this capacity to receive knowledge, he becomes an eager disciple of the Lord. . . . His *admiration prompts him to believe*. Proceeding from this point he does his best to learn in every way" (*Stromateis* VII.11).

Admiration requires freedom, and the condition of freedom is detachment: "We ought to behave as strangers and pilgrims . . . as people who are not passionately attached to the created world but use it with all gratitude and with a sense of exaltation beyond it." The sensible world, riches, and the bodily beauty of one's friends can be enjoyed with gratitude when all of human life is ordered to "Life itself." The quality of life as spiritual discipline is joy. "Throughout the day and night one is filled with joy, uttering and doing the precepts of the Lord. Not only at dawn, on rising, and at midday, but also when walking and lying down, dressing and undressing . . . carrying God within and being carried by God" (*Stromateis* VII.12).

The final objective of Christian life is deification: "The Word of God became human that you may learn from him how it may be that humans can become God." Clement put daily advance in the place of apocalyptic expectations. Meantime, he says, we live joyously: "all our life is a festival; being persuaded that God is everywhere present on all sides we praise him as we till the ground, we sing hymns as we sail the sea, we feel God's inspiration in all that we do."

READING

Clement of Alexandria, *Stromateis*, Books III and VII

Origen of Alexandria (d. 254)

Two of the most interesting men of the third century, Plotinus and Origen, were taught by the same teacher, Ammonius Sacchas, of whom little is known. The Platonic philosopher Plotinus (d. 270) focused and developed the mystical strain of Platonism. His influence has extended through medieval Christian thought to Renaissance thinkers and beyond them to our own time. The Christian Origen (d. 254) developed a highly influential method of scriptural exegesis and a distinctive theology. His method of scriptural interpretation established the importance of reason in Christian faith. He also continued and extended the work of Irenaeus and Clement in describing a cosmic and temporal setting for human existence.

Origen's life

Most of the details of Origen's life come from the fourth century historian, Eusebius. After several generations in which there were no persecutions in Alexandria, and churches had become large and secure, the Severan persecution broke out in 202. Origen's father was martyred, along with many other Christians. According to Eusebius, the young Origen's zeal to share his father's martyrdom was so great that his mother hid all his clothes so that he could not leave the house. At this time, Clement was head of the catechetical school in Alexandria. When Clement died in 215, Origen became head at the age of eighteen. At least seven of his pupils were martyred. He visited them in prison; he was in court when they were tried; he embraced them when they were about to be executed; and he accompanied their bodies to the cemetery, and then returned to resume his teaching.

Later, Origen expressed nostalgia for those "good old days." It used to be easier, he said, to tell who was a real Christian and who was not.

> Those were the days when Christians really were faithful, when the noble martyrdoms were taking place, when after conducting the martyrs' bodies to the cemetery we returned to meet together, and the entire church was present without being afraid, and the catechumens were being catechized during the very time of the martyrdom and while people were dying who had confessed the truth unto death. . . . Then we knew and saw wonderful and miraculous signs. Then there were true believers, few in number but faithful, treading the straight and narrow way that leads to life. But now when we have become many, out of the multitude that profess piety there are extremely few who are attaining to the election of God and to blessedness.
>
> (*Homily in Jeremiah* 4.3)

Origen wrote these words in a period of peace before the outbreak of persecution in which he was imprisoned, tortured, and subsequently died of his injuries.

Origen was an enthusiast, an ascetic, and a passionate Christian. Eusebius reported that he castrated himself in order to be undistracted by sexual desire. However, Origen's own exegesis of Matthew 19.12 ("some have even made themselves eunuchs for the sake of the kingdom of heaven") makes this doubtful. This passage, Origen said, is clearly one that has no literal interpretation, but only a spiritual sense. Yet some Christian men either strongly considered or actually practiced this extreme measure, for church councils well into the fourth century repeatedly forbade self-castration. Clearly, some zealous third-century Christians considered management of sexuality critically important to a Christian life.

Like Irenaeus and Clement, Origen explored the complex implications of Christian faith. He was influential in three areas: 1) biblical exegesis; 2) speculative theology; and 3) Christian piety. Yet in spite of the tremendous influence of his method of scriptural exegesis, he was never sainted or given the title "doctor of the church," for his theology came under suspicion at the end of the fourth century and was formally condemned by three Councils. His writings were subsequently largely destroyed, surviving only in

Greek fragments and Latin translations. Methodius, his contemporary, accused him of teaching the eternity of creation, the pre-existence of souls, and that the resurrection body is spiritual. Methodius said that Origen taught that since the circle is the perfect shape the resurrection body will be spherical. The fragmented condition of his writings makes it impossible to tell whether he actually taught the doctrines ascribed to him.

Origen himself was strongly concerned with orthodoxy. "My wish," he wrote, "is to be truly a man of the church, to be called by the name of Christ and not by the name of any heretic, to have this name which is blessed over all the earth. I desire to be, and to be called, a Christian in my works as in my thoughts." Despite the condemnation of his theology, Origen had an influence on Christian thought comparable to that of Augustine or Thomas Aquinas. He learned Hebrew in order to consult with contemporary rabbis about historical and linguistic problems. He worked for 40 years on an edition of the Hebrew Bible, the *Hexapla*, in which the Hebrew text, a Greek transliteration of the Hebrew text, and four different Greek versions of the text were arranged in parallel columns. He also presented double commentaries on many texts in the Jewish manner. His massive *corpus* of expositions of scripture includes close to a thousand titles.

Scriptural exegesis
Origen used two methods of scriptural interpretation whose goal was to reveal scriptures' richness of meaning, typology, and allegory. Typology refers to the interpretation of characters and events from the Old Testament as types, or symbols of characters and events in the Christian scriptures. For example, Adam was a type of Christ, the "second Adam." Typology provided the basis for a "supersessionist" theology that understood history as the progressive unfolding of God's redemptive purpose, begun in the Jewish people, and continued and completed in Christianity. In this view, Christianity has superseded, or taken the place of, Judaism so that Judaism no longer exists as an independent religion. Throughout Christian history, many authors, even those who, like Origen, respected Jews and learned from them, subscribed to supersessionist theology. For example, Augustine stated, "The whole content of [Hebrew] scriptures is either directly or indirectly about Christ." After Christ's coming, he said, Jews became "a desk for the Christians, bearing the law and the prophets, and testifying to the doctrine of the Church" (*Contra Faustum Manichaean* XII.7. 23). Supersessionist theology has been decisively criticized and rejected only in the later half of the twentieth century.

The second method of scriptural exegesis Origen introduced was allegory, a method introduced by the first-century Jewish philosopher, Philo of Alexandria. Origen taught that the *whole* of scripture, not only certain difficult passages, has several layers of meaning. Scripture often uses figurative language, he said, that cannot be taken literally. He explained his system of interpretation and his reasons for it in *On First Principles*.

> There are three ways in which the meaning of the Holy Scriptures should be inscribed in the soul of every Christian. First, the simpler sort are edified by what may be called the "body" of scripture. . . . Secondly, those who have made some progress are edified by, as it were, the "soul." Thirdly, the perfect . . . are edified by the "spiritual" law. . . . Thus, as a person consists of body, soul, and spirit, so also does the scripture which is the gift of God designed for human salvation.
>
> (*On First Principles* I.11.4)

The "body" of scripture contains the literal or historical meaning; the "soul" carries the moral lesson to be gathered from the passage; the "spirit" conveys the spiritual meaning. The "simple" are capable of understanding the moral sense when it is pointed out to them. For example, the moral meaning of Paul's statement in I Corinthians 9.9, "Thou shalt not muzzle the threshing ox," applies, Origen said, to the right of Christian teachers to financial support. Little of the literal or moral senses appear, however, in Origen's writings. Origen thought the spiritual meaning was by far the most interesting and important.

Origen taught that the Holy Spirit has buried rich truths in scripture to instruct those who are in the process of ascent. The spiritual sense requires a skilled interpreter, for it must be consistent with the whole of Christian teaching. Origen repeated Irenaeus' insistence that tradition was the only trustworthy key to interpreting scripture. He believed that the Holy Spirit deliberately placed difficulties and impossibilities in scripture in order to make people search diligently for the deeper meanings.

Preoccupied with the richness of scripture, Origen thought it quite impossible for any scripture to have *only* literal or historical meaning. He wrote, the "*logos* is incarnate in the flesh of the holy text." He thought of scripture as a vast ocean or forest, limited only by the interpreter's ability. He taught that the interpretation of scripture was a grace or "charisma." When the interpreter's whole being is absorbed, and every faculty exercised, in understanding the scripture, the interpreter enters a spiritual passion in which interpreter and object are united.

Origen's theology   Origen believed that, taken literally, the Bible contained too much human activity and too little about spiritual cosmic forces. He said that the gospels *conceal* the eternal Christ within the life and record of the historical Jesus. His theology focused on the supernatural plane, sharing philosophers' and Gnostics' excitement with bold visionary and speculative constructions, relating human life to universal space and endless time. He believed that human minds are capable of grasping truth simultaneously in personal, historical, and cosmic dimensions.

Origen's theology began with the premise that on "points not clearly set forth in scripture," speculation is appropriate. However, speculation should be subject to two limitations: nothing may be attributed to God that is incompatible with scriptural descriptions of God's goodness; and "we must be careful always to strive to preserve reverence to God and Christ and to avoid subordinating reverence to intellectual inquiry" (*On First Principles* III.1.17).

Origen began with God, the source and summit of the chain of being – "the fount from which originates all intellectual existence or mind." Using a popular Platonic metaphor, he pictured God as the sun whose first, most immediate splendor or ray, is Christ. The Holy Spirit is the brightness of God at second remove. A hierarchy within God is evident in this description as in Origen's instruction that Christians should pray *to* God *through* Christ.

Before the creation of bodies and the sensible world, God surrounded Godself with "a world of pure minds;" *this* was God's intentional creation. But the pure minds "were seized with surfeit of the divine love and contemplation and turned toward the worse." Origen speaks of a "cooling" of the attraction by which the minds clung to God. This process, once begun, became a "gradual sinking, a decline by degrees." The fall away from the One introduced diversity: "By reason of the faculty of free will, variety and diversity had taken hold of individual souls, so that one was attached to its author by a warmer and another with a weaker or feebler love." However, the fall, caused by the individual will, can also be reversed by the will.

The creation of the sensible world followed automatically from "what the minds had already done with themselves." "In proportion to their particular sins they were enveloped in bodies as a punishment, either finer in substance or grosser, ethereal, aerial, or fleshly." The devil fell farther than the other minds, but his place at the outer reaches of being is not permanent. Origen did not believe in divine punishment; rather, "Each sinner kindles for himself the flame of his own fire and is not plunged into a fire that had been previously kindled by someone else or which existed before him. Of this fire, the food and material are our sins." Individuals are disposed to good or evil through upbringing and the influence of environment as well as by Adam's example.

For Origen, punishment and "learning experiences" were identical. Learning, which began with the soul's fall into a body, is temporary and remedial: "This training of ours in the body extends over a very long period, namely up till the time the bodies themselves with which we are encompassed are found worthy of incorruption and immortality" (*On First Principles* II.3.2). God brings fire into the world, Origen wrote, "as the benefactor of them who stand in need of the discipline of fire." This purifying fire is "chastisement and healing at the same time." He said that scriptural descriptions of punishment are not to be taken literally except "in order to terrify those who cannot by any other means be saved from the fire of their sins" (*On First Principles* II.10.4).

Origen's universe was *dynamic*, constantly in motion. Free will, which originally initiated mind's descent into body, continues to determine its cosmic position. "The will's freedom always moves in the direction either of good or of evil, nor can the rational sense ever exist without some movement." Origen's universe was also a *connected* universe: "All rational natures, including God, the Son, and the Holy Spirit, all angels, authorities, dominions and other powers, and even human beings by virtue of the soul's dignity are of one substance, of one nature, but of different wills." The temporal world is not immense enough to contain this process. Origen envisioned a "cycle of worlds" in which human souls are moved by their own momentum, and "last judgments," far from final, are simply the impetus for new movement. There *is* an end, Origen said, a great last judgment which will annihilate matter and restore the perfect unity of the original creation in which "God shall be all and in all." But he also suggested that perhaps the end is not really the *end*. A new falling away will occur; free will requires it, and the process will begin again.

Piety

How did Origen understand redemption? The incarnation of Christ was necessary, he said, because "no created being can approach God without a guide." Christ's redemptive work broke humans' fall, interrupting the downward momentum and reversing its direction. By identification with Christ, Christians can begin the long climb. Christ's real humanity was able to bind together "both the weakness of human flesh and the willingness of the spirit." Origen was the first theologian to emphasize the human soul of Christ as the faculty that connected God and humanity: "[Of] this soul, then, acting as a medium between God and the flesh (for it was not possible for the nature of God to mingle with a body apart from some medium) there is born the God-man, the medium being, that existence to whose nature it was not contrary to assume a body."

Origen's homilies exemplify early Christian preaching. They demonstrate his emotional love for the human Jesus, sharer of human burdens, yet in a unique way suffering *productively* to release human beings from the power of death. Origen's God is not an unchanging, unfeeling God. "All who wish to follow Christ can do so, though overcome by death, since death has now no strength against them; for no one who is with Jesus can be seized by death. . . . He does away with the irrationality and deadness in us" (*Commentary On John* I. 20).

Origenism
Origen's writing and his passionately committed life exemplified his statement, "He does away with the irrationality and deadness in us." Yet by the end of the fourth century, "Origenism" came to be seen as a heresy. The following teachings, ascribed to Origen, were condemned: the pre-existence of souls; the subordination of the second and third persons of the trinity; universal salvation (which prohibited belief in a permanent afterlife of reward or punishment); denial of the identity of mortal and resurrection bodies; and metempsychosis, or transmigration of souls. "Origenism" was condemned by a Council in Alexandria in 400; the condemnation was reiterated by a Council in Constantinople in 543 and again by the Second Council of Constantinople in 553.

Yet Origen's influence was enormous. The medievalist Beryl Smalley said, "To write a history of Origenist influence on the West would be tantamount to writing a history of western exegesis."

READING

Origen, *On First Principles*, Books I and II

Trinitarian controversy in the second and third centuries

One of the most central Christian beliefs was belief that God is triune, but strenuous efforts to find an acceptable description of the trinity continued for a century and a half. Our understanding of trinitarian debates is complicated by the fact that geographical and linguistic diversity makes it difficult to differentiate positions that seem very similar. Proposed descriptions of the trinity not only use different languages – Greek or Latin – but they also use different metaphors, models, and images. The debates were intense because the stakes were high. How was Christ, through whom Christians received salvation, related to God?

The *Oxford Dictionary of the Christian Church* describes the trinity as a mystery; it can "neither be known by unaided human reason nor cogently demonstrated by reason after it has been revealed." Yet trinitarian controversy was not "academic," meaning (in current public usage), of no practical importance. The various trinitarian positions featured different emotional, psychological, and political perspectives. The way the trinity was conceptualized also intimately affected preaching and prayer.

Before we discuss trinitarian positions, trinitarian and Christological controversies, though related, must be distinguished. Trinitarian debates concerned the relationships within and among the persons of the trinity; they were attempts to understand and articulate God's unity in three persons. Until the end of the fourth century, the relationship of Father and Son focused the debate. The Holy Spirit was not definitively integrated into the Creed until the Council of Constantinople (381). Christological debates occurred a bit later, and were focused on the relationship of human and divine in Jesus Christ.

From the earliest writings, Christians affirmed that Christ the Redeemer was God, not a lower order of being. The earliest surviving sermon after the New Testament began: "Brethren, we ought to think of Jesus Christ as of God, as the judge of living and dead." The earliest martyrdom account, that of Polycarp, said, "It will be impossible for us to forsake Christ. . . . For him, being the son of God we adore, but the martyrs we cherish." The earliest outsider comment on the Christian Church, that of the provincial governor Pliny, described Christians gathering before sunrise "singing a hymn to Christ as though to a god."

These statements seem unambiguous enough; what, then, were the problems that generated the struggle for precise definition? First, the claim that God *suffered* was problematic to many Christians. Second, it was difficult to translate the language of devotion into *teaching* about Christian belief. The poetic language of sermons or hymns can appear contradictory when an attempt is made to *explain*. Hymns characteristically pile one image on another without concern for the divergent meanings conveyed. Third, different audiences required different emphases. Against Roman polytheism, Christians affirmed monotheism. Against Jewish monteheism, however, Christians insisted on the triadic nature of God. The Platonic description of the cosmos of being as flowing from its source by a ranked series of emanations provided an explanation that was attractive to many, but at the cost of picturing Christ as less than God. Using this image, Origen described God as the sun whose first ray was Christ.

Trinitarian descriptions were also intimately related to Christian experience. Christians agreed that Christ came as *logos* to reveal *knowledge* of God; if the redeemer is thought of as an enlightener, it is important to describe the content of that enlightenment. But Christ also brought *life*. The double focus on Christ as *knowledge* and as *life* made it necessary to describe how Christ affected both thought and experience.

Scripture did not help. There is no explicit doctrine of the trinity in the New Testament although references to God frequently take a three-fold pattern. But there are also passages that seem to be mutually contradictory – passages that emphasize Christ's adoption by God, usually at his baptism or resurrection; passages of identity in which Jesus Christ is identified simply as "Lord;" passages of distinction refer to two Lords, as when the Father talks to the Son. Finally, passages of derivation refer to the Father as "greater;" these passages imply that Jesus Christ came *from* God and thus must necessarily be *less than* God. So questions emerged: Was the divine that appeared on earth identical with the supreme divine who rules heaven and earth? Or should Christ be thought of as a demi-god? How is the divine in Christ related to the divine in the Father?

By the third century, different theological interests began to appear in the Greek East and the Latin West. The main trinitarian positions are discussed in the following sections.

Economic trinitarianism

Economic trinitarianism had two major representatives, Hippolytus (d. c.236), who was the last western author to write in Greek, and Tertullian (d. 225), the first western author to write in Latin. Tertullian, who first used the term "trinity," explained what he meant by the trinity: The Father is the sole source of deity, but God's unity is a philosophical, not a mathematical unity, the unity of one principle rather than one entity. Thus: "God's unity is subject to the disposition of the single godhead into Father, Son, and Holy Spirit in order to create and redeem."

> Now all the simple people – and they are always in the majority of believers – are dismayed by the idea of "economy." For the rule of faith brings them from the polytheism of the world at large to the one and only God, and they do not understand that while believing in the unity of God they must believe it together with his "economy." They assume that the plurality and distribution of the trinity implies a division of the unity: but the truth is that the unity in deriving the trinity from itself is not destroyed thereby but dispensed. And so they make a fuss about our preaching "two or three gods," and claim that they are worshippers of one God, not seeing that a unity reasonably distributed constitutes the truth. . . . "Monarchy" means simply the rule of one individual; but that monarchy, because it is the rule of one, does not preclude the monarch, who enjoys that rule, from having a son . . . or administrating his monarchy by agents of his own choosing. . . . Do you consider that the component parts of monarchy, its outward proofs, its instruments, and all that gives a monarchy its strength and prestige – do you consider these are destructive of it, as the rule of one? Of course not. I wish you would concern yourself with the *sense* and not with the *sound* of a word.
>
> (*Adversus Praxean* 3)

Tertullian's picture of the trinity was based on a temporal model in which differentiation occurred at different times and in different activities. The three-foldness of God's being was made explicit in creation and redemption: "God engendered the Word, using the Word to create the universe, and God's Wisdom to adorn or order it." He described the Spirit as "third from the Father and the Son, just as fruit derived from the shoot is third from the root."

A concept as abstract as that of the trinity necessarily depends heavily on the metaphors used to explain it. Tertullian used metaphors of root, tree, and fruit; river and fountain, sun and rays, and ruler and agents. These metaphors implied a hierarchical arrangement of the persons of the trinity. Hippolytus also argued against the assertion that the Father and Son are identical, for that would mean that the Father was born, suffered, and died. Hippolytus avoided this by saying that God's *power* is one, but differentiated according to God's activities. Both Tertullian and Hippolytus used another image that balanced their model of one God with several functions or activities. The Word or Son, Tertullian said, is a *person*, "a second in addition to the Father."

The idea of God as three "persons," however, should not assume twenty-first century ideas of "person." By "person," we usually refer to an integrated complex of mental, physical, and psychological functions. But the Latin word *persona* (Greek *prosopon*) means face, expression, role, or mask. The emphasis is on the external aspect of God, on God's concrete presentation to human beings. For Tertullian the word "person" connoted a *distinction*, not a separation between individuals, as when the same actor, putting on a mask, plays a role; putting on another mask, she plays a different role. The one "person" has not been divided, but extended.

Tertullian used two other words that became important in later stages of the controversy, although Terullian himself did not place special emphasis on them. The Greek word *hypostasis* (Latin: *substantia*) is a biblical term. It indicated an external concrete object, an object in relation to other objects. (Hebrews I. 3 calls Christ the image of the Father's *hypostasis*.) The second term, *ousia*, is more abstract; it indicates an object whose individuality is revealed by an internal analysis. Originally, *hypostasis* and *ousia* were synonymous; they meant real being, existence, or essence. They were differentiated in the process of trinitarian debate.

Subordinationist trinitarianism

The second Trinitarian position explicitly subordinated the Son to the Father. Origen exemplified this position. He emphasized the distinctiveness of each aspect of the trinity, claiming that the Son is both *agenetos* (uncreated), participating directly in the substance of God's being, and *genetos* (created), in that he is not himself the source of that being. However, this formulation was either too confusing or too subtle to have the same influence as his practical instruction to pray *to* the Father, but *through* the Son: "We should not pray to any generate being, not even to Christ, but only to the God and Father of the universe, to whom our Savior himself prayed" (*De orat.* 15.1). He also said that "the Son is transcended by the Father in as great or greater a degree than that by which he himself and the Holy Spirit transcend the best of all other beings."

Origen's student, Dionysius of Alexandria, went beyond Origen's teaching to assert something close to tritheism, separating God into three powers, three separate hypostases – three divinities. Dionysius of Rome censured Dionysius of Alexandria, revealing the different concerns of Eastern and the Western theologians. To Western theologians, the divine *unity* was entirely clear, and important to protect. They found the distinctions between the persons of the trinity "mysterious," although they affirmed the reality of these distinctions. In the strongly platonic climate of the East, the instinct for locating the "rung," or distinctiveness of each entity was strong. These different interests confused the debate.

Monarchian trinitarianism

Monarchianism was based on the fear that God's unity was endangered by emphasis on God's threeness. There were two kinds of Monarchianism: Sabellianism (modalistic) and dynamic (or adoptionist) monarchianism.

In the early third century Sabellians taught that Father, Son, and Spirit are one and the same; they are *modes* or aspects of the same being, perhaps temporary and successive. The distinctions do not correspond to anything in the ultimate nature of God.

Sabellius (d. c.217) is reported to have said, "As there are 'diversities of gifts but the same spirit,' so also the Father is the same, but is expanded into the Son and the Spirit." (Ps. Athanasius, *Fourth Oration*: 25). Sabellius wanted to call God the "Sonfather."

Adoptionist (or dynamic) monarchianism taught that Christ was a human being on whom God's spirit descended in a unique way. Adoptionist monarchians quoted Psalm 2.7: "You are my Son, this day have I begotten you." Paul of Samosata (fl. third century) taught that the Incarnate Christ could be compared to the prophets on whom God's Word had also rested.

None of these positions were formally excluded by scripture or by third-century creeds. The old Roman Symbol, which later became the Apostle's Creed, read simply: "Do you believe in God the Father the Almighty?" And "Do you believe in Christ Jesus the Son of God?" By the end of the third century, the second phrase read (as today): "His only Son, our Lord." In short, creedal definition did not constrain theological speculation on the nature of the trinity. Rather, Trinitarian debates led to efforts to make creeds more precise.

Although third-century differences of perspective in the East and the West should not be exaggerated, Eastern theologians tended to understand the trinity as connected, mutually engaged yet *different* beings. Eastern theologians affirmed unity, but *described* differentiation. In the West, on the other hand, theologians emphasized unity, differentiating within the unity of God only roles or activities. These may appear to be two sides of the same coin, but a monistic view of God implies that *ultimately* the relationships within the source of reality are not *real*, but collapse into unity. Emphasis on the distinctiveness of the persons within the trinity implies that relationships, not simply qualities, are to be found at the level of ultimate reality. If God's essence is relationship, different but related entities are assumed.

Trinitarian conflict was not settled in the third century. It was to be the major issue at the Council of Nicaea in 325. Even then, the council was able to achieve resolution only for as long as Constantine lived to enforce the resolution.

READING

Tertullian, *Against Praxean*

3   Constructing Christian Churches

Church organization

Third-century Christian communities struggled to define themselves, a process that consisted of difficult and contested decisions about what could be included and what must be excluded. Christians attempted to integrate what they considered the best of their society's cultural and intellectual resources, and they excluded aspects they found incompatible with Christian faith. Sometimes identification *with*, and distancing *from*, occurred simultaneously. For example, Christians were eager to be seen as continuous with Judaism in order to benefit from the respect Jews enjoyed as an ancient and honored religion. Yet they did not want to be confused with Jews; every Christian author wrote a treatise or a large section of a treatise against the Jews.

Christians' other-worldly orientation functioned as criticism of, and resistance to, "this world." But although Christians considered their beliefs and values to be counter-cultural, they also appropriated some of the values of the surrounding culture. For example, the social arrangements of Christian communities reflected rather than over-turned or challenged those of contemporary society. Male leadership in Christian churches, a debated issue in the first and second centuries, was firmly in place by the middle of the third century. On the other hand, Christians rejected their culture's belief in fate or determinism, insisting on human freedom and responsibility.

In deciding which aspects of Roman culture to include or exclude, Christians responded to particular social circumstances, not to abstract principles. Against popular belief in astrology, against Stoic theories of necessity, and against Gnostics, Christians emphasized the ability to *choose*. Irenaeus accused Gnostics of believing that "everything passes away by necessity into that state out of which it was created. And they even make God the slave of this necessity, so that even God cannot add immortality to that which is mortal" (*Adv. Haer.* II.14). Tertullian wrote: "God sets before human beings good and evil, life and death. The entire order of disciplines is arranged through precepts, as God calls, threatens, and exhorts. This could not be so if human beings were not free, endowed with a will, and capable of obedience and resistance" (*Adv. Marcion* 2.5.7).

Because of their insistence on humans' ability to choose, third-century Christians did not develop a doctrine of original sin. Irenaeus pictured the human race in solidarity with Adam's disobedience, but he insisted that this condition was already overcome by Christ's obedience. He wrote: "All people are of the same nature, able both to hold fast to what is good, and on the other hand, having also the power to cast it from them and not to do it" (*Adv. Haer.* IV.37).

Practical questions about the nature of the Church were related to understandings of human nature. Was the Church composed only of the "pure," or did it also include noticeably imperfect people? What was the Church's function in salvation? How should authority be organized and recognized? How should penitence be conducted? Conflicting points of view developed on each of these questions.

Prophecy

Supported by scriptural writings and Christian experience, the existence of ecstatic prophecy was undeniable. Yet a high respect for prophecy was at odds with the establishment of orderly communities. Prophecy was notoriously unpredictable and volatile, erratic both in the chosen prophet and in what was prophesied. Ignatius of Antioch, bishop, prophet, and martyr, was the first Christian author to assign legitimate prophecy to bishops. As a prophet and bishop himself, he testified to the ultimate authority, not of prophecy, but of the bishop:

> I cried out while I was with you, I spoke with a great voice, with God's own voice, "Give heed to the bishop and to the presbyters and deacons." . . . I had no knowledge of this from any human being, but the Spirit was preaching and saying this: "Do nothing without the bishop."
> (*Ad Philadelphians* 7.11)

Ignatius's claim that the Spirit insisted on vesting its authority in bishops came to be generally accepted. But the question was far from settled.

Montanus, founder of the Montanist movement, began to prophesy in Phrygia (Asia Minor) in about 172. Two women prophets traveled with him, Prisca and Maximilla. The first regional synods were called to deal with the claims of Montanism, but recordings of their decisions are not extant. Clearly these synods condemned the "new teachings," but Montanism spread across the Roman world. In North Africa, Tertullian became a convert to their teachings.

Prophecy is based on the belief that because the essence of the human person is spirit, other spirits can enter the body and speak though it. The metaphor frequently used to describe prophecy was that of a musician playing an instrument. Against leaders who sought to establish clear lines of institutional authority in Christian communities, Montanist groups argued for the volatile and unpredictable leadership of the Holy Spirit. The introduction to the *Actae of Perpetus and Felicity* (probably written by Tertullian, who developed Montanist sympathies in about 207), summarized Montanist contentions.

> The deeds recounted about the faith in ancient times were a proof of God's favor and achieved the spiritual strengthening of people as well; and they were set forth in writing precisely that honor might be rendered to God and comfort to people by the recollection of the past through the written word. Should not then more recent examples be set down that *contribute equally* to both ends? For indeed, these too will one day become ancient and needful for the ages to come, even though in our own day they may enjoy less prestige because of the prior claim of antiquity. Let those, then, who would restrict the power of the Holy Spirit to times and seasons look to this: the more recent events should be considered the greater, being later than those of old, and this a consequence of the extraordinary graces promised for the last stage of time. For in these last days, God declares, I will pour out my spirit upon all flesh and their sons and daughters shall prophesy and on my manservants and my maidservants I will pour my spirit and the young men will see visions and the old men shall dream dreams (Acts 2, 17–18). So too we hold in honor and acknowledge not only new prophecies, but new visions as well, according to the promise. And we consider all the other functions of the Holy Spirit as intended for the good of the church; for the same Spirit has been sent to distribute all his gifts to all, as the Lord apportions to everyone. (emphasis added)

Conflicts are evident in the passage. Against the view that the early days of Christianity were normative, the author claims that "last days" are even more instructive and authoritative than "the times of the apostles," or "ancient times." This contention supports his advocacy for the value of "new prophecies" and the continuing role of the Holy Spirit in the churches.

Should prophets be thought of as belonging to a past era? Or should ecstatic prophecy in the present be expected and valued? Both of these views were defended. The argument for on-going prophecy was supported by 88 New Testament references. Moreover, in Roman culture, oracles were highly respected, and a long tradition of ecstatic prophecy existed in Judaism. The second century *Didache*, a manual on church order, stipulated that prophecy should be respected if the prophet's behavior demonstrated Christian commitment. In short, Montanists felt themselves on firm ground when they claimed that prophecy should continue to be authoritative in the churches.

Cyprian (d. 258), bishop of Carthage, represented the culmination of a process by which prophecy came to be the prerogative of bishops. Cyprian had revelations that he recorded as oracles and circulated for everyone to read. He condemned Montanists, not for advocating prophecy, but because they did not agree that prophecy should be confined to bishops. "They have separated themselves from the church of God . . . where the elders preside," he said.

Authority

Western

Conflict over the role of prophecy was part of a more general issue, namely, the establishment of formal authority in Christian congregations in which both formal and informal authority had formerly been tolerated. In the West, at the beginning of the third century, an experiment in distributing authority was initiated. The office of *seniores* was established. *Seniores* administered church property and monitored the conduct of clergy. The office disappeared in the third century as bishops gained authority and took over these functions.

It is not known exactly where or when the office of bishop originated. There is no mention of bishops in Jesus' teachings, but St Paul refers to bishops. The model for the Christian bishop may have been the Jewish patriarch who held lifelong, or even hereditary, authority. Tertullian claimed that the apostles had appointed bishops, and Cyprian assumed that the apostles *were* bishops. In North Africa, one of the few places for which evidence exists, lists of hundreds of third-century bishops are extant; every small town had a bishop.

The third-century *Teaching of the Twelve Apostles* described the ideal of good Christian leadership. Bishops were to be men of blameless character, over fifty years of age, but if the church was small and all the members knew him, he could be younger than fifty. A bishop should be married to a Christian woman and not remarried (even if widowed). A bishop's children must be good Christians, and he must be meek, chaste, merciful, and adept at peace-making. He should be learned and lettered, but if not, he must at least know the scriptures well. Once appointed, the bishop could serve for the rest of his life.

The primary requirement, however, was that bishops must be men of keen discernment. Their duties demanded this quality, for they must investigate potential donors and refuse their support if they were unrepentant sinners. Problematic sources of church finances was one of the most frequently mentioned problems faced by third-century bishops. In addition, bishops must supervise the education of orphans, and discern false teachers and expel them. The apostles had told Christians not to go to secular courts with their disputes, and bishops were charged not only with making just decisions but also with reconciliation of the quarreling parties. Members who did not yield to their bishop's guidance must be excised from the congregation, at first for two to seven weeks; if after that time they were still unrepentant, they were to be excommunicated for life.

Bishops accumulated many other duties and powers, but the sobering bottom line was that at the Last Judgment a bishop was personally responsible for the members of his congregation. Augustine (d. 430), not otherwise a timid bishop, admitted that he trembled at the thought of that awesome responsibility.

Bishops' authority, and the power to assert that authority, was established during the second and third centuries. A bishops' power was institutional and judicial, but it was also spiritual, the authority to include or exclude individuals from Christ's body. Bishops imposed penalties ranging from temporary denial of admission to the Eucharist to excommunication, ejection from the community, and a curse (*anathama*). Bishops ruled "in the place of God," as one third-century text says. The *Didascalia Apostolorum*, a third-century Syrian church order, instructs: "Love your bishop as a father; fear him as a king; honor him as God."

Abuses of power were not unknown. Origen, not himself a bishop, characterized (or perhaps caricatured), bishops as saying: "We terrify people, and make ourselves inaccessible, especially if they are poor. To people who come and ask us to do something for them, we behave as no tyrant, even, would. We are more savage to petitioners than any civil rulers are. [Origen concluded] You can see this happening in many recognized churches, especially in the bigger cities" (*In Matt.* 16.8).

Nevertheless, bishops' powers were not uncontested. The letters of Bishop Cyprian, written in the mid-third century from his place of hiding during the Decian persecution, reveal his struggle to maintain his authority over rebellious clergy, confessors who were usurping his authority by liberally granting absolution to Christians who had lapsed in persecution, and communities of celibate women. The latter is a particularly interesting moment in the development of ascetic communities of women. Having left fathers and refused husbands, these women thought they should be able to choose their own dress and the details of their lifestyle. They must have heard with some dismay Cyprian's words: "Obey your bishop as a father." Establishing his control over celibate women was apparently quite crucial to Cyprian's authority as a bishop, and he was ultimately successful in dictating the details of their dress and activities.

There were two checks on bishops' power. First, bishops were elected by the clergy with the consent – by acclamation – of the congregation. Second, once elected, bishops were in a high-risk position. Until the mid-third century no widespread systematic persecution of church members occurred; rather, bishops were consistently targeted. Although Cyprian hid and attempted to administer his church by letters during the first part of the Decian persecution, he was arrested and martyred by beheading when he returned to Carthage in 258.

Some of the most vexing problems relating to authority were generated by persecutions. As evident in the *Acts of Perpetua and Felicity*, the confessors – those who had confessed Christian faith and been condemned to death – enjoyed great personal power, prestige, and authority. Frequently, a persecution would cease as suddenly and unpredictably as it began leaving some confessors alive and well. These Christians were often more popular than the local bishop, many of whom had withdrawn into hiding during the persecution. Yet bishops held institutional power, so the two different kinds of power came into conflict.

The Decian persecution in the mid-third century left crowds of lapsed Christians eager to be reunited with the Church. Faced with thousands of penitents, the issue of their restitution became church-wide. Two Roman priests differed over how severe churches should be with Christians who had lapsed. Hippolytus (d. c.236) maintained the hard line that Christians who had lapsed could be readmitted to communion only on their deathbeds. Callixtus (d. c.222), a former slave who became bishop of Rome, thought that people who had sinned in major ways should be reunited with the Church as soon as they had confessed and endured a period of exclusion. He quoted the parable of the wheat and the tares as the model for inclusion of the struggling and imperfect. He also cited Paul's question: "Who are you to judge another man's servant?" The mixture of animals in Noah's ark was also a precedent for a church of the imperfect. Callixtus argued that the holiness of any and all Christians was based, not on their sinlessness, but on God's forgiveness.

Schism and heresy

Christians' beliefs have usually been considered central to their religious loyalty. "Orthodoxy," or right belief increasingly defined Christian communities as councils pronounced on differing interpretations of scripture, theology, and practice and new members were required to recite and assent to creedal statements of belief. The word "heresy" comes from a Greek word simply meaning "choice," or something chosen, but Christians reshaped the word to indicate tenacious adherence to dissident doctrines or beliefs – "holding false opinions about God" – *as defined by bishops*. Not all disagreements pertained to doctrine, however. "Schism" refers to differences in matters of church order. Schismatics withdrew from established churches to organize separate communities and congregations. They held different opinions about matters of practice, "although they may believe just what we believe." In spite of the commonly accepted distinction between schism and heresy, Christian authors often polemically escalated accusations against opponents by calling schismatics "heretics."

Some bishops could see that heretical beliefs were actually useful to the Church. "Heresies" identified ideas and beliefs that needed clarification, or moral teachings that needed more precision. Bishops claimed that heretics and schismatics had become fascinated with a *part* of Christian faith, which they exaggerated in such a way as to distort traditional faith and practice. Montanists provide a good example.

In addition to their esteem for continuing prophecy, Montanists proposed a "new discipline," one that was sorely needed, Tertullian thought, in a time of moral laxity. They fasted Wednesdays and Fridays until sunset. They also held that no repentance could occur after baptism, that second marriages were not permitted, and that flight in the times of persecution was not allowed. Montanists also continued one of the earliest Christian interests, apocalypticism. They thought themselves to be living in "last days" in a church that had become more interested in "unity" than in moral rigor or prophetic utterance. Montanists believed that the Church should be thought of as the bride of Christ, "without spot or wrinkle," as a ship sailing through the storms of the world, and as a "holy society, living in righteousness."

By contrast, other Christians had largely lost interest in an imminent apocalypse. Their notions of purity had changed too. Origen's nostalgia for the astringent effect of imminent martyrdom was replaced by strategies for the long term. Clement responded to the variety of moral styles he saw about him in the Alexandrian Church by differentiating a "visible" and an "invisible" church. The visible church was defined objectively by a succession of bishops from the apostles, he said, but only the invisible church can claim to be "one." It is the invisible church that is the "body of Christ." The visible church attempts – at best – to approximate the invisible, but the match between the ideal and the real is, and will always be, less than perfect. Clement's concept of the church accounted for the embarrassing imperfection in the visible church without relinquishing the *idea* of purity.

Two other issues appear in the records of third-century conflicts: sexual morality, and behavior in times of persecution (or the problem of the lapsed). In the 309 Synod of Elvira, 46 percent of the canons (rulings) had to do with control of sexuality. These dealt with questions concerning who could marry whom, and condemnations of adultery and incest. There were continuous debates throughout the third century about whether clergy should be celibate.

The establishment of formal penance was prompted by disagreements about readmission to communion of those who had lapsed in persecution. Standardization of penitential practices was attempted but not completed in the third century. Left to the discretion of individual communities, penance could be either too severe or too lax. Because adequate provision for securing forgiveness for sins committed after baptism was not in place, baptism was often postponed until a person was near death. Individuals were expected to atone for trivial sins by prayer, almsgiving, and mutual forgiveness. Larger sins, like theft or embezzlement, required a *public* penance consisting of confession and a period of exclusion from communion, followed by formal absolution and restitution. In the third century, Church leaders considered sins such as homicide, adultery, and idolatry/apostasy beyond the Church's authority to forgive. Gradually, however, they assumed the right to forgive these sins.

For third-century Christians the purity of the sacraments was largely an issue for the future. By tradition, baptism by water and in the name of the trinity was valid, and the sacrament was not seen as depending on the priest who dispensed it. But the question of which Christian communities could share communion emerged in Cyprian's church. Cyprian's response was to sacrifice rigorous notions of purity in order to insist on an objective standard for church membership. For him the criterion of membership was not the acceptance of certain beliefs, but *submission to the bishop*. From Cyprian came the startling and unprecedented statement, "The one who does not have the Church for mother cannot have God for father" (*The Unity of the Catholic Church*: 6).

Unity

The historical circumstances in which Cyprian spoke the above words help to explain his intransigence. In March 251, there was a schism in Carthage in which a rival bishop, Fortunatus, was elected. In 253, after the Decian persecution, another schism developed over the readmission to communion of those who had lapsed in the persecution. The Roman presbyter Novatian (martyred in 258) maintained Hippolytus's rigorist stance, insisting that lapsed Christians should be excommunicated until shortly before their death. In Carthage, Maximus was elected the Novatianist bishop. Cyprian's statement, "The one who does not have the Church for mother cannot have God for father" was written in an embattled situation.

Where was the "true Church?" Which of the rival bishops was authorized to speak for it? There were no doctrinal disputes among the contenders. Cyprian claimed his authority as bishop on the basis of an alleged unbroken succession of bishops from the apostles. But questions remained. Should the Catholic Church admit to communion people who had been baptized in Christian groups considered heretical or schismatic? In 256 the African bishops sided with Cyprian's view that rebaptism was necessary for those who had been baptized in schismatic or heretical groups. However, Stephen, bishop of Rome, thought that rebaptism was unnecessary. The issue remained unsettled at the time of Stephen's martyrdom in 257, and Cyprian's in 258. The struggle itself, however, highlighted another issue that remained unsettled in the third century: Was episcopal authority to be collegial among bishops, or did the Roman bishop have primacy?

Cyprian's treatise *On the Unity of the Catholic Church* proposed several different bases for the unity of the Catholic Church. He claimed a historical unity based on a presumed unity at the beginning of Christianity. He also claimed a metaphysical unity, "one God, one Christ, one Church." And he claimed an existential unity, the Church as "one people fastened together in a solid bodily unity by the glue of concord." He pictured the Church as streams flowing from a single spring; as light emanating from a single source; as a fetus in the mother's womb ("Whoever leaves the womb cannot breathe apart."); as a coat that is "not cut or rent;" and as the unity of a single body. For Cyprian, however, the visible and objective symbol and reality of the Church's unity was vested in the person of the bishop: "The bishop is in the church, and the church is in the bishop, and if anyone is not with the bishop, he is not in the church." Even martyrdom, the ultimate test of Christian commitment, did not "count" if the martyr was not "with the bishop." Schismatic confessors existed, he said, but they "are not good men," despite appearances. He went so far as to compare them to Judas.

Cyprian acknowledged that heresy and schism were increasing; "with us the vigor of faith has withered." How was this to be explained? Because, he said, these are last days, when chaos and error must be expected. Apparently some schismatics had quoted scripture against him, for Cyprian argued *against* the verse, "Where two or three are gathered together, there I [Christ] am in the midst of them." Clearly, Cyprian argued for a unity that did not exist.

Readers of Cyprian's treatise can discern in the midst of his passionate plea for unity the pain of persecuted and embattled Christian communities. Cyprian's experience of personal and communal peril and the threat of dissolution is revealed in his treatise. His harsh language responded to the desperate circumstances in which he wrote.

READING

Cyprian, *On the Unity of the Catholic Church*

Women in second- and third-century Christian movements

Many women in the privileged classes of the Roman Empire, like Perpetua, were educated. Some – a few – were influential in their society and enjoyed freedom in public life. Literature of the period indicates that women achieved recognition as poets, writers, and historians, and there is one reference to a woman engineer. Seneca wrote, "Women have the same inner force and the same capacity for nobleness as men." But Musonius commented, "Only a woman trained in philosophy is capable of being a good house-wife." Until the fourth century, most women were under the legal guardianship (*potestas*) of a father, even when they married; a woman only became legally dependent on her husband when her father died.

The picture is complex. There was a trend, evident in laws concerning property, divorce, and inheritance, toward greater freedom for women. But there was also a reaction to women's increasing economic and social mobility. Popular writers often associated greater freedom for women with a breakdown in general moral standards. Curiously, the strongest statements in support of women's abilities and activities often appear in the same societies and at the same time as the strongest statements against women. Local differences further complicate the task of anyone who strives to understand women's situation in the later Empire. Generalizations based on laws, literary evidence, and church canons are inadvisable; the evidence, according to historian Gillian Clark, is irreducibly "geographically patchy, class-biased, and male-biased."

Societies and communities may agree about what the issues are, but they seldom agree about how they should be resolved. If, for example, we find strong statements about women, their dress, and their roles in Christian communities, we should not conclude that male leaders and authors, to a man, had no esteem for women. On the basis of the evidence, we can, however, recognize that male leaders considered it essential to their credibility as leaders to define and establish women's public and private roles. Apparently, Christians did not significantly alter their assumptions about women from those of their society. Activities permitted by law and custom to Roman women were similar to those allowed Christian women. In different geographical and temporal settings, Christianity both undermined and subverted *and* strengthened traditional attitudes toward women.

The Platonist Celsus, writing about 178, accused Christians of subverting social conventions. He cited Roman patterns of authority within the family by which the *paterfamilias* had the legal power of life and death over his wife, children, and slaves. What did Celsus see in Christian communities that prompted his criticism?

Part of the excitement of the early Christian movement was the possibility it held of restructuring family and social relationships. Jesus himself had shocked his disciples by treating women with attention and respect. Moreover, Paul's statement in Galatians 3.18, "In Christ there is neither male nor female," (from an early baptismal formula), authorized a new spiritual equality that seemed to imply social equality. Apocalyptic expectations also encouraged Christians to work hastily and effectively for the coming kingdom. In the earliest Christian movement, men and women worked together, traveled together, and in some cases, lived together in order to facilitate missionary activity. Men and women who were vowed to celibacy experimented with "spiritual marriage" (*subintroductae*, or *agapatae*), for mutual companionship, protection, and support.

By the beginning of the second century, churches repeatedly outlawed spiritual marriages, apparently finding them an insupportable strain on the commitment of the participants, the credulity of the community, or both. Church legislation continued to prohibit these relationships; 24 synods condemned them in the third and fourth centuries, suggesting that spiritual marriage still attracted adherents. Spiritual marriages demonstrate the struggle of women and men to find new relationships that would support and strengthen cooperative work.

In the second century, women sometimes occupied official ministry positions in churches. They were called "deaconesses," or "widows." Women's ministries focused on assistance of the sick, care for orphans, strangers, prisoners, and assisting at the baptism of women, though male clergy were required to say the words of baptism. Women who held ministry roles were invariably women who were not sexually active at the time. Yet married priests were told not to sleep with their wives only at the beginning of the fourth century, and until the end of the fourth century no enforcement of clerical celibacy was attempted.

A prayer of ordination for deaconesses is recorded in the fourth century *Apostolic Constitutions*, which claims to be a compilation of earlier documents. In this prayer, God's authorization and protection of Jewish women is cited as precedent for Christian women's ministries.

> O eternal God, the Father of our Lord Jesus Christ, the creator of man and woman, who replenished with the spirit Miriam and Deborah and Hulda and Anna; who did not disdain that thy only-begotten child should be born of a woman; who also in the tabernacle of the testimony and in the temple, did ordain women to be keepers of thy holy gates; do thou now also look down upon this thy servant that is to be ordained to the office of a deaconess, and grant her thy holy spirit, that she may worthily discharge the work that is committed to her to thy glory, and the praise of thy Christ, with whom glory and adoration be to Thee and the Holy Spirit forever. Amen.

Women regularly appeared in leadership roles in heterodox communities. Gnostic communities had prophetesses who held both authority and sacramental functions. Since women have usually been associated with body (and men with rationality) in the West, it is striking that Gnostics combined ultimate rejection of body with acceptance of women's ministries. The second-century Gnostic "Gospel of Mary" described a conflict among the disciples over Mary Magdalene's teaching role. Before his ascension, Christ taught his disciples, but after his ascension, they found that they were not very clear about what he meant on some matters, so Mary Magdalene undertook to clarify Jesus' meaning by revealing to them some private revelations he had made to her. Peter was outraged at her presumption: "Did he then speak with a woman in preference to us, and not openly? Are we to turn back and all listen to her? Did he not prefer us to her?" Levi tried to mollify Peter, saying that the disciples should not miss the opportunity to hear Jesus' secret teaching from Mary.

In the second century, however, there were few clear lines between heterodox and orthodox communities. A growing consensus that Jesus Christ came to earth in the flesh differentiated incarnationist Christians from Gnostic Christians, but outsiders often overlooked doctrinal differences. The association of women in leadership roles with communities labeled "heretical" meant that one obvious way for incarnationist Christians to differentiate themselves from rival groups was to proscribe leadership by women. Before his conversion to Montanism Tertullian wrote, "And the women of these heretics, how wanton they are! For they are bold enough to teach, to dispute, to enact exorcisms, to undertake cures, maybe even to baptize!" By the mid-third century, the mainstream view was – in Origen's words – "For it is improper for a woman to speak in an assembly, no matter what she says, even if she says admirable things, or even saintly things, that is of little consequence, since they come from the mouth of a woman."

Feminine imagery for God was used at the same time that women were excluded from leadership roles in the churches. Clement of Alexandria wrote, "And God himself is love. . . . In his ineffable essence he is father; in his compassion to us he became mother. The father by loving became feminine." Clement, like Tertullian, used "bad mother – good mother" language to introduce his description of the atonement. Eve, the virgin, introduced sin into the world, while Mary, the virgin, introduced the Word of God: "What had gone to destruction through the female sex was by the same sex restored to salvation." This parallelism, however, did not result in esteem for actual women, who were rebuked in strong and sarcastic terms for their desire to participate in Christian ministry. Referring to I Corinthians 14.35 Tertullian remarked sarcastically, "How very likely that he who consistently refused to allow a woman even to learn should have granted a female authority to teach" (*De baptismo* 17). He insisted, "A woman may not speak nor baptize, or offer the Eucharist, nor claim the right to any masculine function, still less to the priestly office" (*De virginibus velandis* 9).

The first Christian images

The earliest extant material evidence of the Christian movements comes from the third century. This evidence has often been overlooked, yet the first Christian buildings, images, and sculpture significantly augment our knowledge of Christians' interests and values. Fragments of Christian meeting-houses have been discovered, all of which were built after 235 and before 400. The oldest extant Christian house was at Dura Europus, near the eastern border of the Roman Empire in the Syrian dessert. The Christian meeting house, a temple of Mithras, and the Jewish house synagogue were on the same street. Ironically, these buildings were preserved because the town was destroyed in the mid-third century. These houses, built against a wall, were buried in the heavy reinforcements needed for an imminent war with Persia. The synagogue and the Christian house are indistinguishable in construction from the houses surrounding them. All had wall paintings, done by several artists, none of whom were especially proficient. Figures are stiff, but subjects seem to have been carefully chosen. The Christian house contained depictions of Adam and Eve, Christ the Good Shepherd bearing a lamb, the healing of the paralytic, Peter walking on water, the three Marys at the tomb, David and Goliath, and the Samaritan woman drawing water.

Fragments of *tituli*, or house churches, are also extant in Rome, Spain, and Britain. But by the second- or early third-century, the basilica design was being adapted by both Jews and Christians for worship. Used in Rome and elsewhere in the Empire since the second century BCE, the basilica is a rectangular hall whose breadth is between a half and a third of the length.

Catacombs

In addition to worship locations, Christians also needed burial sites. Christians rejected the common Roman practice of cremation, though they gave no (written) reasons for this preference. Perhaps burial was attractive to Christians because, according to scripture, Jesus had been buried in a rock-cut sepulcher. Their secular neighbors thought it remarkable that Christians buried not only their family members, relatives, and members of their communities, but also many of the urban poor who would otherwise have been buried *en masse* in huge pits for promiscuous burial.

Until about the mid-second century, Christians had no private cemeteries; like their neighbors, they used the underground excavations called catacombs. After about 150, long series of Christian catacombs were dug in the relatively soft volcanic rock, or *tufa*. The Roman catacombs were built about two miles outside Rome, obeying the prohibition against burying the dead in the city.

"There at the tomb of Polycarp," one early text reads, "the Lord will permit us as shall be possible to us to assemble ourselves together in joy and gladness to celebrate the birthday of his martyrdom, alike in memory of them that have fought before, and for the training and preparation of those who will fight hereafter." Christians visited the catacombs to commemorate the dead, both kin and local martyrs, but they did not habitually worship in the catacombs. The early catacombs have few rooms of any size; the largest could have held about 50 people, packed in. It would also have been impractical to walk back and forth from the city for regular worship. Moreover, there is no evidence that Christians hid in the catacombs in times of persecution, for the location of Christian catacombs was known to everyone.

Christians frequented the catacombs for occasional communal gatherings, but also for private devotions. According to the fourth century Christian, Jerome, Christians often strolled and prayed in the catacombs. He described the ambiance and effect of the catacombs.

> When I was a boy in Rome, and was being educated in liberal studies, I was accustomed, with others of like mind and age, to visit on Sundays the sepulchers of the apostles and martyrs. And often did I enter the crypts, dug deep in the earth, with their walls on either side lined with the bodies of the dead, where everything is so dark that it almost seems as if the Psalmist's words were fulfilled, "Let them go down alive into hell." Here and there the light, not entering through windows but filtering down from above through shafts, relieves the horror of the darkness. But again, as one cautiously moves forward, the black night closes round.

> (*Commentary on Ezekiel* 60)

The presence of death is well-known to "concentrate the mind," and to intensify and focus consciousness. Jerome described how inspired his prayers were in this environment. Scenes painted on the ceilings and walls presented scriptural stories of miraculous deliverance, mostly from the Hebrew Bible (figure 1.1, see CD Rom figures 1.1 and 1.2). A third-century collection of prayers from North Africa cites most of the same scriptural incidents that are pictured on catacomb walls. Catacomb paintings may have served as memory aids for reciting certain prayers.

Paintings are not unique to the Christian catacombs, and much of the painting in Christian catacombs had little to do with Christianity, but used a repertoire of images common to Jewish, secular, and Christian tombs (see CD Rom figure 1.3). Flowers and foliage, naked *putti* harvesting grapes, Orpheus playing his lyre, and Cupid and Psyche gathering flowers are common subjects. Similarly, inscriptions owe more to a common

Figure 1.1   Three Hebrew Children in the Fiery Furnace, Catacomb of Priscilla, third century. Daniel's three friends are depicted as *orantes* in the midst of flames. They represent peaceful and trusting *pietas* in the midst of overpowering threat.
Orantes were common in classical painting, sculptural art, and coins before Christians adopted the representation. Usually a female figure with upraised arms, the figure represented prayerful piety and supplication. No figure appears more frequently in catacomb art. Photo AKG/Erich Lessing.

repertoire than to Christianity. Jewish and Christian inscriptions are often indistinguishable: *In pace*, or "in peace thy sleep." Catacomb art provides another reminder that Christians, Jews, adherents to Roman religions, and others shared a broad secular repertoire of ideas and images.

Human figures were the primary subjects of catacomb art. *Orantes*, figures with arms lifted in prayer, had a long pre-Christian history in Roman art. They were often representations of the deceased (see CD Rom figures 1.4 and 1.5). The style of catacomb art was surprisingly standard across the Roman Empire. It is striking that at the same time that martyrs' blood was flowing, Christian art expressed only deliverance and peace. Apparently Christians sought images that compensated rather than reflected their experience. Bodies are expressive; the bodies of dozens of *orantes* figures found in the catacombs strain to enter their prayer, as described by the early third-century Clement of Alexandria.

> For this reason also we raise the head and lift the hands in the closing outburst of prayer, following the eager flight of the spirit into the spiritual world, And while we thus endeavor to detach the body from the earth by lifting it upwards along with spoken words, we spurn

Figure 1.2   Banquet, Catacomb of Priscilla, Capella Greca, eighteenth century.
Banquets were depicted often in the second- and third-century catacombs. Here seven people recline on a couch in preparation for eating a meal of bread, fish, and wine. There is some ambiguity about the gender of the figures. Amusingly, the eighteenth-century chapel above the catacomb repeats the fresco in mosaic *tesserae* – with one correction. The figure at the left of the group, the main celebrant, has been given a beard, although the ankle-length skirt characteristic of women's dress has been retained. Photo SCALA, Florence.

the *fetters* of the flesh and constrain the soul, winged with desire of better things, to ascend into the holy place.

(Stromateis 7.7.40; emphasis added)

Depictions of banquets were common in catacomb painting. Three overlapping interpretations have been proposed for these scenes. They might represent the customary family meal (*refrigerium*) at the tomb of a loved one on the anniversary of their death, a eucharistic celebration, a heavenly banquet, or all of the above (figure 1.2; see CD Rom figure 1.6).

In about 120 catacomb images Christ is shown as a shepherd, bearded or unbearded, carrying a sheep. A small marble sculpture from the third quarter of the third century shows Christ as Good Shepherd (see CD Rom figure 1.7). Christ was also occasionally depicted as a philosopher teaching his disciples.

Scenes from the Hebrew Bible dominate catacomb painting and other art (see CD Rom figure 1.8). The most frequent subjects were Noah and the ark, Abraham's near-sacrifice of Isaac, Moses striking the rock (see CD Rom figures 1.1 and 1.2), and Jonah's encounter with the "great fish" (see CD Rom figure 1.9). Daniel in the den of lions and the three Hebrews in the fiery furnace occur several times (Figure 1.1; see CD Rom figure 1.10). Adam and Eve, coyly covering their genitals, appear at the Catacomb of Peter and Marcellinus (see CD Rom figure 1.11).

Less frequently, there are New Testament scenes, such as the arrival of the Magi, Christ and the Samaritan woman, the annunciation of the angel to Mary, the baptism of Jesus, and various miracles, the most common of which is the resurrection of Lazarus. And there are symbols like loaves and fishes (see CD Rom figure 1.12). The catacomb of Callixtus has two baptism scenes in which the baptized are smaller than the baptizer, indicating that they are *infans* or *neonates*, newly born Christians. They are also naked, as later baptismal instructions direct.

Who painted these scenes? Historians' best guess is that it was the *fossores* or diggers who excavated the catacombs. Several roughly contemporary church orders mention the *fossor* as a minor clerical grade, but nothing further is known about them. (see CD Rom figure 1.13)

What was *missing* from the earliest Christian images? There was no naturalistic portrait of Christ (see CD Rom figure 1.14), and no depiction of the crucifixion until 432. Constantine outlawed crucifixion in the first quarter of the fourth century, but it was not used as a Christian symbol until associations of a dishonorable and gruesome death faded from living memory. Christians preferred to concentrate on themes of life and deliverance rather than on Christ's death or the deaths of more contemporary martyrs.

Much more imagery from pre-Constantinian Christianity has been lost than is extant. Some images are still faintly visible, but are impossible to decipher. Until the nineteenth century, exploration of the catacombs was not done in a scientific manner, and from the early medieval period forward, graves were repeatedly ransacked. There were also attempts to remove frescoes that damaged or destroyed them.

In addition to catacomb images, all existing fragmentary house churches show evidence of painting. The common misinterpretation of early Christianity as imageless and antagonistic to images cannot be sustained. Christians of the second and third centuries apparently needed images that sustained them in persecution, accompanied their worship, and offered alternatives to secular images that often featured popular gladiators, and the images of competing Roman religions.

Liturgy

Christian liturgies reveal Christians' insistence on the engagement of bodies and senses in the worship of the incarnated God. Second and third century texts and visual images indicate that attention was given to forming Christian bodies as well as Christian souls. We must not, however, attempt to identify a "Christian attitude" toward bodies, for a wide range of attitudes, ideas, and images existed. Bodies, sexuality, and gender assumptions lay at the heart of the experience of the Word made flesh, and thus were frequently the subject of conflicts in Christian communities.

Before theologies were articulated, people *practiced* Christianity. Complete liturgical manuscripts are not extant until the eighth century, but bits of information, suggestions, and hints found in letters, sermons, and legislation from early councils and synods can be pieced together to sketch second-century liturgical practices. We cannot, however, assume that everything mentioned was actually practiced in Christian communities. These sources are also difficult to interpret since they may have been prescriptive rather than descriptive. Moreover, liturgies were in constant use, so they were constantly altered, revised, and added to. Like contemporary Italian cathedrals, they contain strata in which the earliest construction is overlaid with many later additions. Local variations also make it impossible to generalize across the Roman Empire.

Christians received few instructions from their founder about how to worship or how to teach converts. This meant that they had considerable latitude for shaping their worship. Christian worship seems to have moved from showing great differences across geographical locations to gradual consensus and standardization. Standardized liturgical practice was the result of concerted efforts by Christian leaders, and occurred slowly.

Second-century Christian worship

The earliest evidence for the worship of Christian communities comes from hearsay. Pliny, a Roman governor, reported his impression of Christians to the emperor Trajan: "The sum total of their guilt or error amounted to no more than this, they met regularly before dawn on a fixed day to chant verses alternately among themselves in honor of Christ as if to a god. . . ." The music of the earliest Christian communities is lost, but from the first century forward, the words of hymns are extant. Some liturgical historians have posited a Jewish origin for Christian singing, but, though this is a likely conjecture, no documentary evidence supports this claim.

Justin Martyr gave the first substantial description of Christian worship. Writing his *First Apology* from Rome in about 150, he described a regular weekly service.

> On the day called Sunday there is a meeting in one place of those who live in cities or the country, and the memoirs of the apostles or the writings of the prophets are read as long as time permits. When the reader has finished the president in a discourse urges and invites [us] to the imitation of these noble things. Then we all stand up together and offer prayers. . . . When we have finished the prayers, bread is brought, and wine and water, and the president similarly sends up prayers and thanksgivings to the best of his ability, and the congregation assents, saying the Amen. The distribution and reception of the consecrated [elements] takes place, and they are sent to the absent by the deacons. Those who prosper, and who so wish, contribute, each one as much as he chooses to. What is collected is deposited with the president, and he takes care of orphans and widows, and those who are in want on account of sickness or any other cause, and those who are in bonds, and the strangers who are sojourners among us, and briefly, he is the protector of all those in need.
>
> (*Apology* 67)

In 100, Christianity was still largely an urban phenomenon in the West. In the East, however, it had spread to small towns and villages. Christian communities were loosely organized with volunteer administrators and little connection with one another. There were overseers (*episcopoi*), stewards (*diakonai*), and migrating preachers, like St Paul. Ritual was also loosely organized. Some congregations assembled at sunrise for prayer and hymn singing, and toward evening for a meal (*agape*).

Christians preached in town squares, competing with Stoic and Platonist preachers for the crowd. Sometimes Christians hired a hall, as the Ephesus congregation did when

St Paul visited. But most Christians met in private homes, a practice they called "breaking the bread from house to house." The first meeting rooms were dining rooms, since a meal was the core of the service and in Roman homes the dining room was often the only large room. It was usually on the top floor, hence the "upper room, high up, open to the light," mentioned in *The Acts of the Apostles*.

Christians met to sing and pray, to teach, to baptize new members, and to eat together. One of the earliest liturgical prayers says simply, "God, we thank you for the knowledge, faith, and immortality you have made known through your servant Jesus." Second-century liturgical prayers described the salvation Christians experienced as revelation and as forgiveness, as life and as light. They seem to have been unconcerned with more precise definitions, an attitude noticed by their neighbors. Celsus, a second-century secular critic of Christianity wrote, "Some will not hear or give reason about their faith, but stick to 'ask no questions but believe,' and 'your faith will save you,' and 'the wisdom of the world is a bad thing and foolishness is good.'"

Creeds, or statements of Christian belief, emerged from baptismal liturgies. There were many variations in different locations in the second century, but there were also several common factors. All creeds invoked the "Father, Son, and Holy Spirit," and they all mentioned the life, death, and resurrection of Jesus. The earliest creeds stated the facts Christians believed without analysis or explanation. How Christians should *act* (*orthopraxy*) was apparently more important than how they should articulate their beliefs.

The earliest descriptions of preparation for baptism are found in fourth-century catechetical instructions. Several meanings are given for baptism. Baptism meant entrance into the Christian community and participation in the hope of everlasting life. Writing in about 155, Justin called baptism "illumination." Sometimes St Paul's strong interpretation of baptism as participation in the death and resurrection of Jesus is cited. Birth imagery is also evident in baptismal rites that described the newly baptized as "neonates," newborns. The gospel account of Jesus washing the disciples' feet (John 13. 1–20), together with references to foot-washing in several later baptismal rites suggests that foot-washing may have been *the* baptismal rite in some Christian communities. The process of becoming a Christian was thought of and expressed in diverse ways.

The eucharistic celebration consisted of a meal, called a "love feast" (*agape*). The name invited conjectures and allegations from unsympathetic neighbors on the nature of this love feast. Joseph Jungmann, a twentieth-century scholar of ancient liturgies, has said that that the greatest change in the history of Christian worship was abandoning the meal in the mid-fourth century when congregations became too large to make a meal feasible.

The *Didache*, or *Teaching*, a Syrian church manual (date unknown) includes several eucharistic prayers. They strongly resemble Jewish blessings that accompanied the third cup of the paschal meal, and there is no mention in them of the body and blood of Christ. The blessing for the cup reads, "We thank you, our Father, for the holy vine of David, your child, which you have revealed through Jesus, your child. To you be glory forever." The blessing for the bread: "As this piece of bread was scattered over the hills and then was brought together and made one, so let your church be brought together from the ends of the earth into your kingdom. For yours is the glory and the power through Jesus Christ forever."

The Greek word *eucharistia* means thanksgiving; this was the primary meaning of the celebration. At the beginning of the second century, Clement of Rome argued against the idea that the eucharist is an offering, though other sources refer to "offering the gift." Clement of Alexandria wrote, "Rightly do we not offer God who has need of nothing a gift. On the contrary, we glorify him who dedicated himself to us, by dedicating ourselves to him."

Yet the Roman liturgy of about 150 included the following eucharistic prayer.

> We therefore offer unto thee this cup for the refreshing of our souls, and this cup of everlasting salvation, making remembrance of his death and resurrection, and giving thanks unto thee. And we beseech thee to send thy holy spirit upon this oblation, and upon thy church, that he may fill us and unite us in thy kingdom. To thee be praise and honor and worship through Jesus Christ thy son, with the Holy Spirit in holy church unto the ages of ages.

Finally, Christian literature exhibits a remarkable lack of fanaticism. The earliest church manual, the *Didache*, recognized a tension between the assumption that Christians are holy people and loving acceptance of actual Christians: "If any person is holy, let him come; if any person is not, let him repent. . . . If you can bear the Lord's full yoke, you will be perfect. But if you cannot, then do what you can."

By the beginning of the fourth century, Christians had achieved informal consensus about the reality of Jesus Christ's incarnation. They had begun to construct creeds that shared common elements. Bishops had gained institutional and spiritual power and authority. But central doctrinal issues were unresolved, and although most Christians did not realize it, persecution was not over. Chapter 2 explores fourth-century Christians' volatile and contradictory excitements.

READINGS

The Didache
Clement's First Letter
The Epistle to Diognetus

2 Inclusions and Exclusions: The Fourth Century

Prologue

Historian Robert Markus has suggested that what was at stake in fourth- and fifth-century Christianity was the historical unity of the Christian churches through time. The sudden change from persecuted sect to empire-wide Church, sponsored by an emperor, was deliriously exhilarating to many Christians, but it also raised questions of identity. Was this triumphant Church identical with the Church of the martyrs? Even the enthusiastic Eusebius, Constantine's staunch supporter and avid recorder of contemporary events, remarked near the end of his life, "We, although not held worthy to have struggled unto death and to have shed our blood for God, yet being the sons of those who have suffered thus and distinguished by our fathers' virtues, pray for mercy through them" (*Comm. In Ps.* 78.11). A generation gap existed between those fathers and sons. Fourth-century doctrinal debates, Markus argues, "sprang from a perceived need to safeguard the continuity of Christian belief . . . at a time when the Church's mode of existence was itself undergoing drastic change." The events that precipitated this change, and their contemporary interpretation, are the subject of this chapter.

The fourth-century Church struggled to enjoy the benefits of imperial patronage without becoming a ward of the state. Throughout the century, Christian bishops accumulated power formerly held by the state in its capacity as a *religious* entity. Historian Hal Drake has called the struggles of the fourth century "one of the most important transfers of power in Western history." The relationship of Church and state was not settled in the fourth century, but a fragile and uneasy balance of powers was established by the end of the century: Constantine's religiously diverse society became state-supported Christian orthodoxy.

However, many Christians did not subscribe to the Nicene orthodoxy established by Constantine and reinforced by Theodosius. To ignore those who withdrew or were ostracized after each theological decision is to confine our sights to the relatively small geographical area surrounding the Mediterranean, for many of those who disagreed, moved out of the Roman Empire. Other dissident Christians moved in. The political future of the Empire would be largely in the hands of Arian Visigoths who called them-selves simply "Christians." Augustine, writing his epic *The City of God*, found himself in the awkward position of trying to explain that the ravages of the 410 Sack of Rome, bad as they were, would have been much worse had the Arians not respected the sanctuary of Christian churches, and also insisting that Arians were, from the perspective of Nicene orthodoxy, heretics.

Dissenting Christians were tireless missionaries. After the 431 Council of Ephesus, those who accepted Nestorius' teaching (judged heretical at the Council) migrated to Persia where they dominated Christianity in Persia by the fifth century. They were established in China by the eighth century. Following the Council of Chalcedon in 451, Monophysite Christians (judged heretical at the Council) left the Catholic communion to form churches (Copts, Syrian Jacobites, and Armenians) that occupied more than six times the geographical area occupied by Catholic Christians. But this is ahead of our story.

The gains and losses of fourth-century Christianity are difficult to assess. Orthodox Christians emerged from the fourth century allied to a state that approved and enforced doctrine and punished dissent, both pagan and Christian. But, as this chapter describes, state sponsorship was costly. The history of Christianity in the fourth century cannot be narrated simply as a triumphal story.

1   "The Evidence of Our Eyes"

Since 240 the Roman Empire was under pressure from northern European tribes who had become aware that the Empire's wealth was vastly disproportionate to its military strength. They began to migrate into the Empire, at first simply to forage for food. Between 240 and 270 every frontier collapsed. In response to these threats, a rapid mil-itarization of Roman society occurred in which the old senatorial class was marginal-ized. Roman emperors were no longer, like Marcus Aurelius, learned philosophers, but soldiers who achieved recognition in battle. Coins from the later third century show emperors in battle dress instead of in the traditional toga. The Empire was decentral-ized as armies were recruited from, and stationed among, frontier populations. The army doubled in size and cost, and civilian taxes doubled. In a desperate attempt to govern more effectively, the Empire was divided into Eastern and Western sectors, each ruled by an emperor and a Caesar. In the first decade of the fourth century, Constan-tine and Maximian ruled in the West; Diocletian and Licinius ruled the East.

By the beginning of the fourth century, Christianity had strong roots in the cities of the Mediterranean world. As it gained adherents in cities and provincial towns, it also changed, simultaneously acquiring self-confidence and becoming acculturated to Roman society. Christianity's "conversion" from persecuted sect to confident Church took many forms, several of which occurred before the fourth century. One of the most fundamental was its self-identification with philosophy as skilled apologists like Justin Martyr, Origen, and Athenagoras explained Christian beliefs and practices to non-Christian Romans. On sarcophagi and frescoes of the late third century Christ appears as a philosopher, lecturing to a circle of disciples. The *cathedra*, or bishop's chair at the center of every fourth-century church was understood as continuous with, and the suc-cessor of, the philosopher's chair. Christianity was no longer seen as a superstition of simple folk; it could now be thought of as a new and more adequate way of living and thinking, the culmination of Greek philosophy and Roman aspirations.

At the beginning of the fourth century persecutions seemed far in the past; Christians had not been persecuted since 261. They were worshipping openly, if inconspicuously. There were at least 25 *tituli*, or buildings specifically for Christian worship, in Rome, some of them of considerable size. As much as a third of the Roman population may have been Christians. Flourishing churches owned land and businesses.

Christians thought of themselves as part of Roman society; they were shocked by the sudden onslaught of persecution in 303. The persecution was initiated at a routine official sacrifice attended by the Eastern emperor, Diocletian. The priests entrusted with foretelling the outcome of a battle by reading the entrails of a slaughtered animal claimed that they could not read the usual signs because some Christians present had crossed themselves. Diocletian then sought advice from the oracle at Miletus, but he received the reply that the oracle was unable to predict because false oracles were being circulated by Christians. These were not new charges, but the episode inaugurated what was remembered as the "great persecution." Historians estimate, on the basis of extrapolations from local records, that in the Eastern Empire 3,000 to 3,500 Christians were executed. In the West, approximately 2,500 to 3,000 Christians lost their lives.

The first object of the persecution was not Christians themselves, but a large church in the eastern imperial capital, Nicomedia. By imperial edict, all churches were to be destroyed, scriptures and liturgical books confiscated, and meetings for worship forbidden. A few months later a second edict ordered the arrest of all clergy, an embarrassment when it was found that existing prisons could not contain so many. In 304 persecution became general when all citizens were ordered to sacrifice to the deified emperor on pain of death. Those who declined were executed. Christians had never before experienced persecution on this scale. Suspects were tortured – racked, scraped, flogged, dragged, and maimed – before being put to death. Whole families and parts of congregations were herded into the arena, ringed with wood, and burned.

It was, however, easy to avoid persecution. The simple act of throwing a few grains of incense on a fire burning before a portrait of the emperor, indicating support for the empire, satisfied the state. Non-Christian Romans considered the sacrifice a civic gesture to gods who had long since lost their religious status and remained as symbols of the state. Christians interpreted this gesture as an act of emperor-worship. It was *the* point at which many Christians could not integrate Roman culture and Christian commitment. The North African Christian Tertullian acknowledged: "Some think it madness that, when we could offer sacrifice here and now and go away unpunished, preserving the same attitude of mind as before, we prefer to be obstinate rather than safe."

Historian Peter Brown has detected a dramatic shift in the imagery of martyrdom in the late third century. Second- and third-century Christians thought of martyrdom primarily as participation in the sufferings of Christ; Christ suffered in the martyr's place, as the martyr suffered for Christ. By the late third century, however, triumphal imagery dominated. Martyrdom was seen as a victorious struggle in which the devil and the powers of evil were overcome. Confessors taunted the crowds as they were led into the arena to be executed. Brown writes, "It was only a step for the potent god of the arena to become a god of battles, and so an imperial god." The imagery that would, a bit later, be transferred into that of a Christianized empire emerged in the

Diocletian persecution, and it is in this context that the triumphal imagery of fourth-century churches can be understood. The martyrs' triumphal overcoming of death became the triumph of Christianity in the cities of the Empire. How did this dramatic change occur?

Constantine

In the 70 years before Constantine; 20 of the 23 emperors who reigned were assassinated. Constantine was proclaimed emperor by the army on July 25, 305 when persecution of Christians was at its most intense. The impromptu acclamation that designated him emperor was followed by violent attempts to gain sole power in the West. In 312 Constantine won the decisive battle of the Milvian bridge against Maxentius, his co-emperor. In February 313, he and the Eastern emperor, Licinius, agreed on a policy of religious freedom. From this time forward, Christianity was a legal and *favored* religion. It was not made the official religion of the Roman Empire until the 380s.

Twenty years after the event, Constantine told the historian Eusebius that before the battle, he saw a cross superimposed on a noon sun and inscribed with the words, "By this conquer." A Roman orator at the *time* of the battle reported that Constantine saw a vision of the sun-god. In any case, Constantine's victory at the Milvian bridge led him to favor the Christian God from then forward.

The so-called "Peace of the Church" brought immediate changes in the policies of the state toward Christianity. It guaranteed the right to profess Christian faith; it restored status to those who had been expelled from imperial service on religious grounds; it brought freedom of assembly and restitution of lands and buildings that had been confiscated. New copies of the scriptures were financed; new churches were built, and buildings were turned over to the churches for their use. A portion of provincial taxes was also given to churches to use for charitable purposes. Eusebius described the change:

> All were freed from the oppression of the tyrants, and being released from the former ills, one in one way and another in another, acknowledged the defender of the pious to be the only true God. And we especially who placed our hopes in the Christ of God had unspeakable gladness, and a certain inspired joy bloomed for all of us, when we saw every place which shortly before had been desolated by the impieties of the tyrants reviving as if from a long and death-fraught pestilence, and temples again rising from their foundations to an immense height and receiving a splendor far greater than that which had been destroyed. But the supreme rulers also confirmed to us still more extensively the munificence of God by repeated ordinances on behalf of the Christians, and personal letters of the emperor were sent to the bishops with honors and gifts of money.
>
> (*Ecclesiastical History* X. 2. 1)

These gifts were largely spent on building churches. According to Eusebius, church buildings extended Christ's incarnation, making it visible to all.

Constantine was never clear about Christian doctrine, but he was very impressed by winning the battle of the Milvian bridge even though he was outnumbered and outmaneuvered. Although he favored Christianity, he did not consider this incompatible with the emperor's traditional status as representative of the sun-god. He continued to preside over the rites of the sun-god throughout his life, placing on his coins *soli invecto comiti* ("to the unconquered sun, my companion"). He was not alone in this: many people found Christianity compatible with solar religion. A fifth-century sermon of Pope Leo the Great rebuked his congregation for paying reverence to the sun on the steps of St Peter's, before turning their back on it to worship in the westward-facing basilica.

Eusebius reported (from memory) Constantine's profession of faith:

> It appears that those who faithfully discharge God's holy laws and shrink from the transgression of his commandments are rewarded with abundant blessings and endued with well-grounded hope as well as with ample power for the accomplishment of their undertakings. On the other hand, those who have cherished impiety have experienced consequences in keeping with their evil choice . . . . I myself was the agent whose services God deemed suitable for the accomplishment of his will. Accordingly, with the aid of divine power I banished and destroyed every form of evil which prevailed in the hope that the human race, enlightened through my instrumentality, might be recalled to a due observance of God's laws and, at the same time, our most blessed faith might prosper under the guidance of the almighty hand.
>
> (*Life of Constantine* II. 24, 28)

Constantine did not permit himself to be deified in his lifetime as earlier emperors had been. Instead he presented himself (slightly more modestly) as God's vice-regent on earth. Eusebius wrote:

> The God of all, the supreme governor of the universe, by his own will appointed Constantine to be prince and sovereign; so that while others have been raised to this distinction by the choice of their fellows, he is unique as the one man to whose elevation no mortal may boast of having contributed.

Like many fourth-century Christians, he was baptized only on his deathbed. Curiously, the defender of Nicaean orthodoxy was baptized by the Arian bishop, Eusebius of Nicomedia.

It is striking that the conversion of one man – even an emperor – could have precipitated the sweeping changes that immediately followed Constantine's victory. Two years before, Christians had been slaughtered in a persecution that exceeded all others in brutality, intensity, and terror. With memories of these times alive in the minds of Christians, Constantine's Edict of Toleration stated that "no one whosoever should be denied the liberty of following either the religion of the Christians or any other cult which, of his own free choice, he has thought the best adapted for himself." By "whosoever" Constantine meant that the male head of a household would choose a religious affiliation for the extended family, including slaves.

Constantine's laws protected children, slaves, prisoners and women. Infanticide became a capital offense. Yet his own household was a center of intrigue and homicide. His son, Crispus, was murdered at home in 326, and in the same year his wife, Fausta (sister of Maxentius), was smothered in the public baths, apparently at his instigation. These murders were followed by the murder of "innumerable friends." Constantine's nephew, the pagan emperor Julian (361–3) claimed that Constantine adopted Christianity because pagan priests, horrified by his deeds, refused to grant him expiation for his sins.

In Constantine's legislation, some traditional offenses and penalties were abolished and new ones were introduced. Gladiatorial contests were prohibited, and replaced with chariot racing. Branding slaves on the face (only) was prohibited on the grounds that the face bears the image of God. Convicts were consigned to mines to "work out their penalties without loss of blood," though as historian W. H. C. Frend observes, "this must have been a minor solace to a criminal who could still be forced to drink boiling oil or molten lead." Blasphemy was fined at the rate of half of one's goods. Sunday, which Constantine called "the Sun's day," was designated a holiday.

Constantine also enacted laws to enforce sexual morality. Elopement was classified as rape, and severe penalties for adultery were enacted. Divorce and remarriage were made more difficult. A woman could divorce her husband only if he was a murderer, poisoner or tomb violator. She could not divorce him on "frivolous grounds," such as drunkenness, gambling, and infidelity. A husband could divorce his wife for adultery, poisoning, or running a brothel.

Constantine's laws attempted to legislate his idea of the kingdom of God. They represented a systematic undermining of traditional family structures in which the *paterfamilias* had power of life and death over family members and slaves. Before Constantine died in 337, "scarcely any facet of private or public life was unaffected by Christianizing legislation."

The Council of Nicaea

Constantine hoped that the Edict of Toleration would reduce antagonisms and unify the empire. He was distressed when disagreements within the Christian movement emerged almost immediately. In the West the North African churches were in the midst of a bitter conflict over the reacceptance of persons who had lapsed in the Diocletian persecution, a conflict complete with elections, counter-elections, and terrorist incidents. In 316 Constantine attempted to force settlement of the disputes, confiscating property and exiling leaders. When this strategy had not worked by 321, he gave it up, and church leaders continued to quarrel.

Another discord raged in the Eastern Empire. It began as a doctrinal difference between Bishop Alexander of Alexandria and a priest in one of the principle churches of Alexandria, Arius. In 319 Alexander gave a disquisition on the trinity at a local synod that stated unambiguously:

> God was always and the Son was always, at the same time the father; at the same time the son; the son coexists with God unbegotten; he is not born by begetting; neither by thought nor by any moment of time does the father precede the son; God always, son always, the son exists from God himself.

Arius preached the opposite:

> Christ was begotten or created or appointed or established, before which he did not exist; for he was not unbegotten. If the father begat the son, he that was begotten had a beginning of existence; hence it is clear that there was a time when the son was not. It follows then of necessity that he has his existence from the non-existent.

"The *logos*," Arius said, "became incarnate by taking the place of the reason in the man Jesus so that Christ was neither fully God nor fully human, but a *third something*" (emphasis added).

Proof texts flew back and forth. Arius quoted John 14.28: "The father who sent me is greater than I;" and Mark 10.18: "Jesus said, 'Why do you call me good; there is only one good and that is God.'" Alexander quoted John 14.10: "I am in the father and the father is in me." Once again, scripture was ambiguous.

Arius's subordination of Christ to the father assumed the hierarchical cosmos of Platonism. Popular Platonism pictured a cosmos in which all beings have their place closer to, or farther from, the source of being – for Christians who used this model, God; for Platonists, the One. The One radiates being, and those closer to the source – the intelligible world and the stars – participate more fully than those at a distance who are more invested in the material world than in the One. The idea of a being, Christ, who belongs fully to divinity *and* fully to the human order made no sense to many intelligent people. If, however, Christ's "place" could be identified as the first emanation from God, closest to, but not quite fully God, that would make sense.

In 320, Bishop Alexander called a synod that excommunicated Arius. But Arius and his followers neither acknowledged nor obeyed the ruling. Constantine sent an emissary to adjudicate, but the situation only worsened. So in 325 Constantine called the Council of Nicaea to explore and decide on the issues. The emperor himself attended, though he understood the politics but not the theology; he called the trinitarian issue "a trifling and foolish dispute about words." With uncharacteristic modesty, Constantine did not judge the outcome of the council, since he was an unbaptized layman at the time, but he did participate in discussions.

What was new about the Council of Nicaea was the claim that the decisions of the council would be *ecumenical*, that is, universally binding on all Christians. There have been only seven undisputed ecumenical councils in the history of Christianity, though numerous local general councils or synods have been held (several of which have later been judged heretical).

The Council of Nicaea was attended by 318 bishops, only six of whom were from the West. What an amazing moment! After centuries of spasmodic but persistent persecution by the Roman state, Christian leaders met at an occasion sponsored, financed, and organized by a Roman emperor. Some of the bishops in attendance were blinded or crippled from torture during the Diocletian persecution. Eusebius reports that Constantine kissed their blinded eyes and their visible wounds.

Three parties quickly formed around the trinitarian issue: a large undecided and uncommitted majority, followers of Arius, and followers of Bishop Alexander. After a brief discussion, the Council rejected the Arian statement. Then a local baptismal creed was offered as a compromise. The creed was amended to satisfy the middle party, and anti-Arian phrases were added: "begotten, not made;" "of one essence with the father" (*homoousion*); "came down and became man." The creed was approved on June 19, 325. Arius and two bishops who did not sign the amended creed were deposed and exiled, and the bishops went home.

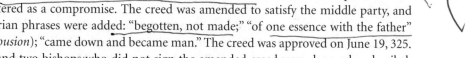

The Creed of Nicaea

We believe in one God, the Father all-sovereign, Maker of all things visible and invisible; and in one Lord Jesus Christ, the Son of God, begotten of the Father, only-begotten, that is, from the substance (*ousia*) of the Father; God of God, Light of Light, true God of true God, begotten not made, of one substance (*homoousion*) with the Father through whom all things were made, things in heaven and things on earth; who for us and for our salvation came down, and was enfleshed, and enhumaned, suffered, and rose on the third day, ascended into the heavens, is coming to judge the living and the dead; and in the Holy Spirit.

And those who say: "There was when he was not," and "before he was begotten he was not," and that he came into being from nothing, or those who say, that the Son of God is of another substance (*hypostasis*) or essence (*ousia*) or that he is created or changeable or alterable, these the Holy Catholic and Apostolic Church anathematizes.

The Creed of Nicaea was an attempt to affirm the relation of the son to the father as simultaneously "begotten, not made" *and* as *homoousios* (of one being) with the father. It is important to notice that the Creed of Nicaea is *not* the so-called "Nicene Creed." In 381 the Council of Constanople made further emendations that created the creed presently known as the Nicene Creed.

The creed had both a positive and a negative agenda. It attempted both definition, and rejection of alternative views. The creed affirms one God, but speaks of three. It mixes personal imagery (Father, Son, Spirit) with abstract, impersonal imagery (visible, essence, light). The creed is hymnic; parts of it can be traced back to the earliest baptismal creed in *Phillipians* 2. Poetic, evocative language is mixed with explanation ("begotten, not made"). It seeks to clarify, to celebrate, and, finally, to pronounce anathema on dissenters. "Anathema," originally a dedication to the gods of Roman religions, was by the fourth century a curse. Christian usage further shaped its meaning to consigning adversaries to Satan and hell.

Until his death in 337 Constantine enforced the Nicene "settlement." The contemporary Roman historian, Ammianus Marcellinus, observed that immediately upon Constantine's death and throughout the fourth century, bishops bustled around to one council after another, each trying to impose on the rest his own interpretation of trinitarian faith. "And the only noticeable result," Marcellinus concluded, "was the imposition of an intolerable burden on the means of public transport."

And yet, for the men engaged in trinitarian struggle, definition seemed crucial if Christianity were not to be so diversely interpreted that little remained of the Church of the martyrs. At stake was nothing less than the *kind* of Savior needed for redemption. The bitter Nicene struggle against an Arian interpretation was based on the conviction that a creaturely Christ could not *save*; only God could save. So Christ must either possess fully divine power, or be fully divine. The Creed of Nicaea did not specify which, but their soteriological concern, the concern for a Savior who could save, carried the day at Nicaea.

The Council of Nicaea reacted only to part of Arius's teaching, namely, his claim that Christ was not fully God. He taught that Christ was both the preexisting Creator of the world, and a creature, neither fully God nor completely human. A surviving 321 letter from Arius to Eusebius of Nicomedia briefly set out Arius's view, which he said he would defend, even if "threatened with a thousand deaths:" "Before he was begotten or created or appointed or established, he did not exist; for he was not unbegotten. We are persecuted because we say that the Son has a beginning, but God is without beginning."

Arius also wanted a savior who could save. He said that precisely because Christ was capable of change – suffering and spiritual development – he saves by becoming an example for his followers. Though labeled a "heresiarch," or originator of a heresy, the ambiguity of this accusation was evident in the support for his theology that continued to emerge after his excommunication. Arius's views are reconstructed from accusations against him; he circulated his theology in popular songs that survive only in fragments. Later councils continued discussion of Arius's view of Christ's saving work. Moreover, Arius was readmitted to communion at least twice after the Council of Nicaea; reinstated to communion by a council convened by Constantine at Constantinople in 336, he died on his way to Bishop Alexander's church. We visit Arius's Christology again later in this chapter.

In the fourth century, Christians had new and different problems as loosely organized local communities now belonged to an empire-wide institution. What was to take the place of persecution as a correction for the flood of barely Christianized converts that flocked to join the Christian churches as it became not only legal but politically advantageous to do so? Christians recognized that self-monitoring, an internalization of rigor, must take the place of external threat. They tried to ensure that converts were serious about their religious commitments by developing strenuous catechetical preparation and by requiring assent to a creed. These practices also had profound effects within Christian communities, shaping them in ways that would remain unchallenged for 1,500 years. Christian communities defined themselves, established leaders and leadership styles, and designated authority. Moreover, a new structure emerged in Christian churches. The separation of clergy in the chancel from congregants in the nave, the order in which catechumens were baptized (children, men, women), and other fourth-century decisions institutionalized a social order that became normative in Christian communities.

How was the creed *used*? It is not known how quickly it became a tool of catechesis across the empire, but by the end of the fourth century, at Augustine's church in North Africa, catechumens were given the creed or *symbolum* at the end of a long period of fasting, introspection, instruction, and repentance. They had *never heard or read it* before. Although parts of the creed may have been mentioned in sermons, the creed as a whole was only "handed over" after intensive preparation. Catechumens were expected to memorize it, word for word; they each recited it alone as a personal statement of faith before the whole congregation during the Easter vigil at which they were baptized.

Canons

The Council of Nicaea declared 20 canons, or decisions on matters of church order and practice. These canons offer glimpses of churches attempting to define themselves in new circumstances. Several canons regulated and standardized clergy, regulating the election and powers of bishops and clergy and prohibiting self-castration. Clergy were also forbidden to move to a more prestigious or more profitable parish. Moreover, a clear hierarchy of clergy was established that forbade deacons to administer the Eucharist to presbyters or bishops:

> Let the deacons remain within their own bounds, knowing that they are the ministers of the bishop and the inferiors of the presbyters. Let them receive the Eucharist according to their order, after the presbyters, and let either the bishop or the presbyter administer

to them. Furthermore, let not the deacons sit among the presbyters, for that is contrary to canon and order. And if, after this decree, anyone shall refuse to obey, let him be deposed from the diaconate.

(Canon 18)

Issues of power and sexuality were intertwined in the canons of Nicaea. Both ascetic extremes (like self-castration or refusing to take communion with twice-married people) and Roman casualness about sex were addressed. Clergy were instructed that they must not withhold communion from married people, or from twice-married people (Canon 8). The power of bishops and clergy was firmly linked to their sexual abstinence.

An effort was made to standardize liturgical practices: "Since there are some persons who kneel on the Lord's Day and in the days of Pentecost, therefore, so that all things may be uniformly observed in every parish, it seems good to the holy synod that prayer be made to God standing" (Canon 20). Periods of repentance and exclusion from communion were stipulated for those who had lapsed in persecution, and clergy were forbidden to deny them readmission at the end of that time. The canons of Nicaea demonstrate that informal, local, and ad hoc decision-making was in the process of being formalized, standardized, and centralized.

Theological controversy and problems of church order were not the only interests of fourth-century Christians. New and lavishly decorated church buildings, liturgy, and music attracted a broad and diverse audience. Some Christians felt ill-at-ease in the sumptuous fourth-century churches, and they left them to pursue solitude and ascetic practices. Ascetic monasticism provided an alternative to triumphal Christianity. We turn to these topics next.

Church building and decoration

A newly visible Christianity altered the skylines and landscapes of ancient cities. The tremendous relief Christians experienced at the end of persecution was evident as they hurried to build impressive churches. By 315, a mere five years after the great persecution, a magnificent new edifice financed by Constantine on some land he acquired through his second marriage was begun, St John Lateran. Other new church buildings sprang up simultaneously in Rome, Trier, Jerusalem, and Constantinople. In the vicinity of Rome alone, churches erected between 313 and 330 included: St John Lateran and its octagonal baptistery; Santa Croce in Gerusalemne; San Lorenzo; SS Marcellinus and Peter; San Sabastiano; Santa Crisogono; and St Peter's.

Eusebius's joy over the new church at Trier, in the province of Belgica, appears less naïve and materialistic when we recall Christians' long experience of more-or-less secret worship and when we recognize that his theology of visibility was founded on belief in Christ's incarnation. Eusebius wrote, "The church is a marvel of beauty, utterly breathtaking" (*Ecclesiastical History* X. 44. 2). At the dedication of the church he remarked:

> Oh God! We have heard with our ears, our fathers have told us the work which you did in their days, in days of old, but now as we no longer perceive the lofty arm and the celestial right arm of our all-gracious God and universal king by hearsay merely or report, but

Figure 2.1   Floor mosaic, Cathedral, Aquileia, Italy, c.318

observe, so to speak, in very deed and with our own eyes that the declarations recorded long ago are faithful and true, it is permitted us to raise a second hymn of triumph and to sing with a loud voice and say, "As we have heard, so have we seen." [Later he added] The testimony of our eyes makes instruction through the ears unnecessary.

(*Ecclesiastical History* X. 44. 2) (See CD Rom figures 2.1 to 2.5)

Christian literature characterized Christ as light-bringer, and light was a major motif of fourth-century churches. Most Constantinian churches had an eastern orientation; the sun rose on the chancel or sanctuary end and set on the atrium end. In some, altars were positioned and services timed so that the sun struck the altar during the mass.

Light was also a common theme of sermons. Augustine preached to catechumens in his North African basilica: "You were once in darkness, but now you are light in the Lord. Walk, then, as children of the light. Keep vigil against the darkness and its rulers in your mother, the light; and from the bosom of your mother, the light, pray to the Father of lights."

Light was vividly brought into play in Christian churches by mosaic decoration (see CD Rom figures 2.6 to 2.8). Mosaic has been called an art of light, but it is also amazingly durable. Black-and-white mosaics originated on the floors of eighth-century BCE Greek homes; by Constantine's time, strongly colored floor mosaics predominated. During the second quarter of the fourth-century, mosaics were transferred from floors to walls and vaults. When mosaics did not need to be walked on, tesserae (tiles cut from colored glass, alabaster, marble, or plain glass embedded with gold or silver foil) could be placed at angles that caught the light, giving the appearance of shimmering movement as viewers moved in relation to the mosaic (see CD Rom figures 2.4 to 2.8).

At Aquileia, an important northern Italy seaport on the Adriatic, the cathedral (begun CE 318) is in the form of a Latin cross, with the nave and two aisles separated by Roman columns. Floor mosaics, preserved because two subsequent floor layers were built over them, are the only part of the church that remains from the fourth century (see figure 2.1). The Aquileia floor is the largest known mosaic floor in Western Europe, covering 760 square meters. Motifs were largely adapted from the Hellenistic East. There are doves drinking, animals (a dancing donkey), fish, pastoral scenes, scriptural stories, and portraits. Sections feature the *asaroton*, or "unswept floor," featuring randomly-placed lobster claws, fish bones, and fruit peelings (see CD Rom figures 2.11 to 2.16). An inscription reads: "Blissful Theodore: With the help of God you completed the construction of this edifice and gloriously dedicated it in the name of God."

Christians brought the subjects and styles of Roman art into churches. Motifs included vine scrolls (now interpreted as eucharistic imagery), peacocks (a classical symbol of immortality), and *putti* or "flying babies." Did Christians copy the motifs of secular Roman art in their churches simply because they had not yet developed a distinctive Christian repertoire of images and styles? Probably not; they apparently felt entitled to use the common repertoire of their culture. It has been argued that these images may even have represented a conscious effort to attract converts and make them feel at home in the church by providing familiar images.

The Cathedral at Aquileia, with its many images from the everyday lives of the sea-faring people who first worshipped in it, suggests that these images were thoughtfully and purposely included. It is not known whether Bishop Theodore or anyone else gave theological reasons for the inclusion of images of octopus, squid, and fish of various sorts, the story of Jonah, and portraits of contemporary people and domestic animals. Lacking supporting texts, we cannot know how the people who built the cathedral chose their images; we can, however, observe the material evidence to learn that they found it appropriate to integrate daily life with scriptural stories in their worship of the incarnated God.

Fourth-century Christian churches made a strong statement about the visibility of Christianity in the world of senses and bodies, the triumph of the Word made flesh. Worship in its many sensory modes – music, images, ritual words and gestures, and incense – was a communal sensory experience, a conversion of the senses. The coordination of sensory engagement with belief in the Christian doctrines of creation, the incarnation of Jesus Christ, and the resurrection of body, combined to produce a vivid experience of the Christian's new life. It is only as we consider the engagement of the senses in worship that we can fully grasp the *physical* dimension of Christianity, with its claim to bring new life to bodies as well as minds. Fourth-century catechetical instructions and practices also support the suggestion that attention to the conversion of bodies and senses was balanced and integrated with instruction in beliefs, placing the convert within a new history and a new community.

READING

Eusebius, *Ecclesiastical History*, Book 10

Liturgy

In *The Power of Myth* (1988), Joseph Campbell wrote:

> People say that what we're all seeking is a meaning for life. I don't think that's what we're really seeking. I think that what we're really seeking is an experience of being alive, so that our life experiences on the purely physical plane will have resonance within our inmost being and reality, so that we actually feel the rapture of being alive in our bodies.

A fourth-century Eucharistic prayer by Serapion of Thmuis (Egypt): "We beg you, make us truly alive," suggests that Christian liturgy sought to produce the sense of aliveness based on strongly engaged senses.

Moreover, attention to the liturgical practices of Christian communities affords some access to otherwise unrecorded Christian experience, that of ordinary Christians. In the nineteenth century, Johann Wolfgang von Goethe remarked: "What can I make of church history? I can see nothing but clergymen. As to the Christians, the common people, nothing can be learned." Laypersons' descriptions of Christian liturgy in the fourth century are not extant, but their music, sermons, and catechetical instruction – what they smelled, saw, and heard – in the worship of the Word made flesh, gives some sense of the experience of worship, the unifying practice of Christian communities.

There is little evidence that most fourth-century Christians argued about the relationship of the Father and the Son, or the human and the divine in Christ. But many of them worshipped in the lavish new basilicas financed by Constantine and his successors. The first detailed descriptions of how people were instructed, baptized, and received the Eucharistic sacrament come from the fourth century. We can also begin to picture various devotional practices at this time.

Membership

Before the fourth century, a person who sought membership in a Christian community had to be recommended by Christian friends who knew her way of life and could testify to its morality. Secret, unwritten instruction was conducted one on one, or in small groups, over a period of two to three years. In the fourth century, however, the number of converts made it impossible to carry on this personalized instruction. Some formalization and standardization was necessary.

A "catechumen" was one who had been scrutinized and accepted for the long and complex process of instruction and practices by which conversion was achieved. In this process, disengaging from one's secular values and socialization was as important as weaving Christian life into mind and body along with new ideas and habits. There was new scripture to absorb, a new history to learn, new authorities to consult, and new ritual activities in which to participate.

Most fourth-century converts probably registered for instruction with little more than a willingness to acknowledge belief in Christ. They then underwent 40 days of moral and religious instruction combined with ascetic practices – daily exorcisms, fasts, prayers, and periods of abstinence from bathing and sexual activity. The process culminated in baptism, usually conducted during the Easter Vigil. But baptism alone was not decisive; rather, it was the *whole* process that gradually produced a conversion of body and mind. Lent, the 40-day period before Easter, was designated in the fourth century as a time for the instruction of catechumens and reevaluation of their lives by members. For members, the only standardized practice was a 40-hour fast just before Easter, incumbent on anyone who could endure it.

Baptism

In the fourth century, infants were baptized if they seemed to be in danger of dying, but adult baptism was the rule. In the early century, many people (like Constantine) postponed baptism until they were close to death. But by the end of the century Augustine and others urgently admonished people not to postpone baptism.

> I must warn you in the words of Holy Scripture: "defer it not from day to day, for his wrath shall come on a sudden." God knows that I tremble myself when I hear those words. I must not, I cannot, be silent. I am compelled to preach to you on this matter and to make you fearful, being myself full of fear.
>
> *(On the Gospel of John* 44. 2)

Convinced as he was that no one unbaptized would be saved, Augustine felt an awesome responsibility to admonish his congregation not to wait until close to death to be baptized.

During the seven weeks preceding Easter, those enrolled for baptism were instructed for three hours every day on the essentials of the faith, the evils of pagan amusements, and sexual morality. They also underwent daily exorcisms; every sizable church had several exorcists whose job was to "blow out" the demons from the body of the catechumen, reciting an ancient prayer: "Come out of him/her, accursed one." While this was done, the person stood on a harsh sackcloth or rough animal skin. A sermon by Theodore of Mopsuestia explained: "You stand on garments of sackcloth so that from the fact your feet are pricked and stung by the roughness you may remember your old sins and show penitence and repentance."

The Easter Vigil was the climax of catechumens' preparation. After a long series of scripture lessons that began with the creation of the world and ended with the passion story, the bishop preached. Baptisms began at first cockcrow. The congregation processed to the baptismal font, singing Psalm 42, "As the hart pants for the fountain of water, so pants my heart for you, O God." Each catechumen recited the creed as her/his personal statement of faith. After taking off the one tunic in which the initiate was clothed, s/he was anointed "from the topmost hairs of the head to the soles of the feet" with oil.

The earliest instructions for Christian baptism stipulate two conditions, invocation of the trinity, and naked baptism. At beginning of the fifth century Cyril of Jerusalem explained to the newly baptized what they had recently experienced:

> Immediately, upon entering [the baptistry], you removed your tunics . . . Having stripped, you were naked . . . Marvelous! You were naked in the sight of all and were not ashamed. Truly you bore the image of the first-formed Adam, who was naked in the garden and was "not ashamed."
>
> *(Mystagogical Lectures)*

Similar instructions and descriptions came from Syria, Alexandria, and Antioch. Naked baptism may have been patterned on the baptism of proselytes in post-biblical Judaism, or on Roman mystery religions' initiations. It also symbolized Christians' belief that the Incarnation of God in Jesus Christ required the explicit acknowledgment of bodies as the site of religious commitment.

Both Jews and Christians prohibited nakedness in other contexts. Christian leaders repeatedly cautioned against the Roman custom of mixed nude bathing at public baths. However, behavior forbidden in a secular context was *required* in a ritual context. Although every extant baptismal instruction specified naked baptism, diverse theological rationales were given, from the example of Adam and Eve in the garden "naked and unashamed," to participation in the death and resurrection of Jesus, to baptism as a preview of the resurrection body. Theology was apparently less important than the practice itself.

When the candidate for baptism entered the pool, she was asked the traditional questions: "Do you believe in the Father? Do you believe in the Son? Do you believe in the Holy Spirit? Do you believe in the Holy Church, the remission of sins, and the resurrection of the body?" After which her head and shoulders were dipped, or water was poured over her head. It is unlikely that candidates were immersed; in Augustine's basilica at Hippo in North Africa as in other fourth-century baptistries, the baptismal pool reached approximately to the chest of a boy, and approximately to an adult's navel. After baptism, the neonates (those newly born) appeared before the bishop and were again anointed. They were then clothed in a white linen robe and slippers; the new Christian's foot must not touch the earth for eight days. Finally they were given a small portion of milk and honey, the ancient ritual food of the newborn.

The power of such a religious experience can only be imagined. Contemporaries often attributed an almost magical effect to baptism. How were the secular meanings of naked bodies disconnected so that bodies could be experienced and *seen* as integral to a new religious life? Part of the answer to this question lies in the long process of instruction and ascetic practices in which catechumens were taught to think of themselves differently than they had as secular people. Congregations viewing baptism had undergone similar instruction, which prepared them to *see* bodies as the site of Christian commitment. Moreover, Roman households were intimately and concretely familiar with births and deaths that occurred in the home, and with accidents and diseases that were cared for at home, giving Christians a familiarity with bodies that allowed for a wide range of meanings. It is important not anachronistically to import twenty-first-century media interpretations of bodies as either sexual or medical to a culture not shaped by modern media.

Baptism was not the same experience for everyone. Despite Galatians 3.18, "In Christ there is neither male nor female . . ." there were three features of fourth-century baptism in which gender differences were evident. First, since women were baptized in Christian churches in which they were not permitted to hold leadership roles, in most geographical areas they were anointed and baptized by men. The mid-third century *Didascalia apostolorum* stated:

> Had it been necessary for women to baptize, certainly the Lord would have also been baptized by his own mother, not by John, or when he sent us to baptize, he would have sent women with us as well for this purpose. But now, nowhere, either by command nor in writing did he transmit this, since *he knew the order of nature and the fittingness of things*, being the creator of nature and the legislator of the arrangement. (emphasis added)

Although the *Didascalia* says that if there is a deaconess, she should anoint the woman being baptized, evidence of deaconnesses is found only in the Greek and Syrian churches; there were apparently none in Egypt or Palestine, and the office is unknown in the West. A rite that could not be conferred by a woman, but in which naked women were anointed by male clergy, made explicit in practice the subordination of women to men in Christian communities.

The order in which initiates were baptized was the second gendered feature of Christian baptism. Children were baptized first, men second, and women last. Sources give no rationale for this practice, but it is repeated in several manuals of church order. Third, Hippolytus' instructions (mid-fourth century) read: "and last, the women, who shall all have loosened hair." In the Roman Empire, the styling of women's hair was linked to the social order; unmarried women and prostitutes wore long, flowing hair, while married women's hair was bound on their heads. Unbound hair at the time of baptism may have signified a symbolic state of virginity at the time of new birth, or it may have signified a state of mourning – the only time that married women appeared in public with loosened hair – for Eve's role in introducing sin into the world. Lacking texts that interpret the practice, possible interpretations can only be suggested.

Eucharist

Newly baptized Christians saw the eucharistic celebration for the first time. Until they were baptized, they were secluded during this part of the worship service so that they could hear but *not see* the ritual. Instruction in perceiving the body and blood of Christ with *spiritual*, rather than physical eyes was an important part of their instruction. Tasting bread and wine, they must *see* body and blood. John Chrysostom (347–407) wrote: "The eyes of the body can see only those things which come under their perception, but the eyes of faith are quite the opposite. . . . This is faith: to see the invisible as if it were visible." Chrysostom described the central moment of the eucharistic celebration, the *epiclesis*, or invocation of the Holy Spirit: "The priest stands before the table, holding up his hands to heaven, and invokes the Holy Spirit to come and touch the elements; there is a great silence, a great stillness. The Spirit gives grace: the Spirit descends, touches the elements. . . . Then you see the sacrifice of the lamb completed" (*Catechetical Lectures* 2.9).

Two interpretations of the eucharistic elements were common in the fourth century. John Chrysostom, Ambrose (339–97), and others described the elements as the literal body and blood of Christ: "Not only ought we to see the Lord, we ought to take him in our hands, eat him, put our teeth into his flesh, and unite ourselves with him in the closest union." Cyril of Jerusalem's catechetical instructions indicate a more symbolic interpretation:

> Christ once said "If you do not eat my flesh and drink my blood you have no life in you." His hearers did not take the meaning spiritually and were shocked; they withdrew themselves, thinking that he was urging a literal eating of flesh. . . . Therefore think of the bread and wine not as merely that . . . for in the symbol of bread his body is given to you, and in the symbol of wine his blood, so that by partaking of the body and blood of Christ you may be made of the same body and blood with him. For in this way we become Christ-bearers, since the body and blood is distributed in the parts of our body.
>
> (*Catechetical Instruction* 22)

Trinitarian controversy both before and after the Council of Nicaea had largely neglected to define the role of the Holy Spirit, though the Spirit was affirmed and invoked. Against those who questioned the Spirit's divinity, Athanasius (296–373) and Basil of Caeserea (330–79) defended its divinity and activity. In doing so, they appealed to liturgical and sacramental tradition, to the Spirit's traditional titles that affirm divinity, and to experiential evidence of the Spirit's work in *making alive*.

Music

Christians recognized the power of music, as had others before them. Plato wrote extensively about music in his description of an idealized state, *The Republic*. He praised the musical modes that invigorate and arouse listeners to the duties of the good citizen, and he banned those that, in his view, led to "softness and sloth." He argued that an excellent musical education was central to the formation of excellent rulers, "because more than anything else rhythm and harmony find their way to the inmost soul and take strongest hold upon it."

As Plato pointed out, powerful sensory experiences are always religiously ambiguous. Worshippers may become attached to the music, or to the religious image, forgetting the spiritual reality to which it points. For this reason some Christians, like Clement of Alexandria, disapproved of the use of instruments in worship. However, in spite of concern over music's potential to divert and distract, most Christians found the dangers to be outweighed by music's capacity to create an auditory sacred space. In the sixth century the Latin author Cassiodorus said that music is intrinsically a spiritual experience in that it induces a joy that "raises our senses to divine realities and charms our ears with its measure."

The immediate roots of Christian music probably lay in synagogue practice, where "psalms and hymns and spiritual songs" were sung. The earliest Christian music was unaccompanied unison chant, but by the fourth century, more complex music filled Constantine's new basilicas. At first unwritten, chants were soon recorded in notation, which allowed the same music (with local variations) to be sung across the Mediterranean world. The liturgy supplied a common framework for church music – prayers, lessons, psalms, and hymns, as well as the processional, offertory, and eucharistic celebration. By the fifth century, the flourishing monastic movement chanted the hours of the daily office. Moreover, the division of the liturgical year into Christmas and Easter cycles required music for the different seasons.

Music was an integral, even foundational, part of Christian liturgy and as Christianity spread, so did its music. Chant traditions developed simultaneously in two directions: preservation of received tradition, and fresh stylization that endeavored to overcome the habituation resulting from hearing the same melodic lines again and again. Because senses fatigue, the ear must be surprised. So chant traditions consist of layers; each new layer resisted, embellished, or replaced the last.

According to Augustine, hymn-singing began in the fourth century:

> The Church of Milan had only recently begun to practice this exhortation and consolation, and there was great enthusiasm among the brethren as they joined together both with heart and voice in the singing. . . . It was then that the practice began of singing hymns and psalms in the manner of the Eastern churches. . . . The custom has been kept from that day to this and has been imitated by many, indeed by almost all of your congregations in other parts of the world.
>
> (*Confessions* 9.7)

Augustine wrote, "What tears I shed in your hymns and canticles! How deeply I was moved by the voices of your sweet singing Church! Those voices flowed into my ears and the truth was distilled into my heart, which overflowed with my passionate devotion. Tears ran from my eyes and I was happy in those tears" (*Confessions* 9.6).

In the West the position of cantor was established and boy choirs were introduced in the fourth century (fifth century in the East). Music schools were begun in large churches to train men and boys as church musicians. Women's voices disappeared in Christian liturgy in the fourth century as worship was formalized. Some church leaders (like Ambrose in Milan and Ephrem in Syria) defended women's participation in liturgical choirs, but others had complaints: women's voices were too seductive; pagan and heretical groups regularly employed women's choirs; women singers shared the bad reputation of all female entertainers; and women's singing was arrogant and incompatible with the humility and obedience required of women. Similar complaints were brought against boys' choirs, but with a different outcome. Women's choirs were disallowed, and the use of boys' choirs increased.

In the early seventh century the English church historian, Bede (called "*venerabilis*") recorded the instructions sent by Pope Gregory I (called "the Great"), to the missionary Augustine of Canterbury (not Augustine of Hippo). Gregory's instructions included teaching the newly converted British tribes how to sing in church. A uniform repertoire of chant was initiated, as well as reforms in style that emphasized the blending of voices rather than solo voices. Although it is unlikely that Gregory composed music, the legend that he did can be traced to the ninth century, and Western church monophonic music came to be known as Gregorian chant. (CD Rom, Music 2.1)

Four kinds of music were used in liturgy: solos, texts sung by a lector with a refrain response sung by the congregation, antiphonal singing (in which the congregation is divided into two groups which alternate in singing the verses of a psalm), and unison singing. The earliest descriptions of unison singing insist that all – young and old, women and men, "sing as with one mouth," a symbol and embodiment of the unity of the congregation.

No theology of music emerged in the fourth century. Its use in the Jewish synagogue, and reports of early Christians' hymn singing was enough to support its continued use. Moreover, the Church's concern with unity made the congregational practice of singing together an important expression of that unity. "Singing together exemplifies exactly what worshipping together strives to accomplish – offering the corporate body to God by breathing at the same time, while lifting the common voice, which has arisen from deep within each individual, in the act of praise" (Victoria Sirota, Lecture October 24, 1990, Harvard Divinity School). Christian authors described church music as a *localization* of the music of the heavenly spheres. Musicologist John Stevens writes, "If this heavenly music is indeed 'real,' then to share in it is not a metaphoric experience; it is rather our earthly music that is the metaphor."

Every liturgy involved music; there were chants for the officiating priest, the assistant or deacon, (possibly) a trained choir, and the congregation. The more solemn the occasion, the more of the service was chanted rather than spoken. Describing a Palm Sunday liturgy of a later period, Stevens describes the weaving of chants with action and procession as "part of a total ritual of movement, color, and gesture."

Meanwhile two clerks carried the relics and the Blessed Sacrament to the first station. There a lesson from the Gospel was read, and the antiphon "*En rex venit*" was sung for the adoration of the sacrament. Two antiphons sung by two alternating choruses, and, if needed, two responds accompanied the procession to the next station at the door to the fourth station at the rood. The cross, which had been covered since the first Monday in Lent, was uncovered and the officiant began the antiphon "*Ave*," the choir singing "*Rex noster*," with a genuflection to the rood. These three words were sung twice more at a higher pitch each time, and at the third time the antiphon was continued and completed by the choir. Then the crucifix on the high altar was uncovered, and the procession entered the choir to the singing of a respond.

By the fourth century, the language of the Western liturgy was Latin, but Greek was the first language of Western, as well as Eastern Christianity. Thus the Greek words, "Kyrie eleison, Christe eleison" were retained, and are still used today.

READING

Ambrose of Milan, *On the Mysteries*

2 Ascetic Monasticism

Ascetics were apparently the only people who criticized fourth-century church building and lavish decoration. At the end of the century, Jerome (the same Jerome who strolled in catacombs on Sunday afternoons) wrote:

> We Christians are supposed to live as though we are going to die tomorrow; yet we build as though we are going to live always in this world. Our walls shine with gold, our ceiling also, and the capitols of our pillars. Parchments are dyed purple, gold is melted into lettering; manuscripts are decked with jewels, . . . yet Christ dies before our doors naked and hungry in the persons of his poor.
>
> (*Ep.* 22.32; *Ep.* 128.4)

At the beginning of the fourth century, Christian asceticism included a wide range of different styles. Some ascetics lived at home, practicing prayer, meditation, and acts of charity. Others lived in community, beginning to develop common patterns – such as prayer at the third, sixth, and ninth hours – keeping a common purse, and wearing distinctive dress. In striking and intentional contrast to the dress of clergy, which was based on the ceremonial court dress of Roman officials, ascetics' dress was adapted from that of the lowest classes of Roman society.

Other ascetics practiced the more flamboyant asceticism of the Syrian desert, Palestine, and Mesopotamia. Simeon Stylites (c.390–459), spent 40 years on top of a 50-foot column. People brought their problems to him and he decided lawsuits, prophesied, and healed. He also scolded and advised bishops, emperors and governors, and converted heretics. His considerable social power was based on his ascetic feats. Simeon exercised a new kind of power in a society increasingly alarmed at the apparent power-lessness of the state in the early fifth century.

Although Simeon had numerous imitators, he was not typical of the large numbers (there are no reliable estimates) of people who dropped out of their societies and went to the Egyptian desert to practice asceticism. Palladius' *Lausaic History* and the *Historia Monachorum* describe a major social movement that was noticed and sometimes regretted by contemporaries, not only by non-Christians, but also by church leaders. Synesius of Cyrene, bishop of Ptolmais at the beginning of the fifth century, objected to the ascetic withdrawal from society of large numbers of people who, he thought, might better spend their energies supporting the fragile structures of church and society.

But contemporary objections to asceticism were rare; even those who remained in society admired the intransigent commitment of those who dropped out. Jerome wrote:

> O desert, bright with the flowers of Christ! O solitude whence come the stones of which, in the Apocalypse, the city of the great king is built! O wilderness gladdened with God's presence! What keeps you in the world, my brother, you who are above the world? How long shall gloomy roofs oppress you? How long shall smoky cities immure you? Believe me, I have more light than you. Sweet it is to lay aside the weight of the body and to soar into the pure bright aether. Do you dread poverty? Christ calls the poor blessed. Does toil frighten you? No athlete is crowned but in the sweat of his brow. Are you anxious about food? Faith fears no famine. Do you dread the bare ground for limbs wasted with fasting? The Lord lies there beside you. Do you recoil from an unwashed head and uncombed hair? Christ is your head. Does the boundless solitude of the desert terrify you? In the spirit you may walk always in paradise. Is your skin rough and scaly because you no longer bathe? He that is once washed in Christ need not wash again. To all your objections the Apostle gives this one brief answer: "The sufferings of this present time are not to be compared with the glory which shall come after them." You are pampered indeed, dearest brother, if you wish to rejoice with the world here *and* to reign with Christ hereafter.
>
> (*Ep.* 14)

Historians have sometimes suggested that the women and men who went to the Egyptian desert in the fourth and fifth centuries did so to escape various problems, such as social pressures, economic difficulties, churches increasingly filled with very minimally Christianized pagans, or disappointing personal situations. Any of these motivations may have played a part for various individuals, but they cannot account for the tremendous fascination and attraction that ascetic life in the desert held for rich and poor, educated and uneducated, women and men alike. Palladius (d. 425) wrote:

> Together with the holy fathers who took upon themselves the yoke of the solitary life, we commemorate also the marvelous women who led their lives in the divine spirit and who waxed exceedingly old . . . *for they wished to lay hold upon their souls* and to bind upon their heads the crown of impassibility and holiness. (emphasis added)

Ascetic women

The ascetic movement gave Christian women new possibilities for the cultivation of a religious subjectivity not available to them in Roman society. About half of Roman women of all classes married between the ages of 10 and 14, committing them from then on to child bearing and household duties. Within the Christian movement, virginity offered an alternative. Yet virginity was not an easy decision for a woman to make for several reasons. A young woman's withdrawal from society could cause problems in the inheritance structure of Roman society. If one daughter in a Christian family vowed celibacy, this was likely to be accepted, perhaps even rejoiced in. But if the only or the last daughter wanted to do so, there was consternation, even among the best of Christians, for if a family line ended without heirs, its wealth reverted to the state. Jerome wrote encouragingly to a young woman who was considering retirement from the world: "Do you fear the extinction of the line of Camillus if you do not present your father with some little fellow to crawl upon his breast and slobber on his neck? Your father will be sorry, but Christ will be glad."

Jerome, an admirer of ascetic women, reports that Marcella, daughter of one Roman counsel and niece of another, introduced the city monastery to Rome. "At that time no great lady knew anything of the monastic life, nor ventured to call herself a nun. The thing itself was strange and commonly accounted ignominious and degrading" (*Ep.* 127.5). Many of the women who entered monasteries were widows. Laws from Augustus' time had limited the period of widowhood to two years, but Constantine abolished those laws specifically to permit the option of monastic life for widows.

Other ascetic lifestyles also attracted women. The letters of Egeria, a pilgrim to Jerusalem from northern Spain, described the Easter liturgy of Jerusalem at the end of the fourth century. Her travel journal, written to her "sisters" at home tells of her excitement in being "on the spot," with direct experience of "places mentioned in the Bible." "I know," she wrote, "that I shall never cease to give thanks to God, but I thank him especially for this wonderful *experience* he has given me, beyond anything I could expect or deserve. I am far from worthy to have visited all these holy places."

For Egeria, the holy places were visible witnesses to accounts of Jesus' life. Her spirituality was based, not on mental concentration or meditation; rather, placing her body at the holy places produced her strong empathy with the events believed to have occurred there. She lived a life of perpetual pilgrimage:

> So loving ladies, light of my heart, this is where I am writing to you. My present plan is, in the name of Christ our God, to travel to Asia since I want to make a pilgrimage to Ephesus, and the martyrium of the holy and blessed apostle John. If after that I am still alive and able to visit holy places, I will either tell you about them face to face, or at any rate write to you about them if my plan changes. In any case ladies, light of my heart, whether I am in the body or out of the body, do not forget me.

A third role for women in the ascetic movement is exemplified by a woman who lived and worked outside the Mediterranean area. Nino, called in Armenia "the apostle, baptizer, and illuminator of the Georgians," missionized Transcaucasia in the fourth century. As we have seen, Christians in the Mediterranean area insisted on male leadership and identified women's leadership with heretical groups. In Georgia, however, Nino baptized on several recorded occasions; she also acted as a "teacher of the faith," a healer and a preacher. The accounts of her saintly life refer frequently to women's activities in civic and religious life. Moreover, Nino had been taught by another woman, Sara. A later hagiography (saint's life) describes Sara as saying to Nino:

I see, my child, thy strength like the strength of the lioness, whose roar is louder than that of any four-footed animal, or like the female eagle which, soaring in the highest air, beyond the male, and with the pupil of her eye seeing all the country, tiny as a pearl, stops, searches, and like lightening perceiving her prey, she plumes her wings and immediately swoops upon it.

The Egyptian desert

"They wished to lay hold upon their souls:" the difficulty of this project was recognized and those considered successful were given the title "great athlete." The prototype and model for solitary asceticism was St Antony, an Egyptian from a wealthy Christian family whose *Life* (356–62) was written by Athanasius. After his parents' death, Antony gave away his (and his sister's) inheritance and withdrew to the desert. Living on loaves of bread "let down from above," Antony fought battering demons for 20 years, never bathing and wearing a fur shirt in the baking desert. According to Athanasius, when he emerged after 20 years, his unchanged appearance amazed people: "For he had the same habit of body as before, and was neither fat, like a man without exercise, nor lean from fasting and striving with the demons, but he was just the same as they had known him before his retirement" (*Life* 14). He then instructed others in ascetic skills, such as identifying demons' tricks; he also healed the sick and, though illiterate, was consulted by philosophers. During the Diocletian persecution he left his solitary retreat to minister to confessors who were in prison or working in the mines. Antony's sage advice to novice ascetics was to approach every day "as though making a beginning daily" (*Life* 16).

What techniques did ascetics use to "lay hold upon their souls"? Evagrius Ponticus, a wealthy and educated man who visited the huge colony of hermits who lived in the Nitrian desert (west of the mouths of the Nile) in the later fourth century and stayed the rest of his life, gives the most detailed report. Evagrius was the first monk to write extensively and his influence on later authors gives him a central place in the history of Christian spirituality. Although his Origenist theology led to his condemnation at several local synods, his analysis of the *practice* of ascetic spirituality remained useful. The first technique of the ascetics, he said, was solitude. Solitude was essential, he said, for examining the soul in order to identify its areas of deadness. The *Sayings of the Fathers* (wrongly so-called, because the sayings of desert mothers, or *ammas*, were included), a sixth-century collection of documents from the Egyptian desert, also placed solitude among tools for the ascetic struggle.

There were three close friends, earnest men, who became monks. One of them chose to make peace between men engaged in controversy; the second chose to visit the sick; the third chose to be quiet in solitude. Then the first, struggling with quarreling opponents, found that he could not heal everyone. And, worn out, he came to the second who was ministering to the sick, and found him flagging in spirit and unable to fulfill his purpose. And the two went away to see the third who had become a hermit and told him their troubles. And they asked him to tell them what progress he had made. And he was silent for a little, and poured water into a cup. And he said, "Look at the water." And it was cloudy. And after a little he said again, "Now look; see how clear the water has become." And when they leaned over the water they saw their faces as in a glass. And then he said to them, "So it is with the man who lives among men. He does not see his own sins because of the turmoil. But when he is at rest, especially in the desert, he sees his sins.

(Sayings of the Fathers, Part II)

The ascetics' second technique was aphoristic advice. Visiting an experienced colleague, a young monk would ask: "Speak to me some word, some phrase." The "word" he sought was not an explanation or an argument, but a "saying" for the student to carry away with him and ponder until it changed his life. Like a Zen koan, the meaning of a "saying" was often not immediately evident. For example, "A brother asked Abba Serapion: 'Speak to me a word.' The old man said: 'what can I say to you? You have taken what belongs to widows and orphans and put it on your window-ledge.' He saw that the window-ledge was full of books" (*Sayings* Part VI. 12).

The third technique was self-observation: the disciple must observe closely the "demons" operating within his own psyche. Demons, Evagrius Ponticus said, act *through thoughts to arouse emotions.*

> If any monk wishes to take the measure of some of the more fierce demons, then let him keep careful watch over his thoughts. Let him observe their intensity, their periods of decline, and follow them as they rise and fall. *Let him note well the complexity of his thoughts,* their periodicity, the demons that cause them with the order of their succession and the nature of their associations. Then let him ask from Christ the explanations of these data he has observed.
>
> *(Praktikos* 50; emphasis added)

Evagrius, like all close observers of the ascetic life, was sensitively aware of the particular temptations the lifestyle was likely to generate. (The following quotation might, however, also apply to twenty-first-century students.)

> The demon of *acedia* (boredom, indifference) – also called the noonday demon – is one that causes the most serious trouble of all. He presses his attack upon the monk about the fourth hour and besieges the soul until the eighth hour, First of all he makes it seem that the sun barely moves, if at all, and that the day is fifty hours long. Then he constrains the monk to look constantly out the windows, to walk outside the cell, to gaze carefully at the sun to determine how far it stands from the ninth hour, to look now this way and now that to see if perhaps one of the brothers appears from his cell. Then too he inspires in the heart of the monk a hatred for the place, a hatred for his very life itself, a hatred for manual labor. He leads him to reflect that charity has departed from among the brethren, that there is no one to give encouragement. Should there be someone at this period that offends him in some way or other, this too the demon uses to further contribute to his hatred. This demon drives him along to desire other sites where he can more easily procure life's necessities, more readily find work, and make a real success of himself. He goes on to suggest that, after all, it is not the place that is the basis for pleasing the Lord. God is to be adored everywhere. He joins to these reflections the memory of his dear ones and of his former way of life. He depicts life stretching out for a long period of time, and brings before the mind's eye the toil of the ascetic struggle, and . . . leaves no stone unturned to induce the monk to forsake his cell and drop out of the fight.
>
> *(Praktikos* 12)

Evagrius suggests that this demon can be vanquished by not taking its insinuations seriously.

Ascetic practices formed the fourth technique: "For those who have attained to purity of heart *by means of the body* and who in some measure have applied themselves to the contemplation of created things know the grace of the Creator in giving them a body." Continence, or renunciation of sexual activity, was the one permanent and non-negotiable asceticism. Other practices Evagrius described were moderate, temporary, precisely chosen, and personally designed to address whatever hinders prayer. He mentioned vigils, prayer, fasting, solitude, limiting one's intake of water, and reading. John Cassian added poverty and nakedness.

Ascetic authors consistently acknowledged the usefulness of ascetic practices, but cautioned against *abuse* of the body. These frequent warnings may indicate that abuses were not uncommon. Palladius, the fifth-century historian of early monasticism and pupil of Evagrius Ponticus, warned: "Our holy and most ascetic master stated that the monk should always live as if he were to die on the morrow, but at the same time he should treat his body as if he were to live on with it for many years to come" (*Praktikos*: 29)

Communal asceticism

By the end of the fourth century the individual asceticism (eremetical) of the Egyptian desert had largely given way to communal (cenobitic) forms of ascetic life. Pachomius (290–346), traditionally known as the founder of monasticism, reported that even though Antony was a hermit, he would have approved. He quotes Antony as saying: "In the early days when I became a monk, there was no community for the nourishment of other souls; . . . each of the early monks practiced asceticism on his own. But afterwards your father embarked upon this enterprise with good effect, helped by the Lord." Community both increased the pressure on the monk to understand his own soul, and provided support and encouragement for the task. John Cassian (360–435) wrote: "For curing the faults I have been talking about, human society, so far from being a hindrance, is useful. The more often people see that they are impatient, the more thoroughly they do penitence and the more rapidly they achieve a sound mind."

The founders of monasticism recognized that secular society functions both to encourage the pursuit of sex, power, and possessions, and to limit the potential destructiveness of these pursuits. Monastic life provided an alternative: Instead of the pursuit of sex, the monk vowed celibacy; instead of the pursuit of power, he vowed obedience; instead of seeking possessions, he vowed poverty. The repeatedly stated object of these renunciations was to overcome the deadness resulting from socialized behavior; the goal was *more life*. Early monastic *Rules* show little interest in the ascetic tools of the desert hermits. The only two practices retained by Basil (330–79) were "withdrawal from the world" and silence.

The sixth-century *Rule* of St Benedict of Nursia (in central Italy) for the lay monks of Monte Cassino, built on earlier *Rules*. It addressed both the administration of a monastery and the spiritual life of its monks. Benedict required a life of obedience, stability of residence, and moral struggle. The abbot was to be chosen by the monks; once chosen, he had full authority over all decisions relating to the monastery and the individuals within it. Obedience, humility, and patience were the supreme virtues of the monk. Study and the intellectual life were not valued: "There [was] no provision in the Rule for works of learning, for the reading of non-Christian authors, for the copying of manuscripts" – all activities that would become important in later monasticism (O. Chadwick, 1958: 28). Monasticism became one of the great institutions of medieval Christianity. We return to it in subsequent chapters.

READINGS

The Pilgrimage of Egeria
Athanasius, *Life of St Antony*
The Sayings of the Fathers
The Rule of St Benedict

3 Christological Controversy

Trinitarian and Christological controversies had overlapping concerns as descriptions of the relationships among the persons of the trinity affected how the relationship of the human and divine natures in Christ was conceptualized and explained. Focusing on trinitarian description, the council of Nicaea largely ignored Christological questions. The Nicene formula, "The Son was made flesh, becoming human," was probably intended to emphasize the reality of Christ's incarnation (against Gnostics) rather than to claim the integrity of both natures.

Both Arians and "Nicenes" (the victorious party at Nicaea) agreed that "the Word was in Christ." But Arius's view that Christ was subordinate to the Father implied that Christ was less than fully divine. On the other hand, the Nicenes' affirmation of the "same substance" of Father and Son seemed to imply that Christ was not completely human. We need to look more closely at both positions in order to understand the different religious sensibilities that underlay them. Athanasius's and Arius's theologies illustrate the connection between trinitarian and Christological description.

Athanasius

Athanasius's (296–373) childhood occurred during the Diocletian persecution. He attended the Council of Nicaea as an aide to Bishop Alexander. In 328 when Alexander died he became bishop of Alexandria, a position he held for the next 45 years. Athanasius was educated in classical philosophy and culture, and he had a profound and subtle mind. But he was obdurate on a point that seemed to him utterly crucial, namely, the equality of Father and Son. Struggle against Arians and their beliefs dominated his life. He was the leader and spokesman for those who found the fully equal status of Christ as God so crucial that they denied the right of any who thought of Christ as subordinate to worship or administer the Eucharist.

Athanasius's opposition to Arius was based on a soteriological concern: what kind of a savior can *save*? His trinitarian concern resulted in a Christology that emphasized Christ's divine nature. He described the human body and mind of Jesus as *taken over* by the divine Word: "It was the Word who performed miracles and who wept, was hungry, prayed, and cried out from the cross." Yet, when he momentarily forgot the Arian conflict, he spoke rather differently about the equality and integrity of the two natures. A monk once asked him, "How is the Son equal to the Father?" Athanasius replied, "Like the sight of two eyes."

During his career as bishop, Athanasius was exiled five times, primarily for the methods he used in fighting rival Christians – Arians, and Melitians (who thought the terms by which the lapsed could reenter the Church too lax). No doctrinal charge was ever brought against Athanasius, but he was formally excommunicated for "acts unworthy of a Christian bishop." His enemies testified that he had threatened to call a dock strike at Alexandria that, had it been carried out, would have blocked the corn supply to Constantinople. He apparently kidnapped a Melitian bishop; when accused of his murder, Athanasius produced him. Historian Timothy Barnes summarized his examination of the evidence of Athanasius's activities in Alexandria: "Despite his protestations of innocence, Athanasius exercised power and protected his position in Alexandria by the systematic use of violence and intimidation" (Barnes, 1993, *Athanasius and Constantine*, 32). Each of his exiles resulted from an imperial edict against the *exclusive* claims of the Nicene party.

Arians, on the other hand, were conciliatory, tolerant, eager to gather all under the Christian banner, and eager to gain Constantine's support by fulfilling his expectation that Christian faith could unite the empire. While Nicene bishops excluded Arians from communion, most Arians wanted inter-communion and an inclusive Christian empire. Nicenes (who after the Council of Nicaea are accurately called Catholics) were skeptical about the possibility that church and empire could be united.

Athanasius's *On the Incarnation*, written when he was about 20 years old, gave no hint of his future terrorist politics. It laid the groundwork for his anti-Arian polemic. Using a direct, unpolished, and sometimes repetitive style, Athanasius proposed a powerful analysis of what is wrong with human beings and how they can be redeemed. Combining strong imagery, *ad hominem* argument, and scriptural quotations, he presented the need for salvation and God's activity in offering it:

> For as, when the likeness painted on a panel has been effaced by stains from without, he whose likeness it is must needs come once more to enable the portrait to be renewed on the same wood, for the sake of his picture, even the mere wood on which it is painted is not thrown away, but the outline is renewed upon it; in the same way also the most holy son of the father, being the image of the father, came to our region to renew human beings once made in his likeness, and find them, as ones lost, by the remission of sins; as he says himself in the gospels: "I came to find and to save the lost" . . . "Except a person be born again," not meaning, as they thought, birth from woman, but speaking of the soul born and created anew in the likeness of God's image.
>
> (*On the Incarnation* 14)

Christ entered human nature, Athanasius said, to achieve solidarity with the human race in order to save it. Asserting Christ's full humanity led him to ask: What is the *normatively* human experience? Tertullian, who had asked the same question over a century before in a different context, had insisted that a fully human *birth* guaranteed humanity. Athanasius identified death as the normative human experience. Death, he said, was woven closely into the human body by the sin of Adam and Eve. Therefore, Christ's *essential* redemptive act was to "put on" a human body in order to "find death in the body and blot it out" (*Incarnation* 44). Christ had to take a body "capable of death" in order to alter the human condition *from the inside*. Once Christ, the "very Life" had entered the human condition,

> The actual corruption of death has no longer holding ground against human beings, by reason of the Word, which by his one body has come to dwell among them. And like as when a great king has entered into some large city and taken up his abode in one of the houses there, such city is at all events held worthy of great honor, nor does any enemy or bandit any longer descend upon it and subject it; but, on the contrary, it is thought entitled to all care, because of the king's having taken up residence in a single house there; so, too, has it been with the monarch of all. For now that he has come to our realm, and taken up his abode in one body among his peers, henceforth the whole conspiracy of the enemy against humankind is checked, and the corruption of death which before was prevailing against them is done away. For the race of human beings had gone to ruin, had not the Lord, the Savior of all, the Son of God, come among us to meet the end of death.
>
> (*Incarnation* 9)

Athanasius believed that human nature is not in need of destruction and reconstruction. The goodness of creation was one of his most persistent themes. For Athanasius, death was evil, a sliding away from the source of life to non-existence. The contradiction at the heart of human nature is that human beings are simultaneously created in God's image *and* from nothing. Death is a weakness that destroys the integrity of human nature.

The fact that death has been overcome is evident, Athanasius said, in the Christian martyrs who accepted death rather than renounce their Christian faith, "for human beings, by nature are afraid of death and the dissolution of the body." But "he who has put on the faith of the cross despises even what is naturally fearful and for Christ's sake is not afraid of death." Death has changed for the Christian: "Henceforth we are *only dissolved*, agreeably to our body's mortal nature, at the time God has fixed for each, that we may be able to gain a better resurrection" (*Incarnation* 45). Death has no power to harm the Christian; it is "a lion teased by children." The Christian is covered and protected (as if) from a great fire by asbestos: "But just as one who has the asbestos knows that the fire has no burning power, so too let him who is incredulous about the victory over death receive the faith of Christ . . . and he shall see the weakness of death and triumph over it" (*Incarnation* 31). As formerly death was "woven closely to the body," so now the life of Christ is woven closely to the body.

Athanasius's Christology and anthropology were interconnected. Just as the divine nature dominates and subsumes the human nature in Christ, so in the Christian the divine life can possess the human body. By "turning one's gaze" to Christ, "we, not merely being clay, may not revert to clay, but . . . being joined with the Word from heaven, we may through him be brought to heaven, that we may transcend and divinize our humanity, using it as an instrument for the energizing and illumination of the divine within" (*Incarnation* 21).

Arius

Christological controversy has largely been interpreted through the perspectives of the victors. From this perspective, Arius and his party seem to be interested merely in attacking Christ's divinity. Yet the early Arian controversy would not have been as heated if it did not involve *two* positive theologies, two passionately held and contradictory views of Christ's nature and work. What did Arius see? What did he miss in Athansius's description of the incarnation of Christ?

Arius was a scriptural exegete who regularly instructed laypersons in scripture. He believed that doctrine should be defined by, and supported from, scripture. And he noticed in scripture many references to Christ's human characteristics. The Gospels are full of accounts of Jesus' physical and psychological suffering. "He bore the marks of true humanity – the body's infirmities, the mind's uncertainties, the soul's troublings, the need for divine empowerment through the spirit" (Gregg and Groh, 1981: 12). Arius emphasized Christ's creatureliness, his participation with Christians in "the full range of [human] psychological and spiritual limitations" (Gregg and Groh, 1981: 4). While Arius described the "closest possible links" between Christ and the believer, Athanasius set "Christ as far as possible from other rational creatures" (Gregg and Groh, 1981: 13).

Arius emphasized Christ's changeability, his growth in learning and spiritual insight, and his dependence on the Holy Spirit. Like the believer, Christ was dependent for his existence and authority on the Father's will, and he was "in" the Father "by mutuality of wills" (Gregg and Groh, 1981: 173). From his reading of scripture, as well as from earlier Christian authors like Irenaeus, the human Jesus who shared every aspect of humanity was the one who could redeem humanity.

Athanasius and his party ascribed scriptural accounts of Jesus' weakness to his *flesh*, assumed briefly during his earthly life, while his divinity remained unchanged. Gregg and Groh conclude their study of Arius's Christology: "The Athanasian Christology was founded in a theology of the differences between divine and human nature. By linking Christ essentially and eternally to God, Athanasius insures that the incarnation will bring the divine nature into contact with the human nature" (180). For Arius, the theological problem was not how to bring salvific divinity to humanity. Rather, Christ's pre-existent adoption as "only-begotten" Son of God gave him the goodness and wisdom believers could learn from and grow in. It was not Christ's *nature* that saved, but his work, his example of faithful practical wisdom and dependence on God's will *on location*, in the human situation.

The death of Constantine in 337 brought renewed trinitarian conflict. In the 340s, three important local councils omitted the *homoousion* (same substance) phrase from the creed. In the 350s, the Arian emperor Constantius was determined to defeat the Nicene definition, but he died before he achieved this goal. In 361 the non-Christian emperor Julian ruled briefly. He neither supported nor banished anyone, hoping that the problem would simply dissolve. Because of the work of Athanasius in the East and Bishop Hilary of Poitiers in the West, the *homoousion* position gradually triumphed.

In 381 the Catholic emperor Theodosius called an ecumenical council at Constantinople. He warned the Greeks in advance that the terms of ecclesiastical recognition would be acceptance of the creed of Nicaea and communion with the Roman bishop.

The council reworded the creed, omitting the clause that curses those who believe differently, and the creed of Nicaea became the Nicene Creed. It contained an article on the Holy Spirit, the first formal statement of the Holy Spirit's deity. The Council of Constantinople effectively ended trinitarian controversy, but Christological controversy continued.

The men most involved in the Trinitarian and Christological controversies occasionally worried about the polemical context that determined the problems addressed as well as acceptable solutions. Some of them deplored the controversy's preoccupation with the correct word. Even the aggressive Athanasius wrote: "Those who accept the Nicene Creed but have doubts about the term *homoousion* must not be treated as enemies; we discuss the matter with them as brothers with brothers; they mean the same as we and dispute only about the word."

Moreover, the definitions of Nicaea and Constantinople caused many people, who had worshipped together when the poetic language of liturgy allowed a proliferation of meanings, to realize that they thought of the trinity differently than stated by the creed. Henceforth, those people were excluded from communion.

Fourth-century interest in definition and exclusion must, however, be understood in the context of a simultaneous (and contradictory) interest in *inclusion*. Christianity was preached as a *via universalis*, a universal way, open and accessible to all. We should notice, however, the ambiguity of the term "universal." It could be understood either as an open and accessible way, or as the *only* way. Both meanings circulated in the fourth century.

Excitement with a *via universalis* could not have been more strongly and directly reflected and communicated than it was in the new architecture and art of the Christian movement. Constantine's dream of unifying the empire under Christianity provided the impetus as well as the funds for making the universal way attractive – visible, audible, and tangible – as an integral part of Christian worship. The inclusivity of fourth-century images and architecture is startling when we note that it was contemporaneous with fourth-century theological debates.

READING

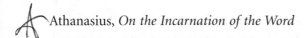

Athanasius, *On the Incarnation of the Word*

4   Church and Empire

From 313 forward, the pope in Rome came increasingly to be considered "first among equals," based on the Apostles Peter and Paul's affiliation with the Church at Rome. At the beginning of the fifth century, Pope Innocent I (402–17) ruled that no religious question should be decided without consulting the pope. But it was not until the papacy of Leo I (440–61) that the full theory of papal primacy was asserted. Leo I claimed that the care of the whole Church had been entrusted to him as Peter's successor. Pope Gelasius I (492–6) set the terms of the struggle by his bold assertion that papal power superseded imperial power and could not be challenged by anyone. Yet resistance to the

Roman pope's supremacy continued. The ever-volatile balance of power between pope and emperor continued to be contested through the Middle Ages. Chapter 3 will explore further the medieval struggle over this issue.

Similarly, questions concerning the relationship between church and state were pressing at the end of the fourth century in the West. Should the state decide ecclesiastical matters? Should the state be called upon to enforce Catholic decisions about doctrine and practice? Should the state prosecute dissidence? Should the church be loyal to the state no matter what the state and its ruler did? Or, should the church be autonomous from the state? In matters of doctrine? In property? Should the state be religiously tolerant, as the Senator Symmachus eloquently urged in 384? Pleading for the reinstatement of the Altar of Victory in the Senate, he said, "What difference does it make how a person searches for the truth? Surely there must be more than one avenue of approach to a secret so vast." These questions were given working solutions at the end of the fourth century, but they continued to plague church–state relations throughout the medieval period.

Theodosius I reversed Constantine's alleged unwillingness to coerce anyone to religion. In his decree that made Christianity the religion of Empire he stated:

> We desire that all peoples who fall beneath the sway of our imperial clemency should profess the faith that we believe to have been communicated by the Apostle Peter to the Romans and maintained in its traditional form to this day. And we require that those who follow this rule of faith should embrace the name of Catholic Christians, adjuring all others madmen and ordering them to be designated as heretics, and condemned as such, in the first instance to suffer divine punishment, and therewith, the vengeance of that power which we, by celestial authority, have assumed.

Constantine's religiously tolerant Empire became the Christian Empire at the end of the fourth century. The "universal way" was no longer the open and accessible way, but the "one way."

Augustine of Hippo

No author in the history of Christianity is as simultaneously revered and resented as Augustine of Hippo (356–430). In no Christian author is the necessity of reading with generosity – what did he *intend*? – and suspicion – what were the effects of his theological vision? – more evident. Because of Augustine's pervasive influence in Western Christianity, it is important to understand his theology, especially his teachings on concupiscence and original sin; his social teachings; and his theological controversies.

Concupiscence
Augustine, Bishop of Hippo in the North African province of Numidia at the end of the fourth century, began his thinking and writing with an analysis of his own experience. "I came to understand," he wrote, "through my own experience" (*Confessions* 8.5). In doing so, he was amazed that his starting point was so distant from the interests of most people: "And people go abroad to wonder at the heights of mountains, the huge waves

of the sea, the broad streams of rivers, the vastness of the ocean, the turnings of the stars – and they do not notice themselves" (*Conf.* 10.8).

When you do stop and take a look at human nature as it is, Augustine said, the first thing you notice is that things are not as they should be. A puzzling and terrifying disjunction lies between every person's concerted efforts to be happy and the overwhelming pain suffered by human beings.

> Everyone, whatever his condition, desires to be happy. There is no one who does not desire this, and each one desires it with such earnestness that it is preferred to all other things; whoever, in fact, desires other things, desires them for this end alone. . . . In whatever life one chooses, there is no one who does not wish to be happy.
>
> (*Sermon* 306.3)

Why, then, Augustine asked himself, was there so little happiness? He found part of the answer in involuntary suffering and lifelong vulnerability to pain. In the *City of God* 22.21 he described the evidence that there is *too much* pain in the world, far more, that is, than one can learn from. He cataloged woes ranging from the discipline children undergo in order to be socialized and educated ("How is it that what we learn with toil we forget with ease?") to the human and environmental sources of pain, terror, and death. He cited the harshness of weather, calamities, storms, floods, earthquakes, and political upheavals, the danger of being crushed by falling buildings, of being attacked by animals, the assaults of demons, and "diseases for which the treatments and medicines themselves are instruments of torture." The list goes on and on – restless dreams, fear itself . . .

But it was not involuntary pain that made Augustine conclude that human life is, in some sense, a punishment. It was the apparently *voluntary* way that people seemed to dismantle their own happiness as fast as they built it. The *Confessions*, Augustine's own story, both illustrated this observation and tried to explain it. Augustine invited his readers to place his theology in the context of his experience, as he did.

Newly elected bishop by congregational acclamation at the age of 40, Augustine wrote a journal. The *Confessions* was therapy, not only in the modern sense of introspection and reconstruction of one's personal past, but also in the ancient sense, an attempt to locate oneself within time and space, history and cosmos, the larger arena of human existence. The *Confessions* also differed from modern journals in that it was not private; Augustine shared it with other interested people, both friends and strangers. The usefulness of hearing about someone else's "journey" was part of his motivation in narrating his life.

He described his early life as a frenzied struggle for happiness, followed by disillusionment that brought him to a burned-out condition. He described his life as a prize-winning public speaker and teacher of rhetoric in the imperial capital of Milan, "I panted for honors, for money, for marriage . . . I found bitterness and difficulty in following these desires. . . . How unhappy my soul was then! . . . I got no joy out of my learning. . . . I was eaten up by anxieties" (*Conf.* 6.6). Augustine called his compulsive grasping at every object that crossed his path in the fear that something would be missed, *concupiscentia*. And he saw its most evident occurrence in the newborn infant. Taking his paradigm seriously helps illuminate what Augustine meant by "concupiscence."

The classical world, the world of Augustine's education, had seen old age as miserable; Augustine wrote, "Who would not tremble and wish rather to die than to be an infant again if the choice were put before him?" (*City of God* 21. 14). Augustine saw the *form* of concupiscence in the infant's behavior. Not content to wait to be fed, the infant screams, tries to grasp the breast or bottle, exhibiting every sign of anxiety. As the child grows, its anxious grasping is not eradicated but extended, given different objects and a wider scope. The anxiety of infancy becomes the anxieties of childhood, adolescence, and adulthood: "For it is just these same sins which, as the years pass by, become related no longer to tutors, schoolmasters, footballs, nuts, and pet sparrows, but to magistrates, kings, gold, estates, and slaves" (*Conf.* 1.9).

Concupiscence pervades and organizes human life, from the first moment in which the infant gasps/grasps breath to the adult's pursuit of sex, power, and possessions. Concupiscence is not, Augustine said, zestful and energizing, but painfully disorienting and joyless. Surprisingly, Augustine said that the appropriate attitude toward concupiscence is *sympathy*. He marveled that "no one is sorry for the children; no one is sorry for the older people; no one is sorry for both of them" (*Conf.* 1.9). Concupiscence was, for Augustine, a sickness or wound, the result of an ancient fall that radically debilitated human nature.

Concupiscence is not nourished by its objects, even in attaining them. The objects are good in themselves, Augustine insisted, but they are consistently unsatisfying to the person who anxiously pursues them: "For those who find their gratification in external things easily become empty and pour themselves out of things seen and temporal and, with starving minds, lick shadows" (*Conf.* 9 4). The incapacity of "things" to provide satisfaction, however, curiously only seems to prompt human beings to redouble their efforts to secure gratification, efforts that spin them deeper and deeper into the ruts of habitual behavior. Augustine analyzed his experience: "From a disordered will came concupiscence, and serving concupiscence became a habit, and the unresisted habit became a necessity. These were the links – so I call them a chain – holding me in hard slavery" (*Conf.* 8. 5).

The only quasi-nourishment of the habit of concupiscence is the momentary gratification of – in Augustine's vivid language – "scratching the itching scab of concupiscence" (*Conf.* 9. 7). Undernourished, the psyche sinks into lethargy and anxiety, a state that combines the inertia of a sleepwalker with frenzied activity. The quality of relationships with other people in this mode is dramatically presented in Augustine's image of "eating one another up, as people do with their food" (*Conf.* 9. 2). The behavior of the infant at the mother's breast is disguised, but structurally unaltered in adult behavior.

Augustine's famous conversion, narrated in Book 8 of his *Confessions*, illustrated his recognition of the "weight" of concupiscence. Conversion was not a simple matter of revising intellectual decisions. It was the transformative experience of coming – being led, he said in retrospect – to the bitter end of his own resources and agenda. The moment of conversion occurred when Augustine realized that the objects he had so strenuously pursued and attempted to possess had instead possessed him, and "a slave cannot enjoy that which enslaves him."

Augustine's conversion, was a conversion of the will. It began with a painful but accurate sight of himself:

Any yearning of the soul for good

> But you, Lord, were turning me around so that I could see myself; You took me from behind
> my own back, which was where I had put myself during the time when I did not want to
> be observed by myself, and you set me in front of my own face so that I could see how foul
> a sight I was – crooked, filthy, spotted, and ulcerous. I saw, and I was horrified, and I had
> nowhere to go to escape from myself.
>
> (*Conf.* 8. 7)

He became aware of a childish voice chanting, "Tolle lege; tolle lege:" (take and read)!
His response was obedience, the trusting acceptance that the message was for him. Trust
replaced the infant's first gasp/grasp response. Augustine did not say that it was easy to
resist a deeply imbedded habitual response and to substitute a new response, but the
message of the *Confessions* was that, with God's grace, it is possible. That is what
Augustine's first readers were interested in hearing about.

Augustine's conversion was to continence, as he had known it must be. His famous
pre-conversion prayer, "Give me chastity, but not yet," expressed his recognition that for
him, an integrated sexuality was impossible. He was keenly and humbly aware that one
who is compulsive in a particular area may not be able to integrate what another person
can enjoy with freedom and gratitude.

Augustine's sharp sense of the suffering of human life led him to conclude that the
whole human race exists in a "state of punishment." "What else is the message of all
the evils of humanity?" The strongest evidence is death. Earlier Christian authors urged
their readers to "despise" or even to embrace death, but Augustine asked, "Is death, which
separates soul and body, a good thing for the good?" He answered, "The death of the
body, the separation of the soul from the body is not good for anyone . . . it is a harsh
and unnatural experience" (*City of God* 13. 6).

Concupiscence, Augustine said, is caused by the soul's insubordination from its
creator, its unrealistic attempt to exist in isolation from the source of its being. Body is
the helpless victim of soul's ruthless pursuit of objects. Augustine objected to the late
classical commonplace of referring to body as a prison:

> You consider the flesh as fetters, but who loves his fetters? You consider the flesh a prison,
> but who loves his prison? No matter how great a master of the flesh you may be, and no
> matter how great the severity with which you are kindled, I am inclined to think that you
> will close your eye if any blow threatens it.
>
> (*On the Usefulness of Fasting* 4)

Involuntary behavior reveals the body's value more than philosophical disclaimers.

Augustine saw that the Christian doctrines of creation, the Incarnation of Christ, and
the resurrection of body all insist that body is an integral and permanent part of human
being. Concupiscence is *perpetrated on*, rather than instigated by body. Yet there was, for
Augustine, a close association of concupiscence, body, and sexuality. While involved in
sexual relationships, Augustine said, he had felt himself unfree, driven, and compulsive.
When a resolution occurred, he renounced all sexual activity, and experienced feelings
of relief and freedom. Nevertheless, he did not advocate his solution for anyone else.

Society

Theologically, Augustine's social teachings were based on his doctrine of original sin, a
dark undertow that vitiates human existence. Until pressed by controversy as an old man,

he did not attempt to say how this taint is communicated to every member of the human race. His model of the human being as hierarchically structured – body controlled by soul, soul controlled by God – reflected, and was also reflected in the society in which he lived. In the social world of newly conquered Rome, he believed that the subordination of some people to others was inevitable. He said that social inequality was not ideal; indeed, it was evidence that human beings live in a state of punishment, the result of the craving of a few for dominance over the many. "God did not wish the rational being, made in God's own image, to have dominion over any but irrational creatures, not human over human, but human over the beasts." Nevertheless, the "ordered harmony" Augustine advocated was hierarchical. It began in the household, where "the husband gives orders to the wife, parents to children, and masters to servants" (*City of God* 19. 14). He rationalized that throughout society the one who gives orders must consider himself a servant, caring for the needs of those to whom orders are given; he must act from "dutiful concern," not from "lust for domination" (*City of God* 19.15).

Augustine thought that the fulfillment of human values must be postponed to another time and space, beyond human life. To understand what Augustine valued, we must look to his detailed fantasy of resurrection that was based on but not defined by scripture. There will be equality among human beings: "all injustice disappears, and God is all in all."

> There, where the greatest peace will prevail, nothing will be unsightly, nothing inharmonious, nothing monstrous, nothing to offend the eyes, but in all things God will be praised. For if *now* in such frailty of the flesh and in such weakened operation of our members, such great beauty of body appears that it entices the passionate and stimulates the learned and thoughtful to investigate it . . . how much more beautiful will the body be *there* where there will be unending eternity and beautiful truth and the utmost happiness?
>
> (*Sermon* 243. 8; emphasis added)

Controversies

Augustine and his opponents argued over their different ideas of humanity. At the time of the controversies, each side offered interpretations that had not been ruled out by consensus or church legislation. However, Augustine's opponents came to be considered "heretical" when councils decided the debates in his favor. Through Augustine its most articulate spokesman, African Christianity effectively defined Christianity in the West from the fifth century through the medieval period and into the Protestant and Roman Catholic reformations of the sixteenth century.

Donatist

The Donatist controversy originated in 311 during the Diocletian persecution. Donatists alleged that during the persecution the bishop of Carthage had relinquished the sacred books owned by the Carthage church to civic authorities for destruction. The same bishop subsequently ordained Caecilian, later bishop of Carthage. Eighty North African bishops condemned this ordination, claiming that the taint of the *traditore*, or betrayer of Christianity, adhered to everyone ordained in his succession. Donatists, named after one of the protesting bishops, separated from the Catholic Church to form their own church, claiming to be "pure" from association with anyone who had been ordained by a traitor. During the fourth century, emperors alternated forcible suppression of

Donatists with laissez-faire expectations that they would coexist peacefully with Catholics. By Augustine's time, Donatists greatly outnumbered Catholics in North Africa, but Catholics were strongly supported by geographically distant Catholic emperors. Donastist strongholds tended to be in the country and Catholics were stronger in the cities than in the country, but the Donatist church in Hippo, excavated in the mid-twentieth century, was larger than Augustine's basilica. No theological differences separated Donatists and Catholics, but different interpretations of church and sacraments stood between them.

In 405, after formal debates, Donatism was outlawed and disbanded by imperial edict. Still Donatism persisted, and in 411, sterner measures were enacted and enforced. Donatists' buildings were confiscated and turned over to Catholics, and those who declined to join the Catholic church were fined (if they were laypersons) and/or exiled (if they were clergy).

In the controversy, two different images of the Church emerged. Donatists understood the Church as the pure "bride of Christ," "without spot or wrinkle," a "shut-in garden." Augustine, who spoke for Catholics, saw the Church as a community of imperfect people defined by their love of God. Was the church to be seen as a place where people were becoming Christians – learning and struggling – or did it consist of people who were "pure" from association with those who had betrayed the Church two generations before? The lintel on a fourth-century Donatist church read: "This is the door of the Lord; the righteous shall enter in." Augustine, on the other hand, wrote of his own congregation:

> One who enters [a Christian church] is sure to see within drunkards, misers, tricksters, gamblers, adulterers, fornicators, people wearing amulets, clients of sorcerrors, astrologers . . . he must be warned that the same crowds that press into the churches on Christian holidays also fill the theaters on pagan holidays.
>
> (*De catechizandis rudibus* 25. 48)

Augustine called the Church a *corpus permixtum*, a mixed body, that would only be sorted, sheep from goats, on the day of judgment. At that time God would decide who was a member and who was not. Donatists' claim to be the only true church was also in conflict with Augustine's sense of the universality – or catholicity – of the Christian Church: "How can the true church be comprised of a small group of Africans?" he asked.

Donatists and Catholics interpreted the sacraments differently. Were the sacraments effective when administered by a priest who had been ordained by a *traditore*? Did contamination magically pass from the priest to those who communicated with him? Augustine argued that the sacraments belong to Christ, not to the priest, so clergy imperfection did not invalidate the sacraments they administered. If the efficacy of sacraments depended on the virtue of the minister rather than on Christ's authority, Christians would need to worry about the priest's personal life instead of their own growth in the Christian life.

Augustine denied, however, that Donatist sacraments, even though performed in isolation from the Catholic Church, were defiling. Donatist baptism and ordination, he said, were simply ineffectual until those who had received them returned to the Catholic Church. From 411 forward, most Donatist churches, complete with their bishops, clergy, and buildings, returned to communion with Catholics. Yet Donatism continued to exist in North Africa until the Muslim invasions of the seventh and eighth centuries obliterated both Catholics and Donatists.

Manichaean

Augustine encountered Manichaeans long before he converted to Catholic Christianity. Manichaeans, founded by Mani, originated in southern Mesopotamia. Mani, who called himself "the apostle of Jesus Christ," claimed that the promised Holy Spirit had descended on him, giving him further revelations beyond the New Testament writings. Manichaeans' claim to possess a higher revelation had appealed to Augustine in his youth. He was a Manichaean "hearer" for nine years. Manichaeans had two grades of members, the "perfect," whose ascetic practices and rituals were believed to release particles of light, and "hearers," ordinary people whose religious duties consisted largely of providing for the *perfecti*. They taught that two kingdoms, one of light and one of darkness, existed permanently, corresponding to spirit and matter. Particles of light from the spiritual world were trapped in the material world, and the goal of Manichaean practice was to free the light particles. *Perfecti* were expected to abstain from sexual intercourse, which produced more flesh to trap light particles. And they were not permitted to kill life, whether plant or animal life.

Manichaeans were frequently found within, or on the fringes of, Catholic congregations. Their dualistic beliefs were not immediately recognized – by themselves or by others – to be incompatible with Catholic belief. Moreover, *perfecti*'s practices were somewhat similar to those of Catholic clergy and monks.

Augustine described Manichaeans as neurotically sensitive to the pain of living beings; he mocked them for saying that a tree hurts when it is cut. They believed that the community for which human beings are responsible is that of all living beings. Augustine argued that the community to which human beings are responsible is that of rational minds: "For we see and hear by their cries that animals die with pain, although man disregards this in a beast with which, as not having a rational soul, we have no community of rights" (*De moribus manichaeorum* 17.52). Manichaean dualism was apparently compatible with sensitivity to non-human suffering and a sense of responsibility for minimizing that suffering.

Manichaeans were repressed and persecuted, the victims of imperial coercion and religious intolerance. Like his predecessors, Theodosius enacted severe laws against them, and local bishops identified Manichaeans and brought them to trial. They were the only Christian dissidents to be executed in the fourth century Christian Empire. They fled from the Roman Empire to Persia, and Manichaean missionaries established Christianity in China in the seventh or eighth century.

Pelagian

Pelagius, a baptized layman from the British Isles, had read Augustine's *Confessions* and was shocked and alarmed by Augustine's statement, addressed to God, "Command what you will, and give what you command" (*Conf.* 10. 29). He thought this statement of dependence on grace condoned what he called a "languid piety," an attitude he saw as the antithesis of the Christian life. Pelagius emphasized each Christians' responsibility to choose the good, to define her/himself, and to grow in Christian commitment. He also wanted reform in the church. Encouraging a young noblewoman, Demetrias, who was about to enter a monastery, he said, "Since perfection is possible, perfection is obligatory." He opposed a double standard for Christians according to which some became full-time Christians, designing a life-style devoted to perfection, while some did the best they could, but lived morally ambiguous lives.

Pelagius taught that the evils of human nature were due to socialization, to culture, and to bad habits from the secular past, a thin veneer that can, with a bit of effort, be scraped off by ascetic practices. Next to Pelagius, Augustine seemed tolerant. Recalling his own experience, he said that progress in the Christian life was not a matter of *will power*. It was, rather, a matter of *will*, the unified energy of the person, a gift of grace. The *struggle* to do good, Augustine said, is the mark of original sin. Only the grace of God can make the practice of virtue *easy*, spontaneous, and effortless.

Augustine's idea of the operation of grace in a human life needs further exploration. In an early treatise, *De musica*, Augustine wrote, "Delight is, as it were, the weight of the soul. For delight orders the soul. . . . Where the soul's delight is, there is its treasure" (6. 11. 29). A person's will is "dependent on a 'capacity for delight,' and conscious actions [are] the result of mysterious alliance of intellect and feeling . . . the outgrowth of hidden processes, processes by which the heart is stirred, is 'massaged and set' by the hand of God" (Brown, 2000: *Augustine of Hippo*, 163). A person cannot *choose* what gives her delight. It is, Augustine said, utterly mysterious why one person makes fruitful and life-giving choices and another makes choices that deaden his life, spinning him deeper and deeper into misery. Both choose what delights them, but the former, by God's grace, delights in the good, while the later lacks this grace. Perhaps the concept could be clarified by translation into a modern idiom. It might be said that God's *direct* influence on a person operates unconsciously, while *indirect* influences are mediated through church-attendance, Bible-reading, study, sacraments, and preaching (Williams, 1930: 114).

The human's role in turning toward, or cooperating with, grace was debated again and again in the history of Christianity. It is worth noticing that it has also been discussed within other religions. In Hinduism, for example, the issue of humans' role in receiving divine assistance has sometimes been pictured as the difference between the cat-carrying method and the monkey-carry method. When the kitten's mother carries it, the kitten goes limp and is picked up by the scruff of the neck by its mother's teeth. The baby monkey, on the other hand, must leap onto its mother's back and hang on for dear life if it is to be carried. For Augustine, the cat-carrying method would have best described God's grace.

It was in the conflict with Pelagius that Augustine earned the title given him by later Catholics, Doctor of Grace. Pelagius did not deny the grace of Christ; rather, he believed that the grace given to human beings at birth was sufficient, along with moral effort, to enable them to act rightly. Augustine insisted that a person's ability to do good is dependent, in every moment, on receiving grace, and that understanding this, psychologically and intellectually, is crucial to the Christian's attitude of humility and gratitude.

Original sin
Augustine's doctrine of grace and his related teachings on original sin and predestination took form in the context of his controversy with Pelagius. Augustine was the first Christian author to make the fall of the human race through the sin of Adam and Eve a central feature of theology. Where did he locate this evil in fallen human nature? Sometimes he spoke like a classical philosopher, saying that evil is a lack of knowledge. But ultimately Augustine did not identify original sin with ignorance. The flaw, he said, lies

in the will. For Augustine, will was, as Peter Brown writes, the "vital capacity to engage one's feelings in a course of action, to take delight in it, that escapes our powers of self-determination." Before the fall of the human race, will was oriented to delight in God. By this delight, objects in the world were valued (effortlessly and spontaneously) according to their intrinsic worth. The original sin was not a substantive evil, but a *defect* by which the will was divided against itself, becoming incapable of unconflicted delight in God and action in the world.

Augustine taught that healing from this condition is a gift of God's grace, but full recovery is not possible in this life. In his debates with Pelagius, he insisted that God's grace is necessary for *every virtuous act*. Pelagius did not deny the necessity of God's grace, but he said that grace, given richly and abundantly in creation, supplied every human being with enough. Combined with their own committed efforts, the grace given in creation would enable Christians to come to Christian perfection.

Augustine asked, Why, then, do some people turn toward the light, becoming more loving, and living more fruitfully and happily, while others seem to pursue destructive behavior, accumulating unhappy relationships and unproductive activities. Is it a matter of inadequate education? Poor parenting? Unfortunate circumstances? Bad luck? Yes, Augustine said, but these are effects, not causes. The real reason is that some people have simply received *more grace than others.* Neither those who receive, nor those who do not, "deserve" what they get. Augustine's doctrine of grace *described* what he saw when he observed humanity. He found it impossible to understand in any other way why people are as they are and do as they do. His doctrine of predestination is an extension of his doctrine of grace, the logical result of humans' complete dependence on God. In some passages he distinguished God's *foreordination* from God's *foreknowledge* of salvation and damnation; in others he suggested that God selected a few individuals for salvation, leaving the *massa damnata* to their fate.

Different understandings of humanity (anthropology) underlay Pelagius's and Augustine's understandings of God (theology). Augustine thought of people as essentially and permanently infants, helpless, and utterly dependent on God's grace. He wrote, addressing God, "What am I at my best but an infant suckling on the milk you give and feeding on you, the incorruptible food" (*Conf.* 4.1). Pelagius urged that Christians should *grow up*, taking responsibility for maturation in the Christian life. Pelagius acknowledged that this would require great effort, but he was optimistic that, given that effort, Christians could fulfill the commandments and practice virtue.

Pope Zosimus officially rejected Pelagius' position in 418; he and his supporter, Celestius, were expelled from Rome and discussion of his ideas was forbidden. Yet controversy over the relationship of God's grace to human effort did not end in Augustine and Pelagius's lifetime. In different contexts in the history of Christianity, people continued to struggle to articulate two seemingly contradictory truths: Grace and salvation are unmerited gift, *and* Christians must work to accept the gift.

The Christian empire

The edict by which Theodosius established Christianity as the official religion of empire in February 380 differs significantly from Constantine's edict, almost 70 years before, by which Constantine made Christianity a legitimate religion of the empire. Constantine exemplified the religious tolerance for which the second- and third-century Christian apologists had pled, accepting their argument that religious belief could not be coerced. Constantine's statement, aptly called the "Edict of Toleration," stated, "No one whosoever should be denied the liberty of following either the religion of the Christians or any other cult which, of his own free choice he has thought to be best adapted for himself." Eusebius said that he was "unwilling to constrain others by the fear of punishment" (Eusebius, *De vita Constantini* 2. 56). Theodosius had no such scruples. He required everyone to be Catholic Christians, labeling others "madmen and heretics."

A word by which Christians differentiated themselves from their non-Christian neighbors appeared (in this usage) for the first time in the early fourth century. "*Pagani*" was a slang term adopted by Christians to insult those who were not "enlisted through baptism as soldiers of Christ against the powers of Satan" (Fox, 1986: 31). "Pagan," as used by Christians (then and now), lumps together many different Roman religions as if they were monolithic, reflecting Christians' rejection of all religions but the "one way." "Paganism" had no doctrines and thus no heresy, but consisted of the performance of cultic rites. Like Christians, adherents of Roman religions used the Greek word *hairesis* (heresy), but they meant by it a school of thought, not false doctrine.

During the last decade of the fourth century, the Christianization of the Roman Empire proceeded rapidly. Theodosius I claimed to be the emperor of a sacred monarchy in which all laws were sanctified by divine authority. Christian clergy were granted special rights, such as immunity from taxes and civic trial. Verdicts against the practice of Roman religions were enacted and enforced; temples were closed and worship prohibited. Within approximately 65 years Christianity went from persecuted cult to a religiously intolerant and politically coercive imperial religion.

Church and state shared a common assumption about power, namely, that power is good. For a society without an internal police force, and for whom food availability was always insecure, a powerful state was very desirable. Yet church leaders thought that the state's power ought to have clear limits; they were unwilling to let the state decide matters of Christian doctrine and practice. Bishops even, on occasion, rebuked emperors.

Ambrose, bishop of Milan, considered the emperor a "son of the church." In 390, the Catholic emperor Theodosius I ordered the massacre of 7,000 people in Thessalonica as punishment for the murder of the provincial governor. Ambrose excommunicated Theodosius, and refused him entrance to the church until he came in repentance, barefoot, dressed in rags, and covered with ashes. When he did so, Ambrose imposed a period of repentance and exclusion from communion before readmitting him (Ambrose, *Ep.* 51). On another occasion, Bishop Ambrose prevented the emperor from requisitioning a Catholic church building for use by Arian Christians. He barricaded himself in the church along with his whole congregation – the first sit-in – until the emperor relented.

Augustine's *City of God* described Christians as intermingled in society, distinguishable only by their motivating love for God. What is the role of the "earthly city" when ultimate hope is transferred beyond human space/time? Augustine proposed an interdependent relationship of Church and state. Unlike others who hoped that the Christian empire could become a kingdom of God on earth, Augustine thought that the most the state could do was to secure the peace that expedited the Church's work. Augustine knew at first hand the alternative to social order, namely the chaos, rape, and murder Roman women and men had suffered in 410 in the Sack of Rome. The Church, in turn, should support the state; Christians should be good citizens.

According to Augustine, imperial laws should prevent and correct religious dissidence. He had urged that Donatists be "compelled to enter" the Catholic Church, and endorsed the use of punitive measures to bring reluctant Donatists to communion with Catholics. The measures he advocated were fines and, if necessary, exile, *not* corporal or capital punishment. He opposed the death penalty for any crime on grounds that it excluded the possibility of repentance. The death penalty was not used against Donatists in North Africa, but Augustine discovered the limit of his power to influence imperial penalties when, in spite of his pleading for a lesser punishment, several pagans were executed.

Augustine rationalized religious coercion on two grounds. In a letter to a friend he said that he had initially been opposed to coercion. After it was established, however, many people returned to the Catholic communion because they feared fines and some of them told him that once they were within the church they learned the former error of their ways and were happy to have been brought back. Augustine urged that coercion be accompanied by education: "for if they were only being terrorized and not instructed at the same time, this would be an inexcusable tyranny on our part." He reasoned, "Why, therefore, should the church not use force in compelling her lost sons to return if the lost sons compelled others to their destruction?" (*Ep.* 185. 7).

Augustine's second reason for endorsing religious coercion was that Christ himself, motivated by love, had used force to compel belief.

> For who can possibly love us more than Christ, who laid down his life for his sheep? And yet, after calling Peter and the other apostles by his words alone, when he came to summon Paul . . . he not only constrained him with his voice, but even dashed him to the earth with his power; and that he might forcibly bring one who was raging amid the darkness of infidelity to desire the light of the heart, he first struck him with physical blindness of the eyes. If that punishment had not been inflicted, he would not afterwards have been healed by it. . . . Towards whom did Christ use violence? Whom did he compel? Here they have the Apostle Paul. Let them recognize in his case Christ first compelling and afterwards teaching; first striking, and afterwards consoling.
>
> (*Ep.* 185. 22)

These rationalizations, developed in the context of a minority church, had a long life in other circumstances. A letter to a friend reveals that despite his acceptance of the value of coercion, coercion was never easy for Augustine.

> What shall I say to the infliction and remission of punishment in cases where we have no other desire but to forward the spiritual welfare of those we have to decide whether or not to punish? What trembling I feel in these things, my brother Paulinus, what trembling, what darkness!
>
> (*Ep.* 95. 3)

Augustine died in 430 in a world vastly different from that of his youth and maturity. As he died, Vandals surrounded Hippo, piling corpses against the city walls. In the hot

African sun, it did not take long for both the air and the water supply to be poisoned. Augustine's life's work seemed to him undone by violence. His biographer, Possidius, a priest and friend of Augustine, wrote:

> The man of God saw whole cities sacked, country villas razed, their owners killed or scattered as refugees, the churches deprived of their bishops and clergy, and the holy virgins and ascetics dispersed; some tortured to death, some killed outright; others, as prisoners, reduced to losing their integrity in soul and body, to serve an evil and brutal enemy. The hymns of God and praises in the churches had come to a stop. In many places the church buildings were burnt to the ground; the sacrifices of God could no longer be celebrated in their proper place and the divine sacraments were either not sought, or, if sought, no one could be found to give them.
>
> *(Vita)*

In the new world in which Augustine died, cities, the achievement of ancient culture, were abandoned as the wealthy took up permanent residence in what had been their resort villas in the countryside, and the poor tried to find a bit of land to farm at subsistence level. Despite civic administrators' efforts to freeze people to their location and occupation, no one wanted to be trapped in a walled city when the "barbarians" came.

READING

Augustine, *Confessions; City of God* 19. 13–15; *Ep.* 185.

5   Theological Resolution

Sexuality and asceticism were hot topics In the Latin West at the end of the fourth century. Jerome (342–420) urged celibacy; his hierarchy placed virgins above married people, and he ranked married people according to whether they had been married once, twice, or to pagans. The monk Jovinian (d. 405) argued against classifying and valuing people according to their sexual choices. Like Clement of Alexandria before him, Jovinian held that whether a Christian is married, widowed, or single makes no difference in the quest for spiritual growth, and that future-life rewards will not be depend on sexual status. Jerome accused Jovinian of acknowledging only two classes of people, Christians and non-Christians. Augustine also argued against Jovinian in his treatise "On the Good of Marriage," calling him a "monster." The mood of the moment was against Jovinian. His protest against enthusiastic asceticism was condemned by synods at Rome and Milan.

While these debates were occurring in the West, Eastern Christians were apparently arguing about doctrine. According to Gregory of Nyssa (c.330–95): "If in this city you ask anyone for change, he will discuss with you whether the Son was begotten or unbegotten. If you ask about the quality of the bread you will receive the answer, 'The Father is greater and the Son is lesser.' If you suggest a bath is desirable, you will be told, 'There was nothing before the Son was created'" (*De filii deitate et spiritu sancti*).

Nicene definitions were still hotly contested. The historian Socrates (c.380–c.450) described the failure of those who argued these positions to understand each other.

> The situation was exactly like a battle by night, for both parties seemed to be in the dark about the grounds on which they were hurling abuse at each other. Those who objected to the word *homoousios* imagined that its adherents were bringing in the doctrine of Sabellius and Montanus. So they called them blasphemers on the ground that they were undermining the personal subsistence of the Son of God. On the other hand, the protagonists of *homoousios* concluded that their opponents were introducing polytheism. . . . Thus, while both affirmed the personality and subsistence of the Son of God, and confessed that there was one God in three hypostases, they were somehow incapable of reaching agreement, and for this reason could not bear to lay down arms.
>
> (*Hist. Eccles.* 1. 23)

Doctrinal debates continued at the Council of Constaninople (381) and the Council of Ephesus (431). They were resolved, at least for the orthodox, at the Council of Chalcedon (451), but for at least 50 years before this, they had been exclusively an Eastern concern. Doctrinal controversy requires a certain amount of freedom from more urgent problems, a freedom that the West – at least since the Sack of Rome by the Visigoths in 410 – had been unable to afford.

Northern European tribes had threatened the West on and off since the end of the third century. At the beginning of the fifth century, however, they demanded attention in a way they had not when they threatened distant borders. The Sack of Rome in 410 was horrifying beyond its actual destruction. "*Roma eterna*" had not been conquered for 800 years, yet less than 30 years after the Empire became Christian, it was vanquished by the Visigoths under Alaric. Augustine wrote *The City of God* to answer charges that Christians' defection had prompted the gods to abandon Rome. Two decades later, the Vandals besieged and conquered Roman North Africa.

In the East the situation was different. Constantinople repeatedly escaped capture and looting by paying the Ostrogoths "protection money." The gold budget of the Eastern Empire in the late fourth century was roughly twice that of the Western Empire. Thus, "barbarians" extracted enormous gold payments from Eastern cities and, still eager for conquest, went West.

The Council of Constantinople

Emperor Theodosius I called the Council of Constantinople in 381 hoping to end the Arian controversy and unite the Eastern bishops to the Nicene faith. One hundred and fifty Catholic bishops (who accepted the decision of the Council of Nicaea) and 35 "heretical" bishops attended, none from the West. The Council declared that Constantinople had "honorary precedence" over all other churches except Rome; it condemned Arianism and Apollinarianism (described below), and appointed several bishops to important cities. Trinitarian controversy was ended by the Council's ratification of the slightly revised Creed of Nicaea (called the Niceno-Constantinopolian Creed), popularly known simply as the Nicene Creed.

We believe in one God, the Father Almighty, maker of heaven and earth and of all things visible and invisible. And in one Lord Jesus Christ, the only begotten Son of God, begotten of his Father before all worlds, Light of Light, very God of very God, begotten not made, being of one substance with the Father by whom all things were made. Who for us men and for our salvation came down from heaven and was incarnate from the Holy Spirit and the Virgin Mary and was made man, and was crucified for us by Pontius Pilate, suffered, and was buried and arose again on the third day, according to the Scripture, and ascended into heaven, and sits at the right hand of the Father, and is coming again with glory to judge the living and the dead; of whose kingdom there shall be no end. And in the Holy Spirit, the Lord, the giver of life, who proceeds from the Father, who together with the Father and Son is worshipped and glorified, who spoke through the prophets. In one holy, Catholic and Apostolic Church. We confess one baptism for the remission of sins. We look for the resurrection of the dead, and the life of eternity to come. Amen.

The largest change was the addition of a paragraph in which the Holy Spirit's role was described.

Although most bishops were satisfied with the settlement of trinitarian disputes, Christological controversy continued. Two understandings of the relationship of the human and the divine in Christ dominated, the Antiochean and the Alexandrian. Theodore of Mopsuestia (c.350–428) championed the Antiochean view. He taught that in Jesus the divine Word was bonded to a human being with mind, soul, and body. In order to protect the humanity of Jesus from being subsumed by the divine nature he maintained a clear and permanent distinction between the two natures. He said that it was not the divine nature that suffered and died; rather, the divine nature "remained with the man Jesus until it helped him to loose the pains of death." Theodore emphasized the redemptive role of Jesus' *humanity*.

The second Christological understanding was the Alexandrian position in which the divine and human in Christ were joined by a "hypostatic union" in which each nature retained its integrity. Cyril, bishop of Alexandria (d. 444), its most articulate fifth-century advocate said, "Christ was incapable of suffering because of his divinity, but took on flesh that could suffer so that the suffering of his flesh could be said to be his own." In this view, sometimes called a "union of predominance," the body of Christ was a tool (*organon*) of his divinity. The formula "in two natures" expressed opposition to statements that collapsed the two natures into one.

Cyril of Alexandria's contemporaries described him as impetuous, violent, and power-hungry; his election to bishop was strongly opposed. During his term of office, Hypatia, a highly esteemed and influential Platonic philosopher, was murdered by a Christian mob that was led by a church lector, Peter. Yet Hypatia respected Christianity and taught both pagans and Christians, and she was the honored and beloved teacher of at least one Christian bishop, Synesius of Cyrene, who studied with her sometime during the last decade of the fourth century. The motive for her murder, then, seems to have been, not religious differences, but her support of Cyril's enemy, Orestes, prefect of Egypt. Indeed, after her death, according to a contemporary, "All the people surrendered to the patriarch Cyril."

Apollinaris articulated the extreme Alexandrian position. Apollinaris said that the divine Word *took the place of* the human spirit in Jesus, functioning in his body as mind and will. He spoke of Jesus as "God incarnate," as "flesh-bearing God." According to Apollinaris, Jesus possessed perfect divinity but not integral humanity.

Each of these positions, and the men who held them, understood different aspects of Jesus as supremely significant and in need of explication, emphasis, and protection. Ongoing differences of religious sensibilities and values were invested in these descriptions. Is salvation provided by a powerful divine savior, undiminished and untroubled by human struggle and pain? Or is the human Jesus, in all his vulnerability, the mediator of salvation to humanity through his fleshly solidarity with them?

Three theologians from Cappadocia formulated a powerful metaphor for the union of human and divine in Jesus. Basil of Caesaria (d. 379), his brother, Gregory of Nyssa (d. 395), and their friend, Gregory of Nazianzus (d. 389) asked: What description of Jesus enables *faith* rather than *argument*? Gregory of Nazianzus answered that the right metaphor assists faith – the poetic, flexible metaphor. He proposed the following:

> The analogy from human experience is one of a unified operation in which biological life, reason, and wisdom are combined. This analogy rests on the teaching that human beings are created in God's image and can, through Christ, actualize that image and participate in God. "Hints and likenesses" of creation in God's image can still be seen in human beings [Gregory says] if we are careful not to project onto God the defects and limitations of human being.
>
> (*Theological Orations* 21)

Gregory of Nazianzus suggested that it is possible to picture the unity of humanity and divinity if, instead of a union of *substances*, one thinks of a unity of *operation*. He explained the unity of the trinity as based on a single operation.

But it was Augustine who explored the doctrine of the trinity most fully in his treatise *On the Trinity*. He approached the topic as a devotional exercise, seeking to understand the trinity as reflected in the human, made in the image of God. Considering and rejecting many possible explanations, he finally isolated a model for the internal relationships of the Trinity in the human functions of memory, understanding, and will.

The rallying point for the last stage of controversy over the description of human and divine in Christ in the years between the Council of Constantinople (381) and the Council of Chalcedon (451) was the Council of Ephesus (431).

The Council of Ephesus

The Asian bishops were late, delayed by sandstorms. Nestorius (d. 451), Bishop of Constantinople and the chief supporter of Antiochean Christology, had arrived, but he refused to participate in the gathering convened by Cyril of Alexandria (d. 444). Nestorius was quickly anathamatized and deposed. Finally the Syrian bishops who supported Nestorius arrived and held their own council, which anathematized and deposed Cyril, the staunch defender of Alexandrian christology. Finally the papal legates arrived from the West and decided that the first council – Cyril's gathering – was authoritative. They added that anyone who copied Nestorius's written works would suffer the amputation of their hand.

Discussions were more complex than is indicated by this quick summary of the actions taken. The issue debated was whether Mary, the mother of Jesus, could be referred to as "God-bearer, *Theotokos*." The term "*theotokos*" had been used for the first time in an official document in a 324 encyclical; by the end of the fourth century it was widely used. But was this title theologically *correct*? How should its liturgical and devotional use be understood? The question was not whether, and how, Mary was to receive recognition for her role in the incarnation; it was over how Christ's divinity and humanity were to be conceptualized. Even so, it is striking that the argument focused on a woman and childbirth.

Cyril of Alexandria supported the use of *theotokos*. He argued that the unity of Christ was safeguarded by a "communication of properties" (*communicatio idiomatum*), so that what was claimed of his divine nature could be also claimed of his human nature, or vice versa. He envisioned a union of *hypostases* (*hypostatic union*) in which Christ's human and divine natures were united, yet distinct.

Nestorius proposed that the term "*christotokos*" was more accurate as descriptive of Mary's role in Christ's birth. He found *theotokos* confusing, he said, and he could not bring himself to say that *God* was born in the normal human way. Nestorius' proposal claimed to protect the purity and uniqueness of *both* Christ's natures. Cyril quoted Nestorius as saying:

> I know that she is august who received God, *through whom* the Lord of all passed, and *through whom* the sun of righteousness beamed. . . . For I have not said *passed through* in the sense of *born* . . . that God *passed through from out* the Virgin Mother of Christ was I taught from the divine scripture; that *God* was born of her I was nowhere taught.
>
> (*Ep.* II; emphasis added)

Cyril added: "Nestorius repeated the well-known blasphemies about our Lord's sacred infancy and childhood, that he would not call him God who was two or three months old, or who was nourished at the breast, or who fled to Egypt." Using Gregory of Nazianzus's argument, Cyril insisted that the unified activity of soul and body in humans is an example of the kind of unity to be found in Christ's divinity and humanity:

> But since we affirm that the Word became as we and took a body like our bodies and truly united this to himself, in a way beyond understanding and speech, and that he was thus made human and born after the flesh, what is there incredible therein and worthy of disbelief? The human soul, being of another nature than the body, is yet born with it, just as we say that it too has been united with it. Yet no one supposes that the soul has the nature of the body as the beginning of its own existence, but God places it in the body and it is born along with it. Therefore the Word was God but was made human too, and, since he has been born after the flesh by reason of the human nature, she who bore him is necessarily Mother of God.
>
> (*Ep.* II)

Cyril proposed that it was the *unity* of the two natures that was primary; the *distinctness* was secondary. Nestorius repeatedly accused Cyril of deifying Mary, but Cyril replied that this was exactly not the point: "For if he had not been born like us according to the flesh, for if he had not taken part like us of the same, he would not have freed the nature of humanity from the blame contracted in Adam, nor would he have driven the decay away from our bodies" (*Ep.* 4).

Because Mary's humanity made the title appropriate, the Council of Ephesus proclaimed Mary "Theotokos." The council's proclamation contains the only generic use of "woman" in the history of Christianity. The all-male Council declared: "The blessed Virgin was woman as we are." Fifth-century women understood that the Council's affirmation of Mary's role in the Incarnation had implications for their own status as women. Contemporary sources describe joyous celebrations led by women at the "triumph of the Theotokos." Eastern Orthodox Churches still celebrate "the triumph of the Incarnation" at the Council of Ephesus, one of the twelve major feast days of the liturgical year.

The Symbol of Union (433), a conciliatory creed by which the Antiochean bishops were brought into formal agreement with those who subscribed to "Theotokos," won Cyril's enthusiastic support, even though it contained important concessions to Nestorius' position. In fact, Cyril's favorite expressions were missing from the document and it contained Antiochene terminology. Why, then, was Cyril pleased with it? There is evidence that he came in the course of the heated debate at Ephesus to understand the Antiochean position's implications for the Eucharist.

> It was necessary for him to be present in us in a divine manner through the Holy Spirit: to be mixed, as it were, with our bodies by means of His holy flesh and precious blood, for us to have him in reality as a sacramental gift which gives life, in the form of bread and wine. And so that we should not be struck down with horror, at seeing flesh and blood displayed on the holy tables in our churches, God adapts himself to our weakness and infuses the power of life into the oblations and changes them into the effective power of his own flesh, so that we may have them for life-giving reception, and that the body of life may prove to be in us a life-giving seed.
>
> (*In Luc.* 22. 19)

The Councils of Constantinople, Ephesus, and Chalcedon were held in the East and they reflected Eastern concerns. Although political loyalties, regional differences, and power struggles were evident, Christological controversy cannot be reduced to politics. The men who argued these issues had strong, and strongly conflicting, visions of the "Word made flesh." Western theologians were content to leave unexplored many issues that troubled Eastern theologians. In the midst of the controversy, Pope Leo I sent a letter (449) to the Patriarch of Constantinople which simply reiterated the ideas of his predecessors. At the time it was ignored, but later it would contribute to a resolution.

For the debate was not over. In 451 the Emperor Marcian convened the Council of Chalcedon. Marcian was a professional soldier, without doctrinal expertise. He was concerned, like his predecessors, to unify the empire. Five or six hundred bishops attended, including only two Western bishops and two representatives sent by Pope Leo I.

The Council of Chalcedon

At the Council of Chalcedon, the successful position formed around Leo's letter (*Tome*), the only Western document in the official documents of the ecumenical councils. The

Tome asserted that the divinity of Christ is identical with the Divine Word, and that divine and human natures co-existed in Jesus without mixture or confusion. It stated that the natures are separate principles, though they always act together: "Each form accomplishes in concert with the other what is appropriate to it, the Word performing what belongs to the Word, and the flesh carrying out what belongs to the flesh" (*Tome* 3).The *Tome* reiterated that the oneness of the persons in Christ is best expressed by the *communicatio idiomatum*, that is, that what can be said of the divinity of Christ can properly also be said of his humanity, and vice versa. In addition to drawing up a formal confession of faith, the Council also canonized two letters on Christology by Cyril and once again revised the Nicene Creed.

> The Chalcedonian creed is less poetic, and more explicitly theological [than former creeds]. It pronounced Christ to be (a) perfect God and perfect man, consubstantial with the Father in his Godhead, and with us in his manhood; (b) made known *in* two natures without confusion, change, division, or separation. The meaning of the preposition 'in' was explained by further clauses: (c) the difference between the natures is in no sense abolished by the union; (d) the properties of each nature are preserved intact, and both come together to form one person (*prosopon*) and one *hypostasis*.
>
> (H. Chadwick, 1967: 203–4)

Many Eastern theologians were still deeply disturbed by what seemed to them a Christology that simply did not say *enough*. Most Copt, Greek, and Syrian Christians considered Christ the prototype of the redeemed person. If human nature could be totally transformed and *made one with God's nature in Christ*, then the average person could also hope to be transformed into the divine nature (deification). Monks especially felt the need for a divine Christ to aid them in their struggle with the demons. At one point in the proceedings at Chalcedon, the Egyptian bishops, referring to the monks said, "We shall all be killed if we subscribe to Leo's *Tome*." The formula of Leo's *Tome*, namely, that Christ was "in two natures" emphasized the reality of Christ's humanity, and his permanent identity with human beings. Greek readers were shocked by its emphasis on the humble human element in Christ and its emphasis on the cross and resurrection, the *work* of Christ, rather than on his cosmic divinity. Should deification best be thought of as "from below" – on the basis of Christ's sharing human nature – or "from above" – human nature caught up into the divine nature? Chalcedon did not specify.

A year after the Council of Chalcedon, in the face of continued unrest, the emperor Marcian promulgated a curious edict: "Christians are to abstain from profane words and cease all further discussion of religion, which is forbidden. This sin, as we believe, will be punished by the judgment of God; but it will also be restrained by the authority of the laws and the judges." Predictably, his decree was ineffective. Debates about Christ's two natures continued to simmer for another two centuries.

After the Council of Chalcedon, the imperial government tried unsuccessfully to reconcile the non-Chalcedonian Monophysites of Egypt and Syria. Attempting this, the fifth ecumenical council at Constantinople in 553 reinterpreted Chalcedon's decisions. They said that Christ is "in two natures," but they also affirmed that he is "one incarnate nature." Using the *communicatio idiomatum*, the Council of Ephesus had said that "God is born;" invoking the same formula, the second Council of Constantinople said that "God died" (Canon 10).

Many forms of Monophysitism emerged in the later fifth and sixth centuries. All were opposed to the decision of the Council of Chalcedon that Christ had two natures, divine and human. For Monophysites, Christ's divine nature swallowed his human nature, becoming one nature, even in the incarnation. An extension of Cyril's Alexandrian theology, for Monophysite Christians Christ's divine power to save was at stake. These often acrimonious debates were not caused by a few theologians' scruples; rivalries between cities and popular piety were also factors in the different theological positions. Nor was intellectual precision the driving motivation; Monophysites claimed strong theological and scriptural foundations. Anthropological assumptions also informed Monophysite theology. The Eastern church's strong respect for asceticism suggested a sharp distinction between body and soul in which soul dominates body. Pholoxenus of Mabbug counseled his monks to "lift up the power of your body upon your soul, and change and mingle the life of it with the life of your soul, that . . . its feeble power be mixed with the might of its spiritual power" (quoted by Chesnut, 1976: 75). Similarly, although Jesus experienced all the limitations of a human mind and body, he experienced them as the divine Word, and it was the divine Word that performed all Jesus' actions. Monophysite Christologies emphasized that God's power acted directly in Jesus of Nazareth.

By 600 the Monophysite empire was vast, geographically much greater than that covered by the Latin and Orthodox churches combined. A permanent division remains within Greek Christianity between Chalcedonians and Monophysites. The results of the theological controversies of the fourth and fifth centuries illustrate the historical fact that precision in doctrine has often resulted in the establishment of separate communions and communities.

It was not only Christians who held dissenting beliefs that were affected by the doctrinal Councils of the fourth century and the first half of the fifth as Constantine's non-coercive Christianity became Theodosius' intolerant Christianity. During this time, Jews were effectively marginalized from public life, and attitudes toward the ancient and honored religion of Judaism changed. Legislation forbade Jews to function in imperial courts in the Christian Empire; synagogues were destroyed by mob violence; and sermons preached supersessionist theology. The mosaics in the Church of Santa Maria Maggiore, funded by a pope and an emperor and built in 432 just after the Council of Ephesus, illustrate this theology. Numerous depictions of Hebrew Bible incidents relating God's protection of the Hebrew people adorn the nave walls, culminating in the prophecies and birth of Christ on the triumphal arch.

The term "pagan" became a stigmatizing label identifying the "other" at the same time that temple worship was forbidden and altars and shrines were closed by imperial edict. The Emperor Julian's brief (361–3) attempt to resuscitate paganism by imperial patronage came to nothing. Bands of monks attacked temples; those that remained standing became museums. Constantine removed from the Senate the altar of Victory on which senators had offered incense at the beginning of each year without provoking a major outcry. The pagan senator Symmachus' plea for its restoration (quoted above) was the last appeal for both Roman tolerance and its ancient religion. No pagan martyrs dramatized the passing of Roman religion, but by the end of the fourth century, paganism was the past.

Non-Chalcedonian Christians

Within 50 years of Chalcedon three churches separated in order to affirm a single nature (monophysite), a *divine* nature in the incarnate Christ. The Copts, the Syrian Jacobites (named after their leader, Jacob Baradaeus), and the Armenians accepted the Council's and the Fathers' teachings prior to the Council of Chalcedon, but differed from Chalcedon's Christology. The history of Monophysites, Nestorians, Manichaeans, and Jacobites carries us away from the Mediterranean and into Syria and Palestine, Central and Southeast Asia, Tibet, Japan, Arabia, Afghanistan, Iran, Armenia and Georgia, India, Mongolia, and China. Merchants and missionaries carried Christianity along trade routes and into marketplaces and throne-rooms. The history of Christianity outside the Roman Empire is obscure, but most non-Chalcedonian Churches claim that one of Christ's apostles brought the Christian faith to them.

Two major groups rejected Chalcedonian orthodoxy. Nestorians moved from Syria to Mesopotamia and Persia. By the end of the fifth century they had become vigorous and effective missionaries across Asia. Monophysites, including Coptic and Jacobite Christians, spread from Egypt and Ethopia to Syria and Persia. Armenian Orthodoxy accepted the decrees of all the ecumenical Councils through Ephesus, but rejected Chalcedon. Messalians and Adoptionists (after Paul of Samosata) became minority Christianities in Armenia and Georgia. "Each of the three parties, Orthodox-Catholic-Chalcedonian; Nestorian; and Monophysite-Jacobite-Coptic, accused the others of heresy, despite the undoubted fact that all three held with enthusiasm to the 'Nicene Creed' " (Gillman and Klimkeit, 1999: 16–17).

Non-Chalcedonians were persecuted on a scale never experienced within the Roman Empire in some of the areas in which they settled. In Iran, Christians were persecuted for 40 years after Constantine's death; Theodosius's declaration of Christianity as the religion of the Roman Empire prompted a new wave of persecution. Incomplete records indicate that by the mid-fifth century under Zoroastrian persecution, ten bishops and 153,000 clergy and laypersons had been executed in Iran.

Finally, non-Chalcedonian Christians also entered the Roman Empire. In the fifth and sixth centuries "barbarians" (literally, non-Greek speakers) who had been Christianized by Arian missionaries held important posts in the Empire. While Arian Christians held power, they neither proselytized nor persecuted.

Leaders like the Visigoth Alaric became simultaneously rulers of a federated people and high-ranking generals in the Roman army. As early as the 380s Arians, supported by the emperor's mother and successfully opposed by Bishop Ambrose, sought to take over Catholic church buildings in the imperial capital of Milan. A century later Arian churches appeared in the imperial capital of Ravenna. Eager, for the most part, to be assimilated into the Empire, Arian Goths, Franks, and Vandals disappeared as a separate people in the sixth century. Islam obliterated Christianity in many parts of Asia, and North Africa in the seventh and eighth centuries.

The fourth century was a time of great changes. Dramatic gains occurred, as persecution ceased and membership in newly built Christian churches became attractive to many Romans. Rich liturgical, artistic, and devotional traditions developed. This chapter has endeavored to convey the exciting sense of Christianity's triumphs as experienced by many fourth-century people without ignoring its critics and dissidents. Some of the critics and dissidents produced new institutions – such as monasticism – that survive to our own time as alternatives to a Christianity adapted to achieve broad consensus. Concurrently, a coercive Empire and an intolerant Church joined forces. But the partnership of Church and Empire was not to survive for long. Chapter 3 explores a West characterized by decentered state power and new religious interests.

READINGS

Gregory of Nazianzus, *Theological Orations* (Orations XXVII–XXXI)
Gregory of Nyssa, *Catechetical Oration*

3 Fleshing Out the Word: Medieval Christianity East and West

Prologue

The early medieval centuries in the West have often been called the "Dark Ages," a time of deterioration and decay, or as the eighteenth-century English historian Edward Gibbon put it, the aftermath of the "decline and fall" of the Roman Empire. But twentieth-century historians challenged that picture. For example, W. C. Bark argues that the sixth century was the time of the greatest technical innovation until the twentieth century. The collapse of the Roman Empire was the collapse of an antiquated bureaucratic system requiring a disproportionate amount of upkeep compared to the services it performed. People served the state, rather than the state serving the people. Similarly, Augustine claimed in the *City of God* that rather than the gods protecting Rome, Rome had protected her gods.

Seen in this context, the reduction of Western societies to the local and agrarian level resulted in more efficient ways of living. "Medieval society was functional in ways not dreamed of in classical civilization," Bark writes. Between the first century CE and the middle of the fifth century, the only new inventions in the West were some devices in the glass industry. But by the sixth century, new inventions responded to the needs of an agrarian society. Even the breakdown of Roman roads and the demise of cities had positive effects, relieving the countryside of providing food for city populations.

The development of local self-sufficiency was also necessitated by the demise of slavery. Lacking the Roman Empire's abundant supply of slave labor, people invented new ways to perform necessary tasks. A breast-collar for horses allowed fewer horses to plow larger fields with greater ease, and horses were shod. A wheeled plow increased efficiency, and a three-field system, by which two fields were planted and one was allowed to remain fallow, regaining nutrients, was used. The water mill, known in antiquity but not used, was now put into operation. Because of these and other innovations, by the tenth century the standard of living was superior to that of the urban masses in the "golden age" of the Antonine emperors of the first centuries of the common era.

Medieval people's religious interests also changed. In the West, theological disputes were confined to monasteries where monks still argued about Augustine's doctrines of grace and predestination and how to describe what transpired in the eucharistic celebration. Popular religious interest, however, was never more vivid. Medieval interest in saints, miracles, and relics, often interpreted by modern historians as "superstition," explored Christianity's claim that God had entered the visible world of bodies and senses. In practices that reveal their thinking, medieval people asked: What can be expected of the material world if God has assumed a human body in Jesus Christ? What can we expect to see, to touch, to hear, and feel since the sensible world has been radically altered by God's presence? How do material objects, bodies, and events reflect and express the power of an incarnate God?

Before examining the medieval West, we will explore the Eastern Orthodox heirs of fourth- and fifth-century theological controversies in the Greek East. How were the decisions made at Nicaea, Ephesus, and Chalcedon interpreted in Orthodox religious practices? Although formal separation between East and West occurred only in the eleventh century, *theological* interests were distinct from the fifth century forward. In the medieval centuries, Eastern and Western Churches increasingly drew apart due to distance and lack of communication. Moreover, the *religious* interests of Orthodox and Catholic Christians were based on theological understandings that were not always clearly articulated. However, their practices provide evidence of medieval people's religious passions.

1   Eastern Orthodoxy

After the Council of Chalcedon, peaceful co-existence between the Greek East and the Latin West was based on mutual misunderstanding and cultural and geographical distance. East and West largely ignored one another, intent on local problems. Pope Leo I (d. 461) rejected Chalcedon's assimilation of the Church to the state, as well as the Council's declaration that Constantinople was equal to Rome in authority. Persian invaders besieged the East in the seventh century as northern Europeans had besieged the West in the fifth century. Jerusalem and Antioch were captured in 638 and Alexandria was conquered in 642–3. Nevertheless, Eastern Orthodoxy expanded. In the tenth century, the Russian Orthodox Church came into communion with the Greek Orthodox Church, and by the eleventh century, the Finnish Church did also.

The first open disagreement between West and East occurred when the Council of Toledo (589) added the word *filioque* to the Creed, specifying that the Holy Spirit proceeds from the Father *and the Son* (the "double procession"). This addition precluded thinking of the Holy Spirit as proceeding from Father *through* Son. The Eastern preference for thinking of the persons of the trinity as hierarchically arranged was intact despite centuries of discussion, as was the Western predilection for a fully equal trinity. Different philosophical, political, theological, and cultural conceptions, too strong to be influenced by the decisions of a church council, underlay the different views of East and West. A formal breach occurred between the Western and Eastern churches in 1054 when the papal legate excommunicated the Patriarch of Constantinople, laying the bull of excommunication on the high altar at Hagia Sophia. In return, the patriarch of

Constantinople, Michael Celularius, excommunicated and anathematized the papal representative.

At the time it seemed just another insignificant quarrel. No Byzantine historian mentioned the mutual excommunication, and some communication went on as before. Yet the separation remained until, at the Council of Florence (1438–45), partially successful efforts were made to unite the two major churches of Christendom.

The points at issue were both theological and practical. In addition to objecting to the double procession of the Holy Spirit, the Orthodox also contested the Western use of unleavened bread in the Eucharist, the doctrine of Purgatory, and the primacy of the pope. Those who sought to reunite the Churches argued that they agreed *in substance* but expressed the faith differently. Their slogan was "unity of faith; diversity of rite." In 1439 a union of Greek Orthodox and Armenians with the Western Church was achieved; the Copts were reunited in 1442; and the Syrians in 1444. All these reunions collapsed, however, when Constantinople was captured by the Turks in 1453.

Theology

In the Eastern Orthodox Church, only three men are called theologians, St John the disciple; Gregory Nazianzan (329–89); and St Simeon (d. 1022), called the "new theologian." These men were mystical or poetic writers, not "systematic" theologians, revealing different understandings of what constitutes theological knowledge in East and West. In the West, theological "knowledge" is primarily analysis, definition, and exploration of the relationship of one theological proposition to another. In the East, theological "knowledge" is gained through the liturgical experience of the worshipping community.

Eastern Orthodoxy recognizes two kinds of theological knowledge, *cataphatic* and *apophatic*. *Cataphatic* knowledge consists of what can be affirmed about God on the basis of revelation (scripture) and experience. *Apophatic* knowledge recognizes the limits of human knowledge of God, acknowledging its metaphoric and imprecise nature. It has been called the way of negation. John of Damascus's (d. 749) *The Orthodox Faith* described the interdependence of *cataphatic* and *apophatic* theological knowledge.

> Now one who would speak or hear about God should know beyond any doubt that in what concerns theology . . . not all things are inexpressible and not all are capable of expression, and neither are all things unknowable nor are they all knowable. That which can be known is one thing, whereas that which can be said is another, just as it is one thing to speak and another to know.
>
> (*The Orthodox Faith* 1.2)

John began and ended his discussion of what *is* known of the orthodox faith with confessions of what is *not* known, reminding his readers that a great deal is not only unknown, but unknowable. Moreover, some things can be known experientially but cannot be described in words. Simeon the New Theologian (d. 1022) wrote: "Do not try to describe ineffable matters by words alone, for this is an impossibility. But let us contemplate such matters by activity, labor, and fatigue. In this way we shall be taught the meaning of such things as the sacred mysteries" (*Orations* 26). In short, theological knowledge is not what can be articulated, but what can be appropriated.

The Orthodox Church balances the personal or subjective nature of theological knowledge with *cataphatic*, or *objective* knowledge, gained from scripture and tradition. Orthodoxy also accepts as authoritative the declarations of ecumenical councils and the teachings of the Eastern Church Fathers. Recognizing that the Fathers differed in their teachings, they identified as normative an area of common agreement among them, a *consensus patrum*. Orthodoxy considers the Fathers perennially contemporary because all believers participate in the same spiritual reality. Each person who gains knowledge of God gains the same knowledge as that of the Fathers. In the Orthodox Church, innovation and blasphemy are roughly synonymous. Orthodoxy has a sophisticated awareness of the fact that different *language* indicates different referents; thus, the language of the Fathers is normative. Maximus the Confessor wrote, "Every formula and term that is not found in the Fathers is shown to be obviously an innovation" (*Theological and Polemical Works* 22). One Western twelfth-century theologian remarked that Eastern theologians, courageous in other respects, are cowardly about transgressing the boundaries of the Fathers.

Within Orthodoxy, councils have a carefully defined authority. In the New Testament book of Acts, when a disagreement broke out between different factions, the apostles were not appealed to. Rather a council was convened. Councils, however, are only orthodox if their doctrines are orthodox. Even the ecumenical Councils lack the absolute authority of the *consensus patrum*.

In addition to the knowledge of God gained through experience ("activity, labor, and fatigue"), knowledge of God is gained through contemplation. Contemplation is the only way to approach God's transcendence and changelessness. Gregory of Nyssa described the experience of God's transcendence. It is, he said,

> like a perpendicular cliff of smooth rock, rearing up from the limitless expanse of sea to its top that overhangs the sheer abyss. Imagine what a man feels when he stands right on the edge, and sees that there is no hold for hand or foot: the mind feels in just the same way when, in its quest for the Nature that is outside time and space, it finds that all footholds have been left behind. There is nothing to "take hold of," neither place nor time, nor dimension nor anything else, nothing on which thought can take its stand. At every turn the mind feels the ungraspable escape its grasp; it becomes giddy, there is no way out.
>
> (*Commentary on the Canticles*)

Nicephorus (758–829) claimed that theological knowledge is more adequately communicated through images than through language. The transcendence, the silence, and the majesty of God are best grasped, not as intellectual concepts, but as sensory experiences. The mind must be dazzled and overwhelmed. Christ as Ruler of the universe is more adequately represented in the gold leaf and rich strong colors, the unapproachable gaze, the position in the height of the dome of an Orthodox church than in verbal descriptions. In the experience of an image, God's impenetrable silence and majesty becomes event (see figure 3.1).

Figure 3.1   Christ in Majesty (Deesis), mosaic, thirteenth century, Hagia Sophia, Istanbul (Constantinople).

Hagia Sophia was built by Justinian (532–37). It became a mosque after the Turkish conquest and the mosaics were hidden under whitewash. The architecture ingeniously combines a longitudinal axis with a huge central dome, abutted by half-domes at either end. Hagia Sophia was the first building to carry the weight of the domes on pendatives, a device that became standard in Byzantine architecture and in the West. The Deesis is made of tiny painted glass tesserae whose shiny and slightly irregular faces act as reflectors. The effect is that of "a glittering, immaterial screen rather than a solid continuous surface" (Janson, 1963: 163). Photo AKG Images.

Faith through works

Members of Orthodox churches are expected to work out their salvation with the help of the Church's mysteries and sacraments. Personal faith is received through the Church and becomes effective by participation in the Church's life. In sum, all theology is contemplation of the Trinity in the language of the Fathers and in the context of the liturgy.

The Orthodox churches take seriously the scriptural statement, "Christ became what we are so that we might become what he is" (see CD Rom figure 3.1). Scripture supports the claim that because Christ shared human nature, humans can be deified: "Ye are gods" (*Psalm* 82.6), and the New Testament promises that believers "become partakers in the divine nature" (John 10.34). Deification is possible, but if it is to occur, humans must also freely will it. Maximus said, "For the Spirit does not generate a will that is not willing, but transforms into deification a will that has the desire" (*Questions to Thalassius on the Scripture* 6). The Orthodox Church did not debate the relationship of grace and free will as the Western Church repeatedly did. They thought of grace and free will as continuously interacting. The human will cooperates with the divine will (*synergy*) to achieve deification, a participation in the *life* of God, not intellectual knowledge of God.

Icons

Icons are portable religious pictures, usually painted on a wooden panel, but there are also many mosaic or enamel on metal icons. Icons do not represent realistically. Instead, they distort the image in order to point to a spiritual reality (*anagogic* representation) (see CD Rom figure 3.2). Eyes – the "windows of the soul" – are large; noses are thin, and mouths are small; bodies are elongated and landscapes and buildings are abstract. Natural light and colors are suppressed and colors are used symbolically. The iconographer sought to represent what is *really* (that is, spiritually) happening. In a crucifixion scene, for example, Christ was not portrayed as a corpse, but reigning from the cross in majesty, victor over sin and death, the redeemer of humanity. Spectators within the crucifixion scene do not exhibit hysterical grief and sorrow; rather, they show restrained, calm sorrow, relieved by the hope of resurrection (see CD Rom figure 3.3).

Each icon has a traditional place in an Orthodox church. The dome is reserved for the image of *Christos Pantocrator*, ruler and judge of all (figure 3.1). The spaces between the windows in the drum of the dome are for prophets; the four pendatives below depict the four evangelists; the vaults and upper walls of the nave carry depictions of the twelve great feasts of the Orthodox liturgical year (see CD Rom figures 3.4 and 3.5); the lower walls are for Christ's miracles and parables. The main eastern apse is reserved for Mary *Theotokos* (God-bearer) (see CD Rom figures 3.6 and 3.7). An *iconostasis*, a wooden or marble screen that supports panel icons, is placed between the sanctuary and the nave on which portable icons of Christ, the *Theotokos* and Child, and the sacred person or event being celebrated are placed. An icon of Christ is placed south of the door into the sanctuary, and the *Theotokos* is placed north of the door (see CD Rom figure 3.1; contrast CD Rom figure 3.7). The same placement scheme has been in use for over a thousand years, since the resolution of the iconoclast controversy.

Iconoclastic controversy

Theological work begins when questions arise about liturgical or devotional practices. Thus, before a theology of images was articulated, images were used to teach and to focus prayer. But controversy over icons convulsed the Byzantine Empire from the 720s to 843, requiring the development of a theology of icons.

Images embody the distinctive spirituality of Eastern Orthodoxy. In the seventh century they were, in fact, so important that complaints began to appear that the images themselves were being worshipped. In the second wave of the controversy, Emperor

Michael II (820–9) complained that the distinction between honoring an icon for its own sake and honoring it for its prototype was too subtle for most people. It was alleged that miracles were ascribed to particular images, and people hung linen cloths on icons, placing their children in them after baptism. Some people scraped off chips of the icons' paint and mixed them with communion wine.

The first wave of the controversy occurred in the reign of Constantine V, a popular ruler and a self-styled theologian. In 754 Constantine held a council that agreed to destroy and forbid religious images in churches. Thousands of monks, the most energetic defenders of icon-use, were slaughtered. Following this decree, a contemporary chronicler wrote,

> Wherever there were venerable images of Christ or the Mother of God, or the saints, these were consigned to the flames or gouged out or smeared over. If, on the other hand, there were pictures of birds or trees or senseless beasts, and in particular horse races, hunts, and theatrical scenes, these were preserved with honor and given greater luster.

Constantine V argued that a genuine image must be "identical in essence" with that which it portrays. The image of Christ in an icon, he said, was a "falsely so-called image;" only the eucharistic elements are identical in essence. He quoted Christ's words, "Do *this* – the eucharistic celebration – in remembrance of me."

Iconodules (or *iconophiles*, lovers of icons) argued that icons are appropriate because of the Incarnation. Christ's visible appearance in a human body altered the status of the material world and showed that the material world can carry divinity. Even before the Incarnation, God was the first to make an image – human beings, made in God's image. John of Damascus wrote:

> The image speaks to the sight as words to the ear: it brings us understanding. . . . I have not many books nor time for study and I go into a church, the common refuge of souls, my mind wearied with conflicting thoughts. I see before me a beautiful picture and the sight refreshes me and induces me to glorify God. I marvel at the martyr's endurance, at his reward, and fired with burning zeal I fall down to adore God through his martyr and receive a grace of salvation. . . . The representations of the saints are not our gods, but books which lie open and are venerated in churches in order to remind us of God and lead us to worship him.
>
> (*Orations on the Images* 1)

Iconophiles like John of Damascus, Theodore of Studios (759–826), and Nicephorus (758–829) argued that iconoclasts denigrated matter by rejecting images as representations of divine power. Nicephorus said, "Why do you worship the book and spit on the image?" Iconophiles pointed out that in the Gospels, sight and hearing were coordinated; similarly, icons and words work together. There were also practical and liturgical reasons for icon-use. The eye comes first, Theodore of Studios argued; sight is more effective than hearing. John of Damascus wrote: "Perhaps you are sublime and able to transcend what is material . . . but I, since I am a human being and bear a body want to deal with holy things and behold them in a bodily manner" (*Orations on the Images* 1) (see CD Rom figure 3.8).

The first wave of the conflict was ended by the Seventh Ecumenical Council, the Second Council of Nicaea in 787. The Council declared:

> We define with all certitude and accuracy that just as the figure of the precious life-giving cross, so also the venerable and holy images, as well in painting and mosaic as in other fit materials, should be set forth in the holy churches of God, and on the sacred vessels and on the vestments and on hangings and on pictures both in houses and by the wayside, that is, the figure of our Lord God and Savior Jesus Christ, of our spotless lady, the Mother of God, of the honorable angels, of all saints, and of all pious people. For by so much more frequently as they are seen in artistic representation, by so much more readily are people lifted up to the memory of their prototypes, and to a longing after them – but not the true worship of our faith which befits only the divine nature – but to offer them both incense and candles, according to the ancient pious custom, in the same way as to the form of the venerable and life-giving cross and other sacred objects.

The Council also defined the kind of honor that is appropriate for saints and holy figures: *dulia* is the veneration properly given to saints and angels; *hyperdulia*, "more than veneration" is given to divine figures; *latria*, worship, is due only to God (see CD Rom figure 3.9).

But the controversy was not over; a second wave of controversy occurred in which paintings were again removed from churches, sacred vessels scraped clean of their embossed figures, and a secret police appointed to search out furtive image-worship. The charge of idolatry, prominent in the first wave of iconoclasm, was no longer the primary argument. Two theological issues were at stake in the second wave: the Incarnation, and the relationship of a picture to its prototype. Nicephorus and Theodore of Studios argued that the image is not *separate*, but it is *distinct* from its original. Thus, the image of Christ should be given "hyper-veneration;" it should not be worshipped as if it *were* Christ. To iconoclasts' arguments that God is uncircumscribed and therefore unrepresentable, Theodore responded that the incarnate Christ *was* circumscribed by taking on the limitations of human nature; therefore it is appropriate to depict him. The second wave of iconoclasm was ended by the death of the Emperor Theophilius in 842. His wife Theodora summoned a Council in early 843 that affirmed the decisions concerning image-use made by the Second Ecumenical Council of Nicaea in 787 and again restored images.

Liturgical needs informed the vindication of icon-use. The liturgy of the Orthodox Church is believed to be a reflection on earth of what is occurring continuously in heaven. In this context, icons embody the *presence* of the spiritual world, reminding worshippers that the liturgy is shared by living and dead (see CD Rom figure 3.10). During the liturgy, a priest recites prayers and censes the icons, acknowledging the saints' presence. The triumph of the icon was understood as the triumph of the Incarnation – the Word made flesh, visible, a sign of the presence of divine energy in the world of the senses. The restoration of images was (and is) celebrated on the first Sunday in Lent (March 11, 843) as the Sunday of Orthodoxy.

In the West a small iconoclastic controversy, unconnected to Eastern iconoclasm, occurred during the ninth century. Bishop Claudius of Turin, a Spaniard by birth, attacked the use of images in his diocese.

People can understand things without seeing images [he wrote], but not without the knowledge of God. Moreover it is a very unfortunate spirit that depends on the help of painters' pictures to remember the life of Christ and cannot draw inspiration from its own powers.

Although the controversy generated a good deal of writing, it did not excite popular and political interests. Hincmar, archbishop of Reims (845–82) ended the controversy by restating the rationale for image-use first suggested by Gregory I in about 600:

Pictures are used in churches so that those who are ignorant of letters may at least read by seeing on the wall what they cannot read in books. What writing does for the literate, a picture does for the illiterate person looking at it, because they see in it what they ought to do. Thus, a picture takes the place of reading.

Avoiding the sophisticated discussions held in the East, Hincmar argued for the *educational* effectiveness of images (see CD Rom figure 3.11).

READINGS

Gregory of Nyssa, *Catechetical Orations* 27–8
John of Damascus, *The Orthodox Faith* XVI, "Concerning Images"

2   The Early Medieval West

The fifth century was a time of rapid and violent change in the Roman Empire as northern European tribes moved into the empire and new rulers laid claim to portions of it. In 404 the Emperor Honorius (ruled 395–423) moved the imperial capital to Ravenna. In 410, after a decade in which the Visigothic chief, Alaric, and his soldiers repeatedly looted the Italian peninsula, they conquered Rome. By 476 Italy was ruled by Vandals and Ravenna became the residence of their chief, Odovacer. Seventeen years later, in 493, Theodoric the Ostrogoth overthrew the Vandal kingdom in Ravenna and ruled Italy until 526 when Belisarius, Justinian's general, reconquered Italy. Invasions by pagan Slavs and Arian Lombards in the sixth century reconfigured the map of Europe.

Islam

With the advent of Islam in the seventh century, a major and permanent force opposed Christianity in Europe, Asia, North Africa, and Persia. Born shortly after Justinian's death, Muhammad was successful in organizing the Arab Bedouin tribes. But it was only after his own death in 632 that the Muslim conquests began. Arab conquests overran the Near Eastern and African provinces of Byzantium and, by a century after Muhammad's death, all of North Africa and Spain had been conquered and southwestern France was threatened.

The Prophet Muhammad did not claim to bring a new religion, but only to reaffirm the truth that had always existed. He taught a simple doctrine of submission to the One (Allah). Like Judaism and Christianity, Islam is monotheistic, and a religion of the book, the Qur'an. Unlike Christianity and Judaism, Muslims have no priests or sacraments; rather, each Muslim is expected to work toward salvation by good deeds and virtue. Religious practices include prayer, fasting, almsgiving, and pilgrimage. Muhammad had several Christian (probably Monophysite) associates, and the Qur'an repeats a number of stories from the Hebrew Bible and the Christian scriptures. Muhammad denied the death of Jesus on the cross, but maintained reverence for the Virgin Mary and supported the immaculate conception 1,200 years before it became Roman Catholic doctrine.

Islam was initially regarded by Christians as a Christian heresy. In the eighth century, the Arabic-speaking Syrian Christian Bishop Theodore Abu-Qurra wrote treatises in which he defended the doctrine of the trinity against Muslim charges of tritheism. Dialogue between Muslims and Christians also occurred in Persia in the last years of the eighth century. By the mid-ninth century it was clear that Islam was not a Christian heresy but a new religion. Nevertheless, Muslim–Christian dialogue continued through the Middle Ages, each side seeking unsuccessfully to correct the errors of the other. Arabs employed Christians as administrators and financial managers in Syria, Arabia, and Egypt. Between 750 and 950, Jacobite and Nestorian Christians instructed Muslims in Syriac scholarship and Greek thought. Occasionally Christians and Muslims also shared buildings for worship.

The new religion brought a new culture. From Spain in the West to the Indus Valley in the East, Muslims avoided the Western conflict between religious and political leaders by combining these offices in one caliph. Baghdad quickly rivaled Constantinople in splendor. Islamic art, architecture, and learning, including Greek philosophy and science and Arabic numerals, came to the West from Muslim scholars. In the twelfth century, a major revision of Western philosophical and theological scholarship resulted from Arab translations and commentaries of Aristotle. The subject of Islam and the West will be revisited in the next chapter.

Justinian, Theodora, and Ravenna

Ravenna, originally a Roman naval base on the Adriatic, was the imperial capital city for over a century, during which it became a treasure house of Christian architecture and art. In Ravenna, Christian imagery was reinterpreted to include the concerns of new rulers who were intimidated by classical antiquity. One of them, Justinian (ruled 526–47), endeavored by the church building and decoration he financed, to demonstrate simultaneously his commitment to Christianity and his imperial authority. His magnificent building program was not confined to Ravenna; it included the rebuilding of Hagia Sophia in Constantinople, and the monastery of St Catherine on Mt Sinai, where the few images that survived iconoclasm were preserved. Not by nature a modest man, Justinian declared at the dedication of Hagia Sophia, "Solomon, I have surpassed you."

Justinian was a strong and effective Byzantine emperor. His goal was to restore the past greatness of the Roman Empire. He reformed administrative abuses in government and arrested a collapse into political, economic, and social chaos. He also collected and codified the legal system, and initiated several military campaigns to win back territories lost to fifth-century invasions. Africa and the coastline of Spain were retrieved from the Vandals (533); Italy, and part of southern Spain were reconquered from the Goths, and the Persians were successfully resisted in the East. Justinian defended imperial supremacy over the Church, asserting the imperial prerogative of legislating orthodoxy. He first persecuted, then reconciled with Monophysite Christians. His conquests were motivated, or at least rationalized, as efforts to exterminate heresy, since Goths and Vandals professed Arian Christianity. These campaigns were costly; to pay for them, Justinian taxed heavily and ruled autocratically.

Justinian's building program also displayed his authority by its scale and grandeur. San Vitale, Justinian's church in Ravenna, is not a basilica; rather, it is an octagonal building with a domed central core. Its vaulting permits large windows that provide brilliant light to the mosaics that cover the walls, their angled tesserae catching the crossing light. The sixth-century historian Procopius described the intricate and dazzling beauty of San Vitale.

> All these details, fitted together with incredible skill in midair and floating off from each other and resting only on the parts next to them, produce a single and most extraordinary harmony in the work, and yet do not permit the spectator to linger much over the study of any one of them, but each detail attracts the eye and draws it on irresistibly to itself. So the vision constantly shifts suddenly, for the spectator is utterly unable to select which particular detail he should admire more than all the others. But even so, though they turn their attention to every side and look with contracted brows upon every detail, observers are still unable to understand the skillful craftsmanship, but they always depart from there overwhelmed by the bewildering sight.
>
> *(Buildings)*

The Ravenna mosaics were the last major work of imperial art before the iconoclastic controversy in the Eastern Empire (see CD Rom figures 3.12 and 3.13).

Procopius wrote two different accounts of Justinian's reign, one that flattered Justinian (*Histories, Buildings*), and one that mocked him, the *Secret History* (*Anecdota*). In the *Secret History*, Procopius represented Justinian as weak-willed and subservient to his wife, Theodora who, he said, was cruel, lustful, and scheming. He claimed that, as a child, Theodora had been a comedian and a child prostitute. Justinian married her despite Roman law that forbade a senator to marry a woman "dishonored by a servile origin or a theatrical profession." Credibility is lent to this part of Procopius' narrative by the fact that Justinian abolished that law when he became emperor.

According to Procopius, a weak-willed Justinian seated Theodora on a throne "as an independent and equal colleague." He required the provincial governors to take an oath of allegiance in the names of both Justinian and Theodora, an annoying innovation. Theodora, a Monophysite Christian, had a stately palace converted into a sanctuary for 500 prostitutes she brought from Constantinople. Procopius claimed that some of the beneficiaries threw themselves out the window into the sea rather than live the monastic life arranged for them by Theodora.

Procopius made no secret of the fact that he hated Theodora. His account of her activities is a rich source of "tasteless historical stories." He delighted in stories of her cruelty, practice of magic (a crime punishable by death), and sexual excesses. Curiously, numerous historians after him accepted and reiterated these stories despite his evident bias. One such story claims that Theodora required the services of ten young men every night to satisfy her sexual hungers. Yet, if Procopius was right about Justinian's dependence on Theodora, the successes of Justinian's reign must be at least partially attributed to her. Procopius did not attempt to resolve this contradiction.

There are only two historical sources for Theodora: Procopius and the San Vitale mosaics. In the mosaics, Theodora and Justinian are depicted in a liturgical procession, accompanied by their retinues, offering the bread and cup. The Justinian and Theodora panels are set under the apse mosaic, which shows Christ enthroned on a globe above the four rivers of paradise. Imperial splendor was presented as a direct reflection of Christ's splendor. Since San Vitale was dedicated in 547, and Theodora died in 548, it is likely that she had influence on how she was represented. If so, her self-representation could not contradict more completely Procopius's stories of her cruel and lustful behavior. But it is possible that both could be more-or-less true; historical people cannot be reduced to saints and villains but, like their modern counterparts, were bewilderingly complex.

Justinian endeavored to maintain the Roman imperial tradition, but new styles of political leadership also emerged in the early medieval West. In the remote northern kingdom of the Franks, Bishop Gregory of Tours (c.540–94) narrated the rule of Clovis, the Frankish king, in his *History of the Franks*. For Gregory, a leader's virtue was demonstrated by his power; if he held power, he must be virtuous. Describing Clovis, Gregory wrote:

> When they [his enemies] were dead, Clovis received all their kingdom and treasures and, having killed many other kings and his nearest relatives, of whom he was jealous lest they take the kingdom from him, he extended his rule over all the Gauls. . . . For God was laying his enemies low every day under his hand, and was increasing his kingdom because he walked with an upright heart before God and did what was pleasing in God's eyes.

Clovis was converted to Catholic Christianity along with 3,000 of his warriors shortly after 500. The Franks' victory over the Arian Burgundians soon resulted in a Catholic Gaul.

Jews

Gregory of Tours described the relationship of Christians and Jews in the early medieval West. According to Gregory, Jews had clearly defined legal and constitutional status, but although Roman emperors had recognized an obligation to protect Jew's legal rights, barbarian leaders did not. Medieval Jews seem to have had little social standing. Occasionally they were forcefully baptized. Although Gregory is not a trustworthy historian where numbers and events are concerned, he probably reflected accurately popular opinion regarding Jews. He found them parasitic, ignorant, and expendable, an "alienated minority" in Christian society.

The earliest restrictive legislation against Jews occurred in Constantine's reign in the 330s. It prohibited proselytizing by Jews, and forbade Jews to own Christian slaves or to hold civic office at an administrative level. Constantine also required that Jewish taxes, formerly sent to the Jerusalem Temple, be paid to the imperial treasury. In the fifth century, autonomous Jewish rule in Palestine ended. The Theodosian Code, compiled in 438, stated that Jew's legal rights must be respected, as long as Jews respected Christian rights. But theologians like John Chrysostom assaulted Jews in sermons and writings, identifying Jews with evil of all sorts. Augustine believed that Jews would be reconciled to Christianity in the last days, but he contributed to Jews' marginalization by emphasizing an opposition between spiritual and carnal strivings, with Jews strongly identified with carnal appetites. By the mid-fifth century, the mosaic decoration of Santa Maria Maggiore in Rome (described in chapter 2) brought together in vivid visual images a Christian consensus already evident in sermons, imperial legislation, and popular destruction of synagogues, that Christianity had replaced and superseded Judaism.

Classical learning

Gregory of Tours began his *History of the Franks* by admitting that liberal culture and learning were lacking in his society. He wrote the Franks' history, he said, because there was literally no one else who could. His acknowledgement of his "rude speech" was not overly modest, as anyone who tries to read his Latin can attest. In order to situate his people, the Franks of Merovingian Gaul, he began with the creation of the world, but he moved very rapidly (within a page) from the days of creation to the history of his own time.

Classical learning was one of the first interests to disappear in the demanding circumstances of medieval life. Almost no one had leisure for it. "If our concern were with secular erudition," one Roman wrote, "we think no one nowadays can boast much learning. Here the fury of the barbarians burns daily, now flaring up, now dying down. Our whole life is taken up in cares, and all our efforts go to beating back the war bands that surround us."

Boethius (c.480–524) was one of the last philosophical minds of his time. He came from a Roman aristocratic family and was made a consul at age of 30 under the Ostrogothic Arian emperor, Theodoric. Boethius, an old-fashioned thinker in a new political world, thought of classical learning as the heritage of Catholic Christendom. A "renaissance man" before his time, he tried to translate all of Plato and Aristotle, and he published works on arithmetic, geometry, astronomy, and theology.

Accused of plots against the emperor, Boethius was imprisoned and executed. In prison, awaiting execution, he wrote *The Consolation of Philosophy*, a thoroughly classical book that lacks any mention of Christianity. Boethius consoled himself with classical ideas of a just and rational universe, *not* a universe he was experiencing.

> I am not so discouraged by what has happened to me that I complain now of the attacks of evil men against virtue; the reason for my surprise is that they have accomplished what they set out to do. The desire to do evil may be due to human weakness; but for the wicked to overthrow the innocent in the sight of God – this is monstrous.

Boethius found this dissonance painful emotionally and intellectually. Profoundly out of sync with popular Christianity, he had no interest in miracles, saints, and relics. "You live in a world which all people share, so you ought not to desire to live by some special law." He wrote *The Consolation of Philosophy* to convince himself and his readers that misfortune is nothing but a test of one's mettle.

Missions

In Ireland, a gentle and tactful form of mission took place in the fifth century under the leadership of St Patrick (c.390–460). There is no record of martyrs, either pagan or Christian. As a boy, Patrick was enslaved and brought from Britain to Ireland. After living in Ireland for six years, he managed to work his way back to Britain. While there, he had a dream in which the "voice of the Irish" begged him to bring them Christianity. So he led a mission to Ireland in the 430s. There is little information about the development of Christianity in Ireland until the beginning of the sixth century; by then, a flourishing church existed.

Irish Christianity was organized around country monasteries ruled by abbots rather than bishops. It was in conflict with Roman Christianity on several points, like the correct date of Easter and the fact that in Ireland the clergy were not required to be celibate as Roman clergy were (however ineffectually). The Irish Church united with the Roman church reluctantly; the union was only finalized in 1172 by the English conquest of Ireland.

There is evidence of the existence of organized Christianity in Great Britain by 314, when several English bishops attended the Council of Arles. When Anglo-Saxons invaded, however, the English Church was dispersed. A new mission, described by Bede the Venerable (673–735) in his *Ecclesiastical History of the English People*, was sent to the British Isles. The mission was led by Augustine of Canterbury (not Augustine of Hippo), under the detailed direction of Pope Gregory I. Conversion in the British Isles, as elsewhere, was communal; rulers chose the religion of their people. The monks who missionized Britain recognized that the tribal leaders were impressed by power, and that they considered miracles a persuasive display of power. Bede's account related the many miracles that attracted and finally convinced them to adopt Christianity. The Synod of Whitby in 664 was the occasion of the official acceptance of Christianity.

Displays of power were not the only attraction Christianity held for Britons. In a society in which corruption, treachery, and violence were everyday occurrences, the most important fact of life was its fragility.

> When we compare this present life with that time of which we have no knowledge, it seems to me like the swift flight of a lone sparrow through the banqueting-hall where you sit with your thanes and counselors. Inside there is a comforting fire to warm the room; outside the wintry storms of wind and snow are raging. This sparrow flies swiftly in through one door of the hall, and out through another. While she is inside she is safe from the winter storms; but after a few moments of comfort she vanishes from sight into the darkness she came from. Similarly we appear on earth for a little while, but we know nothing of what went before this life, or of what follows.
>
> (Bede, *History* 2. 13)

One Anglo Saxon leader concluded: "Therefore if this new teaching can reveal any more certain knowledge, it seems only right that we should follow it."

One of the most contentious issues of the medieval West was evident in Charlemagne's relationship with Pope Leo III (d. 816). Charlemagne (742–814) was crowned "Holy Roman Emperor" in Rome on Christmas Day 800. The ambiguity concerning who held the greater power was acted out in his coronation. The pope crowned him, implying that the pope had the greater power. But after crowning him, Leo knelt before Charlemagne in a gesture of submission. The question of who had the ultimate authority remained unresolved.

Charlemagne's palace chapel at Aachen (dedicated in 805) was inspired by San Vitale in Ravenna. It illustrates the delicate balance between emperor and Church. Charlemagne's monumental marble throne sat in the *westwork* directly facing the sanctuary and eastern apse where the bishop celebrated the mass (see CD Rom figure 3.14).

Charlemagne's reign had two goals: to reestablish classical learning and to exterminate paganism. In pursuit of the former, he brought the finest scholars in Europe to his court. Alcuin, a pupil of Bede, who had been head of the cathedral school at York, became the leading scholar of Charlemagne's court, practicing scholarship that endeavored to revive the scholarship of an earlier time. Two scholars, the monk Einhard, and Notker, called "the stammerer," wrote biographies of Charlemagne – the first medieval biographies of a layman. One of them revealed that although Charlemagne was illiterate, he slept with a copy of the *City of God* under his pillow. Motivated by the shortage of parchment, Charlemagne's scholars developed a new miniscule script. The liturgical developments they initiated will be discussed in the next section.

Charlemagne's method of missionizing was forced baptism. Alcuin protested vigorously, citing Christ's precept of love, but Charlemagne persisted. On one occasion, three thousand Lombards who resisted baptism were slaughtered. Charlemagne also attempted to Christianize his society by laws. The death penalty was legislated for a range of offenses that included killing a bishop, priest, or deacon, burning an alleged witch, robbing a church, refusing to be baptized, and eating meat during Lent.

There is little information about missions outside the Roman Empire. As discussed in chapter 2, various kinds of Christianity existed in Persia (Nestorians), India, Central and southeast Asia, and China. By 900, Christianity was established in Gaul, Germany, Britain, and Ireland. On the eve of the Muslim conquests, Christianity was distributed across the known world.

The Church

The Christian Church survived the collapse of the Roman state with which it was often optimistically identified during the fourth century. This was partly facilitated by Ambrose's political stands and by Augustine's theological work. Neither envisioned a Christian Empire in which Church and state were synonymous. Christian leaders' flexibility in interpreting and addressing new situations was also a factor in the Church's survival. For example, two fifth-century popes were successful in keeping barbarian armies from looting Rome.

In 451, Pope Leo I (d. 461), author of the *Tome* on which the Chacedonian resolution was based, persuaded the threatening Huns to retreat beyond the Danube River. The Greek historian Priscus reported that Pope Leo went with a small unarmed delegation to the Hun's camp outside Rome, negotiated with their leader, and returned with Attila's agreement that the Huns would not attack Rome. Again in 452, when the Vandals conquered Rome, Leo was able to secure concessions that minimized the damages. Gregory I conducted similar successful peace negotiations with the Lombards. Leo and Gregory were Christian leaders who exercised a kind of power that was recognized and valued in a frightening world.

Gregory I ("the Great," 540–604) was prefect of the city of Rome before entering religious life. He reluctantly left the peaceful life of the monastery to become pope when his predecessor died of a plague that was ravaging Rome. In his *Dialogues* Gregory complained of his loss of monastic peace when he was pressed into ecclesiastical service:

> But now all the beauty of that spiritual repose is gone, and the contact with worldly men and their affairs, which is a necessary part of my duties as a bishop, has left my soul defiled with earthly cares. I am so distracted with external occupations in my concern for the people that even when my spirit resumes its striving after the interior life it always does so with less vigor. Such, in fact, is the way our mind declines. First we lose a prized possession but remain aware of the loss; then, as we go along, even the remembrance of it fades, and so at the end we are unable any longer to recall what was once in our possession.

The first act of Gregory's pontificate was to conduct a liturgy of intercession for deliverance from the plague. During the liturgy, it is reported, no less than 80 members of the congregation fell down dead. In a time of multiple crises – plague, famine and devastation, and threat from invaders – Gregory ransomed captives, provided food and water, and founded hospitals. He also wrote a Pastoral *Rule*, a treatise on the book of Job, other scriptural commentaries, and the *Dialogues*, originally called *The Miracles of the Italian Fathers*. The latter was one of the first examples of a new literary genre, medieval hagiography, or saints' lives.

In addition to the dramatic courageous acts of several Christian leaders, quieter forms of stabilization and consolidation of the Church occurred. The early medieval Church also reformed liturgy. Alcuin and his scholars established the liturgical year, along with a lectionary of scripture and hymns. In the seventh century the *Gregorian sacramentary* shortened the service from three hours. Charlemagne, ignoring the rivalry between Gallican and Roman liturgies, adopted the Gregorian reforms. The service still included choir music and choral responses, lectionaries of hymns and readings from the four gospels, intercessory prayers, responses, and a sermon.

Attention was given to improving the quality of sermons. At Charlemagne's request, Paul the Deacon (d. c.800) wrote a broadly circulated compilation of sermons for the purpose of providing clergy with material for effective preaching. Rabanus Maurus (d. c.856), archbishop of Mainz, similarly concerned for clergy education, wrote a manual on liturgy, prayer, fasts, and other topics requisite to clergy's informed functioning. In short, Charlemagne's interest in liturgical and ecclesiastic reform, learning, and doctrine constituted his contribution to medieval Christianity, not his conquests.

Various musical instruments were used in early medieval churches: lyre, zither, harp, flute, horns, percussion instruments, cymbals, castanets, and hand bells. Charlemagne had an organ installed in the palace chapel at Aachen. Notker the Stammerer wrote: "This admirable instrument, with the aid of brass vats and leather bellows, chases the air through brass tubes as if by magic, its roaring equaling the sound of thunder and its sweetness the light sounds of lyre and cymbal."

The Church performed important social functions in the violent and volatile medieval world. In an attempt to minimize murders, numerous saints' days were added to the calendar. Since murder on a saint's day was a mortal sin, a person bent on murder might think twice if he had to wait a day in order not to lose his immortal soul. Churches also offered sanctuary to political enemies, criminals, battered wives, and members of feuding families. The Sirmondian Constitutions (419) formalized what was already practiced in the 410 Sack of Rome when the Arian Goths respected sanctuary in Christian churches. Title 13 of the Sirmondian Constitutions stipulated that "persons who flee for sanctuary to the churches shall be safe within fifty paces outside the doors." Similar legislation was repeated throughout Christian lands. The fifth century Spanish *Lex Visigothorum* stated, "No one shall dare to remove by force any person who has sought sanctuary in a church unless said person shall attempt to defend himself with arms."

The first marriage rituals appeared at the end of the fourth century when the Church endeavored to regulate marriage. In the fifth century, men paid a large dowry to the bride's father; Justinian tried unsuccessfully to equalize the contributions of both families to the new household, but by the eighth century, a reverse dowry or bridewealth was established.

In the fifth and sixth centuries in the West, women were scarce due to the frequency of death in childbirth, female monasticism, and the common practice of polygamy among wealthy men. In order to distribute women, kinship requirements were legislated. By 821 marriage partners were not permitted to be more closely related than seven degrees of kinship. Marriage by kidnap was prohibited, and *public* weddings were required in order to ensure the absence of coercion. Women and men were usually in their middle-to-late twenties when they married.

Marriage customs developed around "church weddings," that is, weddings that occurred on the church steps. Tenth century canon law states that a couple could not enter church for 30 days after marriage, and then only after a ritual penance. The strong implication of these stipulations was that even in marriage, sex was tainted. But reproduction was valued. In the West a nuptial blessing was conducted while the couple was in the marriage bed. In a society scantily populated, the potential of childbearing was blessed, not the relationship itself. The custom of placing martyrs' crowns on the heads of the couple developed in the East to indicate the demands of marriage on both partners.

Birth control must be counted as one of the social services provided by the medieval church. The only *official* means of birth control was abstinence, and days were stipulated on which abstinence was mandatory. These included 40 days before Christmas, 40 days before Easter, eight days after Pentecost, the eves of the Great Feasts, Sundays, Wednesdays, and Fridays, during pregnancy, 30 days after giving birth (if a boy), 40 days (if a girl), during menstruation, and for five days before taking communion (three times a year was required). It is difficult to see how medieval societies populated themselves, if not by transgressing canon law!

Finally, the Church's social services included the provision of feast days. Communities without weekends needed regular breaks from relentless agrarian labor. At Corbie (east of Amiens in France) in 822, in addition to Sundays, peasants had 36 non-working days a year. In sum, early medieval Christianity in the West was characterized by alertness to people's needs, as well as to Church protocols.

Piety

New religious interests appeared in the early medieval West as saints, miracles, and relics generated popular excitement. In his *Dialogues*, Gregory the Great described the amazing abilities of St Benedict of Nursia: "Of course he knew God's secrets since he followed God's teachings. For it is written, 'He who is united to the Lord becomes one spirit with him.' Holy men are not ignorant of God's thoughts insofar as they are one with God" (*Dialogues* 2). Holy persons enjoy a God's-eye view. Gregory wrote:

> To a soul that beholds the creator, all creation is narrow in compass. For when a person views the creator's light, no matter how little of it, all creation becomes small in his eyes. By the light of the inmost vision, the inner recesses of his mind are opened up and so expanded in God that they are above the universe. In fact, the soul of the beholder rises even above itself. When it is caught up above itself in God's light, it is made ampler within. As it looks down from its height it grasps the smallness of what it could not take in its lowly state.
>
> Therefore, as Benedict gazed at the fiery globe, he saw angels too returning to heaven. To say that the world was gathered together before his eyes does not mean that heaven and earth shrank, but that the mind of the beholder was expanded so that he could easily see everything below God since he himself was caught up in God.
>
> (*Dialogues* 2. 25)

According to Gregory, Benedict's abilities included making predictions (including the time of his own death), healing, raising the dead to life, and controlling and/or eliminating demons (including permitting them to return if certain conditions were not met). He had intimate knowledge of the material world, and could detect when someone was trying to poison him. Astral projection was also within his repertoire. Gregory explained this "reasonably": since "spirit is more mobile in nature than body, Benedict appeared in spirit to monks he wanted to instruct spiritually." He was able to release the souls of the damned, and to change the weather – not by magic, Gregory says, but by love. Moreover, Gregory said, holy people exercise these powers even after death. Saints "grant greater favors through their relics than through their living bodies."

Interest in relics was not confined to popular superstition. Gregory of Nyssa, a superbly educated and subtle late fourth-century thinker, wrote:

> Those who behold the relics of the saints and martyrs embrace, as it were, the living body in full flower. They bring, eye, mouth, ear, and all the senses into play and then, shedding tears of reverence and passion, they address to the martyr their prayers of intercession as though he were present.
>
> (*On Theodore the Martryr*)

Similarly, Jerome, the most renowned and prolific Christian scholar of his time, said, "Whenever I have been angry or have had some bad thought upon my mind, or some evil fantasy has disturbed my sleep, I do not dare to enter the shrines of the martyrs . . . I quake."

Until the fifth century, shrines containing the relics of saints and martyrs were in the countryside. Bishops, complaining that people were more interested in shrines than in churches, energetically appropriated the cult of saints and martyrs, placing the bones of holy people under the altars of newly built churches. In doing so, they ensured the availability of relics to the community. By the end of the sixth century, the graves of saints were centers of ecclesiastical life. Families of deceased persons competed to bury their loved ones close to holy bones. One fifth-century inscription read: "Here I lie at the chapel door; here I lie because I'm poor; the farther in, the more you pay; here lie I as warm as they."

The holy people Gregory of Tours described in his *History of the Franks* were extremely practical and had strong social consciences. Many of the "miracles" he reported had a non-dramatic, everyday quality. In Gregory's harsh world, in which mothers kill daughters, husbands wives, and old friends in sudden drunken rages stab each other, many things that might, in a gentler time, be considered coincidental or natural seemed miraculous. Gregory's "miracles" include a headache getting better, a sudden change of heart in a person bent on revenge, the turning of a plague, and a prisoner's escape. Gregory's world had little room for the ordinary; most occurrences were either miraculous or diabolical.

Gregory described an ascetic recluse who had two specializations, driving demons from the bodies they possessed, and curing pimples. He also "often rather ordered than requested judges to spare the guilty. For he was so attractive in his address that they could not deny him when he asked a favor." But one prisoner for whom he pled was clearly guilty of numerous thefts and murders, and the people of the region demanded his execution for their own safety. The prisoner was executed, and the holy man had to content himself with bringing the dead man back to life.

Holiness was itself considered miraculous. There was, for example, the parish priest who, while plague was raging, "never left the place, but remained courageously burying the people and celebrating mass . . . a priest of great kindness and friend of the poor." Moreover, *witnessing* a miracle was a mark of sanctity; not everyone present at the occurrence of a miracle recognized it. Gregory tells of a chalice that left the hand of an adulterous deacon and flew back to the altar, admitting, "It was only granted to one priest and three women to see this; the rest did not see it. I was present, I confess, but I had not the merit to see this miracle."

It is well to remind ourselves that early medieval people's fascination with miracles emerged from their interest in God's activity *within* the world of bodies and senses. Since the "Word became flesh," the flesh of ordinary people might find healing in unpredictable settings. Moreover, miracles were democratic. Church leaders like Gregory the Great, bishop of Rome and Gregory, bishop of Tours, far from managing miracles, were, like ordinary Christians, participant-observers of the supernatural occurrences of everyday life.

READINGS

Boethius, *The Consolation of Philosophy*
Gregory of Tours, *History of the Franks*
Bede, *Ecclesiastical History of the English People*

(margin, handwritten) Dark Ages

3   The Ninth and Tenth Centuries in the West

The last decades of the ninth and the first half of the tenth centuries are, with some justification, called the "dark ages," a time of disorganization and decay. Charlemagne's empire, distributed among his sons, disintegrated into tiny warring fragments; renewed invasion by Vikings from the north, Magyars from the east, and Saracens from Spain put territories from Ireland to the Mediterranean under siege. Yet even in these times of social and political chaos, Christianity spread. The conversion of Denmark, Norway, Sweden, Bohemia, Poland, and Hungary occurred during the second half of the tenth century, and Russia converted to Greek Orthodox Christianity in 989.

Feudalism developed as a response to the chaos of society; weaker landowners put themselves into the protection of stronger lords, and in return made contributions in the form of service in the lord's army. The economy was based on agriculture, with little commerce, scarce money, and few towns. Serfs, half free, because they could not be sold, and half slave, because they could not leave, cultivated the land. Feudalism, not yet fully established in the tenth century as its hereditary character was not yet in place, will be considered further in the next section as the social context for the eleventh-century monk Anselm's theology. In Anselm's writings the two main institutions of medieval life, feudalism and monasticism, were brought together.

The papacy

Historians agree that the papacy reached a nadir in the tenth century. Under the first Ottonian emperors popes swore allegiance to the emperor, but Emperor Otto III (983–1002) was successful in removing the papacy from the control of Roman nobles. During the prior 250 years, there had been only two popes who were not Romans, but under Otto men who were not Romans or even Italians were elected to the papacy. From then on, popes were chosen from around the world, thus establishing the universal character of the papacy. One of these new popes was Otto's former tutor, Sylvester II. "During his brief pontificate the medieval ideal of harmonious cooperation between pope and emperor was close to being a reality" (Strayer and Munro, 1942: 151). Problems were not over, however. After Otto's death the Roman nobility regained control of the office until Emperor Henry III (1017–56) succeeded in deposing rival popes who admitted to simony and appointing a German, Clement II, as pope. Repeating Charlemagne's coronation in reverse on Christmas Day 1046, the pope was consecrated whereupon he immediately crowned Henry emperor.

The Gregorian reform of church and papacy began under Pope Leo IX (in 1049 at the Council of Rheims) and ended at the First Lateran Council (1123). Named for Pope Gregory VII (1073–85), its two primary initiatives were 1) deriving from scripture "a pattern of life in which the priesthood was set aside from and over the laity;" and 2) teaching that church unity was based on papal leadership (Morrison, 1985: 177). One of the Gregorian reform's primary targets was the time-honored tradition by which laypersons (monarchs and wealthy landowners) elected and installed priests and bishops. Early in the twelfth century the Investiture controversy ended with the establishment of the Church's prerogative in selecting church office-holders in England, France, and Germany.

Medieval women writers

Two woman writers flourished in the ninth and tenth centuries in the West, the noble laywoman Dhuoda (b. 803) and the nun Hrothwitha (b. c.935) of Gandersheim. Dhuoda married Bernard of Septimania in Charlemagne's palace at Aachen, but sometime later he sent her away, subsequently sending for their two sons to live with him at the imperial court – one was 14, the other an infant. When her eldest son William was 16, Dhuoda wrote a devotional manual for his use, the first Christian manual written for a layperson. The manual, together with her letters and poems, have preserved her name. Literary historian Peter Dronke states that "none of the major Carolingians . . . can match Dhuoda in showing a mind and presence of such sensitive individuality" (Dronke, 1984: 36).

Dhuoda's manual contained religious, moral, and practical advice. She instructed her son on how to achieve serenity and salvation in the midst of secular life and in spite of worldly cares. She wanted her son to understand his duties and proper loyalties in a harsh world of men. She urged him to be loyal to his father, the man responsible for her exile and separation from her children. Yet she also revealed her own feelings:

> Moreover, though I am besieged by many anxieties, the only one in the foreground, if God wills and judges it right, is that I may be able at some time to see you face to face. I would have wanted this indeed if the power to fulfill it had been given me by God; but since fulfillment is far from me, sinful as I am, I want it still, and in this willing my spirit utterly fails me.

Dhuoda's husband was executed for treason by Charlemagne's successor Charles the Bald in 843. William joined the rebels; he was captured and executed four years later.

The tenth century German noblewoman and nun, Hrothwitha of Gandersheim wrote plays patterned on those of the Roman author, Terence. Her plays narrated the miraculous protection of consecrated Roman virgins from the lust of soldiers. Hrothwitha's plays are unusual in presenting men's bodies as simultaneously repugnant and threatening to the spiritual life, as a voluminous monastic literature of male monasticism regularly presented women's bodies.

Monasticism

Monasticism originated in the fourth and fifth centuries, but its "great age" occurred in the ninth through the twelfth centuries, guided exclusively by Benedict's *Rule*, drawn up for the monks of Monte Cassino about 540. Female monasticism was as numerically significant as male monasticism. The main duty of monks – a *social* duty – was the maintenance of a continuous life of prayer and liturgy that provided the foundation for, and supported, society. Monasteries were not self-supporting until a later period, and thus they needed lay patrons. Wealthy lords and kings endowed monasteries; in exchange prayer was offered for their well-being in life and safe-passage in death.

In medieval monasteries almost all the time not needed for eating and sleeping was devoted to communal worship. Benedict said that private prayer, manual labor, and communal worship should be roughly balanced. Services occurred throughout the day, from shortly after midnight until late in the evening. In the middle of the night, bells summoned monks to Matins, in the early hours to Lauds, at dawn to Prime, two hours later to Terce, at noon to Sext, early in the afternoon to None, early in the evening to Vespers, and later to Compline. Medieval monks did not have clocks, only sun-dials and hourglasses, so these hours are approximate.

The monk's day began about 2 a.m. and closed at 6:30 p.m. in the winter. In the summer, an afternoon siesta allowed for a longer evening. In winter and Lent, monks ate only one meal a day; in the summer, two meals. The monastic diet was sparse and usually vegetarian, but exceptions were made for youth, age, and illness.

Benedict prescribed reading for monks, but he did not urge them to pursue learning. The monk's primary discipline was continuous prayer, stimulated by reading and by a repertoire of mental images that acted as an aid to memory. Not all monks could read, however, so reading aloud, during meals and in liturgy, was an important part of monastic life. The Bible, Augustine, John Cassian, and Gregory the Great were at the core of monastic reading materials.

In medieval monasteries, theology was primarily meditation. The twelfth-century monk, Hugh of St Victor, wrote: "Meditation has its foundation in reading. It rejoices to run freely in an open space where it can fix its gaze upon the truth without hindrance and investigate now this now that problem until nothing is left obscure or doubtful." Historian Jean Leclercq describes reading as monastic meditation:

> In the middles ages, as in antiquity, [people] usually read, not as today, principally with the eyes, but with the lips, pronouncing what they saw, and with the ears, listening to the words pronounced, hearing what was called "the voices of the pages." It is a real acoustical reading. ... When *lectio* and *legere* are used without further explanation, they mean an activity which, like chant and writing, requires the participation of the whole body and the whole mind. ... [T]o read a text is to learn it "by heart" in the fullest sense of this expression, that is, with one's whole being: with the body, since the mouth pronounced it, the eyes saw it, and the ears heard it, with the memory which fixes it, with the intelligence which understands its meaning and with the will which desires to put it into practice.
>
> (*The Love of Learning and the Desire for God*: 19–22)

Carolingian manuscript illumination developed in monasteries roughly from the reign of Charlemagne and his successors to the end of the ninth century. Part of Charlemagne's program of reviving classical art and cultural life, manuscript illumination was done primarily in the process of copying manuscripts of the Bible, the Psalter, and sacramentaries (instructions and texts for the mass). Master copies were made and circulated throughout the empire in an effort to inspire further copies. By the mid-ninth century, court competed with monastery in the production of illuminated manuscripts (see CD Rom figures 3.15 to 3.17).

Cathedral schools and monastic schools provided the only available education. In cathedral or "bishop's schools," boys and young men received religious instruction and basic skills of reading and writing. Monastic schools usually had two curricula – religious training for children and young monks, and an external school for clerks (anyone whose duties required literacy).

Eadmer's *Life* of Anselm describes one monastic school:

> Once . . . when a certain abbot who was looked upon as a very fine monk was talking with Anselm about some of the problems of monastic life, he threw in some remarks about the boys who were being brought up in the cloister, and added: "What, I beg of you, is to be done with them? They are perverse and incorrigible. We beat them constantly, day and night, and they keep getting worse than they have ever been." When Anselm heard this he was astonished. "You never stop beating them?" he said. "And when they grow up, what are they like?" "Dull," he replied, "and like brutes." "With all your effort, you have been rather unfortunate in their upbringing, if you have only succeeded in turning human beings into brutes." "But what can we do?" the abbot asked. "We restrain them in every way for their own benefit, and we get nowhere with it." "You restrain them? I beg you, my lord abbot, tell me this. If you were to plant a young tree in your garden, and to hem it in right away on all sides, so that it could not stretch out its branches at all, if you released it after several years, what kind of tree would result?" "A quite useless one, of course, with gnarled and twisted branches." "And whose fault would that be but your own, for shutting it in without using any judgment? But surely this is just what you are doing with your boys."
>
> (*The Life and Conversation of Saint Anselm* I. 22)

Theology

The kind of academic work done by some monks is largely responsible for the debates that occurred in the ninth and tenth centuries. Scholarship consisted of compilation and commentary. Monks compiled texts from the classics, scripture, and earlier Christian authors and collected commentaries on scripture. By the end of the ninth century commentaries, pieced together from the church fathers, circulated. Scholars compared, discussed, and commented on, or "glossed," them, offering synonyms, etymologies of words, and comments on the construction of sentences, and noting discrepancies, inconsistencies and gaps.

Medieval scholars pored over Augustine, finding him frustratingly vague in his sacramental theology and contradictory in his teachings on predestination. Augustine had refused to say that God foreordains anyone for damnation. He focused, rather, on God's mercy by which a few are designated for salvation, leaving without appeal the *massa damnata*. He made a careful distinction between God's foreknowledge and God's foreordination, claiming that God foreknows and foreordains the elect from before the foundation of the world, but merely foreknows the damned.

Questions emerged: What was the relationship between God's grace operating through the sacraments of the church and offered to all, and predestination? In 529 the Synod of Orange reacted against Augustine's teaching that humans are completely dependent on God's grace. The Synod declared that "all who receive baptism can, if they labor faithfully, *do* those things that belong to the salvation of the soul." Augustine's doctrine of grace seemed to them both to slight the sacraments and to encourage laziness.

The most heated controversy of the ninth century was over predestination. The monk Gottschalk (d. 868) of the Abbey of Orbais stated the logical extension of Augustine's teaching, never spelled out by Augustine himself, namely that "without grace, freedom is like an eye that is blind." He said, "God constrains every person in such a way that it is vain and useless for the person by their free will to do any works of their own toward salvation." Christ himself had claimed to be a "ransom for many," he argued, not for all.

Hincmar (d. 882), bishop of Rheims, was alarmed. He said, "Gottschalk teaches the doctrine of grace without teaching the doctrine of free will, with the result that, under the pretence of piety, he preaches sheer negligence and produces a vicious complacency." He argued a technical point: "Sinners who have been foreknown in their own sins before they were in the world have not been predestined, but their *punishment* has been pre-destined for them on the basis of their having been foreknown." Augustine had insisted on *both* free will and predestination. For him, they solved different theological problems. Free will explained sin, and grace explained how anyone could achieve salvation and virtue. But how could the grace of God act efficaciously in the life of an individual and still not compel anyone? Even when extolling grace, Hincmar stressed its secondary function. After the Fall, he said, free will was sluggish and weak, but not dead.

The debaters' institutional affiliation influenced their theology. Gottschalk assumed that he and his fellow monks were elect; from this perspective the most fruitful attitude was to acknowledge dependence on God and to feel gratitude to God. Hincmar, parish bishop with pastoral concerns in mind, wanted a theology that encouraged people to *work* toward salvation.

Neither position could be vindicated by appeal to Augustine. Florus of Lyons (d. 860), observed, "it is easy for the devoted and simple reader to become confused by the great and multiple arguments of Augustine and to weary of the question" (Pelikan, 1978: 95). A synod convoked by Hincmar in 853 decreed a doctrine of predestination *of* punishment, rejecting predestination *to* punishment. Another synod two years later reversed this decision, and the matter remained unresolved.

The predestination controversy demonstrated the need for more refined theological tools. John Scotus Erigena (810–77) an Irishman who headed the palace school at Laon, placed the question in a philosophical context. Contemporaries were horrified, but his *method* was to be the way of the future.

Scotus knew Greek as most Latin theologians of his time did not, and thus had access to Eastern authors. He regarded the sixth century Greek mystical theologian, Dionysius, as the "supreme theologian." He had also read Gregory of Nazianzus, Gregory of Nyssa, Basil of Caesarea, Maximus the Confessor, and Origen. Through these authors, John retrieved the orderly universe of the Platonically influenced Greeks, a conceptual universe that contrasted sharply with the collapsed and chaotic universe of Western medieval theology. Gregory I, Gregory of Tours, and Bede inhabited a universe in which divine power acted directly in the visible world. In Scotus's universe, all creation is a theophany, or manifestation of the divine nature, the reflection and, in the case of human beings, the *image* of the creator. Dionysius wrote:

> Love which works good to all things, pre-existing, over-flowing in the Good, moved itself to creation. The Good by being, extends its goodness to all things. For as the sun, not by choosing or taking thought but by merely being enlightens all things, so the Good, by its mere existence sends forth upon all things the beams of its goodness.

Dionysius's emphasis was on God's continuous gift that holds all living beings in existence. The connecting link to being is the rational mind. Thus, it is not by sanctity or asceticism that one can participate in God's energy, but by developing her rational capacity, by *thinking* well.

John Scotus developed a tool for theology – dialectic – which he called "the discipline of disciplines." Dialectic demonstrates the relationship between propositions, clarifying their meaning. It can operate on any content to show either its self-contradiction or its cohesiveness. The best analogy is a chess game. Each theological proposition has implications for every other proposition, so that after affirming one proposition, one can only move in certain directions. Skillfully applied, dialectic can block counter-moves, demonstrating the incompatibility of an opponent's statements.

Using dialectic Scotus addressed the ninth-century predestination controversy, but his approach was so new that not only did it not *help*, but it outraged the other debaters. His method came into use only in the twelfth century. In its own time, it was condemned at two synods (852 and 859) for its "intellectuality" and for its pantheism.

John said, "Predestination is synonymous with God's foreknowledge of his own works." He thought it heretical to speak, as Gottschalk did, of *two* predestinations, one to eternal reward and one to damnation. In John's universe, evil and sin are *no thing* (not "nothing," because they have real effects), that is, not a force or substance, but a falling away from full participation in being. Therefore, John said, God could have no foreknowledge of evil, since the foreknowledge of God pertains only to existing things. It follows that "if no one is elected to punishment, how can the punishment be predestined?"

His intervention in the ninth-century eucharistic controversy was similarly futile. The monks Radbertus and Ratramnus in a Benedictine monastery at Corbie argued over whether the bread and wine of the Eucharist were literally or symbolically the body and blood of Christ. Scotus said, "This visible Eucharist, which the priests of the Church confect daily upon the altar from the sensible material of bread and wine . . . is a type and analogy of spiritual participation in Jesus," not *mere* symbol, but what he called the "communication" of divine and material and thus in reality the *presence* of Christ. The Christian, John said, "spiritually" sacrifices Christ and eats Christ's body "*mente non dente*" (spiritually, not with the teeth) (Pelikan, 1978: 96). Hincmar was offended by this interpretation, not only for its intellectualism, but also for its suggested pantheism.

Like his hero Dionysius, Scotus did not answer directly the question of the relationship of faith to reason. He affirmed, knowing Augustine, that faith precedes rational comprehension. But he also thought that many scriptural passages needed philosophical elucidation before they could be accurately understood. So he *affirmed* the primacy of faith, but what he was interested in exploring was rational process. He even said that when one reaches a stage at which faith and reason are in conflict, the teachings of reason must prevail. He understood faith as the "beginning," from which one ascends to reason. For him, faith came first, but reason was more important.

Romanesque architecture

In an astonishing flurry of building activity, the first distinctively European architecture appeared in the tenth century. Romanesque churches are large with ambitious vaults, rather than wooden roofs, and decorated exteriors. They are more complex and integrated than earlier churches, with walls articulated horizontally by tiers, arches, galleries, and windows. Columns and piers define the vertical space. Stone sculpture that had disappeared after the fifth century reappeared, usually as bas relief.

The first Romanesque church was part of a Benedictine abbey, Limburg an der Haardt, and the style spread rapidly. The cathedral at Speyer, begun about 1030 and completed in the twelfth century, is one of the largest churches in the West. Its uncluttered aisles exhibit its powerful simplicity and its series of arches and niches are typically Romanesque (see CD Rom figure 3.18).

4   Early Scholasticism

The eleventh century saw the first increments of Western civilization not subsequently lost due to invasions and internal disorder. Monasteries grew dramatically both in numbers and in size. Church government and the papacy underwent much-needed reform. The most often-lamented offenses of the secular clergy were simony (buying and selling church office) and concubinage. At the beginning of the eleventh century Pope Silvester II described bishops as saying: "I gave gold and I received the episcopate; but yet I do not fear to receive the gold back if I behave as I should. I ordain a priest and I receive gold; I make a deacon and I receive a heap of silver. Behold, the gold which I gave I have once more unlessened in my purse." In the eleventh century, however, emperors concerned with reform appointed popes who initiated reform. Under the leadership of the Benedictine monastery at Cluny, monastic reform also spread. For two and a half centuries new monasteries sprang up and many monasteries formerly isolated and independent formed affiliations and developed central administrations.

In 1095 Pope Urban II called for a "pilgrimage" to liberate Christ's tomb and to free Christians in Jerusalem from Islamic rule. Although Urban hoped to attract well-equipped knights and soldiers, thousands of ordinary people volunteered. A motley and untrained army set out from northern France, the Rhineland, the Low Countries, and Saxony. The so-called "People's Crusade" was poorly organized, fed, and clothed, and the crusaders ransacked villages and countrysides, spreading plague as they went. Along the way, crusaders killed many Jews along the Rhine River in Germany, the first medieval pograms, and an event still mourned by modern Jews. Few members of the People's Crusade reached Constantinople; almost all of those that did were slaughtered by the Turks.

In 1096 organized armies under the leadership of knights and counts set out, fighting their way through Asia Minor. They captured Constantinople, and took Jerusalem on July 15, 1099, putting many of its inhabitants to the sword. For the following three centuries, frequent crusades set out to liberate Jerusalem.

Anselm

John Scotus's study of theology as a logical discipline had no immediate successors. But more than a century after his death a monk from a poor monastery in the small Norman town of Bec used a similar theological method. Anselm (later Archbishop of Canterbury) was steeped in the monastic tradition of meditation. In a letter accompanying a "little meditation" which he sent a friend, he emphasized loyalty to authority:

> It was my intention throughout the whole of this disputation to assert nothing which could not be immediately defended either from canonical writers or from the words of St. Augustine. And however often I look over what I have written, I cannot see that I have asserted anything other than this. Indeed, no reasoning of my own, however conclusive it seemed, would have persuaded me to presume to be the first to say these things. St. Augustine proved these points in the great discussions in his *De trinitate* so that I, having as it were uncovered them in my shorter chain of argument, say them on his authority.

Yet there was a difference in Anselm's meditation. His meditation was not *only* private prayer; it was also *philosophical inquiry*. Indeed, Anselm found prayer and philosophy highly compatible, since the aim of both was to shake off the sluggishness of the mind and to see things as they are in their essential being, that is, in God. Anselm's meditation was considerably more energetic than most monastic meditation. In fact, the form of meditation initiated by Anselm did not rely either on free-associating with reading, or on "letting the mind roam freely." For Anselm, meditation was a highly active and disciplined *exercise*. He struggled – often an anguished struggle – to understand. He innovated within an institution that did not value innovation. Thus, he sought to conceal his creativity.

> I want everything I say to be taken on these terms: that if I say anything that a greater authority does not support, even though I seem to prove it by reasons, it is not to be treated as more certain than is warranted by the fact that, at present, I see the question in this way, until God somehow reveals something better to me.

Despite this claim, he didn't actually *cite* either scripture or earlier Christian authors. It is difficult to imagine a more decisive break than this with the monastic past. A hundred years later, Thomas Aquinas, quoting Boethius, said, "Authority is the weakest form of proof." It was Anselm who first opened the possibility that theology need not rely on the authority of scripture or patristic authors.

For Anselm, reason was the natural activity of faith, "faith seeking understanding." "Reason is the eye of the spirit," he wrote, "and faith is the most glorious of the objects presented to it." Yet intellectual discipline was not an end in itself for Anselm. His devotion was also a new style of monastic piety. Neither intellect nor strong emotion were features of traditional monastic piety. Rather, the virtues of obedience and humility channeled the subjective, introspective piety of individual monks into communal liturgical expression. Monastic piety was focused on the hard work, the full-time job, of seeking salvation and on the life of discipline and discipleship necessary to it. Anselm did not abandon traditional monastic piety, but he integrated it with philosophical inquiry, blending devotional fervor and intellectual passion:

> For it is true that the more richly we are nourished in Holy Scripture by the things that feed us through obedience, the more accurately we are carried along to the things that satisfy through knowledge. For indeed it is vain to say "I have understood more than

all my teachers," if he does not dare to add "because thy testimonies are my meditation."
And he is a liar when he recites "I have had understanding above the ancients," if he is not
familiar with what follows, "because I sought your commandments." Certainly this is just
what I say: He who will not believe will not understand. For he who will not believe will
not *experience* and he who has not had experience will not know. For experience surpasses
hearing about a thing, as greatly as knowledge by experience excels acquaintance by
hearing.

(Letter to Urban II; emphasis added)

Proslogion

Anselm believed that God is to be known through experience, but understanding was
also a form of experience of God. He repeatedly advised his monks that knowing *about*
God was useless unless they also *know God*. For Anselm, thinking about God was always
preceded by prayer that established a *relationship* with God. Threaded through the
Proslogion's philosophical discussions, Anselm interjected prayers. He wanted, in a single
work, to know God through prayer and also to establish what can be known about God.
He believed that prayer and philosophical inquiry can unite in a knowledge of God that
is simultaneously discursive, logical, intuitive, and independent of scriptural or ecclesiastical authority. In the *Proslogion* Anselm did not fuse the two approaches – prayer and
rational inquiry. They simply alternate. Nevertheless, two approaches that could have
occurred in different authors, or even in different texts, are used together in a single
treatise.

The *Proslogion* begins with an impassioned prayer:

How long, O Lord, will you forget us? How long will you turn your face away from us?
When will you look upon us and hear us? Look upon us, O Lord, hear us, enlighten us,
show us your face, show us your own self. Take pity on our efforts and strivings toward
you. O Lord, in my hunger I began to seek you; I beseech you, let me not, still fasting, fall
short of you . . .

After this, the reader arrives abruptly at Anselm's ontological argument. If we were to
suppose that God did not exist, Anselm said, we would be involved in a contradiction,
since we could conceive of an entity greater than a non-existent God – namely, a God
that exists. But Anselm was still uneasy about whether having said that, he had found
anything useful. Indeed, in chapter 15 he concluded happily that the question of
God's existence does not depend on the fact that human beings can think of a being
"than which nothing greater can be conceived." God is, rather, "something greater
than can be thought" by human beings. He concluded where he began: The human
mind cannot prove God's existence, a real existence that can ultimately only be known
experientially.

Yet, even though God cannot be logically "pinned down" by a human mind, Anselm
found philosophical inquiry a fruitful *method* of seeking God. By overcoming the false
dichotomy of reason and experience, Anselm was satisfied that he had solved the question of how God can be known. Intellectual process *is* experience. The words "delight,"

and "joy" occur again and again in the final chapters of the *Proslogion*: "If there are many great delights in delightful things, what wonderful and great delight is to be found in God who made the delightful things themselves."

Anselm's exercise in philosophical argument left him somewhat chastened, recognizing the limitations as well as the value of the philosophical search for God. For the first two decades of his career his writings address philosophical problems, but in the next two decades (beginning in the 1090s), he abandoned philosophical questions and focused his writings on explicitly doctrinal and scriptural matters. Traces of his youthful interest in philosophy can be found in these later writings, but by 1098 when he wrote *Why God Became Human*, he had returned to the monastic preoccupation with salvation.

Why God Became Human (Cur Deus Homo)

Anselm's *Cur Deus Homo* (1098) was the first Christian treatise devoted to explaining how salvation was accomplished. In the treatise, Anselm's method, the problem he addresses, and his explanation of the mystery of salvation were closely tied to the society he knew. Although all theology reflects its social and institutional location, as well as other factors that combine to create a theologian's perspective, Anselm's roots in a feudal culture are particularly evident in his theology.

Feudalism was not primarily a social or economic system, but a form of local government in which political functions were performed according to private contracts. The king was the first lord (*dominium*), but he could issue direct commands only to his immediate vassals, that is, to knights pledged to his service. In turn these knights could issue direct commands only to those pledged to serve them. And so on to the lowliest vassal/serf who ultimately obeyed the king through the long chain of vassals. Feudalism entailed responsibilities for both parties. The lord was bound to protect his vassal, to secure justice for him, and to give him such aid as he might need. In return, the vassal swore "to give aid and counsel to his lord," a phrase which covered many undefined services. Primarily responsible for military service, vassals were also obliged to farm the lord's estates. Lords were dependent on the service pledged them by their vassals, even up to the king, whose vassals could, and frequently did, rebel.

Feudalism also played a role in the first crusade. Pope Urban II preached the crusade specifically as correcting a slight against God's honor. God, as feudal lord, required the obedience of all people, but Muslims, who held the holy places, and Jews, the descendants of those who had crucified Christ, were understood as disturbing God's honor and thus subverting the created world.

Anselm wrote *Cur Deus Homo* two years after the first crusade was preached on these terms. Both Anselm and Pope Urban II participated in a mentality common to people of the eleventh century. "It is impossible for God to lose his honor," Anselm wrote, "for if a sinner does not freely pay what he owes God, God takes it from him against his will." In the case of the crusades, Urban II reasoned, it was up to God's faithful vassals to rally to God's support.

The mentality of honor, violation, and restitution or satisfaction appeared also in eleventh- and twelfth-century penitential practices. The sinner must give "satisfaction" for wrongdoing, must *pay back* offenses against God's honor. Purgatory, the final chance to make restitution, was thought of as a place of punishment in which Christians endured the fires of judgment until the sins they carried with them to their death were expiated. An attitude of religious pessimism encouraged the belief that the "population of heaven was small, and consisted mainly of monks." The doctrine of purgatory, which according to historian Jacques Le Goff did not exist before 1170, had a positive effect; more people could hope for heaven if they would have opportunity, even after death, to expiate their sins.

Indulgences, the Church's forgiveness of sins, also arose in response to a need for assurances of forgiveness and salvation. Indulgences were given to those taking part in a crusade; if they died while on the crusade, they were assured of being spared purgatorial cleansing before entering heaven. There was no sale of indulgences until later in the Middle Ages, when indulgences became a precipitating cause for the Protestant reformations of the sixteenth century.

Anselm described *Cur Deus Homo*, as a hastily compiled treatise, published before it was ready. In it Anselm claimed to bracket revelation in order to address "unbelievers" who find Christian faith contrary to reason. However, he modified this claim shortly after making it, saying that he is "talking over" the question with monastic colleagues (who could hardly have qualified as unbelievers)!

Prior to Anselm, theories of salvation were remarkably undeveloped, relying primarily on images of Christ deceiving the devil, who had "rights" over the human race due to its sin. Augustine had described Christ as the bait in a mousetrap; the devil, reaching out to snatch Christ, was instead caught and paralyzed in God's trap. Other authors proposed images of snaring birds and catching fish or mice. Anselm's reaction to theories of redemption based on deception of the devil was: "Did Christ carry out the work of redemption so as to deceive the devil who, by deceiving humankind, had cast them out of paradise? But surely the truth does not deceive anyone."

Anselm sought to define redemption as objective in order to address pessimistic views in which salvation was limited to a few, requiring the hard, full-time work of monks. His account of redemption is the following: By their sin, human beings *voluntarily* put themselves in the power of Satan. Since God had created human beings in God's own image and likeness, intending them to serve him happily and voluntarily, human sinfulness constituted a violation of God's honor. Thus, God could not simply *forgive* humans without restitution for this violation.

Anselm used the feudal society of his time as an image of the human situation: "Nothing is less tolerable in the order of things than for a creature to take away the honor due to the creator and not repay what he takes away." Yet the rational order of the universe prohibits God from simply overlooking human sin. This situation put God in a double bind: God cannot complete what God began in the creation of the human race without finding a way to overcome this wrong turn of events. Anselm referred repeatedly to aesthetic considerations, to the beautiful and the "fitting." Sin disturbs "the beauty and order of the universe," causing "a certain ugliness, derived from the violation of the beauty of order."

Humans have nothing with which to repay God. How, then, is restitution to be made? The second part of Anselm's treatise describes the payment of this debt:

The debt was so great that, while humans alone owed it, God alone could pay it, so that the same person must be both God and human. Thus it was necessary for God to take both God and human into the unity of God's person, so that humans who ought to pay and could not should be in a person who could.

But a problem appears. Anselm recoiled from saying that God demanded the death of God's son as the payment for the sins of humanity, so he insisted that Christ's self-sacrifice was voluntary, "in no sense an obligation." He added that it was not that God demanded Christ's death to God as retribution for humanity; rather, being simultaneously God and human, "Christ offered himself to himself." Christ as human offered himself to Christ as God.

Anselm's innovations consisted of rejecting the devil's rights over humanity, and attempting to demonstrate the *objectivity* of redemption by the *necessity* of logical argument. Of Anselm's twelfth-century successors, only Peter Abelard agreed with him that the devil has no rights over humans.

Anselm insisted that it was *necessary* for salvation to occur in the manner he described. In the context of popular fascination with fate and astrological determinism, earlier theologians – Irenaeus, Clement, Origen, and Augustine – had vigorously denied necessity. They emphasized the voluntary nature of God's redemptive activity. Anselm, however, worked in a culture dominated by the monastic sense of the frighteningly arbitrary and unpredictable nature of salvation; he equated logical necessity with "inexpressible beauty."

A reluctant saint

Anselm's colleague Eadmer wrote a biography of Anselm, but being a modest man, Anselm ordered Eadmer to destroy it. Eadmer did, according to monastic obedience – but not before he made a copy. Eadmer would have liked to write a conventional biography, replete with the requisite miracles, the essential ingredient of hagiography (saints' lives) in his time. Saintliness was usually demonstrated by signs at the saint's birth, miracles and prophecies during her/his life, a dramatic death-bed scene, and posthumous miracles associated with the saint's relics. But Anselm did not supply Eadmer with such material, and Eadmer was too honest to invent it. Two other biographers of Anselm, Alexander and Baldwin, felt justified in supplying from their own imaginations "proof" of Anselm's saintliness. But Eadmer, puzzled by what he *experienced* as saintliness in Anselm, yet without many miracles, had to largely content himself with showing the winsomeness of Anselm's personality.

Anselm was a reluctant saint. Eadmer told of journeying with Anselm when the brother of a madwoman accosted the party, begging Anselm to cure her. At first Anselm "passed by as if he were deaf," but upon further urging by a crowd that had gathered, Anselm hastily made the sign of the cross over her and rode quickly away, bewailing her plight. They learned later that the woman had been cured (*Life* xlii).

Anselm's reluctance to heal the woman shows an unusual modesty, or, perhaps, a fear of failure. In any case, Eadmer's *Life* of Anselm exhibits a new style of saintliness, one that was not focused on miracles, but rather on Anselm's wisdom (demonstrated by the story of the recalcitrant boys) and gentleness.

READINGS

Anselm, *Proslogion*
Anselm, *Why God Became Man*

4 The Voice of the Pages: Incarnation and Hierarchy in the Medieval West

1 Twelfth-century Theology, Scholarship, and Piety
2 The Thirteenth Century: Theology and the Natural World
3 Thomas Aquinas
4 Gothic Cathedrals

Prologue

> We had a different idea of the marvelous; we thought that if everything happened
> naturally, that would always be the most marvelous.
>
> Rainer Maria Rilke, *The Notebooks of Malte Laurids Brigge*

A new intellectual excitement, based in part on new interest in the natural world and its orderly workings, is noticeable in twelfth-century authors. Miracles and relics came on occasion to be explicitly doubted, at least by those who recorded their thoughts. In 1162 the Bishop of Orleans bluntly announced that he had his doubts about the relics of St Geneviève, and Peter Abelard (d. 1142) was driven from St Denis for having expressed some reservations about whether the abbey's most precious relic, the body of Dionysius the Areopagite, was actually what it was thought to be. Guibert of Noigent (d. 1124) pointed out that there was one head of John the Baptist in the East and another in the West. He said: "It is on the one hand certain that there has been only one John the Baptist, and on the other, that no one can say without sin that one man had two heads." Guibert was not a skeptic; he believed as sturdily as the next person in genuine relics, but he protested challenges to credulity.

The new intellectual interests occurred in the context of widespread heightened excitement about miracles, understood as evidence of God's direct activity in the world of bodies and senses. Even as Guibert complained, relics multiplied. Fragments of the "true cross," vials of the Virgin's milk, Christ's umbilical cord, and saints' bones and clothing were carefully housed in elaborate reliquaries. Proto-saints were kept, by force, if necessary, in their towns of residence so that the town could be sure of having their relics when they died. The largest number of relics were in Rome at the basilicas of Peter and Paul. Their only rival in the west was St James at Santiago de Compostela.

Churches with fewer relics became "rest stops" for pilgrims making their way to a major center.

The most valued relics were those associated with Christ – fragments of the cross, or pieces of his garments. In 1239 the Latin emperor of Constantinople sold Louis IX of France the crown of thorns, and St Louis built the beautiful Sainte Chapelle in Paris as an architectural reliquary to enclose it. Relics of the Virgin were the second most-valued relics. Fragments of her clothing on the occasion of the annunciation and birth of Christ were the precious property of cathedrals like Chartres, dedicated to her honor. Other saints provided an endless supply of bones for medieval people to purchase, steal, and fight over.

The "buzzword" among twelfth-century intellectuals was "*universitas*," the universe seen as one rich and harmonious whole, in which human beings are reassuringly ensconced in a cosmic order under God's direct providence. Curiosity, in disrepute since Augustine's insistence that "God and the soul" were the only legitimate objects of interest, was the prevailing attitude. Twelfth-century intellectuals began to lose interest in miracles; a century later Thomas Aquinas wrote his treatise on divine governance without discussion of miracles as a primary mode of God's activity in the world.

Efforts were made to overcome any perceived disjunction between the supernatural and the natural. Because spirit and matter are joined in human beings, it was argued, matter has significance. Answering the question of why human beings were created, Alan of Lille said, "For it was fitting that corporeal as well as incorporeal nature should come to participate in the divine goodness, should relish that goodness and live in joy."

Twelfth-century monks recorded a range of interests, from Guibert of Nogent's practical instructions on "How to Make a Sermon" to the scholarship and mystical theology of Hugh of St Victor. Some twelfth-century monks developed an interest in mystical experience; by the fourteenth century, this became a popular interest. In the fourteenth century the first vernacular books were treatises on mystical experience such as the *Book of Margery Kempe*, Lady Julian's *Showings*, Richard Rolle's, *The Fire of Divine Love*, Jan von Ruysbroeck's *Sparkling Stone*, and the anonymous *Cloud of Unknowing*.

1   Twelfth-century Theology, Scholarship, and Piety

The monks

Anselm's suggestion that God acted in ways consistent with human logic struck many of his contemporaries, including the Cistercian, Bernard of Clairvaux (d. 1153), as dangerously arrogant. Anselm had insisted that God could not be known by reason alone, but only by prayerful experience. Yet once reason and prayer were distinguished, people began to have more interest in one than the other.

Hugh of St Victor's (d. 1142) theology combined the best of both *scholare* (scholar) and *claustrale* (monk). Hugh, along with Richard, Andrew, Adam, and others of the abbey of St Victor in Paris (founded 1110), created a rich and diverse literature that included historical chronicles, geography, grammar, philosophy, psychology, sermons, commentaries, and manuals.

Like Anselm, Hugh was not known to have performed any miracles, but the brothers who wrote about him called him a "second Augustine" because he was "gentle, pious, humble, and good." "Learn everything," he told his pupils, "You will find nothing superfluous; a narrow education displeases . . . but learn at leisure, 'more haste, less speed.' It does not matter if you have not read everything; the number of books is infinite; do not pursue infinity" (quoted by Smalley, 1983: 61).

Hugh reacted against "reading with glosses in the feverish manner of the schools." He wanted to call learning back to what he considered its proper activity, the meditative study of scripture. He described an ideal program of study that began with the arts and sciences and gradually proceeded to wisdom: "Do not despise these lesser things. They who despise lesser things will gradually fail. . . . I know there are some who want to philosophize immediately . . . their learning is asinine. Do not imitate such men" (quoted by Smalley, 1983: 62).

Hugh distinguished three senses of scripture, the historical, the moral, and the spiritual sense, as had Origen. But Hugh did not contrast the "lowly letter" with the "higher" spiritual sense. He saw the letter, or literal sense, as crucial for giving access to the spirit. By "letter" Hugh meant not only the literal sense of the words, but also the historical events of scripture, so hastily passed over by his contemporaries in their eagerness to find a spiritual meaning.

Like the letter, the picture also gives access to the spirit. In his treatise, *Noah's Mystical Ark*, Hugh's subject was "how to prepare the heart for the divine in-dwelling." His method was pictorial. Hugh described an image-based lecture in which the picture did not illustrate the text; rather, the text was a commentary and illumination of the picture.

> First I find the center of the flat surface where I mean to draw the ark. There, having fixed the point, I draw round it a small square. . . . Then I draw another rather larger square around the first, so that the space between may appear to be the border of the cubit. Then I draw a cross inside the inner square so that the ends meet each of the sides; and I paint it gold. Then I paint in the spaces between the cross and the square, the upper ones flame-color, the lower sky blue.
>
> *(De arca Noe Mystica)*

Hugh then proceeded to give each shape and color a spiritual or mystical meaning.

Hugh's disciple Richard of St Victor (d. 1173) addressed the awkward question of what to do when inconsistencies are discovered in the writings of the Fathers. Correct the fathers, he said, for they are best honored by decent scholarship, not by slavish copying. "Do you wish to honor and defend the authority of the fathers? We cannot honor the lovers of truth more truly than by seeking, finding, teaching, loving, and defending the truth. Do not ask whether what I say is new, but whether it is true" (*Prologus in visionem Ezechielis*). Following his own advice, Richard's text is interspersed with such phrases as "I wonder how Jerome can say . . . We follow the Jews and Josephus rather than Bede here . . . Blessed Augustine seems to hold, but . . . Men of great authority give this opinion . . . They are misled."

Bernard of Clairvaux (d. 1153), "the greatest master of language of the middle ages," reformed monasteries and taught future popes. He was a major figure in a developing devotion to the human Jesus, advocating what he called a "carnal love for Christ."

"Notice," he said, "that the love of the heart is, in a certain sense, carnal because our hearts are attracted more to the humanity of Christ and the things he did while in the flesh." Love of the human Jesus is stimulated, he said, by visualizing various events in Jesus' life. Bernard saw in Christ's patience and love not merely a revelation of God's love, but *saving work*. He claimed that Christ's *life* was redemptive, as well as his death.

Bernard's *Sermons on the Song of Songs* pictured Christ as the bridegroom of the soul and the church. He also wrote many hymns, prayers, and sermons on the Virgin Mary. He called Mary the "*mediatrix*" between humans and a Christ pictured as too awesome and too just to be approachable. Mary's attributes, according to Bernard, are humility, love and pity. Calling Mary "the mother of the judge in the day of need," he said: "Let him deny your mercy who can say that he has ever asked for it in vain."

Bernard was not alone in his esteem for the Blessed Virgin. Anselm and Adam of St Victor wrote hymns to her, and in the following century another great monk – Thomas Aquinas – decided in her favor the question: "Whether the blessed virgin possessed perfectly the seven liberal arts." We will discuss twelfth-century attitudes toward the Virgin Mary later in the chapter.

Based in monasteries but not confined to monasteries, interest in mystical experience spread by personal contact. But monasteries also served society in several ways. Monks maintained the fabric of prayer considered crucial for sustaining secular society. They also provided public liturgies and acted as confessors. Monasteries were also becoming important economically. By the twelfth century, supported by wills and bequests, monasteries owned huge amounts of arable land adjacent to towns and villages.

Hildegard (1098–1179), abbess of Rupertsberg, near Bingen, was one of the most prolific authors of a time rich in new movements in spirituality and theology. Tenth child of noble parents, she was raised, like many other children, in a monastery. Lacking formal education, she educated herself. In addition to theological writings, she wrote a medical encyclopedia that discussed herbs, trees, mammals, reptiles, fish, and birds, "elements," gems and metals – all with reference to their wholesome or toxic properties and medicinal uses. Another volume in the encyclopedia dealt with mental and physical diseases. She wrote a morality play, and she traveled extensively, preaching and prophesying. She wrote six major books, founded two monasteries, and corresponded extensively with bishops, abbots, princes, and others. Called the "Sybil of the Rhine," Hildegard became famous in her own time.

She was also a visionary. From early childhood Hildegard had a supernatural power of vision that she described as a "non-spatial radiance that filled her visual field at all times without impairing her natural vision" (Newman, 1987: 6–7). When she was 43, a voice commanded her to "tell and write" what she saw and heard in her visions. Her major theological work, the *Scivias*, is filled with colored pictures (see CD Rom figures 4.1 and 4.2). It was, however, her poetic and musical composition, "Symphonia armonie celestium revelationum" ("Symphony of the Harmony of Celestial Revelations"), that described the content of her mystical experience (CD Rom Music 4.1).

Hildegard wrote music for liturgies at her monastery. A friend wrote after her death that "after [Hildegard] had enjoyed the sweetness of celestial harmony in her visions, she would 'make the same measure – more pleasing than ordinary human music – to be sung publicly in church,' with sequences composed in praise of God and in honor of the saints." Spiritual truth, joy, and music were closely linked in Hildegard's imagination. Contemporaries who knew her music commented on its beauty and strangeness, calling it a "chant of surpassingly sweet melody . . . with amazing harmony, . . . a strange and unheard of (*inaudite*) melody" (Newman, 1988: 12; CD Rom Music 4).

Music evoked nostalga for the garden of Eden; "A person often sighs and moans upon hearing some melody, recalling the nature of the celestial harmony," Hildegard wrote. She said that Adam, before the Fall, "possessed a voice that rang with the sound of every harmony and the sweetness of the whole art of music. And if he had remained in the condition in which he was created, human frailty could never endure the power and resonance of that voice." When Adam sang with the angels, "he had a resonant voice, like the sound of a monochord."

Hildegard's music required an enormous range; many of her compositions used two and a half octaves, considerably beyond the capability of an average singer. The wide melodic leaps are also distinctive, and ascending and descending fifths are frequent.

Like her music, Hildegard's poetry was unlike any other poetry written in the twelfth century. Her style was free verse, non-metrical (like the Psalms); liturgical prayer was her model. Compare, for example, a poem contrasting Mary and Eve by Adam of St Victor, Hildegard's contemporary. Adam wrote in rhyming trochaic meter:

> Eve once destroyed us/ But Mary redeemed us/ By means of her son
> One mother bore sadness/ The other with gladness/ Fruit second to none.

On the same theme Hildegard wrote:

> O most radiant mother/ of sacred healing/ you poured/ ointments/through your holy son/
> on the sobbing wounds of death/ that Eve built/ into torment for souls.

Hildegard's unusual imagery confuses separate metaphors, mingling them into a mystical synesthesia. Hildegard wrote of the prophets:

> O you fortunate roots/ with which the work of miracles/ and not the work of crimes/ was
> planted/ through a rushing course/ of transparent shadow.

Hildegard's theology required several media – poetry, music, and art to communicate its richness.

The masters

In the twelfth century the first professional Western scholars taught in the first institutions that existed exclusively for the purpose of advancing learning. Scholasticism created its own setting, the university; it discovered its own method of argument, dialectic; and it generated the problems on which it operated. In the new universities academic guilds conferred a certificate, or *licentia docendi*, awarded by the chancellor when a student had mastered a body of learning. Originally designed to protect students from incompetent or unorthodox teachers, these certificates were the first academic degrees.

Universities emerged from the medieval bishops' schools attached to cathedrals. At the close of the eleventh century the course of study in a university included the seven liberal arts of the traditional curriculum, divided into the *trivium* or literary studies (philosophy, grammar, ancient poets and rhetoricians) and the *quadrivium* (scientific studies). By the end of the twelfth century, Aristotelian logic (dialectics), mathematics, and astronomy had been added to the curriculum.

Until the thirteenth century, universities were private, and students roamed from school to school seeking the most interesting ideas, companions, and teachers. Lively exchanges of ideas occurred as students followed teachers of good reputation, much as fourth century ascetics had sought out spiritual masters. It was cheaper to go from Oxford to Paris to hear a famous teacher than it was to buy his books. At the beginning of the twelfth century there were three important universities in Western Europe: Paris, where logic and philosophy were studied; Salerno, where medicine and law were featured, and Bologna, which specialized in law.

Universitas was a common name for medieval guilds or trade unions. Thus, the "university" was a guild of academic masters organized, like other trade guilds, for two purposes, the defense and advancement of the art and the training of young people. By the thirteenth century, schools were well established and teachers circulated among them. In 1215 the Chancellor of the University of Paris complained of an overload of bureaucracy, and desk and committee work: "In the old days when each master taught for himself and the name of the university was unknown, lectures and disputations were more frequent and there was more zeal for study." Examinations were oral, and were "so difficult that at some institutions it was necessary to make rules against knifing the examiners" (Strayer and Munro, 1942: 263).

The method of scholarship at universities was dialectic, the art or science of determining the logical relationship of propositions within a discourse. Operating on propositions of Christian belief and natural philosophy, students and teachers examined the logical ties that connected propositions. They aimed at nothing less than creating a synthesis of theology and natural philosophy that would mirror the whole of intelligible reality.

The most heated philosophical debate of the early twelfth century was the problem of universals. Are objects in the sensible world the primary existing entities? Or are being, reality, and value stronger in the general classes to which they belong? Is "humanity" the real entity in which individuals participate? Or are individuals the primary existing reality that can subsequently be labeled "humanity?" Nominalists like Peter Abelard (d. 1142) answered that since universals are derived from our observation of individuals, individuals are the primary reality; universals are without content in the absence of individuals. Realists like William of Champeaux (d. 1121) answered that individuals derive their reality from the class in which they participate; humanity precedes and constitutes individual human beings.

The problem, as stated, was insoluble. No one was willing to claim that individuals create and possess their own existence, the implication of the nominalist position. And yet it seemed inadequate to describe the people and objects of the sensible world as derived from the general categories in which they participate, the realist position.

Peter Abelard, a man who described himself as stimulated by controversy, dominated the first four decades of the twelfth century. He is not remembered primarily for his theological or philosophical work, however, but for his *Story of My Misfortunes* and for correspondence with his student and later wife Heloise. Although Abelard and Heloise's story is often described as romantic, it bears little relation to romance based on mutual attraction. It is, rather, a story of violence and sexual abuse. Abelard wrote to Heloise: "Even when you were unwilling, and resisted to the utmost of your power, and tried to dissuade me, as yours was the weaker nature I often forced you to consent with threats and blows." When their story became known, Heloise's uncle castrated Abelard, and Abelard and Heloise both entered monasteries. The twelfth-century expectation that violence accompanied love relationships is indicated by the fact that, despite his harsh treatment of her, Heloise repeatedly professed her love for Abelard.

Although Abelard himself was not a thorough-going rationalist, his theology stimulated rational inquiry and pioneered a theological method. His introductions and summaries of Christian teaching were an important precursor of the thirteenth century *summa*, or survey of theology. He was also first to use the word '*theologia*' for the study of God.

Abelard believed that "careful and frequent questioning is the basic key to wisdom; by doubting we come to questioning and in questioning we perceive the truth" (*Exposition on the Epistle to the Romans*). In his best-known work, *Sic et Non*, texts from scripture and the Fathers are juxtaposed to contradictory texts. Did Abelard intend the work as a demonstration of the contradictions in authorities in order to make way for a more rational approach? Or was his work an exercise in harmonizing the discrepancies and difficulties of authorities? It is likely that contemporaries thought of it as the latter, since they did not object to the book. Nevertheless, by comparing different authors on the same topics, Abelard laid the groundwork for a "hermeneutics of suspicion."

In his "Exposition of the Epistle to the Romans," Abelard took up the question of the meaning of redemption. Like Anselm, Abelard rejected the theory that the devil had "rights" over humankind: "The devil possessed no right against humans except perhaps insofar as it was a case of the Lord's permitting it by handing humans over to the wretch who was to be their jailer." Abelard reluctantly conceded that God the Father was the recipient of the price paid by Christ, but he could not accept this conclusion.

> Indeed how cruel and wicked it seems that anyone should demand the blood of an innocent person as the price for anything, or that it should in any way please God that an innocent man should be slain – still less that God should consider the death of his own son so agreeable that by it he should be reconciled to the whole world!
>
> (*Exposition* II. 2)

Abelard's psychological redemption contrasts Anselm's legal account of redemption. Abelard described the death of Christ as efficacious in generating in humans the *love* whose existence guarantees predestination to salvation: "Everyone who now honestly and purely loves the Lord for his own sake is predestined to life, and will never be over-taken by death until the Lord shows him what is of obligation concerning the sacraments and also gives him the ability to understand it" (*Exposition* II. 4).

Bernard of Clairvaux opposed Abelard's view of redemption. He charged that Abelard's theology denied the reality of original sin and weakened the concept of redemption to enlightenment and example: "Abelard says that the purpose and reason of the Incarnation was that Christ might illuminate the world with the light of his wisdom and kindle it to love of himself. Where then is the *redemption*?" (quoted by Pelikan, 1978: 130). Against Abelard and Anselm, Bernard affirmed that the devil had rights over humans and Christ's life and death redeemed them.

It is not possible to draw a sharp distinction between the twelfth-century "religion team" and "reason team." If a twelfth-century thinker chose reason as primary, he was careful firmly to integrate faith. Those who, like the Victorines and St Bernard, insisted on the primacy of faith and doubted the mind's capacity to apprehend reality, nevertheless spent their time in painstaking scholarship and scriptural exegesis. And Abelard, the "rationalist," expounded an intensely personal appropriation of the saving work of Christ. For the moment, Bernard's defense of faith as primary dominated. Within 50 years, however, both Albertus Magnus (d. 1280) and Alexander of Halles (d. 1245) valued reason sufficiently to write a *summa*, or summary of theology.

READINGS

Bernard of Clairvaux, *On the Song of Songs*, selections
Peter Abelard, *The Story of My Misfortunes*
Hildegard of Bingen, *Scivias*, "Vision Two," "Vision Five"

Pilgrimage

One of Western medieval Christians' most engaging, often entertaining, and frequently dangerous religious practices was pilgrimage. The three most frequent pilgrimage destinations were Rome, Jerusalem, and the so-called "great pilgrimage" to the Cathedral of St James, Compostela, in northern Spain.

Church architecture of the twelfth and thirteenth centuries responded to the need to accommodate large crowds of pilgrims. Pilgrimage churches typically have a spacious nave (usually with five aisles) for liturgies (see CD Rom figures 4.3 and 4.4). Ambulatories with radiating chapels where saints' relics could be displayed and pilgrims could circulate were also requirements of pilgrimage church architecture. Moreover, churches built along pilgrimage routes were placed on the highest hill in the town so that they could be seen from a distance, inciting pilgrims to continue toward their goal (see CD Rom figure 4.5). They also have elaborately detailed tympanums, usually depicting Christ as judge, surrounded by saints and angels (see figure 4.1, and CD Rom figure 4.6).

The first famous pilgrim to Jerusalem was St Helena, the Emperor Constantine's mother, who claimed to have discovered there a piece of the true cross. It was she who initiated interest in the long and hazardous trip to holy places. By the end of the fourth century, large numbers of Western Christians were traveling to the "Holy Land" to express and renew their devotion to Christ. Some pilgrims went on one or several pilgrimages in their lifetime, while others adopted a life of continuous pilgrimage. Many pilgrims found pilgrimage exciting as well as edifying. In writings by and about them, there is a strong note of thirst for experience.

Dangerous Practice of Pilgrimage [margin handwritten annotation]

Figure 4.1 Creation of Adam, north transept façade, Chartres Cathedral, France, c.1220.
Christ's hands tenderly encircle Adam's head as Adam clings to Christ with childlike affection.
The sculpture is part of a later embellishment of the program of the tripartite porch that narrates
in stone the whole story of the creation and fall of humankind.

In the Middle Ages, a pilgrimage might be undertaken for any of several reasons. It might be penitential, either self-imposed or assigned by a confessor. Or it could be ordered by a civil judge in recompense for a crime; even capital offenses were often punished by judicial pilgrimage. In 870, a certain Rathbert battered his mother to death and was sentenced to two pilgrimages, one to Mont-Saint-Michel, and one to Rome. In the eleventh century, on his way to the French war, John of Arundel carried off sixty women and girls from a convent near Southampton for the pleasure of his soldiers. As he crossed the English channel a storm broke out and it was necessary to lighten the load, so he ordered the women tossed into the sea. He expiated for this crime by a pilgrimage to Jerusalem and by posthumous penance; he was buried naked and in chains. Most medieval pilgrimages, however, were undertaken for the excitement of physical proximity to martyr's shrines and the holy bones they contained, the sites of miracles one could see with one's own eyes.

Preparations for a medieval pilgrimage emphasized the seriousness and potential danger of a major pilgrimage. The pilgrim acquired the pilgrim's dress, a long, coarse tunic, and a large cross, staff, and pack in which food and other essentials were carried. The pilgrim was exhorted to bring no money, but to depend on the charity of others. Her clothing and equipment were blessed by a priest. The pilgrim also made a will, and made amends with anyone to whom he owed anything or with whom he had unhappy relations. Finally, he might secure a safe-conduct document for passage through territories reputed to be dangerous, although these first "passports" were usually ineffective.

In addition to emphasizing the seriousness of a major pilgrimage, elaborate preparations indicated its danger. Sickness caused by contaminated food or water and unaccustomed exertion was an inevitable feature of pilgrimage. A twelfth-century *Guide for Pilgrims to Santiago* lists common dangers: wild animals, bad roads, natural catastrophes, and bandits. One fourteenth-century pilgrim reported that half of the pilgrims who set out for Rome in 1350 were robbed or killed on the way – probably an exaggeration, but nevertheless an indication that major threats were routine. Moreover, there was the constant problem of finding food for themselves and fodder for their animals. Even church attendance along the way could be hazardous. Urging the need for expansion of the Church of St Denis (outside Paris), Abbott Suger (d. 1151) cited the terrible crush of pilgrims on feast days that sometimes caused fatalities. In 1120 a fire broke out in the Church of Sainte Madeleine in Vezelay on the feast day of Mary Magdalen; 1,127 pilgrims were burned to death.

The most hazardous pilgrimage was to Jerusalem. Many pilgrims walked 3,000 miles, or endured six weeks in small boats in order to reach Jerusalem or perish in the attempt. The fourteenth-century English pilgrim Margery Kempe described a sea voyage to Jerusalem whose conditions were little improved from those of centuries before. Together with the grave consequences of conducting a pilgrimage without the appropriate inner commitment, these formidable conditions constituted both physical and spiritual dangers.

There were also moral dangers. Pilgrims traveled in groups, both for self-defense and for mutual help and amusement. Sermons were their only organized recreation, but they often found more lively amusements. Songs from the pilgrimage route to Santiago de Compostela are still extant (CD Rom Music 2). Clearly, pilgrimage could be morally uninhibiting as frequently as it could be spiritually reviving. Even during the times of greatest interest in pilgrimage, medieval authors repeatedly expressed concern over the frequency with which pilgrimage was treated as an escape from both the problems and the moral strictures of daily life at home.

The only planned "entertainment" on a pilgrimage was frequent sermons. The following excerpt from a sermon, "*Veneranda Dies*," was to be read to pilgrims heading to Compostela on December 30, one of two twelfth-century feasts of St James.

> The way of St. James is fine but narrow, as narrow as the path of salvation itself. The path is the shunning of vice and the increasing of virtue. . . . The pilgrim may bring with him no money at all, except perhaps to distribute to the poor along the road. Those who sell their property before leaving must give every penny of it to the poor, for if they spend it on their own journey they are departing from the path of the Lord. In times past the faithful had but one heart and one soul, and they held all property in common, owning nothing on their own; just so the pilgrims of today must hold everything in common and travel together with one heart and one soul. To do otherwise would be disgraceful and outrageous. Goods shared in common are worth much more than goods owned by individuals. Thus it is that the pilgrim who dies on the road with money in his pockets is permanently excluded from the kingdom of heaven. . . . [Wealthy pilgrims who take the journey in comfort] are not real pilgrims at all, but thieves and robbers who have abandoned the way of apostolic poverty and chosen instead the path of damnation. . . . If St. Peter entered Rome with nothing but a crucifix, why do so many pilgrims come here with bulging purses and trunks of spare clothes and eating succulent food and drinking heady wine? St. James was a wanderer without money or shoes and yet ascended to heaven as soon as he died; what, then, will happen to those who make opulent progress to his shrine surrounded by all the evidence of their wealth?
>
> (Quoted by Sumption, 1975: 124)

Doubts about the value of pilgrimage were not aimed solely at potential physical or moral dangers. Pilgrimages were also questioned on theological grounds. At the end of the fourth century, in his *Treatise on Pilgrimage*, Gregory of Nyssa wrote, "When the Lord invites the blest to their inheritance in the kingdom of Heaven, he does not include a pilgrimage to Jerusalem among their good deeds." In the fourteenth century, Berthold of Ratisbon wrote, "What is the point of going all the way to Compostela to see some bones, for the real St. James is not there, but in heaven. Also, all you have to do to enter into the presence of God is to go to the parish church." Yet great numbers of people went on pilgrimage for at least a thousand years of Christian history. Interest in relics and miracles seemed valid to people who were taught that their God became flesh, walked the earth, and shared human vulnerability. Because he had shared their susceptibility to accident, disease, and death, God could be expected to sympathize with and heal their frequent illnesses and pains.

Hospitals were built along pilgrimage routes for the care of ailing, needy, and weary pilgrims. Regulations varied in these hospitality sites; in most of them, a pilgrim could have free lodging for a limited time, and be fed or have facilities for preparing food. He could wash, have a haircut, get clothing mended or boots repaired, and if sick, could have medical attention. If a sick pilgrim died – and many did – she would be buried in the graveyard adjoining the hospital. Many monasteries from the tenth century forward, opened hospitals, and many saints were created by caring for pilgrims in them.

Even the most uneventful pilgrimage resulted in physical and emotional change as pilgrims were removed from their accustomed environment, relationships, work, nourishment, and habitual behavior. Pilgrimage was also a strong reminder that the unpredictability of human life is not adequately recognized in a sedentary lifestyle. Travel over dusty countrysides, steep and slippery mountain passes, through dark and dense woods, and over hills and valleys more accurately represented life's realities (see CD Rom figure 4.7). Life as spiritual pilgrimage to a destination, the most insistent message of medieval Christianity, was concretized by pilgrimage.

According to medieval reports, pilgrimage sometimes resulted in physical cures. The belief that physical diseases had spiritual causes was a strong incentive to experience a cure when spiritual restitution had been made. A range of illnesses twenty-first-century people might consider psychosomatic could be cured by proximity to a powerful relic. Medieval reports of the spiritual and even the physical benefits of pilgrimage can often be credited without credulity.

In about 810 Bishop Theodimir found three bodies in the northwest corner of Spain. He believed that the bodies were those of St James and two of his disciples because, according to legend, St James the Apostle had conducted a preaching mission in Spain. The town of Santiago de Compostela was built over the spot where the bodies were found. The body assumed to be that of St James proved miraculously immoveable so a church was built over it. Boatloads of pilgrims set out for Compostela from Scandanavia across the Baltic; boatloads came from Hamburg and Bremen, and from the English ports. The French and Swiss came across land. By the twelfth century Santiago de Compostela was, along with Rome and Jerusalem, one of the most frequent goals of pilgrimage (see CD Rom figure 4.8). St Francis of Assisi and St Brigitta of Sweden both made the pilgrimage to Compostela. The present baroque cathedral contains the twelfth-century church (see CD Rom figure 4.9).

Pilgrimage reached its peak of popularity in the later Middle Ages, but by the fifteenth century, it was frequently questioned. Its popularity led to loss of its religious austerity; it sometimes became the sort of lark recounted in Chaucer's *Canterbury Tales*. In seventeenth-century Protestant circles, largely due to John Bunyan's devotional manual, *The Pilgrim's Progress*, pilgrimage became a major metaphor for the Christian life. Literal pilgrimage continues to be practiced in most Roman Catholic countries.

The mendicant orders

The growing wealth of medieval towns and the landed affluence of monasteries generated a reaction in the twelfth century. In the 1170s a wealthy merchant, Valdes (often incorrectly called Peter Waldo) of Lyon, gave away his wealth and organized a community of poor preachers, men and women. Pope Alexander III recognized Valdes's vow of voluntary poverty, especially when he proved orthodox in doctrine and agreed to swear that he did not believe that all the rich are in hell! However, the pope forbade Valdes and his followers to preach except by specific invitation of clergy, a prohibition they soon ignored. Soon clergy considered vows of poverty virtually synonymous with heresy.

Francis of Assisi (1181–1226) challenged the rejection of poverty. Son of a wealthy merchant, he renounced riches and began to preach and live in apostolic simplicity and poverty with a few followers (see CD Rom figure 4.10). Their lifestyle was modeled on Jesus's instructions to his disciples to go out two by two, without money or possessions, to preach the gospel. In 1210 Francis convinced Innocent III to approve a *Rule* specifying that Franciscan friars would wander in poverty. Those of his followers who were educated preached, but most of his followers worked among the poor, teaching the Christian life by living it. By 1220 there were two orders of friars, Franciscans, or "Friars Minor," and Dominicans, or "Preachers."

Dominic (1171–1221), a Spaniard, was an Augustinian canon who engaged in missionary work among the Cathars (further discussed in chapter 5) in the south of France during the Albigensian Crusade initiated by Innocent III. Discouraged by the ineffectiveness of his labor, he wanted to establish a monastic Order, but was prevented by the Fourth Lateran Council's (1215) prohibition of new Orders. Undeterred, Dominic based his Order on the *Rule* of St Augustine, arguing that because of this, the Order was not new. Probably influenced by St Francis, he soon convinced the 16 members of his order to adopt the lifestyle of wandering missionaries. Dominic traveled extensively organizing new branches of the Order. His last year was spent in Bologna, urging university students to join the Order of Preachers.

Both the Friars Minor and the Preachers differed from conventional Orders by their commitment to poverty and an itinerant lifestyle. However, these commitments barely outlived their founders. The Franciscan Order was permitted corporate ownership by Pope John XXII in 1317–18, and in 1475 Pope Sixtus IV allowed the Dominican Order to own property and permanent income. In this and the following chapter, we will continue to notice Franciscans' and Dominicans' activities and theological interests as their numbers and influence increased through and beyond medieval Christianity.

2   The Thirteenth Century: Theology and the Natural World

St Francis of Assisi (d. 1226) and his younger contemporary, Bonaventure (d. 1274), answered differently the medieval question: What is ultimately real? The question might also be phrased: Where should our attention be if we want to grasp the most significant thing about God, the world, and ourselves? Each answer must be considered in its integrity and profundity.

Incarnational theology: Francis of Assisi

Medieval people were fascinated by miracles – displays of God's power in evidence available to the senses, interruptions of the normal course of events. People believed that the Incarnation of God in Jesus Christ had caused a dramatic alteration of the status of the sensible world, so that one could expect God to act directly in and on the sensible world. From this perspective, the place to put one's attention is on the natural world of bodies and objects. Francis of Assisi was the greatest of the medieval religious leaders who gave what we may call the incarnationist answer to the question of what is ultimately real. For Francis, the natural world is the arena of God's direct activity. He did not think of people and the natural world as distracting him from a stronger reality.

Thus he did not endeavor to free himself from the delights and burdens of the sensible world in order to contemplate; he and his disciples understood Francis' *activity in this world* as his holiness. An immensely charismatic leader, Francis was declared a saint only two years after his death. Recently he was appropriately proclaimed the patron saint of ecology by Pope John Paul II.

Francis was a popular preacher, practical consultant, and saint, one of very few saints in the history of Christianity who is reported to have enjoyed a good laugh from time to time, and who even made his audiences laugh on occasion. He and his disciples were street performers who caught people's attention in order to preach to them. He traveled extensively, preaching in Italy, France, Spain, Syria, and he reached the court of Sultan al-Kamil in Egypt where he had long conversations with the caliph, but ultimately failed to convince him to convert to Christianity. Francis left 28 writings, including the *Earlier Rule*, the *Later Rule*, the *Testament*, and dictated letters. In his *Testament*, written shortly before his death, he described his conversion as the result of an experience with lepers. In the thirteenth century, lepers inspired horror, fear of contagion, and moral censure. Francis wrote:

> The Lord granted me, Brother Francis, to begin to do penance in this way: while I was in sin, it seemed very bitter to me to see lepers. And the Lord himself led me among them and I had mercy upon them. And when I left them, that which seemed bitter to me was changed into sweetness of soul and body; and afterward I lingered a little, and left the world.

Living among the poor and powerless, Francis said, helped him "to follow the humility and poverty of our Lord Jesus Christ."

Francis combined the personal winsomeness of Anselm with the saintly power (*virtus*) of St Benedict. His intimate relationship with the natural world was his medium. *The Little Flowers of St. Francis*, published a hundred years after his death, represents the way he was remembered rather than a literal account. In it the story of the wolf of Gubbio is reported by Brother Ugolino of Monte Santa Maria. A fierce wolf regularly devoured livestock and small children and threatened the safety of the town. When Francis visited Gubbio, the people begged him to address the problem. So Francis left the town alone to seek out the wolf. Soon the wolf ran toward him fiercely, as if to devour him. But Francis reasoned with the wolf, eventually establishing a plan to which the wolf nodded agreement. In return for leaving them alone, the townspeople would feed the wolf. All ended happily, and for the rest of the wolf's life he was fed and did not prey on the town.

The saintliness of Francis' life, however, lay not only in his ability to act as a peacemaker between conflicted parts of the natural world. He also inaugurated a new, and very literal, interpretation of the imitation of Christ. Practicing severe asceticism and keeping his body at the point of death for many years at a time, he denied himself sleep, shelter, and food to such extremes that those of his followers with less robust physiques could not imitate him. According to his first biographer, Thomas of Celano, as Francis lay dying he apologized to his body for his harsh treatment.

Francis vowed poverty in imitation of Christ who was "poor as he lay in the crib, poor as he lived in the world, and naked on the cross." In the context of the new commercial culture of thirteenth-century Italian towns, he resisted the values of secular society. But Francis' imitation of Christ went further. He is the first saint reported as receiving the stigmata, open wounds miraculously inflicted in the hands, feet, and side – the places Christ was wounded in the crucifixion. After a vision on Mt Alverna, Francis' biographer wrote, Francis retained "a most intense ardor and flame of divine love in his heart . . . and a most marvelous imprint and image of the passion of Christ in his flesh." These wounds gave Francis "very great joy in his heart . . . [and] unbearable pain to his flesh and physical senses." Francis' stigmata were attested by all thirteenth-century Franciscan writings. In his *Major Life of St. Francis* Bonaventure wrote, "Francis was totally transformed into the likeness of Christ crucified, not by the martyrdom of his flesh, but by the fire of his love consuming his soul." Francis believed that to imitate Christ was to participate in his physical, as well as his spiritual, suffering. Francis' delight in, and sensitivity to, the natural world contrasts sharply with his cruelty to his own body. Yet his companions and followers insisted that his stigmata were the direct result of the "habitual ecstasy" in which he lived.

Francis' companion, Clare of Assisi (d. 1253), was 12 years younger than Francis. On Palm Sunday, 1212, Francis himself gave her the monastic clothing, or habit, of the Order of Poverty and took her to the small church of San Damiano where she lived with her nuns, the Poor Clares, for the rest of her life. Francis did not allow the Poor Clares to wander about begging as he and his male followers did, but insisted that they be cloistered. After Francis' death (at the age of 45), Clare struggled for years to achieve what she called "the privilege of poverty" (without land or regular income). Only two days before her death, Pope Innocent IV approved a *Rule* for the Poor Clares that honored their wish to be unencumbered by property or income.

St Francis founded an Order, yet soon after his death the Order developed different values, organization, and interests. Even before his death Franciscan friars arrived at the University of Paris; by the next generation there was a permanent Franciscan Chair at the University. By the early fourteenth century, there were about 1,400 Franciscan houses, mainly around the Mediterranean; one-fifth of these were female communities. Bonaventure has been called the second founder of the Franciscan Order because of his reinterpretation of Francis' values. But not all Franciscans were happy with Bonaventure's reinterpretation of Francis' teachings.

In Francis' lifetime there was already a split in the Franciscan Order between those who continued to advocate Francis' radical poverty and those who thought poverty should not be the essential issue. The "Spirituals" split with the Franciscan Order, adopting Francis' flamboyant asceticism and the teachings of Joachim of Fiore (d. 1202). Joachim analyzed human history into seven ages, saying that the present age, the seventh age, just before the apocalyptic end of the world, was the age of perfection in the Spirit. His teachings were popular in central Italy, Provence, and southern France. Spiritual Franciscans were implicated in the destruction of Conventuals' (Franciscans who favored the common holding of property) possessions and accused of questionable political loyalties. The group was condemned in several papal bulls and several of its members were burned as heretics. The group persisted, however, and eventually formed a rigorous group within the Franciscan Order, The Friars of the Strict Observance.

Spirituals Peter John Olivi (d. 1298) and Olivi's disciple, Umbertino da Casale wrote a popular devotional treatise called the *Tree of the Crucified Jesus*. It advocates and outlines a meditative practice by which the Christian imaginatively enters the interior suffering – the suffering spirit – of Christ, providing a meditative parallel to Francis' stigmata and substituting a spiritual participation in Christ's physical sufferings for Francis' literal participation.

The hierarchical view: Bonaventure

Bonaventure was deeply influenced by Francis. According to tradition, Francis healed him when he was a child. He thought, however, that Francis lived on another level of being than most people – the ecstatic. What Francis lived and felt, Bonaventure *thought*. He translated the six-winged seraph that wounded Francis with the stigmata on Mt Alverna into six stages of "the mind's road to God."

Bonaventure entered the Franciscan Order in 1217. He became a regent master of the Franciscan School at the University of Paris in 1257, a position he held for a quarter of a century. In the same year he was elected Minister General of the Order. He wrote commentaries on scripture as well as on particular topics. His *Defense of the Mendicants* praised poverty as the basis of gospel perfection.

There was, however, considerable cultural distance between Francis' band of followers, preaching and performing street theater, and the Franciscan masters at the University of Paris. How did this transformation occur so rapidly? Francis had never quite condemned learning, but neither did he have any desire to see it developed in his Order. He thought of learning as at best unnecessary and at worst, dangerous. On one occasion he is reported to have torn apart a copy of the New Testament, distributing several pages to each brother so that each could enjoy it at once! Yet because of Francis' deep respect for the natural world, some of the greatest scholars and scientists of the time were Franciscans: Roger Bacon (scholar of Aristotle and works translated from Arabic), Duns Scotus (theologian and "Doctor *subtilis*"), and Robert Grostesste (who taught astronomy, optics, mathematics, and other scientific subjects, as well as theology).

Francis prohibited the instruction of lay brothers in the Order, and on one occasion, he called learning "practically synonymous with pride." Faced with this clear direction from the founder, Bonaventure asked himself: What was Francis' *intention* in forbidding laypersons to read and write? Obviously, he answered, to check vain curiosity. If, then, instead of *themselves* desiring education, they received it by order of their superiors, not only would they not be breaking the rule by receiving instruction, but they would actually be strictly bound to do so. This interpretation of Francis' intention reshaped the Franciscan Order. Bonaventure did not comment on the difference between knowing enough to preach a sermon on virtue or the Last Judgment and knowing enough to be a master at the University of Paris. In effect, Bonaventure replaced Francis' harsh physical asceticism with intellectual discipline.

Bonaventure's *The Mind's Road to God* described a process, a path. But it was not a pilgrimage in time, but a method for journeying in meditation to God *now*, in the present. It is also a hierarchy. Since "hierarchy" has a negative value in the minds of many twenty-first-century people, we must carefully note why Bonaventure valued it. A hierarchy, Bonaventure wrote, "is an ordered power of sacred and rational realities which *preserves for those who are subordinated* their proper authority" (emphasis added).

He did not primarily seek to demonstrate the greater beauty and reality of the higher rungs of a metaphorical ladder; he wanted to protect the lower rungs from losing their integrity, absorbed in the higher rungs. In fact, his attention was not on the *rungs* of the ladder at all, but on its uprights, or sides, that hold together the whole ladder. The rungs, or stages, provided a discursive *access* to the highest levels of reality. They show where to start and how to proceed. Body and the sensible world hold the ambiguous position of being the foundation, the *first step*, the place to start, *and* the lowest rung. Bonaventure *began with* "the whole sensible world . . . by which ladder we may mount up to God." On Bonaventure's journey of the mind to God, knowing and feeling must be closely interwoven, "lest one should believe that it is enough to read without passion, speculate without devotion, examine without joy, work without piety, understand without humility, be zealous without divine grace, see without wisdom, divinely inspired."

Succinctly stated, Bonaventure's method was: "we must mount Jacob's ladder before descending it." In the *process,* the mind's eye is cumulatively trained to recognize the connectedness of the whole universe. He paired each rung of the ladder with a corresponding human capacity and activity. On the first rung, one contemplates the beauty of the sensible world. The opening of the senses is the activity that guarantees the understanding appropriate to this level.

> The one, therefore, who is not illuminated by such great splendor of created things is blind; the one who is not awakened by such clamor is deaf; the one who does not praise God because of all these effects is mute; the one who does not note the first principle from such great signs is foolish.
>
> (*Mind's Road* 1.15)

Attentiveness to the sensible world, Bonaventure said, produces delight, and delight provides the energy for the ascent. The capacity for delight, exercised on sensible things, leads to the object of supreme delight, God. Starting with delight, Bonaventure next noticed the interconnection of all objects of delight.

> If, then, delight is the conjunction of the harmonious, and the likeness of God alone is the most highly beautiful, pleasant and wholesome, and if it is united in truth and inwardness and in plenitude which employs our entire capacity, *obviously it can be seen that* in God alone is the original and true delight, and that we are led back to seeking it by all other delights.
>
> (*Mind's Road* 2.8; emphasis added)

At the second stage of ascent, God is contemplated *in* sensible things, as their creator. While the first stage focused on the surface beauty of sensible objects, the second stage looks more deeply into them, noticing their structure and the intricacy and skill of their composition. The third stage moves the contemplator to recall the image of God in the mind. In considering the mental capacity by which the mind knows, loves, and remembers, "you will be able to see God in yourselves as in an image." "When the mind pauses to consider itself," Bonaventure wrote, "it rises through itself as through a mirror to the contemplation of the blessed trinity."

Bonaventure insisted that each progressive stage gathers in or incorporates the previous stages. He wrote a treatise called *The Reduction of the Arts to Theology* in which he argued that theology collects or distills all the other intellectual arts or fields of inquiry, summing up the best of their insights in theological knowledge. What did he mean by "reduction"? His ladder image did *not* mean that one must discard the lower rungs as soon as one achieves a higher rung. Similarly, the sciences, history, and philosophy are not discarded when one turns to theology. Rather, the arts are "reduced" to theology as a cook "reduces" a sauce, that is, by boiling it to its essence. Nothing is discarded, and all the flavors are distilled to their strongest intensity.

Bonaventure said, "We must mount Jacob's ladder before descending it." The last stage, the stage in which the mind's eye is dazzled in a "stupor of wonder" is the *gathering of all the stages into a unified vision.*

> While, therefore, you consider these things one by one in themselves, you have reason to contemplate the truth; when you compare them with one another, you have the wherewithal to hover in the highest wonder; and therefore, that you mind may ascend in wonder to wonderful contemplation, *these things should be considered all together.*
>
> (*Mind's Road* 6.3; emphasis added)

At the beginning of the thirteenth century, Sts Francis and Bonaventure vividly summarized the two medieval descriptions of how God acts in the world. The next section discusses St Thomas Aquinas, whose theology integrated Francis's attention to the natural world of bodies and senses with Bonaventure's theological hierarchy.

READINGS

Bonaventure: *The Mind's Road to God*
St Francis of Assisi: "The Canticle of Brother Sun;" "First Letter to the Custodians;" "A Letter to St Anthony;" "The Earlier Rule"
St Clare of Assisi "the *Rule* of St Clare;" "The Testament of St Clare"

3   Thomas Aquinas

Thomas of Aquino (d. 1274), *Doctor Angelicus*, was given by his parents to the Benedictine Abbey of Monte Cassino when he was five or six. He learned piety and grammar there, but he never mastered calligraphy and his friends called his handwriting "*littera inintelligibilis.*" He studied at the University of Naples; it was there that he was introduced to Aristotle's writings. He was attracted to the Dominican Order's ideals of evangelical poverty, study, and service to the Church and became a mendicant Dominican in 1244 at the age of 19. His horrified family abducted him, but after he spent some months convincing them that he had no wish to become the wealthy and influential prelate for which they hoped, they resigned themselves to his choice. At the University of Paris where he studied (under Albert the Great) and taught (from 1256 on) conflicts between the secular masters and masters of the mendicant Orders led to attacks on Thomas. Pope Alexander IV had to order the chancellor of the university to grant Thomas the *licentia docendi*. When Thomas gave his inaugural lecture, he and the audience were protected by soldiers.

Throughout his life, controversies arose over Thomas's use and interpretation of Aristotle. He and Bonaventure disagreed on the matter; Bonaventure argued that the "godless philosopher" should not be used in theology. In 1270, four years before Thomas's death, a list of 18 theological propositions influenced by Aristotle was condemned. Thomas himself was not mentioned and his ideas were never condemned during his lifetime, but conflicts surrounding the use of Aristotle continued. Three years after his death, several propositions from Thomas's teaching were condemned. Yet a year later, in 1278, his teachings were officially imposed on the Dominican Order by their General Chapter. Thomas was canonized in 1323, and declared a Doctor of the Church in 1567. In 1879, Pope Leo XIII made Thomas's theology mandatory for all students of theology.

Aristotle

In the late twelfth- and early thirteenth-century West, universities were stimulated by a new body of knowledge. Knowledge of Aristotle, together with scholastic method, altered education radically. Trilingual Jewish scholars in Spain translated the works of Aristotle and his Muslim commentators into Latin, making them accessible to Western scholars. The Spanish Jewish philosopher Maimonides (1135–1204) anticipated Thomas in teaching that the creation of the world was probable, but could not be demonstrated. It would be difficult to exaggerate the excitement surrounding this new learning. One Spanish Christian, Mozarab Alvaro of Cordova, complained about it:

> My fellow Christians delight in the poems and romances of the Arabs; they study the works of Muslim theologians and philosophers, not in order to refute them, but to acquire a correct and elegant Arabic style. Where today can a layman be found who reads the Latin commentaries on Holy Scriptures? Who is there that studies the gospels, the prophets, the apostles? Alas! the young Christians who are most conspicuous for their talents have no knowledge of any literature or language save the Arabic; they read and study with avidity Arabian books; they amass whole libraries of them at immense cost . . . On the other hand, at the mention of Christian books they disdainfully protest that such works are unworthy of their notice.
>
> (Quoted by Makdisi, 1981: 240)

Most of Aristotle's works had been unknown in the West since antiquity, while Plato's thought (based on a few of his treatises) was adopted and adapted by Christian thinkers from the early centuries of the common era forward. Aristotle's central emphasis was attention to the world as it presented itself to the senses and intellect. "See how it *acts*," he had insisted. When he considered the mind or soul in itself he became imprecise. Moreover, he said little, and did not develop what he did say, about the "First Cause" of the universe. Aristotle's God was an unknown, uncaring source whose only role was to guarantee the unity of the universe. Plato, on the other hand, was little interested in the world of senses and bodies, seeing them as epiphenomena of eternal ideas. Thomas Aquinas's teacher, Albert the Great (d. 1280) said, "One can be a perfect philosopher only if one knows both Plato and Aristotle; if we consider the soul in itself, we follow Plato; if we consider it as the animating principle of the body, we follow Aristotle."

Despite the excitement over Aristotle, some of his works were condemned for alleged pantheism in 1210, and their use was strictly limited within the university. At the University of Paris in the same year, the Theology faculty demonstrated its hegemony over the Arts and Sciences faculty by formally prohibiting the Arts and Sciences faculty to discuss Aristotle. In 1229, the University of Toulouse decided that Aristotle's books on natural philosophy could be used "to look into the very bosom of nature" – and thus they were condemned. The same author that Thomas Aquinas called simply "the philosopher," was referred to by many bishops as "the godless philosopher," for *Aristotle provided the conceptual possibility of analyzing the world without any reference to God.* It is difficult to exaggerate the importance of this startling new perspective. For over 800 years, from Augustine to Bonaventure, theologians had looked at the world *in order to* see God in and through it. Aristotle was attractive to many Jewish, Muslim, and Christian scholars as the first author who was not valued simply for supporting religious beliefs.

Study of Aristotle introduced new questions about the human soul and its capacities. From Augustine forward, knowledge of God had been thought of as essentially subjective. Bonaventure was the first to attempt a synthesis of subjective and objective knowledge of God. The mind's journey to God began by looking at things and delighting in them, a preliminary to engaging subjective and intellectual capacities. By constructing a hierarchy for the express purpose of preserving the integrity of the world of the senses, Bonaventure implicitly authorized empirical scientific exploration.

Scholastic method

Two teaching methods dominated the new universities, both of which had been practiced two centuries before in Islamic scholarship. They were the lecture (*lectio*) or exposition, and the disputation (*disputatio*).

Thomas Aquinas said that teaching is the only profession that does not break contemplation. Perhaps this was due to his lecture style. Thomas' *lectio* consisted of reading aloud from a text, a phrase, line, or paragraph at a time, stopping to comment on, or "gloss," the text as he read. In the absence of printed books, the primary responsibility of teaching was to transmit to students the content of ancient texts. This method was still in effect in Luther's time, except that by then students were expected to read the text to be discussed in the library. Luther dictated his lecture, word for word, and students wrote it down. Student notebooks, extant from Luther's lectures, record every word of the lecture. Thomas' method may have been livelier. His comments and glosses sought to recover the energy and excitement of the text. Medieval glosses, whether written or spoken, were the way medieval people considered, or "tried on", the author's thoughts. Glossing the text, they interacted with it, weaving the author's thoughts into their own thinking, asking questions of it, free-associating from it, or suggesting a practical appropriation. Strange interpretations sometimes emerged, but Thomas' method did not foster dullness.

The second method of academic instruction was the disputation. Used first in the field of law, it was quickly taken up by theology. In medieval universities disputations occurred at least twice a year, at Christmas and Easter. They were public events, participated in by townspeople, students, and masters. The formal debate, still practiced today in high schools and colleges, is the closest modern equivalent to the disputation. Anyone could propose any topic: *quodlibet* – literally, "whatever." The question could be a profound theological question, an ethical question, or even something quite trivial. The master arranged the topic as a formal question: *quaestiones disputatae*. Then the students "divided" and examined the question. Arguments *pro* and *con* were given. Then the audience and participants took a break while the master prepared an answer, a *responsio*, including in his answer parts of the various arguments that could be salvaged and woven into a cohesive answer. Next, he answered any objections that arose. At first the disputation was mainly an exercise for students but it was soon formalized. In the thirteenth century participation in a number of disputations was a requirement for the licentiate.

Theological method

Scholasticism began with Abelard's juxtaposition of contradictory sentences from the Church Fathers in his *Sic et Non*. At the beginning of the thirteenth century Alexander of Halles (d. 1245) composed the first *summa* or collection of theological knowledge by compiling, discussing, and reconciling sentences from the church fathers. One of his contemporaries observed that Alexander's *summa* was "about as much as one horse could carry." Using as his text Peter Lombard's *Sentences*, Alexander listed quotations under four headings: trinity, creation and sin, incarnation and the virtues, and sacraments and last things. In adopting this theological method, Alexander broke the early medieval identity of theology and scriptural exegesis, opening theology to rational investigation of matters of faith. Yet medieval theologians, even those who practiced scholastic methods, did not abandon exegesis; Thomas Aquinas wrote exegetical commentaries on the gospels, the Epistles, Isaiah, Jeremiah, the Psalms, and Job.

Scholastic method can be studied in its most developed form in Thomas Aquinas' *Summa Theologiae* (in which Thomas quoted Aristotle 3,500 times). Thomas introduced his project in this way:

> Because the master of Catholic truth ought not only to teach the proficient but also to instruct beginners, we propose in this book to treat of whatever belongs to the Christian religion, in such a way as may tend to the instruction of beginners. We have considered that students in this science have not seldom been hampered by what they have found written by other authors, partly on account of the multiplication of useless questions, articles, and arguments; partly also because those things which are needful for them to know are not taught according to the order of the subject matter, but according as the plan of the book might require, or the occasion of the argument offer; partly too, because frequent repetition brought weariness and confusion to the minds of the readers. Endeavoring to

avoid these and other like faults, we shall try, by God's help, to set forth whatever is included in this sacred science as briefly and clearly as the matter itself might allow.

The *Summa* follows the form of the public disputations. It is divided into Parts, which are then divided into Questions and further divided into Articles in question form. For example, in "Concerning the External Principle of Human Actions, that is, the Grace of God," Thomas set out ten questions. In each article, he gave several possible answers, drawing upon scripture and patristic authors. His "I answer" followed, in which he responded to anticipated objections ("On the first point," "On the second point," etc.). He then took up related questions in the following articles. The best strategy for reading the *Summa*, is to read the heading that sets out the question to be dealt with; then skip to the "I answer;" from there, go to the articles that articulate his reasoning. Finally return to read "on the first point," and so on.

Thomas' theology

A question that had been asked in various forms from the earliest days of Christianity was clearly articulated in the thirteenth century: What is the relationship between God and the visible world? Christians believed that the integration of God and human in Christ's Incarnation had altered the sensible world; what, then, could they expect to experience in the world of bodies and senses? Thomas's theological project needs to be placed within this larger question as well as in its immediate intellectual context.

The earliest disagreement occurred between Christians who believed that Jesus of Nazareth was born, suffered, and died in the normal human way, and those who found God's full participation in the human condition unthinkable. The doctrinal controversies of the fourth and fifth centuries argued the question in the abstract, formally deciding that Christ was fully God and fully human. In medieval paintings, the Virgin Mary presented the barefooted infant Jesus, his human flesh derived from her body, making God's Incarnation visible. People recognized that the implication of the Incarnation was that God actively intervened in the world of bodies and senses; they expected miracles and they treasured physical objects they believed contained divine power, such as saints' bones and garments. Eastern Christians defended icon-use on the basis of Christ's appearance in the visible world, making it appropriate for icons to represent the presence of sacred figures and saints in the liturgy.

St Francis, Thomas' older contemporary, believed that attentiveness to the natural world was the perfect form for contemplation of God. He understood body as form of the soul. Francis saw a world in which the power of God was continuously evident in the graceful play of spirit in matter.

Bonaventure, who died a month before Thomas in 1274, had a different analysis of God's activity in the world. For him, the power of God always radiates through a metaphysical ladder of being in an orderly way – from God, through the ranks of angelic beings, to the rational soul, and from soul to body. This non-collapsible ladder is continuous, the gradations of being intimately connected. There are no blank spaces and no shortcuts. For example, there must be angels in Bonaventure's universe, because between God, who is pure spirit and uncreated, and humans, who are created combinations of spirit and matter there must be created, purely spiritual, beings. Evil did not – and cannot – appear on Bonaventure's hierarchy of being, for evil is no-thing, and therefore has no positive existence.

Recognizing that it is perennially unlikely that a question or problem will be settled in the form in which it arose and came to an impasse, Thomas changed the question. His predecessors had asked an ontological question, namely, how is being distributed? In other words, what is ultimately more real, the spiritual or the sensible world? Thomas asked instead an epistemological question: He asked, how can humans *know* reality? By what activity can humans *investigate* being?

He answered that the rational mind can understand the sensible world. The mind's tools – observation and measurement, are the appropriate way to investigate sensible objects. He learned this from Aristotle's "see how it acts." Just as Bonaventure protected the lower ranks' "sphere of authority" from engulfment by the higher ranks, Thomas protected the authority of reason *in its proper sphere of operation*. Reason is exactly the right tool, he said, for investigating the sensible world.

But the rational mind is not the right tool for understanding revelation. Mysteries like the trinity or the incarnation are not susceptible of proof, of comprehension, or even of approximate explanation. The appropriate human capacity for approaching revelation is *faith*. Mysteries of faith can be illuminated by apt analogies, but they cannot be explained or proven.

> A philosopher and a theologian pursue different interests; one looks for inherently natural characteristics, the other for relations opening out to God. Even when they look at the same thing their point of view is different. The philosopher starts from proximate causes, the theologian from the first cause as divinely revealed; his concern is the manifestation of God's omnipotence and glory. . . . They also follow different courses, for philosophy takes creatures in themselves and thus infers truth about God; creatures come at the start, God at the end. The movement of theology is the reverse; God comes first, the creature afterwards.
>
> (II *Contra Gentes* 4)

By identifying the different starting points and content of faith and reason, revelation and the natural world, Thomas distinguished God and the sensible world. Yet these different contents are not separate. How did Thomas *hold together* the two realms he so carefully distinguished? What connects revelation as found in scripture and the sensible world as observed and experienced? "Our enterprise", Thomas wrote, "should be to draw out the *analogies* between the discoveries of reason and the commands of faith." "We have to take hints," he said, "from the workings of nature."

> We know incorporeal realities, which have no sense images, by analogy with sensible bodies, which do have images, just as we understand truth in the abstract by a consideration of things in which we see truth. God, we know according to Dionysius, as Cause about which we ascribe the utmost perfection and negate any limit. Furthermore, we cannot, in our present state, know other incorporeals except negatively and by analogy with corporeal realities. Thus, when we understand anything of these beings, we necessarily have to turn to images of sensible bodies.
>
> (*Summa Theologiae* 1a. 84. 8)

The theologian's *imagination*, he said, is critical: "The image is the principle of our knowledge. It is that from which our intellectual activity begins, not as a passing stimulus, but as an enduring foundation. When the imagination is choked, so also is our theological knowledge" (*Opusc. Xvi, De trinitate* vi. 2). Thomas used analogy consciously and self-critically, careful to define its limits: "Analogies do not amount to demonstration or provide complete understanding." Rather, they suggest, enable, and illuminate; *analogies support faith.* The ability to know God, however, is a gift of grace, not of reason. Grace is the condition in which God is known. Thomas offers an analogy: "Grace is a glow of soul, a real quality, like beauty of body" (*Summa* 12ae, Q. 110, art. 2).

The sensible world can be explored by reason, while faith and divine grace are necessary in the sphere to which reason unaided has no access. Analogy is not proof or identity. Thomas said, "Divine help is the influence of the first cause on secondary causes, and of a principle cause on instrumental causes; in both cases the *nature of the subordinate cause is respected*" (*III Contra Gentes* 149). In short, although Thomas recognized that miracles sometimes occur, divine help does not usually leap from heaven to earth, but makes use of the ladder.

Like Bonaventure, Thomas was concerned to protect the lower orders from being overwhelmed by the higher. Thus he argued for human freewill, entailing the ability to resist divine grace. Without human choice, grace is necessary but not sufficient. People must *prepare themselves* to receive God's grace, but even this cannot be done without the prior operation of grace. Thomas insisted on the necessity of grace *and* the autonomy of nature *in the arena of human life*, rather than as philosophical/theological propositions – in *practice*, that is, not in metaphysics. In experience when one takes responsibility for her/his life, choosing to deal gracefully with other people and the circumstances of life, when one learns to expose oneself to influences that nourish and heal, one then experiences oneself as "receiving" the strength and courage to act lovingly. The careful definitions of types of grace Thomas gave are all explications of the activity of grace *in real life.*

Having relinquished reason's effort conceptually to grasp God, Thomas found that there actually are some things that can be known of God by unaided reason. The existence of God, God's eternity, and God's creative power and providence can be discovered by natural reason, he said, completely apart from revelation.

Étienne Gilson, one of Thomas's most eloquent modern interpreters, has remarked, "While the depth of a theology may be measured by the pleasure with which it talks of God, its firmness and consequent durability as a structure will always be measured by its analysis of the human." Examination of the human, according to Thomas, requires the use of both approaches outlined above. A philosophical or rational approach is needed to explore body and the natural world, and a theological or revelation-based approach is necessary for understanding the human soul. Thomas observed and interpreted human experience within his own society, but humans were not only created from the dust of the earth, but also by the breath of God. Therefore some important features of human nature can be investigated only by theology. Thomas wanted to integrate an incarnationist with a hierarchical view, to protect physical nature from being subsumed into spiritual or metaphysical description. Thomas's account of creation, the Fall, and redemption demonstrated both the distinctiveness and the complementarity of soul and body, faith and reason, theology and philosophy.

In order to describe the unity of humanity, Thomas adopted Aristotle's formula: "the soul is the form of the body."

> The reason for this is that what a thing actually does depends on what it actually has to give. . . . Now it is obvious that the soul is the prime endowment by virtue of which a body has life. Life manifests its presence through different activities and different levels, but the soul is the ultimate principle by which we conduct every one of life's activities; the soul is the ultimate motive factor behind nutrition, sensation, and movement from place to place, and the same holds true of the act of understanding. So that this prime factor in intellectual activity, whether we call it mind or intellectual soul, is the formative principle of the body.
>
> (*Summa* Ia. 76, 1)

According to Thomas, soul, though distinguishable from body, is intimately engaged in all human functions, not merely with the so-called "highest" activities, thinking and contemplation. Soul is engaged in digestion no less than intellection. The implications of this assertion are enormous. For one thing, Thomas cannot say, as Plato did, that the soul is the person. Nor can he use Augustine's formula that the person is a soul *using* a body as its instrument of sensation. Rather, for Thomas, to analyze humans into "body" and "soul" is to distinguish two realities, a spiritual and a material, *neither of which could exist without the other*. Thus, "it is not the soul . . . that belongs to the species, but rather the composite of soul and body." Moreover, soul's connection to body is permanent:

> It belongs to the very essence of the soul to be united to a body, just as it belongs to a light body to float upwards. And just as a light body remains light when forcibly displaced, and thus retains its aptitude and tendency for the location proper to it, in the same way the human soul, remaining in its own existence after separation from the body, has a natural aptitude and a natural tendency to embodiment.
>
> (*Summa* Ia 76, 1)
>
> The soul will not be without the body forever. Since the soul is immortal, the body will be joined to it again. This is resurrection. The immortality of the soul, then, would seem to demand the future resurrection of the body.
>
> (IV *Contra gentes* 60)

Thomas's sense of the permanent mutual dependence of body and soul had some startling effects in his theology. First, the accuracy and adequacy of the mind's activity depends on the health and well-being of its body: "There is no free play of the mind except when the senses are fit and vigorous." Furthermore, in a culture that considered sight the "queen of the senses," Thomas defined touch as the highest human sense:

> Touch, [he wrote], is the foundation of all the other senses. A good touch results from a good complexion or temperament. Excellence of mind follows from bodily complexion, for every form is proportioned to its matter. People with a good sense of touch are therefore of a higher soul and clearer mind.
>
> (Commentary II, *De anima*, lecture 19)

A theology that seeks to demonstrate the integration of soul and body must include a treatment of sexuality. Thomas did not to say, as Augustine had, that original sin is transmitted at the moment of conception. Rather, for Thomas, lust of all kinds (power, possessions, and sex) is a *symptom*, not a cause, of sin. Rather, the effect of original sin can be observed directly, not in any positive agenda, but in its debilitating effect on humans. Inertia, listlessness, torpor: these are Thomas's evidence of original sin. Sexuality shares in, rather than transmits, the debilitation caused by sin. Nor, for Thomas, is sex the result of the Fall.

> For everything that is natural to human beings is neither withdrawn from nor given to them by sin. Now it is plain that it is natural to human beings in their animal life (which we had even before sin), to procreate by copulation, as it is to other perfect animals. And this is indicated by the organs assigned by nature to this function. And therefore it cannot be said of these natural organs, any more than of any other organs, that they would not have been used before sin.
>
> (*Summa* 1a. 98, 2)

Thomas said that sex, since it is not the cause or the result of sin would be unimaginably more pleasurable were it not affected, along with the whole human being, by that lassitude or enervation caused by original sin: "Not that the pleasurable sensation would have been any less intense before the Fall as some say, for the pleasure of sense would have been all the greater, given the greater purity of human nature and the greater sensibility of body" (*Summa* 1a. 98, 1).

Thomas was also concerned not to reduce soul to body. The main reason for the existence of human bodies, he said, is that bodies are necessary for reason; the senses are needed to collect data from the sensible world. Soul then works with this data to construct ideas and to illuminate revelation by identifying analogies.

Thomas noticed, given his genuine interest in bodies and the natural world, that it is incorrect to speak of "the body," since a generic human body is never seen or touched in experience. Rather there are at least two varieties of "the body" – male and female bodies. Thomas's principle, following Bonaventure, is that two different *natural* entities cannot inhabit the same rung on the hierarchy of being, reality, and value. Thomas claimed (supported by philosophical and theological antecedents) that male and female are "naturally" different. According to Aristotle, female bodies are failed, or incompletely formed, male bodies. According to the creation account of Hebrew scriptures, woman was derived from man, and paintings and cathedral façades pictured an adult Eve floating upward from a slit in the side of the sleeping Adam. Thomas agreed with a long line of predecessors that women have fewer rational capacities than men.

Sex difference, for Thomas was not caused by sin, but is a "natural" created feature. Since the death of bodies is natural for created beings, sex is also natural for the continuation of the race. Death without sex would be tragic for the human race, and so would sex without death. According to Thomas, the main reason for the creation of "woman" is procreation. For, Thomas said, another male would have been better, stronger and more companionable at "helping man" in any other way than procreation.

Thomas concluded that because "woman" was created after and derivative from man and because women "lack" male genitals, "woman" is a created being who simultaneously lacks rationality and full embodiment. If evil is a falling away from full being, and woman is a falling away from normative (male) being, then "woman" is inevitably associated with evil, a conclusion Thomas believed to be scripturally supported by Eve's initiation of sin in the world.

It is evident that Thomas' teachings reflected and reinforced rather than challenged the social arrangements with which he was familiar. Étienne Gilson, wrote: "The way to keep anything from being lost is to put everything in its place." As we have seen, that was Thomas's *intention*. The *effects*, however, have supported the exclusion of women from ordained leadership roles in the Roman Catholic Church to our own time.

Like Augustine, Thomas believed that human beings were capable of achieving happiness and that happiness was the goal of their creation. But it was not only that a part of humans could be happy. Influenced by Aristotle, Thomas posited human integrity as essential to happiness.

> In speaking of perfect happiness, some have said that no bodily conditions are present, indeed, they would have the soul entirely disembodied. . . . But this is unseemly: it is natural for the soul to be united to a body, and one perfection should not exclude another. Therefore we conclude that *integral happiness requires a perfect disposition of body.*
>
> (*Summa* 1a-2ae. iv. 6; (emphasis added))

Thomas' identification of the goal of human being was neither Bonaventure's "stupor of wonder," nor Francis' ecstasy. Thomas' goal was *happiness* – he called it beatitude. Happiness integrates incarnationist vividness with hierarchical orderliness.

> We are bound to affirm that the blessed see God's very being. Happiness is the ultimate achievement of rational nature. A thing is finally complete when it finally attains its original purpose, and without being forced. . . . A thing reaches God by what it is and by what it does. First, by likeness. This is common to every creature, and the rule is that the closer the likeness to God the more the excellence. Second, by activity . . . by which I mean the rational creature's knowing and loving God. The human soul comes directly from God, and therefore finds its happiness by returning direct to God. God must be seen for what God is in Godself; seen, that is, without a medium which acts as a likeness and representation of the thing known, such as a sense-image in the eye or reflection in a mirror; but not without a medium, called the light of glory, which strengthens the mind to have this vision.
>
> (*Quodlibets* viii. 1)

Thomas' contemporary, Bartholomew of Capua, described the close of Thomas' writing career. On December 6, 1273, the Feast of St Nicholas, Thomas celebrated mass. Apparently something extraordinary occurred, for "after the mass, he never wrote nor dictated anything. In fact he hung up his writing instruments." Since Thomas usually spent the whole day writing, dictating, or teaching, this was an abrupt and surprising change. His colleague Reginald asked him why he had given up his work. Thomas replied, "I cannot go on . . . All that I have written seems to me like so much straw compared to what I have seen and what has been revealed to me."

Thomas' statement has been variously interpreted. Some say that he had a "breakdown," others that he saw the utter futility of verbal communication. Another interpretation must be considered: Fifty years after Thomas's death the German Dominican Meister Eckhart (d. 1329) said that from the perspective of mystical vision, all language, time, theological knowledge, and ordinary experience seems paltry and ineffectual.

Yet, Eckhart insisted, the indefatigable pursuit of knowledge is a way to *get to* mystical vision.

Thomas died on February 12, 1274, not yet 50 years old. Although the University of Paris pled for his body, in the best medieval custom his corpse was boiled and his bones/relics distributed to various cathedral treasuries. The University of Paris got his *corpus*, not his corpse. In 1299, less than 25 years after Thomas' death, Pope Boniface VIII's *Detestande feritatis* prohibited the practice of dividing, embalming and boiling bodies, calling the division of bodies monstrous and detestable.

4   Gothic Cathedrals

Devotion to the Blessed Virgin Mary was not new in the twelfth century, but songs, devotional manuals, stories, sacred drama, painting, sculpture, stained glass, and architecture were dedicated to her as never before. In *Mont Ste-Michel and Chartres* (1900), Henri Adams explained the popular attention to Mary as the result of the majestic depictions of Christ in Romanesque art. In tympanum sculpture, Christ is shown as an inaccessible judge. "In the eyes of a culpable humanity," Adams wrote, "Christ is too sublime, too terrible, too just, but not even the weakest human frailty could fear to approach his mother." Whether or not this conjecture is correct, the 580 cathedrals built between 1170 and 1270 were almost all dedicated to Mary. At Chartres Cathedral (built 1194–1220) 175 representations of Mary depict her both in majesty and as a humble maiden. Hymns were also addressed to Mary as "*Coeli Regnam*" (Queen of Heaven); she was called "*Imperatrix supernorum*," "*Templum Trinitas*," and even "*Redemptrix*." The three-aisled cathedral itself was said to symbolize Mary containing the Trinity. Chartres was dedicated to the Assumption of the Virgin although her assumption was not Roman Catholic dogma until 1950.

The medieval period was the time of the greatest learned, as well as popular, devotion to Mary. Theologians of various religious orders argued about the Virgin's attributes and powers as well as about what bodily fluids she possessed. Councils invoked Mary's presence and wisdom. Jean Gerson, chancellor of the University of Paris at the beginning of the fourteenth century affirmed her implicit appointment to the priesthood, calling her the "Mother of the Eucharist." The most popular Tuscan preacher of the first half of the fifteenth century, Bernardino of Siena, praised Mary in the most extravagant terms in his lengthy and passionate sermons, waxing eloquent over the "unthinkable power of the Virgin Mother."

> Only the blessed Virgin Mary has done more for God, or just as much, as God has done for all humankind. God fashioned us from the soil, but Mary formed him from her pure blood. God impressed on us his image, but Mary impressed hers on God. God taught us wisdom, but Mary taught Christ to flee from the hurtful and follow her. God nourished us with the fruits of paradise, but she nourished him with her most holy milk, so that I may say this for the blessed Virgin (whom, however, God made himself), God is in some way under a greater obligation to us through her, than we to God.

People of the twelfth and thirteenth centuries were not interested in a new kind of church architecture; they were interested in the worship experience stimulated by the new churches. In a single century the French built 80 cathedrals and nearly 500 churches of cathedral class, costing (according to a crude translation into contemporary coinage) several thousand million dollars. A complicated mixture of devotion, chauvinism, plea-sure, and fear motivated the building activity (see CD Rom figures 4.11 and 4.12).

The term "Gothic" came from later Italian Renaissance humanists who used it to label scornfully what they considered a barbarian art form. "Gothic" refers to architec-ture originating in the Îsle-de-France (i.e., Paris and vicinity) between 1150 and 1250. A bit later, Gothic architecture also developed internationally. A great deal of regional variety existed until about 1400 when a style called "international Gothic" was stabilized.

St-Denis

The origin of Gothic style can be located in one building, the abbey church of St-Denis outside Paris. The burial place of a long line of Carolingian kings, St-Denis was also the private oratory of a closed monastic community. Both Charlemagne and his father were consecrated as Holy Roman Emperors at St-Denis. Between 1137 and 1144, St-Denis was rebuilt by its abbot, Suger, chief advisor to King Louis VI. Suger established and made visible a strong alliance between monarchy and church at St-Denis.

St-Denis was also a pilgrimage church (see CD Rom figure 4.13). When Suger became its leader it was an eighth-century building, much too small, he claimed, for the hordes of people who crowded into the church on a feast day. He gave the following argument for the necessity of rebuilding:

> As the numbers of the faithful increased, the crowds at St.-Denis grew larger and larger until the old church began to burst at the seams. On feast days it was always full to over-flowing, and the mass of struggling pilgrims spilled out of every door. Not only were some pilgrims unable to get in, but many of those who were already inside were forced out by those in front of them. As they fought their way towards the holy relics to kiss and worship them, they were so densely packed that none of them could so much as stir a foot. A man could only stand like a marble statue, paralyzed and free only to cry aloud. Meanwhile the women in the crowd were in such intolerable pain, crushed between strong men as if in a wine-press, that death seemed to dance before their eyes. The blood was drained from their faces and they screamed as if they were in the throes of childbirth. Some of them were trodden underfoot and had to be lifted above the heads of the crowd by kindly men, and passed to the back of the church, and thence to fresh air. In the cloister outside, wounded pilgrims lay gasping their last breath. As for the monks who were in charge of the reliquaries, they were often obliged to escape with the relics through the windows. When first as a schoolboy I heard of these things from my monastic teachers, I was saddened and conceived an earnest desire to improve matters.
>
> (Quoted by Sumption, 1975: 213–14)

The interior of St-Denis is distinguished from Romanesque churches by its lightness, both literal and architectural (see CD Rom figure 4.14). The windows were enlarged so that they no longer pierce a heavy wall, but fill the whole wall, becoming themselves translucent walls. The first of the large rayonnant-style (so called for their radiating patterns) rose windows appeared at St-Denis (see CD Rom figure 4.15). The architectural lightness was made possible by heavy buttresses that carry the outward pressure of the walls. The buttresses are visible only from the *outside*, where they jut out between the chapels of the double ambulatory.

Romanesque architecture had included an ambulatory around the choir that made the movement of large crowds of people possible. Pointed arches also existed in Romanesque churches (in the choir at Vezelay, for example), and so did the ribbed groin vault that featured two vaults carried by arches at intersecting right angles. But all of these had never before existed in the same building. Their combined effect is geometric harmony and maximal luminosity.

Abbot Suger's two books on the rebuilding and refurbishing of the church give a carefully reasoned argument for beauty as a trigger of mystical experience. His treatises, *De administratione* and *De consecratione*, were probably written to refute the acerbic objections of his contemporary, St Bernard (1090–1153), abbot of Clairvaux, who had forbidden the use of figural painting and sculpture in churches, except for wooden crucifixes. Bernard advocated vestments of the crudest linen, and iron candlesticks; only chalices were permitted to be of silver or silver-gilt. Bernard wrote: "But we who, for the sake of Christ, have deemed as dung whatever shines with beauty, enchants the ear, delights through fragrance, flatters the taste, pleases the touch – whose devotion, I ask, do we intend to incite by means of those things?" Bernard's criticism is worth quoting at length:

> I shall not mention the astonishing height of your oratories, their exaggerated length and excessive width, the sumptuous manner in which they are decorated and painted, so that the onlooker is curious to gaze on them, and the attention of the faithful is distracted and they are less disposed to meditation – no, I shall not mention any of these things, . . . for I am perfectly willing to believe that all this is intended only to glorify God. I will merely use the same terms, in speaking of other religious, like myself, as a certain pagan used in speaking to other pagans, like himself. O pontiff, said he, what is the good of displaying all this gold in the church? And I, changing only the verse, but not one whit of the poet's thoughts, I will say to you, what is the good, among poor people like yourselves – if, that is, you are truly poor – of all the gold that glitters in your churches? You display the statue of a saint, male or female, and you think that the more overloaded with colors it is, the holier it is. And people throng to kiss it – and are urged to leave an offering; they pay homage to the beauty of the object more than to its holiness. Likewise in the churches, it is not crowns that are hung from the ceiling but wheels covered with pearls, surrounded by lamps, encrusted with precious stones that gleam more brightly than the lamps. And the candelabra are like veritable trees of bronze, most admirably worked, and the gems that adorn them are no less dazzling than the taper that they bear. O vanity! Vanity! Vanity! And folly even greater than vanity! The church sparkles and gleams on every side, while the poor huddle in need; its stones are gilded while its children go unclad; in it the art lovers find enough to satisfy their curiosity, while the poor find nothing there to relieve their misery.
>
> (Quoted in Duby, 1981: 122–3)

Suger responded with a theological argument for the use of beautiful objects in churches. He cited the patron saint of St-Denis, Dionysius, a sixth-century mystical writer, to support his argument that objects of beauty can lead directly to experience of

God, the Great Beauty. Since all created things participate in "the process through which divine light flows down until the rays are dispersed in matter and broken up into a welter of physical bodies," this process can be reversed by an ascent from multiplicity to oneness. We need not, he said, be ashamed to depend upon sensory perception: "instead of turning one's back on the physical world, one can transcend it by absorbing it, by seeing the beauty and giving thanks to the author of beauty." Indeed, he said, our minds can only rise to that which is not material under the "manual guidance" of the material. All visible things mirror the creator. Dionysius wrote: "Every creature, visible and invisible, is a light brought into being by the Father of lights. . . . this stone or that piece of wood is light to me . . . For I perceive that it is good and beautiful in its existence." Moreover, Suger described mystical vision as *democratically* accessible. Illiterate and uneducated people, he said, are more likely to attain it than people whose heads are cluttered with words and ideas.

Abbot Suger explained that the windows at St-Denis have a three-fold function. They are bearers of holy images; they are beautiful in themselves, being made of intrinsically rich materials resembling precious stones, and their light is mysterious, glowing with a divine light, for "natural light passed through them and was transformed into a mystical, icon-bearing light" (Calkins, 1979: 173).

The church building was for him an extension of the ritual of the church, especially the eucharistic celebration, in which "thou joinest the material with the immaterial, the corporeal with the spiritual, the human with the divine." Suger loved not only the building but also the ceremonies that took place in it. The benediction of the holy water, he said, is "a wonderful dance, with countless dignitaries of the church, decorous in white vestments, splendidly arrayed in pontifical miters and precious amulets embellished by ornaments, walking round and round the vessel as a celestial rather than terrestrial chorus." The mass is an "angelic rather than a human symphony." Even the activity of building the cathedral was itself a spiritual exercise: "In God we too are builded together for a habitation of God through the Holy Spirit in a spiritual way, the more loftily and fitly we strive to build in a material way."

Suger understood himself as building theology, and the dedication rites of St-Denis include the vision of the celestial city of Revelations 21. 2–5. He was not alone in understanding the cathedral in this way. The Gothic cathedral was designed, mystically and liturgically, to transport the worshipper to the spiritual universe. In depictions of the Last Judgment in frescos or stained glass, the heavenly mansions are often represented as a Gothic cathedral, making this association explicit in people's minds.

Amiens

Amiens Cathedral (built between 1220 and 1280) is one of the tallest and largest Gothic cathedrals, its height supported by flying buttresses (see CD Rom figure 4.16). Flying buttresses transformed the size and appearance of Gothic cathedrals, placing the heaviest parts of the building's skeleton on the outside. At Amiens, a lower tier of flyers resisted the outward thrust of the stone walls and vaulting over the nave, while an upper tier of flyers braced the high clerestory wall and the tall timber roofs above the vaults against the wind loadings that created a greater lateral load on the walls (see CD Rom figure 4.17). High winds became worrisome due to the new heights of Gothic buildings.

Chartres

The present church was begun in 1194 after a fire destroyed most of the town as well as the entire cathedral except for two towers, the royal portal between them, and the crypt. It was rebuilt in less than 25 years, and roofed in 1220 (see CD Rom figures 4.18 to 4.21). The architect is unknown. In the nineteenth century, after another fire in which the roof and belfries were burned and the bells melted, it was roofed with iron covered by copper plates. It was to have seven steeples, but these have never been completed. The building of a cathedral was a costly venture, and not all medieval people were eager to use resources in this way. It would be wrong to think of cathedral building only in Suger's terms, that is, as a fulfilling spiritual discipline. Conflict surrounded cathedral building. It is discussed further in the next section.

In 876 Charles the Bald, Charlemagne's son, gave Chartres its priceless relic, the Virgin's tunic. According to different legends, the Virgin wore it either on the day of the annunciation or on the night of the nativity. When the church and town burned in 1194, the tunic was thought to be lost but it was found in the rubble (miraculously) undamaged and is presently in the cathedral treasury.

A contemporary chronicler, Haimon, abbot of St-Pierre sur Dives, wrote: "Has anyone ever seen or heard of powerful lords and mighty princes . . . and even women of noble birth bowing their necks to the yoke and harnessing themselves to carts?" Robert de Torigny, abbot of Mont-Saint-Michel reported that men and women dragged wagons loaded with wood, stone, and grain "through deep swamps on their knees, beating themselves with whips, numerous wonders occurring everywhere, canticles and hymns being offered to God. Even King Louis IX (called "St Louis") participated in the building of Chartres (Duby, 1981: 119).

Medieval pilgrims slept in the nave at Chartres. Its paving stones allowed washing, and panes of the stained glass could be taken out to air the cathedral. A famous labyrinth on the floor of the cathedral spans the entire width of the central nave, more than forty feet in diameter, repeating the pattern of the western rose window of the same diameter. The maze has a flower at its center as does the rose window. Medieval pilgrims made their way to the center of the labyrinth on their knees (see CD Rom figure 4.20).

Stained glass, a vivid feature of the new cathedrals was a peculiarly French medium. In England as late as the fifteenth century, greased linen or paper was used instead of stained glass. Stained glass windows act as "huge multicolored diffusing filters that change the quality of ordinary daylight" as incense changes ordinary air. The art historian Viollet-le-Duc wrote,

> After studying our best French windows, one might maintain as their secret of harmony that the first condition for an artist in glass is to know how to manage blue. The blue is the light in windows. . . . It is a luminous color that gives value to all the others. If you compose a window in which there is no blue, you will get a dirty or dull or crude surface

which the eye will instantly avoid; but if you put a few touches of blue among all these tones, you will immediately get striking effects if not skillfully conceived harmony. So the composition of blue glass singularly preoccupied glass workers of the twelfth and thirteenth centuries.

(Quoted by Adams, 1933: 133.)

The twelfth-century windows at Chartres contain "Chartres blue," a color that later became impossible to duplicate.

The theology of stained glass was described by Durandus of Mende, a thirteenth-century French theologian:

The glass windows in the church are holy scriptures which expel the wind and the rain, that is, all things hurtful, but transmit the light of the true sun, that is, God, into the hearts of the faithful. These are wider within than without, because the mystical sense is fuller, and precedes the literal meaning. Also by the windows the senses of the body are signified, which ought to be shut to the vanities of the world, and open to receive with all freedom spiritual gifts.

(Durandus of Mende, *Symbolism*: 24.)

The physical effects of stained glass also had theological meaning for medieval people. Art historian Otto von Simpson wrote:

Light could pass through glass without breaking it and thus was a demonstration of the Immaculate Conception, when Christ entered the Virgin's womb, yet leaving her virginity intact. . . . Christian theology is centered in the mystery of the Incarnation, which in the Gospel of John is perceived as light illuminating the world. Before the end of the thirteenth century it had become general custom to read the opening passages from the Gospel of John at the close of every mass. In the physical light that illuminated the sanctuary, that mystical reality seemed to become palpable to the senses. The distinction between physical nature and theological significance was bridged by the notion of corporeal light as an analogy to the divine light. (see CD Rom figure 4.21)

The two main elements of a Gothic Cathedral are the heaviest of material, stone, and the lightest, light itself. Just as stone was transformed to become a cathedral, human life, medieval people believed, must be transformed by the integration of body and spirit. This is the central message of cathedrals, a balance between, and integration of, heavy and light, material and spiritual.

How did the first worshippers experience Chartres? Lacking their testimony, we can only speculate. Was human life in the here and now marginalized by history and eschatology, pressed to nothingness between a problematic past and a terrifyingly unknown future? Or was human life in the present enhanced by the insistent message that there is something of the first importance that can happen *only* in the present life, namely salvation? We will understand historical people only if we notice their focus on death and an afterlife of reward or punishment. Yet, next to the tympanums featuring Christ in majesty and judgment, Gothic cathedrals present a gentler message, focused on the Virgin's tender care for all humanity.

Religion and politics

We will not see the new French cathedrals "in the life" unless we attend not only to the intentions of their builders, but also to the social and political circumstances in which cathedrals were built. Cathedral building signaled major changes in ecclesiastical power and socioeconomic conditions, largely relating to do the growth of towns. Cathedrals represented not only bishops' power and organizational abilities, but also the growth of trade guilds and bourgeois wealth. Historians have also noticed connections between Gothic cathedrals, with their systematic and encyclopedic visual exposition of Christianity, and the new universities in which scholastic philosophers ordered human knowledge and built comprehensive systems of theology. Gothic cathedrals and universities revealed similar interests in the enterprise of mastering and systematizing theology.

Other connections are less easy to recognize. Cathedrals were built by people eager to achieve self-definition (see CD Rom figure 4.16). They identified the "other," the outsider, the alien, and the dangerous in order to frame their own identity. Both self-definition and identification of the excluded were aspects of the same impulse.

An 1179 council convened by Pope Innocent III had ordered that "all impure creatures, carriers of purulent diseases, and all madmen, possessed by the devil, be shut up in leper colonies far from God's people, whom they contaminated." Pope Innocent III, elected in 1198 at the age of 38, defined himself and his office on his coronation day:

> I am he to whom Jesus said, "I will give you the keys to the kingdom of heaven, and everything that you shall bind up on earth shall be bound up in heaven." See then this servant who rules over the entire family; he is the vicar of Jesus Christ and the successor of St. Peter. He stands halfway between God and man, smaller than God, greater than man.

During his reign a council held at the Lateran palace stated as its agenda "eliminating heresy and reinforcing the faith, reformation of morals, uprooting of vice, and warding off all excess." It also decreed that Jews must wear the *rouelle*, a distinctive round cloth badge, identifying them as outsiders in Christian society.

A century earlier Pope Urban II had preached the First Crusade from the porch of the Romanesque church at Clermont-Ferrand (1095), a sermon that has been called "the most effective oration recorded in history." The project was to expel Moslems from the "Holy Land" as a first step toward creating a Christian world. William, archbishop of Tyre, reported that the natives of Antioch knew the crusaders had arrived when a shower of several hundred heads of slaughtered Turks were thrown over the town walls. For four hundred years, vivid preaching kept the crusading mentality alive. In 1464, Pope Pius II failed to gather any support for preaching yet another crusade.

The first holocaust against European Jews accompanied the "People's Crusade." Crusaders made no distinction between Jews and Muslims as enemies of their faith. "In France, they are reported as saying that 'it was unjust for those who took up arms against rebels against Christ to allow enemies of Christ to live in their own land'" (Riley-Smith, 1999: 54). "Between December 1095 and July 1096 there took place a series of events so distressing to the Jewish people that rumors of them reached the Near East in advance of the crusade, [and] dirges in honor of the Jewish martyrs in the Rhineland are recited in synagogues to this day" (Riley-Smith, 1999: 50). The Jewish communities at Worms and Mainz were massacred; then crusaders marched on to Cologne, Trier, Metz, Regensberg, and Prague where the massacres continued. Synagogues, Torah scrolls, and cemeteries were desecrated and Jews were forcibly baptized, a practice directly contrary to canon law. Many Jews killed themselves and one another to escape Christian baptism. A Jewish chronicler represented the murdering crusaders as saying: "You are the children of those who killed our object of veneration, hanging him on a tree; and he himself had said: 'There will yet come a day when my children will come and avenge my blood.' We are his children and it is therefore obligatory for us to avenge him" (Eidelberg, 1977: 33–4).

Often, Christian bishops tried to protect Jews, taking them into their fortified palaces or dispersing them to hiding places in the country. The papal bull *Sicut Judaeis* (1119–24) decreed "that no Christian shall use violence to force Jews into baptism." Yet, ironically, *if* forced baptism occurred, it was held to be effective, making the forcibly baptized Jews Christians and thus liable to prosecution for "heretical" behavior or beliefs. The fact that the decree was reissued by more than 20 popes during the next 400 years indicates that it was not obeyed. But church leaders, even those who, like Hugh of St Victor consulted with Jews about biblical interpretation, and those who protested violence against Jews, were at best ambivalent, often citing Augustine's idea that Jews' continuing existence was justified on the grounds that they were living witnesses to the prophecies about Christ in the Hebrew Bible.

The Fourth Lateran Council (1215) made the first universal laws requiring Jews to wear distinctive clothing. The Council also forbade Jews to hold public office, to appear on the streets during holy week, and it assigned special taxes to be paid to the Christian clergy. The Council declared in its opening canon: "There is indeed one universal church of the faithful, outside of which nobody at all is saved, in which Jesus Christ is both priest and sacrifice" (quoted by Carroll, 2001: 282).

Thomas Aquinas's *Summa Contra Gentiles* (1259) added learned argument to anti-Jewish laws and violence against Jews. The *Summa Contra Gentiles* used arguments from "natural reason to which all are compelled to assent," rather than revelation, to show the logical consistency and coherence of Christian faith. Thus, Jews could no longer be excused from Christian faith on the basis of "invincible ignorance." They were now believed to have known that Jesus was the Messiah and to have crucified him anyway in deliberate defiance of the truth (Carroll, 2001: 306). Crusader violence against Jews, together with theology and newly restrictive laws, created a new and dangerous situation for European Jews.

Throughout the ninth to eleventh centuries, numerous efforts had been made to curb local violence and private wars of vengeance and acquisition that ravaged society. Councils in France and Germany arranged truces for specific periods of time, for particular days of the week, for saints' days, and for feast days. However, all efforts were ineffective until the Crusades vented the violence of a violent society onto external foes, foes that could be considered God's enemies. A way had been found externalize the violence.

In addition to Muslims and Jews, a third enemy existed, the Cathar (or Albigensian, after their stronghold in southern France) "heretics" from the county of Toulouse and northern Italy. Cathars were dissident Christians who believed that spirit and matter are two separate and warring powers. These beliefs spread rapidly and created panic in the

Catholic hierarchy. It is known that Cathars practiced asceticisms of diet and abstinence from sexual activity, but Cathar's beliefs cannot be reconstructed from their perspective; the repressive campaign that wiped them out also burned their books.

Albigensian doctrine apparently rejected the incarnation of Christ, finding it incomprehensible that the divine glory could ever have sunk into the darkness of the flesh, or that the God of light could have experienced physical suffering. The Fourth Lateran Council of 1215 defined the doctrine of transubstantiation specifically to rebut Cathar's rejection of Catholic sacraments on the grounds that they combined matter and spirit. Cathars will be discussed further in chapter 5.

In *The Age of the Cathedrals*, Georges Duby (1981) suggests that the art of Gothic cathedrals was a "weapon against heresy, in its meticulous depiction of the ancestors of Christ, the Incarnation, and in its exaltation of Mary, the human mother from whom Christ received flesh." It was not the only weapon. In 1209 the Pope summoned the knights of the Île-de-France to a crusade to exterminate the Albigensian heresy. The crusade was largely successful in the short term, but in its wake, growing popular unhappiness with a worldly, wealthy church carried forward the critical aspect of Albigensianism without its dualistic doctrine. The Inquisition, topic of future chapters, originated to deal with the Cathars.

The other, the enemy, the dissident – these all figured strongly in the self-definition of the so-called "age of belief." An intense sense of aesthetic and religious beauty, a systematic and comprehensive theology, and a powerful affective piety co-existed with rejecting, fighting, and killing those whose beliefs and religious practices differed. To look squarely at this uncomfortable synthesis of beauty and murderous hatred, *denying neither*, is to see the age of the cathedrals in the life.

Epilogue

Thomas Aquinas, "the greatest of the schoolmen," described an integration of the concrete, the natural, and the material with the spiritual – body with soul, rational knowledge with revelation, philosophy with theology. Art historian Erwin Panofsky (1979) compared the medieval *summa* (summary of theology) to the Gothic cathedral. Cathedrals, he wrote, exhibit the same fascination with orderly arrangement of parts and the same interest in the way the parts are related to the whole as did the *summa*. Both forms – medieval scholasticism and medieval architecture – were born in the same place, the Île-de-France, at the same time, the twelfth and thirteenth centuries. Both are concerned with cohesiveness – the parts distinct yet balanced – and comprehensiveness – the inclusion of everything in an articulated unity. In Gothic architecture, for example, the bones of the building must show; just as, in the scholastic mind, "a maximum of explicitness" must be evident. In both, the structure conveys the beauty of orderliness. The attraction of orderly beauty explains the enormous influence, to our own time, of both Gothic architecture and systematic theology. In each, no part is incidental or accidental to the harmoniousness of the whole.

Communal habits of thought are evident in the institutions and social arrangements of a society, whether we look at scholastic thought, the systematic theology of the *summa*, the crusades, or a Gothic cathedral. Social arrangements and politics are interconnected with aesthetic, religious, and philosophical ideas. The *effects* as well as the intentions, the problems *and* the beauty must be recognized.

READING

Thomas Aquinas, *Treatise on Grace*, Prima Secundae, Questions 109–114 (in A.
   M. Fairweather (ed.), (1954) *Aquinas on Nature and Grace*)

Interlude

A first glance at Christianity, the religion of the "Word made flesh," might suggest that bodies disappeared from view as theologians continually talked about the soul. Why didn't people with fragile and vulnerable bodies talk about them more? Didn't they expect their religion to help them conceptualize and manage physical life? A more attentive study of the historical evidence, however, reveals that historical people did, in fact, talk about bodies constantly, both directly and indirectly. People who thought of themselves as the "body of Christ" engaged their bodies and senses quite consciously and purposefully in their liturgies and devotional practices, the religious images they placed on the walls of their worship places and burial chambers, and in the buildings they gathered in for communal worship. The history of Christianity can be read as a struggle to *differentiate* body and soul while nevertheless *keeping body and soul together*.

Many articulate and literate historical people described this project. Many others simply acted out the distinction and integration of soul and body woven into devotional practices, liturgies, and church buildings. In the thirteenth century, when Gothic cathedrals were springing up in French towns and villages, Durandes of Mende wrote:

> The arrangement of a church resembles a human body; the chancel, or place where the altar is, represents the head; the transepts the hands and arms, and the remainder – the nave towards the west – the rest of the body. The sacrifice of the altar denotes the vows of the heart.

What did it mean to historical Christians to believe that God had entered the same visible, touchable, audible world that human beings inhabit in a body? Christians answered this question differently in different times and places – in times of persecution and martyrdom; when Christianity was the official religion of the Roman state; when medieval people's horizons shrank to the local, the immediate, to survival in a precarious world; and in later medieval times when Western institutions still alive in our own day – churches, monasteries, and universities – were forming.

Early Christian literature reveals a struggle to maintain highly energetic but conflict-ridden Christian communities, to achieve and maintain a balance between the new *life* they experienced and orderly communities. Christians struggled over issues surrounding authority, clarity, and leadership roles as Christian ideas and practices, social arrangements and relationships, were gradually institutionalized.

In the fourth and fifth centuries, controversies arose over describing the meaning and implications of the Incarnation. Many late-classical people felt discomfort and embarrassment over the disruption of cosmic order implied in the claim that God became human. How could this God-man be made intelligible? Would a Platonic hierarchy be used to "place" Christ as the first emanation of God, one step removed from God? And just *how* did Christ participate simultaneously in humanity and divinity? Surely not, some people said, to the point of being born in the normal way and suffering and dying in pain and distress. A modified and, to the classical mind collapsed, hierarchy of being was finally defined in which the three-persons-in-one of the trinity were both differentiated and united.

In the early medieval centuries, people asked how the material, sensible world of everyday experience was changed by God's appearance in a body. Surely, they decided, they could expect to see miracles, to touch and experience God's power in bodies and in the natural world. God's activity was not predictably and evenly distributed throughout the world of the senses; rather, it irrupted dramatically and unexpectedly. A person's holiness, a relic, a place, or a religious image could be the lightning rod that collected and dispensed God's power. John of Damascus put it this way: "Perhaps you are sublime and able to transcend what is material . . . but I, since I am a human being and bear a body, want to deal with holy things and behold them in a bodily manner" (*The Orthodox Faith* IV. 16).

In the eleventh century, the monk Anselm used the relationships of his feudal society to picture the redemption of the human race. God's honor, offended and insulted by sin, required that restitution be made. And restitution could be made only by one who had the power and sinlessness of God and yet shared humanity with human beings, the God-man. Two years before Anselm wrote *Cur Deus Homo* the First Crusade had been preached on exactly these terms. Penitential practices similarly emphasized the idea of restitution for sin, while theologians like Hugh of St Victor developed the doctrine of purgatory by which people were given a chance to make restitution even after death.

Thomas Aquinas's project was to hold apart – differentiate – and hold together – integrate – the spiritual and the material, soul and body, faith and reason, theology and philosophy. Thomas's distinction of the spheres of faith and reason gave the natural world of bodies and senses priority in the order of discovery; the spiritual world and revelation had priority in the order of value. In Gothic cathedrals an integration of spiritual and material, stone and light, was sought. A hierarchical conception of the universe guaranteed that both spiritual and material retained what Bonaventure called their "proper spheres of authority." Similarly, Thomas believed that God *can* produce miracles, but he thought of miracles as secondary:

> Miracles lessen the merit of faith to the extent that they argue an unwillingness to believe the scriptures, a hardness of heart that demands signs and wonders. All the same, it is better for people to turn to the faith because of miracles than to remain altogether in their unbelief. Miracles are signs, not to them that believe, but to them that believe not.
>
> (*Summa* 3a. 43, 2)

Thomas was much more interested in an orderly, predictable world: "Divine help is the influence of the first cause on secondary causes; in both cases the nature of the secondary cause is respected." (*Contra Gentiles* III: 149)

The later thirteenth and fourteenth centuries to which we turn in the next chapter discussed the question of God's relationship to the sensible world in a different social, economic, and intellectual world. Scholastic theologians, and saints and mystics with popular followings, brought new and fruitful terms to the question of the metaphysical and practical meaning of God's Incarnation.

5   Death and the Body in the Fourteenth-century West

1   Late Medieval English Mysticism
2   German Mysticism
3   Mysticism in Italy and Flanders
4   Fourteenth-century Realism and Nominalism
5   Medieval Piety and Heresy

Prologue

Late medieval religious thought and practice contained two newly prominent currents, mysticism and scholastic theology. Neither involved great numbers of people, but both initiated major redistributions of religious interests and allegiances. Regional differences continued to be important, since most people were engrossed in ideas and events in their immediate vicinities rather than in ideas generated in major cultural centers such as Rome or Paris. English mysticism has a different tone from German, Flemish, or Spanish mysticism.

Preaching, literature, and the paintings and sculptures before people's eyes as they worshipped, vividly depicted death and the Last Judgment (see CD Rom figures 5.1 and 5.2). In the rigidly hierarchical late medieval societies of Western Europe, images of death were symbols of the ultimate equality of human beings. Moreover, religious terror matched the harshness of everyday life. In his 1949 *The Waning of the Middle Ages*, historian Johan Huizinga described medieval life as permeated by violence and by violent contrasts between fierce liveliness and cruel death. In the middle of the fourteenth century plague swept Western Europe. In the wake of this major disaster, people were emotional, excited, passionate, and violent. People who were moved to tears of great devotion at a procession carrying the image of the Blessed Virgin would then adjourn to the town square to watch a criminal drawn and quartered. One medieval chronicler reports that a public execution was "a scene at which the people rejoiced more than if a new holy body had risen from the dead." Towns purchased criminals from other towns for execution – the more extended and gruesome the better – if none were locally available.

Councils in France and England renewed several times Pope Clement V's 1311 decree forbidding refusal of extreme unction (the ritual of final confession and forgiveness) to criminals before their execution. It was difficult to enforce the decree against the brutal wish of the populace to intensify the drama of execution with the certainty of eternal damnation.

Plague broke out in the 1340s and spread through Western Europe within a short time. The plague originated with wild rodents, was ingested by fleas, and thus passed to domestic animals and finally to people. The plague was pandemic, occurring at least once in a generation until the seventeenth century, but gradually diminishing in virulence. Germ warfare contributed to the rapid spread of plague. During a war waged between Italians and Tartars in central Asia over control of important trade routes, the Tartar army, disseminated by plague, threw corpses of the dead into the Italian camp. Within three or four days, plague struck. Many soldiers fled the camp and returned home, carrying infected fleas. Between a third and a half of the population of Europe died. Many speculated that the disease was God's judgment on the sins of society. Paintings of the time depict Christ throwing thunderbolts of pestilence into the world. One medieval chronicler wrote, "There was no escaping the sight and stench of putrifying corpses piled high on the streets."

Reminders of death were ubiquitous, and the notion that a person's entire life passes before their eyes at the moment of death originated in the fourteenth century. *Ars moriendi* (art of dying) literature presented death as the moment of ultimate self-knowledge. Stages of putrification, complete with worms were featured in prayer books illustrated with the "dance of death," on church walls and apses, and in cemeteries. In spite of constant burials and exhumations, the churchyard of the Holy Innocents in Paris was a popular place to stroll while contemplating garish depictions of aged, diseased, dying, and dead bodies. Shops lined the outer walls, prostitutes solicited, and people enjoyed picnics.

Were medieval people morbidly fascinated with death? Were images of death a way to domesticate death, to become accustomed to it? While affirmative answers to these questions may be partially true, it is important to recognize also that reminders of death are known to evoke an intense and poignant sense of *life*. Placed in the context of death, the transitory world becomes all the more precious for being precarious and temporary. A fourteenth-century painting of a dead woman in a shroud has the following inscription:

> Once I was beautiful above all women, but by death I became like this. Once my flesh was very beautiful, fresh and soft. Now it is altogether turned to ashes. My body was very pleasing and very pretty; I used frequently to dress in silk. Now I must rightly be quite naked. I was dressed in grey fur and miniver; I lived in a great palace as I wished. Now I am lodged in this little coffin. My room was adorned with fine tapestry; now my grave is enveloped by cobwebs.
>
> (Quoted by Huizinga, 1949: 141)

At St-Denis, the traditional burial place of the French kings, inscriptions and effigies began to appear on tombs. At first the effigies were stylized figures, but by the fourteenth century, death masks were incorporated (a practice that continued to the seventeenth century). Depictions of the deceased often address the spectator. The tomb of Cardinal Lagrange is inscribed: "Wretch, why are you so proud? You are nothing but ashes, and will, like me, be food for worms." "*Et in arcadia ego*," read many tomb inscriptions, informing the viewer: I too was once in the land of beauty and plenty that you now inhabit, and where I am, you will soon be.

A new style of tomb sculpture for the wealthy began in the fourteenth century. Transi (from Latin *transire*, to cross over) tombs were built from the late fourteenth to the seventeenth centuries. The tomb of Francis de Serra (d. 1360), one of the earliest, shows toads eating away the corpse's mouth, while worms emerge from within the corpse. On the more elaborate tombs, several likenesses of the deceased appear, kneeling *priant* figures; recumbent *gisant* figures, fully clothed and with open eyes; and naked and decomposing *transi* figures. These images of the "real body," that is, the decaying body, go at least part of the way toward explaining one of the most puzzling features of medieval mystics, namely their insistence on "despising the body."

1   Late Medieval English Mysticism

New styles of holiness, together with lay-centered religiosity flourished in the chaos of plague-ridden Europe. Franciscan monks were the most frequent pastors to city populations. Franciscan preaching, in town squares as well as churches, aimed at eliciting strong feelings and strengthening piety. The preaching of doctrine was left to Dominicans.

Educated men were often suspicious of the new popular piety. Jean Gerson, chancellor of the University of Paris at the end of the fourteenth century, said that nothing is more dangerous than ignorant devotion: "The contemplative life has made numbers of people melancholy or mad." He believed that the world was in its senile old age, with all the delusions, fantasies, and paranoia that trouble extreme old age. He listed cases he knew personally – a person who fasted "with vain and arrogant obstinacy," and then ate with insatiable voracity, and a man who thought that each twinge in his corns was a sign that a soul had descended to hell.

Some of the richest documents of the spiritual life came from the fourteenth century. Mystical treatises, written in vernacular languages rather than in Latin so they would be accessible to all who could read, were the *first* vernacular literature in Western Europe. Before the invention of the printing press at the end of the fifteenth century, they were copied and recopied; many manuscripts are extant for the most popular.

Three English mystics, laypeople who managed to keep in the good favor of the church while doing and saying startling things, are explored in this section: Richard Rolle (d. 1349), called the hermit of Hampole, and the leading medieval English hymnwriter; Margery Kempe (d. 1433), a married woman with 14 children; and Lady Julian of Norwich (d. after 1413), an anchorite who lived in a tiny cell attached to her parish church.

Richard Rolle

Richard Rolle dropped out of Oxford University in order to pursue contemplation. He died in the first wave of plague to hit England in 1349. Rolle's *The Fire of Love* begins with the standard disclaimer of fourteenth-century mystics:

> I offer this book for consolation not by philosophers, not by the worldly-wise, not by
> great theologians ensnarled in infinite questionings, but by the unsophisticated and the

untaught, who are trying to love God rather than to know many things. For God is loved in doing and in loving, not in arguing. . . . For this reason I have decided not to write for [the learned], unless, having put aside and forgotten all things which have to do with the world, they burn to be enslaved by single-minded desires for the Creator.

Rolle has been called the first master of Middle-English prose. His images are sensual and dramatic. He speaks of mystical experience as ravishment, sweetness, fire, heat, and exquisite music. He preferred "love in the feeling of the flesh" to intellectual excitement, the rapture *of* the bodily senses to being rapt *from* "bodily feeling to a joyful or dreadful sight." He wrote of the "endless mirth of love," saying "nothing is more profitable, nothing merrier than the grace of contemplation." The soul's memory of Jesus, he wrote, is like "a song of music in a feast of wine."

He saw no conflict between his intensely sensuous language and his insistence that the soul must be converted from its orientation to things of the world; "our soul dies to things loved or sought in the world." He wrote of "despising the world," explaining this phrase by saying that one who seeks the contemplative life must "pass through this world *without the love of* temporal and passing things," that is, without attachment to the constant supply of sensory stimulation on which most people depend.

Fourth-century ascetics and monks had written about diverting attention and desire from pursuit of objects to scrutiny of one's own interior life, and ultimately, directing the energy of desire to God. The three channels into which people in all societies, they said, are socialized to direct their desire are the pursuits of sex, power, and possessions. Thus the vows taken by a monk created a monastic counterculture: celibacy was substituted for the pursuit of sex, obedience for power, and poverty for possessions. Why, then, did Richard Rolle not simply enter a monastery, take vows of celibacy, poverty, and obedience, and undertake a traditional contemplative life?

In the fourteenth century, a lay piety that sought alternatives to the monastic life emerged. Rolle's contemplative practice was essentially private and individual. He was a hermit. He designed for himself a personally tailored spiritual exercise: "Therefore, I can tell thee *my* meditations, but which is most effectual *for you*, I cannot know, for I see not your inward desires." He had no standard repertoire of ascetic practices: "Truly, by itself poverty is no virtue, but only wretchedness." For people who can "hold not the goods they have with full love, but *having them, forsake them*," an asceticism of poverty has no value. However, if one desires wealth, an asceticism of poverty may be necessary.

For Rolle, the soul/self is constituted in its activity of listening and speaking to God, not in events, practices, or the pursuit or possession of objects. It is the *inner* occupation that is important, and Rolle believed that shaping the inner life was a full time commitment, as it was for monks. He advocated active choice and discernment based on intimate self-knowledge. Rolle's idea of an informal, individual program gathered momentum in the fourteenth century. In many mystics and would-be mystics, new values were forming that would soon permeate society.

Margery Kempe

Margery Kempe exemplified a very different lifestyle. Margery, by profession a brewer of ale, was married and the mother of 14 children. She was the illiterate author of the first (dictated) autobiography in English. Her autobiography, titled simply "Book," was also an early – perhaps even the first – example in English prose literature of dialogue based on memory of past conversations. In spite of her habit of referring to herself in the third person as "this creature," her autobiography is strongly personal. Margery confessed to her besetting sin of lechery, and she told some embarrassingly frank stories as examples.

Margery Kempe had visions, comprised mostly of dialogues with Christ, in which, according to her account, she took an active, even garrulous, part. But her primary spiritual discipline was pilgrimages. The discomfort and danger of a long trip jarred Margery into altered and vividly heightened states of consciousness. Her husband accompanied her patiently, even agreeing while still quite young to Margery's demand for mutual celibacy. Perhaps her demand was related to the fact that she had already given birth to fourteen children!

Margery often went into a strange town or village, stood in the public marketplace, and began to exercise her peculiar gift, the gift of tears. She always drew a crowd: "The crying was so loud and so wonderful that it made the people astounded." And the "cryings" frequently went on for two or three hours at a time. Margery reported that she cried at the thought of Christ's passion or anything that reminded her of it:

> When she saw the crucifix, or if she saw a man with a wound, or a beast, whichever it were, or if a man beat a child in front of her, or struck a horse or other beast with a whip, if she saw it or heard it, she thought she saw our Lord being beaten or wounded, just as she saw it in the man or the beast . . .

She experienced Christ's suffering in human suffering. Sometimes she also cried at the thought that "heaven is so merry."

Margery Kempe's tears may not seem to be a mark of sainthood to twenty-first-century people, but her gift was highly esteemed in a society that valued intensity of feeling above everything. Nevertheless, her behavior was, as she faithfully reported, annoying to many people. What better proof of intensity of feeling than tears? The social role she created for herself dramatized a vividly experienced relationship with God, and her culture was fascinated with her visible (and audible) personal piety.

Lady Julian of Norwich

Like Richard Rolle and Margery Kempe, Julian of Norwich began her *Showings* with the claim that she was unlettered. Unlike Margery Kempe, Julian was not illiterate, but she may not have known Latin. At the age of 30, she had an illness that brought her to the point of death. Staring at a crucifix with a darkening gaze, she saw a colorful vision of the crucified Christ. Her pain suddenly evaporated, and in the next several days she had a series of visions, 15 in all. She had no further visions, but she meditated for the rest of her life on the visions she had in those few days. Her meditations moved from the visions, which she calls "bodily sight," to a lifelong effort to interpret and understand them. She did not consider the visions ends in themselves, but only as an impetus to her sustained activity of translating the pictorial language of the vision into personal spiritual knowledge:

All the blessed teaching of our Lord was shown to me in these parts . . . that is to say, by the bodily sight, and by words formed in my understanding, and by spiritual sight. For the bodily sight, I have said what I saw as truly as I can. And for the words formed, I have said them right as our Lord showed me them. And for the spiritual sight, I have said somewhat, but I could never fully tell it.

(*Showings*, Short text: vii)

Medieval mysticism cannot be understood without noticing medieval fascination with pain and its religious uses. Julian, although not the most extreme example, shared her society's common understanding of pain as religiously useful. Her revelations came at the point of death during an almost fatal illness. In retrospect, she said that she had prayed for the illness as for a grace. A contemporary of Julian said, "if people knew how useful diseases are for self-discipline, they would purchase them in the marketplace." When Julian recovered from her illness she had herself immured (enclosed, walled-up) in a small cell, leaving only a small opening through which food and other essentials were passed, and she lived there for the rest of her life, approximately 35 years.

Pain and its religious uses

Lady Julian's illness is an example of the frequent difficulty in discerning whether the pain that was actively used by mystics and others was voluntary or involuntary. Mystics often claimed, in retrospect, to have sought disease or pain when they recognized how much they had learned, *from experience*, the value of pain. Living in a society in which pain can be prevented, masked, or hidden makes medieval attitudes toward pain difficult to comprehend. We find their insights attractive and would rather forget that they were produced by suffering. In fact, many or most medieval mystics went beyond using involuntary pain to causing their own pain.

A massive change in cultural assumptions about pain makes it difficult for modern people to credit medieval reports concerning pain's uses. The nineteenth-century discovery of relatively safe and effective anesthetics and other pain medication made it possible to alleviate most, but not all, pain. But if we do not reconstruct the values medieval people associated with pain, we will not understand medieval mystics, let alone ecclesiastical and juridical torture and punishment, both of which were facts of social life until the nineteenth century.

Ariel Glucklich's (2001) *Sacred Pain: Hurting the Body for the Sake of the Soul* demonstrates that "sacred pain" is a cross-cultural phenomenon. Possession (by gods or demons), initiation rites, and mourning practices involving planned and controlled pain were (and are) used in most cultures. Glucklich argues that modern Western societies are virtually alone in ignoring the recognized uses of pain. The discovery of anesthetics and the medicalization of pain effectively ended common assumptions about "good pain." Yet even in twenty-first century Western societies in which pain can be more effectively "managed" than at any previous time in history, pain that cannot be alleviated still exists and might be "used." Glucklich writes, "The task of sacred pain is to transform destructive or disintegrative suffering into a more deeply valued level of reality than individual consciousness."

Pain is a social phenomenon; its interpretation, and thus the experience of pain, is mediated by common assumptions. Pain never acts on a body, but always on a self socialized to certain interpretations, and for whom other interpretations are remote or impossible. The same acts that medieval people thought productive – for example, self-flagellation or fasting – in modern Western cultures are usually considered symptomatic, "sick." In short, the "same" acts, in different cultures, are not the same.

Julian's theology

The theme of Julian's theology is divine love. Her writings communicate a strong sense of the greater power of divine love than that of evil and sin. "All shall be well, and all shall be well, and all manner of thing shall be well," she wrote. She found metaphors of divine love in a mother's continuous, intimate, and tender care for her infant, and in a tiny child's trusting dependence on its mother:

> Jesus, our mother in nature, our mother in grace, because he wanted altogether to become our mother in all things, made the foundation of his work most humbly and most mildly in the maiden's womb. The mother's service is nearest, readiest, and surest: nearest because it is most natural; readiest because it is most loving; surest because it is truest. The mother can give her child to suck of her milk, but our precious mother, Jesus, can feed us with himself, and does, most courteously and most tenderly, with the blessed sacrament, which is the precious food of true life.
>
> (*Showings*, Long text: 59)

Julian did not originate the concept of God as Mother. Clement of Alexandria (d. 215), wrote about the Christian's nourishment at God's breasts, and other authors also used mother imagery to emphasize God's loving care. But Julian interpreted God's mothering care on a more profound theological level than had earlier authors. Julian described the significance of the Incarnation of God in Jesus as "a taking on of our physical humanity . . . a kind of creation of us," as a mother gives her flesh and blood to the fetus she bears: "The second person of the Trinity is our mother in nature in our substantial creation, in whom we are founded and rooted, and he is our Mother of mercy in taking our sensuality" (*Showings*, Long text: 58).

Lady Julian's mother imagery, however, did not affirm human mothering, but contrasted human and divine mothers: "We know that all our mothers bear us for pain and for death. But our true mother, Jesus, he alone bears us for joy and for endless life." Human mothers are simultaneously honored and dishonored in Julian's theology: "This fair lovely word 'mother' is so sweet and so kind in itself that it cannot truly be said of anyone or to anyone except of him and to him who is the true mother and life of all things" (*Showings*, Long text: 60).

Nevertheless, Lady Julian's repertoire of images from domestic life imply that personal life is the place to look for analogies to God's activity. Thinking of God as mother and as father – Julian used both images – gives an intimate and balanced picture of God's care for human beings: "God almighty is our loving father, and God all-wisdom is our loving mother. I contemplated the work of the blessed trinity and I saw and understood the property of the fatherhood and the property of the motherhood."

Julian commented on pain and its uses:

> And after this our Lord revealed to me a supreme spiritual delight in my soul. In this delight
> I was filled full of everlasting surety, and I was powerfully secured without any fear. . . .
> And then again I felt the pain, and then afterwards the joy and delight, now the one and
> now the other, again and again, I suppose about twenty times. . . . It is not God's will that
> when we feel pain we should pursue it, sorrowing and mourning for it, but that suddenly
> we should pass it over and preserve ourselves in endless delight, because God is almighty,
> our lover and preserver.
>
> (*Showings*, Long text: 9)

Richard Rolle, Margery Kempe, and Lady Julian could hardly have been more different
from each other, yet they had commonalities. Each of them engaged in practices of piety
outside a communal liturgical or ecclesiastical setting. They occasionally referred to participation in the life of a worshipping community, but they largely took the Church for
granted. Their excitement centered on individual contemplative experience, individual
piety, and individual methods of achieving mystical insight.

READINGS

Richard Rolle, "The Mending of Life", in R. C. Petry (ed.) (1957) *Late Medieval
    Mysticism*
The Book of Margery Kempe, selections, trans. B. A. Windeatt (1985)
Julian of Norwich, *Showings*, trans. E. Colledge, OSA and James Walsh, SJ
    (1978)

2   German Mysticism

Meister Eckhart

Reading medieval mystics can be difficult for people trained by their academic experience to read quickly in order to identify the main ideas in a text. In an academic context,
we read mystics at the wrong pace and usually with the wrong interests – with historical or literary critical interests. Readers interested in a text's assumptions, its claims to
authority, its imagery, metaphors, and its rhetorical strategies, are not the ideal readers
of mystical literature, even though the richness of mystical texts rewards such study.
Some mystical treatises describe their ideal reader. For example, the anonymous English
Cloud of Unknowing begins by saying that no one should read the book unless s/he is
committed to "perfection;" otherwise, the book will seem nonsense. Mystics' frequently-
expressed hostility to learning may also have related to the kind of learning practiced at
the time in European universities, discussed later in this chapter.
    Meister Eckhart, fourteenth-century Dominican priest, teacher, and mystic was con-
sidered in his own time very difficult to understand. Son of a noble family, Eckhart
studied and taught in Paris before coming to the Dominican monastery in Thuringia.

Both the laypeople he regularly preached to in the monastery chapel and the theological authorities of the Catholic Church complained of his difficulty. Yet he was one of the most famous preachers of his time. Like other mystics of his time, Eckhart assumed that understanding required a virtuous life.

> Someone complained to Meister Eckhart that no one could understand his sermons. Whereupon he said: "to understand my preaching, five things are needed. The hearer must have conquered strife; he must be contemplating his highest good; he must be satisfied to do God's bidding; he must be a beginner among beginners; and, denying himself, he must be so a master of himself as to be incapable of anger."
>
> ("This is Meister Eckhart from whom God hid nothing," Blakney, 1941: 93)

In 1329, a year after Eckhart's death, Pope John XXII declared that Eckhart, "deceived by the father of lies who often appears as an angel of light" had sown "thorns and thistles among the faithful and even the simple folks." He was accused of teaching 28 errors, among them the claim that unity with God could be achieved in mystical experience. His accusers charged that he made "unity" sound like identity. Eckhart's imagery lent itself to this interpretation; the Christian, he said, can become "more intimate with God than a drop of water in a vat of wine, for that would still be water and wine; but here one is changed into the other so that no creature could ever again detect a difference between them" (*Talks* 20). His image of the drop of water in the vat of wine soon came to be considered symptomatic of heretical claims.

Eckhart was difficult to understand because of the esoteric experience he described. But the difficulty is increased by the fact that his descriptions of the experience of union also seem to contradict one another. He sometimes said that body, intellect, and "works" are to be totally rejected; in other passages all of these seem to be affirmed. Eckhart's teachings become coherent only when they are understood as a *method* for achieving mystical apprehension of God. He was not careful to distinguish moments in a discursive *process* toward mystical union from the perspective gained in the experience of union, though he talked differently about each. He left his hearer/reader to sort one from the other.

Before examining Eckhart's method, two preliminary questions must be addressed: Why did Eckhart think union with God is important? Because, he wrote in *The Aristocrat*, "the seed of God is in us." A capacity is a need. Why, then, is the unitive experience not more frequently actualized? Eckhart replied, "Because so much is required to that end. The principle requirement is that one should get beyond phenomenal nature and in this process a person soon begins to be weary" (*Sermon* 25). Fatigue is caused by the fact that "the soul has two eyes – one looking inwards and the other outwards." The inner eye of the soul looks into essence and takes being directly from God, but it fatigues rapidly because it receives little exercise. On the other hand, "the soul's outward eye is directed toward creatures and perceives their external forms." *This* eye is highly trained and minutely developed because it is exercised constantly on objects in the world. Since it is painful to exercise the unexercised eye, what motivates anyone to do so? Eckhart's answer is that people were created for union with God: "The seed of God is in us." Motivation is also supplied by God's love that *draws* a person to God. God's grace *translates God's love into individual experience*: "Grace is not a stationary thing; it is always found in a becoming" (*Fragment* 12).

Eckhart's method consists of systematically stripping oneself of everything that clutters and obscures the "core of the soul" where the "seed of God" exists. "The more ourselves we are," Eckhart wrote, " the less 'self' there is in us" (*Talks* 11). "Begin, therefore with yourself and forget yourself" (*Talks* 3). Clearly, Eckhart used "self" ambiguously as he described a deconstruction proceeding from outer "self" to inner "self." The first feature of the "self" to forget is the socialized self, constituted by birth in a particular time and place and by one's formative experiences. This is not the self that can experience God. The socialized self is essentially a defense against the "simple stillness" at the core of the soul that conceals the very existence of this core. Emotions, no less than ideas, are part of the socialized self; they should not be taken with inappropriate seriousness, Eckhart said.

> Second, "practices" must be stripped away. Any devotion to any practice that limits your freedom to wait upon God in this present moment and to follow God into the light, by which God may show you what to do and what not to do – how to be as new and free with each moment as if you had never had – or wanted, or could have – another.
>
> *(Sermon 24)*

From this perspective, even religious ritual is a "practice" of the outer self: "To seek God by ritual is to get the ritual and lose God in the process" (*Sermon* 5).

Third, one's body must be "forgotten." In Eckhart's words, soul must "break away from body and seek God." What is the problem with body?

> Body is too strong for the spirit and so there is always a struggle between them . . . The body is bold and brave here, for it is at home and the world helps it. The earth is its homeland and all its kindred are on its side: food, drink, and comforts are all against the spirit. Here the spirit is alien. Its race and kin are all in heaven. It has many friends there. They assist the spirit in its distress, to weaken the flesh for its part in this struggle *so that it cannot conquer the spirit*; penances are put upon the flesh like a bridle to curb it, so that the spirit may control it.
>
> *(Sermon 4; emphasis added)*

Fourth, will and knowledge, "the soul's agents," must be "forgotten." These govern external as well as intellectual activity. Will, that governs external activities, must be surrendered "or else there is no traffic with God" (*Talks* 11). Intellect lies closest to the "core of the soul," but is still "outer" to this core; it too must be laid aside.

> But perhaps you will say, "Alas, sir, what is the point of my mind existing if it is to be quite empty and without function? Is it best for me to screw up my courage to this unknown knowledge which cannot really be anything at all? For if I know anything in any way, I shall not be ignorant, nor would I be either empty or innocent. Is it my place to be in darkness?" Yes, truly. You could not do better than to go where it is dark, that is unknowing (*unwissen*).
>
> *(Sermon 4)*

Finally, the movement from outer to inner requires forgetting space, time, and self-consciousness. "As long as one clings to time, space, number, and quantity, he is on the wrong track and God is strange and far away" (*Sermon* 25).

The "self" that takes its being from God is identified only when all phenomenal nature is stripped away. At that point the union of God and the soul occurs. *This union is the true self.* Eckhart described a "simple stillness," in which, in the "now-moment," "the Father begets his only-begotten son and in that birth the soul is born again." When the soul's customary activities are stilled, a "void" is created that God is *obligated* to fill.

> Do not imagine that God is like a carpenter who works or not, just as He pleases, suiting his own convenience. It is not so with God, for when he finds you ready, he must act . . . God may not leave you void. That is not God's nature. He could not bear it.
>
> (*Sermon* 4)

The soul is automatically organized into self-unity at the same instant in which it comes into union with God. Deconstruction is the human task; reconstruction occurs spontaneously. *Now* Eckhart moves to inclusions as dramatic as the exclusions he described at an earlier stage. What can be gathered into the unified soul? Everything that has been stripped away.

> I am often asked if it is possible, within time, that a person should not be hindered either by multiplicity or by matter. Indeed it is. When this birth really happens no creature in all the world will stand in your way, and what is more, they will all point you to God and to this birth. . . . Indeed, *what was formerly a hindrance becomes now a help.* Everything stands for God and you see only God in all the world.
>
> (*Sermon* 4; emphasis added)

Inclusions occur immediately and spontaneously in the unified soul. Body is returned. "Our hearts and God's are to be one heart; our body and God's, one body. So it shall be with our sense, wills, thoughts, faculties, and members, so that we feel with God and are made aware of God in every part of the body and soul" (*Talks* 20).

But the relationship of soul and body is altered. Whereas before the birth, soul was experienced as a tiny kernel or core in the body, after the union the body is experienced as *in* the soul: "My body is more in my soul than my soul is in my body, but both body and soul are more in God than they are in themselves" (*Sermon* 25). Moreover, the body can be so thoroughly integrated into the unified soul that "the light in the soul's core overflows into the body which becomes radiant with it" (*Sermon* 2).

Activities are returned. When "good works" result from the new birth in the soul, they occur effortlessly, spontaneously.

> One may test the degree to which one has attained to virtue by observing how often one is *inclined* to act virtuously rather than otherwise. When one can do the works of virtue without preparing . . . and bring to completion some great and righteous matter *without giving it a thought,* when the deed of virtue seems to happen by itself, simply because one loves goodness and for no other reason, then one is perfectly virtuous and not before.
>
> (*Talks* 21; emphasis added)

Intellect is returned. Freed from "irrelevant ideas" and its own self-talk and fantasies, it can now attain "pure and clear knowledge of divine truth." Eckhart made strong claims for the capacities of the reborn intellect: "Intellect draws aside the veil," he wrote, "and perceives God naked" (*Sermon* 26).

At the birth of God in the soul, the urge to evil is disassembled into the raw energy that comprises it that can then be used for good. Eckhart did not suggest that one should repress "evil urges" or even "sins:"

> If you have faults, then pray to God often to remove them from you, if that should please God, because you can't get rid of them yourself. If God does remove them, then thank him; but if he does not, then bear them for him, not thinking of them as faults or sins, but rather as great disciplines, and thus you shall exercise your patience and merit reward; but be satisfied whether God gives you what you want or not.
>
> (*Talks* 23)

From the perspective of the unified soul, one's faults and sins become spiritual discipline, the occasion of renewed and strengthened love for God.

Eckhart's definition of the self as defined by relationship with God was not new in the Christian West; it had been in constant use since Augustine. But the idea that the self is defined in relationship is not an obvious one. "Relationship" ordinarily assumes and implies the initial separateness of unconnnected entities between whom bridges need to be built, abysses crossed, or chasms spanned. Some Christians did not express their religious subjectivity as a "relationship" with God.

Eastern Orthodox Christians were, and are, critical of western mysticism's focus on the individual and its tendency to intellectualism, a tendency that is strong in Meister Eckhart. Instead of positing a radical separateness between God and human beings, Orthodox thinkers describe becoming aware of and exploring a *connection*. God, other human beings, and the natural world are seen as intimately interconnected, interwoven, and interdependent with one another. For Orthodox Christians, the project is not to overcome separation, but to realize and actualize a bond that already exists, to strengthen this bond by attention and exercise.

Moreover, "darkness" has different roles in Eastern and Western Christianity. In the East, the metaphor of "darkness" was used to describe the incomprehensibility of God's essence. It refers to the fact that one cannot grasp God intellectually and explain God discursively. This is not experienced as painful; it is merely a fact. The idea common among western mystics that darkness is a painful, even terrifying, sense of isolation or separation from God does not exist in Eastern Orthodoxy.

Eckhart's identification of the "true self" as the individual self that listens and speaks to God was highly influential in the Christian West. The idea of individual religious responsibility and authority came to full articulation two centuries later in Martin Luther. Other constructions of the "true self" will be discussed in the sections that follow. We will notice especially the social experiences and the habits of thoughts that formed the context of transcendent experience.

Meister Eckhart was the "intellectual" of the fourteenth-century mystics. He repeatedly denied that either emotion or will were adequate routes to union with God. His methodical stripping to the core of the soul where God "happened" was unusual in his time. Other mystics were more optimistic about feeling and will. Even those of his immediate successors who used Eckhart's mystical method – like Tauler, and Ruysbroeck – emphasized intense longing and love as necessary for the union.

Most fourteenth-century mystics focused on cultivating desire for God. They taught that desire for God is to be gathered at the direct expense of desire for objects in the world. They urged detachment from, or renunciation of, the beauties and pleasures of the world. But, like Richard Rolle, Margery Kempe, and Lady Julian, they often used language of sensuous beauty and pleasure to describe their experience of God.

The people we call "mystics" left written records of their experiences. In the West, they practiced the devotion that produced mystical experience within church communities, but outside liturgical settings. All mystics were not designated "saints." The next section begins with a discussion of the qualities that medieval societies recognized as indicating sainthood.

READING

Meister Eckhart, "Sermon on the Eternal Birth;" "Another Sermon on the Eternal Birth;" "A Sermon on the Contemplative and Active Life;" "On Solitude and the Attainment of God;" "Love Cannot Be Lazy," in Ray C. Petry (ed.) (1957) *Late Medieval Mysticism*

3   Mysticism in Italy and Flanders

Sainthood and society

Saints lived in societies that defined and shaped the attributes of sainthood. What qualities were fourteenth-century saints expected to demonstrate? *Processi*, or canonization documents, reveal that the attributes considered essential for sainthood were demonstration of supernatural power; asceticism, including fortitude in illness; charitable activity; and evangelical activity. However, these attributes shifted in relative importance in different times and places. Class was also a factor in sainthood expectations. In the eleventh and twelfth centuries saints were primarily drawn from the upper classes, but in the thirteenth and fourteenth centuries saints were predominantly urban artisans and workers, or peasants and rural workers. Women saints became statistically significant for the first time in the fourteenth century. In the eleventh and twelfth centuries, one in twelve saints was a woman; in the fourteenth century, 23.4 percent of all persons with cult followings were women. Even then, however, women saints did not outnumber men; three of every four saints were male. The broadening of the class base, as well as the rise of the mendicant orders that appealed to women as well as men – third order Franciscans, Dominicans, and Carmelites – substantially increased the numbers of women saints. If informal sainthood, or those with unauthorized cult followings were added, the number of female saints would rise even further.

Sociological analysis can provide valuable information. It does not, however, reveal anything about the specific attraction of saintly behavior, both for saints themselves and for those observing them. More intimate details of medieval sainthood, found in literature by and about saints, reveals that, while many mystics were saints, not all saints were mystics. A person could also become a saint by self-sacrificial work to ease the sufferings of others. Catherine of Siena is a good example.

Catherine of Siena

Catherine de Benincasa, daughter of a Sienese dyer and twenty-second child of her family, is one of two women who the Catholic Church has declared a "doctor of the Church" (in 1970). (St Teresa of Avila is the other.) Childhood visions moved her to vow virginity when she was seven, and she entered the Sisters of Penitence of St Dominic at the age of fifteen. She combined an extremely active life with a passionate spirituality, engagement in ecclesiastical politics, and extensive writing and preaching throughout Italy. Her preserved writings include 380 letters, her Dialogues, and two dozen prayers. She reported receiving an invisible stigmata, and is shown in numerous paintings receiving from Christ a ring – his circumcised foreskin – signifying her marriage to him. Catherine was canonized in 1461, less than a century after her death.

The plague was raging in Siena while Catherine lived there. Her vocation was influenced by the terrifying need she saw about her. During the first decade of her life Siena's population dropped from about 100,000 to 13,000; four-fifths of its population died of plague between early spring and the end of August 1493. A contemporary chronicler, Agnolo di Tura, wrote:

> Father abandoned child, wife husband; one brother, another; for this Illness seemed to strike through the breath and the sight. And so they died. And no one could be found to bury the dead for money or for friendship. . . . And in many places great pits were dug and piled with huge heaps of the dead. . . . And I, Agnolo di Tura called the Fat, buried my five children with my own hands, and so did many others likewise. And there were also many dead throughout the city that were so sparsely covered with earth that the dogs dragged them forth and devoured their bodies.
>
> (*Cronaca Senese*; quoted by Aberth, 2001: 109)

Plague was not the only cause of the deaths in Catherine's environs. She had a twin who died shortly after birth, and her favorite older sister died in childbirth as a teenager when Catherine was ten. Catherine believed mystical experience to be valuable, not as an alternative to an active life, but because from it she gained energy to serve the neighbor. Death – its frequency and immediacy – was an important context for medieval mysticism.

Catherine was also intensely concerned about the Church's perceived failure to meet people's religious needs. The Great Schism (1378 to 1417) divided the Church by the election of two and, for a time, three popes. The legitimate pope resided in Avignon under the protection of – some said "kept" by – the King of France. Catherine considered this so-called "Babylonian Captivity" of the Church shameful.

Catherine's food practices and her public career show that fourteenth-century saints were not all alike. Some saints were accused of demon possession, witchcraft, monomaniacal pride, and extraordinarily vigorous will power. In fact, it was not clear to all her contemporaries that Catherine was a saint; for example, she was accused of heresy by the Inquisition. The line between holiness and heresy, craziness, and sainthood was difficult for contemporaries to discern.

Catherine's food practices illustrate the ambiguity of sainthood. From before she was 16, she ate only bread, uncooked vegetables, and water; by the time she was 24, she reportedly ate "nothing," saying that she felt stronger and healthier when she didn't eat. For weeks at a time the only nourishment she tolerated was eucharistic bread. Her detractors accused her of being a fraud because of her claim to subsist on virtual nourishment. Her confessor and biographer, Raymond of Capua described Catherine's eating habits:

> Her stomach could digest nothing and her body heat consumed no energy; therefore anything she ingested needed to exit by the same way it entered, otherwise it caused her acute pain and swelling of her entire body. The holy virgin swallowed nothing of the herbs and things she chewed; nevertheless, because it was impossible to avoid some crumb of food or juice descending into her stomach and because she willingly drank fresh water to quench her thirst, she was constrained every day to vomit what she had eaten. . . . She maintained this life-style until her death.
>
> (Quoted by Bell, 1985: 27–8)

Historians interpret this behavior variously. In *Holy Feast and Holy Fast*, (1987) Caroline Walker Bynum focused largely on the religious and social power that an otherwise powerless woman accumulated because of the fascination these practices held for Catherine's contemporaries. Rudolph Bell (1985) used a psychoanalytic and medical interpretive lens. Susan Bordo (1993) used gender as an analytic category, noticing continuities between historical and contemporary fasting practices in societies designed and administered by men. Bordo proposed that in patriarchal cultures in which young women are valued for their bodies, taking control of one's body by strict regulation of food intake may represent longing for more control of one's life. How did Catherine herself explain her motivation?

> The more a soul possesses the love of God, the more holy hatred it has for the sensory part, for its own sensuality, because the love of God naturally begets hatred for sins committed against God. For the soul sees that concupiscence, the origin and source of every fault, reigns within and plunges its roots into the sensory part. Then it feels itself seized with a great hatred for this life of the senses, and it exerts every effort, not to kill this life, but to pluck out the source of corruption that is rooted in it. That cannot be done without a long, total war on sensuality itself. Furthermore, it is not possible that there should not remain some roots capable of producing at least light faults, which is a new motive for the soul to be displeased with itself. Nothing ensures the security and strength of the soul as much as this holy hatred. Sensuality absolutely must be killed because it robs us of the life of grace by making us resist God.
>
> (*Legenda minore* I. 10)

However Catherine's extreme fasting is interpreted, it must be placed in the context of her remarkable achievements in the public world. She counseled and scolded popes and cardinals; she taught, traveled, preached, and tended the sick and dying when plague broke out in Siena again in 1374. Using her influence to intervene in the politics of various Italian city-states, she went to Avignon to plead with Pope Gregory XI to return to Rome. She also founded a women's monastery in Siena. Ironically, in spite of her own public activity, it was a monastery of strict observance and enclosure. Catherine used her body harshly, yet there was a connection between her asceticism and her ability to act in roles for which she was not only untrained, but vigorously socialized to consider beyond her reach. As a third order Dominican (living in community, but without taking monastic vows), Catherine worked within the ecclesiastical structures of her time. But a new, and far more dangerous, kind of piety was in the air. Operating outside the control of the Church, the new piety placed those who practiced it in danger of being accused of heresy. Church leaders also perceived the communities and individuals we discuss next as dangerous to social order and ecclesiastical authority.

The Devotio Moderna

The most popular book of the fifteenth century, Thomas á Kempis's *Imitation of Christ*, came from the Devotio Moderna (modern devotion) movement. The founder of the *Devotio* was a Dutch Carthusian monk, Geert Groote (1340–84), who left his monastery about 1380 to become an itinerant preacher. Before Groote died of the plague in 1384 at the age of 44, he traveled throughout Flanders preaching both institutional and individual reform. Those who followed his teaching began to live together, the better to inspire, challenge, and encourage each other to greater devotion. But Groote did not intend to originate another monastic Order (the founding of new monastic Orders had been forbidden at the Fourth Lateran Council in 1215). The charter of the first community of the *Devotio Moderna* (1379) was for a community of "poor women, living alone" (this is, without oversight by an established Order), laywomen who took no religious vows, had no special dress, no common purse, and no common religious exercises. Each woman earned and cooked her own food, having in common only the house and its maintenance. What was new about the *Devotio* was the claim that piety could be practiced as effectively outside as inside a monastery.

Groote originally envisioned communities bonded by an inner resolve and shaped by their life in community, but as the movement grew and hundreds of sister-houses and brother-houses spread across the Netherlands and through the German Empire, France, and Italy, the sisters and brothers were forced to abandon the freeform communities intended by their founder. To escape the charges of heresy that threatened religious groups whose social and religious loyalties were unclear to outsiders, they affiliated with recognized religious orders. The sister-houses began to take vows; at first they only vowed chastity, but by the end of the fourteenth century they became Third-Order Franciscans and were called "Sisters of the Common Life." The "Brethren of the Common Life" became Augustinian monks in 1394. As Third-Order Franciscans, the Sisters of the Common Life retained their lay status, while the Brothers largely became priests.

Both brothers and sisters practiced what they called "inner devotion." Even though inner, however, it was not individual, but profoundly shaped by the community. Attention was paid to bodies as well as minds: Actions and gestures were recognized not only as expressing inner dispositions and revealing them to others, but also as *producing* the attitudes they expressed.

> Our bowing at the gospel and the bodily posture of reverence are symbols of the reverence of our minds. Moreover, the outward observance is *a means to induce inward reverence.* A bent posture does admirably befit devotion of mind, *for the motions of the spirit do bear a relation to the posture of the body.*
>
>   (Thomas á Kempis, *Opera omnia*, ed. Pohl (1902–18): 7: 97; emphasis added)

The *Devotio Moderna* movement recognized bodies' communicative power:

> The greatest utility of bodies is in their use as signs. For from them are made many signs necessary for our salvation. Nor do we know the movements of one another's souls but by sensible signs.
>
> (Guigo I, *Meditations* 46)

Although medieval authors often used harshly disparaging rhetoric about bodies, they also recognized bodies as *method* in the religious life. The interconnection of body and soul meant that when body is affected (as in fasting), so is soul. Thus, the management of food and sex was considered central to piety.

Criticism of the medieval Church developed in the *Devotio Moderna* based on a comparison of an imagined ancient church and the present church. Adherents of the movement desired a Christian life patterned after that of the apostles, without dependence on ecclesiastical authority, but nevertheless obedient to the Church.

Jan van Ruysbroeck (1293–1381), a follower of Meister Eckhart, was prior of a monastery before he became an adherent of the *Devotio*. He did not, however, consider monastic life essential to the "perfect life." He taught that the working life of an ordinary person could be a form for the practice of piety. Like Eckhart, Ruysbroeck was concerned to integrate contemplation and action. Unlike Eckhart, Ruysbroeck emphasized the importance of feeling for what he called the "God-seeing life."

> When we possess the God-seeing life, we *feel* ourselves to be living in God; and from out of that life in which we *feel* God in ourselves there shines forth upon the face of our inmost being a brightness which enlightens our reason, and is an intermediary between ourselves and God. And if we, with our enlightened reason, abide within ourselves in this brightness, we *feel* that our created life incessantly immerses itself in its eternal life, there we *experience* the transformation of our whole selves in God; and thereby we *feel* ourselves to be wholly enwrapped in God. And after this there follows the way of *feeling*: namely, that we *feel* ourselves to be one with God; for through the transformation in God, we *feel* ourselves to be swallowed up in the fathomless abyss of our eternal blessedness, wherein we can nevermore find any distinction between ourselves and God. And this is our highest *feeling*, which we cannot *experience* in any other way than in the immersion in love. And therefore, so soon as we are uplifted and drawn into our highest *feeling*, all our powers stand idle in essential fruition; but our powers do not pass away into nothingness, for then we should lose our created being. And as long as we stand idle, with an inclined spirit, and with open eyes, but without reflection, so long we can contemplate and have fruition. But at the very moment at which we seek to prove and to comprehend what it is that we *feel*, we fall back into reason, and there we find a distinction and an otherness between ourselves and God, and find God outside ourselves in incomprehensibility.
>
> (*The Sparkling Stone*, "How We, though One with God,
> Must Eternally Remain Other than God," 10; emphasis added)

Ruysbroeck emphasized reason's secondary role in mystical apprehension of God. The quotation also corrects Eckhart's condemned teaching that it is possible to achieve full union with God in this life, a union so complete that creature and Creator became more indistinguishable than a drop of water in the vat of wine. Ruysbroeck avoided the question of whether the union of the mystic with God is an actuality by defining the union as a state of consciousness, a *feeling*:

> And if we, with our enlightened reason abide within ourselves in this brightness, we *feel* that our created life incessantly immerses itself in its eternal life. But when we follow the brightness above reason with a simple sight, and with a willing leaning out of ourselves, toward our highest life, there we *experience* the transformation of our whole selves in God, and thereby we *feel* ourselves to be wholly wrapped in God.

The *Devotio Moderna* emphasized mystical union as a source of energy for both the active and the contemplative life. Each individual's "highest feeling" occurred, not in private contemplation, but in the context of the "common life" of the sisters or brothers. Mystical experience was the foundation of the active life-in-community. When recognized and affirmed by a community, Ruysbroeck said, mystical contemplation becomes "second nature," as "natural" as "life according to nature." "And *from these riches there comes the common life.*"

The Merode altarpiece

At the height of interest in the *Devotio Moderna* and in the same geographical location, a new art developed in response to new devotional requirements. The new style was aided by a new medium, oil paints. In the thirteenth and fourteenth centuries artists used tempura paint, made by mixing ground pigments with egg yoke. In Flanders in the early fifteenth century, the invention of oil-based paints produced glazes that allowed subtle variations of tone, luminous highlights, and richer shades than had previously been possible. The Merode Altarpiece, painted in 1425 by the so-called "Master of Flemalle" (probably Robert Campin), exhibited the capability of oil paints to reproduce and heighten visual reality (see figure 5.1).

Viewers are invited to be present, as the donors are present in the left wing of the altarpiece, at a scriptural event occurring in a Flemish domestic interior. The integration of spiritual and familiar occurs in a spatial world of everyday reality in which a supernatural event occurs. A tiny infant Christ carrying a cross on his shoulder descends toward the Virgin. Mary is not yet aware of Gabriel's presence, though a candle has already been extinguished by Gabriel's breezy entrance. The annunciation is about to occur (see CD Rom figure 5.3).

In the left wing, the donors of the altarpiece wait. The arms of the city of Malines appear on the badge of the messenger, hat in hand, just behind them. In the right wing, Joseph, surrounded by the tools of his trade, prepares a mousetrap with which to trap the devil. The miracle of Christ's incarnation appears in the midst of an ordinary (if rather wealthy) room, viewed by ordinary people, surrounded by objects of daily life. The sacred event has been given a new immediacy even as it conflates the entire Christian story from the annunciation to Christ carrying his cross. Significantly,

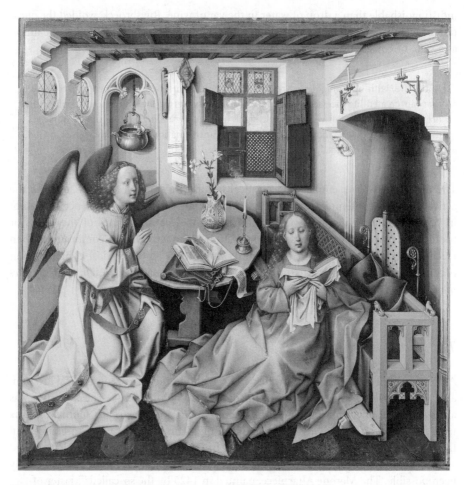

Figure 5.1 Merode Altarpiece, *The Annunciation Triptych*, Robert Campin and assistant, oil on wood, c.1425.
The illusion of naturalness disguises the symbolic character of the details of the altarpiece. The rosebush, the violets, the daisies and the lilies symbolize the Virgin's attributes – charity, humility, and purity. The washbasin and the towel also symbolize Mary, the "vessel most clean" and "well of living waters." The Hebrew letters on the vase symbolize the "old," out of which the "new" lilies spring. The Metropolitan Museum of Art, the Cloisters Collection, 1956 (56. 70). Photograph, all rights reserved, the Metropolitan Museum of Art.

contemporaries simultaneously praised the piety and the realism of the Flemish painters.

READING

Jan van Ruysbroeck, *The Sparkling Stone*
Catherine of Siena, *A Treatise of Divine Providence*; Catherine of Genoa, *Treatise on Purgatory*, in Ray C. Petry (ed.) (1957) *Late Medieval Mysticism*

4   Fourteenth-century Realism and Nominalism

A common cluster of ideas is discernible among fourteenth-century mystics, popular proverbs, and scholastics as scholastic philosophers explored common concerns and reworked common questions, articulating them philosophically. Problems and questions are often more significant than the proposed answers because it is the problems that motivate, provide the energy, and often shape the answers or, more frequently, direct a transition into other questions.

Popular realism

Most fourteenth-century people were neither mystics nor scholastic philosophers, but all seemed to be "realists." Realism refers to the conviction that ideas have reality in themselves. From a realist perspective, particular experiences are instances or examples of the ideas that order human experience. Thus, realists believe that individual experiences can be classified according to already-established categories; they can even be summarized and interpreted in a parable to illustrate a general truth. Medieval proverbs proliferated. Hundreds are attested in every European nation or territory. A few originated in classical literature, but most had medieval origins. The tone is largely resigned, accepting whatever happens. For example:

The big fishes eat the smaller.
The poorly dressed put their backs to the wind.
In need one accepts the devil's help.
No one is chaste unless he can't help it.
No horse is so well shod that it cannot slip.

It is interesting to imagine the occasions to which these proverbs were applied. Other proverbs exhort:

Onward!
Better next time.
The Lord helps those who help themselves.
Not somehow, but triumphantly.

Medieval proverbs simultaneously expressed a rigidly stratified social and ideological world and offered a response to that world. To the few who tried to think in a rigorously systematic way, the same question occurred, namely, whether one should begin with general ideas, deducing from them the meaning of particular experiences; or whether one should start with individual experiences and *build up* conceptions of reality from them.

Scholasticism

Scholastic philosophers occupied a different social location than that of the brewer of ale, Margery Kempe; the hermit, Richard Rolle; or the anchoress, Julian of Norwich.

Meister Eckhart, academic and monk, was closer to the social niche of scholastic philosophers since both he and John Duns Scotus (d. 1308, at the age of 42) lectured at the University of Paris early in the fourteenth century. John Scotus was given the derogatory nickname "duns" (dunce) in the seventeenth century. In his own time he was called the "subtle doctor" (*doctor subtilis*). William of Ockham (d. 1349) was called the "venerable inceptor" (*inceptor venerabilis*). Both were Franciscans. Their thought is precise, highly technical theology.

The "scholastic doctors" were Luther's villains. He caricatured them, making them the foil for his own theology. Partly due to Luther's scorn, the lore about the scholastics that has reached our time pictures them arguing about how many angels can dance on the head of a pin, a canard that appears nowhere in scholastic literature. Scholastics are also accused of arguing about how many teeth a horse has, rather than simply counting a horse's teeth. This too is false. The first experimental scientists were scholastics – for example, Roger Bacon and Robert Grosseteste – who would have been the first to count, rather than argue. Scholastics combined philosophical inquiry with experimental science in the fields of medicine, optics, radiation, and mathematics.

Scholasticism had several important forebears. Its foundations were laid by Augustine's statement that "to believe is to ponder with assent" (*De doctrina christiana*). His formula was "understand so that you may believe; believe so that you may understand" (*De praedestinatione sanctorum*). Boethius' commentaries on Aristotle provided medieval thinkers with their knowledge of logic. His principle that philosophy should serve theology, enabling belief, was fundamental to scholasticism. In the ninth century John Scotus Erigena distinguished authority from reason, saying that authority (revelation, scripture) is the main source of knowledge of God, but that reason has the crucial task of investigating and expounding the data of authority. John Scotus also supplied the method of dialectic, by which theological statements were compared with one another and contradictory statements reconciled. In the eleventh century, Anselm demonstrated that reason could explore theological truths without endangering faith. Abelard also contributed to scholasticism's dialectical method. Thomas Aquinas, the master of dialectic, was the immediate forebear of scholastic philosophy. His writings presented a question and possible responses, followed by a discussion into which he wove together an answer from various strands of the several responses, rejecting incompatible strands. He sought to demonstrate that faith and reason, clearly distinguished, complement and complete one another.

The cohesive universe of earlier thinkers was conspicuously missing from fourteenth-century philosophy. In Augustine's, Bonaventure's, or Thomas Aquinas' universe, one could start with the sensible world, the world closest to hand, and ascend to God by logical steps. In the fourteenth century, a *contingent* universe emerged (at least in the minds of a few educated men), a disturbing world, in which nothing exists by necessity. A new arbitrariness, gaps between the steps of Bonaventure's "mind's road to God," appeared. Thomas' synthesis, in which reason operates on sensible data and faith on revelation, was no longer conceptually compelling. It was not clear that reason could simply be added to faith without any conflict between the two. Nor was it clear that faith can yield knowledge of God except perhaps a vague sense of God's absolute, arbitrary and unknowable power, for God's power could not be expected to operate according to human logic. New questions were asked: Is human reason capable of *any* knowledge of God? Is the world a trustworthy place for humans? For philosophers, as well as people who were not philosophers, these questions were made immediate and intense by the raging of the plague, in which philosophers met painful and premature death along with everyone else.

Similarly, fourteenth-century mystics agreed that the categories of human reason were suspended in mystical experience. They sought to experience God directly, beyond or outside of rational processes. Some, like Catherine of Siena and Meister Eckhart, used the word "reason" in odd ways – not to indicate logical process, but to identify an interior "place" at which God could be encountered in vivid dialogue. Others denied reason's ability to know God. Why did these changes in perceptions of human being, the world and God occur? Like mystics, the scholastic theologians must be understood in the context of the pandemic plague of the mid-fourteenth century.

Plague

From early in the fourteenth century, severe crises of food supply were frequent. The food surplus of the preceding centuries had allowed the European population to increase by 30 percent since the tenth century. But in 1309, crop failures caused food shortages and brought about a continent-wide famine, the first famine in over 250 years. By mid-century, plague swept across western European populations weakened by 50 years of endemic malnutrition.

Yet already high fertility rates continued to increase. Townspeople seized harvests from the surrounding countryside, leaving rural people to starve. Even the wealthy and competently administered city of Florence could not avoid the terror and social chaos caused by hunger. In 1347, although bread was issued daily to 94,000 people, chroniclers estimate that 4,000 people died every day. The Florentine chronicler Giovanni Villani wrote:

> The famine was felt not only in Florence, but also in Tuscany and Italy. And so terrible was it that the Sienese, the Luchese, the Pistolese, and many other townsmen drove from their territories all the beggars because they could not support them. The agitation of the Florentine people at the market of San Michele was so great that it was necessary to protect officials by means of guards fitted out with an axe and block to punish rioters on the spot with the loss of their hands and feet.

Sienese chronicler Agnolo di Tura buried his five children with his own hands. "No one wept for the dead," he wrote, "because everyone expected death himself." In a world in which the arbitrary power of disease reigned, scholastics' attempt to understand God's power was not remote from common interests. Their theologies are discussed below.

The Condemnations of 1277

The intellectual world of the fourteenth century was centered in universities. In 1277, three years after Thomas Aquinas' death, 219 theological propositions, influenced by Aristotle, mediated to the West by Arab commentators like Averroes and Avicenna, were condemned by the bishop of Paris. The bishop's list was crude, taken out of context, hastily compiled, and sometimes inaccurate. Several of Thomas Aquinas' teachings were condemned, but they were reinstated after his canonization in 1325. Two teachings, derived from Aristotle, were especially targeted for condemnation: first, the idea that an individual's distinction from other individuals is based on *matter* (the physical component), rather than on separate souls or intellects; second, that intellect is more important than will. Also condemned was the proposition "that God acts of necessity and not freely." The Condemnations of 1277 formulated the intellectual questions for the next generation of scholars, among them John Scotus and William of Ockham.

The via antiqua: *John Duns Scotus*

John Scotus represented what William of Ockham, roughly 40 years later, called the *via antiqua*. A realist, Scotus believed that ideas are the primary existing realities. He used the Aristotelian vocabulary of the thirteenth century – terms like matter, form, universal, individual, and will. His innovation was to introduce *discontinuity* into the structures of thought.

Scotus rejected Thomas's position that every individual in a species has the same "nature," differing only in matter. Scotus wanted to identify some determinate character of each individual through positive and necessary characteristics, not through an accidental one (matter). He called individual character *haecceity*, this-ness. Each individual being, Scotus said, has a unique and unrepeatable "character" that is not reducible either to intellect or to matter, but is securely located in ultimate reality itself, namely in God. He described *haecceity*: "This entity is included neither in specific form, nor in the matter to which it is linked; we must look for it outside form, outside matter, outside composite being . . . *We must look for haecceity in ultimate reality.*"

Scotus disagreed with Thomas's identification of reason as the primary human faculty, saying that the will has primacy over understanding because the will "commands understanding," directing reason to consider this or that object. It is, therefore, the will that is the direct expression of the individual's *haecceity*. The will is not irrational, but neither is it primarily directed by knowledge.

Insisting that things could be other than they are, Scotus rejected the determinism that earlier thinkers had found reassuring. Against Anselm's teaching that God acts *of necessity*, Scotus taught that God acts *freely*, and could have acted otherwise than he did in creation, Incarnation, and other activities. "There is no cause for the divine will to have willed this or that, other than the fact that the divine will is the divine will." Scotus was concerned to protect God's *freedom*.

The via moderna: *William of Ockham*

To the problem of what can be known in a contingent universe, a universe in which things could be other than they are, the nominalist, William of Ockham (d. 1347), proceeded in the opposite direction from Scotus. While Scotus wanted to establish the conceptual order (including individuals) in ultimate reality, William sought to guarantee the reality of what lay *outside* the conceptual order. Scotus sought a metaphysical basis for all concepts; Ockham reduced all concepts to individual occurrences, rejecting as unreal anything that could not be found in individual existence.

As a nominalist, William of Ockham believed that only the name is common to things called by that name. He did not coin the term "nominalist," but he revalued it and used it in a different intellectual climate from that of its earlier advocates. For William, the "universals" were not the primary reality; the concept "humanity" is not more real than the individual humans from whom the concept is collected. Are there universals, then? And if so, what is their function? William answered that universals are the *signification of words that designate ideas*. Universals are used in propositions, he said, to replace the things they designate. Primary knowledge, however, is *intuition of individual things*.

William's designation of the individual as the primary reality entailed different values from those of a realist. For nominalists, knowledge of genus, understood as a collection of individuals, is certainly possible. But there is a loss of precision in knowing a genus. The concept of genus is less distinct than knowledge of species, which is closer to individual entities. The modern sense of "abstraction" as something removed from particular reality comes from fourteenth-century nominalists. One nominalist wrote, "It is nobler to know an individual than to know it in an abstract universal manner."

Outside the mind with its ability to collect and group entities, William said, everything is singular. His famous "razor" referred to his refusal to acknowledge anything but individuals as actually existing. His idea was not to complicate thought by admitting more steps than are absolutely necessary to a logical process. William narrowed the arena of philosophical inquiry to "what is accessible to experience and susceptible of analysis."

What did this mean for theology? William taught that there is no "natural" knowledge of God or of God's attributes. There is only faith in revelation. As with Scotus, William's God acts freely, without necessity, but William distinguished between God's "absolute power" and God's "ordained power." God's ordained power acts in orderly ways to maintain the created world. In the exercise of his absolute power, however, God is not limited but could, at any moment, decree otherwise than he has decreed. By his absolute power, God can do anything at all except what is contradictory; God could also perform directly what is now performed through secondary causes.

William's religious interest was in protecting God's transcendence – God's freedom to act in unanticipated ways. Extreme nominalists, like the Englishman Robert Holcot (d. 1349), took God's freedom to the extreme of divine arbitrariness. In order to emphasize God's absolute freedom he said, "Someone loving God less could be loved by God more; God could deceive or mislead a person, making him believe what is not true."

The Church: Marsilius of Padua

Both philosophers and mystics were increasingly critical of the state of the Church. For nominalists who believed that only individuals actually exist, more pressure was placed on the actual Church than on a transcendent entity called "the Church."

Two nominalist philosophers criticized the contemporary Church, Marsilius of Padua (d. 1343) and William of Ockham. Marsilius was the first to suggest that lay intervention was needed to correct the Church's abuses of power. He denied that the Church was autonomous as an institution and demanded that the Church be accountable to its members. He also advocated that papal and ecclesiastical jurisdiction should be governed by scripture.

This critique would occur repeatedly in the next two centuries. Comparing the "early Church" and the present Church, Marsilius said that the disciples and apostles lived in poverty, simplicity, and equality, and thus that spiritual power should not be equated with temporal power. Differences between clergy and laity should be minimized, he said, and the Christian community as a whole should decide matters of faith and doctrine. The pope, elected by the people, should merely represent the community's decisions, up to and including excommunication. Marsilius was excommunicated for these teachings. He was an early victim of the plague, as was William of Ockham, who was also excommunicated for his criticism of the Church.

William was less extreme than Marsilius. He believed that the Church was indispensable to the Christian because it provided the sacraments necessary for salvation. He denied, however, that the Church in its existing state was adequate. His views apparently resonated with many others, since they were condemned twice – during his lifetime in 1339–40, and again in 1473.

Like Marsilius, William advocated the apostolic ideal. Christ had renounced all temporal possessions, he said, so his successors had no right to wealth. He extended this principle not only to the Church as an institution, but also to all individuals exercising spiritual power. The pope is not different from other men; he too is liable to sin and error. The office confers no special graces, but makes lapses from grace more visible and shocking. A pope who falls into error, he said, should be deposed by the emperor.

William maintained the idea of a universal Church, but it differed considerably from the realist idea of the Church. For nominalists, the Church was made up of individual Christians; it was not an abstract idea or an institution. William's "Church" was composed of all believers from the time of the apostles forward who did not err against the faith.

These thinkers, the religious movements examined in the following section, and mystics had in common a reinterpretation of the source and nature of spiritual power. Each sought an authority alternative to the Church, whether scripture, an idealized picture of the "early Church," or the subjective authority of a vivid relationship with God. In the fourteenth century, the Church was criticized for its institutional and temporal power and wealth and for its leaders' abuses.

READING

Excerpts from John Duns Scotus's *Commentary on the Sentences* and William of Ockham's *Eight Questions on the Power of the Pope*, in Ray C. Petry (ed.) (1957) *Late Medieval Mysticism*

5 Medieval Piety and Heresy

Complaints about the fourteenth-century Church were matched by clergy complaints about poor church attendance and widespread unbelief. In 1311 the preacher Giordano of Pisa said:

Who nowadays believes in the good things unseen, the good things of paradise? Who cares about them? They do not know what they are. Today the whole world is full of this sin. Nowadays they feel no fear of the threats and pains of hell. They simply do not believe in them. They do not place hope in any other life than the present.

Which beliefs and doctrines were doubted? Sermons indicate that many found it diffi-cult to accept the Fourth Lateran Council's (1215) declaration that the eucharistic bread and wine are changed in substance (transubstantiated) into the body and blood of Christ. Other frequently doubted doctrines included the resurrection of Christ from the dead and the general resurrection. Moreover, Franciscan and Dominican preachers agreed that voracious thirst for money, arrogance, and lust were common.

Piety and heresy were often difficult to distinguish in the fourteenth century. No leaders dominated; rather, people were thinking religiously for themselves. The concept of heresy as dissident belief had always been a feature of Christianity. In the early church it was even thought to have some positive effects; no less an authority than St Paul had said, "There must be heresies." Heresy provoked the refining of theology and tested the faithful. Early church heresies were usually alternative interpretations of Christian belief. They originated with men Augustine acknowledged as "great minds." But dissident theology and doctrine did not prompt most fourteenth-century heresies; instead they were usually motivated by a desire to return to apostolic simplicity and zeal. "Heretics" were often *more*, rather than less, religious than their neighbors.

In the fourteenth century as in the early church, church leaders did not think of heresy as either "alternative interpretations" of Christian belief and practice, or as devo-tion to a higher religious standard but, quite simply, as the work of the devil. A four-teenth-century "type" of the heretic was drawn: heretics exhibited pride, a superficial appearance of piety, sexual libertinism and, in contrast to the openness of Catholic preaching and worship, heretics were secretive. Robert Grosseteste's (1175–1253) defin-ition of heresy was widely quoted. A heresy, he said, is an opinion contrary to scripture, publicly avowed, and obstinately defended.

Heresy was deeply frightening to people who believed in a last judgment that would result in an eternity spent in heaven or hell. Heresy was considered contagious, spread-ing in families and communities. There was also a physiology of heresy. It was thought that the same imbalance of bodily humors that caused illness affected moral and cog-nitive functions. This theory was supported by the spread of heresy through Europe at the same time that "leprosy" – anything showing unpleasantly on the skin, including lesions, boils, rashes, and ulcers – was spreading. Both leprosy and heresy appeared sud-denly, spread rapidly, were seldom cured, were passed on from parents to children, and were most virulent among the poor.

All heresies were assumed to be ancient, their structures well known and predictable. In the twelfth century, Bernard of Clairvaux wrote: "For I do not recall having heard anything new or strange in all their mouthings, numerous as they are, but that which is worn by use and long agitated by the heretics of old, and which has been well threshed and winnowed by our theologians." Since the devil had no new ideas, four-teenth-century theologians copied out descriptions of heresies from patristic authors rather than expose themselves to risk of contamination by observing contemporary heretics.

Inquisition

The French philosopher Michel Foucault analyzed power in a way that provides insight into the medieval Church and state. "Strong power," he said, is power that *attracts*, making people want to adopt the requirements and rewards of the institution. Weak power occurs when strong power fails; it forces or compels people to submit. The medieval Church had lost its attractive force for large numbers of people; it thus resorted to weak power.

Religious coercion existed in the fourth century, but penalties were limited to excommunication, exile, and refusal of burial in consecrated ground. Medieval people, however, believed that it was the duty of the Church and the state to protect society by exterminating heresy. It appears to have been widely believed that a stubborn heretic's only chance of salvation lay in torture and execution during which, *in extremis*, s/he might repent and be converted. The first stage of medieval inquisition was the episcopal inquisition, conducted by bishops. In 1184 Pope Lucius III established guidelines for the detection of heresy and procedures for dealing with it. He required bishops to visit parishes at least twice a year to identify and prosecute heretics. Since heresy was also considered treason against the state, the death sentence was mandatory for persistent dissenters.

The thirteenth century saw the origin of the papal Inquisition. In the early thirteenth century, Pope Innocent III had accepted new groups – like the Franciscans and Dominicans – that sought acknowledgment and authorization by the Church; he also permitted laymen to preach, provided they limited themselves to moral exhortation and left doctrine to the clergy. But in 1241 Pope Gregory IX initiated a different policy. Rather than integrating religious energies into the Church, he appointed special agents to hunt out heresy. These agents were much more efficient than bishops, and the papal Inquisition was born. It officially ended only in 1854. Within about a half century from the origin of the inefficient episcopal inquisition, a centralized, efficient, and effective Inquisition was in place.

Yet the Inquisition was not the massive, centralized bureaucracy it later became. In the fourteenth century, inquisitors (usually Dominicans) traveled to places rumored to harbor heresy in order to discover and exterminate it. They often had a difficult job convincing communities to support their investigations and interrogations, and their success was limited. Bernard Gui acknowledged this in his handbook, *The Conduct of the Inquisition of Heretical Depravity* (1324). He wrote:

> For it is extremely difficult to catch heretics when they themselves do not frankly avow error but conceal it, or when sure and sufficient evidence against them is not at hand. Under such circumstances, serious problems beset the investigator from every side. For on the one hand, his conscience torments him if an individual is punished who has neither confessed nor been proved guilty; on the other, it causes even more anguish to the mind of the inquisitor, familiar through much experience with the falsity, cunning, and malice of such persons, if by their wily astuteness they escape punishment, to the detriment of the faith, since thereby they are strengthened, multiplied, and rendered more crafty.

The papal Inquisition was the first international police force. Inquisitors were appointed for long periods so that their knowledge and skills could be developed and refined.

Records were kept, and handbooks outlining questions were written. Witnesses were examined secretly so that accusers were not seen by the accused, nor was the accused informed of the charges against her/him. True repentance could be demonstrated only by full confession of all facts and accomplices, and torture was used.

From the Church's perspective, the Holy Office of Inquisition was considered a penitential office, aiming at spiritual reconciliation and the restoration of the wayward to the community of the faithful. Based on the common assumption that pain can produce religious insight, the Inquisition's methods were modeled after ascetic practices. "The fasts, vigils, scourging, and every other form of voluntary self-torture that the mystics inflicted on their own persons were turned against the heretics as an instrument of law" (Glucklich, 2001: 163). Inquisitors sometimes sincerely desired the restitution of the accused and hesitated to condemn them. Those found guilty of small offenses, like respect for a heretical preacher, might make atonement by a pilgrimage. Those who confessed serious doctrinal errors were imprisoned. Those who refused to recant their errors, or who, having recanted were again accused, were handed over to the secular authorities for execution, since the Church was forbidden to shed blood.

The most numerous fourteenth-century groups pursued by the Inquisition were Jews, Cathars (or Albigensians), Waldensians, and adherents of the Heresy of the Free Spirit.

Jews

Handbooks that circulated from the thirteenth century forward included Jews in inquisitors' jurisdiction in certain cases. These included alleged blasphemy against Christians or Christian beliefs, practicing usury, magic and sorcery, proselytizing among Christians, or aiding and receiving Jews who had converted to Christianity and "relapsed" to Judaism. Although Jews were routinely and haphazardly persecuted in the eleventh and twelfth centuries, it was mostly by mobs. Local bishops and the pope protected Jews when they could. Repeated papal injunctions stipulated that Jews' lives must not be endangered, that they were not to be baptized by force, nor should their cemeteries be desecrated – acts that occurred frequently enough to prompt these reiterations. Pope Gregory IX, who appointed official inquisitors, blamed the crusaders for slaughtering over 2,500 Jews.

Accusations against Jews were stimulated by the malnutrition, plague, and religious unrest of the fourteenth century as scapegoats were sought to vent the general fear and anger of the Christian population. Accusations that Jews committed crimes (like killing children and poisoning wells) date from the time of the crusades. Moreover, it was widely thought that Jews were deceitful, wicked, dangerous and, since rationality was thought to be identical with Christianity, irrational. Accusations were also encouraged by the existence of a prosecuting institution.

Medieval anti-Jewish legends were folklore, but the religious hatred that motivated them had concrete social effects. Historian Christopher Ocker (1998) relates the increase of accusations in the fourteenth century to new popular devotion to the passion of Christ. Encouraged by Franciscan preaching imaginatively to suffer with Christ, it was apparently a short step to blaming contemporary Jews for Christ's suffering. Peter the

Venerable said (in 1156), "Christ still feels completely Jewish insults." Ironically, Ocker writes, "love prompted hatred and the desire for vengeance."

Cathars

Cathars (from Greek "cathari," pure), also called Albigensians (from the town of Albi, their center) in Southern France, were also numerous in northern Italy and along the Rhine Valley in southern Germany. Cathars were dualists; they believed in warring cosmic powers of good (spirit) and evil (matter). They taught that creation originated in a battle in heaven between Satan and God in which Satan trapped the angels in bodies. (The angels wept when they discovered themselves in sexually differentiated bodies, foreseeing how much difficulty it would cause!) Cathars believed that soul and body are utterly opposed to one another. Souls wander from body to body until they arrive at the body of a *perfecti* (a Cathar who had reached perfection) and are redeemed.

Eversin of Steinfeld represents the Cathars as saying:

> We are the poor of Christ, wandering people; fleeing from city to city like sheep in the midst of wolves, we suffer persecution with the apostles and the martyrs. We lead a holy life, fasting, abstaining, working and praying by day and night, seeking in these things the necessities of life. We live thus because we are not of this world; you are lovers of the world, at peace with the world because you are worldly. False apostles have corrupted the word of Christ for their own ends and have led you and your fathers astray. We and our fathers, the successors of the apostles, have remained in the grace of Christ, and will remain so until the end of the world. To distinguish between you and us Christ said, "By their fruits ye shall know them." Our fruits are following in the footsteps of Christ.

Because they believed the material world to be evil, they condemned marriage, rejected the sacraments, refused to eat meat, milk, eggs, or any other foods coming from animal bodies. They also rejected orthodox doctrines of purgatory, hell, and the resurrection of body. Like the Manichaeans of the fourth century (with whom they were frequently identified) there were two classes of members, believers who lived ordinary secular lives and the *perfecti* or elect who practiced rigorous asceticism. A sermon against the Cathars by Eckbert of Schonau lists (among others) the following beliefs: infant baptism is useless until the child seek baptism of its own volition; there is no baptism by water; instead, there is a secret baptism by fire and the holy spirit; purgatory is denied, saying that the souls of the dead pass to eternal happiness or eternal damnation at the moment of death; they deny the efficacy of the mass; they alone can consecrate the elements into the body and blood of Christ; they deny that Christ was born of a virgin and deny the true flesh of Christ; and they believe human souls to be apostate spirits which can deserve salvation through good works, but only in their sect.

Women in early Cathar communities had opportunities not available to them in society or the Church. They preached, taught, and held *perfecti* status. As the movement matured, however, women were gradually excluded from leadership roles. After practicing various asceticisms during her lifetime, a member received the one Cathar sacrament on her deathbed, the *consolomentum*, or baptism of the Holy Spirit by the laying on of hands.

In certain geographical areas, Cathars were a major threat to the Catholic Church. By the fourteenth century, however, they had been exterminated by ruthless persecution, counter-preaching, and by the first crusade (1208–18) against heretical Christians. Clearly, Cathars held different beliefs and practices than Catholics. It is less easy to see why the Waldensians were not accepted and integrated into the Church.

Waldensians

An inquisitorial handbook, the *Passau Anonymous* (1260), described the Waldensians' social location and values:

> Heretics are to be recognized by their morals and their words. In moral behavior they are composed and modest. They take no pride in their clothing, which is neither too rich nor too abject. They do not undertake any business because they seek to avoid lying and oaths and fraud, but they make their living by the work of their hands, as craftsmen; their learned men are weavers and textile workers. They do not increase their riches but are satisfied with necessities. They go neither to taverns, nor to shows, nor to any such vanities. They avoid anger; they are always working, teaching, or learning, and therefore they pray little. They may also be recognized by their words, which are precise and modest.

Waldensians, also called Humiliati, or simply "the Poor," were founded by Valdes (d. 1218). Waldensians were a gospel-based movement without formal structure that might, in another time, have been integrated into the church, but in the thirteenth century, were excluded and radicalized. Valdes (later sources prefix the name "Peter") was a wealthy merchant from Lyons who distributed his wealth to the poor after settling his wife and daughters in a convent. He wanted to preach against Cathars and against the Church's worldliness, but canon law restricted preaching to the clergy. So Valdes appealed directly to Pope Alexander III, who granted him an audience. The pope was apparently much impressed by Waldo's piety and energetic commitment to the gospel, embracing Valdes at the conclusion of the interview. But he forbade him to preach unless invited by local clergy. Later, under Pope Lucius III, both Cathars and Waldensians were placed under the ban of excommunication, but the Waldensians survived and still exist in the Piedmont district of Italy.

The Waldensians were the first popular literacy movement. Valdes taught himself to read vernacular translations of scripture and the Fathers, and it was said of them that "men and women, adults and children, learn and teach unweariedly by day and night; the workman devotes his day to his work, the night to religious instruction." It was also a missionary movement; "the newly converted, after a few days, seek to draw others into the sect." Whatever beliefs and practices were not found in scripture, they said, should be rejected. The religious engagement and activism of Waldensians contrasted sharply with the passivity of most Catholic laypeople. Women were important within the movement, as members, as preachers, and as financial supporters.

The existence of women preachers may reveal part of the appeal of these new religious groups. The *Decretum Gratiani* (1140) had forbidden women to preach, but despite the prohibition, women's preaching was not unknown within the Catholic

Church. Abbesses like Hildegard of Bingen, and saints like Catherine of Siena preached both within their own communities and more broadly. But usually, women listened to male preachers. Perhaps Waldensian women preachers were encouraged by contemporary paintings that depicted legendary women like Catherine of Alexandria, and scriptural women like Mary Magdalene, preaching.

In heretical groups women participated actively in leadership roles. Cathars acknowledged that "good women," like "good men" had "received from Christ and the apostles the power not only to absolve sinners by baptism in the Holy Spirit but also to confer it upon others" (Brenon, 1998: 114). Waldensians were repeatedly accused of unauthorized preaching. Evidence for women's preaching comes from Waldensians' opponents and thus gives no information about women preachers' topics or concerns. Condemning women's preaching, Geoffroy of Auxerre cited Paul's instructions that women are not to speak in churches and that they should ask questions of their husbands at home. The questions are to be asked, he wrote, not "of each other," but "of husbands," and not any husbands whatsoever, but "their own" husbands (Kienzle, 1998: 101). Valdes' women followers, Geoffroy said, are "wretched little women, burdened with sins . . . curious and verbose, forward, shameless, and impudent." He said that women preachers, by reversing the social order, indicated that the end of the world is at hand.

In belief and practice, Waldensians represented an effort to simplify Christianity to what they considered its essentials. They taught that there are only two ways, one of life and one of death, one way leading to heaven and the other to hell. They wanted to eliminate what they considered "excrescences," by which they meant the doctrine of purgatory, religious images, prayers for the dead, and pilgrimages, teaching that it was the responsibility of each individual to work for her own salvation without the help of the institutional Church.

Clergy feared Waldensians' enthusiasm and their evangelism, saying "They are making their first moves now in the humblest way, because they cannot launch an attack. If we admit them, we shall be driven out." As they were excluded from churches, Waldensians' criticism of individual immoral clergy extended to rejection of the sacraments they dispensed. As their criticisms became more and more fundamental, they were increasingly persecuted. As they were increasingly persecuted, they became more and more insistent on preaching and on criticism of the Church that excluded them.

Heresy of the Free Spirit

There were often very minimal differences between mystics who managed to keep the esteem of church authorities and those who came under inquisitional scrutiny. No movement better exemplified the fragility of the line between orthodoxy and heresy than the so-called "heresy of the Free Spirit." The movement, named only by the papal bull (*Ad nostrum*) that condemned it, was not an organized sect. Similar to the early Brothers and Sisters of the Common Life (*Devotio Moderna*), the "movement" was composed of individual mystics who sometimes joined together in informal communities.

Mystics, often themselves accused of heresy, sometimes took the initiative in accusing others. For example, Jan van Ruysbroeck frequently preached against "Free Spirits," and cooperated with inquisitors to identify them. Undeniably, piety had its radical fringes. Some of the Free Spirits, for example, went naked to exemplify their belief that to be without property is to be without sin.

Treatises from the Free Spirits movement were often attributed to Meister Eckhart. Jan van Leeuwen, of the *Devotio Moderna*, wrote: "Before Eckhart's time no one knew of these awful Free Spirits nor of their teachings which all originate in the stupid doctrine he used to preach that we are God's children like Christ without distinction." Free Spirits were accused of teaching 1) autotheism: that complete and permanent identity with God is possible on this earth, that "they could be one with God to the same extent that Christ was one with God;" 2) that people did not need the sacraments of the church; and 3) antinomianism: that after the union with God a person was freed from all restraints and could indulge in or take whatever they needed without sin.

The Frenchwoman Marguerite Porete's lengthy work, *The Mirror of Simple Souls*, was in its time, ascribed to Jan van Ruysbroeck. It was a devotional classic for several centuries; five medieval translations of the original Middle French text exist, as well as two Latin and two Italian translations and an English translation. (In the twentieth century it was published by the Benedictines with official Church approval, the *nihil obstat* and *imprimatur*). Yet its author was burned at the stake for heresy on June 1, 1310 in Paris.

Marguerite was accused of the usual beliefs associated with the Free Spirits, but her careful description of what she believed in *The Mirror* reveal that the accusations caricature her beliefs. She used Eckhart's image of the union of the soul with God as a drop of water in a vat of wine, encouraging accusations of autotheism. The image signaled heresy, but orthodox mystics also used it. One fourteenth-century commentator, referring to the image, wrote: "You can also find it in Tauler, but you must understand him nicely." Marguerite also asked to be understood "nicely": "I beg you who read these words, try to understand them inwardly, in the innermost depths of your understanding, with all the subtle powers at your command, or else you run the risk of failing to understand them at all."

The medium of the soul's union with God, Marguerite said, is love:

> Being completely free and in command on her sea of peace, the soul is nonetheless drowned and loses herself through God, and with him and in him. She loses her identity as does the water from a river when it flows into the sea. Her work is over and she can lose herself in what she has become: love. Love is her only delight and pleasure.
>
> (*Mirror* 17)

Yet Orthodox authors of both the Western and the Eastern Churches taught that Christians participate in God's essential energy, love. No less an authority than St Augustine said that whenever a person loves, she necessarily participates in the God who *is* love.

Porete was accused of believing that the sacraments were unnecessary because she taught that life can have a pervasively sacramental quality: "People . . . who see God as bound by his sacraments and works . . . are silent and miserable for not finding him. But those who find him everywhere through uniting their will to his have a happy and enjoyable life." The liberated soul, she wrote, "does not seek God by penance nor by any sacrament of the holy church, nor by thought, words, or works." She did not advise people to abandon the sacraments, but she did suggest that they were not the only avenue to knowledge and experience of God.

Finally, Porete was accused of antinomianism, of believing that she was above law. She taught that the experience of God's love simultaneously *transcends and incorporates* virtues and religious practices. If the soul, at the "highest stage of her perfection," is "beyond noticing the rules of the church," she wrote, it is because "she has assimilated [each of these] to the point where they are part of her."

If Marguerite Porete had entered a cloister like Mechthild of Magdeburg, a mystic with whom she is often compared, she would probably have attracted little attention. Her active life and the politics surrounding her arrest seem to have contributed more than her teachings to her execution.

By 1334, many "heresies" existed in Western Europe. Some can be differentiated only by location: Bogomils, Apostolics, Free Spirits, extremist Spiritual Franciscans, and mystics of all stripes. No group was powerful, and none had powerful leaders and spokespersons. They existed alongside religious movements that were accepted by the Church, like the *Devotio Moderna*, the Camoldolese, the Capuchin Franciscans, and third-order Franciscans and Dominicans. Together, these religious movements – "orthodox" and "heretical" – represented a great deal of the religious energy and passion of the time.

Italian devotional painting

The fourteenth century was an age of unusual suffering. Catastrophic floods and earthquakes occurred in addition to endemic malnutrition and pandemic plague. "There is evidence of a general shift of climate around 1300 that disrupted long-established ways of life: rivers that had not frozen in living memory now did so; recurrent flooding damaged fields, and a severe deluge of 1315 made people compare it to Noah's flood" (Kieckhefer, 1987: 78). These troubles stimulated new forms of devotion, for conditions of physical vulnerability – hunger, disease, and pain – demand strong spiritual and psychological resources. For example, a new subject in painting depicted the Virgin with one bared breast, either feeding the infant Christ, or pointing to her breast to appeal to Christ for the salvation of sinners huddled in her cloak. The nourishing breast of the Virgin was apparently a highly meaningful image for undernourished and starving people.

New devotions were added to those already practiced: the rosary, stations of the cross, eucharistic devotions, the (literary and artistic) image of the sacred heart, and the Feast of Corpus Christi. Devotional literature proliferated: *ars moriendi*, or art of dying manuals, popular religious songs, vernacular saints' lives, mystical literature, meditations on Christ's sufferings and passion, and particular devotions to a saint, the Virgin, or the Eucharist. Sermons were preached in the open air or town squares, accompanied by histrionic gestures calculated to elicit crowd response.

In societies in which later distinctions between sacred and secular realms did not exist, these devotions were participated in by ecclesiastical and secular rulers, nobles, merchants, and paupers alike. Although highly trained theologians argued the finer points of eucharistic doctrine, it did not require sophistication to recognize that the doctrine of transubstantiation described "a wonderful miracle . . . on which their material and spiritual well-being depended" (Elwood, 1999, 12–13). In colorful Corpus

Christi processions, Christ's body and blood were carried out of the church into streets and town squares, sacralizing the common social world. Hymns summarized the complexities of the doctrine, emphasizing the importance of faith to bridge the gap between what could be seen by the eyes and what must be believed. One hymn read, in part:

> So, the Christian dogma summeth,
> That the bread his flesh becometh,
> And the wine his sacred blood:
> Though we feel it not nor see it,
> Living faith that doth decree it,
> All defects of sense make good.
>
> (Quoted by Elwood, 1999: 16)

Numerous ecclesiastical attempts were made to control popular piety. In order to limit the devotions paid to local and unauthorized saints, the pope claimed the sole right to designate who was a saint. A complex canonization procedure was designed, "an elaborate quasi-judicial process involving scrutiny of witnesses and the composition of a canonization biography or *vita*." In 1215 the Fourth Lateran Council required laypersons to regularize church attendance. Annual confession was required and penalties were imposed; anyone failing to carry out their penances would be denied entrance into church or, on death, denied ecclesiastical burial. Clergy were given greater power over the lives of parishioners than ever before. It was stipulated that confession must be to one's own priest; only with his permission could one confess to another priest. The priest must be careful to inquire about all aspects of the sin confessed, give proper counsel, and assign penance. The priest must keep confession secret under pain of deposition and sentencing to perpetual punishment in monastic confinement. Finally, these newly strict requirements were to be declared frequently in church so that no one could claim ignorance.

New and newly popular themes appeared in paintings such as the *pietà* and the man of sorrows. A study of 700 fourteenth-century Italian panel paintings found that Christ was depicted in 35 percent, the Virgin in 55 percent, unidentified saints in 15 percent, and identified saints in 9 percent of the paintings. Among identified saints, Francis of Assisi, apostles and early martyrs, and Clare of Assisi and Dominic were the most frequently represented. Extra-canonical literature like Jacobus da Voragine's *Golden Legend* and pseudo-Bonaventure's *Meditations of the life of Christ* provided stories that were elaborated in paintings.

What religious sensibilities did fourteenth-century paintings elicit and train? Who were the first viewers? In what context did viewers see religious paintings? What scenes, persons, gestures, moments seem (because of their repetition) to have fascinated people? Did the noticeable increase in realistic painting itself carry religious meaning? Viewers seldom recorded their responses, but by comparing contemporary texts and images, several tentative suggestions can be made about contemporary responses.

By the fourteenth and fifteenth centuries distinctive devotional emphases had emerged from the Friars Minor, or Franciscans (originated in 1223), and the Friars Preachers, or Dominicans (originated 1216). Both Orders understood their mission as outreach and ministry to people's religious needs. But Dominicans and Franciscans cultivated religious engagement differently. Dominicans' chief interest was preaching and education; for several centuries most of the leaders of European thought were Dominicans. Dominicans, specifically ordered to preach against heresy, were educated in theology and philosophy. Francis and his early followers were not priests, and they were not authorized to preach doctrine; instead, they preached penitence, charity, and reform of life. Franciscans' chief interest was conversion of the heart and training of religious affections. Dominicans attempted to persuade minds.

Both Orders had a Second and a Third Order for women. The Second Order were cloistered monks, but the Third-Order Franciscans and Dominicans, halfway between cloister and secular life, led an active life in the secular world. Third-Order Franciscans and Dominicans vowed virginity but, like Catherine of Siena, lived at home, engaged in prayer and service.

Dominicans and Franciscans departed from traditional monastic spirituality by placing less emphasis on the development of an interior life than had earlier medieval monks. Love of neighbor *as a way to love God* was thought essential to religious life. Francis insisted on a lifestyle of complete poverty, not only for individuals but for the whole order, an insistence that barely outlived Francis himself (discussed in chapter 4). Francis's conversion, begun when he gazed at a crucifix in the little Church of San Damiano, continued as he served lepers, overcoming his own disgust and aversion (see CD Rom figure 5.4). He encouraged his followers to similar service: "And they must rejoice when they live among people who are considered to be of little worth and who are looked down upon, among the poor and the powerless, the sick and lepers, and the beggars by the wayside."

A revival of preaching was a strongly felt need in late medieval Europe. The constitutions of the "Order of Preachers" state: "Our order is known to have been founded from the beginning for the sake of preaching and the salvation of souls, and our effort ought above all to be directed primarily and enthusiastically toward being able to be useful to the souls of our neighbors."

Dominicans prepared for preaching by study and meditation. The Dominican Thomas Aquinas' systematic account of Christian faith demonstrated the integrity of intellect and the validity of contemplation as a form of the spiritual life. After his time many other Dominicans, including Meister Eckhart and St John of the Cross, followed the path of the intellect.

Dominicans and Franciscans used the visual arts differently according to their different missions. In religious images influenced by Franciscan spirituality, identification with Christ, especially with his suffering and death predominate. Dominicans used the visual arts to illustrate theological relationships – mystical, moral, or dogmatic. Dominicans taught through painting.

Franciscan devotional painting

The Arena (or Scrovegni) Chapel, Padua, was painted by Giotto di Bondone around 1305. It stands next door to a large, austere Cistercian abbey-church that was dark and forbidding, with little painting. The Scrovegni Chapel was the private chapel of a noble family, but apparently townspeople were not excluded, because shortly after Giotto painted the Scrovegni Chapel, a letter to the Scrovegni family from the abbot of the Cistercian church complained that the abbey-church was deserted as people flocked to the colorful new chapel. To contemporary eyes, Giotto's paintings were startling in their realism. Boccaccio, author of the *Decameron*, wrote: "Giotto was able to paint all natural and artificial subjects in a completely lifelike manner, so that many persons considered them to be real." Moreover, Giotto's paintings are not posed photographs, but *moving pictures* in that they depend on the viewer's knowledge of the actions before and after the "snapshot" (see CD Rom figures 5.5 to 5.8).

In the Arena Chapel, Giotto painted scenes from the life of Mary in four main groups: 1) scenes from Mary's childhood and youth before Christ's birth, based on the Apocryphal *Protoevangelium of James* and the *Gospel of Pseudo-Matthew*; 2) scenes relating to Christ's birth and infancy; 3) Mary's presence at the passion of Christ; and 4) events occurring after Christ's death, like Mary's dormition or death, assumption, and coronation. Abbreviated architectural settings place the focus on the emotional responses of the participants in the sacred scenes (see figure 5.2).

An anonymous fourteenth-century devotional manual, the *Meditations on the Life of Christ* instructed viewers to "meditate on the humanity of Christ, which is given you in this little book," to imagine themselves eye-witnesses and participants in the events described and depicted, and to imaginatively adopt the *feelings* of the sacred figures. Only about a third of the illustrations were completed; the picture sequence ends in the middle of Jesus's public life. The whole passion sequence is missing, but frames for additional illustrations continue throughout the manuscript. In the *Meditations*, images were used to enhance the reader's identification by stimulating her imaginative presence in the events of Christ's life (see CD Rom figures 5.9 to 5.11).

The Upper Basilica of St Francis at Assisi provides a third example of Franciscan painting. Painted in the 1320s or early 1330s, Giotto (and his assistants) depicted Francis' life and ministry in simple yet vivid scenes (see CD Rom figures 5.12 to 5.15).

Dominican devotional painting

Frescos painted by Fra Angelico (Giovanni da Friesole; d. 1387) in monastic cells at the Dominican monastery of San Marco in Florence show scenes from Christ's life that are differently focused than those influenced by Franciscan piety. These are not "moving pictures," but posed scenes. Their purpose is not to arouse emotion, but to stimulate contemplation. Dominican monks appear in the sacred scenes, both observing and modeling the responses expected from the viewer. Meditation on these scenes was preparation for preaching vividly and persuasively on them (see CD Rom figures 5.16 and 5.17).

De modo orandi, a thirteenth-century devotional manual for Dominican novices, instructed novices in the use of gestures and postures to accompany and intensify prayer, many of which are also found in the Dominican figures in Fra Angelico's paintings. The manual states, "specific states of mystical consciousness can be stimulated by deliberately assuming bodily postures" (Hood, 1993: 205). By imitating the founder of the Order, who himself imitated Christ, the novice could begin to preach with his life even before he was permitted to preach with words.

Figure 5.2   Crucifixion, Arena Chapel, Padua, Giotto, 1304–5.
Giotto's *Crucifixion* in the Arena Chapel is very different from contemporary depictions of the crucifixion. In thirteenth-century crucifixes, Christ's body either takes the shape of a graceful S-curve with schematic rendering of the muscles, or an upright figure appears to reign from the cross. Giotto's crucified Christ sags into his knees, which take the weight of his body. The anatomy of his body is naturalistic, suggesting Christ's physical pain rather than his triumphal salvation of the world. Photo AKG Cameraphoto.

The scenes, painted in the cells lived in by their Dominican viewers, are often only slightly related to biblical events. Their goal is not accurate narration but contemplation of the event. By contrast with the emotionally charged narratives Franciscans provided for lay people, the cell frescos at San Marco represent a contemplative and intellectual approach to painting and developed an art that directed viewers to the Orders' specific mandate and goal.

Humanity was made in the image of God, but was the image reflected in the mind, with its capacity for contemplation and mystical experience? Or was God's image to be found in fragile and vulnerable bodies, like Christ's body susceptible to suffering and death? Both interpretations were maintained in the thirteenth and fourteenth centuries. Suffering societies required the strong religious comfort offered by a suffering God. New devotions, new religious movements, strengthened images, and vernacular descriptions of mystical experience arose to meet the need. These resources arose both within and outside the institutional Church. But criticism was also increasing. In chapter 6 we explore continuing and increasing demand for reform of the Body of Christ.

READING

Marguerite Porete, *The Mirror of Simple Souls*, selections, trans. Ellen Babinsky (1993)

6 The Suffering Body of Christ: The Fifteenth Century

Prologue

The fifteenth and sixteenth centuries were the first "space age." New lands were discovered, leading to a new sense of the size and shape of the world and the human place within it. Copernicus, who has been called the father of modern astronomy, was a Polish priest whose writings were published posthumously. He taught that the sun, not the earth, was the center of the universe, thus decentering the earth in space. It was unlikely, he said, that a large body like the sun revolved around a small body like the earth. Copernicus' description of the earth as whirling about the sun, along with the other planets, created a dizzying sense of an infinite universe. The tidy, knowable, and comfortable universe was gone, and with its disappearance religion was increasingly called into question.

Among the authors who participated in Italian renaissance culture, the dominant strain is the individualism that permeated religion, philosophy, and theology. What prompted this attention to the individual? The divorce of the medieval authorities of reason and faith may have been part of the cause. Reaction to the plague's disrespect for human life could have created a "*sauve qui peut*" (usually translated "each man for himself") mentality. But these might equally have led to renewed respect for religious institutions and heightened reverence for authority.

Whatever combination of factors brought about the new interest in the individual, Renaissance men, in common with late-medieval mystics, held the conviction that personal experience was a valid starting point for the acquisition of knowledge. Criticism of received ideas, institutions, and politics, combined with new ways of reading texts and new images in the visual arts, created a shift from external to subjective authority. The opinions of one Renaissance man, Laurentius Valla, were characterized admiringly by one of his friends: "He finds fault with Aristotle's physics. He finds Boethius' Latin barbaric. He destroys religion, professes heretical ideas, scorns the Bible. . . . And has he not taught that the Christian religion is not based on proofs but on belief?" In spite of these views, Nicholas, Cardinal of Cusa, recommended Laurentius Valla to the pope for entrance into the Roman curia, or papal court.

A vivid sense of the value of "man" also characterized the new men of the Italian Renaissance. Marsilio Ficino, a fifteenth-century Florentine humanist wrote: "To him the sky does not seem too high, nor the center of the earth too deep. Time and space do not prevent him from going anywhere at any moment. . . . On all sides he strives to dominate, to be praised, to be eternal, like God."

Yet Renaissance humanists were religious men, even though they were often labeled "atheists" because they criticized the Church. None of them ever professed a through-going philosophical atheism, and the most outspoken among them made his confession and received extreme unction when death approached.

It is important to notice that the Italian Renaissance was a highly class- and gender-affiliated movement. One historian has estimated that "the Renaissance" involved perhaps one or two hundred educated and/or artistic men. Feminist historian Joan Kelly (1985) demonstrated that during the Renaissance, women's family and public roles were significantly curtailed. It was not a renaissance for everyone.

In this chapter, we begin to consider sixteenth-century changes as they emerged from late-medieval societies. By the sixteenth century the population of Europe had recovered from the plagues of the fourteenth century. Although plague recurred about once in every generation into the seventeenth century, it had less and less virulence as populations developed resistance. The sixteenth century saw the beginnings of a distinction between sacred and secular spheres in music, art, and literature. Cervantes wrote the first novel. Montaigne created the essay form to present ideas or argue a thesis. And Shakespeare composed his dramas with no mention of religion.

Twentieth-century British philosopher, R.G. Collingwood, defined "progress" in a way that is useful for considering fifteenth- and sixteenth-century changes. "Progress," he said, is "gain without corresponding loss." Progress, according to this definition, is rare; significant losses accompany most human progress. The fifteenth-century is no exception. There were gains, but corresponding losses must be noted as well. An example will illustrate.

The invention of the printing press by Johann Gensfleisch of Gutenberg at the end of the fifteenth century was an important gain. The printing press spread ideas and values among broader and broader populations as literacy increased. Scholars have claimed that the Protestant reformations of the sixteenth century could not have occurred without the printing press. Hundreds of thousands of pamphlets explaining reformation theology were circulated. Historian Steven Ozment has found over 10,000 titles of such pamphlets. Even people who could not read – still around 80 percent in the sixteenth century – heard pamphlets read aloud in town squares and churches. From reformers' perspective, the printing press represented a significant gain.

What about "corresponding loss?" Printing presses also made possible the circulation of the first broadsheets or newspapers. These regularly featured descriptions of the alleged deeds, trials, and executions of accused witches. Historian Elizabeth Eisenstein (1980) has claimed that the popular large-scale witch persecutions that accompanied *all* the reformations – Catholic and Protestant – depended on the printing press. In these broadsheets, people were *told* that witches caused myriad ills – miscarriages, crop failures, impotence, disease, and accident. When they were also *shown* what witches looked like in the crude woodcuts that illustrated the broadsheets, they learned to look for the cause of their miseries in women familiar to them. It was then that the witch persecutions occurred on a massive scale. The loss of human life on the scale of the witch persecutions must be counted a significant loss.

1   The Conciliar Movement

The Great Schism

The medieval Church in the West never fully recovered from the Great Schism (1378–1417) in which there were two, and for a short time three, rival popes, men of war and diplomacy. The confidence of a Church whose self-definition and self-image was unity was demoralized by the spectacle of rival popes anathematizing one another. The conflict between popes also reflected conflicting interests between states. A popular saying held that no one had gone to heaven since the Great Schism.

The Great Schism was preceded by the "Babylonian Captivity" of the Church (1309–77), in which popes resided in Avignon under the protection of the French king. This was the situation against which Catherine of Siena preached. She is credited with playing an important role in ending the Babylonian captivity. The return of Pope Gregory XI to Rome did not, however, end the problem, but rather initiated the Great Schism, which ended at the Council of Constance in 1417, with the election of Pope Martin V. The "Babylonian Captivity" and the Great Schism made evident the need for more trustworthy governance of the Church.

The Conciliar movement constituted a major effort to wrest the ultimate authority of the Church from the pope and to place it in a general council. As discussed in chapter 5, both Marsilius of Padua and William of Ockham had advocated this change. In the fifteenth century its primary spokesman was Jean Gerson, chancellor of the University of Paris. His short treatise, "On the Unity of the Church," argued that a general council could be called by bishops, secular princes, or even by members of the Church. Prepared for the Council of Pisa, the document is a careful discussion of such questions as: Where does the unity of the Church lie? What needs reform? Who should take responsibility for reform? And: What powers should a general council have? However, when the issue was argued at the Council of Pisa in 1409 the only result was the election of a third pope.

Agitation for reform on every level continued, and took many forms, from Erasmus of Rotterdam's urbane and scholarly humanism to Savanarola's flamboyant apocalyptic preaching in Florence. At the same time, devotional movements (discussed in chapter 5) incited people to take personal responsibility for apostolic living and experience of God's presence.

In spite of the optimism of authors like Jan van Ruysbroeck about the "mixed life" (combining piety and secular responsibilities), contemplation and mystical devotion proved too time-consuming for most laypeople. Contemplative movements tended to create quietists, people who retreated from the ordinary activities of everyday life, shunning political or social activism. On the continent, contemplatives produced no schools of thought, no organizations, no official leaders, and no advocacy base. But for many

Christians they presented a welcome alternative to Church observances, the hierarchical chain of religious authority, and the organization men of the fifteenth-century Church. Widespread interest in contemplation continued in Western Europe into the sixteenth century, but the only extra-ecclesiastical religious movements to survive in recognizable form were the Lollards in England and the Waldensians.

2   Italy: Fifteenth-century Preaching

Savanarola

In Florence, the Dominican preacher Savanarola (1452–98) enjoyed a brief popularity. His sermons ranted against wealth, learning, and privilege as "vanities." They often ended in bonfires of luxury and amusement items. Renaissance historian Jacob Burckhardt described the scene:

> On the lowest tier were false beards, masks, and carnival disguises; above came volumes of Latin and Italian poets, among others, Bocaccio and Petrarch, some of which were valuable printed parchments and illuminated manuscripts; then women's ornaments and toilet articles, scents, mirrors, veils, and false hair; higher up, lutes, harps, chessboards, playing cards; on the two uppermost layers were nothing but paintings, especially paintings of beautiful women – sometimes paintings of classical women; Lucretia, Cleopatra, or Faustina; partly portraits of contemporary beauties: Bencina, Lena Morelli, Bina, Maria de'Lenzi.
>
> (Burckhardt, 1960: 337)

Savanarola also attacked both the ruler Lorenzo the Magnificent and the current state of the Church. In 1495 Pope Alexander VI forbade him to preach, a prohibition that Savanarola ignored. But by then his severity had created a backlash among Florentine citizens. He was imprisoned, tortured, and hung as a schismatic in 1498.

While Savanarola was preaching in Florence, the painter Luca Signorelli included his portrait in an epic cycle depicting the end of the world and the resurrection of the flesh. Signorelli "preached" to a highly visual society in paints rather than words.

Signorelli's Resurrection of the Flesh *at Orvieto*

Signorelli's *Resurrection of the Flesh* was painted in the Chapel of the Madonna of San Brizio as part of a series on events predicted to occur at the end of the world. In some ways, Signorelli's paintings are unique, but they also belong in a long tradition of visualized theology. Every medieval and Renaissance church attracted viewers to belief with images of the Last Judgment and the resurrection of bodies to eternal reward or punishment.

The Cathedral at Orvieto was begun on November 13, 1290, though its façade was not completed until the seventeenth century and the bronze door of the main portal was put in place only in 1970 (see CD Rom figure 6.1). In the San Brizio Chapel, the first chapel on the right facing the altar, Signorelli painted scenes depicting the appearance of the Antichrist, the Last Judgment, Purgatory, and the resurrections of the blessed and the damned.

On the entrance arch, scenes from the end of the world show the Antichrist thrown head over heels from heaven. Rust-colored rays sweep the scene, representing God's angry judgment (see CD Rom figure 6.2). Straight ahead of the entrance on the altar wall at left, angels lead the elect to heaven, while on the right, sinners are led by a demon with a white banner to hell. The damned act out their despair as they see Charon's boat drawing near to ferry them to hell. Above, two angels watch the pitiful scene impassively.

The Antichrist scene on the right wall of the San Brizio Chapel features contemporary scenes – executions, murders, and armed fights, incidents that happened in Florence in living memory, peopled with figures (like Savanarola, Fra Angelico, and Signorelli himself) recognizable to contemporaries (see CD Rom figure 6.3). Next to the Antichrist on the right wall is the *Crowning of the Elect*, the earliest painting Signorelli executed in the chapel (see CD Rom figure 6.4). His fresco of "The Damned in Hell" is energetic and violent. Devils and damned, in spite of their grotesqueness are still recognizably human – some of them are livid purple like the plague victims who were dying daily in Orvieto as Signorelli painted (see CD Rom figure 6.5).

Signorelli's *Resurrection of the Flesh* is on the left wall of the chapel. His resurrected bodies are marked in three ways to specify their difference from mortal bodies. Each of these characteristics of resurrected bodies was discussed by Augustine centuries before in the last book of his *City of God*. Bodies are weightless, freed from the downward pull of gravity; they display affection for one another without sexual lust; and these naked figures retain sexual difference, but without the markings of gender socialization.

The *Resurrection of the Flesh* focuses on the moment just after the horns of trumpeting angels have called the blessed to resurrection (see CD Rom figures 6.6 and 6.7). Bodies in various stages of enfleshment appear, struggling to climb out of graves where they have slumbered, awaiting the day of resurrection. Figures emerging from the earth are pulled by their eyes, which according to Augustine, are now capable of *seeing* God. Some figures have not yet put on flesh; on some, like the figure on the right standing next to the skeletons, one can still see through the flesh to backbone, hip sockets, and thigh bone (see figure 6.1). The naked figures have fully muscled bodies, *real* bodies, as Augustine had insisted, even though spiritual bodies and thus, like the angels' bodies, weightless. Several of the figures are experimenting with their new weightlessness as they stretch out their arms to test the lightness of the air or to hug each other gently.

Signorelli's female nudes are not the standard erotic female body of the (male) "period eye." In the Renaissance, and until the seventeenth century, the erotic female body was characterized by small high breasts, a short waist, and large belly. Signorelli's female nudes exhibit neither the small high breasts nor the exaggerated belly that was considered erotic. Moreover, male and female nudes touch each other with infinite tenderness but without lust. They enjoy one another's beauty for its own sake, as Augustine had described.

In order to eliminate the marks of gender socialization from his resurrected bodies, Signorelli removed differences of posture, gesture, stance, size, and musculature, so that female and male bodies appear equally strong, flexible, and expressive. His treatment of

Figure 6.1   Detail, *Resurrection of the Flesh*, Signorelli, The San Brizio Chapel, Orvieto Cathedral, 1502. Photo AKG Nimatallah.
The moment just after the horns of trumpeting angels have sounded is depicted. Bodies in various stages of enfleshment struggle to climb out of graves, pulled by their eyes.

female bodies is unprecedented in Christian tradition in which female nakedness repetitiously symbolized sex, sin, and death, and only male nakedness signified spiritual athleticism, aspiration, and achievement.

Signorelli's *Resurrection of the Flesh* provides a vivid example of a theologically informed visualization of resurrected bodies. It influenced Michelangelo's *Last Judgment*, painted 40 years later in the Sistine Chapel.

Italian Renaissance religion and learning

In fifteenth-century Italy new styles of learning created new environments for learning. The medieval universities were no longer the location of the most exciting thinking. Humanist salons were protected by princes and popes. Salons credentialed no one and had no practical concerns. They existed for the love of learning, to *advance* learning, not to rework or catalog traditional material. In these informal academies a different kind of reading emerged. People read in order to understand the text itself, not primarily to use its ideas to support scripture and tradition. They studied languages, even Asian languages. Petrarch initiated a revival of Latin literary culture, and in 1462 an Academy was established in Florence, headed by Marsilio Ficino.

Renaissance humanists were fascinated with classical antiquity. Bishop Nicolas of Cusa (1401–64), who has been called the best mind of his time, was an ardent humanist. He wrote: "Everywhere we see the minds of people turning back to antiquity with extreme avidity." He taught that God is a circle, whose circumference is everywhere and whose center is nowhere. The implications of his doctrine are evident: If God is everywhere, then everything is interesting and important; everything reveals God's "traces, footprints," and image.

Humanist scholars liked to debunk ideas "universally" held, that is, ideas held in Western Europe among educated men. At least three humanist scholars independently demonstrated that the so-called "Donation of Constantine" was a forgery. This document was believed to be a fourth-century deed in which Constantine ceded to the pope all the Roman lands and territories. The "Donation" was frequently cited as legitimation for the church's extensive ownership of property and wealth. Nicholas of Cusa, Laurentius Valla, and the English humanist, Reginald Pecock, simultaneously and independently proved the "Donation" to be an eighth-century forgery.

3   England: John Wyclif and the Lollards

English opposition to the papacy and reforming impetus took a directly political form. An increasing sense of nationalism merged with opposition to papal power and to the extensive property held by the pope in England. A series of English laws attempted to limit the pope's right to appoint bishops and the right of the English clergy to appeal to Rome. At the same time, the Hundred Years War between France and England led to the creation of the French state (1339–1453).

Social and religious movements

John Wyclif launched his attack on the papacy in an atmosphere of concern about the relationship of pope and king. He would remain the inspiration of English "heresy" until the 1520s, when Luther's writings began to appear in England. A complex set of personal, religious, and political issues were interwoven in this influential forerunner of sixteenth-century reformations. With only one important exception, John Wyclif anticipated every doctrine of the Protestant reform by over a hundred years. The exception is the doctrine of justification by faith alone.

Wyclif was an Oxford don, a university master, who turned "heretic." Although heresy charges were a perennial occupational hazard of university life on the continent, Wyclif was alone in England in his deliberate defiance of the Church. He had a popular following, though he never encouraged such a following. The Lollards had several heroic political moments, like the Peasant's uprising in 1381 and the Lollard march on London in 1414. Lollards successfully withstood vigorous persecution for over a hundred years, surviving as a movement to join the English reformation in the sixteenth century.

Later sources like *Foxes' Acts and Monuments* (usually called *Foxes' Book of Martyrs*), say that most Lollards were common people – weavers, wheelwrights, smiths, carpenters, shoemakers, tailors, and other tradespeople. Few or none, Foxe wrote, were learned, "but it pleased the Lord to work in them knowledge and understanding by reading a few English books, such as they could get in corners." Some who could not read memorized large portions of scripture.

Contemporary lists of the Lollard's "false opinions" included: They 1) say that the bread of the eucharist is not the identical body of Christ; 2) reject confession to a priest, preferring to confess to God in the heart; 3) repudiate images; 4) reject belief in the intercession of the saints, saying: "the best saint in heaven has enough to do to pray for himself;" and 5) reject the authority of the pope.

Like the Waldensians, Lollard laypeople preached. Their opponents said: "Lollards preach out of their heads on matters of faith." One sermon against Lollards complains that Lollards ask the question: "Why should not women be enabled to celebrate and preach like men?" The sermon responds to this question: "Because Our Lady, who was sinless and full of grace, was given no such powers," concluding with advice to women: "Take thee to thy distaff, covet not to be a priest or preacher."

Like the Waldensians, the Lollards were regularly accused of "good works." They gave alms, paid their debts, and abstained from oaths and swearing. Their opponents apparently needed to explain the attractiveness of Lollards' beliefs and practices: "The Lollard is like a poisoner who does not administer his poison neat, but mixed with sweet tasting food and medicine."

Lollards had many complaints against the English church and clergy. Their two positive teachings were that the clergy should emphasize preaching rather than the sacraments, and that the vernacular Bible should be given freely to laypeople. The English clergy were not known for their poverty or their apostolic living. Their exclusive right to administer the sacraments necessary for salvation, together with their "soft livings," created resentment. On the political side, these resentments led to communistic beliefs; on the religious side, they led to attempts to minimize the necessity and value of the sacramental ministry of the church. Preaching and lay access to vernacular scripture were urged as the primary correctives to priestly control of the sacraments.

Medieval tradition saw scripture as a difficult, almost incomprehensible, text that could be understood only by trained clergy with the use of handbooks. Even for monks, the study of scripture was not generally advocated. Fifth-century monks had understood study of scripture as an ascetic discipline. By the twelfth century monks were instructed that the study of scripture could be a temptation to neglect one's prayer life, and it was the prayer life of a medieval monk that was her/his primary duty. The twelfth century Cistercian, Gilbert of Holland, had reproved monks: "Reading ought to serve our prayer and prepare our mood for contemplation, not encroach on our time and weaken our character." By contrast, Lollards believed that common people could receive from scripture a direct sense of the knowledge and presence of God.

Wyclif also saw the vernacular Bible as an antidote to the clergy's exclusive possession of scripture and sacraments. He believed that an authentic sense of the person and spirit of Christ was mediated primarily through scripture, not through the Church. In his last years, he and his assistants began, but did not finish, a translation of the Bible into Middle English. Wyclif's translation was a very wooden and literal rendering, translated word by word in the Latin word order. A century and a half after Wyclif, a complete translation of the Bible into English was accomplished, the Coverdale Bible (1535).

Theology

Wyclif had been influenced by nominalism at Oxford, one of the strongholds of nominalist teaching in his time. But his views of the Church and sacraments reacted against nominalism; he was an *ultrarealist*. He understood scripture as a divine exemplar conceived in the mind of God before creation. Every word of scripture, he taught, is a divine idea; every part is authoritative.

His view of the Church was also ultrarealist. Wyclif rejected the visible Church in favor of the archetypal Church that had existed eternally in the mind of God. The authority of the visible church, he said, derives from the degree to which it resembles the invisible Church. Wyclif's views on predestination also undermined the importance of the visible church and sacraments. The salvation of each Christian, he said, depends on the inscrutable will of God, *not* on the sacramental provisions of the visible church. He stated that no one, not even a pope, "knows whether he be of the church or whether he be a limb of the fiend." Only God, who has decreed his salvation or damnation, knows. Wyclif guarded his doctrine against some of its more libertarian interpretations by warning that "each person must hope that they are safe in bliss," and, most importantly, must *act* as if they are "limbs of holy church." By 1378, Wyclif had moved from an agnostic position about the pope to one of outright rejection. After 1371, he became a hunted and endangered man, living under the protection of the notorious "Black Prince," John of Gaunt.

Wyclif's teaching on the Eucharist was a reaction both against nominalism and against what he saw as "materialism." Against the nominalists' complex analysis of the material properties of the eucharistic elements, he developed an intricate theory of symbolization. He argued that the efficacy of the eucharistic sacrament depends on the spiritual condition of the participant; bread and wine only become the body and blood of Christ for believers. Therefore, he claimed, it is impossible that "a hog, a dog, or a mouse" can "eat our Lord."

In 1215, the Fourth Lateran Council had decreed that every Catholic must believe the doctrine of transubstantiation, that is, that at the consecration of the bread and wine, two events occurred, the bread and wine disappeared, and the body and blood of Christ appeared. Wyclif described Catholic transubstantiation in this way:

> Transubstantiation is the passage of one substance according to its entirety into another with the whole multitude of accidents remaining, so that neither matter nor substantial form which were in the bread and wine remain after consecration, but all material or formal substance which was in them is destroyed. The body of Christ succeeds through conversion under the same accidents, and thus there is no annihilation of any substance, both, because of the conversion of the whole substance into a better one, and also because the accidents that were previously in the bread and wine remain; for idolatry would be committed toward those remaining accidents by adoring bread and wine as the Lord's body, and thus as God. It seems to me that the primitive church did not teach thus, but the modern church does.
>
> (*The Eucharist*: 2.30–1)

Wyclif disagreed with the first of these claims, insisting that bread and wine remains bread and wine. Both his realist philosophical commitments and his wish to de-mystify, and thus to minimize, priests' sacramental power prompted this view. Beyond his opposition to Catholic doctrine, however, his positive theology of the eucharist eludes understanding. A clear understanding of Wyclif's understanding of the presence of Christ in the elements of the mass cannot be drawn from his later writings. He believed in the Real Presence, but did not explain what he meant by that. In the heat of debate with Nominalist philosophers, he took several positions, none of which clarified his views.

Wyclif was concerned about what he called the "pagan" or magical view that the bread and wine after consecration become body and blood in objective reality so that "a hog, a dog, or a mouse can eat our Lord." Opponents objected that "common folks" would lose their faith if exposed to a symbolic interpretation. Wyclif replied that if so, their faith was materialistic, magical, and "the vilest disbelief because it is a form of idolatry whereby a creature (the bread and wine) is worshipped as God."

"When we see the host," he insisted, "we ought to believe not that it is itself the body of Christ, but that the body of Christ is concealed in it." Observing the variety of opinions concerning the Eucharist, Wyclif drew the conclusion that the Church, in affirming the doctrine of transubstantiation, had "advanced by deteriorating." There is no mention of transubstantiation in scripture, he said, and the Church "ought still to believe as at first." It was clear to him that the saints of the primitive church and their children after them understood that the bread and wine became the body and blood of Christ *figuratively*. Moreover, Wyclif questioned the significance of the sacrament as the center of Christian life. He wrote, "to meditate upon Christ is infinitely better than to celebrate the sacrament."

John Wyclif died on December 31, 1384. His curate stated on oath that on December 28 Wyclif, while hearing mass in his church, at the elevation of the host, fell down, smitten by a severe paralysis in the tongue, so that he could not speak from then to the moment of his death. On May 4, 1415, 150 years after his death, 45 articles from Wyclif's writings were condemned at the Council of Constance. Among the condemned articles are the following: that no one after Urban VI (1378 – the occasion of the Great Schism) should be accepted as having been pope; that temporal lords can take temporal goods away from the church at their discretion, when those who hold them are habitually sinful; anyone who enters any sort of religious order makes himself less apt and suitable for observing the commands of God; universities, places of study, colleges, degrees, and the exercise of the master's degree in the same are vain since the introduction of pagan writers, and are only of as much use to the church as the devil is; it is not necessary for salvation to believe that the Roman Church is supreme among other churches; and Augustine, Benedict, and Bernard are damned, unless they repent of having had property and of having founded and joined religious orders. He concluded, "From the pope down to the lowest order they are all heretics."

4   Reform in Bohemia

The Bohemian reform movement, largely under the leadership of John Hus, was the most successful "failure" of any reform movement before the sixteenth century Protestant reforms in southern Germany and Switzerland. The Bohemian reform rejected papal authority in matters of doctrine and, between 1419 and 1436, established religious toleration in which a remarkable range of beliefs and practices flourished. Stimulated by John Wyclif's ideas, Hus went beyond Wyclif who had argued that secular lords were responsible for reforming the English church. Hus thought that the prerogative and the program of reform should come from the common people.

John Hus was chaplain of the Bethlehem Chapel, founded for preaching in the national language, of the University of Prague. Hus, a powerful preacher, was also an agitator and a writer. In the 12 years he was chaplain of the Bethlehem Chapel, he preached over 3,000 sermons to overflowing crowds. A contemporary reported that listeners sometimes climbed out the windows to escape the intense compunction and conviction his preaching provoked. The walls of the Bethlehem Chapel featured vivid paintings in pairs; in one, a scene from Christ's life or apostolic times was depicted; the other showed a scene involving contemporary ecclesiastical corruption. Hus' sermons followed similar themes, contrasting the poverty and simplicity of the early Church with the abuses of the modern Church.

The Bethlehem Chapel was a liturgical center in which congregational singing was given a high priority. Hus himself translated scores of Latin hymns into Czechoslovakian. The importance of singing in reforming movements cannot be overestimated. Music effectively bonded people with common beliefs and purpose and created active engagement in liturgy. In Catholic liturgy at this time, singing was done by choirs; even the responses within the mass were sung by the choir rather than the congregation. For the congregation, worship was largely a passive experience.

Social protest and activism were stimulated by the high level of poverty in Bohemia. The poverty of about half the population (40 percent indigence) contrasted sharply with the obvious wealth of the church and evident clerical abuses. To be a real Christian, Bohemian agitators insisted, you must be poor. Reform in Bohemia was also intimately linked to Czech nationalism. The two major reforming agenda were addressed to the abuses of simony and indulgences, but other abuses were also listed, such as the abuse of popular credulity in relation to relics and their quasi-magical properties, and avarice and laxity in religious orders. There were public demonstrations, in which demonstrators carried large placards with pictures and slogans like those in the Bethlehem Chapel, contrasting scenes from the New Testament and the contemporary Church. In one such scene, Christ carries his cross, while the pope rides on horseback adorned with all the symbols of his power and accompanied by corps of magnificently attired cardinals on horseback. The demonstrations gathered momentum and increased in violence and three agitators were beheaded, the first Hussite martyrs.

The Jena Codex

The *Jena Codex* is a Hussite tract, compiled from various manuscripts, with text added later. A supplement published in 1495 included four of John Hus' letters and two woodcuts depicting John Hus' death (see figure 6.2). The first parts were written in Latin, the rest in Czech. Paired pictures carry the tract's reforming message. Events in the lives of the apostles at the time of the "true" church are contrasted with a scene depicting the wealth and corruption of the contemporary Church (see CD Rom figures 6.8 and 6.9).

Figure 6.2 The Martyrdom of John Hus, Workshop of Janichek Zmiley, before 1525. Prague, National Museum.
Hus was burned at the stake (1415) as a heretic for his advocacy for reform in the Church. An eyewitness reported that he died singing.

Paintings for the tract were done by Janichek Zmilely and his workshop. Nothing is known of Zmilely's life, except that he painted for Utraquist hymnals and graduals as well as for the *Jena Codex*. The colors used in the *Jena Codex* are intentionally didactic: glistening colors, the "new colors" of the present-day sinful world of the Antichrist are contrasted with subdued "old colors" illustrating the "true" church. The scenes need little interpretation. Their message was clear and gathered support for reforming activities in Bohemia.

John Hus' "On Simony"

"Simony" was named after Simon the magician (in the New Testament book of Acts) who offered the apostles money if they would give him spiritual power. It was one of the most frequently lamented vices of the late medieval Church. Wyclif had also written a treatise "On Simony," which was brought to Prague by Hus' close friend, Jerome of Prague. Hus' definition of simony as "the conscious intent to buy or sell anything spiritual," made clear that simony was not only the clergy's sin, though he believed that the court of Pope Boniface IX was the source of the vice. In "On Simony" a common theme of fifteenth-century reform protest appears, namely that popes are not immune from serious sin; the office does not grant holiness to the pope. Rather, the "greater the office, the more the damnation of a sinful incumbent."

Laypeople were also guilty of purchasing sacramental rituals – private baptisms, marriages, burials, and masses for the dead. Hus compared simony to leprosy, a highly contagious and fatal disease. Hus' opponents argued that even Judas, when his entrepreneurial activities were discovered, was not deposed and ejected from the company of the disciples; Jesus himself ate dinner with him on the night before his death, though he knew of Judas' simony.

Hus knew about simony from personal experience; he acknowledged that he originally wanted to become a priest in order to secure an abundant and sure livelihood. Hus thought of simony as the model of all sins. Everyone who commits mortal sin is a simoniac because they sell their soul to the devil in exchange for a temporal gain of pleasure, money, or power. Hus described in detail how each order of the clergy participates in simony, analyzing different kinds of simony in detail. Apparently he felt that there was no danger of suggesting forms of simony that people were not already practicing!

How should simony be avoided? The pope could reform the Church, Hus said, but if he did, "his apostles would not let him remain alive for long!" So he had three further suggestions. First, he advocated elections rather than appointments for episcopal and parochial offices. Second, he called on secular princes to intervene: "When you oppose those who steal cows," he wrote, "you should much more oppose those who, having guilefully extracted money from the poor, destroy the souls of the poor and their own as well." Third, he urged that church communities withhold revenues from simoniac priests and bishops. He did not suggest that uneven distribution of wealth is a social evil; rather it was a *theological evil* in that by it, souls are harmed.

The question of indulgences that was to play so significant a part in the Lutheran reformation was an issue addressed by Hus. "Indulgences" were temporal remissions of sins by the church in exchange for confession, contrition, and penitential acts. Indulgences originated in the crusades, when crusaders were offered full (plenary) indulgence if they died in a crusade. The theology of indulgences assumed a "treasury of merits" deposited by Christ and the saints over which the Church has earthly jurisdiction for the forgiveness of sins. Indulgences did not remove all penalties, however; sins have penalties even after the penitent is reconciled, for the Church claimed no jurisdiction beyond the grave.

How were indulgences thought to benefit medieval people? First, the active appropriation of forgiveness had psychological benefit. Prayer, charitable deeds, pilgrimage:

any of these penitential practices helped people to appropriate and *experience* forgiveness. Second, the sale of indulgences (a late stage of the practice) seemed to make sense in late medieval societies. One's money represented one's life, an offering symbolic of the giving of self. Yet abuses were perhaps inevitable. The later Middle Ages saw the rise of professional "pardoners" who sold indulgences without restriction or supervision. In 1567, Pope Pius V, in response both to vigorous objections by reformers and to a changed world, prohibited indulgences.

Hus considered indulgences a form of simony. Because of his advocacy for reform, John Hus was condemned by the Council of Constance in 1415 to be burned at the stake as a heretic. He was a different kind of martyr than the heroic martyrs of the early Christian centuries. About 30 of his letters, written from the Franciscan monastery where he was imprisoned, date to the month before his death. They describe Hus' convictions and fears as his execution approached. In prison he suffered from headaches, toothaches, fever, and kidney stones and he vomited blood. He brooded on earlier martyrs, both biblical and historical, now in a position to recognize their anguish. Hus was an anti-heroic, or perhaps simply human, martyr. He was not ashamed to acknowledge the anguish of anticipating martyrdom. Two weeks before his death on July 6, 1415 he wrote to a friend:

> O most kind Christ, draw us weaklings after thyself, for unless thou draw us, we cannot follow thee! Give us a courageous spirit that it may be ready; and if the flesh is weak, may thy grace go before, now, as well as subsequently. For without thee we can do nothing, and particularly to go to a cruel death for thy sake. Give us a valiant spirit, a fearless heart, the right faith, a firm hope, and perfect love, that we may offer our lives for thy sake with the greatest patience and joy.
>
> (Letter to Lord John of Chlum, June 23, 1415)

Three days later he wrote to the same friend: "I suppose that this is my last letter to you because tomorrow, I think, I shall be purged of sins, in the hope of Jesus Christ, by a dreadful death. I cannot describe what I have passed through this night." An eyewitness account related that John Hus died singing, "not convicted and not confessed."

Taborites and Utraquists

Hus' death both consolidated and radicalized the Hussite movement. After his death the movement split into two camps, a moderate party of aristocrats called Utraquists and the radical Taborite party. The Taborites, a well-organized army, led a revolt with both a religious and a political agenda in and around Prague. The Taborite army used banners with a red chalice on a black field, protesting the current practice of withholding the cup from laypeople and symbolizing their demand for communion in both kinds. They destroyed images, baptized in streams and ponds, and held mass in barns and stables. The issue of the chalice for laypeople focused their demands, called Utraquism (*sub utraque species*). Hus had supported the demand that lay people receive communion in both bread and wine. In the week of his death he wrote:

Do not oppose the sacrament of the cup of the Lord that the Lord instituted in himself and through his apostle. For no scripture is opposed to it, but only a custom which I suppose has grown up through negligence. We ought not to follow custom, but Christ's example and truth. Now the Council giving "custom" as the reason, has condemned the lay participation as an error. Whoever should practice it, unless he recover his senses, shall be punished as a heretic. Alas! Now malice condemns Christ's institution as an error!

(Letter to Havlik, June 21, 1415)

By 1416 all Prague churches were in the control of reformed clerics, but a series of papal crusades to Bohemia between 1420 and 1431 resulted in a general restoration of churches to Catholic jurisdiction. King Wenceslas (not the "good King Wenceslas" of the Christmas carol; "Good King Wenceslas" was murdered by his brother in 929, and considered a martyr) permitted three Utraquist churches to remain in Prague. Under the next king, Utraquist leaders again resisted royal armies that tried to suppress them. In 1419 the Taborites adopted the Four Prague Articles that stipulated freedom of preaching, the sacrament in both kinds for all Christians, exemplary living and no secular power for priests and monks, and secular punishment for all mortal sins of the clergy. Hussites, a combined group of Taborites and Utraquists, controlled the throne of Bohemia from 1457 to 1471, and the movement spread across Europe. It was to be the last major reforming crisis before Luther's protest against indulgences a hundred years after Hus' death.

5   The Isenheim Altarpiece

The Isenheim Altarpiece, a masterpiece among late Gothic polyptychs, was built and painted for the monastery of St Anthony, Isenheim. It was commissioned by the superior of the Order, Guido Guersi, to be placed in the choir of the monastery chapel on the high altar (see CD Rom figure 6.10). The altarpiece was the first stage of a healing program for victims of the so-called burning sickness and other skin diseases treated at St Anthony's monastery, including leprosy and the newly epidemic syphilis, for which no medical remedy existed. Patients were regularly taken to view the altarpiece to assure themselves of either the possibility of miraculous healing or the strength and courage to bear the fatal disease.

According to a sixteenth-century chronicler, Aymar Falco, miracles of healing did occur:

In the year 1530 we witnessed that many who suffered from this terrible illness were completely cured through imploring the patron saint and through the holy wine in which the relics of the saint's body had been immersed, and which was then applied locally to the diseased parts of the body.

What was burning sickness? A fifteenth-century chronicler wrote: "The victim's blood was affected by a poisonous inflammation that consumed the whole body, causing tumors which developed into incurable ulcers and caused thousands of deaths." Burning sickness was also known as "holy fire," "hell fire," and "St Anthony's fire." Abscesses all over the trunk of the body gradually spread to the arms and legs, detaching them little by little from the torso. In 1597 it was discovered that the disease was caused by ergot, a poisonous fungus growth in grains of rye.

In the late medieval world diseases often took on epidemic proportions; their causes and cures were equally unknown. Soothing efforts, compresses, potions, and other procedures for alleviating symptoms ranged from blood-letting to amputation. Disease was considered a punishment for sin and a testing of faith, an earthly purgatory in which the sufferer could, by patience and trust in Christ, expiate her/his sins.

In its closed position, the altarpiece displays a crucifixion, flanked by wings (see CD Rom figures 6.11, 6.12, and 6.16). The closed position was displayed on weekdays, in Lent, and during Holy Week. St Anthony in the right wing holds his symbol, the Tau cross, while a demon breathes the breath of pestilence through a window. In the left wing, St Sebastian, the plague saint, stands pierced with arrows. Christ's body is a sickly green shade, flecked with bleeding sores. He hangs heavily from the cross, bending ankles and causing fingers and toes to curl. Fifteenth-century descriptions of the now-extinct burning sickness correspond in every detail with Grunewald's depiction of the crucified Christ. Grünewald apparently used the patients as models and painted with meticulous accuracy.

On Christ's left, John the Baptist is standing before the healing waters of baptism. He points calmly to Christ, holding a book that states, "He must increase; I must decrease." On Christ's right, the Virgin swoons, and Mary Magdalen, in frenzied grief, kneels before the cross. The kneeling Magdalen, the swooning Virgin, and St John, bending to support her, form a group united in their grief. The lamb at John's feet bleeds, reiterating Christ's sacrifice.

The crucifixion scene is painted on two hinged panels that, when opened, cover the fixed wings and reveal strikingly different scenes. The first opening of the altarpiece was reserved for joyous feast days like Christmas and Easter, as well as appropriate Sundays throughout the liturgical year. Representations of (left to right) the Annunciation, the nativity (with angels' concert), and the resurrection appear. These scenes, filled with glowing, brilliant colors, contrast strikingly with the somber exterior (see CD Rom figures 6.13 to 6.15, 6.17).

The center scene of the first opening is (like the crucifixion scene of the closed position), painted on hinged wings that open to the third position of the altarpiece. The second opening was reserved for the feast day of St Anthony. The central scene consists of wooden, polychromed sculptured figures. This sculpted group had been done by Nicholas of Hagenau in 1503 as part of an earlier altarpiece. Grünewald's paintings are an ingenious addition, amplifying the program of the altar but conforming to its frame. St. Anthony is seated enthroned in the central panel, flanked by St Athanasius, his fourth-century biographer, and St Jerome (see CD Rom figures 6.18 to 6.20).

The painted wings are devoted to two hermit monks, Sts Anthony and Paul of Thebes (d. c.350), traditionally the first hermit. Anthony is said to have visited Paul when he was 113 years old, a scene depicted in the left panel. In this scene, the promise of peace and salvation are symbolized by the doe and stag drinking from the water of eternal life. Medicinal plants grow in the foreground, implying the possibility of cure for the patients. The plants have been identified and their properties described from contemporary sixteenth-century manuals and herbal handbooks. The Anthonite hospital had two staples for soothing burning sensations. One was a kind of wine vinegar;

the other was an ointment. Grunewald included the herbs used in these recipes in this scene. On the right, the scene is the "Temptation of St Anthony" (as described by Athanasius in his *Life of St Anthony*,") The saint is assailed by horrible demons, some covered with pustulant sores while angels repeat Anthony's battle in the skies above.

It seems that the Isenheim Altarpiece was as preoccupied with death as its first viewers. The crucifixion displays imminent death; the entombment shows the state of death; the first opening looks into, *through*, and beyond death to the healing, hope, and bliss of resurrection. According to the popular *ars moriendi* (art of dying) manuals of the time, every dying person must wrestle with three predictable temptations, despair over sins, pride over good deeds, and passionate attachment to persons and things. The temptations of the dying inform the second opening on the St Anthony side, while the much longed-for happiness of a tranquil and holy old age is the subject of the "Meeting of Sts Paul and Anthony."

The grotesque suffering body of Christ of the Isenheim Altarpiece was not created for casual viewing. Rather, its first viewers could identify with it through their own suffering bodies. By converting involuntary suffering into a *voluntary spiritual discipline*, the patient could receive hope and comfort. For people for whom even the temporary alleviation of suffering was unlikely, it was seen as crucial *either* for healing or for managing a "good death" to work actively with one's suffering rather than suffering passively.

Medieval theologians insisted that Christ's suffering and death was voluntary, consciously chosen in obedience to God, a purposeful redemptive act. Yet the visual message of the crucifixion scene (not only this one) contradicts the voluntary nature of Christ's death. Christ did not put himself in this position of cruel torture; he was put there, literally, nailed there. In the gospels' account, his mockers scornfully incited him to come down from the cross, and he did not, or could not. The theological message of the crucifixion is that Christ's spirit volunteered to suffer for the sins of the world, but the *visual* message is his vulnerable human body, suffering helplessly. Similarly, patients who lived with the Isenheim Altarpiece, by spiritual strength and courage, were offered the possibility of integrating their physical suffering into the quest for physical and spiritual healing as they entered in hope through the crucifixion of their own suffering into the joy of resurrection.

6   Erasmus and Luther on the Human Condition

A reappraisal of the human condition was one of the themes of the Italian Renaissance as scholars discovered in the classical texts of ancient Greece and Rome new esteem for human capacities. Humanists struggled to integrate faith in human goodness with Christian beliefs. Vives, a representative humanist, wrote:

> Our mind is a victim of its own darkness; our passions, stirred by sin, have covered the eyes of reason with a thick layer of dust. We need a clear insight, serene and undisturbed. All the precepts of moral philosophy can be found in the teachings of Christ. In his doctrine and in his words, man will find the remedy to all moral diseases, the ways and means to tame our passions under the guidance and power of reason. Once this order has been secured, man will learn proper behavior in relations with self, with God, and

with neighbor and will act rightfully not only in the privacy of the home but also in social and political life.

This statement combined pessimism and optimism, a high evaluation of humans' potential with a low evaluation of human nature as it is. Typically, humanists neglected the question of *who* could realistically aspire to the social conditions necessary for rational development.

Erasmus

The early sixteenth-century debate between Erasmus of Rotterdam (1469–1536) and Martin Luther (1483–1546) reflects a fundamental disagreement between Renaissance and Reformation assumptions about humanity. Erasmus was ordained an Augustinian canon in 1492, but he left the monastery in 1495 to study at Paris and Oxford. He refused a professorship at Paris in order to work on a Latin translation of the New Testament, and he became the first teacher of Greek at Cambridge. Erasmus lived the life of an academic migrant worker, repeatedly refusing offers of a more secure and stationary existence in order to maintain his academic freedom. The most renowned scholar of his age, he not only supported reforming movements within the Catholic Church, but he also wrote satires on the doctrines and institution of the church. Erasmus loved peace, however, and he did not participate in the more dramatic efforts for reform. He remained within the Catholic Church until his death, hoping for reform without revolution.

Erasmus wrote the most popular devotional manual of his time, the *Enchiridion militis christiani* (Handbook of the Christian Soldier). Addressed to an actual soldier, it pictures the Christian life as a continual battle in which the soldier's sword is scripture. Erasmus characterized his devotional manual as a "little dagger" against the wiles of the enemy, namely the "flesh," figured as "Woman."

His treatise *On the Freedom of the Will* emphasized man's abilities, capabilities, and possibilities. Working to assimilate humanism to Christianity, he thought Luther's preaching was fatal to the humanist cause: "While I was fighting a fairly equal battle," he wrote, "Luther suddenly arose and threw the apple of discord into the world." While Erasmus and other Christian humanists found testimony of God's presence and will in the perfectability, power, rationality, and wisdom of "man," Luther found this same alleged "wisdom" to be an abyss of helplessness, pride, and ignorance.

The full elitism and individualism of Renaissance humanism can been seen in Erasmus' essay *On the Freedom of the Will*. He began by reiterating the medieval idea that scripture is obscure. While it may be good for learned individuals, it was not intended for "common ears." Erasmus' estimation of most humans was low: "For the most part, people are dull-witted and sensual, prone to unbelief, inclined to evil, and with a bent to blasphemy." Because of this condition, scripture must be carefully and respectfully interpreted *by experts*:

> For there are secret places in the holy scriptures into which God has not wished us to penetrate more deeply, and if we try to do so, then the deeper we go, the darker and darker it becomes, by which means we are led to acknowledge the unsearchable majesty of the divine

wisdom, and the weakness of the human mind. . . . Many things are reserved for that time when we shall no longer see through a glass darkly or in a riddle, but in which we shall contemplate the glory of the Lord when his face shall be revealed.

("Prefatory Observations," Rupp and Watson, 1966: 39)

Erasmus was frustrated with Luther and his followers who claimed that the message of scripture could be grasped by ordinary people:

> If there is any controversy concerning the meaning of scripture, when we bring forward the authority of the early fathers, they chant at once, "Ah! but they were only men." And if you ask them by what arguments the true interpretation of scripture may be known, since both sides were "only men," they reply, "By the sign of the Spirit." If you ask why the Spirit should rather be absent from those who have illuminated the world by their published miracles than from themselves, they reply as if for 1,300 years there had been no gospel in the world. If you seek of them a life worthy of the Spirit, they reply that they are just by faith, not by works. If you look in vain for miracles, they say that the age of miracles is past, and that there is no need of them now that we have so much light in the scriptures. And if you deny the scriptures to be clear in such a point that so many great men have stumbled in darkness, the argument returns full circle.

(*Freedom*, Rupp and Watson, 1966: 45)

Erasmus publicly disagreed with Luther over the issue of freedom of the will. Erasmus largely framed the issue as one in which the *effect* of belief in freedom of the will is paramount. He asked, in essence, is it more *productive* to claim that the human will "can apply itself to the things which lead to eternal salvation or turn away from them?" or to claim that "the power of the will is wholly extinguished"? Erasmus wrote: "Let us then suppose that there is some truth in the doctrine which Wyclif taught and Luther asserted, that whatever is done by us is done not by free choice but by sheer necessity. What could be more useless than to publish this paradox to the world?" He concluded: "Free will is damaged by sin but not extinguished by it."

The pace of Erasmus's treatise is leisurely, using metaphors and analogies from everyday life. He resisted the oversimplification of complex ideas (like grace); instead of definitions, he provided images. He was against extremism and passivity. He was troubled by the violence to the human will implied by a theology of grace that described grace as compelling a person without their assent. He also opposed a concept of God as a cruel and arbitrary tyrant, damning some and saving others without cause or merit. He agreed with Luther that God must "draw" or attract the person who is to become a Christian, but, he wrote:

> The word "draw" sounds as though it implied necessity and excluded freedom of choice. But in truth this drawing is not an act of violence, but it makes you will what yet you may refuse, just as if we show a boy an apple he runs for it, and as we show a sheep a green willow twig and he follows it, so God knocks at our soul with his grace, and we willingly embrace it.

(*Freedom*, Rupp and Watson, 1966: 80)

Erasmus was also against passivity: "This I do not see: how [Luther and his followers] maintain a free choice that is quite inactive":

Nobody denies that apart from the grace of God no one can hold a straight course in life.
... Nevertheless, we too meanwhile exert ourselves as best we are able ... One who seeks
help does not cease from trying ... And how are people to prepare their hearts, since
Luther says that all things happen by necessity?

(Freedom, Rupp and Watson, 1966: 77)

Luther

The 2003 film *Luther* tells the traditional story of the colorful and violent events and
"characters" of the early German reformation. It describes Luther as joining the
Augustinian friars when he was frightened by lightning that came close to hitting him.
Luther's real motivation was more complex. He may have been attracted to the
Augustinian friars because of their interest in Bible studies, but he also had a pressing
personal reason for placing himself beyond the jurisdiction of the Erfurt authorities
who sought to arrest him for participating in a duel and allegedly killing another
student, Jerome Buntz, in January 1505. Luther referred to the event much later:
"Because of God's extraordinary decision I was made a friar, so that they could not
capture me. Otherwise, I very easily would have been captured. But now they could not,
because the entire Order took care of me" (quoted by Posset, 2003: 91–2). Sheltered
within the monastery, Luther was exempt from the jurisdiction of local governments.

Luther (the film) focuses on the appeal to ordinary people of the young Luther's
theology of a merciful and gracious God. In doing so, it follows many traditional scholars in exaggerating the corruption of the late medieval Catholic Church and failing to
show its spiritual resources. The extent to which Martin Luther's reforming agenda
emerged from, and was continuous with, reforms of the fifteenth-century religious
Orders has only recently been adequately recognized and acknowledged. Luther's
spiritual father was Johann von Staupitz, vicar general of the Friars Hermits of St
Augustine (wrongly so-called, since the Augustinian friars were not hermits, but itinerant preachers who were sent where they were needed). Luther repeatedly and throughout his career thanked Staupitz, calling him his "closest friend" and crediting Staupitz
with "giving birth to me in Christ." It was from Staupitz, Luther acknowledged, that he
learned his theology of "grace and the cross." The young monk Luther, tormented by
his inability to feel that he was accepted by God, learned from Staupitz to rely on Christ,
quoting Psalm 119. 94: "I am yours, save me" – the verse Staupitz's biographer calls "the
motto of Staupitz's life and work" (Posset, 2003: 1).

Staupitz did not break with the Catholic Church as Luther did, but he gave Luther
several of the most central insights of the Lutheran reformation. Staupitz was a scriptural preacher; it was he who instigated Luther's opposition to indulgences; his conviction that theology should serve piety influenced Luther's pastoral emphasis; and both
Staupitz and Luther were anti-papal (though to different degrees). Most importantly,
Staupitz's emphasis on God's "sweetness" that attracts like a magnet, rather than on God
as stern and angry judge informed Luther's insistence on God's trustworthy mercy. In
short, no sharp distinctions can be drawn between Luther's theology and that of his
spiritual father.

In 1505, at the age of 22, Martin Luther entered the Augustinian monastery at Erfurt.
As a monk, he studied theology, becoming a doctor of theology at Wittenberg

University in 1512. From then on until the end of his life (1545) he taught at the University of Wittenberg, commenting systematically in his courses on the Psalms, the epistles to the Romans, Galatians, and Hebrews. At the same time he engaged in academic debates, many of which involved scholastic theology and reform of the church. Luther wrote voluminously; his *corpus* amounts to approximately 600 titles; the English translation collects them in 100 volumes.

As a young monk, Luther experienced spiritual anxiety over whether he had done enough to accomplish salvation. He wrote later:

> I made a martyr of myself through prayer, fasting, vigils, [and] cold. . . . What was I looking for in all that if not God? He knew how well I observed my rules and what a severe life I led . . . I no longer believed in Christ; rather I took him for a severe and terrible judge, the painted kind that one sees in paintings sitting on a rainbow.
>
> (Luther, *Weimarer Ausgabe*, vol. 45: 482; also Thulin, 1966: 17)

His conscience was not at ease until he understood the meaning of the scriptural words, "The just shall live by faith." These words were the powerful insight that became the basis of his theology. Henceforth, he said, whenever he read scripture, he saw in it only this one idea: "The just shall live by faith." He called this verse the "gospel" or "Word of God," the *key* to scripture.

According to tradition, Luther published his famous "Ninety-Five Theses" in 1517 by tacking them on the Wittenberg Castle Church door. This account is a legend; Luther hand-copied the 95 theses, giving copies to his fellow academics for discussion. They also copied and distributed them, and had them printed for further circulation. Within two weeks they had spread over Western Europe. The public attention was a surprise to Luther, who continued to think of reforming ideas as belonging within academic disputations. He wrote in a letter to a friend:

> It is a mystery to me how my theses, more so than my other writings, indeed, those of other professors, were spread to so many places. They were meant exclusively for our academic circle here. They were written in such language that the common people could hardly understand them. They . . . use academic categories.

In 1525 Luther responded to Erasmus' *Freedom of the Will* with his own treatise, *The Bondage of the Will*. The two treatises differ markedly in style. Erasmus's style is leisurely and moderate, full of elegant metaphors. Luther's style is polemical, sarcastic, biting. Luther accused Erasmus of not taking the subject seriously due to feeling "no personal interest" in it. "He never has his heart in it and finds it wearisome, chilling, or nauseating; how, then, can he help saying absurd, inept, and contradictory things all the time since he conducts the case like one drunk or asleep. . . . *Theology requires such feeling as will make a person vigilant, penetrating, intent, astute, and determined*" (*Bondage*, Rupp and Watson, 1966: 178–9; emphasis added).

Erasmus appealed to humans' capacity to control their behavior according to rational principles. Luther was convinced that ignorance and contempt for God are not isolated to "the lower and grosser passions," but are thoroughly and intimately incorporated in "the highest and most excellent powers of humans, that is, the reason and the will." So he found it impossible to rely on precisely those aspects of humanity that are most deeply and disastrously affected by sin: "Scripture presents man as not only bound, wretched, captive, sick, and dead, but in addition to its other miseries it is afflicted with this misery of blindness, so that he believes himself to be free, happy, unfettered, able, well, and alive." Luther accused humanists of twisting scripture to apply judgment "to the brute part of human being so that the rational and truly 'human' part may be left untouched." But if reason and the will are part of the problem, he says, they certainly cannot be part of the solution.

Luther and Erasmus differed over the issue of the accessibility of scripture. Erasmus thought that scripture is difficult and obscure; Luther found scripture "wholly clear." "Christ has opened our minds," he said, so that "the subject matter of scripture is all quite accessible, even though some texts are still obscure owing to our ignorance of their terms." However, if one lacks the "key," justification by faith, "no one perceives one iota of what is in the scriptures."

Second, while Erasmus thought that freedom of the will was "not a subject for common ears," it seemed crucial to Luther:

> It is not irreverent, inquisitive, or superfluous, but essentially salutary and necessary for a Christian to find out whether the will does anything or nothing in matters pertaining to eternal salvation. . . . on this question both knowledge of oneself and the knowledge and glory of God quite vitally depend. It is fundamentally necessary for a Christian to know that God foresees and purposes and does all things by his immutable, eternal, and infallible will. Here is a thunderbolt by which free choice is completely prostrated and shattered.
> (*Bondage*, Rupp and Watson, 1966: 118)

Luther repeatedly said that whether or not one thinks the will is free to choose the good affects what he called "the bottom of the heart." Luther, no less than Erasmus, asked the pastoral question, what is the *effect* of belief in freedom of the will? Their answers were diametrically opposed. Erasmus said that belief in free will prompts people to "study and strive." Luther said that belief in free will leads to nothing but "outward works."

Indulgences

Cardinal Albert of Mainz, a young man in his twenties, precipitated Luther's outrage (and thus, the Lutheran reformation) by arranging with the Roman curia to sell indulgences throughout Germany to pay for his installation fee for the archbishopric of Mainz. Half of the money raised was to go to Rome for the rebuilding of St Peter's, the other half to repay Albert's debt. The indulgence was advertised in extravagant terms. "Those who assisted were promised the remission of all their sins, and, apart from any contrition on their part, the release of their friends from purgatory the moment the money clinked in the chest" (Bainton, 1952: 38). Albert did not advertise the fact that he would also gain through the sale of indulgences.

Luther was not alone in his outrage over the indulgence preachers that soon began to work in Germany. His 95 theses were immediately successful because many others were also provoked. He wrote the theses in order to provide Albert with a simple and forceful description of the issues. The theses contained three arguments. His leading argument was the poverty of the German people. "If the pope knew the poverty of the

German people he would rather that St Peter's lay in ashes than that it should be built out of the blood of his sheep" (*Indulgences* 50, 51). But this was actually the least of Luther's objections. His second objection was to the pope's assumption that he had jurisdiction over souls in purgatory. Like other conservative theologians, Luther believed that "the pope could only remit penalties imposed by himself on earth. Indulgences do not affect purgatory, and do not forgive sins" (Bainton, 1952: 40). His third object went to the heart of his theological convictions, namely, that a sinner who is focused on escaping punishment is lost. No attitude but that of horror at his sins could lead to salvation. Luther's insistence that God saves only when the sinner is at the point of abjection and despair is discussed in chapter 7.

The archbishop acknowledged receipt of "treatise and theses by an impertinent monk in Wittenberg touching the holy business of indulgences" (quoted by Haile, 1980: 177). By 1521, shows of support for Luther frightened Albert, leading to Luther's excommunication on January 3, 1521 at the Diet of Worms. Luther did not remove his monastic cowl, however, until 1524. After his excommunication his life was in danger; he was put under the "ban of the empire," meaning that anyone could at any time seize him for punishment and burn his books. He remained for the rest of his life under imperial ban, but was protected by Frederick the Wise, Elector of Saxony and founder of the University of Wittenberg.

We continue to explore Luther's theology in its religious, social, and institutional setting in chapter 7.

READING

Erasmus, *On The Freedom of the Will*; Luther, *The Bondage of the Will*; in E. Gordon Rupp and Philip S. Watson (eds.) (1966) *Luther and Erasmus on Free Will and Salvation*

7 Reforming the Body of Christ: The Sixteenth Century, Part I

1 **Luther's Theology**
2 **Radical Reformations**
3 **Calvin's Theology**
4 **Protestant Developments in the Later Sixteenth Century**

Prologue

> This experiment in individuality is, for the historian, of great interest. But for one aware of the suffering, it is appalling.
>
> (Saul Bellow, *Mr Sammler's Planet*)

Perhaps the most painful aspect of the sixteenth-century reformations was that the new authorities of scripture and individual conscience produced no agreement among people. People for whom religious authority had been clearly and unambiguously posited in the "one holy Catholic and apostolic Church" now struggled to identify and establish religious authority. No one in the sixteenth century questioned the necessity of religious authority, but each group decided differently what that authority should be. Tensions arose almost immediately and mutual persecutions began among different branches of the reformations.

[handwritten annotation: Could not agree on the religious Authority]

The individual in the Protestant reforms

Individuals, in the modern sense – people who understand themselves as more-or-less autonomous, self-consciously self-creating individuals – were virtually unknown before the fifteenth century. Moreover, Western European "individualism" reveals its Renaissance roots in being a highly gendered construct. Male socialization in Western societies has tended to feature "rugged individualism" as a characteristic of maleness, while female socialization has emphasized the value of relationships. Some men actively resist the myth of male autonomy, just as some women resist thinking of themselves as defined by their relationships. Yet there are, and have been, many women and men who accept their socialization, and all women and men are affected by the social world constructed around these assumptions.

Renaissance humanism and the popular vernacular writings of late-medieval mystics revealed a new sense of the individual's inner authority. Although faithful to the Church, mystics valued the inner strength of personal conviction, ultimately finding a new basis from which to question the authority of the late-medieval Church. The individual rather than the religious community was seen as primary. In order to understand why, for the next hundred years or so, people were willing to die and kill for their beliefs, we consider in this chapter each of the most numerically significant of these reforms.

Vision in the Protestant reforms

Protestant reformations brought a massive paradigm shift within Christianity, a new identification of which sense should be centrally engaged and exercised in Christian worship and devotional practice. In Protestant movements, the ear and hearing assumed new importance, while the eye lost its privileged role in religious practice. Martin Luther wrote: "The ear is the only organ of a Christian." He taught that the Word of God enters consciousness through the ear, exposing the "shelters" that conceal a person's complete dependence on God. The Word of God creates the condition of terror in which the person cries out to God, the *only* condition in which God saves. *Sola scriptura* became the slogan of the Lutheran reformation, affirming the authority of scripture for belief and practice.

By contrast the primary ancient and medieval theory of vision underlay the medieval view of the importance of vision in worship and devotion. This theory stated that a visual ray, a concentration of the fire that animates and warms the body, reaches out to *touch* its object. The viewer initiates the act of seeing, chooses the object of vision, focuses, and provides the energy for the act of vision. The visual ray is also a two-way street; an image of the object travels back up the visual ray to be imprinted on the mind and retained in memory. Visual ray theory emphasized the viewer's *activity* in the act of vision. Medieval congregations were required (by the Fourth Lateran Council in 1215) to *ingest* the eucharistic bread and wine at least once a year because they were inclined to think that they had communicated when they gazed on the bread (touching it with their visual ray) elevated by the priest. Most medieval people considered concentrated vision full participation in the sacrament.

Luther accepted the common theory of the visual ray, but he did not think that the Christian *should* be active in worship and devotion. Rather, the worshipper should be *passive*, the Word of God being the active agent. Two centuries before Luther, Meister Eckhart, whose writings Luther knew, had written:

> Hearing brings more into a person, but seeing one gives out more, even in the very act of looking. And therefore we shall all be more blessed in eternal life by our power to hear than by our power to see. For the power to hear the eternal word is within me and the power to see will leave me; for hearing I am passive, and seeing I am active. Our blessedness does not depend on the deeds we do but rather in our passiveness to God. . . . God has set our blessedness in passivity.
>
> (*Sermon* 2; Blakney, 1941: 108)

Some Protestant reformers rejected religious images, but even those (like Zwingli in Zürich) who distrusted the sensuousness of life-sized oil paintings, nevertheless used engravings and woodcut images on printed pamphlets to inform, inspire, and educate a largely illiterate public. Luther privileged the ear, but he did not think that religious images should be discarded. Images should be stripped from the heart, he said, not removed from sight.

Even for those Protestant reformers who retained images, the reformation was an oral event. Yet a new use of vision accompanied the reformations as printing made reform ideas accessible to large numbers of people. The Lutheran reformation was "the first major, self-conscious attempt to use the recently invented printing press to shape and channel a mass movement" (Edwards, 1994: 1). Historian Mark U. Edwards, Jr. has estimated that literacy in German cities was "about thirty percent, greatly exceeding an overall literacy rate of perhaps five percent." Printed documents influenced "opinion leaders" – preachers and teachers – who then passed ideas along orally to large numbers of people. Luther was Germany's best-selling vernacular author. The first of his works available in print was his "Sermon on Indulgences and Grace," which urged people to choose good works over indulgences, arguing that indulgences were not scriptural. Luther, who had never seen a complete Bible until he was 21, translated the New Testament, thereby placing matters of religion before "ignorant common folk." The written word informed and supported the spoken word, carrying and conveying the Word in Protestant reformation culture.

Nevertheless, in discussing a fundamental shift in religious perceptions from image to word, the abruptness of the change should not be exaggerated. The monks of Luther's Augustinian Order, like those of the other mendicant Orders (Franciscans and Dominicans), were preachers to the populations of late medieval towns. Concerned with accessibility, they typically preached in the vernacular on Sunday afternoons to large crowds "in complete separation from the celebration of the Eucharist." The mendicants' preaching activities may have been the "forerunner of the worship practice of Protestants which consisted primarily of liturgies of the Word that were then returned to Sunday morning worship settings" (Posset, 2003: 14).

Luther's teaching on the relationship of Gospel, scripture, and the Word of God exemplifies his attempt to clarify and simplify Christian faith, to reject the obscurities that could puzzle "common folk." For Luther the "Word of God" was not identical with scripture; scripture *contains* the Word of God, but it *becomes* the Word of God only when it acts in a certain way, that is, as a confronting presence: "It is one thing when God is present, and another thing when he is present *for you*. But he is present for you when he adds his Word to scripture and declares 'here you shall find me.'"

According to Luther, the Word of God confronts the individual, exposing the system of hideouts from reality the person has constructed. These inadequate shelters mask the reality that a person never possesses her life; it is, at every moment, received. Luther's analogy is the pitifully inadequate blankets under which a child huddles when she is afraid of the dark. The Word of God effectively strips away that imagined protection and places the person in the presence of God who asks, "Where are you in your life?"

Personal confrontation by the Word provokes the personal response to the Word that is the central activity of faith. Once an opponent quoted a verse of scripture to support an argument; Luther responded, "I know that is the word of God, but is it the Word of God *to me*?" Similarly, in his Latin *Commentary on Jonah* he wrote: "We must not content ourselves to inquire whether a certain word is of God, but we must also ascertain whether this word is intended for us and so apply it to ourselves or not" (1. 2).

Although Word and scripture are not identical, Word and Gospel are synonymous. In 1517 Luther stated, "The true treasure of the church is the most holy gospel of the glory and grace of God" (quoted by Pelikan, 1959: 128). Luther always thought of the Word of God as *spoken* word: "Christ did not command the apostles to write, but only to preach, "he said; and "The Gospel should not be written, but screamed." The written word has less confrontational power than the spoken word. Yet Luther's own tremendous literary output as well as his translation of the Bible into German reveals that although he privileged the spoken word, he was not indifferent to written words and their potential for communicating the Word.

Luther's esteem for words and their power to localize the Word became a hallmark of the Lutheran reform. His esteem for words began when, as a young monk, he used to confess for hours at a time, irritating his confessor, Staupitz, who remarked, "Look here, Brother Martin. If you are going to confess so much, why don't you go and do something worth confessing? . . . Stop coming in here with such flummery and fake sins!" (quoted by Posset, 2003: 112). In the Lutheran reform, preaching became more important than it had been in many medieval churches, and hymns became more important than religious images as a means of focusing religious feeling. Luther himself wrote about 36 hymns (scholars differ on the exact number) and he translated many more from Latin to German.

The idea that images should be used to illustrate rather than stand on their own (accompanying worship and shaping devotion), came from the Lutheran reformation. Twenty-two woodcuts were included in Luther's 1522 German New Testament. In 1524 he designated further episodes he wanted illustrated from the Old Testament. By the 1530s a new school of Protestant biblical illustration was flourishing in Wittenberg. Luther wrote in an introduction to an illustrated prayer book: "And what harm would there be if someone were to illustrate the important stories of the entire Bible in their proper order for a small book which might become known as a layperson's Bible? Indeed, one cannot bring God's word and deeds too often to people's attention."

Luther's own regard for images is summed up in the follow quotation:

> It is possible for me to hear and to bear in mind the story of the passion of our Lord. But it is impossible for me to hear and bear it in mind without forming mental images of it in my heart. For whether I will or not, when I hear of Christ, an image of a man hanging on a cross takes form in my heart just as the reflection of my face naturally appears in the water when I look into it. If it is not a sin but a good thing to have the image of Christ in my heart, why should it be a sin to have it in my eyes?
>
> (*Against the Heavenly Prophets in the Matter of Images and Sacraments*, LW 40, 82)

Luther's colleagues did not all agree with him. His senior colleague at the University of Wittenberg, Andreas Bodenstein von Karlstadt, separated from Luther, insisting on the immediate destruction of images. Karlstadt began with Luther's argument for the power of images, but arrived at a different conclusion:

My heart since childhood has been brought up in the veneration of images and a harmful fear has entered me which I would gladly rid myself of, and cannot. . . . When one pulls someone by the hair, then one notices how firmly his hair is rooted. If I had not heard the Spirit of God crying out against the idols, and had not read His Word, I would have thought thus: "I do not love images. I do not fear images." But now I know how I stand in this matter in relation to God and the images, and how firmly and deeply images are rooted in my heart.

(Quoted by Christensen, 1979: 25)

Despite the rejection of images by some Protestant reformers, images were influential in both Protestant and Roman Catholic reforms in the context of new institutions, new forms of worship, and differently focused beliefs. We examine Lutheran reformation art and architecture later in this chapter.

1   Luther's Theology

Luther distinguished between law and gospel, but he did not simply identify "law" with the Hebrew Bible and "gospel" with the New Testament. Both law and gospel, he said, are scattered in all the books of the Bible. Nor did he differentiate law and gospel temporally: "every age is a time of law and a time of gospel." In fact, Luther said, "grace cannot be preached without law."

> To God alone belongs that sort of seeing that looks into the depths with their need and misery, and is near to all that are in the depths. . . . And this is the source of men's love and praise of God. For no one can praise God without first loving him. No one can love him unless he makes himself known to him in the most lovable and intimate fashion. And he can make himself known truly only through those works of his which he reveals in us, and which we feel and experience within ourselves. But where there is this experience, namely, that he is a God who *looks into the depths and helps only the poor, despised, afflicted, miserable, forsaken, and those who are naught,* there a hearty love for him is born, the heart overflows with gladness, and goes leaping and dancing for the great pleasure it has found in God.
>
> (*Magnificat*)

Luther's famous phrase, *incurvatus in se* describes the habit of sin that vitiates human life. The person is curled in on himself, feeling that he must, by good works, achieve his own salvation. But until law reveals the sinful state of human nature, "Nature per se cannot even recognize the filth of sin." The law's work is "to kill and to damn, to reveal the root of our sin." It is a "power of wrath, not of correction." There is nothing positive about law, except that it destroys all protection from an angry God, dismantling human defenses to the point of abjection. It is *only* at this point that the gospel can begin its work of *recreation*. Two examples help to illustrate Luther's idea of the relationship of law and gospel – the story of Jonah, and the pedagogy of the Lutheran movement.

The story of Jonah, Luther said in his German commentary, is a puzzling biblical story unless one sees in it the paradigm situation of law and gospel. "It is about how powerful, active, and effective God's Word is . . . otherwise it seems an insignificant story." Luther reminded his readers that the outcome of Jonah's story was not predictable to Jonah as it is to us for whom it is a familiar story. Luther analyzed Jonah's situation in the belly of the great fish:

> It is impossible for nature to act or conduct itself contrary to what it feels. And now that it feels God's anger and punishment, it cannot view God otherwise than as an angry tyrant. Nature cannot surmount the obstacle posed by this wrath; it cannot subdue this feeling and make its way to God against God and pray to him, while regarding him as its enemy. . . . The second lesson that we derive from this is that we must feel our crying to God is of a nature that God will answer. . . . That means nothing else but to cry to God with the heart's true voice of faith; for the head cannot be comforted, not can we raise our hands in prayer, until the heart is consoled. And as I have said, the heart finds solace when it hastens to the angry God with the help of the Holy Spirit, and seeks mercy amid the wrath, lets God punish, and at the same time dares to find comfort in his goodness. *Take note what sharp eyes the heart must have,* for it is surrounded by nothing but tokens of God's anger and punishment and yet beholds and feels no punishment and anger, though in reality it does see and feel them, and it must be determined to see and feel grace and goodness, even though these are completely hidden from view. Oh, what a difficult task it is to come to God. Penetrating to him through his wrath, his punishment, and his displeasure is like making your way through a wall of thorns, yes, through nothing but spears and swords. The crying of faith must feel that it is making contact with God.
>
> *(German Commentary on Jonah 2.2)*

Luther called faith "a sort of knowledge or darkness that can see nothing," and a "joyful bet." Preaching and the sacraments are the "means by which faith is created." "It was one thing for God to be present, but quite another for God to be present 'for you.' He was present 'for you' when he added his Word and bound himself to it, saying, 'It is here you can find me.' And so when you have the Word, you can take hold and grasp him with certainty.'"

No single treatise of Luther's described his entire theology, but his "Preface" to the *Epistle to the Romans* laid out the essentials. He began with definitions: law, sin, grace, faith, righteousness, flesh, and spirit, then moved to a précis of the content of Paul's *Epistle to the Romans,* which he called "the most important document in the New Testament, the Gospel in its purest expression." God's law, he wrote, demands that it be fulfilled with "pleasure and love," not with a "reluctant and resisting heart." But this is an impossible demand; people cannot simply produce on demand "a heart that is free and eager and joyful." Sin occurs when a person attempts to obey the law by "doing its [external] works," rather than meeting its requirements "gladly and lovingly." In brief, the "inmost heart" moves to "outer works." When "becoming righteous is taken entirely out of our hand and put into the hand of God," however, grace "makes the law dear to us." The Christian's part is faith, but "no one can give himself faith;" faith is not a person's "doing," but "a divine work in us, a living, busy, active, mighty thing" that makes it impossible "not to do good works incessantly."

What have faith and grace to do with predestination? Luther insisted that predestination is a "comforting" doctrine, and only by following his thought carefully is it possible to see how the potentially terrifying doctrine that God decides "before the foundation of the world" which individuals will be saved or damned could possibly be comforting. Luther used the order of the *Epistle to the Romans* to illustrate the psychological point at which the doctrine alleviates rather than increases fear. Romans, he said, "gives the richest possible account of what a Christian ought to know;" it sets out "the whole of Christian doctrine in brief." "You must study this epistle chapter by chapter, he said. "Concentrate first on Christ and his gospel." Then, in chapters 1 to 8, the problem of sin will arise. Chapter 8 gives the perspective necessary for understanding that predestination is part of the providence of God as revealed in the passion and death of Christ. "If we do not feel the weight of the passion, the cross, and the death, we cannot cope with the problem of providence without either hurt to ourselves or secret anger with God." Predestination, in this context, reassures the Christian that her eternal destiny is completely in the hands of the *God who wills to redeem humanity*. Cautioning that the doctrine of predestination is "strong wine" that must not be drunk by "suckling infants," Luther concludes his preface by admiring Romans' placement of its discussion of predestination at precisely the point in the text that it can be understood as comforting. Luther repeatedly said: "He deserves to be called a theologian who comprehends the visible and manifest things of God seen through suffering and the cross," insisting that the "Christ in whom God was revealed was Christ crucified." The Christian knows Christ "hidden in suffering" (*Heidelberg Disputations*: 21).

God must be distinguished from God's masks, Luther said: on the one hand God is revealed in scripture, that is, through God's Word, but God is also "a supernatural inscrutable being who exists at the same time in every seed, whole and entire, and yet also in all and above all and outside all created things. . . . Nothing is so small but God is still smaller, nothing so large but God is still larger" (*Confession Concerning Christ's Supper*). In order to see the hidden God, one must make use of his self-revelation in his Word.

Like the story of Jonah, Lutheran pedagogy sought to stimulate the crisis situation in which God responds to the sinner's desperate call. Children's catechisms, which began to appear in the 1520s, were intended to be memorized from as early an age as possible. They begin with long lists of moral, physical, and spiritual sins and their punishments. The 1538 catechism of Caspar of Aquila, the Superintendent in Saxony reads in part:

> Question: What have you learned from the Ten Commandments? Answer: I have learned the knowledge of our damnable sinful life. For the Ten Commandments are a book of vices to us in which we read clearly what we are before God without Grace, namely: idol worshippers, miscreants, blasphemers and despisers of God's divine name, cursed robbers of his holy temple, and renegades to his eternal word. We are disobedient abusers of our fathers, we are child murderers and envious dogs, killers, whoremongers, adulterers, thieves and rogues, deceivers, dissemblers, liars, perjuring tale bearers, false witnesses, insolent misers. In sum, we are wild insatiable beasts against whose evil nature God erects the commandments as if they were high walls and locked gates.
>
> Question: Show me out of scripture what will happen to those guilty of ingratitude. Answer: Jeremiah says in the 11th chapter, 'cursed be the one who obeys not the words of this covenant; even his prayer is an abomination to God.' God will scorn such a one in his deepest anguish and not hear him; he will punish him severely with many diseases, to wit: fever, swellings, pestilence, inflation, war, fire and hailstones, sores and boils, and altogether so much terror, misery, suffering, curses, confusions, and frustrations that he must fall into despair.

The method and goal of pedagogy was made very clear in Lutheran catechisms:

> Use the knife of God's word to cut off the branches of their contumacious will. Raise them in the fear of God. And when their wild nature comes up again – as weeds always will – and the old Adam sins in them again, kill it and bury it deep in the ground, lest the newly grown good nature once again revert to its wild state.
>
> (Quoted by Gerald Strauss in Trinkhaus and Obermann, 1974: 291)

This is only half the picture, however. Lists of abuses and threats were followed in each catechism by strong and moving assurances of God's forgiveness and love for the "miserable offenders." Reformation historian Gerald Strauss writes, "[God's love] is always invoked at emotionally powerful junctures in the religious message when the bereft, forlorn human victim of his own wrong instincts sees the restoration of divine love as the *only* remaining hope of comfort, peace, and solace."

Luther and the first Lutherans sought a "consciousness" and not simply a new ordering of ideas. For this, education was essential, and the first carefully planned and unified education, in contrast to the poorly supervised, uncoordinated education available in medieval cathedral and monastic schools, took place in Protestant schools. Modern education began with Lutheran standardization of education. Pedagogy was seen as the only hope, both for individuals and for society. The prologue to one Lutheran catechism read:

> If we wish to increase the kingdom of Christ and populate our community with God-fearing Christians we must make our beginning with children. They are the seed which we must cultivate. As for their elders, they are too far gone in sin. There is no longer any guiding or teaching them, as daily experience with them tells us.
>
> (Strauss, 1978: 293)

Luther had used scripture and conscience to challenge the authority of the Roman Church, but he was not prepared to reject all external authority. Lutheran pedagogy existed in tension with emphasis on the individual and her/his Bible as the locus of religious authority. Perhaps only individuals who had been so heavily trained in childhood could be expected to interpret the scripture in conformity with Lutheran theology and practice.

Luther's insistence on the Christian's freedom needs to be understood in the context of strong pedagogical and political counter-balances. Shortly after his excommunication, he became aware that his teachings on spiritual equality contained the potential for anarchy. He saw how readily this exhilarating concept could be translated into notions of social equality. In 1525 when the Peasant's Revolt erupted, Luther advised political rulers to smash the revolt, urging them to "strike, kill, squash, and burn" the "lawless beasts."

The volatile religious and social situation in southern Germany resulted from lack of a religious authority on which all could agree. On both psychological and social levels, the Lutheran reform was the most disorienting and disturbing event since the Sack of Rome in 410.

Luther's critique of Scholasticism

Luther accused the "scholastic doctors" of creating a highly technical theology that was concerned with definitions rather than with addressing and engaging the "bottom of the heart." The task of theology is not to explain, he said, but to convert, and scholastic theology did not have a doctrine of sin that resonated in "the depths of the heart" with power to convert. Luther rebelled against his own education in which he had memorized long passages from a follower of Wiliam of Ockham, Gabriel Biel. Biel taught that sin consists in single acts of wrongdoing that can be cancelled through penance. For Luther, on the contrary, sin is forgiven and covered, not expiated and cancelled. The Christian *remains*, Luther said, simultaneously righteous and a sinner (*simul justus et peccator*). Rather than removing the person's sin, Christ covers it with *his* righteousness, so that instead of the inadequate blanket of good works, the Christian is covered with the asbestos sheet of Christ's righteousness. The Christian must remain aware of this double state: "Nothing could be so harmful to them as the presumption that they are healthy, for it would cause a bad relapse."

> Man, before he is regenerated into the new creation of the kingdom of the Spirit, does nothing and endeavors nothing toward his preservation or toward his continuing in his creature existence . . . and after he is recreated does nothing and endeavors nothing toward his preservation in that kingdom; but the Spirit alone effects both in us, regenerating us and preserving us when regenerated, without ourselves.
>
> (Rupp, *The Bondage of the Will*, 1966, p. 137)

Luther's critique of Roman sacraments

Luther defined the church as "the assembly of all believers, among whom the gospel is preached in its purity and the holy sacraments are administered according to the gospel" (*The Babylonian Captivity of the Church*). He saw the visible church as functional, providing for Christians' spiritual needs. Only God knows who is a member in the "church of the predestined," however. Based on his theology of sacraments, Luther rejected all but two of the seven sacraments of the Roman Church, baptism and the "Lord's Supper." For Luther a sacrament was composed of two elements, a promise made by God, and a sign. The sinner brought to baptism, he said, "does not so much need to be washed as he needs to die." Luther preferred baptism by immersion, "not because I deem it necessary but because it would be well to give a thing so perfect and complete a sign that is also complete and perfect" (*Treatise on Baptism*). The promise of the Lord's Supper was nourishment, its sign the elements of bread and wine. Luther rejected the doctrine of transubstantiation on grounds that it did not appear in scripture, but he believed that the "real presence" of Christ is objectively given with the bread and wine. (Luther's eucharistic doctrine will be further discussed in chapter 8.)

All the other Roman sacraments – penance, marriage, ordination, and confirmation – Luther said, simply return the Christian to God's promise in baptism; they do not constitute separate sacraments. Luther retained penance as private confession, however, because "it is a cure without equal for distressed consciences." He wrote of ordination,

"Not a single word is said about it in all the New Testament." Christ is the only true priest, but by identification with Christ in baptism, all believers share in Christ's priesthood. Ministers are chosen from among the Christian people to perform certain duties as representatives of all Christians.

Lutheran Reformation art and architecture

Although Luther claimed that the ear was "the only organ of the Christian," painted images played a large part in the Lutheran reformation. Early in the reform, Lucas Cranach the Elder's *Passional Christi und Antichristi* (1521) contained antitheses, paired pictures contrasting the "early Church" and the contemporary church (see CD Rom figure 7.1). The Jena Codex, discussed in chapter 6, used similar images but apparently had no direct influence on the *Passional Christi und Antichristi*. Antitheses were also used in sermons of the time, imaginatively describing the imagined purity of New Testament times and the corruption of the contemporary Church.

Cranach was closely associated with Luther, and a keen supporter of the reform. He painted several portraits of Luther and altarpieces for Lutheran reform churches. He also helped to finance Luther's translation of the New Testament and printed Lutheran pamphlets on his own printing press from 1523 on, though artists, like other adherents of Luther's ideas, were in danger. In his *Passional*, Cranach illustrated Luther's 1520 accusation of the pope as Antichrist.

The "scriptural" scenes in Cranach's *Passional Christi und Antichristi* were set in Germany in the 1520s, not In Rome or Jerusalem, thus encouraging viewers' identification with Christ. In each scene, the poverty of Christ is contrasted with the pope's wealth, and Christ's humility with the pope's pride. The text for a depiction of Christ driving the moneychangers from the temple reads:

> Jesus found in the temple those who were selling/ Oxen and sheep and pigeons, and the moneychangers./ And making a whip out of cords, he drove them all out./ And he poured out the coins of the moneychangers / And overturned their tables;/ And he told those who sold the pigeons, "take these things away!/ You shall not make my father's house a house of trade./ You received everything freely. Therefore give freely."

The inscription for a depiction of the pope selling indulgences reads:

> Here sits the Antichrist in God's holy temple/ Overturning everything God has ordained./ He suppresses the Holy Scripture/ And sells remission of sins,/ Indulgences, and churchly offices./ He burdens consciences with his laws./ He declares sainthood for some/ And condemns others unto the fourth generation./ He commands obedience to his own voice/ As if it were the voice of God.

The closing text offers readers a choice between following the pope and following Christ. The consequences of following Antichrist are clearly explained: Antichrist and his followers will be "killed by Christ's breath and fall by virtue of the glory of his coming."

The pamphlet closes with a quotation from Luther, "Persevere for now. It will soon be better." Within a few years there was a Latin edition of the *Passional* and ten German editions of a thousand copies each.

The Zürich branch of the Protestant reformation was iconoclastic. Zwingli's parish church, the Grössmunster, was a Carolingian church (completed in 1215, with Gothic towers added at the end of the fifteenth century). Its interior decorations had been finished between 1500 and 1518. In response to demands that its images be destroyed, all art was methodically removed from the church by a committee headed by Zwingli and two other priests between June 20 and July 2, 1524 (see CD Rom figure 7.2).

Throughout the sixteenth century the Protestant reformations produced little new church building. Lutheran reformers usually achieved the kind of space needed for worship by altering existing churches. The earliest example in Europe of a surviving Protestant church is the small Schloss-Hartenfels Chapel in Torgau, Germany, dedicated by Luther in 1544 (figure 7.1). This rectangular building with galleries is white-plastered, its only color consisting of moldings and ribs of gray stone. Its furnishings are plain, consisting of an altar, baptismal font, organ, and pulpit. The altar, supported by four carved pillars, holds no relics. A painted altarpiece depicting the Last Supper was added sometime after the dedication of the building. The only other decorations in the church called attention to the spot from which the Word was preached, the pulpit. Polychromed carvings on the pulpit by Simon Schröther depict three scenes: Simeon and the infant Christ; the child Jesus preaching to the doctors in the temple; and Christ driving the moneychangers from the temple.

Lutheran reformation churches included altarpieces with some remarkably (some said blasphemously) different features than medieval altarpieces. The reformers and their families, as well as Protestant princes are placed within the sacred scenes, often taking the place of disciples and apostles (see CD Rom figures 7.3 and 7.4). On the Wittenberg altarpiece, painted by Lucas Cranach the Elder in 1547, the central panel depicts a Last Supper with reformers pictured as the apostles (see also CD Rom figure 7.5). On the predella, Luther preaches Christ crucified to a congregation that includes the painter Lucas Cranach the Elder who points to Luther's wife Katarina and their son, Hans (see CD Rom figures 7.6, 7.7, and 7.8).

Lucas Cranach was a leading citizen and artist in Wittenberg. In 1504 he became the court painter for Frederick the Wise, Elector of Saxony and Luther's protector. He was on the City Council from 1519 to 1549. He was also godfather of one of Luther's children. Between 1520 and 1568, he and his son (Lucas Cranach the Younger) painted Luther's theology, creating a specifically Protestant reformation iconography. Two kinds of paintings were done, single panels, often hung on or near the front of the pulpit, and commissioned winged altarpieces.

The Cranachs also painted the Weimar altarpiece whose central panel is a complex composite scene that includes the crucifixion as well as the resurrection (see CD Rom figures 7.9 and 7.10). The lamb standing at the foot of the cross does not bleed into a chalice as in many pre-reformation paintings (like the Isenheim Altarpiece), but holds a banner of victory, thus substituting the theme of victory for that of sacrifice. On the right of the cross John the Baptist, Lucas Cranach, and Martin Luther attend the cruci-fixion. The stream of blood flowing from Christ's side, arches directly to Cranach's head, claiming a new role for the artist: the artist as believer, interpreter of the Gospel, and

Figure 7.1   Schloss-Hartenfels Church, Torgau, dedicated by Luther October 5, 1544.
A painted altarpiece depicting the Last Supper was added some time after the dedication of the
building. The only other decorations in the church were the polychromed carvings on the pulpit
by Simon Schröther, depicting three scenes: Simeon and the infant Christ; the child Jesus preaching to the doctors in the temple; and Christ driving the moneychangers from the temple. Photo
AKG/Stefan Drechsel.

worshipper. Luther holds an open Bible inscribed with texts cited by Luther in his
sermons on the crucifixion (John 1.7; Hebrews 4.16; and John 3.14–15).

In the background the devil stokes the fires of hell while a condemned man is forced
toward the flames. Hebrews are camped on a hillside with the serpent on a cross pre-
figuring the crucifixion. On Christ's right, prophets appear with Moses holding the
tablets of the law. An angel announces the birth of Christ to shepherds on a distant hill.
Lucas Cranach's placement of the crucifixion within this complex set of images created
a full scriptural context for the reformed faith.

On the left panel, the donors, John Frederick, former Elector of Saxony, and his wife appear; their three sons are on the right panel. Contemporaries would not have found it novel to see donors represented in the wings, and small Dominican figures had appeared on the edges of Fra Angelico's paintings at San Marco. But it was quite new, and must have been startling (and to some, blasphemous) to place recognizable living figures in the center of the sacred scene. Other altarpieces feature the Baptism of Jesus with reformers (Lucas Cranach the Younger 1565) (see CD Rom figure 7.11), and the Resurrection of Christ with reformers (Lucas Cranach the Younger, 1556) (see CD Rom figure 7.12). Reformation artists painted a strong statement about reformers' access to sacred figures and events, implying that Protestant preachers interpreted scriptures from the vantage point of participants in Christ's earthly life.

The Second Wittenberg Altarpiece, completed in 1569 by Lucas Cranach the Younger, contains a vine-covered mountain that stands for the Christian Church (see CD Rom figure 7.13). The left side represents the "old" church, on the verge of being destroyed in spite of all the busy work going on. Workers fill its dried-up well with stones. On the right side, in the vineyard of the Protestant reformation, Luther and other reformers till Christ's vineyard, receiving (at lower center) the same wage as the pope and Roman clergy, who have labored longer (Matthew 20) – an important theme to reformers! On the reformation side, since no worker supposes that he is earning merit with God, the vines flourish.

Reformation theology was communicated visually as well as verbally. In the Dessau Altarpiece, painted by Lucas Cranach the Younger in 1565, the central panel depicts the Last Supper occurring in a renaissance dining hall (see CD Rom figure 7.5). The donor kneels at the front, while reformers and princes surround Christ. To Jesus' right sits Prince George of Anhalt; on his left, Luther, Bugenhagen (pastor in Wittenberg), Justus Jonas, and Caspar Cruciger, superintendent of Lutheran churches in Little Poland and Lithuania, and others. The painter, Lucas Cranach the Younger, is the cupbearer at the right. The painting reiterates the Real Presence of Christ in the Lord's Supper as Luther formulated it. However, Christ's presence was associated with a new ecclesiastical authority – the sixteenth-century "disciples" surrounding him.

Albrecht Dürer (1471–1528) referred to Luther as "a Christian man that helped me out of great distress." Although he was eager to "draw a careful portrait of him from the life and to engrave it on copper," he never met Luther. Dürer appreciated Luther's view that religious images were useful. In 1525 he wrote:

> For a Christian would no more be led to superstition by a picture or effigy than an honest man to commit murder because he carries a weapon by his side. He must indeed be an unthinking man who would worship picture, wood, or stone. A picture, therefore, brings more good than harm, when it is honorably, artistically, and well made.

Dürer presented his *Four Apostles* to the City Council of Nurnberg in 1526, a year and a half before his death (see CD Rom figure 7.14). The *Four Apostles* consists of two tall matching panels, the left depicting a larger than life-sized John and Peter, with Paul and Mark on the right panel. The most important roles in the composition are not given to the traditionally most important apostles, but to John and Paul. Because of Paul's emphasis on faith and grace, Paul was *the* apostle of the Lutheran reform; early

Protestants were sometimes called "Paulines." Luther wrote: "Paul was the wisest man that ever lived after Jesus Christ." He also called Paul "the very best teacher." John, "a master above all other evangelists," was Luther's favorite evangelist.

Peter, holding a key, and Mark are subordinated. Ludwig Grote commented: "By showing St Peter, the first bishop of Rome and the rock of the old church reading the gospel according to St. John, he is saying in plain Lutheran language that the only valid authority in the government of the church is the Word of God – not the fathers, popes, or councils of the church." Three of the four figures hold gospels. John reads from a manuscript that starts, "Im Anfang war das Wort" (John 1:1: "In the beginning was the Word").

Protestants also used non-representational symbols. Luther's seal (see CD Rom figure 7.15) was a visual statement of his theology; he described it in a 1530 letter to a friend. The black cross on a white heart, he said, was meant to signify that:

> although the cross is black and mortifies and must also cause pain, it nevertheless leaves untouched the color of the heart. . . . it does not kill but gives life. . . . However, this cross must be set in a white rose to indicate that faith gives joy, consolation, and peace and, in brief, places us in a pure and joyous rose. . . . The rose is set against a background of heavenly blue. . . . And around the field there is a golden ring as a sign that the bliss of heaven lasts for eternity and is endless . . .

Luther's teachings and the Lutheran reform will continue to engage us. In chapter 8 we return to Luther's theology of the Lord's Supper and his views on marriage, the family, and society. First, however, we look at the several other Protestant reformers.

READING

Luther, *The Freedom of the Christian*; *Preface to the Epistle to the Romans*; *The Babylonian Captivity of the Church*

2   Radical Reformations

The so-called "radical reformations" must be distinguished from the "magisterial" reformations." The term "magisterial" refers to the branches of the Protestant reform in which princes decided the religious loyalty of people in their territories. These include the Lutheran and the Reformed traditions, including Zwinglian and Calvinist groups, and the English reformation. Radical reformers agreed that the separation of religion from the control of national or territorial states was a fundamental necessity if religion was to be religion. They believed that religion should be by *voluntary association*, not by secular princes' choice. Many denounced war and all forms of coercion except the "ban" by which disobedient members were excluded from communion. Magisterial reformers had initiated the use of vernacular languages in propaganda against Roman Catholics; radical reformers used it in polemics against magisterial reformers.

Within the radical reformation, Anabaptists and Spirituals can be differentiated by their different choices of an ultimate authority. Both were considered politically as well as religiously dangerous, and they were vilified and persecuted by magisterial reformers and Roman Catholics alike. Their geographical distribution was focused in Switzerland, Austria, Moravia, and South and Central Germany. Calvin called them fanatics, scatterbrains, deluded, and mad dogs. Bullinger, the Swiss reformer, called them "devilish enemies and destroyers of the church of God;" Luther called them fanatics (*Schwärmer*). The radical reformation, never an organized movement, consisted of local groups, some of which are still in existence in North America: Hutterites, Amish, Moravians, Mennonites, Schwenfeldians, Polish Brethern, and less directly, Unitarians.

Anabaptists

For Anabaptists, ultimate religious authority lay in the individual's relationship with God, unmediated by church, sacraments, or doctrines. Anabaptists were anti-clerical, opposed to both magisterial reformers' and Roman Catholic clergy's claim to act as mediators between the believer and God. For radical reformers, Christianity was "personal, experiential, immediate, and individual." They valued scripture and made extensive use of the New Testament, but neither scripture nor the sacraments were absolute authorities for them. They thought of the Lord's Supper as a "commemorative banquet" or a "fellowship meal." They rejected infant baptism; as one Anabaptist, Pilgram Marpeck (d. 1556), said: No one can believe for anyone else, "neither husband for wife, wife for husband, children for parents, or parents for children." They were called "Anabaptist," or rebaptizers, but the name was inaccurate since they believed that they had only been efficaciously baptized once – as adult believers.

Radical reformers rejected what they considered unwarranted additions to the simple community-centered worship of early Christians. Their services were "genuine fellowships of believers, sharing in Bible study, prayer, and mutual admonition, without formal liturgy." They were committed to spreading their beliefs by informal, usually one on one, missionizing. They have been called "the Protestantism of the poor," because their beliefs spread rapidly among the poor they regularly cared for. And, more than any other reforming groups, they were persecuted heavily for their beliefs.

Anabaptists had a different starting point from that of the magisterial reformers. They began, not with a crushing experience of sin, but from the experience of rebirth. Original sin, they said, does not condemn, except as a person "makes it his own." Anabaptists were primarily interested in sanctification rather than justification. The Anbaptist Balthasar Hubmaier said that Luther's teaching on justification by faith alone is an oversimplification. Some people, he wrote, "have grasped only two articles from all the preaching: 'we believe, faith saves us;' and 'we cannot do anything good; God works in us the willing and doing and we have no free will'" (Williams and Mergal, 1952: 114). He wrote his "little book" to "show what a person *can do*." It outlines a complicated dualistic anthropology as support for his belief that people can – and must – do *something*.

Anabaptist groups differed enormously among themselves on many matters of church discipline and authority, but they held in common the doctrine of an *inwardly disciplined* and *externally free* "apostolic" church. Seeking direct access to the divine, they called the magisterial reformers "new popes." Anabaptists were the first religious group to practice separation of church and state.

Origins

The largest group of Anabaptists emerged from the Zwinglian reform of Zürich. Another sizable group left the Lutheran reform at the time of the Peasant's War in 1525 in the south German principalities.

The Swiss Anabaptists contested Zwingli's policies in Zürich. Zwingli (see CD Rom figure 7.16), a Catholic priest and humanist scholar, began his gradual conversion to reform by setting aside the lectionary and expounding scripture, verse by verse. By 1525, he had preached his way through the whole New Testament. Reform began in Zürich in 1522 when Zwingli preached against compulsory Lenten fasts. The town council agreed not to impose Lenten fasts, but said that they should be followed for the sake of good order. Not satisfied, Zwingli and his followers pressed for the ruling that "all religious customs should be based on the pure word of God." This undermined the authority of the Roman Catholic bishop in Zürich, and it established civil rule.

In 1523, Zwingli prepared his *Sixty-seven Articles*, comprised of by-then familiar Protestant statements. They asserted the authority of the Bible over that of the church, salvation by faith, and the right of nuns and priests to marry. They denied that good works merit salvation, that monastic vows are binding, that there is a purgatory, and that anything is required of a Christian except what the Bible states. Zwingli also softened the traditional understanding of original sin: "Original sin is not sin but disease, and the children of Christians are not condemned to eternal punishment on account of that disease."

In 1525 the city council forbade religious images and abolished the mass. In its place, a "love feast" was instituted as a memorial and remembrance of Christ. Zwingli believed that the elements of bread and wine of the Lord's Supper are symbolic and commemorative. All ornaments, clerical robes, tapestries, frescoes, relics, crucifixes, and images were removed from the Grössmunster, and bell-ringing, organ-playing, and singing ceased. In 1527 the great organ in the cathedral was dismantled. No music, even hymn-singing, occurred in worship in Zürich for over a hundred years. The exclusion of music was highly uncharacteristic of Protestant reforms.

Zwingli was cautious about too many precipitous changes in church practice. The issue over which radical reformers split from the Zwinglian reform was infant baptism. Zwingli said that infant baptism was not clearly taught in scripture, but he feared that abolishing it would be too radical. He concurred when the city council ordered parents to have their infants baptized or leave the city. After several public debates, some colleagues withdrew from Zwingli and began preaching their own convictions, namely that baptism could only be properly administered to adults who freely believed the gospel. They began "rebaptizing," at first by sprinkling, but immersion came to be the accepted form. In 1527 leaders of the "rebaptizers" met at Schleitheim and drew up the seven articles of the Schleitheim Confession:

1   Baptism shall be given to all who have learned repentance and amendment of life, and who believe truly that their sins are taken away by Christ, and to all those who walk in the resurrection of Jesus Christ and wish to be buried with him in death, so that they might be resurrected with him.

2   The use of the ban after secret admonition twice so that all who partake of the Lord's Supper may be one in mind and love.

3   Exclusion from the breaking of bread of any who are not united by baptism in the one body of Christ which is the Church of God and whose head is Christ.

4   Separation from the evil and wickedness of the world, from all popish and anti-popish works, meetings, and (Catholic) church attendance, drinking houses, civic affairs, and abominations, from all use of the sword and weapons of force.

5   Pastors who have good standing in and out of the communion, to read, admonish, teach, warn, discipline, ban, pray, and lead the faithful, who shall be supported by the church, and disciplined by the church if they fall into sin, and who in case of martyrdom shall be succeeded by others chosen and ordained in the church in the same hour.

6   Non-use of the sword in connection with the ban, refusal to serve as a judge in worldly disputes, or to serve as a magistrate or a prince, since they employ the sword.

7   Rejection of all swearing and oath-taking.

(Quoted in Raitt, 1987, *Christian Spirituality* II: 346.)

Most of the radical reformers refused to bear arms, serve in the military, swear an oath, or hold any civic office. Many, like the Hutterites also refused to pay war taxes or revenues for executioners' wages, although they were obedient to authorities in all matters that did not violate their consciences.

The second largest group of Anabaptists came from southern Germany. Luther's denunciations of the corruptions and abuses of monasticism were interpreted by many German townspeople and peasants as a mandate to seize church properties. The name "Peasant's War" is a misnomer in that not all, and perhaps not most of the participants, were peasants. In 1525, the Twelve Articles, a list of demands addressed to the church and the German nobility was written. The Articles demanded release from serfdom on the grounds that all Christians are free and equal. Luther's ideas of the priesthood of all believers seemed to protesters to mandate a more egalitarian society. The Twelve Articles, based on Luther's *The Freedom of the Christian*, included the right the choose and depose their own pastors, withdrawal of the cattle tax, communal ownership of fields, forests, and meadows, and hunting and fishing rights.

Luther replied to the Twelve Articles in his treatise *Admonition to Peace*. He said that Christian freedom is a spiritual, not a social, status and he deplored the externalization of an interior and spiritual condition. Christians, he said, were obliged to bear wrongs patiently. Rewards for longsuffering would be forthcoming in the next life. But 300,000 Germans – townspeople, peasants, knights, even priests, who had very little to lose – were already ravaging and pillaging. Luther believed that the sword had been given to secular princes for the purpose of keeping order; in 1525 he wrote *Against the Robbing and Murdering Hordes of Peasants*, urging princes: "Smite, slay, and stab, secretly or openly, as if among mad dogs, lest the whole of the land be ruined." An estimated 100,000 Germans perished in the subsequent suppression. Luther's position lost him much of his popularity, and two of his senior colleagues and friends, Andreas Bodenstein Carlstadt and Thomas Müntzer, left him to support the revolt. As a result of the War, peasants' situation deteriorated further. Peasants became the personal property of the landlord, and had no political rights until the early nineteenth century.

Between 1525 and 1535 the radical reformation spread rapidly and persecution fell heavily. Anabaptists were feared politically because they were thought to endanger the union of church and state by seeking to establish a counter-culture based on the Bible. It was feared that toleration of religious differences would lead to civil war as, in fact, it did in France and England. Moreover, all of northern Europe was in terror of attacks by the Turks who had advanced through Hungary and as far as Vienna, Austria, by 1541.

In this political climate, Anabaptists' refusal to support or fight for the state seemed treasonous. In sixteenth-century Switzerland there was no paid standing army. Instead, every man was expected to be armed and ready for defense. To refuse military service was to refuse citizenship. One Anabaptist, Michael Statler said:

> If the Turk should come, we ought not to resist them. For it is written "thou shalt not kill." We must not defend ourselves against the Turks and others of our persecutors, but are to beseech God with earnest prayer to repel and resist them. If warring were right, I would rather take the field against so-called Christians who persecute, capture, and kill other Christians than against the Turks. The Turk is a true Turk, knows nothing of the Christian faith, and is a Turk after the flesh. But you who would be Christians and who make your boast of Christ persecute the pious witnesses of Christ and are Turks after the spirit!

Anabaptist women were imprisoned, tortured, and martyred along with men. Historians estimate that by 1535, 50,000 Anabaptists had been martyred. In 1529 and 1530, the diets of Speyer and Augsburg made membership in an Anabaptist group punishable by death. In many places informers and bounty hunters were employed to identify Anabaptists. After 1563, in imperial territories, a bonus was added; information leading to the arrest and conviction of Anabaptists was rewarded with a third of the accused person's property. Many territories required that baptisms be registered, so it could more easily be seen who *did not* baptize children.

Roman Catholics still burned at the stake for heresy in the medieval manner; Protestant princes primarily decapitated or drowned in the eight Protestant territories in which Anabaptists were executed. Drowning was considered an especially apt punishment for people who insisted on rebaptizing those who came into their movement. In Roman Catholic territories, heresy laws were executed with severity, while in evangelical (Lutheran) territories, Anabaptists were usually treated as seditionists rather than heretics and allowed to emigrate. They were imprisoned or executed only if they persisted publicly in their faith. Some German territories rejected the death penalty for heresy and some town councils refused to condemn to death familiar neighbors known to be gentle, upright, and charitable. In merely imprisoning or banishing Anabaptists, they violated the imperial law that demanded their death.

Entrance into an Anabaptist group was by baptism or rebaptism, if one had been baptized formerly. Adult baptism was interpreted as an imitation of Christ's baptism: "In baptism," Balthasar Hubmaier wrote, "one pledges oneself to God, in the Supper, to one's neighbor, to offer body and blood in the neighbor's stead as Christ did for us." In later Anabaptism, baptism was thought of as the decisive appropriation of salvation. The Lord's Supper became the ritual of communion with like-believers.

The ban was the exit from an Anabaptist community. Menno Simons, founder of the Mennonites and a former Roman Catholic priest, wrote a treatise *On the Ban* that exhibits the painful obedience of people committed to obey all the scripture. "The scriptures show that it is a command," Simons wrote. Fragile, mobile, rapidly changing groups needed to be able to define themselves, to eliminate, as one Anabaptist said, "extraneous matter." "The church without this power is a monstrous body lacking the faculties and instruments of evacuation and expulsion of excrements, or other noisesome things, and therefore is never appointed by God to life, but to death and destruction." The ban was a final reinforcement of church discipline, the result of their view that the church is a visible community needing protection from contamination. Menno Simons endeavored to show that the ban is necessary, but that "true Christian love takes precedence." The point of the ban was the reformation of lives; this objective was to inform every exercise of the ban: "The ban was instituted to make us ashamed *unto reformation*. Let it be done with all discretion, reasonableness, and love."

Simons said that it is ultimately *unloving* not to cooperate with the ban, even if it is placed on one's spouse or child, because to comply with the ban is "to seek the reformation of my own body." Simons was careful to specify that the ban is a withdrawing of *spiritual* communion, not the refusal to "give a worldly greeting." Neither is the ban intended to preclude care for someone who has been banned: "I would care for them, provide the temporal necessities of life, so far as it be in my power."

Simon's treatise, although addressed to those who might overzealously apply the strictures of the ban, was also a polemic against the Roman Catholic "greater excommunication," which deprived the excommunicated of the "right to administer or receive the sacraments, and of all public and private communion with Christians, and all the rights and privileges of the church except last rites." By contrast, Simons insisted: "we are not to deny necessary services, love, and mercy to the banned [for] the ban is a work of divine love, not of perverse, unmerciful heathen cruelty."

Spirituals

"Anabaptists" and "Spirituals" have often suffered by association with one of the most dramatic of Anabaptist groups. The so-called "Münster event" was directed by its leader, Jan Matthijs, formerly a Haarlem baker. The "revelations" he received daily indicated to him that he should rule despotically, crown himself King David, drive out the sick and the aged, and execute critics. After Matthijs's death, the new leader, Jan of Leiden, introduced polygamy. Sins punishable by death in Münster included blasphemy, seditious language, scolding one's parents, adultery, lewd conduct, backbiting, spreading scandal, and complaining. But the Münster event was only the lunatic fringe of Anabaptism. Obbe Philips's "A Confession" (1957) gives a contemporary account of the Münster group.

Instead of looking to the past, to apostolic times, for their beliefs and values, as did Anabaptists, Spirituals looked to the future. In his "Letter to John Campanus," Spiritual Sebastian Franck insisted that the real church died out shortly after the time of the apostles. Since then the visible church has been nothing but a hollow shell of the spiritual church. Anything that remains from the real church is "all in the Spirit and no longer outward." The truth is intact, but is not available in outward form. Casper Schwenckfeld's treatise, "An Answer to Luther's Malediction" extends Franck's argument, saying that the sacraments are suspended until it is revealed that they are to be reinstated. The sacraments, he said, are too important to celebrate externally. Rather they must, for the present – and the present is still in effect in the Schwenckfelder Church based since 1734 in Pennsylvania – be construed solely as *inner* nourishment.

Spirituality of the radical reformations

The spirituality of the radical reformation was characterized by a strong emphasis on discipleship, on *following* Christ. Radical reformers rejected both Luther's tenet of justification by faith alone and predestination to salvation or damnation (double predestination). They placed emphasis on the passion of Christ as a present event in which all are called to participate. They spoke of following the "bitter Christ," rather than the "sweet Christ" of the magisterial reformers. By "following the bitter Christ" they meant that one cannot be saved

> other than by suffering and tribulation. If someone needs an animal it must first be killed, prepared, cooked, and roasted and the animal has to suffer according to the will of the one who uses it. If God would use us, we have first to be justified and cleansed within and without. And this can only take place under the cross and suffering.
>
> (Quoted in Raitt, 1987: 340)

Radical reformers emphasized solidarity in suffering with Christ and also in the suffering of all creatures. Their "gospel of all creatures" saw the natural world as a paradigm of suffering and the complete abandonment of self: "letting loose of oneself" (*gelassenheit*).

> In the "gospel of all creatures" is nothing else signified and preached than simply Christ crucified, but not Christ alone as Head, but the whole Christ with all members. . . . He did not direct the poor people to books, but he taught them and showed them the gospel by means of their work. . . . From such parables people are diligently to mark how all the creatures have to suffer the work of men, and come through the suffering to their end, for which they were created, and also how no one can come to salvation, save through the suffering and tribulation which God works in them.
>
> (Hans Hut, *The Mystery of Baptism*)

Clearly, the spirituality of the radical reformations was influenced by the constant threat and reality of martyrdom. From this reality, a literature and cult of martyrdom arose, complete with relics, saints' lives, stories, hymns, and poems describing martyr's deaths.

The Anabaptist woman, Janneken Munstdorp, in prison awaiting execution wrote to her infant daughter a short summary of Anabaptist values. Speaking of herself and the child's father she wrote:

> Let it be your glory that we did not die for any evil doing, and strive to do likewise, though they should also seek to kill you. And on no account cease to love God above all, for no one can prevent you from fearing God. If you follow that which is good, and seek peace, and follow it, you shall receive the crown of eternal life; this crown I wish you, and the crucified, bleeding, naked, despised, rejected, and slain Jesus Christ for your bridegroom.
>
> (Quoted by George, 1987: 345)

Second to the Bible, the most important document of Anabaptism was a book entitled: *The Bloody Theater or Martyr's Mirror of the Defenseless Christians Who Baptized only upon Confession of Faith, and Who Suffered and Died for the Testimony of Jesus Their*

Savior. Published in Dutch in 1660, it ran to 1,290 pages. The first section described martyrs who were beheaded for administering the "true baptism of repentance," beginning with John the Baptist and concluding with the death of Savanarola in 1498. The author sought to establish a connection with the martyr church throughout the ages, uniting Anabaptist martyrs to this long tradition (George, 1987: 343). It may seem odd that descriptions of trials, torture, and excruciating deaths would attract converts. Nevertheless, it is a well-documented historical phenomenon, and not only in the radical reform. In the English reformation, John Foxe's *Acts and Monuments of the Christian Martyrs* played a similar role (discussed in chapter 8).

In hymnals like the Swiss Brethren's *Ausbund*, major themes were patience in suffering and suffering as the way to salvation. Among the 84 hymns appear 24 songs about martyrs' trials, torture, and executions. These were sung to standard tunes that must have been memorized since they have no musical notation.

Economic justice was a preoccupation of the radical reform, perhaps because many of them were poor. Reformers like Menno Simons specifically differentiated his church from those of the mainline reformers by care for the poor:

> True Christians, he wrote, do not allow a beggar among them. They have pity on the wants of the saints. They receive the wretched. They take strangers into their houses. They comfort the sad. They lend to the needy. They clothe the naked. They share their bread with the hungry. They do not turn their face from the poor, nor do they disregard their decrepit limbs and flesh. This is the kind of Christianity we teach.
>
> (Quoted by George, 1987: 363)

Some groups, like the Hutterites in Moravia, lived in pacifistic communes in which all goods were shared and property held in common.

The disappearance of common authority in the sixteenth and seventeenth centuries resulted in the deaths of hundreds of thousands of people. Why were people willing to die (and kill) for their beliefs? It is difficult for twenty-first-century people, familiar with terrorism claiming religious motivation, to sympathize either with martyrs or their executioners. We should, however, attempt to understand both, if only as an exercise in historical imagination. For sixteenth-century Christians of all persuasions who believed in the reality of eternal punishment for wrong beliefs, the stability of society as well as religious integrity depended on the maintenance of orderly communities with common beliefs. Most late-medieval cities had places for execution outside the city gates, visually announcing to all who entered the city that social order and religious conformity would be enforced within the city walls.

READING

Thomas Müntzer, *Sermon before the Princes*
Balthasar Hubmaier, *On Free Will*
Menno Simons, *On the Ban*
Sebastian Franck, *A Letter to John Campanus* (in G.H. Williams and A. Mergal (eds.) (1952) *Spiritual and Anabaptist Writers*)

3   Calvin's Theology

The designation "Protestant" was not used until 1529, but reformation spread rapidly in Western Europe from southern Germany and Switzerland. Cities were reformed under the direction of different reformers: Zwingli and Bullinger in Zürich; Wolfgang Capito and Martin Bucer in Strasburg; Oecolampadius in Basel; Zwingli in Zürich; and Farel and Calvin in Geneva. Calvin's reform produced both what has been called "Protestantism's most comprehensive theological system," and a model community.

John Calvin (1509–64) (see CD Rom figure 7.17), was a second-generation reformer. In his youth he prepared for a legal career, but changed to humanistic studies. His first book was a commentary on the Latin author, Seneca, written to imitate and compete with Erasmus. Calvin's early attitude toward reform of the Church, like that of Erasmus and other humanists, was that the church could be reformed without creating a new institution. Calvin was radicalized when his friend Nicholas Cop was inaugurated as rector of the University of Paris. Cop's address advocated salvation by faith and a return to the "pure Gospel." The address so incensed its audience that Cop and Calvin (his close friend) were obliged to flee Paris. Calvin, dressed as a vinedresser, escaped in a basket.

Calvin did not offer many autobiographical vignettes in his voluminous writings. His only reference to a conversion experience is embedded in his *Commentary on the Psalms*, written in 1557. His description reveals no sense of a sharp break with the past. Describing his early career change from law to theology, Calvin remarked, "God turned my course in another direction by the secret rein of his providence. What happened first was that by an unexpected conversion he tamed to teachableness a mind too stubborn for its years." Calvin's greater interest in sanctification than in the moment of "quickening," seems to have come from his experience: "We are converted little by little to God, and by stages," he wrote (*Commentary on Jeremiah* 31.18). William Bouwsma, one of Calvin's biographers, comments: "Calvinism was the creation of a devout sixteenth-century French Catholic."

In 1536 Calvin went to Geneva, which Guillaume Farel was already in process of reforming. Calvin urged further reforms, but his proposals did not attract Genevans, and he was expelled in 1538. However, in 1541 the town magistrates invited him back to Geneva to "restore order" and to stop the ever-increasing flow of people returning to the Roman Catholic faith. From then until the end of his life he worked, with varying degrees of success, to create a godly community in Geneva.

In Paris, advocates continued to urge reform. Their opponents responded with zealous persecution. In 1536, Calvin addressed the first edition of his *Institutes of the Christian Religion* to the king of France, Francis I, to explain the need for reform within the context of a comprehensive theology. He continued to revise, enlarge, and rewrite the *Institutes* until shortly before his death (the 1559 edition). In a prefatory "Address to King Francis" he appealed for tolerance for French Protestants. His preface to the reader states that the *Institutes* were addressed to "candidates in sacred theology." "Those who have received from God fuller light than others," he said, should help "simple folk by lending them, as it were, a hand in order to guide them and help them to find the sum of what God meant to teach us in his Word." Some passages of the *Institutes* may have been too difficult for either candidates in sacred theology or "the simple," but endeavoring to make the *Institutes* broadly accessible, Calvin translated each Latin edition (except the first) into French.

> The right way to seek God and the best rule we can follow [Calvin said] is not to force ourselves with too bold a curiosity to inquire into his majesty, which we ought rather to worship than to investigate too curiously, but *to contemplate God in his works*, by which he renders himself near and familiar to us and, we might say, communicates himself.
>
> (*Institutes* I. IV. 1; emphasis added)

Calvin began with the premise that self-knowledge and knowledge of God are interconnected. What, then, do human beings need to know about themselves in order to know God? What do they need to know about God in order to know themselves? He answered that the first thing people need to know is that:

> what is noblest and most to be valued in our souls is not only broken and wounded, but altogether corrupted, that perversity is never idle in us, but continually produces new fruits; just as a burning furnace ceaselessly throws up flames and sparks, and as a spring spouts its water. Wherefore, those who have defined original sin as a *lack* of the original justice which ought to be in humankind, although in these words they have comprehended all the substance, still they have not sufficiently *expressed the force of it*. For our nature is not merely empty and destitute, but it is so productive of every kind of evil that it cannot be inactive.
>
> (*Institutes* II. I. 9; emphasis added)

Contrast this view of human nature with Renaissance humanists' rhetoric about the greatness of "man." To these claims, Calvin replied, "The scriptures show us what we are in order to reduce us to nothing. It is true that human beings will intoxicate themselves all the more, deluding themselves with belief in their great dignity. They may well think highly of themselves, but God in the meantime knows them to be only a lot of stinking refuse" (*Institutes* II. I. 8).

Yet Calvin was a humanist, one of the best Latinists of the sixteenth century. Did he simply invert humanism in his doctrine of a fatally flawed human nature, or did vestiges of humanist theory remain in his thought? Humanism and human sinfulness are somewhat awkwardly combined in Calvin's theology. In spite of his belief that human nature was fundamentally corrupt, he cataloged many human achievements, citing as examples of human goodness that humans demonstrate the "light of reason" concerning the government of this present life; they excel at mechanical arts, philosophy, and all the liberal arts; and they have a "natural propensity" for orderly societies. In short, Calvin believed that humanity contains considerable beauty and goodness, and his examples of human goodness did not refer only to Christians.

> When we see in a pagan writer this admirable light of truth which appears in their books, it ought to admonish us that the nature of humanity, fallen though they be from integrity and much corrupted, does not cease still to be adorned with many of the gifts of God. If we recognize the Spirit of God as the unique fountain of truth, we shall never despise the truth wherever it may appear. We cannot read books that have been written on all these subjects without wonderment.
>
> (*Institutes* I. III. 3)

Moreover, despite its perversity, humanity retains the image of God; "we find God a hundred times both in body and in soul" (I. V. 4). The natural world also exhibits strong evidence of its creator, the "elegant structure of the world serving us as a kind of mirror." At the same time, humans have "no more power of loving God than a stone, a tree-trunk, or a piece of mud." Why? Because all human beings participate in original sin.

> It must not be said that this obligation is incurred solely by the fault of another, as though we were answering for the sin of our first father without having deserved anything. For what has been said, that by Adam we are made accountable to the judgment of God, does not mean that we are innocent and that, without having deserved any punishment, we are bearing the unmerited effect of his sin: but that since, by his transgression, we are all involved in confusion, he is said to have laid us all under obligation.
>
> (*Institutes* II. I. 8)

Providence

Both Calvin's intense awareness of human depravity and the many goods he saw in human nature must be understood in the context of his central concern with recognizing, maintaining, and heightening the "glory of God." Calvin thought it "cold and life-less" to see God merely as original creator. Providence *perpetually* creates the world: "All events whatsoever are governed by the secret counsel of God." There is, in fact, "no random power or agency or motion; nothing happens fortuitously; not a drop of rain falls without the express command of God." "Fortune and chance," he said, "are heathen terms;" Providence pervades the universe.

Is God responsible for evil then? Calvin distinguished God's "permission" from God's "will." He gave an example:

> Whence, I ask you, comes the stench of a corpse, which is both putrified and laid open by the heat of the sun? Everyone sees that it is stirred up by the sun's rays; yet no one for this reason says that the rays stink. Thus, since the matter and guilt of evil repose in a wicked man, what reason is there to think that God contracts any defilement, if he uses his service for his own purpose?
>
> (*Institutes* I. XVII. 5)

Anthropology

Calvin's strategy for accentuating and dramatizing the glory of God and God's activity was to use the human race as a foil. He described all human capacities as vitiated, enervated, and so corrupted that it is useless to seek salvation in some capacity of human being. Calvin was explicit about his use of the human race as a contrast for God's glory: "Our insignificance," he said, "is God's exaltation." Anything human is "naturally averse to God." This was Calvin's vision, the impetus for his theology. It was also the foundation for some of his most difficult teachings.

Calvin called consciousness of God's glory and its effects in the world "quickening" (*vivificatio*). Quickening does not result from a new intellectual understanding of God, but from recognition of an intimate *connection* of the believer with Christ by which "Christ's life passes into ours and becomes ours, just as bread when taken for food becomes vigor for the body." Quickening enables a person to see particular events and individual lives as *concrete forms or localizations* of God's glory. A supernaturally heightened consciousness is needed to perceive the glory of God.

Calvin frequently used images of change speeded up to a terrifying rate. "Everything rushes headlong," he said, even though "everything longs for permanent existence, that fixed condition that nowhere appears on the earth" (*Institutes* III. IX. 5). He called the world of human experience a "slippery place," not only externally, but also in intellectual and physical experience. The body is "unstable, defective, corruptible, fading, putrid, and pining." The mind is not spared the same evaluation: it is equally untrustworthy in its "boiling restlessness, fickleness, contradictoriness, and ambition" (*Institutes* III. X. 6).

Calvin's idea of salvation was powerful and complex; it requires careful interpretation. In the Latin and French editions of the *Institutes*, he characterized the sinful state of humanity in various ways. His favorite term was "sluggishness," but he used many synonyms: torpor, lethargy, intoxication, dullness of apprehension, drowsiness, coldness, and deadness. These words indicate that Calvin's "depravity" was similar to what a modern person might call depression. It makes a person "so lazy that instead of taking only a minute to move our foot, we need an hour before we can stir; for every step we take forward, we stumble and fall back two, or suffer some pitiful setback" (*Institutes* III. XII. 8; see also I. XV. 3). The problem is that life rushes along, but human faculties fatigue and are unable to *stay with it*.

The problem is how to adjust to the speed of reality. What must happen in order to move a person from "sluggishness" to "quickening?" Picture a person busily engaged in weaving a piece of carpet on which to stand. By the doctrine of total depravity, Calvin suddenly whisks the carpet from under her, and she sees, in the dizzy seconds between losing her balance and falling, that there is nothing to do, nothing to be, nothing to own, but all is the "glory of God." This is simultaneously knowledge of oneself and knowledge of God. But there is a further step. Quickening happens when a person responds to this beauty and terror with faith:

> When a person is laid low by the consciousness of sin and stricken by the fear of God, and afterwards looks to the goodness of God – to God's mercy, grace, and salvation, which is through Christ – he raises himself up, he recovers courage, he takes heart and, as it were, he returns from death to life.
>
> (*Institutes* III. III. 3)

In the split second in which one realizes one's worthlessness, one instantly emerges into participation in the glory of God. Fully understood, this gives new meaning to "worthlessness" or "total depravity."

But quickening does not provide a *method* by which the experience of quickening can be incorporated into a Christian life. *Sanctification*, a lifestyle of continuous and cumulative appropriation of quickening, must occur. Sanctification is the process by which quickening becomes a lifestyle characterized by holiness. This *process* interested Calvin more than the sudden momentary flash of quickening. Sanctification is "not accomplished in a moment, a day, or a year," but by interrupted, slow progress. Two attitudes energize sanctification: repentance – awareness of one's continuing failures and inadequacies – and gratitude for the new life in Christ. Each attitude corrects the other. Repentance prevents the slackening of attentiveness that Calvin has called "sluggishness;" gratitude guards against too much focus on repentance, which would bring discouragement. "The Spirit is called the spirit of sanctification, because the Spirit quickens and cherishes us, not merely by the general energy which is seen in the human race as well as other animals, but because the Spirit is the seed and root of heavenly life in us."

Scripture

Calvin was a biblical theologian. He bracketed philosophical questions, but his commentaries on scripture fill 45 volumes in the English translation. He wrote commentaries on nearly every book of the Bible, most of them preserved as lecture notes by students at the Academy of Geneva. He was a modern biblical scholar in his concern to establish an adequate text and his insistence on the study of original languages.

According to scripture, God can be known in two activities: in nature as creator, and in scripture as redeemer. "Therefore, while it becomes a person seriously to employ his eyes in considering the works of God, since a place has been assigned him in this most glorious theater that he may be a spectator of them, his special duty is to give *ear* to the Word that he may the better profit" (*Institutes* I. XV. 6).

Like Luther, Calvin assumed that scripture is heard rather than read – or that reading is a kind of hearing. Although God revealed Godself to the patriarchs and prophets of the Hebrew Bible by oracles and visions, now that these have been written, Christians must learn from scriptures:

> It is impossible for anyone to obtain even the minutest portion of right doctrine without being a disciple of scripture. God, foreseeing the inefficiency of his image imprinted on the fair form of the universe, has given the assistance of his word to all whom he has ever been pleased to instruct effectually, we too must pursue this straight path if we aspire in earnest to a genuine contemplation of God; we must go, I say, to the Word, where the character of God, drawn from his works, is represented accurately *and to the life.*
>
> (*Institutes* I. VI. 1; emphasis added)

Scripture was a self-authorizing starting point, an authority, Calvin said, that Christians must believe "to have come from heaven as directly as if God had been heard giving utterance to them." He believed that the canon of scripture was an achievement of the Spirit, not the Church. Like Luther, he opposed the Roman Church's claim to authoritative interpretation of scripture by insistence on the clarity of scripture. He did not mean by this that the meaning of every verse is evident; rather he meant that scripture's salvific message is clear and accessible.

Spirit

Calvin taught that Spirit and scripture must be considered together because Spirit works *through* scripture. Scripture and Spirit refer to and imply one another. He was adamant on this point, opposing radical reformers who advocated the authority of visions and direct personal illuminations. He recognized *interpreters of scripture* as prophets, not visionaries.

> Let it therefore be held as fixed that those who are inwardly taught by the Holy Spirit acquiesce implicitly in scripture; that scripture, carrying its own evidence along with it, deigns not to submit to proofs and arguments but owes the full conviction with which we ought to receive it to the Spirit.
>
> (Institutes I. VI. 1)

If scripture is clear and its meaning evident, why is the Spirit necessary for accurate interpretation? The Spirit is needed, Calvin said, to produce *conviction and certainty*: "In vain were the authority of scripture fortified by argument or supported by the consent of the Church or confirmed by any other helps if unaccompanied by an assurance higher and stronger than human judgment can give" (*Commentary on Isaiah* 45.19).

> Read Demosthenes or Cicero, read Plato, Aristotle, or any other of that class; you will, I admit, feel wonderfully allured, pleased, moved, enchanted; but turn from them to the reading of the sacred volume, and whether you will or not, it will so affect you, so pierce your heart, so work its way into your very marrow, that, in comparison of the impression so produced, that of orators and philosophers will almost disappear.
>
> (Institutes I. VIII. 1)

The Spirit produces *existential conviction*, because "we feel a divine energy living and breathing in it, an energy by which we are drawn and animated to obey it, willingly indeed, and knowingly, but more vividly and effectively than could be done by human will or knowledge." Calvin was openly contemptuous of any theological system that fails to generate the energy, motivation, and incentive for appropriation. The Spirit infuses this energy into scripture, which, without Spirit, would be nothing but black marks on a page.

Neither creation nor redemption can be known without the Spirit, which applies inwardly the external meaning of creation and the historical incarnation of Christ. The Spirit is also essential for the Christian's sanctification.

Christ

As we have seen, Calvin polarized God and human being, attributing all goodness to God and abject sinfulness to human being. He made these distinctions in order ultimately to describe a *unity of God and human*, of Christ and the Christian. Lacking such clear distinctions, "unity" is confusion. Once he had differentiated, even polarized, God and human, Calvin used such phrases as the following to describe the unity of Christ with the Christian: Christ has "riveted us to himself;" Christ "dwells in us;" Christ "not only unites us to himself by an undivided bond of fellowship, but by a wondrous communion brings us daily into closer connection until Christ becomes altogether one with us." "We are united with him more closely than are the limbs with the body." And "the union that we have with Christ belongs not only to the soul, but also to the body, so much so that we are flesh of his flesh and bone of his bone."

In Christ, the image of God is renewed in the Christian and the Christian receives "an assurance which leaves no doubt that the goodness of God is clearly offered to us. This assurance we cannot have without truly perceiving its sweetness and experiencing it ourselves." Calvin's appeal to vivid religious experience characterized the Calvinist tradition, as Luther's ultimate appeal to God's promises was fundamental to the Lutheran tradition.

Predestination

Calvin's most difficult doctrine is his teaching on predestination. By predestination he referred to an absolute, irrevocable, election to salvation or damnation. "The grace of God does not *find*, but *makes*, persons fit to be chosen" (III. XXI. 8; emphasis added). Calvin was the first Christian thinker to teach consistently and without equivocation that God actively damns as well as saves (double predestination). Although Augustine and Luther had preferred to speak of God's *foreknowledge* of who would be saved, they sometimes acknowledged scriptural warrants for a doctrine of double predestination. Calvin recognized that it makes little logical sense to say that an omnipotent God foreknows rather than foreordains.

> We rightly say that God foresees all things even as he disposes them; but it is confusing to say that God elects and rejects according to his foresight of this or that. When we attribute foreknowledge to God we mean that all things have always been and eternally remain under his observation, so that nothing is either future or past to his knowledge. He sees and regards them in the truth as though they were before his face. We call predestination the eternal decree of God by which he *decided* what he would do with each person.
>
> (*Institutes* III, XXI. 8; emphasis added)

He defined predestination in *Institutes* III. XXI. 5: "By predestination we mean the eternal decree by which God determined within himself whatever he wished to happen with regard to every person. All are not created on equal terms, but some are preordained to eternal life, others to eternal damnation; and accordingly as each has been created for one or the other of these ends, we say that he has been predestinated to life or death."

Predestination was not Calvin's most central theological interest, however. In 1552 he wrote a short treatise "On Predestination;" in the 1556 edition of the *Insitutes* he mentioned it twice; and he devoted four chapters of the 1559 *Insitutes* to it. The importance of the doctrine for Calvin was that belief in predestination emphasized God's absolute omnipotence and the Christian's total dependence on God. He wrote, "It is plain how greatly ignorance of this principle [predestination] detracts from the glory of God and impairs true humility" (*Institutes* III. XXI. 1). He gave a curious reason for the limitation of election to a few: "The better to display God's liberality in this most excellent gift, God does not bestow it on all promiscuously, but by special privilege God imparts it to whom God will."

Calvin considered predestination a necessary support for the doctrine of justification by faith. God, throwing works entirely out of view, elects those whom he has predestined . . . to make it appear that our salvation flows entirely from the good mercy of God, we must be carried back to the origin of election . . . there being no other means of humbling us as we ought, or making us feel how much we are bound to God. . . . We shall never feel persuaded as we ought that our salvation flows from the free mercy of God as its fountain until we are made acquainted with his eternal election.

(*Institutes* III. XXI. 1)

Unlike Luther, Calvin did not fear that meditating on election and predestination might cause despair. On the contrary, Calvin thought that one could be assured of election:

The election of God is hidden and secret in itself, but the Lord manifests *by the calling*, that is, when he does this good to us by calling us. Wherefore, people are being fantastic or fanatical if they look for their salvation or the salvation of others in the labyrinth of predestination instead of keeping to the way of faith that is offered to them . . . *to each one his faith is a sufficient witness* of the eternal predestination of God, so that it would be a horrible sacrilege to seek higher assurance.

(*Institutes* III. XXI. 7; emphasis added)

Predestination is usually described from the perspective of those who feel some confidence that they are elect (John Bunyan, discussed in chapter 9, is an exception). *Assurance of election* is the context for Calvin's theology of predestination.

Whoever finds himself in Jesus Christ and is a member of his body by faith, he is assured of his salvation; and when we want to know this we do not need to go up on high to inquire about something that must now be hidden from us. For behold! God himself comes down to us; he shows us enough in his son; it is as though he were saying, here I am; contemplate me and know that I have adopted you as my children.

Calvin made a casual suggestion that was placed in a different theological context and emphasized by his followers, the New England Puritans. He said that Christian "works" are a sign or demonstration of "the Spirit of adoption that has been given to us." He also said that works are an "inferior sign," and he insisted that people should not try to figure out whether others are elected by observation of their works. Elect and reprobate exist together in church and society until God separates them at the Last Judgment.

We ought never to expunge the excommunicated from the number of the elect or to despair of them as if they were already lost. And the more we perceive pride and obstinacy in them instead of humility, the more we ought to commit them to the hand of God and commend them to his goodness, hoping better for the future than we can see for the present.

(*Institutes* IV. XII. 9)

Seeking to determine who is elect and who is reprobate would disastrously undermine the church and society. Calvin advocated what he called " a certain judgment of charity" by which Christians *ascribe* election and church membership to all who profess faith.

Church

Church and society were the two arenas in which sanctification occurred. Calvin thought of the church as a halfway house between fallen human nature and God's intention for human beings, a place to begin to restore the order lost in the fall. The Church's job is, by the Spirit's energy, the *renovatio imago dei*, the restoration of the image of God. The Church dispenses aids to generate and nurture faith, the "means of grace." Calvin had many images for the Church, but none occurred as frequently as the image of the mother. He spoke of the Church as "the mother through whom alone we enter into life; away from her bosom one cannot hope for any forgiveness of sins or any salvation."

The Church is also a community of grace and salvation. Calvin defined the Church as the "Word truly preached and sacraments rightly performed" – in that order. But isn't there a contradiction between belief in predestination and the need for the preaching and sacraments of the Church? To answer that question we must take into account not only what Calvin said but also what problems were solved for Calvin by the doctrine of predestination. Calvin held the doctrine of predestination because he found it in scripture, but it also had a more immediate benefit.

Predestination explained a perplexing, even anguished, question that came from Calvin's experience. He asked, "Why does the preaching of the Word not move equally all who hear it?" His answer was "because it bears fruit only in the elect." In short, the doctrine of predestination explained to Calvin why not everyone responded to his preaching. But why preach at all, if every person's eternal destination is already decided? Because it is through preaching that the elect are moved and drawn to recognize their election. Preaching is for the purpose of awakening faith and enabling sanctification.

For Calvin, sacraments were secondary in importance to preaching. He referred to sacraments as "another aid, near and similar to the preaching of the gospel, to the sustaining and confirming of the faith," but he always insisted that the sacraments merely supplement preaching. The gospel alone would be sufficient. He discussed sacraments at length in *Institutes* IV. XV. A sacrament is "an external sign by which the Lord seals on our consciences his promises of goodwill towards us, and we, in turn, testify our piety towards him." Like Luther Calvin retained only two sacraments, baptism and the Lord's Supper: "For baptism bears witness that we are purged and washed and the supper of the Eucharist that we are redeemed."

Although he largely accepted Luther's reasoning about the sacraments, Calvin weakened Luther's interpretation. Luther had said that the primary meaning of baptism was death and rebirth; Calvin thought of baptism as washing. He defended infant baptism as "conferring blessing toward salvation," but having difficulty supporting the practice from scripture, he had to be content with quoting Jesus' words, "Let the children come to me." He wrote of the elements of the Lord's Supper, "the bread and wine are visible signs which represent to us the body and blood: the name and title of body and blood is attributed to them because they are instruments by which our Lord Jesus Christ distributes them to us." However, in 1540 he wrote to Martin Bucer:

> Although the body of Christ be in heaven, we nevertheless truly feed on it here on earth, because Christ, by the unfathomable and omnipresent virtue of his Spirit, makes himself so much our own that he dwells in us without change of place. I can see nothing absurd in saying that we are truly and really receiving the flesh and the blood of Christ, and that thus he is food to us substantially, so long as it is agreed that Christ comes down towards

us not only in the outward symbols but also in the hidden working of his Spirit so that we can ascend to him by faith.

(Treatise on the Lord's Supper)

The Lord's Supper was celebrated four times a year in each parish in Geneva.

Calvin's Geneva

Calvin believed that temporal and spiritual governments should be separate, but he also held the medieval idea that the state should protect and cooperate with the Church. These ideas, together with his insistence that there are no criteria by which to determine who is a true member of the Church and who is not, resulted in a concerted effort to extend the discipline of sanctification to the entire city. In the *Institutes* he gave the following reasons for discipline: "to ensure that the church of Christ was not dishonored, to prevent the good members of the church from being corrupted by the bad, and to help the bad mend their ways" (Benedict, 2002: 97). The Genevan "experiment" undertook nothing less than the dramatic transformation of society.

Calvin met resistance to all his efforts to reform Geneva, and he was never the absolute dictator that caricature has invented. In 1541 the secular magistrates called Calvin to return to Geneva. Calvin's Geneva in 1541 was a small town, pressured by crowding, plague, and the challenge to its government caused by a large influx of refugees from persecution of Protestants in France (after 1530, the population of Geneva more than doubled, numbering 21,000 people in 1560). Calvin's mandate was to restore order in the church, and he took on the job with characteristic energy and determination. Calvin was first and foremost a minister in Geneva, hired and paid by the secular rulers of Geneva, the magistry. The power he wielded in the city was based on his control of "the only means of mass communication and public indoctrination in Geneva – the pulpit" (Naphy, 1994: 154). He also controlled directly the personnel of the Genevan churches. Soon after his arrival in Geneva, Calvin undertook to rid the churches of incumbent ministers in order to replace them with "educated, socially prominent, hand-picked foreigners who could be expected to give Calvin their wholehearted support" (Naphy, 1994: 223).

The pulpit, not the governing bodies of Geneva, was the "single most important means available to Calvin for shaping Genevan minds and mores" (Naphy, 1994: 153). Calvin's sermons were often vitriolic, "specific personal attacks," directed at Geneva's rulers as well as its people. He complained pointedly that "the rulers of Geneva refused to accept correction and behave as they were told" (Naphy, 1994: 161). In short, "the consolidation of the Reformation in Geneva along lines consistent with Calvin's idea of a godly state was a long and difficult process. The result was never a foregone conclusion" (Naphy, 1994: 222).

One of Calvin's first acts in Geneva was to write a set of ecclesiastical ordinances specifying the establishment of a consistory of pastors and elders to examine people reported to hold dissenting religious opinions, who did not attend church services, or who were accused of vice or crime. The ordinances also required children to attend weekly catechism classes and admitted no one to communion who could not recite the catechism. As a *church* board, the consistory heard reports of religious irregularities and moral infractions once a week and assigned penalties consisting of fines, imprisonment, banishment, and excommunication. The secular board, the magistry, alone could pronounce the death penalty.

Calvin dominated the consistory like a tyrant (according to his enemies) or like an angel of God (according to his friends). The scriptural injunction to "judge not," Calvin wrote in his commentary on the beatitudes, refers only to judgments inspired by malice. Despite Calvin's concern for the separation of church and civic jurisdictions, the establishment of the consistory duplicated some of the tasks of the magistry, causing confusion and resentment among the citizens of Geneva. In 1542 the body heard 320 cases, 161 of which involved religious infractions. In 1550 the consistory heard 584 cases; only 86 involved alleged magical or Catholic practices and other religious problems. The majority of cases heard by the consistory involved interpersonal disputes (238 cases) such as family quarrels and domestic violence. Of the cases heard, 160 concerned alleged sexual improprieties. "Thirty-eight people were summoned in 1550 to answer reports that they had spoken ill of the church's ministers or the growing numbers of French refugees in the city." Three kinds of punishment were used in the first years of the consistory's operation: "private admonition before the consistory, usually by Calvin himself; exclusion from communion; and referral of serious offenses against civic morals legislation to the secular magistrates" (Benedict, 2002: 97).

The consistory's activities were contested – sometimes quite vigorously – until at least 1555. The conflicts were exacerbated by people's resentment of ministers from France, imported and paid by the magistrates, who zealously endeavored to reform Genevans' morals. Although the banning of "Catholic" names may not seem major, in a society in which families named their children after relatives and ancestors, this caused significant opposition to Calvin and the ministers. In 1555 an uprising against the French refugees was harshly punished (by exile and execution), effectively ending internal opposition, but costing Calvin his reputation in other cities.

Social reform

Between 1541 and 1550, 48 people were executed in Geneva, and 42 were banished. In 1545–6, 37 people were executed as plague-spreaders. Between 1551 and 1557, 35 people were executed; 96 were banished. Between 1550 and 1557 (the year of Calvin's death), sexual immorality was the most frequent crime (Naphy, 1994). Other infractions included profanity, fighting, dancing, playing cards, carousing, laughter or loud noises in the church, coming late to church, gambling, theatrical performances, not attending church, obstinacy, baptism by midwives, charging interest in excess of 5 percent, pilgrimages, reciting the Lord's prayer (considered a Catholic practice), idols, celebrating papal feasts, saying the pope is a good man, and fasting. Taverns were made into restaurants and equipped with vernacular Bibles, and private homes could be checked at any time without notice for immorality or "Catholic paraphernalia." In 1553 the consistory excommunicated 16 person; by 1560, it excommunicated more than 200 person each year, showing a steep increase in its activities after 1555. Historian Robert Kingdon has estimated that the number of morals cases called before the consistory between 1541 and 1563 is approximately equal to one case against every citizen of Geneva.

It is important to notice that the consistory's zeal against immorality apparently was not prompted by any hostility to sex on Calvin's part. He approved of sex, eating, and drinking. "It is permissible to use wine," he said, "not only for necessity, but to make us merry." He professed himself "carried away in admiration" by the miracle of human reproduction, an especially poignant emotion given the deaths in infancy of all his own children (Bouwsma, 1988: 137).

Vigorous efforts to legislate sexual morality were a prominent feature of Calvin's Geneva. Attempts to regulate sexuality were not new in Geneva, but former laws and social arrangements had tended to be lenient on sexual offenders and permissive of prostitution – except when opportunity arose to make examples of prominent citizens. Under the consistory's jurisdiction, newly intensified regulation of sexual behavior was part of the reconstruction of society. Sexual relations outside of marriage, accepted and regarded as inevitable through most of the fifteenth and early sixteenth centuries, were now condemned and prohibited. Those accused of adultery and fornication were punished harshly. The consistory was largely successful in its goal of regulating morality, protecting marriage, and supporting families. "The city's parish registers [c. 1555] reveal astonishingly low rates of illegitimate births and of prenuptial conceptions" (Benedict, 2002: 103). However, in *Adultery and Divorce in Calvin's Geneva*, Robert Kingdon (1995) argues that although the consistory endeavored earnestly to reconcile unhappy marriage partners, it became apparent that one way to lessen adultery (considered a crime) was to allow partners with differences that could not be reconciled to divorce and remarry. "During the period of Calvin's ministry, it is clear that divorce of the modern type, allowing both partners to remarry, became possible in Geneva" (Kingdon, 1995: 175). Divorce did not become common in Geneva until two hundred years later, late in the eighteenth century.

Calvin did not envision the consistory as a repressive jurisdiction but rather as a "cure for souls," albeit rather more efficient and far-reaching than the medieval discipline that went by that name. "There should be no strictness that may burden anyone," he wrote, "and even none but medicinal corrections, in order to recall sinners to our Lord." He also insisted that "corrections" should be balanced with teaching. His catechisms familiarized children and adults with theological problems and positions and their moral implications that until then had been left to the experts.

Calvin's attitudes toward women and Geneva's treatment of women were those of most sixteenth-century male-governed societies. Genevan women were not educated beyond basic literacy, and thus were marginalized from significant roles in cultural life. However, Calvin went beyond the teachings of other reformers in stating that "Paul's advice for women to be silent in the church" should be included among the *adiaphora* (incidental matters, not central to Christian faith and practice) in which the church should be open to change.

Yet Calvin's Geneva was repressive. Convinced that he was acting as God's representative, Calvin did not tolerate criticism well, let alone personal attack. In Calvin, personal idiosyncrasy combined with power in an age that encouraged people to identify with their religious ideas and to shape the self ruthlessly around them. Several historians have argued that Calvin's intransigence was caused by personal anxiety. They cite the death of his mother when he was four, his father's immediate remarriage and Calvin's banishment from the household (to live with a noble family). However, Calvin's writings do not encourage psychological speculations; they reveal very little about him.

Social explanations of Calvin's agenda are more helpful than psychological explanations. He lived in an age that almost universally believed that persecution of religious and social dissidents was necessary in order to preserve the orderliness and cohesiveness of society. From a twenty-first-century perspective, Calvin was clearly intolerant. But toleration, if it was known at all in the sixteenth century was considered laziness – failure to preach, cajole, or force adherence to ideas that they believed came directly from God, "as if God had been heard giving utterance to them." Calvin wrote, "Being assured in my conscience that what I have taught and written did not grow in my brain, but that I hold it from God, I must maintain the same if I do not wish to be a traitor to the truth."

Moreover, the persecuted became persecutors at the first opportunity. Anabaptists, the most brutally persecuted of the Protestant reform groups, persecuted other Anabaptist groups whenever they had the power to do so. One historian calls them "markedly more intolerant than the institutional Church." Persecution of dissidence was standard religious behavior in the sixteenth century. Indeed, it could be argued that Calvin's regime exhibited far more clemency than did other city governments in executing only one person for heresy in the entire period of Calvin's leadership in Geneva (Michael Servetus). Calvin recognized that he was himself continually at risk; he was, in fact, informally but publicly accused of heresy by several opponents.

Such considerations do not condone Calvin's harsh attempts to legislate morality and religious assent in Geneva. They do, however, embed Calvin's intolerance for dissent in the almost unquestioned matrix of commonly accepted ideas of his time. It is difficult to differentiate between Calvin's personality and the social values of his world. Tolerance would have entailed "a compromise with conscience." The French proverb, "To understand all is to forgive all" is not necessarily true. If we accept it as true, we are less likely to do the difficult work of understanding, assuming that understanding commits us to "forgive." Forgiveness is, after all, wholly irrelevant, but understanding is not, because understanding how a historical situation worked, or failed to work, can alert us to the possible effects of present loyalties and advocacy.

Michael Servetus

The execution of Michael Servetus (1553) was one of Geneva's most deplorable episodes. Servetus, a renowned physician and a self-taught critical theologian entered into violent controversy, by mail, with several of the reformers concerning the relationship of the eternal Word to the historical Jesus. Servetus said that he did not find the Trinity in the Bible and he denied that God took human substance in Christ. His book *On the Errors of the Trinity* (1531) exposed him to punishment by death for antitrinitarianism; after writing it he lived for 22 years in France under an assumed name.

In 1545 Servetus sent Calvin a draft of his *Restitution of Christianity*. Calvin replied by sending a copy of his *Institutes of the Christian Religion* to Servetus for his instruction. Servetus returned the copy with copious marginal notes, many of them scornful and sarcastic. Calvin reported him to the Inquisition in France. Servetus escaped from France and fled to Geneva; why he did so remains a mystery. He attended Calvin's church, the Cathedral of St Pierre (the so-called Grössmunster), in Geneva, where he was arrested and subsequently tried by the magistry (Servetus was not brought before the consistory). At his trial Servetus answered accusations of heresy with counter-accusations of heresy against Calvin, demanding that Calvin be expelled and his goods turned over to him, Servetus. On October 27, 1553, he was burned at the stake, despite Calvin's pleas for a less painful death.

The morality of putting to agonizing death the man (Servetus) who is credited with being the first to discover the circulation of the blood did not go entirely unnoticed. The event motivated Sebastian Castellio (1515–63) to write his anonymously published treatise, *Concerning Heretics and Those Who Kill Them*. In it he argued that burning heretics is far removed from Christ's spirit and words. "To kill a heretic," he wrote, "is not to defend a doctrine, but to kill a person." He concluded, "The Christian's entire life has only one purpose, which is that declared by Jesus: to translate into reality the love of God and fellow human beings." Almost no one agreed with Castellio. In reply, Theodore Beza of Lausanne wrote a defense of Serevtus's execution, *Of the Punishing of Heretics by the Civic Magistrates*. Later, in his *History of the Life and Death of Calvin* (1565), he wrote:

> There are few towns in Switzerland or Germany where Anabaptists have not been put to death, and rightly; here [Geneva] we have been content with banishment. Here Bolsec blasphemed against the providence of God, here Sebastian Castellio derogated the very books of the holy scriptures, here Valentin blasphemed against the divine essence. None of these is dead; two were only banished, the third got off with formal amends to God and the government. Where is this cruelty? Servetus alone was sent to the fire. And who was ever more worthy of it than this wretch who, for the space of thirty years in so many ways blasphemed against the eternity of the Son of God . . . ?
>
> (Quoted by Cottret, 2000: 207–8)

The ministers and magistrates of Basel, Zürich, and Bern, consulted by Genevan authorities, were unanimous in agreeing that Servetus should be executed. Luther's colleague, the gentle, scholarly Melanchthon, who had met Servetus, wrote to Calvin:

> I have read the writing in which you refute the detestable blasphemies of Servetus, and I return thanks to the Son of God who was the arbiter of your combat. I am in entire agreement with your judgment. I affirm also that your Magistry was acting justly in putting this blasphemer to death after a regular trial.

Servetus was also burned in effigy by Roman Catholics in France.

Sixteenth-century punishment

A good deal of scholarly attention has focused on the repressive aspects of Calvin's Geneva. However, Geneva was not unique among sixteenth-century cities in seeking to enforce its citizens' good behavior. Close study of most, if not all, cities of the time reveals similar strategies. Castellio's wisdom may seem obvious to many twenty-first-century people; in its own time it advocated that cities abandon a policy of spectacular punishment they counted on for achieving stable societies. Indeed, public punishment itself was a statement about the state's authority, replacing private vengeance for private wrongs. Moreover, if – as was believed – punishment deters, then punishment provided a teaching opportunity. Thus, moralizing sermons were preached at executions, and the conduct of the condemned carefully scrutinized for signs of exemplary contrition. Stripped of humanity by tortures that rendered his body grotesque, the condemned was removed by death from the company of the living. In southern Germany and Switzerland, the late-medieval sentencing formula stated:

> This poor man shall be hanged on the high gallows by a new rope between heaven and earth, so high, that his head shall almost touch the gallows and beneath him the leaves and grass may grow. Here he shall be strangled to death by the rope so that he will die of it and be undone and his body shall remain on the gallows so that it shall be given over to the birds in the air and taken away from the earth so that furthermore neither persons nor property may be damaged by this man and others shall witness his punishment as a fright and a warning.
>
> (Quoted in Merback, 1998: 139)

A message about the state's power to avenge was not, however, the only or perhaps even the primary message received from spectacular punishment. Rather, in viewing a hanging, beheading, burning, drowning, or breaking with the wheel, spectators beheld a Christian drama of repentance, purification by suffering, and salvation. By torturing and executing the condemned, "in their own eyes a community had 'paved the way to eternal life for a soul seemingly beyond redemption.' . . . The entire community saw it as its responsibility to ensure that the poor sinner's conversion and repentance was complete and satisfying" (Merback, 1998: 144–5). Far from being an accidental effect of punishment, pain was the medium through which repentance and salvation were thought to occur. "Good pain" (discussed in chapter 5), could produce not only mystical experience but also the salvation of the obdurate and the community's stability. Centuries would pass before Castellio's advocacy that the ritual of publicly visible punishment be forfeited seemed praiseworthy to large numbers of people. Even today some urge (for various reasons) that executions be televised.

READING

Calvin, *Institutes of the Christian Religion* I, II–V; II, VII–XI; III, XXI–XXV

4 Protestant Developments in the Later Sixteenth Century

In Western Europe the early sixteenth century was a time of religious excitement about various proposals for the reformation of Christian life and practice. In the later sixteenth century the new religious groups settled down to defining, articulating, and in some cases legislating, exactly what they believed.

The sixteenth century was a time of unprecedented religious anxiety. The loss of a stable religious authority and disagreement over what authority might take the place of the One Church led, in the public arena, to devastating wars and mutual persecutions. In the private sphere, a malady virtually unheard of in the fifteenth century reached epidemic proportions. Historian H. C. Eric Midelfort describes the increase of melancholy and its treatments. Melancholy, he writes, became "the premier disease of the sixteenth century." It was thought of as a religious disease: "As the level of theological argument rose . . . so did the apparent level of religious madness and demonic possession, that is, of resolute and stubborn error" (Midelfort, 1984: 134).

Luther's friend and successor, Philip Melanchthon, wrote a treatise on melancholy, and Andreas Planer wrote: "The devil can make one melancholic. Melancholy persons are healed not by the use of drugs, but by prayers. The melancholy are authors of their own death. . . . Old women with melancholy tend to become witches" (*De morbo Saturnino seu melancholia*; quoted by Midelfort, 1984: 123). The young Luther suffered from melancholia, attributing despair to attacks of the devil and finding in Bible study "medicine against depression" (Posset, 2003: 94).

Protestants and Roman Catholics treated melancholy differently. Protestants did not practice exorcism, despite clear references to it in the New Testament. They believed that although Christ and the apostles had cast out demons, the age of miracles was over. Demon possession still occurred, they acknowledged, but it should be treated by increased reading of the Bible and prayer. Catholics practiced exorcism and thus had a cure that often worked well for a range of psychosomatic illnesses.

Mental disease is a cultural artifact that tends to be diagnosed relative to an available cure. In sixteenth-century Germany, melancholy was a disease increasingly identified with learned men and princes. When poor people suffered from mental illness their disease was characterized by "silliness and nonsense," inability to work, and regression, both socially and legally, to the status of children. They were instructed to read their Bible and pray. When wealthy and learned people were melancholic, however, they received medical attention based on physicians' assumption that the cause of all illness was physical in origin. Thus, wealthy sufferers were bled to adjust the balance of humors in the body. The roots of modern psychiatry lie in sixteenth-century approaches to melancholy. (After a brief hiatus in the twentieth century during which the "talking cure" was the approved way to address mental illness, doctors once again tend to adjust the body by the use of prescription drugs to address mental illness.) While historians concentrate on the wars and persecutions resulting from sixteenth-century religious turmoil, there is evidence that the personal psychological effects were equally vast.

Protestantism was established in many parts of Western Europe in the later sixteenth century. In no two countries was the pattern the same. This chapter explores the spread and consolidation of Lutheran and Reformed churches and the origins of Unitarianism. Chapter 8 discusses reform in the British Isles and Roman Catholic reform, recovery of some areas initially lost to Protestantism, and the beginning of Catholic missions.

Unitarians in Poland and England

Antitrinitarianism was the direct result of Protestant emphasis on individual Bible study. Some, like Calvin's opponent Michael Servetus, said that they didn't find either the word "trinity" or the idea of a divine trinity in scripture. Antitrinitarianism as a *movement*, however, began within the reformed churches of the Netherlands. It migrated, largely driven by persecution, to Poland and England. One of the first records of antitrinitarian beliefs in Poland was the 1539 burning of a jeweler's wife, Catherine Vogel (80 years old), for believing in the existence of "one God, creator of all the visible and invisible world, who could not be conceived by the human intellect."

On January 22, 1556, Peter Giezek (Latin: Gonesius), a former lecturer in logic at the Padua Academy, faced a synod of Polish Calvinists and stated his creed. He declared that the trinity did not exist, and that the word "trinity" was an unscriptural invention; he criticized the Athanasian Creed (used by Lutherans), rejecting it as a human invention; he said that God the Father is the sole God, and that there is no other; and he said that Christ is inferior to his father, his father's servant. He supported these statements from scripture and the writings of Irenaeus with great erudition. The synod formally denounced him, but some of the attending pastors were convinced, and they formed the nucleus of the Unitarian organization in Europe, although the official break with the reformed church came only in 1563.

Unitarians migrated to Poland. At a time when religious wars were raging in Europe, Poland was enjoying a cultural renaissance, largely attributable to the political and religious freedom tolerated there. Many religious groups flourished in the second half of the sixteenth century in Poland. In the latter half of the seventeenth century, Calvinist Andrew Lubieniecki wrote the first *History of the Polish Reformation*. While we might see a laudable "pluralism" in this religious picture, Lubieniecki saw Poland as "seething with heresy, a mass of various worships, the like of which could have been seen only in heathen times."

A religious consensus gradually formed around the concept of God's unity, though antitrinitarians, originally called "Socinians," differed among themselves on how to describe Jesus Christ. Meanwhile groups with unitarian beliefs were heavily persecuted and died out in many places, or, as a Calvinist chronicler said: "they were wiped out by Jesus Christ through his servants." But by the second generation – after 1600 – the Unitarian movement spread, becoming influential in England and the Netherlands.

The founder of European Unitarianism, Faustus Socinus, was an Italian from Siena, a person of great learning who went to Poland to seek sympathizers. Socinus was heavily criticized by his followers, some of whom thought that he overestimated the role of Christ while some accused him of underestimating that role. Within 40 years of his death, his followers said they found errors in his thought and objected to being called "Socinians." Instead they accepted the originally pejorative name given them by their Calvinist opponents, Unitarians.

Unitarians held three tenets, which can sound as startling to us as they did to sixteenth-century people only by a heroic effort of historical imagination: freedom of religious thought; the principle of applying reason to the interpretation of scripture; and tolerance of all creeds. They exhibited a remarkable humility in matters of doctrine and theology and a willingness to rethink any belief. George Schomann, author of the earliest Unitarian catechism (1570), advised: "From Catholicism through Lutheranism, Calvinism, and Anabaptism I have come to the true catholic faith. If a still purer church should arise at any time, then at once join it."

Written statements of faith never held the prominence in Unitarianism that they did in Calvinism. Unitarians wrote catechisms because they wanted to demonstrate the rationality of their beliefs, not in order to demand adherence to those beliefs. The Racovian catechism (1605) described God as omnipotent and with free will, but fundamentally inscrutable to the human mind. Socinus had written: "To speak of three persons [by which he meant three individuals] is to speak irrationally; only one God can possess supreme dominion over things." Unitarians held that human beings have the freedom to will, but difficulty in *performing*, the good. Unitarians did not believe in predestination and original sin. The Racovian catechism emphasized human beings' capacity for obedience or disobedience.

Unitarians thought of the Holy Spirit as the energy of God. They described Jesus as a mortal man while he lived on earth but, at the same time, the only begotten son of God, distinguished from other people by his perfect holiness of life. At his resurrection he was given the "office" of chief director of human salvation. Jesus is humanity's high priest, not because of the sacrifice of his life, but because of his *present* mediation and intercession since his return to heaven. Polish Unitarians baptized by immersion, interpreting baptism simply as a rite of initiation. They also practiced the Lord's Supper, calling it a feast of remembrance.

Unitarians held strong views on society. Governments should not compel Christians to bear arms, they said, and they rejected the concept of "just war." They also believed that Christians should not go to court, but that civic magistrates were to be obeyed in everything that did not conflict with conscience. Like Anabaptists, they advocated the separation of church and state. Unitarians embraced pacifism, even if one had to die for it. Initially Socinians were mainly ruling class people, but social radicalism is a difficult stance for the rich. Fairly soon this radicalism was interpreted simply as a command to love other people. Yet many Unitarians voluntarily freed their own serfs at great cost, even though they did not advocate the abolition of slavery. Some sold their estates to assist the poor. They originally condemned all criminal laws, but later demanded only the relaxation of the more severe penalties.

English Unitarianism was founded by John Biddle, but it was not until 1773 that Unitarianism ceded from the Church of England and became a separate denomination. Some English Unitarians went to the United States at the end of the eighteenth century to found King's Chapel, Boston, the first Unitarian congregation in the New World. In 1961 the American Unitarian Association joined with the Universalist Church in America to form the Unitarian Universalist Association.

Lutheran

In 1518 Philip Melanchthon taught Luther Greek at the University of Wittenberg, though Luther was 15 years his senior. After Luther's death in 1546, Melanchthon, his companion and colleague of 28 years, emerged as a leader in his own right. Luther had called Melanchthon "the greatest theologian that ever lived," but it was *Luther's* theology that fascinated Melanchthon. He wrote the *Loci Communes* (1521) in order to record it. The *Loci* highlighted Luther's view of humanity as "mired in a cess-pool of self-love, too sinful to be capable of anything but hypocrisy." Luther said that the *Loci* should be canonized.

Melanchthon authored the basic creed of Lutheranism, the *Augsburg Confession* (1530). He also had ecumenical interests and participated in most of the major ecumenical colloquies of his day. In 1548 when the Emperor Charles V tried unsuccessfully to impose Catholicism on Saxony, he engaged Melanchthon to edit a conciliatory document that integrated the major tenets of Catholicism and Protestantism. Melanchthon desperately wrote and rewrote the document, trying to make it acceptable. But he succeeded only in drawing criticism from both sides, even when he added an *adiaphora* clause that placed certain practices, like bells and the distinctive dress of priests, in the realm of non-essentials of Christian faith. Nevertheless, the idea that some aspects of faith and practice were "indifferent" recurred as reformers attempted to identify essential elements that all might agree on, relegating to "non-essentials" (*adiaphora*) matters where differences could be tolerated without necessitating separation of communions.

Perhaps because of his willingness to enter into respectful dialogue with Christians of other persuasions – entirely uncharacteristic for Christians of his time – Melanchthon was denounced by some as a humanist, a rationalist (not intended as a compliment), and even called a traitor to Lutheranism. C. L. Manshreck, wrote in his Preface to an edition of the *Loci*:

> Through his reorganizing efforts, his promotion of classical arts, his textbooks, and the hundreds of teachers trained under his tutelage, he allegedly introduced into the evangelical school system principles of reason that conflicted with the religious principle of justification by faith alone. He is accused of weakening the evangelical stand at Augsburg in 1530 by his compromising negotiation with the Roman Catholic contingent; and he appeared to be theologically subversive by changing successive editions of the Augsburg Confession.

So-called "Philippist" views, characterized by Melanchthon's antidogmatism and humanism, split the German Lutherans for a generation in the mid-sixteenth century. After his death "Melanchthonism" became a derogatory term, denoting humanistic deviations from Luther. Yet in contrast to Luther's powerful but unsystematic theology, Melanchthon was the first systematic theologian of the Lutheran reformation; he gave the first Protestant description of systematic theology in the 1555 edition of the *Loci*.

> Whoever wished profitably to teach himself or intelligently to instruct others must first comprehend from beginning to end the principle pieces in a thing, and carefully note how each piece follows the one preceding, just as a builder, when he wishes to build a house, must first construct the entire building in his thoughts and himself project a picture. . . . Thus it is very necessary, in every art and teaching, to note all the principle pieces, beginning, middle, and end, and carefully to consider how each and every piece fits with the others, which pieces are necessary, which are false additions, and which are contrary to the right foundation; and the teacher and the hearer must accustom themselves to comprehend this in a very orderly totality. For if one is careless about doctrine and omits a few necessary pieces, delusion and error follow in other parts; and if one does not keep the end in view, it is the same as if one undertook a journey and gave no thought to the city to which one desired to go.

Melanchthon gradually altered three aspects of Luther's theology. First, during the early conflicts surrounding Luther's theology at Wittenberg, as well as the social conflict that led to the Peasant's War in 1525, Melanchthon began to modify Luther's emphasis on justification by faith alone. He included in the *Loci* a careful description of law and natural reason as binding all people to certain ethical requirements. While external disciplines did not result in justification, he said, they are important for life in the world. When a conflict arose with a fellow Lutheran, George Major, over the role of good works, Major and Melanchthon could agree to reject the statement that salvation was "by good works." But Major insisted that good works were necessary for salvation. Melanchthon, demonstrating his mediation skills, proposed, "One could not say that good works were necessary for salvation, but that *good works were necessary*."

Second, the debate between Luther and Erasmus over freedom of the will caused Melanchthon to rethink and minimize the doctrine of predestination. The 1521 *Loci* had stated Luther's view of predestination, but avoided discussion, saying that people should not be curious about God's mysteries. Similarly, in 1530 Melanchthon omitted discussion of predestination from the *Augsburg Confession* on the grounds that "any attempted explanation of predestination might lead to increased confusion."

Third, Luther's view of the Lord's Supper, as represented in the *Augsburg Confession* was the following: "Of the Supper of the Lord, we teach that the body and blood of Christ are truly present and are distributed to those who eat the Supper of the Lord." Ten years later Melanchthon wrote, "The body and blood of Christ are *truly tendered* to those who eat in the Lord's Supper." Melanchthon believed in what he called the "real spiritual presence" of Christ in the elements of bread and wine. After Luther's death he stated that Luther's view of an objective "real presence" was "bread idolatry."

In short, Luther's teaching on justification by faith alone, his teaching that humanity is completely unable to establish a relationship with God, and his doctrine of predestination – all doctrines that lay at the heart of his theology – were modified when their theological and practical implications became evident. The *Formula of Concord*, drawn up in 1577 by a number of Lutheran theologians, attempted to reestablish Luther's views on these doctrines. It is a definitive statement of Lutheran orthodoxy, but it was never uncontested, and it was immediately rejected by some Protestant princes.

Reformed

"Although Martin Luther towered over the initial decades of the Reformation, Calvinism superseded Lutheranism within a generation as the most dynamic and widely established form of European Protestantism" (Benedict, 2002: xv). Around the middle of the sixteenth century, Reformed churches sprang up in France, Scotland, the Netherlands, Hungary, the Holy Roman Empire (Germany), and the Polish-Lithuanian Empire. In each of these countries, persecution followed. A greater number of Reformed churches appeared in France after 1559 than in any other country. Persecution and civil wars (in 1562, 1567, 1568, 1572, 1574, 1577, and 1580) resulted. In the Netherlands, the scale of persecution was vast and intense. Between 1523 and 1566, 1,300 people were executed for heresy. Despite persecution, evangelical reformed faith continued to attract adherents. In Germany, a "second reformation" occurred along Reformed principles, convincing several princes (who imposed it on their subjects) that Luther had not gone far enough in reforming worship. Elements of the "popish mass" seemed to the Reformed to be maintained by Luther's view of the bread and wine as containing Christ's presence.

Different kinds of formal theological agreement were sought by reformers in different locations. In the English Reformation (discussed in chapter 8), conflicts focused around a book of "common prayer." The Lutheran and Reformed traditions focused on creeds, or confessions of faith. Originally intended to serve as *guides*, they came to be thought of increasingly as defining right belief. A short list of the most important sixteenth-century Calvinist confessions includes the Second Helvetic Confession (Swiss, 1566); the Gallican Confession (French Hugenots, 1559); the Confession of 1560 (Scotland); the Heidelberg Catechism (1563), and the Belgic Confession (1561).

In Eastern Europe, Reformed Protestants adopted the Second Helvetic Confession in the huge Polish-Lithuanian territories (which had adopted Christianity in 966). By the end of the sixteenth century separately governed Reformed churches existed in Little Poland, Great Poland, and Lithuania. Two hundred and sixty-five Reformed churches existed in Little Poland alone. In Great Poland, German Lutheran churches were more common than Reformed. The Polish-Lithuanian nobility led a martyrless reform in these territories that were already accustomed to religious diversity. In 1573 the Warsaw Confederation formalized a practice in effect since the 1550s, the nobility's freedom to specify worship on their domains. This measure, unique in the sixteenth century, "pledged the nobility not to spill blood or invoke penalties of confiscation, imprisonment, or banishment against one another 'for differences of faith or church' and to oppose anybody who tried to do so" (Benedict, 2002: 264).

Calvinist Confessions emphasized the doctrines that distinguished Calvinist from Roman Catholic beliefs. They also reflected contemporary theological controversies within the Reformed tradition. Predestination was the primary point of contention.

The Amsterdam minister and Dutch reformer, Jacob Arminius (1560–1609), was led by his study of Romans to doubt individual predestination to salvation or damnation. A year after Arminius's death, his followers wrote a "Remonstrance," stating that predestination refers to God's general plan for humanity, but that individuals' acceptance or rejection of Christ determined their destiny. Divine grace is not irresistible, and even after choosing Christ, one can lapse into sin. The "Remonstrance" rejected the idea that Christ died only for the elect; Christ died for all, but only believers benefit.

Against Arminians, orthodox Calvinists argued (as did Calvin) that God decreed *for individuals* who would be saved and who would be damned. But they took several different positions on the issue of how predestination related to the Fall of humanity. Supralapsarians believed that God decreed the salvation or damnation of every individual "before the foundation of the world." In their view, God's eternal decrees were not a response to God's foreseeing the fall of humans into sin. Creation itself existed for the purpose of living out God's judgments.

Infralapsarians related predestination to the Fall. They said that God decreed the fate of individuals before creation, but foresaw the Fall and took it into account as part of the larger plan. There were two types of infralapsarians. Double predestinarians believed (as did Calvin) that God relegated every individual to salvation or damnation. Single predestinarians believed that God made no decision to damn, but simply left those *not chosen* to their own devices.

Debates sprang up around these issues. Did Christ die for *all*, or only for some? In order to protect their interest in human freedom, Arminians said that he died for all. In order to protect God's omnipotence, orthodox Calvinists said that he died only for the elect. Can a person lose God's grace once it is operative in her life? Arminians said yes, and gave scriptural examples, like Judas. Orthodox Calvinists said that God's grace, once given, was irresistible and permanent. In short, while Arminians emphasized human volition, Calvinists emphasized faith and the experience of God's grace in a transformed life (evidenced both subjectively and externally).

In 1619 the Synod of Dort was called to deal with issues raised by Arminius. Composed mostly of Dutch theologians, the Synod decided these issues, taking an orthodox Calvinist position on each. The five articles of the Synod of Dort famously summarize their statement under the acronym TULIP.

Total depravity: only corruption and helplessness is attributable to humans;
Unconditional election; salvation and damnation reside in God's free decision;
Limited atonement; efficacy extends only to the elect;
Irresistible grace; grace cannot be rejected when given;
Perseverance of the saints; God preserves the elect so they do not fall away from grace.

At the conclusion of the Synod, 200 Arminian ministers were suspended; eight were exiled. Orthodox Calvinism won the day.

It is easy to ridicule these debates as trivial. Yet the different views have significantly different religious effects. Was the integrity and free will of humans to be thought of as a primary religious value? Or was God's sovereignty the primary value? Echoes of Luther's debate with Erasmus and Calvin's concern to extol the glory of God can be heard in these debates.

The terms "Calvinist" and "Reformed" are not synonymous. "Reformed" acknowledges the fact that after Calvin's death, Calvinist beliefs and practice spread geographically and were interpreted and reinterpred "on location" by many reformers. By the end of the sixteenth century, Reformed Protestantism had made astonishing progress within a short period of time. Historian Philip Benedict estimates that although there were approximately a half million Reformed Protestants in 1554, by 1600 ten million people were members of Reformed churches.

> Each national confession of faith had its nuances and points of emphasis. The Scottish and Dutch churches identified discipline as one of the marks of the true church, but the French mentioned only doctrine purely taught and the sacraments properly administered. The Belgic and French confessions of faith included lucid statements of double predestination; the Heidelberg Confession avoided the question. . . .
>
> (Benedict, 2002: 282)

In this chapter we have focused on the debates and persecutions by which Protestantism in its various forms came to be established in Europe. Women's voices have not appeared in recordings of the synods where men argued theological points; nor can they be found in accounts of the wars in which men killed and died for interpretations of Christian faith. Did women have a distinctive experience in the reformations? Certainly, women shared the risks as well as the convictions that prompted the establishment of new religious groups. In the sixteenth century, Christians' bodies were more at risk on the basis of their religious convictions than ever before as women and men of every persuasion were martyred in large numbers. In addition to shared experiences, however, there were also several distinctive roles for women in the sixteenth century. Chapter 8 begins by examining these roles.

READING

Melanchthon, *Loci communes*, selections: "Justification and Faith;" "Signs;" "Baptism;" "Participation in the Lord's Table" (in W. Pauck (ed.) (1969) *Melanchthon and Bucer*)

8 Reforming the Body of Christ: The Sixteenth Century, Part II

1 **Sixteenth-century Women**
2 **Roman Catholic Reformations**
3 **Reformations in Scotland and England**

Prologue

Terminology surrounding sixteenth-century reformations is often confusing. In common usage, "the Reformation" is usually intended to indicate the Lutheran reformation. Yet the sixteenth century saw many reforming movements, among them very significant reforms within the Roman Catholic Church. The term "Counter-reformation" was first used to indicate any local reversal of the Protestant reformations; then Leopold von Ranke (d. 1886) used it to indicate a general movement of Catholic reform and resistance to Protestantism. "Counter-reformation" is presently used to refer to those elements of the broader movement of Catholic reform that responded directly to Protestant reformations. Moreover, although reform within the Roman Catholic Church was more centralized than Protestant reforms, Catholic reformations should also be thought of in the plural. After the Council of Trent, with its specific agenda of reform of doctrine and practice, the diversity and complexity of Catholic initiatives is referred to as Early Modern Catholicism.

Like Protestant reforms, Catholic reforms had roots in fourteenth and fifteenth century movements (like the *Devotio Moderna*) and in late medieval spirituality and mysticism. Like Protestant reforms, they arose out of the religious confusions, uncertainties, and aspirations of the sixteenth century. In fact, reforming movements within the Catholic Church began earlier than, and independent of, Protestant reformations. Catholic reforms were also highly successful; sizeable geographical regions that became Protestant in the early to mid-sixteenth century returned to the Roman Catholic Church by the mid-seventeenth century. Catholicism remained strong or regained strength in virtually every culture where it had been present before the Protestant reformation, with the exception of England, Scotland, and Scandanavia (O'Malley, 2000: 124). The success of Catholic reforms insured the survival of a persuasive, expanding, global form of Christianity under centralized control.

Protestant and Catholic reforms were both attempts to Christianize the West. The Middle Ages was not a monolithic "age of faith" as it has sometimes been presented.

Diversities of belief and practice existed among Christians; Jews and Muslims were part of medieval societies, and various local beliefs existed alongside more formal religion. Historians of the French *Annales* school, using trial transcripts, have reconstructed many folk beliefs and practices. Often these practices focused on the "evil eye" and fertility cults, that is, on avoiding harm and the reproduction of people, animals, and crops. In the medieval centuries, Christianity camouflaged rather than suppressed these beliefs.

Both the educated and people without formal learning believed in a powerful devil. Pierre Bérulle (d. 1629) agreed with Luther, who lived almost a century before, that "Satan, who before the Fall had no rights over the world or any power over human beings, has despoiled him (Christ) victoriously of his kingdom and arrogated to himself (Satan) the power and empire of the world which had belonged to human beings from their birth. He (Satan) even sometimes invades a human body so that where, before sin, he was incarnated in the serpent, now he is incarnated in human beings." The devil was believed to have power to spawn vermin, lizards, insects, and toads; he could change himself into a goat, wolf, cat, or man. He was thought of as master of the hidden treasures of the earth, knowing all the secrets of nature.

Protestant and Catholic reformations shared common problems, common books of prayer, common religious aspirations, and common assumptions about how to Christianize society. Each attempted to control theaters, begging, and prostitution. Each sought to educate priests and to teach people religion. Both were concerned with church–state relations. As late as the 1560s German and Italian villagers often did not know whether they were Catholics or Protestants. A few miles outside Rome in the Abruzzi, Jesuit missionaries found people crossing themselves who had no idea what it meant.

Because of their similar sources and goals, Catholic reformations should not be understood as a defensive action that would not have come into being at all without the stimulus of the Protestant reforms. Yet styles of Protestant and Roman Catholic reform differed in many respects; it is important to understand the particularity of each. The seventeenth-century worldwide Catholic missions, for example, had no Protestant counterpart.

1   Sixteenth-century Women

How were women's lives affected by the religious turmoil of the sixteenth century? We have already noted Anabaptist women martyrs, but equality in persecution and martyrdom was not new in the sixteenth century. The Renaissance historian Joan Kelly (1982) wrote: "We must look at ages or movements of great social change in terms of their liberation or oppression of women's potential, their impact for the advancement of *her* humanity as well as his." Some scholars of the sixteenth-century have claimed that as a result of the social changes accompanying the reformations, women achieved new status, new and more satisfying roles and opportunities, and new respect within their communities. The historical reality is more complex.

Two kinds of historical evidence are available, women's writings and men's prescriptive admonitions; the latter are more numerous than the former. The diversity of perspectives and values in this literature cautions against generalizations. A few humanists like Erasmus advocated that women should be educated, but there was not a great deal for an educated woman to *do* with an education except to try not to exhibit it. Were women to be thought of as superior, inferior, or equal to men? The published discourse on the subject reveals lively disagreement. Christine de Pisan's (1365–1430) *City of Women* argued that women were naturally superior to men. This book began a four-century-long debate over women's virtues, capabilities, evils, equality or inferiority. Few authors can claim to originate a discussion that continued for four centuries.

John Knox (1513–72), the Scottish reformer, disagreed. While Mary Tudor was queen of England he wrote *The First Blast of the Trumpet Against the Monstrous Regiment of Women* (1558). In it he argued that, while some women may be exceptions to the rule,

> Nature, I say, doth paynt [women] further to be weake, fraile, impacient, feble and foolish; and experience hath declared them to be unconstant, variable, cruel, and lacking the spirit of counsel and regiment. And these notable faultes have men in all ages espied in that kinds, for the which they have not onlie removed women from rule and authoritie, but have also thought that men subject to the counsel or empire of their wyves were unworthy of all publick office. For who can denie that it is repugneth to nature, that the blinde shall be appointed to lead and conduct such as do see? That the weake, the sick, and impotent persons shall nourish and kepe the hole and strong?

Bercher's *Nobilyte of Women* (1552) argues for the equal capacity of women.

> I have noted in some women learning, in some temperance, in some liberality . . . and I have compared them with men who have been endowed with like gifts and I have found them equal or superior. The upbringing of women is so strait and kept as in a prison, that all good inclination which they have of nature is utterly quenched. We see that by practice, men of small hope come to good proficiency so that I may affirm the cause of women's weakness in handling of matters to proceed from the custom that men have appointed in their manner of life, for if they have any weak spirit, if they have any fickleness or any such thing, it cometh of the divers unkindness they find in men.

Certainly, women had several *different* roles in the sixteenth century. Some of these roles were more positive and prestigious than most earlier roles; some were far more painful and dangerous. For example, the abolition of the convent in Protestant territories removed one of the few socially accepted and respected ways for a woman to follow a way of life that cultivated her spirituality, an aspect of a woman's life that could easily be submerged in a life of marriage and motherhood. According to Luther and Calvin, monasticism was rejected by Protestant reformers because it implied a lack of respect for one of God's good gifts, sexuality. Yet the closing of monasteries removed a traditional option for women and changed the lives of many women.

Nuns

For many medieval women a religious vocation was a way to pursue knowledge of God and self in a disciplined spiritual life. It also had the considerable benefit, in a time before effective contraceptives, of freeing women from constant and debilitating childbearing.

In the sixteenth century, many men outlived three wives who died in childbirth or from infections and diseases traceable to childbearing. Catherine of Siena vowed virginity at the age of seven when her beloved teenaged sister died in childbirth. Teresa of Avila's mother married at 15, bore 12 children, and died at the age of 33, when Teresa was 13. For many medieval women who chose a religious vocation, the alternative was immediate and vivid.

In German Protestant territories at the time of the Lutheran reformation, nuns found themselves in a difficult situation. A Genevan nun of the Order of St Clare, Jeanne de Jussie, wrote a chronicle of her experience during the years 1526 to 1535, *The Leaven of Calvinism, or the Beginning of the Heresy of Geneva*. Jeanne was educated in Geneva during the years immediately prior to Genevan reformation. Her convent eventually left the hostile environment of Geneva and moved to Annecy in France.

Jeanne described many women's loyalty to the Catholic faith. She reported battered wives whose allegiance to Catholic Christianity was resented by their Protestant husbands. She described a Catholic woman who died of sadness when her husband had their newborn child baptized by the Protestant pastor. She told of Protestant men breaking into convents, pillaging and destroying, attempting to persuade or force nuns to renounce their vocations. She gave an eyewitness account of Catholic women and children participating in pitched battles against Protestants:

> The wives of the Christians (Catholics) assembled, saying that if it happens that our husbands fight against these infidels (Protestants), let us also make way and kill their heretic wives, so that the race may be exterminated. In this assembly of women there were a good 700 children of twelve to fifteen years, firmly decided to do a good deed with their mothers. The women carried stones in their laps and most of the children carried little swords; others had stones in their pockets, hats, and bonnets.
>
> (Quoted by Douglas, 1974: 99)

Before this battle, some Catholic women came to warn the sisters that if the heretics won, they planned to force all the sisters, young and old, to marry. But a truce was eventually arranged.

Jeanne reports no violence from Protestant women, but she says that they enraged Catholics by sitting in their windows where everyone could see them, spinning and weaving cloth, or doing their wash on feast days. Protestant women also visited Jeanne's convent and tried to talk the nuns into abandoning the convent. One visitor was a former abbess who was now married and "meddled with preaching and perverting people of devotion." She said to the nuns:

> O poor creatures! If only you knew how good it is to be with a handsome husband, and how agreeable it is to God. I lived for a long time in that darkness and hypocrisy where you now are, but God alone made me understand the abuse of my pitiful life, and I came to the true light of truth.
>
> (Quoted by Douglas, 1974: 100)

From Jeanne's perspective, reformation teaching centered on "contempt for the sacrament, iconoclasm, and the new insistence on marriage." Her chronicle gives evidence of the importance of women's participation, on both sides, in sixteenth-century reformations.

Many Spanish nuns found that Luther's idea of justification by faith freed them from a tormented conscience. They frequently experienced confusion and pain over the dissonance between their religious experience of a conscience unappeased by penances, no matter how harsh, and their Church's rejection of reformation ideas. The trial transcript of one such nun, Marina de Guevara, at the height of the Spanish Inquisition, 1558, illustrates this painful quandary. Under inquisitorial questioning, Marina responded:

> Did I say that at the mass for the dead it is better to pray for the living? I don't remember what I said. My memory is weak. I do think the living are in greater need than the dead. If you want to condemn me because of my words it is easy. I express myself poorly. I don't know how to make myself clear. Have I said that Christians are Pharisees? Yes, including myself. . . . My memory is poor and my soul is troubled. For the love of God, show me how I can save my soul and relieve my conscience. I confess that inner works are better than outer. Better than the castigation of the flesh is the overcoming of pride and anger. To bring the heart into tune with God is better than audible prayer. I told one sister not to practice so many penances but to take refuge in the wounds of Christ and not to trust so much to the Virgin as to her son. When a sister was upset over losing her rosary, I said maybe God had hidden it from her to keep her from interminable babbling. Some inferred that I rejected all oral prayer. I have not and do not desire to depart from the faith of Mother Church. In whatever I have erred I ask God's pardon and grace.

Marina de Guevara was judged guilty of heresy, turned over to the secular authorities, and executed, October 8, 1559.

The Spanish nun Teresa of Avila's (1515–82) spirituality had much in common with many nuns condemned by the Inquisition. Yet she had a successful career. She did not criticize or reject "outward observances," although she emphasized inner spirituality. Her rhetoric was shrewd, denying that she was anything but "a poor weak woman." Nevertheless, Teresa was denounced to the Inquisition, accused of heresy and immorality. Her most questionable practice was her practice of inner prayer, called by contemporaries "illuminism." Teresa managed to evade the fate of other Spanish nuns who were saying virtually the same thing.

In Catholic Spain, mental prayer, with its focus on a private spirituality and mysticism, was strongly associated with Protestantism, and therefore with heresy. It was also associated with women and with *conversos*, forced converts to Christianity from Judaism. Teresa of Avila was a first-generation Christian. Her grandfather, a wealthy Jewish cloth merchant, was denounced to the fiercely anti-semitic Castillian inquisition and, with his sons, forced to go in penetential procession to all the churches in Toledo while the Christian populace cursed, threw stones, and spat.

In spite of being a woman, from a *converso* family, and one who advocated mental prayer, Teresa founded a Carmelite monastery where a strict rule was followed. She also wrote an autobiography, *The Interior Castle*, as well as many letters and treatises on spiritual perfection addressed primarily to her sisters in monasticism. She was an active and vocal reformer of the Carmelite Order. In the papal bull that declared her a saint, the pope said that she had "rendered inestimable services to the church by reforming the Carmelite Order, not only for women Carmelites, but also for men, and not only in

Spain, but likewise in other lands." Advising the nuns of her convent against harsh aus-terities, she wrote, "God prefers health and obedience to your penances. Get enough sleep and enough food. What is the point of mortification? The real point is the love of God."

Teresa experienced a conversion to the "Way of Perfection" at the age of 42 as she prayed before a statue of Christ scourged at the pillar. *The Interior Castle*, written in obedience to her spiritual director, was the first detailed description of the stages of prayer from meditation to mystical marriage. She and her friend and disciple, St John of the Cross (1542–91), differed from fourteenth-century mystics in that they described, not mystical experience itself, but a graded method for it. John's treatise adopted the metaphor, *Ascent of Mt. Carmel*, while Teresa thought of the life of prayer as progress through an "interior castle." St Teresa was canonized in 1622; she was named "Doctor of the Church" in 1970.

Witches

Only in the last two decades has witch-hunting received the scholarly attention it deserves on the basis of the large numbers of women affected. Witch persecutions accompanied the reformations, both Catholic and Protestant, but reached their "height" between 1570 and 1630; during this time an estimated thirty to fifty thousand witch burnings occurred in Western Europe. By comparison, the number of heretics burned was infinitesimal.

The numbers are difficult to estimate. Records are extant for some periods and geo-graphical locations, but not for others, and generalization across Western Europe from local figures may mislead. The best estimates suggest that between 1400 and 1700, 80 percent of the seventy to two hundred thousand victims were women. In Trier, one location for which records are extant, between 1587 and 1593, 368 witches were burned in 22 villages. In two of these villages the craze for witch persecution did not abate until there was only one woman left in the village.

Yet in the so-called "dark ages," there was little or no witch persecution. In the ninth century, Pope Boniface VI declared that "to believe in witches was unchristian." And canon law throughout the medieval centuries stated that "whoever believes in witches is an infidel and a pagan." Witch beliefs were folklore, not a theology of witchcraft sup-ported by the organized, methodical, detection and persecution of witches that occurred after 1400. In the fifteenth century earlier declarations were reversed; the "doctrine" of witchcraft was in its final form by 1490. One professor at the University of Sorbonne wrote in 1601 that the fact that witches existed could be *disbelieved* "only by those of unsound mind."

In 1484 Pope Innocent III published a papal bull deploring the spread of witchcraft in Germany and authorizing two Swiss-German Dominican inquisitors to root it out. They began by writing a manual for inquisitors that suggested lines of questioning that would reveal whether a suspect was a witch, signs by which witches could be recognized, and tortures that were especially effective in producing confessions. The *Malleus Malefi-carum*, or *Hammer of Witches*, first published in 1486 went into 14 editions between 1487 and 1520, and at least 16 editions between 1574 and 1669. Although it could only be read by those who read Latin, this document was to play an influential role for the next two centuries in the development of a complex and highly scatological mythology of witchcraft. It included detailed descriptions of witches' Sabbaths and of pacts with the devil, who might join the festivities as a goat, a toad, or a man. Witches' feasts, according to the authors, consisted of anything from boiled turnips to boiled children or exhumed corpses, preferably of kinsfolk. Fricassees of bat, or even, in sensible England, roast beef and beer were also thought to be favorite foods of witches. But the featured agenda item of the witches' Sabbath was always the mandatory sexual orgy.

There is no evidence to suggest that any ritual devil worship actually occurred either on the European continent or in England. Witchcraft seems to have been neither a religion nor an organization, but a massive collective fantasy. It was a fantasy often shared by accused witches, many of whom confessed even without torture to the activities described in broadsheets and witchcraft manuals. Everyone knew what witches did. As the *Malleus Maleficarum said*:

> They raise hailstones and hurtful tempests or lightning; cause sterility in men and animals; offer to devils or otherwise kill the children they do not devour. They can see absent things as if they were present; turn the minds of men to inordinate love or hatred; make of no effect the generative desires and even the power of copulation. They cause abortions, kill infants in the mother's womb by a mere exterior touch. They can at times bewitch men and animals by a mere look without touching them, and cause death.

The *Malleus* claimed to be a collection of witches' confessions. Its title page carried the epigraph: "to disbelieve in witches is the greatest of heresies." In 1468 on the continent, all legal limits on the application of torture in the case of suspected witches were suspended for inquisitional courts. Torture was not yet in use in secular courts, and historian H.C. Lea has pointed out that "certain of the more extravagant and obscene details [about witches' Sabbaths] did not appear in the records of secular tribunals but only in records of inquisitional courts." England is the only country that did not use judicial torture either in cases involving ordinary crime or witchcraft. In England, the more lurid details of witches' activities are also conspicuously missing. Without torture, one historian wrote, "the great witch panics of the 1590s and the late 1620s are inconceivable."

Witch persecutions of the fifteenth to seventeenth centuries cannot be attributed to ignorant superstition. Witchcraft beliefs were taken seriously and participated in by learned scholars and religious leaders, and by erudite and cultured political leaders of Europe. Protestants and Catholics wrote and preached repeatedly on the importance of detecting and executing witches.

Moreover, the witch craze followed the movement of reformations. Historian Trevor Roper documented the increase of witch burnings – often quite dramatic increases – with the movement of Protestant missionaries into Transylvania, Denmark, Brandenburg, Baden, Bavaria, Wurtemberg, Scotland, and England. Witch persecution accompanied the movement of Catholic missionaries, especially Dominicans and Jesuits, through Germany, Flanders, and Poland. Roper's argument is supported by literary evidence as well as court records; the Protestant clergy preached frequently on the text, Exodus 22.18: "Thou shalt not suffer a witch to live."

Luther declared that witches should be burned "even if they did no harm, merely for making a pact with the devil." He also extended the scope of persecution in Lutheran territories by saying that all witchcraft is heresy, and that all heresy and *false interpretation of the Bible* was witchcraft. Parish visitations once a year by Lutheran authorities began in the 1520s to check on the administration of parishes and to examine parishes for "sooth-sayers, cunning women, crystal gazers, casters of spells, witches, and other practitioners of forbidden arts." Villagers were instructed under threat of severe punishment to report such persons to the inspectors. Calvin wrote, "The Bible teaches us that there are witches and that they must be slain. . . . God expressly commands that all enchantresses shall be put to death, and this law of God is a universal law." Alone of the magisterial reformers, Zwingli never showed any signs of belief in witchcraft, and Zurich under his jurisdiction remained largely uninvolved in witch persecution, though his successors instigated it after his death.

Witchcraft was simultaneously a new role for women and a new view of women as powerful *and* evil. Historian Stanislav Andreski has suggested that the witchcraze was connected to the first epidemic of syphilis in Europe at the end of the fifteenth century. Syphilis was a terrifying disease that men associated with prostitutes and, by extension, with all women. Ultimately, there is no single satisfactory explanation for witchcraft persecutions, though misogyny, print, and religious anxiety all played a role in the scapegoating of women.

Christian wives

A new status for the Christian wife was created in the Protestant reforms. Luther taught that the work of every Christian is a vocation if it is exercised in faith and with commitment. Many sixteenth-century women found new self-esteem in the duties of wife and mother, understood as equal in value to that of a magistrate or a clergyman. Moreover, Luther's insistence that married life was not only a good gift of God, but *superior* to the celibate state revalued the status of wife.

Before his own marriage, Luther identified three benefits of marriage: marriage makes the best of humanity's fallen condition; marriage is a spiritual discipline; and marriage is a physiological necessity. In his 1523 *Exhortation to the Knights Templar* he wrote: "Physicians are not amiss when they say that if sexual intercourse is forcibly restrained, it necessarily strikes into the flesh and blood and becomes a poison, whence the body becomes unhealthy, enervated, sweaty, and foul-smelling." Yet, far from denigrating celibacy, he thought of it as a miracle, and "if God has worked a miracle, there is no need of a vow." But most of those who claim to be celibate, according to Luther, shirk the duties and responsibilities of marriage "that [they] may have an easy time of it and be spared the troubles and necessities of married life, and yet, at the same time, neither live chastely nor serve God, but carry on more freely [their] fornication and other wickedness."

The early Luther thought of marriage as a spiritual discipline, a hindrance to "pleasant, lazy living;" it regularly challenged the patience and commitment of both partners. Before his own marriage his writings emphasized the "insignificant, distasteful, despised duties of family and home which, if performed faithfully and with endurance, just as a martyr would endure, would be more valuable than all pilgrimages and masses" (*On Monastic Vows*, 1520) It was, however, the wife's role that required the greater discipline.

The Christian wife must be self-controlled; "she must accept herself as an inferior creature and give over her will to her husband and God."

Luther contrasted two types of women, the Christian wife and the witch. He frequently framed his sermons on the Christian wife with cautionary remarks about the
"unruly" wife, synonymous in his mind with the witch. He warned husbands not to beat
their wives, not because it is cruel or immoral, but because it doesn't *work*: "If she does
not let herself be enticed by her role as housewife, she will not be helped in any other
way, for you will accomplish nothing with blows; they will not make a woman pious
and submissive. If you beat one devil out of her, you will beat in two" (quoted by
Brauner, 1989: 38).

Luther married Katarina von Bora on June 13, 1525. He married, he said, "to please
my father, to spite the pope and the devil, and to seal my witness before martyrdom."
After his marriage, Luther's view of marriage changed. He never called Katarina a
"remedy for sin," and passages in his exegetical work hint at the depth of their relationship. Commenting on Genesis 3.23 he said that marriage "expresses most beauti-
fully the affection of a husband who feels his need for a delightful and full cohabitation
in both love and holiness . . . an overwhelmingly passionate love." In discussing the
gospel account of the marriage at Cana, he wrote:

> Youthful infatuation does not last, just as, at the wedding of Cana, the wine gave out. Mary
> then went to Jesus and told him the wine was emptied. He answered, as it were, "Do you
> have to drink water . . . and is it bitter? See, then, I will make it sweet and will turn the
> water into wine. I will not pour out the water; it will have to stay, but I will perfect it. I will
> not take the vexation out of marriage. I may even increase it, but it will turn out wonder-
> fully, as only they know who have tasted it."

Watching Katarina with their son Martin at her breast, Luther found a new understanding of God: "Surely God must talk with me even more fondly than my Katie with
her little Martin." The *experience* of marriage had changed Luther's esteem for it. On
occasion, he said, he had to scold himself "because I give more credit to Katarina than
to Christ, who has done so much more for me." Unfortunately, Katarina's views have
not been preserved.

Less is known about Calvin's marriage to Idelette de Bure because Calvin did not
often mention his personal life. In a letter to a friend he wrote, "The only beauty that
attracts me is this: if she is modest, accommodating, not haughty, frugal, patient, and
there is hope that she will be concerned about my health" (letter to Farel, May 19, 1539;
quoted by Bouwsma, 1988: 22–3). Idelette de Bure was a widow with two children, a
member of Calvin's congregation. They married in August 1540, and she bore at least
three more children, all of whom died in infancy. After her death, Calvin wrote to
another friend: "Although the death of my wife has been bitterly painful to me, yet
I restrain my grief as well as I can. And truly mine is no common grief. I have been
bereaved of the best companion of my life who, if any severe hardship had occurred,
would have been my willing partner, not only in exile and poverty but even in death"
(letter to Viret, April 7, 1549; quoted by Bouwsma, 1988: 23).

Not all women associated with the Protestant reformations were content to work in
their homes. The new Protestant public education was for girls as well as boys, at least
at the elementary level, and women sometimes took very active, much criticized and

sometimes persecuted, roles in their communities. They wrote tracts, conducted private services, and complained to town councils about prison and hospital conditions. Divorce and remarriage, though never easy in Protestant territories, was at least possible.

It was extraordinarily hazardous to be a woman in the sixteenth century. If a woman was not burned as a witch or a heretic, she was likely to die in childbirth. Yet many women worked successfully with the changing religious and social patterns to live energetic and fruitful lives.

READING

Teresa of Avila, *The Interior Castle*

2   Roman Catholic Reformations

In 1497 Ettore Vernazza, a disciple of Catherine of Genoa, founded a religious confraternity in Genoa devoted to personal piety and good works that attracted prominent clergy and laypeople. Sometime between 1514 and 1517 he founded a branch of the "Oratory of Divine Love" in Rome. Later, Paul III (1534–49) commissioned the Oratory to investigate clerical abuses. In March 1537, they reported a list of abuses that was subsequently placed on the Index of Forbidden Books. Clearly, there was need for reform.

The Council of Trent (1545–63)

Earlier struggles for supremacy between councils and popes made Paul III reluctant to convene a council. After the Council of Constance (1414–17) successfully asserted its supremacy over the pope, councils were either not convoked or were closed for lack of attendance. In 1470 Pius II issued a bull setting aside the supremacy of councils and making the call for a council an affront subject to excommunication. Nevertheless, after 25 years of advocacy for a reforming council, the Council of Trent (located 200 miles northeast of Rome) was convoked. It met intermittently between 1545 and 1563. Its purpose was twofold: to pronounce on theological and practical controversies, and to reform the church.

Fewer than 30 bishops were present at the first session of the Council of Trent; there were no representatives from the universities or from the middle or lower clergy. A few Protestants had been invited to attend as observers but they had no vote; they attended only briefly. The voting delegates were archbishops, bishops, influential abbots and heads of religious orders, dominated by an anxious papacy and its emissaries. The register was signed by 255 prelates, but only 50 to 70 were in attendance for some of the most important sessions. The 25 sessions of the Council were marked by heated debate, and sometimes by fist fights.

A sermon by the Bishop of San Marco in Calabria initiated the first session. After a lurid description of the general decay of morals, he delivered a stirring call to reform:

"The eyes of the whole world are upon you," he told the Council, "Holy Church, Christ's bride, clings to your knees; comfort ye God's people, plant anew, build up, pull down." In a similar vein, Cardinal Pole addressed the company. Referring to the Protestant reformations he said, "We ourselves are largely responsible for the misfortune that has occurred, the rise of heresy, [and] the collapse of Christian morality, because we have failed to cultivate the field that was entrusted to us. We are like salt that has lost its savor. Unless we do penance, God will not speak to us" (Jedin, 1957–61, II: 25–6). The Council decided to take up issues of doctrine and reform alternately since both were equally pressing.

The Council of Trent did not make a single concession to Protestant doctrine; conservatives consistently blocked conciliatory statements. The Council concerned itself with Luther and Lutheranism, either ignoring Calvin or failing to differentiate Calvinist teaching from Lutheran. Trent's most important clarifications of Catholic faith dealt with the status of the Bible, definitions of original sin and predestination, justification by faith, and the role of the sacraments.

Scripture

Trent placed tradition on a par with scripture as authoritative in faith and morals. In the case of conflicting interpretations, the pope's authority was declared final. Responding to the Lutheran idea of *sola scriptura* (the sufficiency of the Bible for doctrine, preaching, and practice), Trent stated that the Bible *as interpreted by tradition* is authoritative. The translation of the Bible into the vernacular was not prohibited, but Trent stipulated that only the Latin Vulgate was to be used for public reading, effectively limiting auditors to Latin speakers.

Although not specifically prohibited by the Council of Trent, the 1559 and 1564 *Index* prohibited reading the Bible in translation. The Holy Office approved translations of the Bible only in 1752, and then only if an approved commentary accompanied the text. By 1800, 71 Catholic vernacular translations of the Bible were in circulation. Trent also declared most of the Apocrypha canonical. (Luther included the Apocrypha in his 1534 German Bible as an appendix, saying that it was "useful and good" to read the apocryphal books. He also wrote commentaries on them, but did not consider them canonical.)

Doctrine

Trent reaffirmed the doctrine of original sin, but defined it cautiously. Against Luther's teaching that after baptism the Christian remains a sinner, clothed or covered with Christ's righteousness (*simul justus et peccator*), the Council of Trent declared: "In those who are reborn, God hates nothing because there is no condemnation for those who are buried with Christ by baptism unto death." Any sinfulness that remains is only "an inclination to sin that can be successfully overcome." Trent emphasized the individual's acceptance or rejection of God's justifying grace, together with insistence that in addition to faith, good works are also necessary for salvation. Trent also stipulated that Christians are not beyond danger of a mortal fall from grace.

Of the 61 general sessions, 44 were devoted to discussions of the doctrine of justification by faith. The final decree, revised three times, defined justification as "the grace of God by which an unjust person becomes just." Justification by faith, it declared, consists not only of "the remission of sins, but also the sanctification and renewal of the inner person by *voluntary* acceptance of the grace and gifts whereby the unjust person becomes just" (emphasis added). The sacraments *inhere* and supply the lack of perfection in the person. Helped by inherent justice, "we are not only called just, but we really are just, each person receiving justice according to their capacities and according to the individual's disposition and cooperation." By combining voluntary assent to salvation and participation in the sacraments, a person *becomes just*, according to Trent. This description maintained the power and effectiveness of the sacraments as channels of grace. The seven sacraments were also confirmed, against Luther's reduction of the sacraments to two.

Trent reiterated one interpretation of Augustine's description of predestination, namely, that God *foresaw*, but did not *foreordain* damnation. Trent declared that salvation is offered to all; "God wills that all be saved, though not all accept."

Practical issues
Trent also affirmed ordination as one of the seven sacraments against Luther's "priesthood of all believers." Celibacy and virginity were declared to be superior to marriage, and divorce was condemned. The existence of Purgatory (defined by the 1439 Council of Florence) was reaffirmed, along with the usefulness of prayers and pious works dedicated to the dead. The veneration and invocation of saints was reaffirmed, as was the honoring of relics, the use of religious images, and the efficacy of indulgences.

Finally, Trent condemned several aspects of Protestant theology, including Luther's view that humans are the passive recipients of divine action: "if anyone says that a person's free will, moved and stimulated by God cannot cooperate at all by giving its assent to God when God stimulates and calls, and that one cannot dissent, if he so wills, but like an inanimate creature is utterly inert and passive, let him be anathema." In sum, Tridentine decrees aimed at making the piety of the Catholic reformation one in which the activity of the Christian was to play a large part in her salvation. Active striving for self-control and virtues, and zeal for works of mercy and charity: all were highly valued and advocated by the Council of Trent.

Preaching, and the requirement that a bishop must reside in his diocese, were two of the most important practical issues discussed at the Council of Trent. Because Catholic liturgies focused on the mass rather than on preaching, the Council acknowledged that services often lacked instruction, admonition, and inspiration. In its twenty-fourth session Trent declared that the "chief duty" of priests and bishops was preaching. In a time before public address systems, pulpits in cathedrals were moved halfway down the nave so that sermons could be heard. But more importantly, recognizing that engaging and effective preaching would not occur simply because it was demanded, the Council established a new form of theological training and professional formation for priests – seminaries.

In the late medieval church, it was customary for a bishop to live at a distance from his diocese. Bishops often considered their diocese a financial asset but left the administration and parish duties to a vicar general. Episcopal residence was not enforced, even though it was stipulated by canon law, so bishops often collected several such "benefices." Trent addressed the problem of absenteeism by stipulating residence; it proved difficult, however, to enforce the ruling. Trent's decisions on the doctrine of the Eucharist are the subject of the next section.

Protestant and Catholic theologies of the Eucharist

More than any other point of theological controversy, eucharistic doctrines focused disagreement both among Protestants and between Protestants and Catholics. Since these doctrines were articulated in a polemical context, it is helpful to consider them alongside one another.

Luther's idea of the status of bread and wine in the Lord's Supper has been called "consubstantiation." He taught that after the consecration of the bread and wine, bread and wine remain, but they become the bearer of Christ's bodily presence: "Christ is in the bread and wine like fire in red-hot iron." "As regards the sacrament of the altar," he said, "our belief is that the bread and wine at the Supper are the true body and blood of Christ." Bread and wine do not change into body and blood, but they nevertheless embody Christ. If a pagan were to participate in the ritual, he would receive Christ's body and blood, but he would receive it unworthily, lacking the faith that justifies. Luther insisted that reception did not depend on a subjective attitude but was an objective fact.

Zwingli, the reformer of Zurich, taught that the Lord's Supper was a memorial rite, a simple remembrance: "The Fathers of the first five centuries understood Christ's words 'This is my body,' in a figurative and not a literal sense" (*On the Lord's Supper*, article 3). He used the following metaphor to explain: "When the father of a family leaves for a long journey he gives his wife a ring with a picture of himself engraved on it . . . The Father represents our Lord Jesus Christ. When he went away he left his spouse, the Church, his own image in the sacrament of his Supper" (*Exposition of the Faith*).

Calvin sought to avoid controversy about Christ's presence in the elements of the Lord's Supper by asking, "what purpose does the Lord's Supper serve?" He answered that the sacrament is for the Christian's nourishment: "Just as bread nourishes, sustains, and preserves the life of our body, so Christ's body is the food and protection of our spiritual life" (quoted by Gerrish, 1993: 13). He affirmed Christ's "real *spiritual* presence" in the sacrament of the Lord's Supper, saying that Christ is "truly exhibited" and "truly received" by faithful Christians. The Holy Spirit is the agent of Christ's presence, and Christians' faith is the means by which Christ is received. On occasion Calvin even used the phrase "substantial presence," but he described the presence of Christ in the elements as "so sublime a mystery that we are incapable of understanding, much less describing, it."

The Council of Trent reaffirmed the doctrine of transubstantiation as defined by the 1215 Fourth Lateran Council. The Council specified that the eucharistic elements of bread and wine are *changed into* the body and blood of Christ. Only the "accidental" properties of bread and wine remained. "If anyone says that in the most holy sacrament of the Eucharist there remains the substance of bread and wine together with the body and blood of our Lord Jesus Christ, and denies that marvelous and singular conversion of the whole substance, let him be anathema." Trent also reaffirmed the Catholic interpretation of the mass as a *sacrifice*, the supreme good work of the Christian community, by which the embodied Christ was offered to God and received by Christians.

The eucharistic debates of sixteenth century restated and extended earlier interests in interpretation of the Word made flesh. Miracles were still an issue in the sixteenth century, as Protestants were forced to answer Catholic accusations that Protestant worship did not produce the contemporary miracles performed through relics. Luther said that sixteenth-century miracles were produced by the Word of God and that they were spiritual miracles. Calvin responded that miracles had occurred in New Testament times as "seals of the Gospel;" since Protestants produced no new gospel, no new miracles were needed. But the primary form in which Christ's incarnation was discussed were debates about how the eucharistic elements of bread and wine become Christ's body in the sacrament. The intensity and durability of Catholic and Protestant reformers' efforts to describe how Christ is present in bread and wine testify to the continuing centrality of the question of Christ's incarnation for Christian faith. Was Christ present symbolically (in the words of consecration), or was Christ's body physically real, in some sense, in the elements of bread and wine? These questions were so central to understanding the Word made flesh that different answers resulted in the establishment of different Christian communions. The next section returns to discussion of Catholic reformations.

Force

Whether a person lived in Protestant or Catholic territories mattered much more than individual religious choice in the sixteenth and seventeenth centuries. The idea of unconstrained religious choice is a modern idea, and even now far from globally accepted. For most of the history of Western Christianity tension has existed between faith by conviction and faith by compulsion. In Catholic territories the Inquisition had been in place for several centuries, but force was not absent in Protestant territories, it simply took different forms.

Garcia de Loaysa, personal envoy to Pope Clement VII (1523–34) advised the pope:

> I never found a better cure for heretics than the force of the Catholic princes, because since heresy originates in the will only, reason has no part in its cure. Following the path of soft dealings, we lost out time, until the sure and only remedy was applied to them – war. Your majesty had better quit that fantasy of converting souls to God and from now on convert bodies to your obedience. Even if they are heretics, let them be your servants. Don't be afraid even of buying their faith.

Pope Paul IV (1555–9) believed that untruth should not have the same social and political privilege as truth, and that persecution of dissidents was a duty. The Inquisition was the first international police force, and in Catholic countries it was virtually absolute. People in high places were not exempt; archbishops were occasionally executed, as were professors like Giordano Bruno who was burned at the stake for teaching the eternity of the universe, heliocentrism, pantheism, an atomic theory of matter, and for rejecting miracles. Thousands of books were also burned in inquisitorial fires. The *Index* of forbidden writings was established by the Council of Trent in 1557. Its first agenda was to condemn Luther's writings. It was abolished only in 1966.

The Roman Office of the Inquisition consisted of six cardinals, headed by the pope. By the mid-sixteenth century it was a formal, centralized institution, much more efficient than medieval inquisitors. The Inquisition could imprison on mere suspicion, confiscate property on arrest, torture, and condemn to execution. In order to protect the rights of defendants in *civil* courts, children under 14, serfs, enemies of the prisoner, women, criminals, and the excommunicated – people considered untrustworthy – were not allowed to testify. In *inquisitorial* courts, anyone could testify, in writing, without identification. The prisoner was allowed to disqualify the testimony of sworn enemies only if s/he could guess who they were. Suspects were not allowed lawyers but defended themselves in a secret court in which the prosecutor and judge were the same person.

Most people's impressions of the Inquisition have come largely from the Spanish Inquisition, which began earlier than the Roman Inquisition and was more ruthless. The Spanish Inquisition tried 49,092 cases between 1540 and 1700. Under Cardinal Ximenes (head of the Spanish inquisition from 1507 until his death in 1517), more than 2,500 people were executed in Spain, and over 40,000 more were imprisoned and tortured. The Spanish inquisition confiscated suspects' property upon arrest, a policy that made the wealthy especially vulnerable to suspicion. Cardinal Ximenes's campaigns for orthodoxy featured combinations of education and propaganda, preaching and persuasion, and force. The Spanish inquisition was suppressed only in 1820.

In Spain, force was aimed primarily at Jews and, to a lesser degree, at the Moorish population of Spain. Yet a Jew could not be brought before the inquisition simply because s/he was a Jew; heresy charges could be brought only against baptized Christians. How, then, could Jews be targeted? The Inquisition was preceded by concerted efforts to convert Jews, including forced attendance at Christian sermons in Hebrew, the offer of material incentives and privileges, and concessions intended to supply evidence of Christian generosity. Once converted, however, the Jews of Italy, Spain, and Portugal were vulnerable to prosecution if they retained any Jewish beliefs or practices. "New Christians" constituted no more than 5 percent of the two million population of Lisbon in 1542; yet they totaled 85 percent of the victims of the Inquisition.

Coercion, the Catholic reform's "weak power" was balanced by its "strong power," or power to attract, to stimulate and convince people to think, believe, and act in ways that conform. Weak power, having lost its ability to attract, relies on force, coercion, and punishment in order to compel assent. Although "weak power" may initially appear effective, it is ultimately ineffective precisely because it inevitably generates resistance. In the rest of this chapter, we turn to Catholic reformations' "strong power."

Ignatius Loyola and the Spiritual Exercises

Ignatius, a Basque nobleman and mercenary soldier, was wounded in a border skirmish in 1521. The only reading matter available to him as he recuperated was Ludolf of Saxony's *Life of Christ*. Convinced of his need for reform of life, Ignatius set out on a pilgrimage to Jerusalem, but he was forced to stop when his leg wound did not heal properly. While he stayed at Manresa for ten months, concentrating on his spiritual life, his leg was rebroken and reset three times. During this time he wrote down whatever he found useful. *Spiritual Exercises*, part of which came from this time and part from a later time, described the way he arrived at the extraordinary spiritual experiences he enjoyed at Manresa. *Spiritual Exercises* provides a method, a carefully graded program, for the religious life, but the goal is not mystical experience but action in the world.

The *Exercises* became the basis for the spirituality of the Order Ignatius founded, the Society of Jesus, or Jesuit Order, which came into official existence on September 27, 1540. Jesuits' tremendous efficiency was immediate evidence of the *Exercises'* effectiveness. Yet in its time this spirituality was shocking; it rejected many traditional features of monastic life, like the chanting of the daily hours of the divine office, special dress, and compulsory ascetic practices. Jesuits were encouraged *not* to mortify their bodies by excessive fasting, loss of sleep, or whatever might harm their studies, activities of service, and missions.

Ignatius's instructions in the *Exercises* describe a relatively short, intensive period of concentrated introspection for the specific purpose of vocational choice. He did not want introspection to be a time-consuming occupation, preferring a method that would rapidly, and with minimal maintenance, provide self-knowledge. On this basis, a choice of vocation could be made, informed by awareness of one's characteristic weaknesses, difficulties, affinities, and strengths. Once the choice was made, the person could devote unconflicted energy to loving service. Ignatius wrote:

> This expression "spiritual exercises" embraces every method of examination of conscience, of meditation, of contemplation, of vocal and mental prayer, and of other spiritual activity. . . . For just as strolling, walking, and running are bodily exercises, so spiritual exercises are methods of disposing the soul to free itself of all inordinate attachments, and after accomplishing this, of seeking and discovering the divine will regarding the disposition of one's life, thus insuring the salvation of the soul.

The *Exercises* were not written to be read, but to be administered by a director. They assume obedience on the part of the monk, and sensitivity on the part of the director. They move the monk through the full range of spiritual emotions, from repentance to the joy of resurrection and new life. Detailed visualizations and meditations on events in Christ's life, together with recall of the monk's memories, connect the monk's life to Christ's. The Spanish evangelical Roman Catholic Juan de Valdes (1516–56) might have been describing the method of the *Exercises* in his observation, "In everything you love and fear, if strictly noticed, you will discover yourself there" (*The Christian Alphabet*).

Art and music of Catholic reformation

The success of the Catholic reformations was due not merely to reform from the top (the Council of Trent) and technologies of repression (Inquisition), but also to its "strong power," attraction. Catholic reforms demonstrate that weak and strong power need not be mutually exclusive. In Catholic lands, the Inquisition coerced, but without the strong power of attraction, coercion would not have been effective in the long term, as coercion inevitably generates resistance. No other religious movement has used its artistic resources so skillfully and so precisely to teach and to evoke a specific religious experience. Catholic reform art engaged the senses in order to awaken, to move, and to guide, in short, to train religious perceptions and sensibilities. Music and the visual arts were used skillfully in the service of the church.

Changing accustomed worship can intensify worshippers' engagement. Many Protestant churches were stripped of their accustomed decorations, altering the worship environment. One enthusiastic admirer of the Zurich Grössmunster remarked after it had been stripped of paintings and sculptures and whitewashed that the church looked "positively luminous." But a new experience of worship can also be achieved by adding richness, surprising the eye and/or the ear. This was the Catholic choice. Music and the visual arts as well as increased attention to effective preaching were used to enhance the worship experience. These changes destabilized and resisted worshippers' expectations, requiring sensory *presence*. Heightened musical and artistic description of the relationship of spirit and sense was one of the Catholic reform's most fascinating aspects.

The Sack of Rome

In 1525, Roman artists were flourishing and the number of artworks in Rome was growing rapidly. But in May 1527, Charles V's army, commanded by Charles de Bourbon, conquered and sacked Rome. The imperial army was composed of 10,000 German Lutherans and about half that number of Spanish and Italian mercenaries. Lacking provisions or resources, the armies lived on looting and extortion. Artworks were destroyed and artists fled. Eager to attack papal power, the imperial troops spat on relics, burned churches, raped nuns, and enslaved young people. The Church's treasure of gold and silver was virtually wiped out, as liturgical objects, precious reliquaries, chalices, monstrances, vestments, and ornaments were stolen. St Peter's was gutted and remained empty for half a century.

Charles V's secretary justified the Sack of Rome as "providential intervention." He said, "Every single horror of the Sack is a precise, necessary, and providential punishment for the iniquities that soiled Rome." One of the terms of surrender required Pope Clement VII (1523–34) to give a plenary absolution for all acts perpetrated during the Sack, adding insult to injury. On February 24, 1529, Charles V had himself crowned emperor in San Petronio, one of the few intact churches in the ruined city of Rome. Systematic restoration of the city was not begun until 1552. It was the dynamism of the Catholic reform that gave Rome a new look.

In its last session (December 1563), Trent reaffirmed the use of religious pictures to accompany liturgy and for devotional practice, defining the precise usefulness of religious images:

> Not that any divinity or virtue is believed to be in them by reason of which they are to be venerated or that something is to be asked of them, or that trust is to be placed in images, as was done of old by the Gentiles who placed their hope in idols; but because the honor which is shown them is referred to their prototypes which they represent, so that by means of the images which we kiss and before which we uncover the head and prostrate ourselves, we adore Christ and venerate the saints whose likeness they bear.

The Gèsu

The Church of the Gèsu in Rome is the mother church of the Jesuit Order and the model for Jesuit churches all over the world (see CD Rom figure 8.1). It was built to honor three teenaged Jesuit missionaries and martyrs, Aloysius Gonzaga, Stanislas Kostka, and John Berchmans. Its foundation in stone was laid by Ignatius in 1550, but construction did not begin until after his death in 1584. In the Gèsu, a simultaneously accessible and transcendent spiritual world is the environment for worship.

Architecturally, the building demonstrates Jesuits' concern for preaching to large congregations. "Churches were to have good acoustics, dispense with side aisles and other complicated designs, [and] be located in a part of the city easily accessible to the populace" (O'Malley, 1993: 357). Moreover, new liturgical needs required innovative features:

> a more spacious, hall-like, and uninterrupted nave to accommodate larger crowds . . . flat or wooden roofs for better acoustics; a large chancel for dispensing communion; shortened transcept-arms to emphasize the centrality of space; more windows for light; and side-altars for the simultaneous celebration of chantry masses.
>
> (Hsia, 1998: 161)

In order to permit greater visibility and audibility, there was no choir screen or barrier between clergy and congregation.

Disagreement occurred over the decoration of the Gèsu. Even though a 1558 ruling had stipulated that Jesuit churches should be "neither lavish not overly decorated," the Jesuit theologian Peter Canisius (1521–97) argued in 1579 that Jesuit churches could be richly decorated. Similarly, Catholic theologian Miguel de Molinos (1640–97) echoed Abbot Suger five centuries earlier when he wrote, "The church is the image of heaven on earth; how should it not be adorned with all that is most precious?" Molinos called the Gèsu an image of heaven on earth and a visible argument for the presence of Christ in the mass.

Others said that Jesuit churches should "inspire contemplation on poverty." Although Jesuits valued and extolled poverty, they were also superb educators, and it was finally the proven capacity of images to inform and train religious sensibilities that decided the issue. Decoration of the Gèsu took nearly a century (figure 8.1) (see CD Rom figures 8.2 and 8.3). Even before it was completed, an English visitor to the church in 1620, Grey Brydges, wrote of the Gèsu:

> Wherein is inserted all possible inventions to catch men's affections and to ravish their understanding, as first, the gloriousness of their altars, infinite number of images, priestly ornaments, and the divers actions they use in that service; besides the most excellent and exquisite music in the world, that surprises our ears. So that whatsoever that can be imagined to express either solemnity or devotion is by them used.
>
> (Quoted by Haskell, 1963: 63).

The Gèsu could not be mistaken for a Protestant lecture hall.

Jesuit churches were the first to be named simply after Jesus, not Christ the Redeemer or some other such title. Over the Gèsu's high altar is a painting of Christ's circumcision, a seemingly minor event in Christ's infancy (described in Luke 2. 21: "Eight days later the time came to circumcise him, and he was given the name Jesus, the name given by the angel before he was conceived"). Christ's circumcision was an unusual subject for the primary place of honor in a church. Its choice is explained by the fact that the

Figure 8.1   Pietro le Gros, *Triumph of Faith Over Heresy*, Ignatius Chapel, Gèsu, Rome.
The propaganda aspect of Roman Catholic reformation art is evident in this sculpture whose message is the reaffirmation of tradition and the defeat of Protestant "heresy." Photo SCALA, Florence.

Feast of the Circumcision is the principle Jesuit celebration. On this occasion, through a ritual operation, the name of Jesus was first associated with his blood. "That is why we Jesuits must be willing to give our blood for his name."

Michelangelo

Michelangelo was commissioned by Pope Clement VII to paint a *Last Judgment* in the Sistine Chapel, the Vatican, Rome (see CD Rom figure 8.4). He began in November 1535 and finished six years later. When the painting was unveiled, Pope Paul III was overcome and broke into prayer, "Lord, charge me not with my sins when thou shalt come on the day of judgment." The eschatological theme of the painting was reinforced by the recent horrors of the Sack.

The multiple naked figures in Michelangelo's painting were controversial. Condivi, a contemporary admirer, said, "In this work, Michelangelo expresses everything that the art of painting can do with the human body." Theatine monks raised objections, but Michelangelo was inflexible, saying, "No other kind of figuration is possible in a representation of resuscitated creatures." Beauty of body signals the higher condition of humanity, he said: "no other proof, no other fruits of heaven on earth do we have." Four centuries before, Thomas Aquinas had similarly found bodily beauty the perfect analogy for grace. "Grace," Thomas had said, "is a quality of soul, like beauty of body."

The *Last Judgment*, a façade with superimposed levels, was entirely painted by Michelangelo, assisted only by a color-grinder. It was the largest fresco in Rome (48 × 44 feet). Painted while preparations were being made for the Council of Trent, it was also a polemic against Luther's theology of justification by faith alone, emphasizing reward and punishment for good and evil deeds. Indeed, in Protestant art, the Last Judgment virtually disappeared. "The Last Judgment is abolished," Luther proclaimed in a sermon on September 7, 1538, "it concerns the believer as little as it does the angels . . . All believers pass from this life to heaven without any judgment" (quoted by Harbison, 1976: 89).

In Michelangelo's *Last Judgment*, Christ, the unmoved mover, draws the elect upward to himself with his right hand; with his left hand he presses the damned down. The figure of Christ (see CD Rom figure 8.5) creates a circle of rising and falling; both blessed and damned are caught in the irresistible momentum of the motion. All look fearfully at Christ, the Judge. Mary huddles beside him, recoiling from the fearsome sight of the Last Judgment.

The painting has three zones: the kingdom of heaven, with Christ as judge of the world in the center occupies the top zone. In the right half of the arch are apostles; patriarchs (and John the Baptist) appear on the left. At the lower end, St Bartholomew (with Michelangelo's face) holds his flayed skin, representing his martyrdom (see CD Rom figure 8.6). The middle zone is the realm of those who have been judged. At the left, an angel raises the elect who cling to a rosary. At the right, the damned fall. In the center, messenger angels blow trumpets of doom. The lowest realm belongs to the underworld and demons. The resurrection of the dead (left) is immediately above the altar. On the right, Minos, prince of hell, ferries the damned to hell.

Michelangelo had also painted the ceiling of the Chapel in 1512 with scenes from the creation of the world (see CD Rom figures 8.7 and 8.8). In the *Last Judgment* the lunettes cover two cycles painted 20 years earlier by Michelangelo, a Moses and Christ cycle, and the ancestors of Christ. Hosts of wingless angels hold instruments of Christ's passion, the cross, and the pillar at which he was scourged, reflecting Catholic reform interest in the flagellation. Former depictions of the scene show Christ bound to a high column, but Michelangelo painted Christ bound by his hands to an iron ring in a low column; without support he collapses under the whips and rods. Athletic angels attempt to raise the cross and the column.

Contemporary painters were strongly impressed by Michelangelo's *Last Judgment*, but most theologians were hostile to its nude figures. During the papacy of Paul IV (1555–9) and Gregory XIII (1572–85) the painting was in danger of being destroyed. The papal master of ceremonies, Biagio, called it a *stufa d'ignudi* (a bathroom of nudes). Pietro Aretino accused Michelangelo of being irreverent. "Such things might be painted in a voluptuous bathroom," he said, "but not in the choir of the highest chapel. Our souls are benefited little by art, but by piety." But artists have ways of repaying their critics; Aretino's portrait was incorporated in the *Last Judgment* as one of the damned, while Biagio was portrayed as Minos, lord of hell. Biago complained to the pope, who replied that he could do nothing, since Biagio was consigned to hell. Had Biagio been in purgatory, he said, the pope's help might have been effective! The disgruntled Biagio carried his criticism to the Council of Trent where, on 3 December 1563, the Council banned the representation of "unsuitable" subjects (like nudes) in religious art. After this, most of the nudes in the Last Judgment were painted over, first in 1559, by a student of Michelangelo, and again in 1572, 1625, 1712, and 1762. The original painted bodies are irretrievable. In the late twentieth-century cleaning and restoration of the fresco, workers found that the original plaster had been chipped off and fresh plaster laid for the overpainting.

Michelangelo's *Last Judgment* with its swirling and weightless bodies influenced an Italian art, largely of the sixteenth century, that tested the limit of efforts to heighten affective piety. Mannerism relies on exaggerated bodies, poses, and gestures to carry its impact (see CD Rom figures 8.9 and 8.10).

> Subjects are treated in ways that make them difficult to understand. The main incident is pushed into the background or swamped with so many figures serving as excuses for displays of virtuosity in figure painting. [There are] extremes of perspective, distorted proportions or scale, and figures are jammed into too small a space. Color is used for its emotional impact rather than naturalistically. There is rich decoration and elaborate illusionism.
>
> (Murray, 1977: 125).

In Mannerist paintings, the balance between spiritual and sensual is tipped heavily in the direction of the spiritual. The artistic forms – music, painting, and sculpture – of the Catholic reform all presented a heightened mystical sensibility. The artworks created for Christian churches contributed to the intensified religious feeling that energized the charitable activities characteristic of the Catholic reformations (see CD Rom figures 8.11 and 8.12).

Music

In 1562 the Council of Trent considered banning music from the Church because of the secular elements in church music. Drinking and love song tunes were often used in masses. The style of sixteenth-century church music was also criticized; in polyphonic settings of the Mass the sacred text was often rendered unintelligible by the elaborate texture of the music. Furthermore, some of the cardinals were worried about the "corruption" of Gregorian chant by embellishments added by the singers. They also voiced objections to the use of instruments other than the organ, and to the "irreverence" of church musicians.

While the cardinals were discussing the appropriateness of music in worship, Giovanni Pierluigi da Palestrina (d. 1594) began to write specifically liturgical music.

Palestrina's music was performed at the Council. Unarguably *religious* in intent and effect, it effectively settled the question of whether music could genuinely contribute to liturgy and worship. A canon was approved that prohibited "all seductive or impure melodies, all vain and worldly texts, and all outcries and uproars" and stipulated that the *words* of church music must be clearly understandable.

Palestrina, who has been called "the father and prince of church music," is credited with saving church music. During a lifetime as organist and choir director at various churches in Rome, he wrote 105 surviving masses. The most important of the several influential musical posts that Palestrina held in Rome was that of composer for the papal choir of the Sistine Chapel. *The Missa Papae Marcelli*, written when Palestrina was Master of the Choir at Santa Maria Maggiore in Rome, incorporated Trent's musical guidelines. Yet much about the composition remains mysterious, including its title. Pope Marcellus reigned for only three weeks in April 1555, before the Council even considered questions relating to music. One clue to the reason for the title might be that on Good Friday 1555, Pope Marcellus spoke to the Sistine Chapel singers about liturgical music, instructing them to enunciate clearly so that the words they sang could be understood (CD Rom Music 8.1).

Palestrina's *Missa Papae Marcelli* seems to aim specifically at making the text intelligible, while demonstrating appreciation for the human voice without accompaniment (*a cappella* – literally, in the chapel). Palestrina divided the six voices into antiphonal responses, interpreting an ancient liturgical practice in an original way. A theme heard first in the soprano voice wanders from vocal line to vocal line, the same theme being heard now in the alto, now in the tenor or bass. Palestrina acknowledged that he sought to compose "music of a new order in accordance with the views of the most serious and religious-minded persons in high places."

Palestrina avoided monotony in his setting of the mass by making a distinction between short texts – the Kyrie, Sanctus, Agnus Dei – and long texts – the Gloria and the Credo. If the text was short, basically the repetition of a phrase, like "Lord have mercy; Christ have mercy; Lord have mercy," he used complex polyphony combining two or more melodic lines, creating a many-voiced texture. However, if a long and less familiar text was involved, he kept the music simple in order to highlight the text.

Gregorio Allegri's (1582–1652) *Miserere* (Psalm 51) was written for nine voices, arranged in two choirs. It alternates polyphonically ornamented psalmody with monodic verses. A startlingly beautiful piece of music, it was sung in the Sistine Chapel during Holy Week. Initially unpublished and guarded by the pontificate, it was passed on from generation to generation of the papal choir until 1770 when it was published. In that year, the 14-year-old Mozart transcribed it from memory after hearing it once. In a letter of April 4, 1831, Felix Mendelssohn gave a description of the ceremony which accompanied the annual performance of the *Miserere*:

> At each verse [of the preceding psalm], a candle is extinguished; then the whole choir intones *fortissimo* a new psalm melody; then the last candles are put out, the pope leaves his throne and prostrates himself on his knees before the altar; everyone kneels with him and says a silent *pater noster*. Immediately afterwards, the *Miserere* begins, *pianissimo*. For me, this is the most beautiful moment of the whole ceremony. . . . During the *pater noster*, deathly silence reigns throughout the chapel, after which the *Miserere* begins with the singing of a quiet chord of voices, then the music opens out in the two choirs. It was this

opening, and in particular the very first sound, that made the greatest impression on me (CD Rom Music 8.2).

At the end of the sixteenth century, Palestrina's music was largely superseded by the new Baroque music. In Baroque music, interest shifted away from the texture of several independent parts to what is called *monody*, literally "one song," that is, a melody written for one singer with instrumental accompaniment, simplifying the complexities of counterpoint. Its most characteristic form was the opera. Palestrina, a composer who deliberately adopted a more restrained manner of composing in order to produce a distinctive sacred music that could not be mistaken for, or confused with, secular music of the time, came to be considered conservative. But his music was perfectly ordered to the Council of Trent's principles. Worshipful music was music that conformed to the mass, and featured intelligible words.

Music and art in the Catholic reform represented nothing less than a skillful reiteration and new vision of liturgical practice. The resources of the Roman Catholic reform were successful to a great degree against the very attractive Protestant rhetoric of the democracy of believers. By 1565 Catholicism had revived at every level. Popes were committed reformers, conservative in theology and self-confident as administrators of a world Church. Piety flourished, and seminaries were established to train competent priests.

READING

Ignatius Loyola, *The Spiritual Exercises*

Early modern Catholicism

Catholic reform theology inspired a host of new charitable organizations and orders. It also prompted a new kind of monasticism, exemplified by the Society of Jesus. The new Orders emphasized *service* – teaching, caring for the sick and the poor, and missionary work, de-emphasizing liturgy, contemplation, and ascetic practices that could interfere with service. New male orders included the Theatines, Capuchins, and the Barnabites.

Cloistered women like Teresa of Avila and laywomen like Catherine of Genoa exhibited the new Catholic reform spirit, characterized by refusal to focus on either contemplation or service at the expense of the other. Rather, contemplation was practiced for the purpose of energizing service. Nevertheless, Trent's reforms included establishing male control of religious women. In 1566 a papal bull reiterated and reinforced Trent's 1563 decree calling for the enclosure of all female religious communities, including Third-Order communities. Late medieval female monasticism had sometimes allowed autonomous and active female communities like the Beguines to flourish; after Trent only a few female Orders like the Ursalines escaped enclosure. In England, Mary Ward, founder of the Institute of the Blessed Virgin Mary, known as "English Ladies," wrote:

> There is no difference between men and women. Fervor is not placed in feeling but in a
> will to *do* well, which women have as well as men. Women may do great things, as we have

seen from the example of many saints who did great things. And I hope in God it will be seen in time that women will come to do much.

The English Ladies were suppressed in 1630, and Mary Ward was imprisoned in the Convent of Poor Clares at Munich.

Sixteenth- and seventeenth-century Catholic missions brought conversions in South, Central and parts of North America, India, China, Japan, the Philippines, Malaya, and a little later in Africa. In each of these locations different missionizing strategies were used. In the New World Franciscan missions often attempted to modify the brutality of Spanish colonization. But unfamiliar diseases and exploitation devastated the native population. In the central Mexican plateau, the indigenous population fell from six million to one million between 1548 and 1605. The most gentle of the Catholic missions was that of the Jesuit Matteo Ricci in China. Ricci became a respected scholar of Chinese culture and Confucianism in order to demonstrate the profound agreement of Christianity as a system of social ethics and individual morality with Confucianism. However, as sources in indigenous languages are studied, it becomes evident that Christian missions were met by widespread resistance. We consider Catholic missions in the New World in chapter 9.

3   Reformations in Scotland and England

Reformation ideas and the growth of nation-states were intertwined in the sixteenth century. Catholic reforms occurred primarily in Italy and Spain. Lutherans, Calvinists, and Anabaptists centered in Germany, the Netherlands, and Switzerland. English reformations, focused by a power struggle between the ruler, Henry VIII (1509–47), and Pope Leo X (1513–21), are perhaps the clearest example of the interconnection of reform and nationalism.

Scotland

Sixteenth-century Scotland was largely rural and feudal, with a weak monarchy and unruly nobility. The universities of Glasgow, St Andrews, and Aberdeen, though long-established, were not up to the standard of continental universities. Generally hostile to England and in alliance with France, Scots had bitterly torn loyalties according to whether their sympathies were Catholic or Protestant.

Little is known of the advance of Reformed theology in Scotland until the 1530s when incidents of iconoclasm occurred and 13 people were executed for heresy. John Knox (d. 1572), who had been a royal chaplain in England and subsequently a disciple of Calvin in Geneva, advocated both Protestant reform and national independence. By 1559 Reformed churches, organized to exercise discipline among the faithful, existed in Scotland, though how many there were is not known. Renewed attempts to repress Protestant worship failed, and in 1560 Parliament voted to adopt the Scots Confession, abolish the mass and "eliminate all previous statutes 'not agreeing with Goddis hoile worde'" (Benedict, 2002: 161). The final stage of the Scottish reformation occurred when the Catholic Mary Queen of Scots abdicated the throne. Reformed Protestantism became the national Church of Scotland by Parliamentary action in December 1567.

England

No single charismatic religious leader led English reformations. Reforms of the English Church were unpredictable, erratic, and, in the sixteenth century, incomplete. Preaching and catechizing for re-educating priests and people, although highly important, were in short supply. Moreover, for most sixteenth-century English people, the commonsense view that worship and works were salvific was unchallenged by the Protestant doctrine of justification by faith alone. In a fictitious 1601 debate, a character articulates this view:

> If a man say his Lord's Prayer, his Ten Commandments, and his Belief, and keep them, and say nobody harm, nor do nobody no harm and do as he would be done to, have a good faith to God-ward and be a man of God's belief, no doubt he shall be saved without all this running to sermons and prattling of the scriptures. . . . we must be saved by our good prayers and our good serving of God.
>
> (Quoted by Haigh, 1993: 281)

The English reform was entangled with a struggle over sovereignty in which England and Scotland became Protestant or Catholic according to the religion of the current ruler. Yet, for all its confusion, English struggles led to the first statement of religious toleration *on a national scale*, namely the Act of Toleration of 1689. The Act did not provide complete religious toleration but intended rather to unite Protestants of various allegiances against Catholics. Nevertheless, its language was more radical than its intentions, contributing to the gradual growth of the idea that religious coercion was unacceptable. But we are not there yet.

During the sixteenth century, as Catholic and Protestant rulers alternated, persecution of dissidents occurred in England and the British Isles as on the Continent. It was an age of violence, an age that agreed that religion was worth fighting over. The suffering is not adequately indicated by the figures. The martyrdom of one man, Thomas Cranmer, exemplifies that suffering. Cranmer, the first Archbishop of Canterbury under the Protestant sympathizer Henry VIII, was martyred in 1556 under the Catholic Mary Tudor. John Foxe's *Acts and Monuments of Matters Most Special and Memorable Happening in the Church* (commonly called Foxe's *Book of Martyrs*) told the story. Cranmer, tortured, tried, and condemned for heresy and treason, recanted and declared his belief in transubstantiation and papal supremacy, signing a prepared statement. However, he shortly recanted his recantation, and was brought to the stake, where he gave a last exhortation to the crowd that had gathered to watch him burn. His statement summarized Protestant faith in God, Christ, and the scriptures, concluding:

> And now I come to the great thing which so much troubleth my conscience, more than anything that ever I did or said in my whole life, and that is the setting abroad of a writing contrary to the truth; which now here I renounce and refuse, as things written with my hand contrary to the truth which I thought in my heart, and written for fear of death, and

to save my life, if it might be; and that is all such bills or papers which I have written or signed with my hand since my degradation, wherein I have written many things untrue. And forasmuch as my hand hath offended, writing contrary to my heart, therefore my hand shall first be punished: for when I come to the fire, it shall first be burned.

Foxe reported that as the fire began to ascend about him, "stretching out his right hand, he held it unshrinkingly in the fire till it was burnt to a cinder, frequently exclaiming, 'This unworthy right hand!'"

In England, powerful narrations of suffering were used effectively to produce social and religious effects. *Foxe's Book of Martyrs* was published in 1563, with 170 illustrations. By 1570, it had gone into a second edition and the Convocation of Canterbury ordered a copy to be placed in every cathedral pulpit. Before 1700, five editions were published. Few if any books have more profoundly influenced English thought, society, and attitudes. Despite Foxe's explicit advocacy that all persecution should cease, the virulently anti-Catholic attitudes expressed in the book combined with vivid stories and pictures of Protestant martyrs maintained English hostility against Catholics for centuries.

Political events also played a large role in influencing English attitudes toward Catholics. In 1588, Philip II with Spain's Armada made a bloody attempt to conquer England in order to enforce Catholicism. The English reacted with the Recusant Act (1593) that denied civil rights to English Catholics. The Act also stipulated penalties (unevenly enforced) of death, banishment, life-imprisonment, forfeiture of estates and goods, double taxation, and monthly fines for not attending Church of England services. The "crime" of not attending services of the Church of England was not revoked until the Catholic Relief Act of 1791, and full civil rights were restored only in 1829.

The reforming ideas that circulated in England were not new, but they had a different flavor. Three circumstances contributed to English reforms. First, English nationalism had a 300 year history, from eighth-century conflicts over the date of Easter and monastic tonsure to the fourteenth-century "Babylonian Captivity" of the Church (during which the pope resided in Avignon, identifying the papacy with France, the traditional enemy of England). The 1215 Magna Carta limited not only the power of the king, but also that of his feudal lord, the Pope. Since the fourteenth-century Lollard movement a national consciousness had formed around resistance to papal supremacy. The fifteenth century saw further gradual erosion of papal supremacy, evident in documents affirming "not some foreign power, not the Pope, but England for Englishmen." Lollardy, although vigorously persecuted, remained an underground movement in the sixteenth century.

Second, a long history of anti-clericalism existed in England. In the fourteenth century, John Wyclif and the Lollards advocated poverty and a scriptural lifestyle for clergy. In the sixteenth century, religious objections to clerical abuses had largely become secular anti-clericalism.

Third, the humanist renaissance in England provided important incentives for reformation. Oxford and Cambridge, where Erasmus taught from 1510 to 1513, were two of the most important centers of sixteenth-century humanist thought. Thomas More, Lord Chancellor of England, pictured an ideal religion based on the dictates of reason and the laws of nature in his *Utopia* (1516).

Each of these factors contributed to interest in the Lutheran ideas that began to filter into England, primarily through the universities, in the second decade of the sixteenth century. Despite massive book burnings and a public excommunication of Luther (in absentia), Lutheran ideas maintained their attraction for many people. But it was not popular evangelical feeling that ultimately created reformation in the English Church, but the decisions of England's rulers. "Change was imposed from above on a largely hostile or indifferent populace" (Benedict, 2002: 232).

Henry VIII, a self-educated theologian, earned the title "Defender of the Faith" for his *Assertion of the Seven Sacraments*, a response to Luther's *Babylonian Captivity* (though the *Assertion*, published under Henry's name, was primarily the work of several university theologians). Henry used reform ideas that supported his *political* program without altering a single Catholic doctrine. In 1538 Henry broke off communication with the German princes; six articles affirmed transubstantiation, communion in one kind, vows of chastity, votive masses, clerical celibacy, and auricular confession. His take-over of every monastery in England by 1540 similarly revealed, not so much a zeal for Protestant reform, as an enhancement of royal power. In short, "Henry VIII did little more than reject papal authority, decree royal supremacy over the national church, and seize a great deal of ecclesiastical property" (Benedict, 2002: 231).

Henry VIII's well-known marriages and divorces played a decisive role in reformation of the English Church. His desire to divorce Catherine of Aragon, and Pope Clement VII's refusal to grant an annulment, "turned the pope's primary English advocate into the pope's foremost enemy" (Elton, 1962: 229). When his petition was refused, Henry and his lawyers initiated a legislative process that undermined the pope's power over the English Church. The culmination of this process, the 1533 Act of Restraint of Appeals to Rome, prohibited English appeals to courts outside England. The 1534 Act of Supremacy, the decisive break with Rome, declared Henry the "Only Supreme Head on Earth of the Church of England." Thomas More was beheaded (1535) for refusing to sign the Act of Supremacy and for his opposition to Henry VIII's marriage to Ann Boleyn.

Religious change in England occurred with a dizzying rapidity. Before 1529 no English cleric doubted that the pope was the supreme head of the English church; after 1534, a mere five years later, no one could assert papal supremacy without placing his life in jeopardy. The mildly Protestant Ten Articles promoted by Thomas Cranmer in 1536, and the publication of William Coverdale's Bible, the first complete Bible in English (1535), did not bring about either reform or the reconciliation of reforming Protestants. In 1543 Henry "restricted Bible reading to members of the upper ranks of society" (Benedict, 2002: 234). His list of those forbidden to read the Bible (and be empowered by it to seek social change) reveals who was likely to be discontented in sixteenth-century England: women, artists, servants, farmers, and laborers.

Yet Bible reading was central to the English reforms. Before 1580 about 30 percent of men and 10 percent of women could read. Some people learned to read in order to read the Bible, but it was also read publicly to large crowds and small gatherings. Printed ballads, affordable by all but the poorest, spread both Reformed doctrine and mockery of Catholic rituals. The centrality of literacy to Protestantism meant that Protestants tended to be from the middle or upper classes. Protestant martyrs tended to be from the middling ranks, since the rich could and did emigrate during Mary's reign. More men than women were attracted by Protestantism, perhaps also due to the greater literacy rates among men; just 50 of the 180 Marian martyrs were women. In England, Protestantism also tended to be an urban phenomenon, spreading from large cities along trade routes.

After Henry's death, Edward VI continued and extended Henry's Protestant reforms, orienting the church in a Reformed direction. But his reign was brief (1547–53), and he died before worship or church polity were reformed. On his death, the Catholic Mary I (1553–8) reversed Edward's reform of doctrine, persecuted and executed Protestants, and restored traditional Catholicism. The personal pain caused by these rapid changes can only be imagined. For example, Henry's 1534 Act of Supremacy had closed all religious orders, and by 1550 clergy were permitted to marry. Under Mary I the attempt to reinstate Catholicism in England forced many clergy who had married to hide their wives in the country for the five years of Mary's reign.

The struggle over a book of *common* prayer focused efforts to define the English church. Elizabethan theologian Richard Hooker described the significance of common prayer in his *Laws of Ecclesiastical Polity*: Common prayer, he said, is preferred to private prayer because of the "vertue, force, and efficacie to help that imbecility and weakness in us, by means whereof wee are likewise of ourselves the lesse apt to performe unto God so heavenlie a service, with such affection of harte, and disposition in the powers of our soules as is requisite" (*Laws* V. 25.1).

In 1549, during Edward VI's reign, Thomas Cranmer's edition of the *Book of Common Prayer* was imposed on churches. It satisfied none of the various Protestant and Catholic adversaries, even though its language was purposely vague on such inflammatory matters as the Lord's Supper. It seemed to deny transubstantiation while retaining "real presence." But it also used memorial language, suggesting that each person might interpret for him/herself. Protestants were unhappy about the retention of prayers for the dead and the celebration of communion in burial services, while Catholics were unhappy about any change at all. Subsequent revisions and counter-revisions of the *Book of Common Prayer* failed to satisfy and, in fact, consolidated the two protesting groups, Catholics and evangelical (Reformed) dissenters, or puritans. John Jewel, bishop of Salisbury and an advocate of the Anglican settlement, opposed both puritan dissenters and Catholics in his "An Apologie of the Church of England."

The *Thirty-Nine Articles* of 1563 contained doctrinal formulae finally accepted as normative for the Church of England. Drafted from earlier versions and personally amended by Elizabeth I, the *Articles* were not a creed; they were instead short summaries of doctrine in direct response to current controversies, but intentionally *open* to various interpretations. The primarily Protestant *Thirty-Nine Articles* were accepted along with a Catholic liturgy.

The reform of the English Church was accomplished by political power rather than by religious arguments. During the long reign of Elizabeth I (1558–1603), stabilization of the religious situation was brought about by the definition of a middle way between Catholics and Protestant extremists. The poet, John Donne (d. 1631) was the first to use the expression *via media*, but the concept of seeking a middle way occurred in the last decade of the sixteenth century; it came to dominate the self-image of the English church sometime in the seventeenth century. Puritans still opposed what they called "popish remnants," but their voice was weakened and their purifying influence lessened by division among them on issues of church government.

Puritans only achieved a capital "P" as a more-or-less coherent group around 1600; before that they were isolated individuals and small groups reacting to different aspects of proposed forms of worship. Puritans – Congregationalists, Presbyterians, Separatists, and Non-Conformists – wanted services that adhered to biblical directives. They wanted more preaching and less ritual, and they wanted religion to be more visible in both lay and clergy lives.

Elizabeth's settlement, characterized by Protestant doctrine and Catholic liturgy, gathered a wide majority of center-of-the-road subjects. In 1593 legislation against both Puritans and Catholics was passed without arousing significant rebellion. In it Puritans were called "wicked, seditious, and dangerous;" Catholics were called "traitorous, dangerous, and detestable." The Elizabethan settlement effectively integrated and modified these two "dangerous" groups. Since the great majority of English people who cared about religion were either Catholics or Puritans; the roots of Anglicanism lie in both camps. The next sections further explore the Elizabethan settlement.

Elizabeth I

Elizabeth I (1533–1603), daughter of Henry VIII and Anne Boleyn, ascended to the English throne in 1558 when she was 25. England was still half-feudal and largely rural, predominantly Catholic, but with a strong Reformed minority. Elizabeth lacked religious fervor, but she had inherited her father's keen eye for political advantage. She disliked both Catholic and Calvinist extremists; her stance has been characterized as a "cool humanism." She dropped the title adopted by her Father, "Supreme Head of the English Church," and took instead the slightly less arrogant title "Supreme Governor." Intelligent and cautious, she exuded an air of authority. Assuming "no small part in controlling the policies of the Anglican Church, she exercised her influence indirectly, often covertly, and with an infuriating reluctance to appear responsible for contentious rulings" (Dickens, 1964: 303).

The broad theological consensus Elizabeth sought formed around revisions of the 1552 *Second Book of Common Prayer*. Eucharistic beliefs were allowed a remarkable latitude by the addition of the words, "The body of our Lord Jesus Christ which was given for thee" . . . to the words, "Take and eat this in remembrance . . ." Commemorative language was combined with a suggestion of real presence, yet short of a declaration of transubstantiation. In addition:

> Regular bread replaced the unleavened communion wafers. A table in the body of the church took the place of the altar. The vestments the officiating minister was required to wear were simplified, although not entirely eliminated. The words of exorcism were removed from the baptismal ceremony. Communicants continued to kneel when receiving the communion elements, but an addendum was added stating that no adoration of the elements was thereby implied.
>
> (Benedict, 2002: 238)

These minor but significant changes met with little opposition. The 1559 Act of Uniformity (which passed in Parliament by three votes) abolished the mass and stipulated the use of a slightly revised *Second Prayer Book* of Edward VI. Forms of service other than the new Prayer Book were forbidden and penalties – up to life imprisonment for a third offense – were placed on clerics who used other forms. The Elizabethan settlement achieved several reforms of worship, including a vernacular liturgy, administration of the sacrament in both kinds (in effect briefly during the reign of Edward VI, but abolished by Mary I), and permission for the clergy to marry. Elizabeth did not change the fundamental doctrines and constitution of the English Church.

But the problems of the English Church were not over. In 1566, after the conclusion of the Council of Trent, Pope Pius V (1566–72) supported Mary Queen of Scots' (1542–87) claim to the English throne. Elizabeth was formally tried, *in absentia*, in Rome, (not surprisingly) found guilty, and excommunicated. The bull of excommunication was carried to England and nailed on the door of the Bishop of London's palace in 1570. Elizabeth's excommunication dispensed her subjects from their oath of allegiance.

Implementation of the bull proved difficult, however. The pope failed to persuade the Catholic European powers to undertake a crusade against England, so specially trained missionaries were sent to England with orders to convert the English people and assassinate the queen. In 1587 after the discovery of a serious plot against Elizabeth, Mary Queen of Scots was executed, thus removing the figurehead of resistance to Elizabeth.

Richard Hooker

Richard Hooker (d. 1600), master of the Temple Church in London and theologian of the Elizabethian settlement, inherited two generations of English reformation debate. He formulated a balanced Anglicanism characterized not only by rejection of the more intransigent Puritan and Catholic elements, but also by the integration of Puritans and Catholics. We should note that "Reformed" and "Puritan" are not synonyms. Tensions existed between people who held varying nuances of Reformed doctrines and practices. At the end of the sixteenth century, most English churchmen were Reformed in theology, but Puritans wanted more reforms of worship. A scholar who has recently examined the contentious question of Hooker's theological loyalties concluded that "though he held a range of distinctive Reformed beliefs," Hooker was "at or near the head of the movement away from the Reformed tradition in the English Church" (Voak, 2003: 320, 323).

Hooker's *Laws of Ecclesiastical Polity* (1594–7) had a specifically polemical purpose. He sought to formulate the philosophical base of the English church primarily in opposition to Reformed theology's radical predestinarianism. Hooker also contested the Reformed picture of the human condition as radically depraved. Addressing the central sixteenth-century issue of "how human reason, human will, and divine grace relate," Hooker de-emphasized original sin. He taught that people can choose either to "know and perform to some degree works that glorify and are obedient to God" or resist God's grace (Voak, 2003: 18, 319). Moreover, Hooker differed strongly from Calvin in putting human reason in place of the Holy Spirit interpreting scripture.

Hooker's theological agenda was ambitious; he wanted to demonstrate that the laws of the Church of England derive from and reflect the grand structure of cosmic law. He believed that the order of the universe is mirrored in the essential core of revealed truth taught by Christ and transmitted by the Church, namely, to own Christ as Lord, to profess the faith Christ conveyed, and to be baptized into the church. Beyond the range of this core, there is a broad area of complexity and obscurity surrounding things that are indifferent (*adiaphora*) to the knowledge and worship of God.

Among "indifferent" things, Hooker included church polity, rituals, and ceremonies as well as ecclesiastical government. In these matters, he said, God-given human authority is sovereign. Melanchthon, Luther's colleague, introduced to sixteenth-century discourse the idea that some features of Christianity are not essential to the faith, but had been in the wings since antiquity, claiming as authority several texts from the writings of St Paul. However, the idea of *adiaphora* did not provide the easy reunion for which its English advocates hoped. Agreement could perhaps be reached on the "indifference" of such things as fasts, feasts, and vestments, but could the doctrines of transubstantiation and purgatory be considered indifferent?

Nevertheless, Hooker's use of the concept of *adiaphora* went at least part of the way toward easing tensions. With Catholics, Hooker recognized the importance of ceremonies that make Christian faith experiential. With Puritans, he criticized the Roman Catholic emphasis on works. "What is the fault of the Church of Rome? Not that she requires works at their hands that will be saved, but that she attributes unto works a power of satisfying God for sin and a virtue to merit both grace here, and in heaven, glory." Works, he said, do not *cause* justification, but they are a necessary expression of gratitude for unmerited justification.

Although Hooker sympathized with Puritans on many theological points (such as justification by faith, election, and perseverance), he criticized them in the *Laws*. First, he said, Puritans had lost a sense of history:

> O nation utterly without knowledge, without sense. We are not through error of mind deceived, but some wicked things hath undoubtedly bewitched us, if we forsake that government the use whereof universal experience hath for so many years approved, and betake ourselves unto a regiment neither appointed by God himself, as they who favor it pretend, nor till yesterday ever heard of among men.

The theological task, as Hooker understood it, was to be faithful to tradition without being bound by it. He saw Puritans' desire to "get back to" the primitive church as being bound by tradition, a literalism that distorted rather than simplified. He thought that contemporary people ought to adopt the apostles' *project*, not their conclusions: "The glory of God and the good of his church was the thing which the apostles aimed at, and therefore ought to be the mark whereat we also level" (IV.1.2). Second, he criticized the puritan principle that "scripture is the only rule of all things which in this life can be done."

Hooker's discussion of the sacraments in Book V. 50–68 of the *Laws* shows how he proposed to hold together a view of the sacraments as communicating the essence of Christian faith with the Reformed emphasis on personal experience. Hooker had thoroughly grasped one of patristic authors' most ubiquitous claims, namely, that the Christian *participates in the Body of Christ*. His definition of participation intensified its meaning: "that mutual inward hold which Christ hath of us and we of him, in such sort that each possesses the other by way of special interest property and inherent copulation" (*Laws* V. 56. 1).

For Hooker participation in the Body of Christ was a two-sided relationship in which neither God nor the Christian is passive:

> Since God has deified our nature, though not by turning it into himself, yet by making it his own inseparable habitation, we cannot now conceive how God should, without us, either exercise divine power or receive the glory of divine praise. . . . It pleases him in mercy to account himself incomplete and maimed without us.
>
> (*Laws* V. 56. 10)

Hooker had no doctrine of predestination to damnation. He posited two wills in God, a general will in which "God longs for nothing more than that all people should be saved," and a mysterious will by which some are damned, "not because God will not save them but because he cannot, though of course their obstinacy cannot be said to defeat or excel the eternal will of God nor call into question his power and goodness." Participation in the Church, the Body of Christ, was the Christian's decisive activity:

> Our beinge in Christ by eternall foreknowledge saveth us not without our actual and real adoption into the fellowship of his Saintes in this present world. For in him wee actualie are by our actuall incorporation into that societie which hath him fore theire head and doth make together with him one bodie (he and they in that respect havinge one name), for which cause by vertue of this mystical conjunction wee are of him and in him even as our verie flesh and bones should be made continuate with his.
>
> (*Laws* V. 56. 7)

The most direct arena of participation in Christ's body is the sacraments. Hooker seems to have thought of the eucharistic elements as symbolic; like Calvin, he was impatient with the various controversies over the mode of Christ's presence in the bread and wine of the Eucharist. The bread and the wine, he said, are "causes instrumental upon receipt whereof the participation of his body and blood ensues." His eucharistic theology was determined and defined by the *experience of participation* in the ritual. Participation involves the whole human being, both a physical ingestion of a material substance, and "that intellectual participation which the mind is capable of."

Hooker valued public devotions over private. His emphasis on public prayer reacted against the idiosyncratic tendencies of private individuals or groups. In Hooker's theology, community was affirmed in the most intimate moments of communion with God. The Christian community is the Body of Christ, the Word made flesh. In a religious climate in which theological opinions and practices were tearing apart nations and destroying lives, Hooker claimed that communal liturgical participation is primary and dogmatic explication of precisely what occurred in participation is of lesser importance. Simplification of doctrine and the acknowledgement that all religious practices are not equally essential permitted people to move gradually toward toleration.

At the end of the sixteenth century, the 1689 *Act of Toleration* was not yet on the horizon. Not until royal supremacy had painfully given way to constitutional sovereignty, and Catholics and Puritans alike were persecuted and emigrated under repressive religious settlements, did cumulative voices advocating toleration begin to be heard. Even then, the rationale for toleration was not specifically religious, but related more directly to seventeenth-century secular interests. Yet many of the first-generation English reformers had already advocated religious toleration and its necessary corollary, simplification of doctrine.

Printed images in England

Massive iconoclasm accompanied Puritan ascendancy as the English Church changed from a culture of images to a culture of the word. London, the center of royal power, was also the center of destruction of images. Many paintings, sculptures, and altars were removed from their locations and brought to London for public destruction. Images were often replaced with the royal arms or with scriptural texts. Pilgrimage sites were also a target for iconoclastic activity. Henry VIII had not urged iconoclasm, but in the reign of Edward VI, the paintings, stained glass windows, rood screens, and sculptures in most London churches were pulled down and broken up, though some were saved and hidden by parishioners who hoped that a Catholic ruler would soon occupy the throne. Some glass was preserved because of the expense of replacing it, and in some windows, glass with idolatrous images was cut out and replaced with plain glass. Many churches were whitewashed. By 1553 the churches of England were "no longer the receptacles of medieval splendor they once had been" (Phillips, 1973: 100).

As visual culture changed to a culture of the word, the flourishing English theater was also attacked. Since medieval theater had focused on Church rituals and biblical stories, it was biblical drama that prompted the most strenuous opposition. By the 1590s, secular drama, though initially protested, had taken its place. But in 1642 theaters were suppressed, a victory for iconoclasts.

Despite iconoclasm, printed images were produced in unprecedented numbers. Within a generation after Gutenberg's invention of the printing press, printing flooded Europe. In England illustrated mass-produced printed broadsheets, sold for pennies, circulated the latest ballads, woodcut pictures, and posters. Penny chapbooks, with both secular and religious topics flooded the marketplace. The first books were devotional manuals, the best-sellers of their time. Several of them, like Foxe's *Acts and Monuments of Matters Happening in the Church* (popularly known as *Foxe's Book of Martyrs*), first published in 1563, and John Bunyan's *The Pilgrim's Progress*, first published in 1678 (discussed in chapter 9), were bestsellers for centuries.

Foxe's *Book of Martyrs* was originally written in Latin, but it was translated when Foxe was persuaded that his book would reach a far larger public if it were available in English. The first edition was illustrated with 170 costly woodcuts that varied in quality. Some are generic scenes of heretic burnings, used more than once to illustrate different martyrdom accounts; some are allegorical; some of the images are skillfully drawn representations of real people and incidents. The final illustration in the volume shows a figure of Justice, blindfolded and holding in one hand an uplifted sword; in the other is a huge pair of scales in which the word of God, silently watched by Christ and his apostles, weighs down one end of the beam. The pope, the devil, and a muscular monk, together with volumes of decrees, images, chalices, bells, censers, and other Catholic paraphernalia are powerless to hold down the other end. Each edition of Foxe's *Book of Martyrs* was newly illustrated (see CD Rom figures 8.13 to 8.15).

In Protestant reform culture recognition of the power of visual images accompanied distrust of vision and its intimate connection to emotion. Words were considered more religiously trustworthy, and printed words flooded European culture as never before. Yet the speed with which images, rood screens, altars, vestments, and chalices were replaced in English churches with the advent of a Catholic ruler demonstrated the affection many English people felt for visible religion. Under Elizabeth, systematic iconoclasm was directed toward removing the images that had emerged overnight when Mary became queen. Parishes were ordered to supply inventories of all their "Catholic" paraphernalia and visitations to insure destruction of such were "marked out by the smoke of bonfires of images and books in marketplaces and church greens throughout the land" (Duffy, 1992: 569).

These attempts to exterminate the "old" worship were only partially successful. Imposed from above and lacking popular enthusiasm, they were met with reluctant obedience rather than communal zeal. Ironically, the prayer-book, intended as a means for eradicating Catholic elements in worship, became the vehicle by which vestiges of traditional religion "slowly, falteringly, and much reduced in scope, depth and coherence, reformed itself around the rituals and words of the prayer-book" (Duffy, 1992: 589).

> As the godly came to see in the prayer-book, with its saints' days, its kneeling, its litany, its prescribed fasts, its signing with the cross, little but the rags of popery, and sought their abandonment, so adherence to the prayer-book became the one way of preserving such observances.
>
> (Duffy, 1992: 590)

Ultimately, the visual richness of late medieval Catholic worship was both challenged and retained in the Elizabethan settlement, even as the Word achieved new status in worship. The genius of English reformations was the maintenance of the rich liturgical tradition of Catholic worship, together with new attention to the Word, read, preached, and believed.

READINGS

Richard Hooker, *The Laws of Ecclesiastical Polity*, Book V
John Jewel, *An Apology of the Church in England*

9 Rationalism and Religious Passion: The Seventeenth Century

Prologue

The last of the early modern wars over religion were fought in the seventeenth century. Scholars estimate that up to three-fifths of Germany's sixteen million people were killed in the Thirty Years War (1618–48) involving Germany, Bohemia, Poland, Denmark, Sweden, Switzerland, and France. The 1648 Peace of Westphalia ended the war by establishing the right of each prince to choose Calvinism, Lutheranism, or Catholicism for his territory. The formula first articulated in the Peace of Augsburg (1555) was repeated at Westphalia, "Let the subject conform to the religion of his sovereign" (*cuius regio, eius religio*, known as the *jus reformandi*).

The Peace of Westphalia did not stop religious persecution within nation-states, however. In France, Louis XIV's determination to have no other than the Catholic faith in his territories brought about the partnership of Church and state, with the state clearly in the superior position. As many as 250,000 French Protestants (Huguenots) emigrated, and thousands more were slaughtered. Twenty-eight thousand were killed in Paris and environs in a single incident in 1572, the St Bartholomew Day massacre, allegedly instigated by Catherine de Medici. Although the Peace of Westphalia provided some protection for religious minorities, Anabaptists were excluded and suffered renewed persecution. The magisterial reformations had reached a more-or-less balanced stalemate.

It was as if people were saturated with religion, with the intolerance, persecution, and strife that accompanied it, weary of fanatical dogmas, witch-burning, heretic hunting, inquisitorial racks, and wholesale slaughter. The authoritative claims of the Roman Catholic Church had been broken, and the equally dogmatic claims of the Protestants seemed to have no more authoritative substantiation than those of Roman orthodoxy. Advocates on both sides put their opposites to death, each side claiming finality for its point of view. But people had grown weary.

(Manschreck, 1974: 276)

Two seventeenth-century movements within Christianity – rationalism and pietism – transcended national and ecclesiastical boundaries. The so-called "Age of Reason," with its appeal to negotiable public standards of judgment, must be seen in the context of the religious wars of the first half of the seventeenth century. Rationalism, the belief that reason could arbitrate intellectual and religious differences, was a direct response and tremendous relief in the context of the massive suffering caused by the religious wars.

Seventeenth-century Christians continued to address the unresolved questions of the sixteenth century: What is authoritative for doctrine and practice? What is the role of reason in religion? What is the role of scripture? What is the relationship between free will, predestination, grace, and the sacraments? These perennial questions were addressed differently in the seventeenth century than formerly.

Twenty-first century Christians have important intellectual and emotional roots in the seventeenth century. For example, it was in the seventeenth century that "religion" began to be thought of as separate from "theology." Many seventeenth-century thinkers would have agreed with twentieth-century theologians' consensus that theology is about thinking, and religion is about praying, and their confusion creates difficulties.

No one before the seventeenth century thought so. From Augustine forward, "faith seeking understanding" was the formula that defined theology's task of explicating and illuminating religion. Theology was essential to religion because, as Thomas Traherne (1636–74) said, "What we misapprehend, we cannot *use*." No seventeenth-century author intended to separate religion and theology; the people (who wrote) simply became more interested in one than the other – more interested either in what could be known about God, the self, and the world, or more interested in the heart "strangely warmed," as John Wesley described his conversion experience. In this chapter we consider several seventeenth-century responses to the "Age of Reason."

1   Descartes and the Method of Doubt

René Descartes (1596–1650), a French Catholic, was born into a family of lesser nobility wealthy enough to secure him in an income that made him independent throughout his life. In his youth he studied languages, humane letters, logic, ethics, mathematics, physics, and metaphysics in a Jesuit school. Later he described his education, the finest that could be obtained in his time: "I found myself embarrassed with so many doubts and errors, that it seemed to me that the effort to instruct myself had no effect other than the increasing discovery of my own ignorance." In the face of this perceived failure of his formal education, Descartes "resolved no longer to seek any other science than the knowledge of myself or of the great book of the world." He became a gentleman scholar and world traveler. He never married, but had a daughter who died at the age of five, the greatest grief of his life.

Several assumptions about knowledge that continue to influence the modern world originated with Descartes. In a religious culture of acrimonious debates over questions of free will, predestination, and justification by faith, Descartes wanted to pause and investigate what can be known *for sure* about human beings and the world. His method reflects weariness with dogma, with appeals to conflicting authorities, and with the vitriolic and abusive *style of the discourse*. He argued that the mysteries of the Incarnation and the Trinity ought not to be explored by reason; being beyond reason, they ought simply to be believed.

Descartes' *Discourse on the Method of Rightly Conducting the Reason* was originally called "The Project of a Universal Science which can elevate our Nature to its Highest Degree of Perfection." The treatise's essentially religious agenda is indicated by its original title. Indeed, Descartes' thought reveals some values not usually thought of as connected to a commitment to reason.

The *Discourse* began with a wry observation about human nature: "Good sense is of all things in the world the best distributed; each person thinks he is so well provided with it that even those who are hardest to please in other things are not in the habit of wanting more of it than they have." Descartes then proposed a new authority in matters of knowledge and, not incidentally, a new audience.

> As it is not likely that everyone is mistaken . . . the ability to judge correctly and to distinguish the true from the false – which is really what is meant by good sense or reason – is the same by nature in all people. Differences of opinion are not due to differences in intelligence, but merely to the fact that we use different approaches and consider different things. For it is not enough to have a good mind; *one must also use it well*. (emphasis added)

Descartes identified "ordinary people" as his audience. To make his thinking accessible to this audience, he wrote in French, in his own name, and with an autobiographical introduction. He stated his confidence in the mind's ability to understand truth: "There is nothing so far removed from us as to be beyond our reach, or so hidden that we cannot discover it, provided only that we abstain from accepting the false for the true, and always preserve in our thoughts the order necessary for the deduction of one truth from another" (*Discourse on Method*: part II).

Other aspects of Descartes' project are similarly novel. First, he presented his ideas as a *method*. Other philosophers certainly had a method; some even described the process and progress of their thought, but none had explicitly presented a rational method that could be used by others. Others presented *conclusions*, leaving it to their readers to identify their assumptions and method. Descartes presented a method, a way to reconstruct his thought processes.

Second, Descartes' claim to understand truth is radically first-personal. His question is not, what can be known?, but what can *I* know? "My aim is not here to teach *the* method that each person should follow in order to conduct his reason well, but solely to show in what way I have tried to conduct my own" (*Discourse* I.4). In a letter to a friend Descartes said that he named the *Discourse on Method* a "discourse" because his aim was not to teach, but "only to talk about it."

Third, far from demanding a disengaged "objectivity," Descartes, the "Father of Rationalism," considered personal interest a necessary component of rational inquiry.

> It seemed to me that I could find much more truth in the reasonings which each person makes about the matters which are of concern to him, and of which the outcome is likely

to punish him soon after if he has made a mistake, than of those which a man of letters makes in his study, concerning speculations that lead to no result, and which have no other consequences for him except perhaps that he will be all the more vain about them the further they are from common sense, since he will have had to spend that much more intelligence and skill in trying to make them seem probable.

(*Discourse* I.6.9–10)

It is impossible for a disinterested observer to grasp truth, Descartes said. Rather, it is *interested* search, combined with the commitment to live out the results of one's inquiry, which constitutes knowledge.

The fourth novel feature of Descartes' thought is that he made no mention of scripture or revelation, trusting reason alone in his search for truth. In fact, he recommended reason for exactly the purpose for which Calvin invoked scripture. Descartes wrote: "I believe that all those to whom God has given the use of reason are obliged to employ it principally for the purpose of acquiring knowledge of him and of themselves. That is why I undertook my studies."

In the thirteenth century, Thomas Aquinas distinguished between truths accessible only to revelation and truths accessible to reason, saying that the two required different approaches. Descartes proposed that the *same* method is applicable to the search for truth, whether applied to the laws of physics or to the search for self-knowledge and knowledge of God. He claimed that philosophy and the sciences are continuous. His image was a tree of knowledge in which the roots are metaphysics, the trunk physics, and the branches the other sciences. His writings exemplified the essential unity of all knowledge. The *Discourse* was written as the Preface to three scientific essays: the *Dioptric*, dealing with problems of optics like refraction; an essay on meteors; and an essay on geometry that laid the groundwork for analytical geometry.

Descartes proposed philosophical method as an *alternative* to theological definitions of humans as created, sinful, unworthy of salvation, and expecting a future resurrection of body and an eternal destiny. He did not offer as colorful a picture of human nature as did Luther or Calvin, yet a close look at Descartes' system and the peculiarities of his exclusions and inclusions reveals that every philosophical idea was prompted by an underlying religious assumption. The only point at which he broke out of preoccupation with God, the self, and the world is in his discussion of the relationship of body and soul, discussed below.

The method

Descartes began by doubting everything doubtable. He rejected all "merely probable knowledge," trusting only "what is perfectly known and cannot be doubted." He adopted four procedural rules: 1) not to accept what is not clearly known; 2) to divide difficulties into parts as far as possible; 3) to work from the easy and accessible to the more complicated; and 4) to omit nothing.

After applying the first rule, Descartes said, he was left with almost nothing. However, instead of giving way to panic, he converted the impression of an abyss into firm ground on which to begin:

I have convinced myself that there is nothing at all in the world, no heaven, no earth, no minds, no bodies; have I not then convinced myself that I do not exist? On the contrary, there is no doubt that I existed if I convinced myself of anything. But [suppose] there is some deceiver, in the highest degree powerful and ingenious, who uses all his efforts to deceive me all the time. Then there is no doubt that I exist, if he is deceiving me; let him deceive me as much as he likes, he can never bring it about that I am nothing, so long as I think that I am something. So, after every thought, and the most careful consideration, I must hold firm to this conclusion: that the proposition *I am, I exist*, must be true whenever I utter it or conceive it in my mind.

(Second Meditation VII. 25; emphasis added)

The location of the "I"

Certain, then, that he – Descartes – exists, and still pursuing knowledge of himself, he asked, "What is this 'I'? I do not yet know clearly enough *what* I am; so that I must take the greatest care from the start not carelessly to take something else for myself."

I noticed that, while I was trying to think that everything was false, it was necessary that I, who was thinking this, should be something. And observing that this truth: *I am thinking, therefore I exist* (*cogito ergo sum*) was so firm and secure that all the most extravagant suppositions of the skeptics were not capable of overthrowing it, I judged that I should not scruple to accept it as the first principle of the philosophy I was seeking.

(Discourse IV.6.32; emphasis added)

Next, Descartes located himself in one precise activity:

Thought alone is of such a nature that I cannot separate it from me. . . . If I were not thinking, I would not know whether I was doubting or whether I existed. And it could even happen that if, for an instant, I stopped thinking, I might at the same time cease to be; so the only thing that I could not separate from me, which I know with certainty to be me, and which I can now assert without fear of error, is that *I am a thing that thinks*. (emphasis added)

The "real Descartes" has been identified. Descartes is a thinking *activity* (not a faculty). Next, Descartes drew the "clear and distinct" implications of his designation of the self as a thinking activity, namely, that the body is not an essential part of human being:

Now from the mere fact that I know for certain that I exist and that I cannot see anything else that belongs necessarily to my nature or essence except that I am a thinking thing, I rightly conclude that my essence consists in this alone, *that I am a thinking thing, a substance whose whole nature or essence is to think*. While it is possible that I have a body which is very closely joined to me; nevertheless, since on the one hand I have a clear and distinct idea of myself as a person that thinks and is not extended, and on the other hand, I have a distinct idea of the body as a thing that is extended and does not think, it is certain that this *I*, that is to say, my soul, which makes me what I am, is entirely and truly distinct from my body, and can be or exist without it.

(Meditations VII. 78; emphasis added)

Mind and body, Descartes said, "come into existence separately." Earlier authors *distinguished* mind and body for the purpose of showing how they can work together; Descartes' *separation* between mind and body was the first thorough mind–body dualism in the history of orthodox Christianity, a *watershed* between the medieval and the modern world.

God's existence

Descartes has proved his own existence to his own satisfaction. The second point that he sought to prove was the existence of God.

> I have always thought that the two questions of God and the soul were the principle questions among those that should be demonstrated by rational philosophy rather than by theology. For although it may suffice us faithful ones to believe by faith that there is a God and that the human soul does not perish with the body, certainly it does not seem possible ever to persuade those without faith to accept any religion, nor even perhaps any moral virtue, unless they can first be shown these two things by means of natural reason. Faith is a gift of God, and the very God that gives us the faith to believe other things can also give us the faith to believe that God exists. Nevertheless, we could hardly offer this argument to those without faith, for they might suppose that we were committing the fallacy that logicians call circular reasoning.

Descartes offered three different proofs of God's existence. First, he proposed a cosmological proof similar to that of Thomas Aquinas:

> Now it is manifest by the natural light that there must be at least as much reality in the efficient cause as in its effect. For where, pray, would the effect get its reality if not from its cause? And how could the cause supply the reality to its effect unless it possessed it itself? From this it follows not only that something cannot proceed from nothing, but also that what is more perfect, that is, contains more reality in itself, cannot proceed from what is less perfect.

The idea of "degrees of reality" was a medieval idea, outmoded by Descartes' time. Thomas Hobbes (1588–1679), Descartes' contemporary, wrote to him:

> Further, I pray Descartes to investigate the meaning of *more* and *less* reality. Does reality admit of more and less? Or, if he thinks that one thing can be more a thing than another, let him see how this can be explained to our intelligence called for in demonstration, and such as he has himself employed on other occasions.
>
> (Quoted by Williams, 1978: 135–6)

Descartes' second proof for God's existence rested on an *a priori* argument. Since Descartes has an idea of a being that is sovereign, eternal, infinite, unchangeable, and creator of everything that is outside himself, there must necessarily be such a perfect being. Hence there must be a being independent of Descartes himself who is the cause of Descartes' idea of God. That perfect being is God. At this point Descartes anticipated an objection: perhaps he could have thought this idea simply by thinking away his own limitations and imagining a being that does not have these limitations. He answered the objection: if it were possible for me to think away these limitations I experience, I could have created myself. But since that is impossible, where can I have gotten the idea of such a being?

Descartes' third proof of God's existence consisted of an argument from causation. Descartes argued that God exists because he (Descartes) has an idea of God; his own ability to think of a God-being proves God's existence: "One must necessarily conclude from the fact that I exist and that the idea of God is in me, that the existence of God is very evidently proved." In other words, Descartes' existence as a thinking entity proves the existence of his creator. But Descartes' ongoing life, his conservation or sustenance, also proves God's existence: "It takes as much power or perfection to preserve a substance in being from one instant to the next as it does to create it from nothing" (Williams, 1978: 149). In short, Descartes made the startling move of deducing God's existence from his own existence.

When he decided to retain only his own thought as essential to his existence, Descartes sacrificed the visible world along with all bodies. Now, content that he has shown that God exists, Descartes deduced the existence of the world from God's existence as Creator.

Body and world

Descartes said, I exist as a thinking thing; the material world exists, and there is one part of the material world that stands in a special relation to the thinking thing that I am, my body. If I am (essentially) my soul, that is, the location of the thinking activity, what, then, is my body?

Descartes described the relationship of soul to body as an "intimate connection." But he also defined both "mind" and "body" differently than had earlier thinkers. Body, for Descartes, was animated body, a body possessing its own life. Augustine and Thomas Aquinas had said that without the soul, body is corpse; soul's "first duty" is to animate body; together soul and body constitute the "I." Descartes identified the soul as the "I." His dying words were, "*Ça, mon âme; il faut partir*" ("My soul, it is necessary to depart"). Soul departs because body dies; body deserts soul.

Descartes sorted all activities into two categories according to whether the mind causes or participates in them or not. For him, "body" (alone) is the location of pains, emotional disturbances, sensations of pressure, emotional stress, and all the processes we call involuntary, such as heartbeat, breathing, digesting, and reflexes. He also identified as belonging to body everything that can be done without thoughtful attention, such as walking, singing, or sleep-walking, for soul, the "I," is a *thinking activity*.

How can two such different entities as body and soul/mind be connected in a living person? Since there are only two kinds of existing entities, *res cogitans* and *res extensa*, the connection could either be mental (consciousness, thought), or physical (material). There must be connection, Descartes said, because if there were not I would not be able to move my body, or register (mentally) changes that happen in my body. Stuck with this apparently insoluble dilemma, Descartes desperately proposed that a "pineal gland" synthesizes all incoming and outgoing data in one center and secretes a subtle fluid that flows through the nerves, conveying information to and from the body.

Rationalism and its founder, Descartes, have received blame for the separation of soul and body, a philosophical assumption that seems to underlie many of the quandaries of the modern world. It is important, then, to understand rationalism as a historical and cultural product of its time. Descartes thought that he had discovered a democratic method that honored every person's capacity for thought. His method was anti-elitist and anti-authoritarian; it placed authority in human beings. Moreover, as suggested at the beginning of the chapter, Descartes' thought must be understood in relation to the frenzy of religious wars, the mania for witch persecution, and the doctrinal disputes of his time. *In the life*, as opposed to in the abstract, Descartes' identification of the thinking self as the locus of authority was both freeing and exhilarating.

Twenty-first century people who have had the "thinking self" around for 350 years often feel more enthusiastic about other cognitive activities, such as perception, intuition, emotion, and sympathy. We have noticed that privileging one cognitive activity simultaneously privileges the human beings who enjoy conditions in which that capacity can be developed, and marginalizes those whose strengths lie in other cognitive activities. In Western societies in which reason has been identified with men and irrationality with women, for example, Descartes' philosophy was, and is, a gendered discourse.

Descartes' dualism reminds us that all historical thought (and all thought is historical), including our own, is ambiguous. What we intend as freeing, empowering, and affirming inevitably creates a new honorific category of activity and people who are good at it, simultaneously marginalizing other activities and people. Finally, we should notice the irony in the fact that the very method – rationalism – that aimed at transcending human interests and religious loyalties strongly reflected those interests. The "Age of Reason" is incomprehensible without the wars of religion.

READING

Descartes, *Discourse on Method*

2   Christianity in Seventeenth-century France

Seventeenth-century France was religiously, socially, and politically chaotic, with religious and anti-religious excitement threatening both the monarchy and the Church. Lively interests within and outside the church took several new forms.

The Catholic reformation in France produced what one historian has called the "feminization of the Church." New roles in the Catholic Church emerged for women (as catechists, for example), and in Church-related charitable and devotional organizations. There were also new forms of social action in hospitals, prisons, and among the poor as women "in remarkable numbers" lived uncloistered but passionately religious lives, combining prayer and service to others. The so-called "devotee" movement ended after 1600 when the government took responsibility for the poor. The simultaneously "other-worldly" and highly practical synthesis fell apart and the movement itself disappeared.

Official procedures for canonization were established by Pope Urban VIII (1568–1644) in the early seventeenth century. All candidates for sainthood (except martyrs) must satisfy three requirements: doctrinal purity, heroic virtue, and miraculous intercession after death. An important distinction was made between "miracle working on earth" (not required), and evidence of "miraculous intercession after death" (required) that demonstrated the saint's ability to advocate for the living.

Among educated men, there was excitement about new scientific discoveries. Scholars battled about Galileo and Copernicus who overturned the cosmological tradition and dramatically reduced the human scale in a universe now recognized as immense. Seventeenth-century scientific excitement was not – like twentieth-century excitement about sending men to the moon – a spectator sport. Many people were engaged in home experiments. As discussed, Descartes' philosophical writings were prefaces to his scientific articles. Pascal's religious writings were journalistic jottings on scraps of paper. What both published was their scientific work. Among Pascal's publications were *New Experiments Concerning the Vacuum*; *Great Experiments Concerning the Equilibrium of Fluids*; and a *Treatise on the Arithmetical Triangle*. He conducted experiments with the vacuum, atmospheric pressure, and probability theory. He invented a calculating machine and designed a system of public transportation for Paris. He was a practical man, not a working theologian, and he raised *religious*, not theological questions. Like many seventeenth-century people, Pascal's scientific pursuits prompted his religious questions.

Three religious groups were prominent in seventeenth-century France: Freethinkers, Jesuits, and Jansenists.

Freethinkers

The term "freethinker," an eighteenth-century designation, referred to small societies and circles of people without central organization or leadership. An estimated 50,000 freethinkers lived in the vicinity of Paris alone. Freethinkers opposed the Church's doctrine of revelation and authority, appealing instead, as their name implies, to the individual's independent thought. They believed that "natural" thought, unconstrained by ecclesiastical loyalties, would lead people to identical conclusions about morality and religion. Although they opposed organized and institutionalized religion, Freethinkers did so from an essentially religious perspective, believing that reason contains a truth that has existed since creation but has been distorted and defaced in Western Christianity.

The existence of a large number of freethinkers in a dominantly Christian society was historically novel.

Jesuits

By the seventeenth century, Jesuits were a powerful group in France. But they also had powerful enemies who regarded them as a group with foreign loyalties (sworn obedience to the pope), and with a dangerous kind and amount of power. They had a centralized, efficient organization, and taught a powerful theology of mysticism and activism. By the early eighteenth century, the Society of Jesus had 176 seminaries and 700 lower schools in France alone, and they taught over 200,000 students in their 800 colleges. Jesuits were also confessors to the rulers in France, Germany, Bavaria, Poland, and Portugal. They held vast properties, and their success aroused suspicion.

Two criticisms were regularly brought against Jesuits: probabilism and mental reservation. "Probabilism" is the confessional policy of declaring any act to be acceptable if there is any probability that it might be. Even if there seemed to be stronger reasons for severity, absolution was granted if *any* grounds against severity could be found. Jesuit confessors were accused of practicing what might be called a "hermeneutic of generosity," or giving the benefit of the doubt. Ignatius Loyola had written: "Every good Christian ought to be more willing to give a good interpretation to another person's behavior or statement than to condemn it as false" (*Spiritual Exercises* 1).

Second, Jesuits were accused of practicing mental reservation. This meant that it was acceptable to withhold part of the truth if the reason for doing so seemed good; in other words, ends justify means. It is probably impossible to get an accurate picture of these accusations. In countries that expelled Jesuits, it was less for specific charges than for the common belief that Jesuits promoted the pope's temporal interests at the expense of the monarch's interests. The emerging nationalism of the time made transnational interests suspect. Jesuits were banned from Portugal in 1759 and from France in 1761. Jesuit schools were closed, foundations dissolved, and property confiscated. In 1767, Jesuits were expelled from Spain for alleged intrigue against the king. The Society of Jesus was dissolved everywhere by papal decree in 1773. The Order was restored in 1814.

Jansenists

Jansenists, the primary theological opponents of the Jesuits in France, represented a reaction within the Catholic Church to the theology of the Catholic reformation. Cornelius Jansen (1585–1638), director of the new University of Louvain, opposed Jesuits' emphasis on freedom of the will and the necessity of good works for salvation. He and his supporters said that emphasis on the individual's free will undermined God's omnipotence, and emphasis on good works denied the efficacy of grace.

Jansen's book, *Augustinus*, claimed to find in the writings of St Augustine of Hippo (d. 430) a doctrine of grace that supported absolute predestination and denied that God's saving will is universal – a doctrine to be found more consistently in Calvin's writings than in Augustine. Jansen's Augustine was based on a very selective reading of suggestions Augustine made in the heat of controversy, taken out of context.

Jansen said that human beings are utterly helpless to turn toward salvation. He denied that a person can perform God's commands without a special grace, and insisted that God's grace is irresistible. Jansen's doctrine was condemned at the Sorbonne in 1649, and by Pope Innocent X in 1653, but it had a widespread following, and it did not simply disappear when condemned. It will be further discussed in chapter 10.

Pascal

The most famous name associated with Jansenist theology was that of Blaise Pascal (1623–62). Pascal was a sickly child; when he was a year old he was said to have been cured from an unspecified disease. The disease was magically turned onto a cat, who died. Pascal's mother died when he was three, and his father, a lawyer, undertook his education. By the age of 12 Pascal had independently discovered the equivalent of Euclid's first 32 theorems of geometry. At 19 he invented a calculating machine. Haunted by illness throughout his life, Pascal died at the age of 39.

Pascal was a traditional Roman Catholic. At 23 he converted to the Jansenist version of Catholicism and wrote his famous *Provincial Letters* – 18 letters over a two-year period – in opposition to the Jesuits' more lenient interpretation of Christianity. Pascal's *Provincial Letters* were placed on the *Index of Forbidden Books* in 1657.

On November 23, 1654 Pascal had a powerful religious experience. After his death a short written record of that experience was found sewn into his clothing. It read, in part:

> From about half-past ten in the evening until half-past midnight: FIRE. God of Abraham, God of Isaac, God of Jacob, not of the philosophers and scholars. Certainty, certainty, heartfelt joy, peace. The world forgotten, and everything except God. Joy, joy, joy, tears of joy. . . . Jesus Christ; Jesus Christ. Total submission to Jesus Christ and to my director. Everlasting joy in return for one day's effort on earth. Amen.

These passionate, barely coherent fragments illustrate the inadequacy of words to convey strong experience. Pascal's readers must supply a sense of his meaning from their own experiences of comparable intensity.

Pascal's so-called *Pensées* (Thoughts) were notes, written "upon the first scrap of paper that came to hand . . . a few words, and very often parts of words only," toward a book in which Pascal intended to defend Christianity against Freethinkers. Strikingly, the *Pensées* offer no account of human knowledge, the natural order, or moral duties. A skeptic on philosophical questions, Pascal had no interest in rational arguments to prove or justify Christian theology. The motivating energy of the *Pensées* could not be more remote from that of his older contemporary and compatriot, Descartes.

Pascal used powerful imagery to describe the human condition. Imagine, he said, that you have only a week to live: "Anyone with only a week to live will not find it in his interest to believe that all this is just a matter of chance." Or:

> Imagine a number of men in chains, all under sentence of death, some of whom are each day butchered in the sight of the others; those remaining see their own condition in that of their fellows, and looking at each other with grief and despair await their turn. This is an image of the human condition.
>
> (*Pensées*, no. 434)

He pictured people struggling in darkness between abysses of infinity and nothingness. Imagine yourself, he said, drowning, half-conscious, spinning helplessly in eddies, unable to resist the current that is sweeping you over the edge of a waterfall into an abyss, unable to reach, or even to see, any bank: this, he said, is the human condition.

Pascal combined Descartes' admiration for human reason with Calvin's vision of humans' utter helplessness. His genius was that he managed to hold both of these apparently contradictory visions simultaneously, and at full strength.

> What sort of freak, then, is human being? How novel, how monstrous, how chaotic, how paradoxical, how prodigious! Judge of all things; feeble earthworm; repository of truth; sink of doubt and error; glory and refuse of the universe.
>
> *(Pensées*, no. 131)

Yet it was not reason as such that Pascal valued, but humans' awareness of death.

> A human being is only a reed, the weakest in nature, but he is a thinking reed. There is no need for the whole universe to take up arms to crush him; a vapor, a drop of water, is enough to kill him. But even if the universe were to crush him, he would still be nobler than his slayer, because he knows that he is dying, and the advantage that the universe has over him. The universe knows none of this.
>
> *(Pensées*, no. 200)

For Pascal, humanity is overwhelmed by both the mental and physical dimensions of existence. On the one side is the mental disorientation of trying to live in a universe of "eternal silences and infinite spaces," a universe in which knowledge of the most important things lies furthest from human experience.

There are three problems with human reason. First, it is woefully inadequate at the most important point, self-knowledge:

> I do not know who put me into the world, nor what the world is, nor what I am myself. I am terribly ignorant about everything. I do not know what my body is, or my senses, or my soul, or even that part of me that thinks what I am saying, that reflects about everything and about itself, and does not know itself any better than it knows anything else.
>
> *(Pensées*, no. 427)

Compare Pascal's uncertainty with Descartes' confidence that a single method will work both for scientific discovery and for self-knowledge. Descartes said: "Nothing is too difficult for human reason to understand if only we are careful not to admit any admixture of things that can be doubted, and always preserve in our thoughts the order necessary for the deduction of one truth from another" (*Discourse* II).

Pascal agreed with Descartes that "all our dignity consists in thought," but Pascal went on to write that "all our reasoning comes down to surrendering to feeling. . . . Reason is available, but can be bent in any direction. *And so there is no rule.*" In response to Descartes' optimism about a universal method, Pascal thought that each object requires its own method.

Pascal's second problem with reason was that reason cannot find God. Therefore it did not, for Pascal, have the calm authority that it had for Descartes. "I cannot forgive Descartes," Pascal wrote, "[because] in all his philosophy he would have been quite willing to dispense with God. But he had to make God snap his finger to set the world in motion; beyond this he has no further need of God." Pascal's alternative proposal: "It is the heart that perceived God and not the reason. That is what faith is: God perceived by the heart, not by reason" (*Pensées*, no. 424).

The third problem with human reason is that one's life situation inevitably governs one's perspective: "Excessive youth and excessive age impair thought; so too do too much and too little learning" (*Pensées*, no. 199).

The mind is not the only unstable feature of human life. Body's vulnerability and fragility is similarly daunting. In the physical world, body occupies an awkward and painful position between the enormous spaces of the universe and microscopic minuteness; the bodily senses are not the best tool for understanding even the physical world.

> For after all, what is a person in nature? A nothing compared to the infinite, a whole compared to the nothing, a middle point between all and nothing, infinitely remote from an understanding of the extremes; the end of things and their principles are unattainably hidden from him in impenetrable secrecy.

In this precarious situation of physical frailty and mental disorientation and instability, humans are nevertheless endowed with a longing for happiness.

> All people seek happiness. There are no exceptions. However different the means they may employ, they all strive toward this goal. The reason why some go to war and some do not is the same desire in both, but interpreted in two different ways. The will never takes the least step except to that end. This is the motive of every act of every person, including those who go and hang themselves.
>
> (*Pensées*, no. 148)

People respond to this intolerable situation by seeking diversion; "a violent and vigorous occupation is wanted to take our minds off ourselves":

> What people want is not the easy peaceful life that allows us to think of our unhappy condition, nor the dangers of war, nor the burdens of office, but the agitation that takes our mind off it and diverts us. . . . Telling someone to rest is the same as telling him to live happily. It means advising him to enjoy a completely happy state which he can contemplate at leisure without cause for distress. It means not understanding [human] nature.
>
> (*Pensées*, no. 136)

Why does the most universal, most powerful urge of humans, the longing for happiness, seem to be the most unattainable? The only possible explanation, Pascal said, is the Christian doctrine of original sin. "It is an astonishing thing that the mystery furthest from our immediate experience, that of the transmission of sin, should be something without which we can have no knowledge of ourselves" (*Pensées*, no. 131).

Pascal asked, Is it not as clear as day that [the human] condition is dual? The point is that if [humans] had never been corrupted, they would, in their innocence, confidently enjoy both truth and felicity, and if they had never been anything *but* corrupt, they would have had no idea either of truth or bliss.

> But unhappy as we are (and we should be less so if there were no element of greatness in our condition) we have an idea of happiness but we cannot attain it. We perceive an image

of the truth but can attain nothing but falsehood, being incapable of [either] absolute ignorance [or] certain knowledge; so obvious is it that we once enjoyed a degree of perfection
from which we have unhappily fallen.

(*Pensées*, no. 131)

Where, then, can one go from paralyzing awareness of the dual condition of humankind? Pascal proposes a wager, the radical form of experiment.

Let us examine, then, this point and say, "God is or he is not." But to which side shall we
lean? Reason can determine nothing here: there is an infinite chaos that separates us.
A game is played, at the end of this infinite distance, where there happens whether heads
or tails. What will you wager? By reason you can do neither one nor the other; by reason
you can defend neither of these. Do not accuse of falsehood those who have taken a choice
for you know nothing of it. "No, but I accuse them for having made not this choice, but a
choice! For both he who takes heads and he who takes the other are both at fault; the right
thing is not to bet at all." Yes, but one *must* bet. This is not voluntary. You are already under
weight. Which, then, will you take? Let's see. Since it is necessary to choose, let's see what
it is that interests you the least. You have two things to lose: the true and the good, and two
things to engage in the wager: your reason and your will, your knowledge and your blessedness. And your nature has two things to flee: error and misery. Your reason is not more
injured in choosing one thing than the other, since it is absolutely necessary to choose. That
is an empty point. But your blessedness? Weigh the gain and the loss, in betting on heads
that God is. Estimate these two chances: if you win, you win all; if you lose, you lose
nothing. Bet, therefore, that God is, without hesitating.

(*Pensées*, no. 418)

The wager was Pascal's answer to Descartes' method. Reason cannot prove God; thus
religion must appeal to fallen human beings through the psychological motivation of
self-interest. The dilemma cannot be resolved, Pascal said, by raising the truth question,
but only by raising the question of self-interest. Did the wager metaphor serve Pascal
well? It must be acknowledged that there is considerable disparity between the intense
and despairing consciousness Pascal evoked and the apparently frivolous solution he
proposed.

What if one bets as Pascal advised? What lies beyond the wager? Is it possible, once
one has wagered, to turn up the cards? Yes, Pascal said, after taking the plunge, there is
evidence that one has gambled correctly. First, Scripture, especially in its testimony to
the incarnation of Jesus Christ, illuminates the immensity of the problem by revealing
its radical remedy. Second, experience of the Christian life justifies the wager. Pascal
even advised "going through the motions," weaving into one's life the liturgical life and
moral requirements of a Christian community in order to experience for oneself the
quality of Christian life. He invoked a Stoic admonition: Act as if you are virtuous, and
by acting as if you are virtuous, you imperceptibly become virtuous; virtue becomes a
habitual response, a lifestyle. (Imagine Luther or Calvin's reaction to this advice!)

Pascal acknowledged that knowledge of self and God can never meet Descartes' criterion of the "clear and distinct" idea, for the clear and distinct idea is necessarily an
abstract idea, uncluttered by the ambiguities of real circumstances. Only by participation in the teachings of Christ is living knowledge possible. This is the kind of knowledge that Pascal calls "self-knowledge":

Not only do we know God through Jesus Christ but we only know ourselves through Jesus Christ; we only know life and death through Jesus Christ; apart from Jesus Christ we cannot know the meaning of our life or of our death, of God or of ourselves.

(*Pensées*, no. 417)

Pascal's God, as the record of his mystical experience stated, was the experiential "God of Abraham, God of Isaac, God of Jacob," not the rational God of the philosophers. Pascal's metaphor for Christian life is that of the infant who confidently leaps into her mother's arms, or stretches upward to be lifted: "Thus I stretch out my arms to my Savior. . . . By his grace I peaceably await death, in the hope of being eternally united with him . . . meanwhile, I live joyfully" (*Pensées*, no. 793).

READING

Pascal, *Pensées*, selections

3 Italy: Baroque Art

Both Descartes, the "father of rationalism," and Pascal, advocate of the heart, were French Catholics. They worshipped in cathedrals decorated by the art that accompanied the spread of Catholic reformations. Based in Italy, baroque art represented a conscious attempt "to make Rome the most beautiful city in the world." Art historian Emile Mâle wrote, "Gothic architecture tries to lift one to the sky, but baroque instead depicts the sky inside the church." Baroque art combines a naturalistic style with subjects preoccupied with religious passion. Illumination is treated naturalistically, but its radiance and luminosity integrate actual light and supernatural light. Baroque art emphasized the fragility and beauty of the passing moment, uniting time and eternity and placing the worshipper in a spiritual universe.

Ecstasy, rapture of the bodily and spiritual senses in mystical experience, was a prominent theme of seventeenth-century Catholicism. Teresa of Avila, a reforming Carmelite saint, wrote of her mystical experience: "The pain was so great that I screamed aloud; but at the same time I felt such infinite sweetness that I wished the pain to last forever. It was not physical but psychic pain, although it affected the body as well to some degree. It was the sweetest caressing of the soul by God."

The Ecstasy of St Teresa (1645–52), sculpted by Gianlorenzo Bernini, in the Cornaro family chapel at the Church of Santa Maria Vittoria in Rome exemplifies baroque interests (see CD Rom figures 9.1 to 9.3). In its setting in the Cornaro Chapel, *The Ecstasy of St. Teresa* integrates sculpture and architecture, creating a "compound illusion." Characteristic of baroque art is the principle of coextensive space, that is, dissolution of the barrier between the artwork and the observer, integration of real and fictional space. On the sides of the Chapel, the Cornaro family lean out of their boxes (into the viewer's space) to view the scene. By transgressing the viewer's space, the figures invite the viewer to enter the space in which the "sweet caressing of the soul by God" takes place.

Michelangelo Merisi da Caravaggio (1573–1610), a renegade, criminal, and artist, mastered the dramatic style and energetic motion valued by baroque sensibilities.

Figure 9.1   Caravaggio, *Supper at Emmaus*, 1602.
The subject of the painting is the moment when the disciples at Emmaus recognized Christ. His right hand, raised in blessing while his left hand gestured toward the bread in front of him suddenly reminded them of the Last Supper. The disciples react with surprise. Caravaggio borrowed Christ's gesture from Michelangelo's Christ in his *Last Judgment* in the Sistine Chapel. Photo AKG/Erich Lessing.

Reacting against Mannerism's pale attenuated bodies, he painted robust muscular bodies, using people he found on the street for models, and painting sacred figures and scenes in the clothing and settings of his own time. Caravaggio's style was immediately copied by other artists, but it also raised controversy over his crude and "irreverent" treatment of sacred figures (figure 9.1) (see CD Rom figures 9.4 to 9.7).

The seventeenth century saw the emergence of women artists in numbers unprecedented in earlier centuries. Although a few names of women artists were recorded in the fifteenth and sixteenth centuries, many seventeenth-century women artists' works are extant. In Italy women artists like Elizabeth Sirani (1638–65) and Artemesia Gentileschi (1593–1652) adopted a style known as Caravaggism, characterized by "naturalism, shallow pictorial space, and dramatic use of light" (Chadwick, 1990: 87). Female heroines whose virtue enabled them to triumph over various evils were frequently painted. Elizabeth Sirani's classical figures and Artemesia Gentileschi's biblical subjects exemplify this theme (see CD Rom figures 9.8 and 9.9; compare 9.10).

Women painters reinterpreted subjects that had repeatedly been used to present "an ideology of [male] dominance over [female] powerlessness, in which a woman's voluptuous body is affirmed as an object of exchange between men" (Chadwick, 1990: 97). For example, Gentileschi's *Judith and Holofernes* treats the apocryphal story in which Judith slaughtered the Assyrian general, Holofernes, thus saving Israel from certain

Figure 9.2   Rembrandt, *Bust of Christ*, 1663.
Painted six years before Rembrandt's death in 1669, his portrait of Christ reflects Rembrandt's
own sadness. His life savings vanished, Rembrandt struggled to earn enough to live on; he had
sold the grave of his wife and model, Saskia the year before. Now, haunted by debt, his themes
ran to tragedy – Lucretia committing suicide, and self-portraits painted the year of his death that
displaying slackened skin that suggest sad self-knowledge. The Metropolitan Museum of Art, Mr
and Mrs Isaac D. Fletcher Collection, Bequest of Isaac D. Fletcher, 1917 (17. 120. 222). Photograph, all rights reserved, the Metropolitan Museum of Art.

military defeat. Gentileschi emphasized Judith's strength and courage rather than the
traditional theme of women's treachery. Her *Susanna and the Elders*, a subject that
commonly depicted a coy and partially draped female nude, placed a naked Susanna,
quivering in apprehensive vulnerability, front and center in the painting. Rather than
enjoying a voluptuous bath (as in Tintoretto's painting of the same subject), Susanna's
cringing fear is emphasized by the crowding presence of the conspiring elders.

Rembrandt Van Rijn (1606–69) interpreted baroque interests in a Protestant setting
in which paintings were not placed in churches. After his wife's death in 1642 and his
bankruptcy in 1656, Rembrandt painted religious subjects with a new feeling. Catholic
subjects (saints and the Virgin) are missing from his repertoire, while Protestant subjects,
such as the Return of the Prodigal and other scenes from Christ's ministry, and portraits,
achieve newly vivid emotional treatment (figure 9.2) (see CD Rom figures 9.11 and 9.12;
compare Peter Paul Reubens "Descent from the Cross" (see CD Rom figure 9.13)).

Baroque pictorial emotionalism contrasted strongly with the Age of Reason. Different sensibilities created these different preoccupations, yet both emerged from Western Europe in the seventeenth century.

The secular breast

In the sixteenth century, sacred and secular spheres were defined in relation to one another. Church music, written specifically for liturgical use, eliminated secular tunes and subordinated musical complexity to clear communication of words. In Protestant territories visual artists had to find new patrons as churches no longer included artistic decoration. Painters like Rembrandt (in the Netherlands) and Dürer (in Germany) painted portraits of reformers, princes, and donors primarily for princes, town halls, and wealthy private patrons.

As both Catholic and Protestant reformers shifted religious attention to words, "the Word," scripture, and preaching, painted flesh acquired secular meanings. In the fourteenth century, depictions of the Virgin with the breast exposed that nourished the infant Christ, pleading with Christ for the salvation of sinners huddled in her cloak, had focused the religious meaning of the breast. Conventions like the placement of the breast high on the shoulder, showing through a slit in orderly clothing, simultaneously engaged erotic interest and insistently directed viewers to religious meanings. By the later sixteenth century, however, the earlier balance of erotic and religious representations shifted; painted breasts now signaled erotic meanings.

Even when a religious subject was painted, erotic meanings outweighed religious meanings. The figure of Mary Magdalen in Catholic reformation art is illustrative. Medieval sources, like Jacobus da Voragine's *Golden Legend* assigned to Mary Magdalen the role of repentant prostitute (without scriptural warrant). She was depicted in scenes from Christ's passion as a histrionic mourner and contrasted with the Virgin's dignified grief. The sixteenth and seventeenth centuries pictured a very different Magdalen, one that is ravaged by grief, in the throes of mystical transport, and overtly sensual. In paintings by Titian, Coccapini, Tintoretto, Giampietrino, and many others, her lusciously fleshy bared breasts, ostensibly intended to focus her intensified religious passion, are seductively caressed by her long hair. In contrast to the carefully revealed breast of the fourteenth-century Virgin, the sixteenth- and seventeenth-century Magdalen's dishevelment suggests the bedroom rather than the church. Images of Mary Magdalen may have been among those images that caused consternation at the 1563 session of the Council of Trent at which "inappropriate" images were banned from churches.

Seventeenth-century artists completed the transition from the sacred to the secular breast. Breasts were depicted as larger and rounder than a century before, eliciting sexual rather than maternal associations. By the eighteenth century, acceptance of explicitly erotic subject matter for paintings "permitted breast exposure without moral excuse" (Hollander, 1975: 199). Breasts, with their evocation of complex delight, had been rejected by religious art and appropriated in secular art. In religious sensibilities, the flesh, as represented in the earliest and most intimate experience of every seventeenth-century newborn, disappeared from church and devotional painting.

4   Christianity in Seventeenth-century England

Puritanism

In England, "Puritan" was used in various senses. Its broadest sense referred to all who wished either to purify the English Church of remnants of "popery," or to worship separately by purified forms. Chapter 8 discussed Puritans in the context of the Elizabethan settlement. After the 1640 English civil war, Puritans divided into Separatists (following heavily persecuted late sixteenth-century Separatists) and Presbyterians, according to the kind of church government they favored. A third meaning of "Puritan" referred to Calvinist clergymen of the Anglican Church. "Puritan" never had a single precise meaning. Often it was used as a term of insult, synonymous with "precisian" (for their strict observance of religious rules and unornamented worship) and "hypocrite."

In spite of differences within Puritanism, Puritans had some common beliefs. Puritan theology insisted that all matters of faith, doctrine, and practice be based on the Bible; tradition, ecclesiastical authority, and reason were all considered secondary authorities. Puritans were the most insistent of all the seventeenth-century English groups on predestination; they were also the most activist. For them, predestination was not a general proposition or a metaphysical description. Rather, it was a category Christians used to explain the existence of their faith. Providence and predestination simply referred to God's determination of all things. For Puritans, the appropriate response to God's call was not passive acceptance, but active redoubling of efforts. They frequently quoted the scriptural text "By their fruits ye shall know them." Virtuous activity was the evidence that faith was not deluded.

Luther and Calvin had described predestination as ultimately mysterious, thereby increasing the Christians' dependence on, and confidence in, God. Puritans expected a stronger *experience* of predestination. But this expectation also made predestination a psychological and religious problem. John Bunyan's autobiography, *Grace Abounding*, vividly describes his tortured anxiety over whether he was one of the elect. Bible verses darted into his mind, either comforting or tormenting him. He had no "critical distance," no ability to discern which verses were "for him."

Later Puritanism showed the importance of Luther's and Calvin's counsels against trying to figure out whether one is elect. The effect of Puritans' emphasis on experience was often that people (like Bunyan) questioned whether the experience of election they had was the right kind of experience, or strong enough, to signify election. Luther and Calvin saw that unless predestination is thought of, not deterministically, but as God's mysterious activity, predestination and personal responsibility are incompatible doctrines. Luther said that predestination is a "comforting" doctrine, and Calvin taught that predestination means that the world and human beings are safely in God's hands, that "nothing pertaining to our safety will ever be wanting" (*Institutes* I. XIV. 22).

In addition to the testimony of experience, Puritans expected *signs* of election. When signs are expected, however, it is difficult to be certain that the signs that appear are clear and unambiguous. One's motivation could always be suspected even if one's activity indicated election. Puritans apparently did not worry about whether or not their neighbor was elect. Oneself was always more than enough to worry about. The self-righteousness often identified with Puritanism was perhaps a compensation for lurking fears of *not* being elect. To address this anxiety, a theology of covenant emerged within Puritanism, especially in the United States. Covenant theology, discussed later in the chapter, emphasized *both* God's initiative and individual responsibility.

Can election be lost? Later Puritans rejected the Arminian emphasis on the individual's free will underlying the belief that election could be lost. Arminians (discussed in chapter 8) believed that predestination was general and did not refer to the individual, leaving the individual free to appropriate it or not. Puritans believed that since God's omnipotence was the sole determiner of individual predestination, election cannot be lost.

Puritans' lifestyle came from their insistence that everything must be seen from the perspective of the absolute majesty of God. They believed that nothing in human life has meaning in itself; only its meaning in God is important. The God's-eye-view, they believed, directed them to be sober, even somber on occasion, but *not* pessimistic. They famously denounced frivolous activities, but this should not be overdrawn. English Puritans believed in wine-drinking and dancing, provided that all activities "contributed to the well-being of the pilgrim on the way to heaven." All things were potentially good, but were not to be thought of as ends in themselves.

Within the broad category of Puritanism different churches interpreted differently the principle that all church practices must be based on the Bible. In England the largest group of Puritans was Anglican Calvinists. The next largest group was Presbyterians, who did not want severance from the Church of England, but did want purification of the "remnants of popish corruption." These two groups wanted a national church together with further reforms. Other Puritans were Independents or Congregationalists. They believed that the churches should be independent bodies of believers, not subject to any bishop or ruling body outside the local church. Separatists left the Church of England, demanding reform of worship and government "without tarrying for any."

Church government

By the mid-seventeenth century issues surrounding church government eclipsed earlier disputes over doctrine and worship practices. At a Parliament called by Charles I at Westminster to negotiate proposals for changing the Church of England, four positions dominated: 1) governance by bishops (the status quo position); 2) congregationals who wanted "self-governing covenanted churches" (including separatists and non-separatists); 3) presbyterial (synodical) government; and 4) those who defended royal supremacy against ecclesiastical government (called by its enemies "Erastianism" after Thomas Erastus, a professor of medicine who had argued in 1569 that the church should not have two heads, thereby creating the possibility that the church could oppose the state).

Political rather than religious considerations decided the outcome. In 1642, bishops were suspended from office, and remaining vestiges of "superstition or idolatry" were ordered removed from churches. The English Church was ordered to bring its practices into conformity with "the example of the best Reformed churches."

The new form of government for England finally decided upon in conjunction with Parliament and spelled out in measures of 1645–6 approximated the presbyterial-synodical churches of Scotland, France, and the Netherlands in its parish-based system of consistorial discipline and four-tiered structure of local, regional, and national synods. But it contained major compromises with Erastian and congregationalist concerns: the decisions of the superior jurisdictions were made advisory rather than binding on individual congregations; government officials conducted the election of parish elders; and sentences of excommunication could be appealed to commissioners chosen by Parliament.

(Benedict, 2002: 401)

The Westminster Confession of Faith (1647) "asserted the high Reformed orthodoxy of limited atonement, irresistible grace, and the perseverance of the saints, while avoiding a stand on the finer points of predestination" (Benedict, 2002: 401). The English civil war and the trial and beheading of Charles I, however, destroyed hopes that the English churches would all accept a common religious practice. Efforts to produce a model that all could follow were abandoned until the Restoration settlements of the 1660s restored the Book of Common Prayer, requiring all ministers to swear consent to everything in it, to conduct services according to it, and to swear loyalty to the king.

Quakers

Quakers were one of the main Separatist groups. George Fox (d. 1691), a shoemaker, was one of their earliest leaders. From 1643 forward Fox occupied himself with a search for truth that was satisfied by none of the many religious groups of his time. He wandered England seeking an "opening from the Lord," but he realized from what he saw that neither "priests nor dissenters nor separatists" had what he longed for, namely, a "sincere and simple manifestation of genuine Christianity." He wrote, "I observed a dullness and drowsy heaviness upon people, which I wondered at." In 1646 he experienced an "inner light" that became his trusted religious authority for the rest of his life.

He declared that "to be bred at Oxford or Cambridge was not sufficient to fit a man to be a minister of Christ." In 1647 he felt a call to preach according to his inner light. Harsh years followed as he frequently interrupted religious services to preach about what he had experienced. He was repeatedly jailed, whipped, stoned, and thrown out of towns. "At Mansfield," he reported in his journal, "the people fell upon me in great rage, struck me down, and almost stifled and smothered me; and I was cruelly beaten and bruised by them with their hands, Bibles, and sticks . . . for preaching the word of life to them."

Gradually people who sympathized with Fox's preaching gathered around him; sometimes whole groups came over to his leadership. The Society of Friends was organized in 1668. They were called "Quakers" because the Spirit often caused them to quake. Fox undertook missionary journeys to Ireland, the West Indies, North America, and Holland, meeting with persecution everywhere.

In 1676 the Scottish Quaker Robert Barclay (d. 1690) wrote *Apology for the True Christian Divinity* expounding Quaker principles and doctrines. The main principle was the Spirit's authority:

> The testimony of the Spirit is that alone by which true knowledge of God has been, is, and can only be revealed. . . . Moreover, these divine inward revelations, which we make absolutely necessary for the building up of true faith, neither do nor can ever contradict the outward testimony of the scriptures or right and sound reason.

Barclay insisted that the Spirit's revelations were not to be tested by either scripture or natural reason as if these were in some way superior. The Spirit is superior to both, and both derive from the Spirit. They rejected formal ministry, rites of baptism and communion, and set forms of worship. Those who are led by the Spirit are to preach without human appointment, "without hire or bargaining," but they may receive gifts for their necessities. Worship was also to be Spirit-directed. Baptism was described as a "pure and spiritual thing," and communion likewise was "inward and spiritual."

Quakers believed that consciences must not be forced. They rejected killing, banishing, or imprisoning for any reason. They also rejected frivolity, including luxurious dress and food. They refused to swear oaths. Emphasizing the sisterhood and brotherhood of all people, they were the first to protest slavery, barbarous prison conditions, and the inequality of women.

In the initial stage of excitement and energy, religious movements often transgress social roles, allowing men and women to work together to spread the word. Quaker women illustrated this pattern; they preached, often suffering for it. "A woman must not speak in church," Dewens Morrey was told in 1657 when she asked why she had been arrested. Her trial report states, "So, in conclusion, they ordered her to go back to Hawkchurch that night and there she was to be whipt until the blood did come, which was done the next morning early, she receiving many cruel bloody stripes."

Historian Kenneth Carroll (1978) describes one Quaker method for attracting attention to their message. Motivated by serious religious purpose, English Quakers in the 1650s and 1660s were the first "streakers!" In 1654 William Simpson passed through the city of Oxford "naked and bare, as a sign to that generation then in being, signifying to you that the day was neare at hand, even at the dore, in which the Lord would strip you naked and bare, both from the rule and authority they were then under in this nation, and also from that covering of religion with which they seemed to be covered." Many others did the same – women and men. In 1655 Thomas Holme went naked as a "sign to this city," reporting afterward to a friend that "I went to the highway naked and great dread fell upon many harts."

Other religious groups flourished in seventeenth-century England. Unitarians were excluded from the Act of Toleration (1689) but their views were represented both within the Church of England and in dissenting groups. Thomas Biddle (1615–62) published *Twelve Arguments Drawn Out of the Scripture* (1647) to demonstrate that Unitarian beliefs were based on the New Testament. In 1719 Unitarians split into two groups, those who agreed with confessional statements, and those who wanted to be governed solely by biblical terms.

Ranters were not numerically important in seventeenth-century England, but they exemplified what people feared about the "new religious movements." Ranters were the left wing of the evangelical groups; they were called an "infection" by the guardians of orthodoxy. Jacob Bottomly, "a great Ranter," wrote in his pamphlet "The Light and the Dark Sides of God" "It is not safe to go to the Bible to see what others have spoken and written of the mind of God. It is better to see what God speaks within me and to follow the doctrine and the leading of it in me."

According to their critics, Ranters had two main characteristics. They were pantheistic, that is, they believed in the essential identity of God with the universe, along with its corollary, God's indwelling in every creature, human, animal, and organic. And they were antinomian, believing that the direct revelations they received from God placed them above human laws. It is difficult, however, to assess their antinomianism as only the witness of their opponents remains. Richard Baxter (1615–91) wrote:

> But withal they enjoyed a cursed doctrine of libertarianism which brought them to all abominable filthiness of life. They taught . . . that God regardeth not the actions of the outward man, but of the heart, and that to the pure, all things are pure, even things forbidden; and so, as allowed by God they spake most hideous words of blasphemy, and many of them committed whoredoms commonly. . . . There could never sect arise in the world that was a louder warning to professors of religion to be humble, fearful, cautious, and watchful.

Heavily persecuted, the Ranters died out by the end of the seventeenth century. The less radical of them converted to Quakerism, in which many of their principles of an individualistic inner religion were preserved, but without the antinomianism that made them a feared and despised group.

Baptists

Baptists were non-Calvinist evangelical Puritans. First organized by John Smyth (d. 1612) while he was in exile in Holland, they affirmed both free will and predestination, but did not define the precise relationship of the two. They were interested in the church as a "gathered community," not in the subtleties of theology. For Baptists, a "calling" to ministry was more important than education or formal appointment. Against the "doctors and priests" mentioned by Bunyan, many Baptist groups thought education for ministry "wholly irrelevant." They wanted equality in the church, and they had observed the tendency of education to produce classes within a congregation. Like earlier continental Anabaptists (but without direct connections) they affirmed "believers' baptism," thinking of baptism as symbolizing, not conferring, regeneration. John Bunyan, a "Particular Baptist" (so called for their belief in God's choice of particular persons for election) expressed Baptists' characteristic anti-professionalism, saying "I preached what I felt – what I smartingly did feel. . . . Besides, sirs, words easy to understand do often hit the mark when high and learned ones do only pierce the air." Bunyan's *The Pilgrim's Progress* is discussed below. "General Baptists," influenced by Dutch Anabaptists, were Arminian in theology, believing that God's general grace was available to all who chose to accept it.

Cambridge Platonists, Latitudinarians

The Cambridge Platonists were a small group of English academics (in the third quarter of the seventeenth century). They were classical scholars, their "Platonism" largely an uncritical mixture of the dialogues of Plato, the metaphysics of Plotinus, and the interpretations of the Renaissance Platonists. Their beliefs on the nature of the soul, the place of reason, and the eternity of moral precepts placed them in the platonic tradition, a tradition they found useful for critiquing what they saw as distortions of thought in their own time.

Cambridge Platonists are noteworthy neither for their numbers nor for their influence, but for their stand against the separation of "religion" and "theology." They opposed Puritans who said, "You cannot understand spiritual things rationally. . . . Reason's self must first be cast into a deep sleep and die, before she can rise again in the brightness of the Spirit." Benjamen Whichcote (d. 1683) wrote:

> What has not reason in it or for it, if held out for religion is man's superstition. It is not religion of God's making. Our reason is not laid aside or discharged, much less is it confounded, by any of the materials of religion; but awakened, excited, employed, directed, and improved by it; for the understanding is that faculty by which man is made capable of God and apprehensive of him, receptive from him, and able to make returns unto him.
>
> (Whichcote, 1901, *Aphorisms*: 459)

Cambridge Platonists distinguished two functions of reason, philosophical thought and reason, as the means by which the soul is inwardly enlightened. They called reason the "organ of supersensuousness." To divorce religion from theology, they said, would be to "put asunder what God hath joined together." Religion, Whichcote said,

> doth possess and affect the whole man; in the understanding it is knowledge; in the life it is obedience; in the affections it is delight in God; in our carriage and behavior it is modesty, calmness, gentleness, candor, and ingenuity; in our dealings it is uprightness, integrity, and correspondence with the rule of righteousness.
>
> (Whichcote, 1901, *Select Sermons*: 53)

They thought of "atheism" as synonymous with materialism, a description of the world that dethrones the mind and replaces it with unthinking arbitrariness. But although they were opposed to materialism, they were infatuated with science, seeing in science a bulwark against atheism. Both Newton and Boyle, influenced by the Cambridge Platonists, argued from the order and beauty of the universe to the existence of its creator. God's role in the universe, though constricted, was essential. Seventeenth-century scientists assigned two ongoing tasks to God, keeping the stars in place and keeping the mechanism of the world in good repair.

Yet the separation of theology and religion carried the day. The Latitudinarians, immediate successors of the Cambridge Platonists, demonstrate that the will to hold together "what God has joined together" dissolved after the 1690s. Latitudinarians are easily distinguished from their mentors by the absence of mysticism in their writings and by their less-than-creative approach to the life of faith. They were prominent churchmen, not scholars, and they valued reason primarily because they considered it the best defense against "unregulated inspiration" or "enthusiasm" – by which they meant fanaticism.

The Pilgrim's Progress

In his autobiography, *Grace Abounding to the Chief of Sinners*, John Bunyan (1628–88) described his family as, "of that rank which is meanest and most despised." He was an itinerant tinker, or mender of pots and pans, when he became a member of the Particular Baptists, one of many Protestant sects in seventeenth-century England. He suffered years of spiritual torment over whether his attention to Christianity had occurred too late for repentance and salvation; perhaps the day of grace was "past and gone." At last he experienced conversion and began to preach. Without training, education, or formal ordination, he was elected minister of a congregation in Bedford. In 1660 he was arrested and imprisoned for religious dissent and released only in 1672. While he was in prison, under conditions of incredible filth, undernourishment, and disease, he wrote *The Pilgrim's Progress*.

   The Pilgrim's Progress has been called the most popular work of Christian spirituality ever written in English. It went into hundreds of editions in the century after it was published and has been translated into over a hundred languages in subsequent centuries. It was liberally illustrated with woodcuts that prompted the reader to visualize the pilgrimage of the protagonist, Christian, and his companions toward the celestial city (see CD Rom figures 9.14 to 9.16).

   Bunyan's book is an extended allegory of the journey of the protagonist, Christian, through the terrors, temptations, and trials of the world to the Celestial City. Leaving the city of this world in order to escape from "the wrath to come," Christian journeyed through the Slough of Despond, Vanity Fair, Doubting Castle, and other places named for their capacity either to encourage or to prevent his progress. He also met many people on the way who either aided or impeded him: Evangelist, Mr Facing-both-ways, Mr Talkative, Worldly Wiseman, Greatheart, Madame Bubble, Vain-Hope, and others. At last, passing through the Valley of the Shadow of Death, he and his companion Hopeful come to the gates of the Celestial City where they are met by shining angels and ushered into the presence of the King, accompanied by "melodious noise."

   Part two of *The Pilgrim's Progress*, published eight years later, recounts the journey of Christiana, Christian's wife, and her children over the same route. When Christian was taught by the Interpreter, he was given weapons and instructed to be on the alert for, and fight against, adversaries of all sorts. When Christiana was given instructions for her journey, she was taken to a shed where a sheep was being slaughtered. The Interpreter said to her, "You must learn of this sheep to suffer, and to put up with wrongs without murmurings or complaints. Behold how quietly she takes her death, and without objecting, she suffers her skin to be pulled over her ears." The gender assumptions of seventeenth-century England are evident in these instructions.

READING

John Bunyan, *The Pilgrim's Progress*

5   Germany: Pietism

Pietism provided a religious alternative to seventeenth-century rationalism. Pietists had theologies, but they were more interested in religious experience than in theological precision. They believed that religion's task was not to "seek understanding," but to "warm the heart," and they sensed that the heart of Christianity was all but lost in dogmatic Protestant orthodoxy. They argued for a faith that was Bible-centered and focused on a sense of human guilt and divine forgiveness through Christ. Personal conversion and a practical daily holiness featuring prayer and devotion, warm concern for people's needs, and the emotional outpouring of religious feeling in hymns were also central to Pietists. Both English and German Pietists remained within existing churches, with no expectation (in the seventeenth century) of forming splinter groups. They had home meetings for prayer and Bible study, for conversation about Christian life, and for mutual reproof and admonition. Pietism was a broadly based movement without central organization.

The beginnings of Pietism on the European Continent are often located in the 1675 publication of Philip Spener's book, *Pia Desideria*. In his book, Spener gave instructions for living a holy life; he thought of himself as seeking to complete Luther's reform of doctrine. Spener's ideas were first published as a preface to an edition of Johann Arndt's *True Christianity* (1606), and there are grounds for considering Arndt the "father" of Pietism on the basis of his emphasis on *practicing* Christianity.

Johann Arndt

Seventeenth-century Lutheran orthodoxy focused on defending Luther's insistence on the Bible as the only and sufficient guide to belief and practice (*sola scriptura*), and justification by faith alone. Luther's vivid descriptions of the moment of justification captured people's attention, causing them to ignore the Christian life. Arndt, reading Luther avidly, discovered another Luther, one who advocated Christian service as the true fruit of a living faith. Arndt was the first author to call attention to Luther's statements on the importance of good works. Arndt wrote in the Preface of his book, *True Christianity*:

> Dear Christian reader, that the Holy Gospel is subjected, in our time, to a great and shameful abuse is fully proved by the impenitent life of the ungodly who praise Christ and his word with their mouths and yet lead an unchristian life that is like that of persons who dwell in heathendom, not in the Christian world. Such ungodly conduct gave me the cause to write this book to show simple readers wherein true Christianity consists, namely in the exhibition of a true, living faith, active in genuine godliness and the fruits of righteousness. I wished to show as well that we bear the name of Christ, not only because we ought to believe in Christ, but also because we are to live in Christ and he in us. I also wished to show how true repentance must proceed from the innermost source of the heart; how the heart, mind, and affections must be changed, so that we might be conformed to Christ and his holy gospel; and how we must be renewed by the word of God to become new creatures. As every seed produces fruit of a like nature, so the word of God must daily produce in us new spiritual fruits. If we are to become new creatures by faith, we must live in accordance with the new birth. It is not enough to know God's word; one must also practice it in a living, active manner.

Arndt's concern, and that of Pietists who followed, occurred in the context of Lutheran orthodoxy or scholasticism in which sermons, as one contemporary wrote, "provided a pretext for a parade of obtuse and irrelevant knowledge." One 1605 sermon on the text "the very hairs of your head are numbered," edified the faithful with the following points: the origin, style, form, and natural position of our hair; the correct care of the hair; reminiscences, warnings, reminders, and comforts to be derived from the hair; and how to wear the hair in a good Christian fashion.

Spener considered Arndt a second Luther. He supported Arndt's concern for a revival of personal religion, simplicity, and evangelical fervor, advocating that pastoral training should be reformed and that sermons should be less disputatious and more devotional. The Pietist movement will reappear, expanded and carried to England and North America, in chapter 10.

Jacob Boehme

Boehme (1575–1624) was a mystic and a highly active Lutheran. Like Arndt and Spener, he opposed theological conflict that distracted people from the duty of Christian living. He was also outraged by the sectarian strife of his time.

Boehme claimed to experience an immediate direct guidance by the Holy Spirit that left "no place for reason." He did not believe that reason was worthless, but rather that it should serve the Spirit. The figure of Sophia, or Wisdom, revealed to Boehme "what God is like in depth." He taught that the Christian's faith is the essential condition for union with God, thus distinguishing his mysticism from that of Catholic mystics who taught that God's grace created the mystical union. Yet he also differed from Luther in his emphasis on effort and commitment rather than passivity before the Word: "No external imputed righteousness that we only believe has happened [has any value]; only an inborn childlike [righteousness] counts" (quoted by O'Regan, 2002: 94). His theology contested Luther's theology on such key concepts as the Trinity, Christ, creation, and grace.

Boehme's *The Way to Christ* was a Protestant mystical treatise. He warned his reader not to read it unless s/he is desperate for new birth. Called "one of the most difficult reads in the history of Christian thought," *The Way to Christ* is too difficult to read for any other reason (O'Regan, 2002: 3). Only passionate love for the incarnated and crucified Christ provides motivation and energy for the undertaking.

The Way to Christ revised Luther's teachings and Lutheran scholasticism in several ways. Like Spiritual reformers, Boehme emphasized the internal transformation of self, an activity in which the Christian must actively and vigorously participate. Beginning with repentance, prayer, and resignation to God, the treatise discussed the experience of new birth and progress in divine contemplation. As the treatise progresses, increments of difficulty in understanding it match ever more difficult stages of "the way to Christ." After publishing the treatise, Boehme was accused of "ungodly theological curiosity" and exiled from his home in Görlitz by Lutheran authorities.

READING

Johann Arndt, *True Christianity*, selections

6   Christianity in Canada and the Americas

Latin America

New histories are presently being written about missions by historians whose primary interests lie in the experience of the missionized – in the *effects* of missionary work, rather than in the intentions of the missionaries. New mission histories examine the social and economic organization of Indian societies before the missionaries arrived and the changes in culture and demography brought about by the missions. In other words, historians seek to understand missions "from the bottom up," rather than from the numerous "self-histories" featuring courageous and self-sacrificing missionaries and their experience with stubborn and rebellious natives. The nearly total absence of Indian testimony makes this difficult, but examined for evidence of native voices, missionary documents and material remains yield information that was disregarded when viewed through the interpretive lens of missionary perspectives.

In 1493 Pope Alexander VI granted to Spain and Portugal the wealth of the newly discovered lands in the Americas as well as the responsibility for the evangelization of millions of new subjects. During the sixteenth century, Portugal and Spain (the most powerful state in Europe), sent Franciscan, Dominican, Augustinian, and later, Jesuit missionaries to convert the Indians. All missions but those conducted by Jesuits were under royal control. Within a century, missions were part of a "fully articulated, multi-faceted imperial program to subjugate and dominate the Indians for religious, political, and economic purposes" (Langer and Jackson, 1995: 138).

Missions began first in Spanish colonies in the Caribbean islands, Hispaniola (1504), and Cuba (1515). With Cortés's conquest of Mexico, conquistadors, settlers, and missionaries moved inland and spread in every direction. The conquest of Peru (1532) completed the Spanish Empire in the New World. Missions played a crucial role in the colonization of frontier areas. Initially, most Indians found the Catholic missions attractive. They were intrigued by new technologies and equipment, European livestock, fruits and vegetables, and distilled alcohol. The missions seemed to many Indians to offer survival and a new way of life in rapidly changing conditions as settlers and soldiers moved into their lands.

In every location, tensions arose over the different goals of missionaries and conquistadors. Seeking gold and other riches, conquistadors expected that the conversion of the conquered peoples to Christianity would guarantee their docility as laborers. From the missionaries' perspective, of course, access to Christianity and the salvation of Indian souls was the overriding purpose of their labors, the primary advantage they offered the Indians, and the cause for which many of them were killed. With the best intentions, the missionaries "sought to instruct [the Indians] not only to understand the tenets of Christianity, but also to live cleaner and better lives and to practice the arts of a higher civilization" (Dunne in Polzer *et al.*, 1991: 541). The chasm between intentions and effects has perhaps never been so evident.

> The Spanish impact proved incredibly disastrous, as was already clear in the first twenty years. . . . The papal bull of 1493 established the character of the invasion as one of evangelization. It was that which justified it. In royal eyes this was never merely a specious

excuse. On the contrary, it was taken extremely seriously, at times agonizingly so. The motivation and behavior of the Conquistadores themselves was something very different. Here
was a gang of adventurers, mostly men quite insignificant at home, risking their lives in
pursuit of gold. Yet there was precious little gold to be found in the Antilles. The growing
population of settlers needed native labour if they were going to achieve anything at all
and, though Isabella had forbidden the enslavement of her native subjects, the Indians were
conscripted into one or another *encomienda*, granted to a Conquistador, whereby they were
compelled to work for him in the mines or the fields, while the women were seized as con-
cubines.

(Hastings, 1999: 330)

Natives were treated brutally and died in great numbers. In the Caribbean, they were
soon almost obliterated, so slaves were imported from Africa to replace them in the
labor force. Epidemic, poor nutrition, removal from their own culture, discipline and
punishment formerly unknown to the Indians (whipping posts, shackles, jail,
and stocks), and chronic illness caused disorientation, depression, apathy, and rebellion.
In short: "All the missionized people experienced severe decline in their numbers, and
in demographic terms none of these peoples anywhere in the Americas has subsequently
recovered" (Langer and Jackson, 1995: 12). Within a hundred years of first contact with
the missionaries, native populations were often reduced by as much as 95 percent. In
the absence of Indian testimony, the suffering can only be imagined.

The Latin American missions were accompanied by great human loss on both sides.
Many missionaries *were* heroic and self-sacrificing, according to the values of their time.
The fact that none of the missions survived when the missionaries left, however, implies
that those values were not successfully communicated to most Indians.

North America

Before any British Protestants arrived in North America, Catholic missionaries from
Spain came to the Southwest to convert Native Americans. Catholic missionaries
from France began missions in Canada and along the Mississippi River. State-church
Episcopalians and Dutch Reformed were also established in New Amsterdam before the
first English Puritans appeared in New England. The European reformations, which
began shortly after the discovery of the New World, dominated Christianity in the English
colonies as people who immigrated brought their religious convictions with them.

Spanish missions in North America accompanied European settlers as they had in
Latin America. By 1630 there were 25 mission stations in what is now New Mexico, with
an estimated 35,000 Christian Indians. By twenty-first-century standards, the missionaries' misogyny, paternalism (at best), and cruelty (at worst), are distressing. One Jesuit
historian, writing in 1936, described all Indians as "the simple fickle savage whose stu-
pidity was sometimes beyond description" (Dunne in Polzer *et al.*, 1991: 10). Disregard
for native customs ranged from discouraging Indians' practice of frequent bathing,
enforcing a sexual division of labor unknown to the Indians, physical punishment, and
"a complete overhauling of the generally open attitude of Indian societies toward the
body and sexuality" (Langer and Jackson, 1995: 25). The regulation of sexual behavior
and punishment of infractions was a major cause of rebellion among the Indians.

French Jesuits and Franciscans led missions in "New France" from the founding of Quebec in 1608 until a British army defeated the French and Quebec came under British rule (1759). Even under British rule, however, Quebec remained a bastion of French Catholic culture. Jesuit missions among the Huron Indians of southern Ontario showed a cultural sensitivity to the Indians unknown in the Spanish missions of Latin America. Jean de Brébeuf, Jesuit missionary to Canada in the early seventeenth century, disagreed with the common attitude among missionaries that Indians should be treated as children, flogged for many minor offenses, and, even when treated with kindness, regarded as unable to conduct their own lives. Brébeuf wrote Christian literature for the Hurons, "not only in their own language, but also (at least to some extent) in the idiom of their culture." For example, Brébeuf wrote the following Christmas carol in the language of the Huron Indians: "Within a lodge of broken bark / The tender Babe was found, / A ragged robe of rabbit skin / Enwrapp'd his beauty round; / But as the hunter braves drew nigh, / The angel song rang loud and high / Jesus your King is born, Jesus is born, / In exclesis Gloria" (quoted by Noll, 1992: 9). Brébeuf was tortured and killed in 1649 by the Hurons' enemies, the Five Nations Iriquois. He was esteemed even by his killers, who cut out his heart and ate it in order to acquire his courage.

Women missionaries were also active in French Canada. Marie Guyart (1599–1672), the first woman missionary to Canada, was an Ursuline nun. She wrote grammars, liturgies, and catechisms for various Indian tribes around Quebec. She also wrote copious letters to France about her experience. After her death, other women missionaries carried on her work.

French Canada, though dominantly Roman Catholic, enjoyed for a time a degree of religious toleration. New France was influenced by the Edict of Nantes (1598) which gave Protestants (Huguenots) in France freedom of worship. Huguenots worshipped openly in Quebec until the mid-1620s when the Edict was revoked (58 years before its revocation in France). Loyalty to the Roman Catholic Church was solidified by the appointment of the first Catholic bishop of Quebec in 1674. Meanwhile, the British colonies to the south of Quebec were experimenting with other forms of religious toleration.

Religious toleration

Since many people came to the English colonies fleeing religious persecution, toleration was a pressing issue. Christianity in North America was obviously pluralistic, but arguments over the desirability of establishing particular denominations occurred from the beginning of the seventeenth century forward. Although initially religious affiliation was considered mandatory for full citizenship, the Massachusetts Bay colony allowed the franchise to men who had been baptized but had not become fully participating members in 1662. In 1691, a New Massachusetts Bay charter provided liberty of conscience to all Christians except Roman Catholics. Colonists "eliminated all church courts, abolished tithes, and made church membership voluntary" (Hall, 1990: 6). Despite this measure of religious freedom (seen by some as religious chaos) there were no consistent atheists in the colonies; "indifference" was more likely to diminish church attendance than hostility.

In 1663, the Rhode Island and Providence plantations received a royal charter that allowed them to embark on the "lively experiment" of complete religious toleration. Carolina, on the other hand, established not one, but several, churches in 1669. The Church of England became the established church in Virginia, the Carolinas, Georgia, and Maryland after 1691, and in parts of New York after 1693. In established churches women were not allowed to participate in church government even though they were in the majority.

The limits of toleration of religious dissidence are clearly evident in the case of Anne Hutchison, a midwife who came under suspicion in Massachusetts for holding weekly meetings in her home, ostensibly to discuss the sermons of their minister, John Cotton. Accused of veering toward antinomianism (the belief that Christians do not need to abide by secular laws), Hutchison was tried by Massachusetts authorities in 1637. Despite her knowledge of scripture and her ability to reason on its basis, she was banished from the colony for claiming that the Holy Spirit spoke directly to her. Envisioning social chaos as the result of such teachings, the Puritan authorities condemned her to exile. They believed that their judgment was confirmed when she and most of her family were killed several years later in an Indian attack in the colony of New York where she had settled.

Quakers came to New England in the mid-seventeenth century. In spite of being consistently fined and whipped in the Massachusetts Bay colony, they kept returning. Between 1659 and 1661 four Quakers were hanged for sedition, disturbing the peace, and blasphemy. Eventually Quakers settled in Rhode Island, where Roger Williams grudgingly allowed them to remain, but their largest settlement was in Pennsylvania where William Penn (1644–1718) championed their acceptance.

Presbyterians from England, Wales, and Scotland established the first Presbyterian Church in 1684. Presbyterians originated twice-annual meetings that lasted several days during which multiple sermons calling for repentance led up to the celebration of the Lord's Supper. These "communion seasons" became the model for the "camp meeting" revivals of the eighteenth century. The Dutch and German Reformed, settling in New York, New Jersey, and Pennsylvania, also contributed to the strong Calvinist strain in American Protestantism.

Baptists settled in Massachusetts soon after the first immigrations; from there they infiltrated other colonies. Exiled from England, their leader John Smyth (1565–1612) was influenced by Dutch Mennonites who, as Anabaptists, believed in adult baptism based on confession of faith. Smyth adopted the practice of adult baptism by immersion. His group was "General Baptists," in that they believed that Christ's death was equally effective for all people. "Particular Baptists" believed that Christ died only for those individuals who were led by the Spirit to accept conversion. The first congregation of General Baptists in America was founded in Rhode Island in 1639; the first organization of Particular Baptists occurred in Pennsylvania in 1707.

The connection between literacy and religion in the English colonies should be noticed. Literacy was high in New England; children and servants were taught to read at home, and they learned to read by reading scripture. Thus, as historian David Hall has said, "Learning to read and being religious were perceived as one and the same thing." But the skill of reading did not necessarily include the ability to write. Based on 1660 wills on which marks take the place of signatures, 40 percent of adult men and

70 percent of adult women were unable to write. Writing became a nearly universal skill in New England only a century later.

Immigrants from Africa arrived in Virginia Colony in 1619. They were not officially slaves, but "slavery had already become an essential building block of European expansion in the New World." "From the first Portuguese explorations in West Africa to the later and more numerous colonies planted in the Western Hemisphere by the Spanish, the French, the Dutch, and the English, human bondage was a central reality – socially, politically, and economically" (Noll, 1992: 7–8).

Curiously, given the Christian preoccupation with missionizing American natives, there were no major efforts to convert Africans. Cut off from their native religions, many adopted the Christianity of their owners. Christian slave owners apparently saw no contradiction between their religion and the fact that they benefited and profited from holding slaves. "The interplay between colonization, slavery, and faith existed from the first" (Noll, 1992: 8).

Witch persecution

The 1692 witchcraft persecution in Salem, Massachusetts was a phenomenon that requires more explanation than the shared worldview of Puritan New England affords. Although prosecution and execution for the crime of witchcraft had occurred in other New England settlements, none of them experienced anything like the scale of the Salem events. In Salem, between mid-January, 1691, and late May, 1693, legal action was taken against 144 people (38 of them males). Fourteen women and five men were hanged; one man was pressed to death, and three women, one man, and several infants died in custody. The next largest witch persecution occurred in Hartford in the 1660s, where only 11 people were accused.

Recent scholarship cites two connected factors that created the conditions in which the Salem witch persecution developed as it did. First, Puritans' worldview "taught them that they were a chosen people, charged with bringing God's message to a heathen land previously ruled by the devil." They inhabited "worlds of wonder," in which God spoke to his people through many large and small "providences" of daily life, such as "signs in the sky, natural catastrophes, smallpox epidemics, the sudden deaths of children or spouses, [or] unexpected good fortune" (Norton, 2002: 295). The devil, irritated by being displaced, especially targeted "God's own Covenant People" through his servants, the witches. The "logic" of witchcraft beliefs was respected by educated and ignorant alike. In a context of belief in a malignant and cunning devil, magic, apparitions, dreams, and physical marks that "proved" witchcraft, conflict between neighbors often resulted in witchcraft accusations. Even the accused frequently believed themselves guilty.

Accused witches were charged with a variety of crimes, from souring fresh milk to killing children and adults. Beyond their specific "crimes," witches were considered heretics in that their power was believed to come from the devil. Perhaps most important of all, witchcraft was thought to undermine communities' solidarity by operating in darkness. People believed that brought to light it lost power.

But the New England Puritans' worldview was only part of a social environment in which the most learned members of the community and its least esteemed members –

young girls, daughters, nieces, and servants, who "resided near the bottom of the social hierarchy" – concurred in judgments that took the lives of over 20 people. Historian Mary Beth Norton has documented that those who played major roles in witchcraft accusations had been recently traumatized by the slaughter of their families and neighbors in what has been called the "Second Indian War" (or "King Williams' War") over control of New England's northeastern frontier, in the early 1690s (and continuing until 1699). "The witchcraft crisis of 1692 can be comprehended only in the context of nearly two decades of armed conflict between English settlers and the New England Indians" (Norton, 2002: 5).

The record of one family's encounter with hostile Indians will serve to indicate the trauma for survivors of these events. The great-uncle of one of the Salem accusers (Mary Walcott) reported finding a farm home outside of Falmouth in which there were six dead and three missing. Investigating "great smoke," he found Thomas Wakely and his wife dead, " 'neer halfe burnt,' lying 'halfe in, & halfe out of the house.' Their adult son had been shot and 'his head dashed to pieces;' their daughter-in-law, 'bigg with Child,' had been scalped; and two of their grandchildren had 'their heads dashed in pieces, & laid by one another with their bellys to the ground, & an Oake plank laid upon their backs' " (Norton, 2002: 87). In March, 1690, French soldiers and Indian warriors attacked the village of Salmon Falls, killing 80 to 100 people, burning houses and killing cattle. Refugees from such raids suspected a connection between the rampaging Indians and the witch crisis. It seemed that God had let Satan out on a long leash in order to punish New England. The Second Indian War and the outbreak of witchcraft in Essex County were Satan's doing.

Moreover, New England's magistrates had made tactical mistakes in the two Indian Wars, failing to move decisively or commit resources to fighting, at critical moments. If God were ultimately responsible for the colonies' punishment by "lengthening Satan's chain," "then the Massachusetts leaders' lack of success in combating the Indians could be explained without reference to their own failings" (Norton, 2002: 299). Such reasoning may have made the Essex judges amenable to witchcraft accusations that they might otherwise have dismissed. Puritans' worldview, *together with* the anxiety of living in sparsely populated settlements vulnerable to attack, or the trauma of seeing one's family slaughtered in an attack one survived, provide an explanation of the unprecedented witch persecutions at Salem village in the 1690s.

Confession was the only completely trustworthy evidence of witchcraft since all other indications rested on the vague testimony of coincidences, apparitions, and dreams. It was believed that confession could also restore community relationships and offer the confessor hope of redemption and forgiveness. Some accused witches confessed falsely, unable to bear the pressure to confess, and then revoked their confession. Some went to their deaths refusing to confess and accusing ministers and magistrates of shedding innocent blood. These scaffold denunciations soured the Salem community on witch persecution. Four years after the last Salem execution the Massachusetts governor called for a day of fasting and prayer to God to pardon those involved in the tragedy of the great witch-hunt (Hall, 1990: 195).

The Salem witch trials occurred toward the end of the witch crises in Europe and the English colonies. The last recorded conviction for witchcraft occurred in 1712, and the last witchcraft trial in 1717. Compared to European persecutions, these are late dates. In Germany, for example, the peak of witch persecution occurred in the 1620s, with the last successful prosecution in 1672. Finally, belief in witchcraft was undermined by improved medical methods for determining the origin of illnesses, by increasing awareness of the fallibility of evidence, and by disillusionment with the effects of witch persecution. Persecution, it was found, did not heal communities, but further strained relationships.

Epilogue

The seventeenth century was a time of contradictions. As witch persecution continued in Europe, and less than 50 years before the witch persecutions in the English colonies, Descartes had placed his faith in reason as capable of identifying the "clear and distinct" idea. Having arrived at knowledge by a foolproof method, he said, one can confidently base one's life on it. Yet New England Puritans also believed in the reasonableness of their identification of evil and its operation in their midst. Missionaries to Latin and North America believed that they brought a reasonable religion and way of life to Indians incapable of reason. Perhaps it was Pascal who best understood the limits of reason: "Reason is available," he said, "but can be bent in any direction."

Has the "Word made flesh" disappeared from Christianity? Certainly, the *effect*, if not the *intent* of Descartes' philosophy shoved body into the wings, ushering a "thinking thing" (*res cogitans*) to center stage. The equilibrium of soul and body, concept and life, by which each was incomplete without the other, seems to have eluded the characters discussed in this chapter. We should not forget, however, that history tends (like media culture), to focus on the most dramatic statements and events of a historical moment, neglecting the "ordinary Christians" who faithfully availed themselves of sacraments and devotions that oriented, challenged, and healed their lives. The "Word made flesh" was alive and well in the lives of Christians, although rhetoric of the time may fail to convey this.

Even when "ordinary" lives cannot be fully documented due to lack of evidence, they must be acknowledged. And, as discussed in the section on Christian missions in the New World, historians are presently finding that attention to conquered and evangelized people reveals formerly ignored material and documentary evidence. "Church history" has usually been "self-history," a history of intentions. Critical historians, examining effects, easily expose the inadequacies of self-histories. But the challenge, to those for whom the history of Christianity is self-history, is to recover a *critical self-history* that mourns the abuses and yet reveals the resources of the Christian traditions.

The eighteenth century saw a widening of the divergence between religion and theology. By the end of the century, Pietism, the religion of the "heart strangely warmed," and the Enlightenment seemed to stand at opposite poles, each claiming exclusive adequacy for human life. Chapter 10 explores Pietism and the Enlightenment, however, not as opposites, but as reactions to one another.

10 Keeping Body and Soul Together: Eighteenth-century Christianity

1 Eighteenth-century Pietism and Revivalism
2 Deism and the Orthodox
3 Religion in Eighteenth-century France

Prologue

The eighteenth-century Enlightenment spread from its original centers in England, France, and Germany throughout Europe and New England. The European population doubled between 1680 and 1800. Average life expectancy also increased from 25 years (in the seventeenth century) to 35 years (in the eighteenth century), reflecting progress in housing, nutrition, hygiene, and medicine, as well as a liberalization of sexual attitudes (Kee *et al.*, 1991: 489, 496). In England, literacy increased from 45 to 63 percent. Book production also doubled in the eighteenth century. Individuals could no longer master the range of intellectual interests available internationally through books, journals, and newspapers.

One historian estimated that the Protestant and Roman Catholic reformations took three centuries to complete. Until the end of the period treated in this book, Catholics were in the process of realizing the Council of Trent's reforms and Protestants were still refining theological ideas and worship practices – preaching, baptism, and the Lord's Supper – within their traditions. Church reforms also affected secular culture. As services among Protestants became more austere, establishments for drinking and dancing proliferated. In England alcohol consumption outside the home increased tenfold between 1690 and 1750. By 1730, about 6,000 alehouses flourished in London alone.

By the late seventeenth century Paris had replaced Rome as the center of visual arts. French baroque, known in France simply as the style of Louis XIV, imitated the subjects and form of classical antiquity. Poussin (1594–1665), the greatest French painter of the seventeenth century, said that the highest aim of painting was to represent noble and serious human actions with balance and restraint. Painting endeavored to engage the mind rather than the senses. With the departure of artistic excitement from Rome to Paris, religious art became secondary.

In the eighteenth century, a shift occurred in French art. Heroic subjects no longer dominated. As if in mockery of classicism with its prominent muscles and large casts of characters, landscape paintings with playful parties, picnics, and portrait paintings

Figure 10.1   The Orgy, Scene III from *The Rake's Progress*, c.1734, William Hogarth (1697–1764),
[Sir John Sloane's Museum, London].
Specifically religious subjects were painted in the eighteenth century, but what was new in that
century was moralizing subjects such as Hogarth's "The Rake's Progress." Hogarth has been called
"the first artist in history to become a social critic in his own right" (Janson, 1963: 451). His paintings "teach by horrible example" the downward "progress" of those who abandon the straight and
narrow path of middle-class virtue. Photo SCALA, Florence.

became popular. In England, Romanticism, with its preference for medieval subjects
and dislike of the establishments of church, society, and state, reacted against baroque
artificiality and excess. Moralistic paintings, like Hogarth's (1697–1764) *The Rake's
Progress* (figure 10.1) replaced religious painting. William Blake (1757–1827) illustrated
his poems and engraved texts with powerful scenes from Biblical and secular subjects.
His *Commentary on Job* imitated medieval illuminated manuscripts with vivid depictions of the trials of Job, combining strong personal feeling with narrative. In the English
colonies of North America, no specifically religious painting occurred until the nineteenth century. Instead, the Word/word extolled by Pietism and Puritanism organized
religious sensibilities as revivals swept New England and Eastern Canada.

New possibilities for mass communication popularized eighteenth-century debates
as Deists and Orthodox (in England) and Jansenists and Jesuits (in France) argued in
public by pamphlet and newsprint. The active French press of the *ancien régime* was
crucial to the circulation of new ideas about culture, society, and religion. In 1789 the

collapse of censorship created a proliferation of newspapers, written in language accessible to those with little formal education. Historian Thomas Munck (2000) credits newspapers with overturning the passivity of most French citizens toward cultural, social, and political affairs so that they became passionately engaged – for better and for worse – with changing society. This social context was critical for the spread of Enlightenment values.

Enlightenment encompassed more than a set of ideas. In his essay "What is Enlightenment?," Immanuel Kant (1724–1804) defined enlightenment as a *process* of discovery in which the individual's active and critical engagement mattered more than the end result. Enlightenment doctrines across broad geographical areas are more difficult to pinpoint than the similar attitudes that existed among Enlightenment thinkers: optimism about human progress through education, utilitarianism concerning society, and realism about politics. Enlightenment culture was characterized by diversity, open-mindedness, empiricism, and curiosity. Reason became a tool for exploring and criticizing inherited beliefs, institutions, and social practices.

Centuries-old assumptions about public punishment were examined and revised. Throughout the enlightened eighteenth century, public executions continued to attract large crowds, but increasingly officials feared outbreaks of protest. In England this fear prompted the refinement (if that is the right word!) of hanging. The trap door (or "drop") that had occasionally been used since 1759, was now made a permanent feature of the raised execution platform. The drop ensured instantaneous death, and thus minimized the chance of crowd intervention (Munck, 2000: 153). Moreover, the public humiliation of being placed in the pillory or stocks for a prescribed time became ambiguous. Offenders against mass morality (like those accused of homosexual acts) were often pelted with stones. But offenders sentenced to the stocks for sympathetic crimes were honored. For example, a man was placed in the stocks for publishing a pamphlet against Dissenters and the crowd decorated the stocks with flowers, turning the occasion into the celebration of a hero.

Eighteenth-century people began to notice the connection between poverty and certain forms of criminality, like theft. Perhaps this was not the first time it had been noticed, but it was the first time enough people noticed and protested to cause reevaluation of the system. More subtle gradations were needed between punishment by death and public humiliation. Where formerly one could be hanged for minor theft, prison sentences were now assigned. However, a prison sentence might not be much better than death for prisoners who could not afford to pay for private rooms and arrange for adequate provisions. In fact, many prisoners died as the result of filthy conditions, contagious diseases (like so-called gaol fever), and malnutrition.

A tract, published in 1764 by the Italian, Cesare Bonesana di Beccaria (1738–94), and soon translated into other European languages, questioned the age-old connection between sin and crime, arguing that the criminal system should devote itself solely to judging the economic or material significance of a breach of the law. Beccaria's *Of Crimes and Punishment* also pointed out confusion within the punishment system on questions of whether prisons should aim to reform and improve the ways of the criminal, whether punishment was primarily for the purpose of deterring others from similar crimes (an assumption that was firmly in place until the mid-twentieth century), or whether revenge for the victim and society was the goal of punishment (Munck, 2000:

152). The Enlightenment raised these questions, even though they were not solved either for the short or the long term.

1 Eighteenth-century Pietism and Revivalism

Germany

Johann Arndt and Philipp Spener (discussed in chapter 9) originated Pietism in Germany. Spener's godson, Count von Zinzendorf (1700–60), was exiled from Saxony for his evangelical interests and his rejection of Lutheran Orthodoxy. He opened his estates, Herrnhut, to evangelical emigrants from Austria, many of them Moravian Brethren. At Herrnhut Pietism's religion of the heart was expressed by strong images in hymns, sermons, paintings, and poetry. Themes of Christ's suffering, blood, and death predominated. Because they sought to stimulate affective piety, paintings – such as John Valentine Haidt's graphic portrayals of Christ's suffering, wounds, and blood – were hung in the houses where the community worshipped. Their preoccupation with Christ's suffering, as stimulus for conversion and the Christian life, led contemporaries to call Moravians the "visible-wound church." Moravian Brethren played an important role in John Wesley's conversion, although he later turned against them because of their mysticism and their alleged tendency to antinomianism.

Zinzendorf visited New England in 1741–3. He helped to found the Moravian community in Bethlehem, Pennsylvania, serving as its pastor. He also wrote and translated hymns. One of them, "Jesus, Thy Blood and Righteousness," was translated into English by John Wesley and became an evangelical favorite. Worship reflected Moravians' interest in personal religious experience. Rather than focusing on doctrinal or moral preaching, women and men were encouraged to express their faith and Christian experience through testimony, song, and prayer.

The Moravian movement also allowed women leadership roles that were unique in seventeenth- and eighteenth-century German Protestantism. In mainstream German Protestantism, the emergence of the sermon as the centerpiece of Lutheran worship effectively required women to be passive listeners (as depicted, for example, in Lucas Cranach the Elder's First Wittenberg Altarpiece (see CD Rom figure 7.2). Within the Moravian movement, however, the critique of mainline Protestantism included accepting women's leadership. Count von Zinzendorf became a spokesman for leadership roles for women, reinterpreting Paul's instruction to women to keep silence in the church. By 1760 in the approximately two dozen Moravian settlements in Europe and North America, women were considered equal to men in spiritual matters (though not in temporal affairs). Women wrote hymns and spoke in the assembled congregation as well as in the women's "choirs," or households. However, Moravians claimed to accept Paul's order that women must not *preach* by making women's sermons exceptional, rather than regular, occurrences.

Moravians' opponents saw women's preaching as threatening ecclesiastical order. In a debate between Zinzendorf and a German Lutheran theologian, Johann Georg Altmann, Zinzendorf defended the practice with texts from the gospel and Paul that suggest women's full participation in the body of believers. Jesus himself initiated equality of women and men, Zinzendorf claimed, concluding, "We act precisely like the Savior, who chose us. After him, we work toward the equality of brothers and sisters." After Zinzendorf's death in 1760, lacking a defender as astute and intransigent as Zinzendorf, women's equality within the Moravian movement was steadily compromised.

Eighteenth-century music of the Lutheran reformation

A brief digression on the history of Christian hymn singing will place in context eighteenth-century Lutheran music. Historical Christians were well aware of the solidarity to be gained by singing together. Music had long been recognized as capable of inspiring and producing strong religious *feeling*. The earliest Christians sang hymns and psalms together in their worship services. One of the earliest hymn collections was of the beautiful fourth-century Manichaean hymns from Egypt and North Africa. The first recorded "sit-in" was a "sing-in." In fourth-century Milan, the imperial capital, Bishop Ambrose's congregation resisted the Emperor's decision to turn their church over to the Arian Christians (whom they considered heretics), by barricading themselves within the church and singing hymns until the emperor relented. Hymns were used to combat heresy, and they were also used by "heretics" to spread their beliefs.

Hymn-singing accompanied and energized reforming movements in medieval Christianity. They also expressed mystical prayer and devotion. Richard Rolle, the English mystic and "hermit of Hampole" was among the leading medieval English hymn-writers. Since only Latin hymns were permitted in church, hymn singing in the vernacular came to be strongly associated with groups outside or on the margins of the Catholic Church. John Hus translated many Latin hymns into the Czech language so they could be understood and sung by his followers.

Calvin and the Reformed tradition preferred to sing the psalms set in metrical versions. Alone among the sixteenth-century reformers, Zwingli considered music in church distracting, though he himself was a skilled musician, playing 14 instruments at professional level. This is puzzling until we consider that, for a professional musician, trained to listen to the structure, performance technique, and interpretation of music, music cannot be simply a background for meditation or prayer. Thus, for a musician, music can distract from worship.

The Lutheran reform had a profound effect on the development of hymnody. Martin Luther understood hymns to be an important form of theological communication. He himself wrote about 38 hymns and he encouraged others to write hymns. Luther did not share Catholic concern with maintaining the purity of church music. He frequently used secular tunes, love tunes and drinking tunes, as settings for scriptural or sacred poetry. In his Forward to the first edition of the *Wittenberg Gesangbuch* (1524), Luther wrote:

> That the singing of spiritual songs is a good thing and one pleasing to God is not hidden from any Christian, for not only the example of prophets and kings in the Old Testament (who praised God with singing and playing and with hymns and with all manner of stringed instruments), but also the special custom of singing psalms, have been known to everyone and to universal Christianity from the beginning.

Accordingly, as a good beginning, and to encourage those who can do better, I and several others have brought together certain spiritual songs with a view to spreading abroad and setting in motion the Holy Gospel which now, by the grace of God, has again emerged. These are set for four voices for no other reason than that I wished that the young might have something to rid them of their love ditties and wanton songs and might, instead of these, learn wholesome things and thus yield willingly, as becomes them, to the good; also, because I am not of the opinion that all the arts shall be crushed to earth and perish through the Gospel, as some bigoted persons pretend, but would willingly see them all, and especially music, servants of him who gave and created them.

Bach

Lutheran chorales and passion oratorios, largely the work of one composer, brought a new beauty and sophistication to hymns. Johann Sebastian Bach began his career at the age of 18 as organist and choirmaster. A pious Lutheran, Bach was inaugurated cantor of St Thomas, Leipzig in 1723, the site of his musical activity for the next 30 years. During these years he wrote over 250 church cantatas together with numerous masses and various pieces for particular parts of the mass.

For Bach, the praise of God was the highest activity of the human spirit; thus, composing sacred music was itself a spiritual discipline. He considered music a reflection of the freedom with which God bound Godself to form in the Incarnation of Jesus Christ (Pelikan, 1986: 121). His library demonstrates that Bach's theological training was informal but seriously pursued. He learned Lutheran orthodoxy from Leonhard Hutter's book, *Compendium locarum theologicorum* (published in 1610). He also owned many other theological books, including Luther's works, Luther's German Bible (in three folio volumes), and several early Pietist works like Johann Arndt's *True Christianity*. His theological interests had two foci, Lutheran orthodoxy with its focus on doctrine, and Pietism with its attention to living a Christian life. These movements within Lutheranism were, in Bach's time, not integrated in public worship, but they could be blended in devotional life. They were also blended in Bach's compositions for the liturgical year. He interwove scripture, doctrinal statement, and the warmly affective piety evident in the chorales.

The chorale

A chorale is a hymn tune specifically associated with German Protestantism. One of Luther's liturgical reforms had been to insist that the congregation participate in the service. He inaugurated services in German and gave congregational singing an important role. He wrote, "I wish to make German psalms for the people, that is to say sacred hymns, so that the Word of God may dwell among the people also by means of song." Luther and his colleagues created the first chorales by adapting tunes from Gregorian chant, popular songs, and Latin hymns. Originally they were sung in unison, but soon they were harmonized in four parts, with the melody always in the soprano voice where it can easily be heard. Typically, a chorale would occur at the close of extended works, like cantatas and masses, resolving the complex voices of the work. After 1660 chorales came to be the most important form of Lutheran church music. Bach wrote cantatas for 35 years.

One of the best known of his cantatas, Cantata 80, "Ein feste Burg ist unser Gott" (CD Rom Music 10.1) has been called the battle hymn of the Lutheran reformation. Written in 1730 for the 200th anniversary of the 1530 Augsburg Confession, Luther's hymn by the same name, "A Mighty Fortress is our God" provided the words. In the chorale, the music reiterates the words: the orchestra plays a whirl of grotesque and wildly leaping figures, through which the chorus makes its way undistracted and never misled (Spitta, 1951: 470–1). Music and words work together to present simultaneously the quintessential Lutheran religious sensibility of extreme threat (Jonah in the belly of the whale), and God's promise to deliver the trusting soul. The counterpoint and contrast between religious anxiety and the celebration of redemption through faith alone were never more vivid than in Cantata 80.

The Passion oratorio

The Passion oratorio is a specifically German Lutheran genre that combines an operatic style with biblical themes. In fact, opera originated in oratorios on biblical themes. Hamburg opened its new opera house with a performance of Johann Theile's "Adam und Eva." Like oratorios, operas featured recitative with interpolated arias. In Bach's oratorios the arias present the emotions of a bystander. For the Mass in B minor, Bach used biblical texts for the Evangelist's narrative; arias represented the persons of the drama; and for the crowds, he used familiar hymn tunes and words sung by the whole congregation at appointed times.

Bach set the text of the Latin Mass to music, thus participating in a liturgical and musical process begun by Luther. In 1523 Luther's introductory remarks to his *Formula missae* state his view of the liturgical tradition of the Mass:

> We therefore first assert that it is not now nor has ever been our intention to abolish the liturgical service of God completely, but rather to purify the one that is now in use from the wretched accretions which corrupt it and to point out an evangelical use.

The Mass in B minor (1747–9) was performed as it was written, a few sections at a time. Bach never conducted or heard it in its entirety in his lifetime. It uses a five-part chorus, and the Latin text is that of the Lutheran liturgy used in Saxony (CD Rom Music 10.2).

The B minor Mass has been called a "case study in Evangelical Catholicity." Luther's doctrines of sin, repentance, and redemption were profoundly expressed in the mass, with its motifs of alternating struggle, gloom, despair and joy, confession and celebration. Since Luther's time, Pietism had interpreted the sense of sin as angst (from the Latin *angustiae*, literally, the sensation of constriction and breathlessness). Pietist hymns and Bach's chorales sought to reawaken the individual's awareness of personal sin by evoking in vivid detail the sufferings of Jesus. They addressed Jesus (rather than Christ) as personal Savior rather than as Lord.

Death was portrayed with a vivid immediacy perhaps never before experienced in church music in Bach's "Mass in B minor." The most dramatic chorus of the mass ("*Crucifixus etiam pro nobis*"), was nearly indistinguishable from opera. In it Bach used two musical strategies to portray grief, chromatic harmony and descending movement. When the lowest tone is reached, there is an extraordinary modulation to G major. Despair gives way to the jubilant chorus of the resurrection in D major, "*Et resurrexit tertia die*" (Machlis, 1955: 407). The seemingly inconsolable grief of the "*Cruxifixus etiam*," ending with the words "*passus et sepultus est*," is directly juxtaposed to the jubilant "*et resurrexit*," expressed by a virtuoso high trumpet.

Pietistism also focused on death, Jesus' death and the Christian's death, and the relationship between them. Between 1648 and 1750, the year of Bach's death, there was a phenomenal growth of literature on the art of dying, stimulated by Pietism and the Thirty Years War. Preoccupation with death is not surprising amidst the precipitous decline of the population of the Holy Roman Empire from about sixteen million to less than six million.

Bach was well known and admired in his own generation. But the following generations found his music florid and pedantic, heavy and overly ornamented. Even his four sons, composers themselves, found it old-fashioned. Some manuscripts of his music disappeared irretrievably. Not until the Romantic age did his work again find passionate adherents. The *St Matthew Passion*, which had not been performed for three-quarters of a century, was discovered and performed by the 20-year-old Felix Mendelssohn in 1829.

It is important to remember that Bach's masses and chorales were not written for concert halls but for church services. Bach's music was – and is – a significant part of Christians' religious resources, an inspiration for Christians who wrote, performed, and heard church music.

England

By the eighteenth century, the smaller seventeenth-century sects (like the Ranters) had largely disappeared. Nonconformist groups (Presbyterians, Congregationalists, Baptists, and Quakers) were quiet. In 1791, Roman Catholics who took the oath of allegiance to the English crown were granted the right to property, education, and the practice of law, rights they had not enjoyed in England for more than two centuries. Tolerance and moderation predominated, though some said that tolerance and conformism were based on indifference rather than conviction.

The larger seventeenth-century religious movements survived and grew. Eighteenth-century Quakers combined interest in social reform, science, medicine, and mental health, with striving for self-transcendence, mystical insight, and radical pacifism (Mack, 1998: 249). They too had seen more radical days. One of the results of religious conformism was the gradual silencing of women in groups like the Quakers that had formerly tolerated women preaching. Quaker women also lost the right to attend business meetings and to hold their own yearly meetings. Instead, they were instructed to cultivate the feminine virtues of domesticity and sensitivity. Nevertheless, eighteenth-century Quaker women spoke out on social reform issues, initiating efforts toward women's suffrage, abolition of slavery, and peace activism that came to fruition only much later.

Shakers, or "The United Society of Believers in Christ's Second Appearing," originated during a Quaker revival in England in 1747. The name "Shakers" derived from their habit of shaking with spiritual exaltation. The original founders were James and Jane Wardley. They were succeeded by Mother Ann Lee, who was regarded by Shakers as "the female principle in Christ," the fulfillment of the Second Coming. Mother Ann led the Shakers to upstate New York in 1774, preaching and conducting faith healing. Shakers placed a high value on celibacy, but marriage was not forbidden. They abstained from alcohol and discouraged smoking. They lived in "families" of 30 to 90 persons, "separated from the world." Communistic and pacifistic, Shakers were persecuted, so a band of women and men fled to Albany, New York in 1774. There were about 5,000 Shakers in the United States at one time; one community has survived to the present.

John Wesley

John Wesley (1703–91) described the beginnings of the Methodist revival:

> Just at the time when we wanted little of filling up the measure of our iniquities, two or three churchmen of the Church of England began vehemently to call sinners to repentance. In two or three years they had sounded the alarm to the utmost borders of the land. Many thousands gathered to hear them; and in every place where they came, many began to show such concern for religion as they had never done before.

Wesley was born in a Lincolnshire parish rectory, the fifteenth child of Samuel Wesley, a clergyman, and his wife Susanna. John's mother was a woman with strong ideas about how to raise children. The first essential, she wrote in her diary, was to break the unregenerate will of the child; having done this, she must guide him in the way he ought to go. This dubious (from a twenty-first-century perspective) child-rearing method produced John and his brother, Charles Wesley. Charles wrote over 5,500 hymns, among them "Jesus Lover of My Soul," "Love Divine All Loves Excelling," "Lo, He comes with Clouds Descending," "Wrestling Jacob", and many, many others. Generations of evangelical Christians learned theology from the hymns of Charles Wesley.

John and Charles went to Christ Church College, Oxford. Together they formed a band of religious seekers other students scornfully called the "Holy Club." They were also called "Holy Moths," sacramentarians, and "methodists." Meeting regularly for Bible study, fellowship, and prayer, they were also faithful in Church of England attendance. They practiced a sort of secular monasticism, praying every hour on the hour, with collects at 9, 12, and 3 o'clock, meditations at 6, and daily self-examination, faithfully recorded in a journal. They pledged themselves to help the needy and destitute.

John and Charles Wesley were both ordained as clergymen in the Church of England. John was an unyielding rigorist, hard on himself and on others. Seeking more strenuous service than that of an English country parish, they sailed to the colony of Georgia in North America. John wrote in his journal, "I hope to learn the true sense of the gospel of Christ by preaching to the heathen." He was eventually driven from the colony for refusing communion to a woman who declined to marry him. On his way back to England, a storm came up, threatening the collapse of the ship and the lives of everyone aboard. Some Moravian Brethren on the ship impressed Wesley by calmly singing and praying throughout the storm. Later, in a journal entry from 1738, Wesley accused himself of tepid religious faith: "In a storm I cry to God every moment; in a calm, not," he wrote. In England, he went to a Moravian meeting where he had the following experience:

> In the evening I went very unwillingly to a society in Aldersgate Street, where someone was reading Luther's Preface to the Epistle to the Romans. About a quarter before nine, when he was describing the change that God works in the heart by faith, I felt my heart strangely warmed. I felt I did trust in Christ, Christ alone for my salvation. And an assurance was given me that he had taken away *my* sins, even *mine*, and saved me from the law of sin and death.
>
> (*Journal* May 24, 1738)

Revivalism

Wesley began to preach in parish churches. But wherever he went, he was told that he must not return. George Whitefield, an old friend and Holy Club member, advised him that if he could not preach in churches, why not preach in the fields? Wesley's *Journal* for April 2, 1739 records:

> I proclaimed in the highways the good tidings of salvation, speaking from a little hill . . . to about 3,000 people. The scripture that I spoke was this: The Spirit of the Lord came upon me because he hath anointed me to preach the gospel to the poor. He hath sent me to heal the brokenhearted, to preach deliverance to the captives and recovery of sight to the blind . . .

Wesley preached an average of two sermons a day; on many days he preached four or five. In 52 years he traveled 250,000 miles on horseback, often accompanied by George Whitefield. They were both powerful preachers. Wesley recorded in his journal: "While I was preaching, one before me dropped down as dead, and presently a second and a third. Five others sank down in a half hour, most of whom were in violent agonies. We called upon the Lord and he gave us an answer of peace."

Revivalism was a new, and not altogether appreciated, phenomenon in the eighteenth century. Many complained that revivals disrupted family life, and services were often interrupted by people forcibly dragging family members out. Yet Wesley's preaching was not revival preaching by later standards. Even though his sermons were long, closely reasoned expositions of doctrine, congregations appeared at any hour of the day. Wesley's own preferred time to preach was 5:00 a.m.

George Whitefield's tour of the North American English colonies in the Fall of 1740 was one of the most remarkable episodes in the history of American Christianity. Whitefield preached to crowds of approximately 8,000 people almost every day for a month (without benefit of loudspeaker). By all accounts, he was a powerful preacher. But Wesley had another talent in addition to preaching; he was an organizer. Wherever he went he left behind him a company of women and men closely knit together to encourage and reprove one another.

Wherever Methodism spread, little bands were organized. They included about 12 people, with a leader to collect the dues (a penny a week) and oversee the group. In 1742 the bands were organized into a Society. In 1746 a further step was taken as bands were organized into circuits or rounds, creating a closely-knit organization in which no member got lost. They practiced rigorous discipline, and expulsion from the bands was common. In Newcastle alone in 1743, 64 members were excluded for such offenses as cursing, swearing, wife beating, frivolity and carelessness, brawling, drunkenness, idleness, lying, and laziness.

On December 25, 1738, Rules of the Band Societies were put into operation. We might recognize Wesley's groups as support, or encounter, groups. Before a member was admitted s/he was asked:

> Do you desire to be told of your faults, plainly and homely? Do you desire that every one of us should tell you, from time to time, whatsoever is in his heart concerning you? Consider! Do you desire that we should tell you whatsoever we think, whatsoever we fear, whatsoever we hear concerning you? Do you desire that, in doing this, we should come as close as possible, that we should cut to the quick, and search your heart to the bottom?

The agenda of the weekly meetings was: "To speak each of us in order, freely and plainly, the true state of our souls, with the faults we have committed and the temptations we have felt since our last meeting."

Wesley's theology

Wesley and Whitefield were close friends, but they had theological differences. Whitefield's Reformed theology found Wesley's insistence on universal salvation fatal to the sense of sin he thought needed to be fostered as preparation for the experience of salvation. Wesley, in turn, told his friend, "Your god is my devil." He argued that belief in predestination killed all hope and led to indifference. The death of Christ *for all* was a constant theme of Charles Wesley's hymns and John Wesley's preaching.

Wesley and Whitefield agreed on a common enemy, however. Both named *indifference* as the enemy of Christian commitment. Both sought to combat indifference by addressing the heart. Their theological disagreement centered on which theology best served the *experience* of conversion and the ongoing work of sanctification. A 1740 sermon by Wesley on free grace brought their disagreement to a final rift. Wesley accused Reformed Calvinists of implying that, since Christ's righteousness is ascribed to Christians, they need none of their own. According to this theology, he said, Christians have no obligation to obey laws, and good works are unnecessary for believers. Indeed, Wesley had seen the doctrine of free grace lead to these conclusions in two of his most able workers. Wesley's strict discipline in his little bands may also have been a reaction to his own early attraction, through the Moravian Brethren, to the doctrine of "free grace," that is, grace unsupported by works.

Wesley's strangely warmed heart was shorthand for a complex program of experiences centered on *personal appropriation* of salvation universally offered. The personal pronoun was ubiquitous in Charles Wesley's hymns as in John Wesley's sermons. Charles' hymn, "Wrestling Jacob," is illustrative: "'Tis Love, 'tis Love! Thou diedst for *me.* / I hear Thy whisper in *my* heart / The morning breaks, the shadows flee / Pure universal love Thou art / To *me* Thy love until the end / Thy nature and thy name is love."

John Wesley outlined a method for personal appropriation of justification and sanctification, a program of *experiences*. His *ordo salutis* (order of salvation) outlined the following stages: 1) conversion; justification by faith; 2) regeneration; the new birth; 3) repentance *after* justification; 4) gradual work of sanctification, the goal of justification; and 5) entire sanctification, or perfection. Wesley urged the goal of Christian perfection on all Christians. But perfection too had stages. In the first stage, all real Christians are made free from outward sin; in the second stage, the mature Christian is freed not only from visible sins, but also from evil thoughts and evil tempers. The third stage brings the actualization of present perfection in one in whom is the mind which was in Christ: "Pure love reigning alone in the heart and life: this is the whole of scriptural perfection" (*Plain Account*: 52).

Wesley taught that Christian perfection is not flawlessness or sinlessness, but perfection in *love*. He advocated a lifestyle of frugality, good deeds, and devotion, strictly enforced. But the rigor of the disciplined life was always corrected by Wesley's insistence on drawing rather than driving, attracting rather than threatening.

Wesley's theology was practical. His interest in structural social change was unique among theologians until the twentieth century in that he envisioned not merely charity to relieve misery, but social change. Throughout his life, and increasingly in his later years when he could no longer travel and preach, his activities centered on raising money for relief programs. He opened a dispensary for the poor; he started a loan society to help those in distress or to finance an enterprise promising a poor person a better way of life. He founded a home for widows and a school for poor children. Moreover, he advocated government's responsibility for poverty. In 1773 he wrote *Thoughts on the Present Scarcity of Provisions* to suggest measures that the government might adopt to end hunger. He also opposed slavery.

John Wesley, clergyman of the Church of England, never broke with the Church despite many disagreements. As late as 1789 (two years before his death), he wrote, "I declare once more that I live and die a member of the Church of England, and that none who regard my judgment or advice will separate from it." Nevertheless, his concern for the evangelization of North America led him to consecrate three ministers as missionaries. Later he also consecrated men to minister in Nova Scotia, Scotland, Newfoundland, Antigua, the West Indies, and even England! He put lay ministers in charge of his circuits that by 1730 had a membership of 30,000. By 1759 the movement was referred to in contemporary literature as the Methodist Church, but the formal break with the Anglicanism did not come until 1795 in England, four years after Wesley's death. In Ireland it came only in 1870.

North America

In 1740, the population in the colonies was about 900,000. Three of the four largest denominations were English and Protestant: Congregationalists; Anglicans; and Baptists. The fourth was Scottish and Scotch-Irish Presbyterians. Twenty-seven Roman Catholic churches clustered in Maryland. By 1750, nine of the thirteen colonies had established churches. The others rejected churches that were affiliated with, and partially supported by, the state. The American colonies' war for independence was prompted in part by the threat that the Church of England, complete with a resident bishop would be established in the colonies (Wilson and Drakeman, 2003: 69). The Bill for the Incorporation of the Protestant Episcopal Church Act was repealed in 1787. In Virginia the Episcopal Church collapsed, reduced from 90 to 13 clergymen.

During the American Revolution, between one-fifth and one-third of the population of the 13 colonies remained wholly or partly loyal to Great Britain. Loyalists were primarily members of the Church of England, but they were also to be found among Presbyterians, Congregationalists, Baptists, and Roman Catholics. Denying that spiritual freedom implied political self-determination, and fearing social chaos, about 35,000 Loyalists fled to Halifax, where some of them founded the Dominion of Canada. Although the French ceded Quebec to Britain by treaty in 1763, Roman Catholics received full civil rights in Canada 50 years before their co-religionists did in England. In Canada in 1763 when the country became formally British, Congregationalists and Roman Catholics dominated. Separation of church and state was never a Canadian principle, though toleration and protection of minority religious groups was guaranteed by law. Religion in Canada remained much closer to European religious patterns than it did in the United States.

The European Enlightenment played a part in the American insistence that religion was not, and should not be, a public, but rather a private matter. Thomas Jefferson and James Madison sought the *independence* (not the separation) of Church and State. The First Congress adopted a clause of the First Amendment stating, "Congress shall make no law respecting the disestablishment of religion, or prohibiting the free exercise thereof." The Congress's intention in adopting this statement is difficult to discern. Did the First Congress intend to sever any remaining bonds between church and state, to allow the government to employ its secular resources to accommodate the religiosity of its people, or simply to exempt itself from legislating on church–state matters, leaving the entire subject in the hands of the individual states? (Wilson and Drakeman, 2003: 54). In any case, Jefferson's "Bill for Establishing Religious Freedom" was framed in 1777, but the Virginia House of Delegates and Senate enacted it only in 1786 due to its lack of clarity and the controversy surrounding it. It stated, in part:

> No man shall be compelled to frequent or support any religious worship, place, or ministry whatsoever, nor shall be enforced, restrained, molested, or burdened in his body or goods, or shall otherwise suffer, on account of his religious opinions or belief; but that all men shall be free to profess, and by argument to maintain, their opinions in matters of religion, and that the same shall in no wise diminish, enlarge, or affect their civil capacities.

Jefferson's Bill was approved in Virginia, with minor emendations, as the First Amendment to the Bill of Rights on December 17, 1791. The other states followed. Evangelical denominations grew rapidly as a result of disestablishment.

The slave trade reached its peak in the second half of the eighteenth century. Between 60,000 and 100,000 Africans were taken as slaves to Europe and the New World *annually* in the 1780s. At the beginning of the American Revolution, the southern colonies held an estimated 430,000 slaves, with another 50,000 in the north. Although slaveholders did little to Christianize slaves, many slaves converted in the Methodist and Baptist revivals after the American Revolution. Between 1770 and 1830 most Christian African Americans attended white churches. In 1785 Lemuel Haynes was the first African American to be ordained in a major white denomination. But relations between blacks and whites within churches reflected and reiterated secular relations, making membership in white churches less than attractive to African Americans. In the Great Awakening, many African Americans became Methodist, but racial tensions led to the founding of three branches of the African Methodist Episcopal Church (by Richard Allen in 1814). The African Baptist Church (Boston, 1805) and the First African Baptist Church (Philadelphia, 1809) were two of the first Black Baptist Churches in the United States.

The First Great Awakening
America's first national event was a series of revivals that occurred in the North American British and French colonies between 1740 and 1743. The First Great Awakening was characterized by flamboyant and highly emotional preaching and strong reactions in congregations – fainting, weeping, and screaming. The Awakening's most significant results were an increase in Baptist and Congregational membership.

George Whitefield (1714–70), the most powerful of the revivalist preachers, visited Georgia with John and Charles Wesley in 1738. Benjamin Franklin's *Autobiography* records that Whitefield "made himself remarkable as an itinerant preacher." However, in the New World as in the Old, local ministers took a dislike to him, and he was forced to preach in the fields. To illustrate the "extraordinary influence of his oratory on his hearers," Franklin told the following story: Whitefield had taken to heart the plight of children who had been orphaned in the harsh conditions of life in the colony of Georgia. He wanted to build an Orphan House for their support and education. So Whitefield "preached up this charity, asking for donations from the large crowds to whom he preached." Franklin disapproved of the plan to build in Georgia, where both materials and workers were in short supply. He thought that the Orphan House should be built in the north where these were more readily available, taking the children to the house, rather than bringing the house to the children.

> This I advised [Franklin wrote] but he was resolute in his first project, rejected my counsel, and I therefore refused to contribute. I happened soon after to attend one of his sermons, in the course of which I perceived that he intended to finish with a collection, and I silently resolved that he should get nothing from me. I had in my pocket a handful of copper money, three or four silver dollars, and five gold pieces. As he proceeded I began to soften and concluded to give the coppers. Another stroke of his oratory made me ashamed of that, and determined me to give the silver; and he finished so admirably that I emptied my pocket wholly into the collector's dish, gold and all. At this sermon there was also one of our church, who, being of my sentiments respecting the building in Georgia, and suspecting a collection might be intended, had, by precaution, emptied his pockets before he came from home. Towards the conclusion of the discourse, however, he felt a strong desire to give, and applied to a neighbor who stood near him, to borrow some money for the purpose. The application was unfortunately made to perhaps the only man in the company who had the firmness not to be affected by the preacher. His answer was: "At any other time, Friend Hopkinson, I would lend to thee freely; but not now, for thee seems to be out of thy right senses."

Whitefield was no less effective in endeavoring to save souls. In 1739, on his second visit to the colonies, he conducted a revival campaign from Philadelphia to New York, and back to the South. In 1740, a crowd of 30,000 people assembled in the Boston Common for his farewell sermon. But this was not the last of Whitefield's many preaching journeys to America. In 1770 he died in Massachusetts, and was buried in the First Presbyterian Church in Newburyport. So greatly was he esteemed that five years later his grave was opened so that American soldiers could divide his garments into small patches to carry with them as amulets as they set off on a dismally unsuccessful expedition to liberate Quebec from the British and the Pope.

Revivalist emphasis on a strongly emotional personal experience of salvation had lasting effects in North America. The evangelist Gilbert Tennent took up where Whitefield left off, preaching to crowds numbering scarcely fewer in number than those who attended Whitefield's sermons. A Great Awakening also occurred in Canada, especially in Nova Scotia in the 1770s, and a Second Great Awakening began in the 1790s in New England, and continued into the first decade of the nineteenth century. By then the revival focused a massive evangelical effort for moral renewal and missions to the "heathen" around the world. Protestant denominations had been slow (with some exceptions, such as the Moravians) to missionize, being too busy maintaining their beliefs and institutions against Roman Catholics and each other to undertake world missions until the end of the eighteenth century. Moreover, Protestants had no ready-made task force like the Catholic monastic orders. The great age of Protestant missions, based in the United States, occurred in the nineteenth century.

Jonathan Edwards' Reformed Theology

Jonathan Edwards (1703–58) a Calvinist clergyman, is credited with originating the First Great Awakening by his preaching at the Congregational Church of Northampton, Massachusetts. His teaching that the church and the world are separate, and that the church must be gathered *out of* the world, made him the "father of modern congregationalism." Edwards was elected president of "New Jersey College" (now Princeton University) in 1757, but he died in 1758. Edwards fused Locke's teaching that all ideas originate in sensation, the Enlightenment view of nature, and Calvin's sense of God's majesty. His *Personal Narrative* described his conversion as marked by a new sense of the beauty and goodness of the created world. He wrote:

> I walked abroad alone, in a solitary place in my father's pasture, for contemplation. And as I was walking there, and looking up on the sky and clouds, there came into my mind so sweet a sense of the glorious majesty and grace of God, which I know not how to express. I seemed to see them both in sweet conjunction; majesty and meekness joined together. . . . The appearance of everything was altered; there seemed to be, as it were, a calm, sweet caste, or appearance of divine glory in everything: in the sun, moon, and stars; in the clouds and blue sky; in the grass, flowers, trees; in the water and all nature.

However, Edwards critiqued the Enlightenment glorification of reason, finding reason incapable of comprehending Christian doctrines like predestination. He wrote his major philosophical work, *The Freedom of the Will* to combat Arminianism (the belief that divine sovereignty and human free will are compatible and that people must *choose* Christ if their election is to be effective) by attacking it on its strongest ground, its affirmation of the will's capacity to choose or resist divine grace. Edwards maintained Calvin's insistence that divine grace is irresistible by distinguishing predestination from compulsion. Clearly, revivals focused attention on the individual's capacity for choice, but Edwards and other Calvinist preachers insisted that God's will precedes and prompts individual choice.

Edwards' theology was influenced by the decisions of the Synod of Dort, the Westminster Assembly, and the Puritanism of his immediate ancestors. Balancing his strong sense of the determinism caused by sin and his belief in humans' ability to choose, Edwards' synthesis managed both to highlight God's omnipotence and to maintain human freedom. Only God enjoys absolute independent identity, he said; created beings have a *dependent* identity. Edwards' moral philosophy emerged from his theology. He taught that the "cordial consent of being to being is the definition of beauty and that spiritual beauty is the essential quality of true virtue" (Ahlstrom, 1972: 309).

Edwards was a powerful preacher. The majority of his hearers were the "Half-Way" covenanted offspring of church members (who could not testify that they had received the experience of being "born again"); church members who were "fully covenanted" by baptism and regular participation; and townspeople, who had no formal affiliation with the church, but were required to attend. The most famous of Edwards' sermons, "Sinners in the Hands of an Angry God," shows why the First Great Awakening began among the young people in his church.

> God holds you over the pit of hell, much as one holds a spider, or some loathsome insect over the fire, abhors you, and is dreadfully provoked: his wrath toward you burns like fire: he looks upon you as worthy of nothing else than to be cast into the fire; . . . you are more abominable in his eyes than the most hateful venomous serpent is in ours. . . . And there is no other reason to be given, why you have not dropped into hell since you arose in the morning, but that God's hand has held you up. O sinner! Consider the fearful danger you are in: it is a great furnace of wrath, and you are held over in the hand of that God, whose wrath is provoked and incensed as much against you, as against many of the damned in hell. You hang by a slender thread, with the flames of divine wrath flashing about it, and ready every moment to singe it, and burn it asunder; and you have no interest in any Mediator, and nothing to lay hold of to save yourself, nothing to keep off the flames of wrath, nothing of your own, nothing that you ever have done, nothing that you can do, to induce God to spare you one moment.

Yet Edwards also frequently (though less memorably) described the "joys of heaven" in vivid detail. He became the chief New England spokesman for a somewhat restrained type of revivalism. His *Treatise Concerning Religious Affections* criticized the emotional excesses of the First Great Awakening, both advocating and reinterpreting religious experience and experiential religion. For Edwards, "true religion, in great part, consist[ed] in holy affections," but he also insisted that true religion is "conformed to, and directed by, Christian rules."

Edwards was forced to resign from his pastorate in Northampton when, distressed by lax standards for church membership, he proposed to preach a series of sermons on the qualifications for admission to communion. His sermon topic was refused and he was asked to resign. Called to the Stockbridge church, he undertook a double ministry, to whites, and to Indians whose exploitation he fought.

For Edwards, experiential faith must always balance doctrine.

Religion in the Western United States

Finally, although it is common to think of religious influences as originating in the East and moving West along with pioneer settlers, it is important to note that some forms of Christianity, as well as other religions, came from the West and moved East. The West, and especially California (which became a state in 1840) was religiously vigorous and diverse. As the gateway to Asia, California also connected Mexico and Alaska. Spanish Roman Catholics, coming west from the Atlantic, and Russian Orthodox Christians, coming east across the Pacific Ocean, brought with them their cultures, meeting on Californian soil (Ernst, 2001: 37). California hosted diverse forms of Christianity: Mormons, Seventh-Day Adventists, Baptists of many stripes, Swedenborgians, and Spiritualists, in addition to Methodists, Episcopalians, Lutherans, Reformed, Disciples of Christ, Quakers, Unitarians, Congregationalists, and Presbyterians. By the end of the eighteenth century, the experiment in religious diversity granted by the First Amendment and the Bill of Rights was firmly established in the West. Immigrations grew exponentially in the nineteenth century, when Buddhists, Hindus, Jews, Taoists, Confusionists, and others immigrated in large numbers, making California a model of religious diversity.

2   Deism and the Orthodox

The Italian Renaissance was a relatively small movement, involving approximately two hundred scholars and artists, but between the Renaissance and the Enlightenment, the printing press was invented. By the eighteenth century basic literacy was widespread, making printed ideas accessible to large numbers of men and women in France, England, Germany, Scotland, the Netherlands, and Scandinavia. Because of the accessibility of ideas, the Enlightenment was more socially inclusive than any previous religious or social movement. Eighteenth-century people questioned core assumptions about religion, society, public affairs, and institutions.

The Enlightenment brought an erosion of certainty about received religious ideas. A new non-dogmatic religion, Deism, attracted a large audience because its precepts were explained without jargon, erudite language, or tortuous arguments. The term "deism" is synonymous with theism (distinguished from polytheism or atheism), but the resemblance to traditional Christianity ends there. Deism, or belief in a supreme divine being (and not much else), was not an academic debate among a few intellectuals over interpretations of doctrine. Characterized by a fresh spirit of iconoclasm, it offered a simple and reasonable religious system, a commonsense, ethically oriented system emphasizing morality and minimizing theology. Moreover, the orthodox response to deism engaged numerous people who were intensely – sometimes fanatically – concerned about religious issues. One pamphlet by the Deist Matthew Tindale drew 150 published replies.

Deism began in England, was exported to the continent and blossomed in Germany, where it took a different character. It then flowered in France as an alternative to the Roman Catholic Church. Deism presented the first popular alternative to orthodox Christianity.

English Deism

Lord Herbert of Cherbury (d. 1648) was the forerunner of English Deism. Although the name Deism did not exist in his day, he summarized its beliefs: 1) God exists; 2) It is our duty to worship him; 3) The proper way to do so is to practice virtue; 4) People ought to repent of their sins; and 5) Rewards and punishments will follow death. Lord Herbert believed that this creed summarized Christianity, providing all its essentials without need of revelation. In an age fascinated by machines, Deism pictured God as a great clockmaker who had created the universe and then left it to run unassisted.

Reason
John Locke (1632–1704) was educated for the ministry, but turned instead to science (as did many men in his time), and then to politics, spending his last years writing about religion. His influence in all these fields was enormous. His *Essay Concerning Human Understanding* laid the foundation for Deism by identifying reason based on sense perception as the basis of human knowledge.

Thus the first capacity of human intellect is . . . that the mind is fitted to receive the impressions made on it, either by the senses through outward objects, or by its own operations when it reflects on them. This is the first step a person makes toward the discovery of anything, and the groundwork whereon to build all those notions which ever he shall have naturally in this world. All those sublime thoughts that tower above the clouds and reach as high as heaven itself, take their rise and footing here. In all the great extent where the mind wanders, in those remote speculations it may seem to be elevated with, it stirs not one jot beyond those ideas which *sense or reflection have offered for its contemplation.* [emphasis added]

Locke distinguished between truths according to reason, truths above reason, and truths contrary to reason. Nothing in Christianity, he said, is contrary to reason, that is, nothing is inherently incredible or improbable. He gave examples: Arguing from effect to cause, he said that the existence of God is according to reason. The resurrection of the dead, he said, is above reason. The existence of more than one God would be contrary to reason. Since God was the creator of reason, revelation cannot be contrary to reason, but supports reason. Revelation, then, must be accepted, Locke said, on the "credit of the proposer."

Others carried Locke's views further. Where Locke *distinguished* truths according to reason and truths above reason, Deists separated them, questioning, and ultimately rejecting, truths above reason or, at best, accepting a few truths above reason that they considered (by reason) to be helpful for the promotion of ethical living.

By the time of John Locke's death in 1704, it was evident that conflict was not going to produce any uncontested geographic religious boundaries. Civil war and the Restoration, persecution of dissidents, and the Church of England's loss of the monopoly of worship: all combined to mark a turning point to religious co-existence. Religious tolerance developed, not by intent, but by "stalemate disagreements between leading political and religious interests" (Munck, 2000: 133).

Enthusiasm

As advocates of reason, Deists opposed "enthusiasm," religious passions best exemplified by Pietist revivalism. John Locke described enthusiasm as "founded neither on reason, nor on divine revelation, but [rose] from the conceits of a warmed or over-heated brain, . . . the notion of some that whatever groundless opinion comes to settle itself strongly upon their fancies is an illumination from the spirit of God." An enthusiast, Locke said, attempts to "take away reason to make room for revelation, but in so doing, puts out the light of both and does much the same as if he would persuade a man to put out his eyes the better to receive the remote light of an invisible star by a telescope." Even if God does, on occasion, enlighten people's minds to recognize certain truths, or to excite them to good actions by the immediate influence and assistance of the Holy Spirit, God does so in ways that are "consonant to the written word of God and . . . [more importantly, for Locke], conformable to the dictates of right reason" (Essay IV. xi. 6).

Who were the "enthusiasts" in the Age of Reason? John Wesley frequently preached against enthusiasm, and reproved itinerant preachers when he suspected them of such excesses. He criticized enthusiasm as "overvaluing feelings and outward impressions; mistaking the mere work of imagination for the work of the Spirit, expecting the end without the means, and underrating reason, knowledge, and wisdom in general" (Letter to Thomas Maxfield, November 2, 1762).

Yet accusations of enthusiasm were repeatedly brought against Wesley's movement. When Thomas Rutherforth, Regius Professor of Divinity at Cambridge, charged that " 'tis a fundamental principle of the Methodist school that all who come into it must renounce their reason," Wesley replied: "Sir, are you awake? Unless you are talking in your sleep, how can you utter so gross an untruth? It is a fundamental principle with us that to renounce reason is to renounce religion, that religion and reason go hand in hand, and that all irrational religion is false religion."

Locke and Wesley (almost a century later) were in full agreement on the centrality of reason in religion. Perhaps critics who accused Wesley's movement of enthusiasm had their eyes more on the style and dynamics of the revival services than on Wesley's disclaimers of enthusiasm.

The Deist attack on Christianity was prompted by Charles Blount's (d. 1693) "amplification" of the Deist creed. Instead of presenting Deism's positive features, Blount used Deism to critique Christianity, saying that revelation was equivalent to superstition, and Jesus was nothing more than a miracle-worker in an age of miracle-workers. The less radical Deist, John Toland (d. 1722), followed with his work, *Christianity Not Mysterious*, claiming that reason must *judge* revealed truths, although he did not argue that revelation was *against* reason, as did Blount. "True religion," Toland wrote, "must necessarily be reasonable and intelligible. *Next*, I show that these requisite conditions are found in Christianity."

> God is pleased to reveal to us in scripture several wonderful matters of fact, as the creation of the world, the last judgment, and many other important truths, which no one left to himself could ever imagine, no more than any of my fellow creatures can be sure of my private thoughts. Yet we do not receive them only because they are revealed: for beside the testimony of the revelation from all requisite circumstances, we must see in its subject the indisputable character of divine wisdom and sound reason, which are the only marks we have to distinguish the oracles and will of God from the impostures and traditions of men.

Matthew Tindal (1655–1733), in *Christianity as Old as Creation*, urged that "natural religion," unadorned by revelation, is "as old as creation." The Bible and Jesus are "republications" of natural religion. Jesus was an example of how all people can conform to the will of God. But more importantly, God established an orderly universe and gave humans reason to discern and the power to practice what nature shows to be true. God made no further revelation. Reason, Tindal said, is the language of nature.

Nature

The second most overused word of the eighteenth century (next to "reason") was "nature." In 1932 in *The Heavenly City of the Eighteenth-Century Philosophers*, the twentieth-century philosopher, Carl Becker, wrote, "In the eighteenth century climate of opinion, whatever question you seek to answer, nature is the test, the standard: the ideas, customs, the institutions of humans, if ever they are to attain perfection, must obviously be in accord with those laws which nature reveals at all times to all people."

In David Hume's (1711–76) *Dialogues Concerning Natural Religion*, one of the characters defended religion from a Deist perspective:

> Look around the world; contemplate the whole and every part of it; you will find it to be nothing but one great machine, subdivided into an infinite number of lesser machines, which again admit of subdivisions, to a degree beyond what human senses and faculties can trace and explain. All these various machines, and all their minute parts, are adjusted to each other with an accuracy that ravishes into admiration everyone who has ever con-templated them. The curious adapting of means to ends throughout all nature resembles exactly, though it much exceeds, the productions of human intelligence. Since, therefore, the effects resemble each other, we are led to infer that the causes also resemble, and that the author of nature is somewhat similar to the human mind, though possessed of much larger faculties, proportioned to the grandeur of the work that he has executed.

Hume criticized this argument, but the argument itself could not be better stated. Since nature is a machine, God is an engineer, and nature's behavior is natural law.

Deists understood the primary characteristic of nature and natural religion to be *orderliness*. On this subject, deists – middle-class men who valued social as well as natural order – often went into suspiciously religious ecstasies. "I believe in God," Voltaire wrote, "not the God of the mystics and theologians, but the god of nature, the great geometrician, the architect of the universe, the prime mover, unalterable, tran-scendental, everlasting." Newton was thought to have banished mystery by discovering a universal law of nature. As Voltaire commented, "Very few people *read* Newton, because it is necessary to be learned to understand him, but everybody *talks* about him."

What about humans in this clockwork universe? Deists were very concerned with moral virtue. Diderot wrote: "It is not enough to know more than the theologians do; it is necessary to show them that we are better, and that philosophy makes more good men than sufficient or efficacious grace."

Orthodox

Orthodox Christians took up the debate with Deism, agreeing on the arbiter of the con-flict, reason. For two decades in England, 1720 to 1740, excited public debate occurred. Every new pamphlet drew dozens of printed replies. But assumptions on both sides made the debate impossible to resolve. While both agreed on the reality of natural reli-gion, the question was whether natural religion was sufficient. Deists said yes; Chris-tians said no. Three orthodox Englishmen, William Law (1686–1761), George Berkeley (1686–1753), and Bishop Butler (1692–1752), addressed the debate by attempting to formulate a new understanding of reason.

In the 1730s, Law noticed that several undefined words bore a great deal of weight in Deists' assertions. "Reason provides the only test of truth," they said, but what *is* reason? Tindal had said that Christianity is a "republication of the original religion of nature," but what *is* nature? Law's queries were less important than the deeply felt belief that informed them. "Why," he said, "should God behave according to the canons of human reason?" But Law went beyond what most of his contemporaries could accept by dismissing the role of reason in religion. His subsequent mysticism reinforced the tacit agreement of friends and opponents alike to pay no further philosophical atten-tion to him, even though his *Serious Call to a Devout and Holy Life* (1728) became a best-selling devotional text.

George Berkeley gave the most extreme orthodox response to Deist's religious views. The most important of Berkeley's works were written before he was 28. They were not, however, composed as an answer to Deism, but as an independent philosophical system (illustrating the axiom that a philosophy is not best criticized by an assault on its ideas, but by the construction of a new and more adequate philosophy). Berkeley proposed that ideas are the primary existing entities and that material things exist only when someone perceives them. Only minds have an active independent existence derived from God, the perfect intelligence. It apparently boggled Berkeley's mind, however, to imagine the consequences of his dictum that objects, when not being perceived, do not exist. He hastily added that God is the ultimate perceiver who *always* perceives the world and everything in it, thus guaranteeing the continuous existence of material entities. Berkeley also accepted, but did not expound on, revelation.

Berkeley's theory of the primary existence of ideas led an English undergraduate, Ronald Knox, to compose the following limerick: "There was a young man who said, 'God/ Must think it exceedingly odd/ If he finds that this tree/ Continues to be/ When there's no one about in the quad.' Reply: 'Dear Sir: Your astonishment's odd/ *I* am always about in the quad/ And that's why the tree/ Will continue to be/ Since observed by/ Yours faithfully,/ God.'"

Bishop Butler's *The Analogy of Religion, Natural and Revealed, to the Constitution and Course of Nature* was the most direct attack on Deism in England. Butler attacked the confident assumption that reason can eliminate all mystery, superstition, ambiguity, and – in society – all inhumanity. His argument, which he saw as against Deists' facile self-confidence, was essentially for modesty in thought. Deists hoped, by staying in an area of well-illuminated knowledge (natural religion), to avoid the mysteries of revealed religion. Butler demolished this by pointing to the mystery of nature itself. He claimed that, because ambiguity and uncertainty are a permanent feature of all human thought, no complete system of thought is possible on the basis of reason alone.

> Have we any right to ask that religion reveal more clarity than nature does? We know the ordinary course of nature and find it pervaded by ambiguity and uncertainty; if the precepts of religion are marked by analogous obscurity and difficulty then it is reasonable to assume that the one kind of knowledge is only as dependable as the other.

An even more drastic statement of the superficiality of confidence in reason came from David Hume (1711–76). Although the full philosophical and theological implications of Hume's philosophy cannot be explored here, its implications for religious thought should be noted. Hume had no positive theological program, but he decisively dismembered the glib rationalism of the first half of the eighteenth century. Deism was not alone in suffering from Hume's attack; Christianity suffered too, as Hume's skepticism questioned *both* reason and revelation. Rejecting Locke's "innate ideas," Hume insisted that the human mind owes everything it knows to perception and to the sensations that shape and form the mind. "Since human beings and their minds were shaped by nature as created by God," it is possible for people "barely by the use of the natural faculties," to bring their ideas, their conduct, and their institutions into "harmony with the universal natural order." Revealed religion is unnecessary.

For Hume, philosophy was essentially critique, an intellectual exercise. It was not, and should not attempt to be, an attempt to outline what can be known. Because he advocated nothing and criticized everything, Hume was not doctrinaire; he had no cause, not even toleration. He proposed a new idea: the *study* of religion. Hume explored people's beliefs, proceeding through analysis and induction to identify the principles around which those beliefs were formed. His method was empirical: observation and the search for structural principles, bypassing metaphysical subtleties, dogma, and revelation.

German Deism

In Germany Deism was shaped by scholarly rather than religious interests. Gotthold Lessing (1729–81), son of a Lutheran pastor, claimed the freedom to form his own ideas of religion, saying: "The true Lutheran does not wish to be defended by Luther's writings, but by Luther's spirit, and Luther's spirit absolutely requires that no one may be prevented from advancing in the knowledge of the truth according to his own judgment" (quoted by Chadwick, 1956: 23). Lessing was uninterested in Christianity as a historically revealed religion. The accidental truths of history can never become the proof of necessary truths of reason, he said. He was interested primarily in morality, and he studied the Old and New Testaments in original languages for their moral instructions.

Lessing was perhaps the first person in history to treat scripture as "texts" to be studied rather than as religious illumination. Although he studied scripture differently, however, his interpretation was remarkably similar to that of generations of Christian preachers, authors, and teachers. He characterized scripture as describing the development of the human race in three stages: the childhood stage of the Old Testament, characterized by rewards and punishments; the youth stage of the New Testament, characterized by ideals of self-surrender and sacrifice; and the adult stage – Lessing's own day, characterized by adherence to the demands and responsibilities of reason.

Lessing's idea of moral stages of humanity was part of a new interest in the critical study of scripture within Lutheranism. German theologians envisioned not only the possibility of new methods of study, but also a far broader area of inquiry. Lessing's liberal Protestantism became the basis for the academic study of scripture, the early history of the Christian churches, the formation of the New Testament canon, and the essential nature of Christian faith. All these came under scrutiny and discussion. German Deism was heavily influenced by Matthew Tindal's words:

> The difference between those who would engross the name Christian to themselves and these Christian Deists, as I may justly call them, is that the former dare not examine into the truth of scripture and doctrine lest they would seem to question the veracity of the scriptures; whereas the latter believe not the doctrines because they are contained in scripture, but the scripture on account of the doctrines.
>
> (*Christianity as Old as Creation*)

Since Christian doctrines were fruitful of humanitarian morality, scripture was worth exploring, the better to elicit its implications for morality.

Eighteenth-century interest in looking at *things*, whether texts or the natural world, led people also to notice society and its ills, and to attempt to do something about them. If God was not responsible for caring for the world, then it was a human responsibility to do so. Thus, most Deists were concerned with social problems. They urged political attention to the daily oppressions of civilized societies. The social conscience and con-sciousness of twentieth-century liberation theologies have precedents in the social sen-sitivity that originated with eighteenth-century thinkers.

READINGS

John Locke, *The Reasonableness of Christianity*
Gotthold Lessing, *The Education of the Human Race*

3　Religion in Eighteenth-century France

In France, the religious picture of the first two-thirds of the eighteenth century – before the French revolution – was "pluralistic." It included Deists, Jansenists, orthodox Roman Catholics, Huguenots, and widespread indifference to matters of religion. It is impor-tant to remember, however, that the Roman Catholics visible to posterity were those who wrote, not the huge majority of faithful believers.

Huguenots

The Huguenot, or Calvinist French Protestant minority, were involved in continuous civil war with the Roman Catholic majority between 1562 and 1598. In 1598 the Edict of Nantes allowed Huguenots full exercise of their religion and even gave them some state support, but the Edict was frequently violated; it was revoked in 1685.

Civil war erupted once again when the Edict of Nantes was revoked, and the Huguenots were considered a disruptive force in France until 1628 when their fortress headquarters, La Rochelle, was destroyed. At that time, about 30,000 Huguenots emi-grated to Holland, Switzerland, England, Prussia, and North America. Others renounced Protestanism and remained in France. By then, Huguenots' numbers were so depleted that they exercised no further influence on French religion and politics. The Huguenot Church was legalized in France in 1802, largely thanks to religious indifference and secularity.

Gallicanism

For a brief time, French Catholics successfully asserted independence from the ecclesi-astical authority of the papacy. The history of Gallicanism, or the struggle for French authority over the French Church, began with the Great Schism of the fourteenth century when Jean Gerson, Chancellor of the University of Paris, and others argued that the state religion of France should not be controlled by an external authority. Gerson even advocated that papal bulls should not be permitted to enter France except with the explicit permission of the king. In 1682 the assembly of the French clergy composed the Gallican Articles, denying the pope's authority over the French Church. The

Articles upheld the decrees of the Council of Constance (1414–17) over those of the pope, and outlined specific freedoms from papal intervention for the Gallican Church. The Gallican Articles were formally withdrawn by the king and clergy in 1693, but Gallican principles continued to be advocated throughout the eighteenth century.

Jansenists

For more than a century, power struggles centered on a papal bull of Clement XI, *Unigenitus*, (1713), condemning Jansenism. Henceforth, Jesuits, Jansenists, and ecclesiastical leaders were grouped around their inclination to support or reject the bull. *Unigenitus* rejected Cornelius Jansen's idea that humans are utterly helpless in relation to God's grace. The disagreement was so intense that *Unigenitus* was enacted into civil law; a ruling was added stipulating that no one could take communion from, or otherwise use the services of any priest who had not accepted *Unigenitus*. Even on his/her deathbed, no one was permitted to receive extreme unction from any dissenting priest. Many dramatic deathbed struggles resulted from this ruling. Finally the king prohibited all discussion of *Unigenitus*, but without effect. Opponents of the bull continued to appeal to Gallican principles, while Jesuits worked against Gallicanism to reinforce the authority of the pope and papal influence (a position known as *ultramontanism* in that authority came from over the mountains). These religious disputes had two results, widespread anticlericalism, and (a century later) the reinstatement of the Jesuit Order (1814).

A Jansenist weekly newspaper, dedicated to relaying developments in the struggle between Jansenists and Jesuits, was a pioneering venture in adversarial journalism. The *Nouvelles ecclésiastiques* informed and directed its public "toward those people and institutions it was supposed to endorse and pitted it against those it was to oppose." The *Nouvelles ecclésiastiques* did not so much find as create its own public. The journal cost only six sols per issue and had a circulation of about six thousand copies, causing the archbishop of Paris to claim that "three quarters of Paris [were] infected with that doctrine" (Van Kley, 1996: 95–7).

No powerful leader rose in France to offer an alternative to popular anticlericalism. Pietism never caught on in France, though the few remaining Jansenists exhibited touches of revival enthusiasm. Enclaves of fanatic Jansenists captured temporary attention as they spoke in tongues, worked themselves into frenzied states in which they prophesied and claimed to perform miracles, practiced self-torture in public, and preached an apocalyptic message. There were also miraculous cures at the tomb of a young Jansenist that excited Parisians briefly until the government intervened and closed the cemetery. The fanatic fringe of the Jansenists, although repudiated by mainstream Jansenists, attracted attention and persisted, despite persecution, for over 40 years. But Jansenism was never the broadly supported religious outlook that its opponents claimed and feared.

Quietism

Quietism emerged at least partly in reaction to seventeenth-century religious conflicts, originated by a Spaniard, Miguel de Molinas (1640–97). Quietism disparaged all religious efforts and advocated passivity, the surrender or annihilation of the will to God. According to Quietist spirituality, no outward works were considered necessary or valuable, neither almsgiving, confession, nor even worship. Quietists believed that it was possible to rest so completely in God that one no longer cared about heaven, feared hell, or even hoped for one's own salvation. This state of quietude was reached by practicing meditative techniques that eliminated thoughts, methods, and secular or religious attachments. One of the movement's advocates, François Fenelon (1651–1715), wrote:

> As to the subject of your meditations, take such passages of the Gospels or of the *Imitation of Christ* as move you most. Read slowly, and when a passage touches you, use it as you would a candy, which you hold in your mouth until it melts. Let the meaning sink slowly into your heart, and do not pass on to something else until you feel that to be exhausted.

Miguel de Molinas wrote, "He who loves God in the way that reason argues or the intellect understands does not love the true God." Quietism was condemned by papal bull in 1687, but it was still attractive to many. It was practiced and promoted in France by Madame Guyon (1648–1717) as well as François Fenelon. A French translation of Miguel de Molinas's extremely popular devotional manual, *Spiritual Guide*, also kept interest in Quietism alive.

Eighteenth-century France was a solidly Catholic nation with a Church possessing extensive wealth, privilege, and authority. It was a Church with intellectual vigor and spiritual vitality, although perhaps more as the result of its history than of its present. It was also, however, a church resented for its wealth and worldliness, with a widening gulf between its preaching clergy and its powerful (and still, despite the Council of Trent's requirements, often absent) bishops. On the eve of the French revolution, only one of 130 bishops was a commoner; these figures were reversed in the case of the working clergy.

French Deism

The tone of Deism in France was different from either that of England, where Deism was primarily philosophical, or Germany, where Deism inspired scholarly exploration of Christian scripture and history. In France, strongly fueled by anticlerical feeling, Deism was a more popular movement than it was in England or Germany.

Voltaire (the pseudonym of François-Marie Arouet, 1694–1778) introduced Deism to France after his sojourn in London in 1726–9. Voltaire was impressed by England as a country of "rationalist philosophy, just social institutions, and religious toleration," an idealistic picture that he presented to his fellow countrymen in his *Lettres sur l'Anglais*. Voltaire had been educated by the Jesuits and *hated* it. He was in the Bastille twice for his heavily sarcastic anti-religious ideas. He abhorred the Catholic Church, accusing it of massive deceit, exploitation, greed, hypocrisy, injustice, intolerance, and persecution of dissidents.

But Voltaire was not simply a reactionary; he also had a positive program. God, in his view, was the impersonal God of nature, not the personal, providential God of

Christians. Voltaire's God was assigned the task of guaranteeing the stability of the universe, not of saving humans, who were never in peril. For Voltaire, God was the wise author of nature, which set a good example for human beings by its orderly behavior. Fascinated by Newton's physics, Voltaire was convinced of the stability of the universe and the natural world – a striking contrast to the foolishness of human beings who will not accept things as they are and learn from them.

Rousseau

Jean-Jacques Rousseau (1712–78) was brought up as a Calvinist in Geneva. He converted to Catholicism in 1728, but in 1754 he returned to Protestantism; finally he became a Deist. He spent much of his adult life in France, and he wrote about religion in the context of a wealthy state church and an impoverished population. His respect and concern for the common people and the humble village priests who served them led him to become one of the most persistent voices raised against abuses. Cumulatively these voices persuaded the government that clerical abuses were so dramatic that the government compelled the church to pay its lower clergy a living wage.

Rousseau was a philosopher and a political thinker as well as a critic of religion. Echoes of Descartes and Pascal appeared in his philosophy, especially Descartes' method of doubt, and Pascal's sense of the simultaneous grandeur and misery of humankind.

> Having thus so to speak assured myself of my own being, I begin to look outside myself, and I observe myself, with a sort of shudder, cast out, lost in this vast universe, and as it were swallowed up in the immensity of beings, without knowing anything of what they are either in an absolute sense, or in relation to one another, or in relation to me. I study them, I observe them, and the first object which is offered me for comparison is myself.
>
> (*The Creed of a Priest of Savoy*: 11)

Voltaire and Rousseau disagreed with each other. Voltaire rejected religion because he found it irrational and unnecessary. Rousseau accepted religion because he found it rational and necessary. Rousseau's "natural man," the so-called "noble savage," his paradigm of goodness, was guided by the natural light to be a good husband and a kind father. Rousseau did not discuss the possibility that his "noble savage" might also be guided by the "natural light" to eat other human beings. In fact, Rousseau valued the noble savage for all the wrong reasons, namely, for his innocence of civilization and lack of reason. Voltaire noticed this problem immediately. In 1754, Rousseau sent his *Essay on Inequality* to Voltaire, who replied:

> I have received your new book against the human race and thank you for it. Never was such cleverness used in the design of making us all look stupid. One longs, in reading your book, to crawl on all fours. But as I have lost the habit for more than sixty years, I feel unhappily the possibility of resuming it. Nor can I embark in search of the savages of Canada, because the maladies to which I am condemned render a European surgeon necessary to me, because war is going on in those regions, and because the example of our actions has made the savages nearly as bad as ourselves.
>
> (Quoted by Russell, 1965: 688)

Voltaire's savages, at least, were guided by reason, to eat only Jesuits!

Rousseau's *Social Contract* opens with the words, "Man is born free, and everywhere he is in chains." This state of bondage was the result of "civilization." Rousseau saw the sciences, for example, as inherently dangerous; even the medical sciences, he said, have not alleviated physical misery, since civilization itself causes many diseases of stress and overindulgence. But most of all, according to Rousseau, the sciences are wasted time and effort because they do not inculcate virtue. The state of nature is the true state of freedom, and the best the civilized state can do is to attempt to reflect this state of nature by legislating laws that limit the damages and destructiveness of man to man. Rousseau advocated what he called "civil religion" which forbids intolerance, recognizing only religion that does not claim to possess absolute truth.

Rousseau was the first author since Augustine to write a detailed autobiography. It was a curious combination of self-admiration and self-flagellation. He wrote about his complicated life, as Bertrand Russell delicately put it, "without any slavish regard for truth," exaggerating both his wickedness and his virtue. Rousseau's own life contrasted strangely with his ideal picture of the "life according to nature," by which he meant natural, spontaneous goodness, and simplicity of motivation and action. Converting to Catholicism, he said, for "wholly mercenary reasons," he then reverted to Calvinism and was "kept" by (and stole from) a wealthy woman. He then became secretary to the French Ambassador to Venice. He finally married Térèse le Vasseur "according to nature" in 1745. Térèse bore five children by him, each of whom (if his account is to be believed) he took to an orphanage.

> My third child was thus deposited in a foundling home just like the first two, and I did the same with the two following: I had five in all. This arrangement seemed to me so good, so sensible, so appropriate that if I did not boast of it publicly it was solely out of regard for their mother. In a word, I made no secret of my action because in fact I saw no wrong in it. All things considered, I chose what was best for my children, or what I thought was best.

Térèse's version may have been different, but we do not have it. Bertrand Russell writes, "No one has ever understood what attracted him to her, since she was uneducated, uncouth, and in later years, drank and ran after stable boys." The question might be put somewhat differently: Whatever attracted *her* to *him*, a man who gave away her babies shortly after birth? Rousseau said that he later repented of abandoning his children and tried to find them, but couldn't.

Rousseau's importance for his own and a future century lay in a subtle but profound shift that occurred in his thinking, a shift of fundamental and pervasive importance. For Rousseau, the essence or most characteristic function of human beings was no longer, as in Descartes (and a host of other authors in the history of Christianity), "I think, therefore I am." Rather, as Rousseau said, "I feel, therefore I am."

> For us to exist is to feel; our sensitivity incontestably comes before our intelligence, and we have feelings before ideas. Whatever the cause of our being, it has provided for our preservation by giving us feelings suitable to our nature; and it cannot be denied that these, at least, are innate. Man does not have an innate knowledge of the good, but as soon as his reason makes him recognize it, his conscience moves him to love it; it is this sentiment which is inborn. Conscience! conscience! divine instinct, immortal and celestial voice; sure

guide of an ignorant and fallible being, but intelligent and free; infallible judge of good and evil, which makes man like God! It is you who makes the excellence of his nature and the morality of his actions; without you I feel nothing in me which raises me above the beasts except the sad privilege of wandering from error to error with the help of an unguided understanding and an unprincipled reason.

(*Creed of a Priest of Savoy*: 42)

Rousseau rejected innate ideas of justice, God, and morality. But he did not propose Locke's *tabula rasa*, or blank slate waiting to be written upon by sense perception. Rather, he advocated "an inborn principle of justice and virtue," which he called "conscience." Conscience is evident, he said, in *feelings*, not in reason. Rousseau's eulogy of conscience in the quotation above might even be considered "enthusiastic."

There were problems with Rousseau's identification of feeling as innate, as Kant was soon to see, but the introduction of a new possibility of essential human activity came at exactly the right time, the time of the greatest discouragement with rationalism. The Jewish philosopher Spinoza, as well as other seventeenth-century rationalists, believed that rationality would preclude violence, especially the violence of religious wars. But, in the last years of Rousseau's life, the French Revolution rationalized civil war and murder in the interest of social justice, demonstrating reason's compatibility with violence and destroying faith in reason's ability to eliminate bloodshed. Rousseau himself was threatened by the Revolution and fled to Geneva. As historian Gerald Cragg wrote, "the age which esteemed reason, order, and stability above all things ended in one of the most convulsive upheavals of human history, the French Revolution."

In the context of discouragement with reason, Rousseau proposed a new authority, feeling. His critique of philosophy occurred most pointedly in his *Discourses*, where he wrote:

General and abstract ideas are the source of the greatest errors in people. I do not draw rules from the principles of a lofty philosophy, but I find them deep in my heart, written by Nature in indelible characters. I have only to consult myself about what I wish to do: all that I feel to be good is good; all that I feel to be evil is evil. . . . Thank heaven [he concludes] here we are freed of all this frightful machinery of philosophy. We can be human beings without being scholars.

(*Discourses* I. 60–1)

Rousseau's claims for feeling went beyond ethics. He proposed a new basis for knowledge: "I know it because I feel it," as well as a new religious authority: conscience.

If rationalism no longer provided a trustworthy basis for religion or politics, there was need for a firm and compelling basis for morality. If reason based on nature was unconvincing, perhaps feeling based on nature would serve as a basis for morality. "Let us obey nature," Rousseau wrote, "which gives us an inborn *feeling* of justice and virtue." The nineteenth-century Romantics extended this to "Let us obey *passion*," but for Rousseau, the first duty of feeling was to accept and reinforce custom and convention. Religion was also to be based on convention rather than conviction! Rousseau's version of the "return of the prodigal son" at the end of the *Creed of a Priest of Savoy*, has the priest urging the prodigal to return, not to the Father, but to conscience!

Rousseau addressed individuals, not communities or society. Just as personal pronouns predominated Charles Wesley's hymns ("it was for *me*, for *me* Jesus died"), so personal pronouns fill the *Creed*. In other contexts Rousseau described convention almost as the original evil, but he thought it is as good a guide as any to religion. Rousseau never doubted that society needs the stabilizing influence of belief in God. Describing what he recognized as the supreme enjoyment (which for former authors had been a mystical, or beatific vision of God), Rousseau did not hesitate to write: "The supreme enjoyment is in satisfaction with oneself; it is to merit this satisfaction that we are placed on earth and endowed with liberty, that we are tempted by passions and constrained by conscience."

Many differences distinguish Rousseau's philosophy of feeling and Wesley's religion of feeling and personal appropriation. Yet both identify feeling as the way to organize knowledge, religion, and morality. Before Rousseau, philosophers gave rational reasons, if not proofs, for the existence of God; Rousseau defended religious belief on the basis of the *feeling* that God exists. After him, philosophers and theologians appropriated this new authority, basing religious belief on feelings of awe or mystery, a sense of right and wrong, feelings of inspiration and aspiration, or a feeling of absolute dependence (Schleiermacher). This way of defending religious belief originated with Rousseau.

READING

Rousseau, *Emile*, "The Creed of a Priest of Savoy"

Jews

Although anti-Semitism was strong in other parts of Europe, French Jews benefited from the Revolution (1789). The Declaration of the Rights of Man and the Citizen stated that "rights resided in individuals, not in governments or institutions" (Carroll, 2001: 414). Since rights are not granted, they cannot be taken away. The French National Assembly's Law Relating to Jews (1791) made it clear that Jews were full citizens of France. However, it also assumed that Jewishness existed only in the private practice of religion. Jews were not thought of as a "people," and the multifaceted complexity of Jewish life was not recognized. Ambiguous as it was, however, the French Revolution provided full citizenship to Jews who had not been full citizens of a state anywhere in the world since before the destruction of Jerusalem in 70 CE (Carroll, 2001: 416).

The eighteenth-century enlightenment affected European Jews differently in different nations. In Austria, a royal edict (1781) protected the religious and civic rights of non-Catholics, including Jews, but English Jews did not obtain full political rights until almost a century later, in 1858–60. Italian Jews were granted citizenship in 1859–70, and Swiss Jews in 1874. In Eastern Europe, Russian Jews suffered increasingly until the Bolshevik Revolution in 1917.

In 1800 only a handful of Jewish congregations existed in the United States. Immigration from Germany during the nineteenth century increased eightfold the number of Jewish congregations and brought new religious and cultural communities to enhance America's religious diversity.

Epilogue

The last quarter of the eighteenth century brought changes so fundamental to politics, religion, philosophy, literature, and social arrangements that it has been called an age of cultural revolutions. Together, the French Revolution, the American Revolution, and the British Industrial Revolution produced modernity. In philosophy and theology, modernity entered with Kant's simultaneous completion and critique of the Enlightenment. But cultural revolutions are not produced by single moments, events, or books. They involve a set of relations that are constantly being made and unmade, contested and reconfigured, that nonetheless produce among their contemporaneous witnesses *"the conviction of historical difference"* (Jones and Wahrman, 2002: 65; emphasis added).

Modernity can be characterized in a number of ways. Politically, national differences became as intransigent as religious differences had been. In the public sphere, the relationship between church and state was no longer characterized as "spiritual" versus "temporal," but as private versus public. On the level of the individual, the "great ideological construct of modernity [was] belief in the individual, centered subject with an essentialized, clearly-demarcated, and always classifiable stable self" (Jones and Wahrman, 2002: 280). The modern individual's identity was private and interior, not public and communal. At the end of the eighteenth century, the conviction of historical *difference* is attested by evidence in diverse arenas of public and private life.

Modernity was a movement toward various forms of liberation, flawed by countermovements that constantly contested and sought to reverse the "progress" attempted and achieved. Eighteenth-century experience was marked "as closely by slavery as by liberty; by racial, class, and gender exclusions as by universality" (Jones and Wahrman, 2002: 66). Newly solidified categories of race, gender, and class excluded most people from the gains fought for by many, but enjoyed by few. For example, among those excluded by the "idea of equality" in the new United States, American historian Ray Raphael lists: "women who could not vote, almost half a million slaves, somewhere between 110,000 and 150,000 Native Americans, [and] about 80,000 to 100,000 loyalists" (Raphael, 2002: 388). Nevertheless, the *rhetoric* of liberation carried a momentum that began a long struggle for social justice.

No single author can fully represent the turn to modernity, but Kant's philosophy amounted to a watershed between what had gone before and the modern world. An Enlightenment Deist, Kant rejected anthropomorphic religion and found revelation unnecessary; he labeled miracles, rituals, prayers, and sacraments superstitious. Moreover, he undermined not only traditional metaphysics, but also Enlightenment reliance on reason. What counts as knowledge, he said, is not knowledge of things in themselves, but the form the mind gives to perceptions that come to it from outside itself. Experience consists both of perceptions, and of what the mind does with them.

Deist predecessors can be detected in Kant's philosophy, but his ideas of religion were distant from the traditional Lutheranism of his childhood and youth. For Kant, religion was primarily about ethics. Rather than basing morality on the premise of a just God who judges and condemns or rewards, Kant proposed reliance on a "categorical imperative" or *intuition* of moral obligation. Starting with a subjective conviction of "duty," Kant deduced a God who produces this conviction. He did not claim to "prove" God's existence, only to present it as a hypothesis. To accept the hypothesis that God is the author of a categorical imperative is to interpret that imperative as a divine command. Although Kant did not develop his ideas of religion into a system, other Protestant philosophers and theologians did. Fichte, Schelling, and Hegel were the best known of the nineteenth-century thinkers Kant inspired.

No nineteenth-century theologian or philosopher could ignore Kant's rejection of metaphysics and revealed religion. Of course, that is not to say that everyone agreed with him; evangelicals, orthodox Protestants, and Roman Catholics reacted strongly against his serene rejection of traditional religion and his concentration on religion as morality. Nevertheless, in philosophy and theology, modernity began with Kant.

Postlude: The Word Made Flesh

For Christians the meaning of the Incarnation of God in Jesus Christ is not that it *transcends* time and place. Rather, in every generation Christians reinterpret the significance of Jesus' life and death in relation to the circumstances in which they live. Commitment to the church as the Body of Christ has not required that others' interpretations must be adopted, but that Christians participate in a centuries-long communal *activity* of interpretation. As Irenaeus, said, tradition is carried forward in warm bodies; it is not fully represented by writings on parchment or paper.

The doctrine that God became incarnate in human flesh states that Jesus accepted the human condition. But what does it mean to accept the human condition? Which features of human experience are quintessentially "human?" Early Christians debated this question. Tertullian said that a normal human birth made Jesus Christ "fully human." Irenaeus said that the essential human experience is progress through various stages of life; thus Jesus became "a child among children, a young man among young people, and a grown man among older people." Athanasius said that death is the normative human experience, and his interpretation, vividly pictured in many crucifixion scenes, has dominated Christian theology. Accepting the human condition has been interpreted primarily as sharing human suffering and mortality.

One of the most significant insights of the latter part of the twentieth century was the irreducible importance of perspective in all human knowledge. Perspective, composed of many elements (such as social location, age, race, ethnicity, gender, class, education, and other variables), both enables and limits one's ability to notice and understand. Using sensitivity to perspective as an interpretive lens, it becomes evident that in accepting human flesh, Jesus also accepted the human limitation of perspective. His words and actions responded directly to the problems of his own society. Speaking and working effectively within the framework of a *particular* social experience, Jesus taught ideas, attitudes, and values that have influenced his followers through the centuries of the common era. His life and teachings have been continually *worked with*, interpreted in relation to the concrete circumstances of particular lives and societies, rather than imitated in any literal way. General principles can be abstracted from Jesus' words and actions to govern Christian behavior in different circumstances than his, but these are useful only when interpreted in the context of particular situations. *Imagination*, trained and exercised by meditating on Jesus' words and actions, is essential to the fresh interpretation of Christian values in the present. Imagination generates "new insights, insights which the Christian may legitimately regard as revelation, not merely human responses but divinely motivated" (Brown 2000: 31).

Studying the history of Christian thought reveals that no single historical moment is normative for "Christian thought," neither its origins nor the present. Christian thought is, rather, an activity conducted within the particular circumstances of Christians' lives. For example, in societies in which the morality of slavery was unquestioned, Jesus' esteem for the marginalized and outcast of his society remained unrealized. In societies in which women's and men's roles were rigidly defined in opposition to one another, Jesus' exclusion of women from the ranks of his immediate disciples went unnoticed. In societies in which pain was common and unrelieved, Jesus' suffering and death were constantly visualized and articulated. Yet each of these traditional interpretations is presently criticized.

To follow the many interpretations of the doctrine of the Incarnation of God in Jesus Christ that lay at the heart of Christianity from the earliest conflicts within Christian communities to the eve of modernity (and beyond), is to notice *both* the pervasive influence of belief in Jesus' "life-bearing flesh," and its inadequate realization. The revolutionary idea of the Word made flesh has carried a momentum that challenges cultural commonplaces, but it is also evident that the implications of the belief that God became human have not yet been fully explored. Wars, persecutions, unjust distribution of wealth, and unjust social arrangements have been, and are, so common as to appear "natural" in the everyday life in Western societies influenced by Christianity.

Noticing the pervasive influence of the "Word made flesh" requires a new sense of what constitutes "Christian thought," making such features as devotional practices, liturgies, images, and music *primary evidence* of Christianity. These represent the ongoing "fleshing out" of the Word, alongside verbal interpretation. The sexism, exclusions, persecutions of dissidence, and self-righteous wars of Christian history, tell yet another story, one that must be held in tension with the triumphal story. Neither can be collapsed into the other as the "real" story.

The religion of the incarnate Word consists of the struggle to "keep body and soul together." It is a *project* of comprehending, incorporating, and participating in the "Body of Christ." Addressing the deep human longing for integrity of body and soul, Christianity makes the wildly counter-evidential, counter-cultural claim that "in my flesh shall I see God." The meaning of that claim can never be definitively articulated, but it forms and informs historical and contemporary Christians who seek to understand it, not only conceptually, but also, and more importantly, *in the life.*

Bibliography

Prelude: Flesh and Word

Carroll, Kenneth (1978) "Early Quakers and 'Going Naked as a Sign,'" *Quaker History*, 67, 69–87.

Darnton, Robert (1984) *The Great Cat Massacre*. New York: Vintage.

Drake, Hal (2000) *Constantine and the Bishops: The Politics of Intolerance*. Baltimore: Johns Hopkins University Press.

Gallagher, Catherine and Greenblatt, Stephen (2000) *Practicing New Historicism*. Chicago: University of Chicago Press.

Glucklich, Ariel (2001) *Sacred Pain: Hurting the Body for the Sake of the Soul*. Oxford: Oxford University Press.

Chapter 1: The Christian Movement in the Second and Third Centuries

1 Christians in the Roman Empire

Benko, Stephen (1986) *Pagan Rome and the Early Christians*. Bloomington: Indiana University Press.

Bowersock, G. W. (1995) *Martyrdom and Rome*. Cambridge: Cambridge University Press.

Bradshaw, Paul F. (2002) *The Search for the Origins of Christian Worship*. New York: Oxford University Press.

Brown, Peter (1971) *The World of Late Antiquity*. New York: Harcourt, Brace, Jovanovich.

Carroll, James (2001) *Constantine's Sword: The Church and the Jews*. Boston: Houghton Mifflin.

Castelli, Elizabeth A. and Taussig, Hal (eds.) (1996) *Reimagining Christian Origins*. Valley Forge, PA: Trinity Press International.

Dodds, E. R. (1965) *Pagan and Christian in an Age of Anxiety*. New York: W. W. Norton.

Foucault, Michel (1985) *The Use of Pleasure*. Trans. Robert Hurley. New York: Pantheon.

Foucault, Michel (1986) *The Care of the Self*. Trans. Robert Hurley. New York: Vintage Books.

Fox, Robin Lane (1987) *Pagans and Christians*. New York: Knopf.

Frend, W. H. C. (1984) *The Rise of Christianity*. Philadelphia: Fortress.

Futrell, Alison (1997) *Blood in the Arena: The Spectacle of Roman Power*. Austin: University of Texas Press.

Garnsey, Peter (1984) "Religious Toleration in Antiquity," in *Persecution and Toleration*. Oxford: Basil Blackwell.

Glancy, Jennifer (2002) *Slavery in Early Christianity*. New York: Oxford University Press.

Miles, Margaret R. (1981) *Fullness of Life: Historical Foundations for a New Asceticism*. Philadelphia: Westminster.

Nussbaum, Martha (1994) *The Therapy of Desire*. Princeton: Princeton University Press.

Perkins, Judith (1995) *The Suffering Self: Pain and Narrative Representation in the Early Christian Era*. New York: Routledge.

Porter, James I. (ed.) (2002) *Constructions of the Classical Body*. Ann Arbor: University of Michigan Press.

Turcan, Robert (1996) *The Cults of the Roman Empire.* Oxford: Blackwell.
Wimbush, Vincent L. (1996) " 'Not of This World': Early Christianities as Rhetorical and Social Formation," in Elizabeth A. Castelli and Hal Taussig (eds.), *Reimagining Christian Origins*, New York: Oxford University Press.

2 The First Theologians

Richardson, Cyril C. (ed.) (1970) *Early Christian Fathers.* New York: Macmillan.
Robinson, James M. (ed.) (1977) *The Nag Hammadi Library.* Leiden: E. J. Brill.

Irenaeus

Donovan, Mary Ann (1997) *One Right Reading? A Guide to Irenaeus.* Collegeville, MN: Liturgical Press.
King, Karen L. (1996) "Mackinations on Myth and Origins," in Elizabeth A. Castelli and Hal Taussig (eds.), *Reimagining Christian Origins*, Valley Forge, PA: Trinity Press International.

Clement of Alexandria

Chadwick, Henry (ed.) (1954) *Alexandrian Christianity*, Philadelphia: Westminster Press.
Grant, Robert M. (1986) "Theological Education at Alexandria," in Birger Pearson and James E. Goehring (eds.), *The Roots of Egyptian Christianity*. Philadelphia: Fortress, Studies in Antiquity and Christianity, pp. 178–89.

Origen

Caspary, Gerard E. (1979) *Politics and Exegesis: Origen and the Two Swords.* Berkeley: University of California Press.
Fox, Robin Lane (1987) *Pagans and Christians.* New York: Alfred A. Knopf.
Origen (1973) *On First Principles*, Trans. G. W. Butterworth. Glouchester, MA: Peter Smith.
Smalley, Beryl (1964) *The Study of the Bible in the Middle Ages.* South Bend, IN: Notre Dame.

Trinitarian controversy in the second and third centuries

Pelikan, Jaroslav (1971) *The Emergence of the Catholic Tradition.* Chicago: University of Chicago Press.
Rusch, William G. (1980) *The Trinitarian Controversy.* Philadelphia: Fortress.

3 Constructing Christian Churches

Church organization

Ash, James L. Jr. (1976) "The Decline of Ecstatic Prophecy in the Early Church," *Theological Studies*, 37(2), June.
Frend, W. H. C. (1984) *The Rise of Christianity.* Philadelphia: Fortress.
Laeuchli, Samuel (1972) *Power and Sexuality: The Emergence of Canon Law at the Synod of Elvira.* Philadelphia: Temple University Press.

Women in Christian churches

Benko, Stephen (1993) *The Virgin Goddess: Studies in the Pagan and Christian Roots of Mariology.* Leiden: E. J. Brill.

Clark, Gillian (1993) *Women in Late Antiquity*. New York: Oxford University Press.

Elliott, Dyan (1993) *Spiritual Marriage: Sexual Abstinence in Medieval Wedlock*. Princeton: Princeton University Press.

Fiorenza, Elisabeth Schüssler (1985) *In Memory of Her*. New York: Crossroad.

Kloppenborg, John S. (1996) "Egalitarianism in the Myth and Rhetoric of Pauline Churches," in Elizabeth A. Castelli and Hal Taussig (eds.), *Reimagining Christian Origins*. Valley Forge, PA: Trinity Press International.

The first Christian images

Finney, Paul Corby (1994) *The Invisible God: The Earliest Christians on Art*. New York: Oxford University Press.

Gough, Michael (1973) *The Origins of Christian Art*. London: Thames and Hudson.

Grabar, Andre (1968) *Christian Iconography: A Study of its Origins*. Princeton: Princeton University Press.

Jensen, Robin (2000) *Understanding Early Christian Art*. New York: Routledge.

Milburn, Robert (1988) *Early Christian Art and Architecture*. Berkeley: University of California Press.

Murray, Charles (1977) "Art and the Early Church," *Journal of Theological Studies*, XXVIII(2), October.

Murray, Peter and Murray, Linda (1996) *The Oxford Companion to Christian Art and Architecture*. New York: Oxford University Press.

Snyder, Graydon F. (1985) *Ante Pacem: Archeological Evidence of Church Life Before Constantine*. Mercer University Press.

Stevenson, J. (1978) *The Catacombs: Rediscovered Monuments of Early Christianity*. London: Thames and Hudson.

Liturgy

Bradshaw, Paul F. (2002) *The Search for the Origins of Christian Worship*. New York: Oxford University Press.

Castelli, Elizabeth A. and Tausig, Hal (eds.) (1996) *Reimagining Christian Origins*. Valley Forge, PA: Trinity Press International.

Church, E. Forrester and Mulry, Terrence J. (eds.) (1988) *Earliest Christian Prayers*. New York: Macmillan.

Church, E. Forrester and Mulry, Terrence J. (eds.) (1988) *Early Christian Hymns*. New York: Macmillan.

Klauser, Theodor (1969) *A Short History of the Western Liturgy*. New York: Oxford University Press.

Chapter 2: Inclusions and Exclusions: The Fourth Century

1 The Evidence of Our Eyes

Abraham, Gerald (1979) *The Concise Oxford History of Music*. Oxford: Oxford University Press.

Barnes, Timothy (1981) *Constantine and Eusebius*. Cambridge: Harvard University Press.

Brown, Peter (1971) *The World of Late Antiquity, AD 150–750*. London: Thames & Hudson.

Campbell, Joseph with Moyers, Bill (1988) *The Power of Myth*, Betty Sue Flowers (ed.), New York: Doubleday.

Chadwick, Henry (1967) *The Early Church*. New York: Penguin.

Drake, Hal (2000) *Constantine and the Bishops: The Politics of Intolerance*. Baltimore: Johns Hopkins University Press.

Frank, Georgia (2001) " 'Taste and See': The Eucharist and the Eyes of Faith in the Fourth Century," *Church History*, 70(4), December.

Laeuchli, Samuel (1972) *Power and Sexuality*. Philadelphia: Temple University Press.

Laeuchli, Samuel (1980) *Religion and Art in Conflict*. Philadelphia: Fortress.

Maguire, Eunice D., Maguire, Henry P., and Duncan-Flowers, Maggie J. (1989) *Art and Holy Powers in the Early Christian House*. Chicago: University of Illinois Press.

Markus, Robert (1990) *The End of Ancient Christianity*. Cambridge: Cambridge University Press.

Matthews, Thomas F. (1993) *The Clash of Gods: A Reinterpretation of Early Christian Art*. Princeton: Princeton University Press.

Miles, Margaret R. (1985) *Image as Insight: Visual Understanding in Western Christianity and Secular Culture*. Boston: Beacon.

Miles, Margaret R. (1989) *Carnal Knowing: Female Nakedness and Religious Meaning*. Boston: Beacon.

Orange, H. P. L. and Nordhagen, P. J. (1958) *Mosaics*. Trans. Ann E. Keep. London: Methuen.

Perkins, Judith (1995) *The Suffering Self: Pain and Narrative Representation in the Early Christian Era*. New York: Routledge.

Sadie, Stanley (ed.) (1980) *The New Grove Dictionary of Music and Musicians, vol. 7*. London: Macmillan.

Sadie, Stanley and Latham, Alison (eds.) (1985) *The Cambridge Music Guide*. Cambridge: Cambridge University Press.

Stevens, John (1986) *Word and Music in the Middle Ages*. New York: Cambridge University Press.

Wilkin, Robert L. "The Nicene Creed in its Historical Setting," unpublished paper.

2 Ascetic Monasticism

Brown, Peter (1988) *The Body and Society: Men, Women, and Sexual Renunciation in Early Christianity*. New York: Columbia University Press.

Chadwick, Owen (ed.) (1958) *Western Asceticism*. Philadelphia: Westminster Press.

Clark, Elizabeth A. (1986) *Ascetic Piety and Women's Faith*. Lewiston: Edwin Mellon Press.

Elm, Susanna (1994) *Virgins of God: The Making of Asceticism in Late Antiquity*. Oxford: Clarendon Press.

Evagrius Ponticus (1978) *The Praktikos*. Trans. John Eudes Bamberger. Kalamazoo, MI: Cistercian Publications.

Harpham, Geoffrey Galt (1987) *The Ascetic Imperative in Culture and Criticism*. Chicago: University of Chicago Press.

Rousseau, Philip (1985) *Pachomius*. Berkeley: University of California Press.

Rousseau, Philip (1988) *Ascetics, Authority, and the Church*. Oxford: Oxford University Press.

Shaw, Teresa (1998) *The Burden of the Flesh: Fasting and Sexuality in Early Christianity*. Minneapolis: Fortress.

Wimbush, Vincent (ed.) (1990) *Ascetic Behavior in Greco-Roman Antiquity*. Minneapolis: Fortress.

Wimbush, Vincent and Valantasis, Richard (eds.) (1995) *Asceticism*. New York: Oxford University Press.

3 Christological Controversy

Barnes, Timothy (1993) *Athanasius and Constantius*. Cambridge: Harvard University Press.

Brakke, David (1995) *Athanasius and the Politics of Asceticism*. New York: Oxford University Press.

Chesnut, Roberta G. (1976) *Three Monophysite Christologies.* New York: Oxford University Press.

Frend, W. H. C (1972) *The Rise of the Monophysite Movement.* Cambridge: Cambridge University Press.

Gregg, R. C. and Groh, Dennis (1981) *Early Arianism: A View of Salvation.* Philadelphia: Fortress.

Hardy, Edward R. (ed.) (1954) *Christology of the Later Fathers.* Philadelphia: Westminster Press.

Pelikan, Jaroslav (1971) *The Emergence of the Catholic Tradition.* Chicago: University of Chicago Press.

Rusch, William G. (1980) *The Trinitarian Controversy.* Philadelphia: Fortress.

4 Church and Empire

Beduhn, Jason David (2000) *The Manichaean Body: Its Discipline and Ritual.* Baltimore: Johns Hopkins University Press.

Brown, Peter (1972) *Religion and Society in the Age of Saint Augustine.* New York: Harper and Row.

Brown, Peter (2000) *Augustine of Hippo.* 2nd edn. Berkeley: University of California Press.

Brown, Peter (1992) *Power and Persuasion in Late Antiquity: Toward a Christian Empire.* Madison: University of Wisconsin Press.

Cochrane, Charles Norris (1968) *Christianity and Classical Culture.* New York: Oxford University Press.

Fox, Robin Lane (1986) *Pagans and Christians.* New York: Knopf.

Gillman, Ian and Klimkeit, Hans-Joachim (1999) *Christians in Asia Before 1500.* Ann Arbor: University of Michigan.

Hardy, Edward R. (1954) *Christology of the Later Fathers.* Philadelphia: Westminster.

Hunter, David G. (1987) "Resistance to the Virginal Ideal in Late Fourth-Century Rome: The Case of Jovinian," *Theological Studies,* 48(1), March.

Lang, David (1976) *Lives and Legends of the Georgian Saints,* Crestwood, NJ: St. Vladimir's Press.

Markus, Robert (1970) *Saeculum: History and Society in the Theology of St. Augustine.* Cambridge: Cambridge University Press.

Miles, Margaret R (1993) "Santa Maria Maggiore's Fifth-Century Mosaics: Triumphal Christianity and the Jews," *Harvard Theological Review,* 86(2), April.

Miles, Margaret R. (1995) " 'Jesus patibilis:' Augustine's Debate with the Manichaeans," in Sang Lee and Wayne Proudfoot (eds.), *Faithful Imaginings: Essays in Honor of Richard R. Niebuhr,* Atlanta: Scholars Press.

Miles, Margaret R. (2000) "North African Christian Spirituality in the Roman Period," in Jacob K. Olupona (ed.), *African Spirituality: Forms, Meanings, and Expressions,* New York: Crossroad.

Rohrbacher, David (2002) *The Historians of Late Antiquity.* New York: Routledge.

Snowden, Frank M. (1994) *Before Color Prejudice: The Ancient View of Blacks.* Cambridge: Harvard University Press.

Tilley, Maureen (1997) *The Bible in Christian North Africa: The Donatist World.* Minneapolis: Fortress.

Van der Meer, Frederic (1961) *Augustine the Bishop.* London: Sheed and Ward.

Williams, N. P. (1930) *The Grace of God.* New York: Longmans, Green and Co.

5 Theological Resolution

Denzinger, Henry (1957) *The Sources of Catholic Dogma.* Trans. Roy J. Defarrari, St Louis: B. Herder.

Dzielska, Maria (1995) *Hypatia of Alexandria.* Cambridge: Harvard University Press.

Fowden, G. (1978) "Bishops and Temples in the Eastern Roman Empire AD 320–435," *Journal of Theological Studies*, n.s. 29, April.

Geary, Patrick J. (1999) "Barbarians and Ethnicity," in Glenn Bowersock (ed.), *Late Antiquity*, Cambridge: Harvard University Press.

Holum, Kenneth G. (1982) *Theodosian Empresses: Women and Imperial Dominion in Late Antiquity*. Berkeley: University of California Press.

Kelly, J. N. D. (1978) *Early Christian Doctrines*. San Francisco: Harper and Row.

McManners, John (ed.) (1993) *The Oxford History of Christianity*. Oxford: Oxford University Press.

Pelikan, Jaroslav (1971) *The Emergence of the Catholic Tradition*. Chicago: University of Chicago Press.

Rusch, William G. (1980) *The Trinitarian Controversy*. Philadelphia: Fortress.

Chapter 3: Fleshing out the Word: Medieval Christianity East and West

1 Eastern Orthodoxy

Baggley, John (1988) *Doors of Perception: Icons and their Spiritual Significance*. Crestwood, NJ: St. Vladimir's Seminary Press.

Barnard, L. W. (1977) *The Graeco-Roman and Oriental Background of the Iconoclastic Controversy*. Leiden: E. J. Brill.

Cavarnos, Constantine (1977) *Orthodox Iconography*. Institute for Byzantine and Modern Greek Studies.

Frary, Joseph P. (1972) "The Logic of Icons," *Sobornost*, 6(6), Winter.

Galavaris, George (1988) *Holy Image, Holy Space: Icons and Frescoes from Greece* (exhibition catolog, Myrtali Acheimastou-Potamianou (ed), Athens: Greek Ministry of Culture.

Galavaris, George (1990) "Early Icons at Sinai from the Sixth to the Eleventh Century," *Sinai: Treasures of the Monastery*. Athens: Ekdotike Athenon.

Le Guillou, M. J. (1962) *The Spirit of Eastern Orthodoxy*. New York: Hawthorn Books.

Lossky, Vladimir (1976) *The Mystical Theology of the Eastern Church*. Crestwood, NJ: St. Vladimir's Seminary Press.

Martin, Edward J. (1962) *A History of the Iconoclastic Controversy*. London: SPCK.

Miles, Margaret R. (1981) *Fullness of Life*. Philadelphia: Westminster Press.

The Painter's Manual of Dionysius of Fourna. (1978) Trans. Paul Hetherington, London: Sagittarius Press.

Pelikan, Jaroslav (1974) *The Spirit of Eastern Christendom, 600–1700*. Chicago: University of Chicago Press.

Rice, David Talbot (1963) *Art of the Byzantine Era*. London: Thames & Hudson.

Weitzman, Kurt (1978) *The Icon*. New York: George Braziller.

2 The Early Medieval West

Bark, William Carroll (1958) *Origins of the Medieval World*. Stanford: Stanford University Press.

Beckwith, John (1964) *Early Medieval Art*. London: Thames & Hudson.

Brentano, Robert (ed.) (1964) *The Early Middle Ages, 500–1000*. Berkeley: University of California Press.

Evans, J. A. S. (1996) *The Age of Justinian: The Circumstances of Imperial Power*. New York: Routledge.

Gillman, Ian and Klimkeit, Hans-Joachim (1999) *Christians in Asia Before 1500*. Ann Arbor: University of Michigan Press.

Harper, John (1991) *The Forms and Orders of Western Liturgy from the Tenth to the Eighteenth Century*. Oxford: Clarendon Press.

Hay, Denys (1964) *The Medieval Centuries*. New York: Harper and Row.

Holmes, George (2001) *The Oxford Illustrated History of Medieval Europe*. Oxford: Oxford University Press.

Muthererich, F. and Gaede, Joachim(1976) *Carolingian Painting*. New York: George Braziller.

Stowe, Kenneth R. (1992) *Alienated Minority: The Jews of Medieval Latin Europe*. Cambridge, MA: Harvard University Press.

Strayer, Joseph R. and Munro, Dana (1942) *The Middle Ages, 395–1500*. New York: Appleton-Century-Crofts.

3 The Ninth and Tenth Centuries in the West

Brooke, Christopher (1982) *Monasteries of the World*. Hertfordshire, England: Omega Books.

Dronke, Peter (1984) *Women Writers of the Middle Ages*. New York: Cambridge University Press.

4 Early Scholasticism

Carroll, James (2001) *Constantine's Sword: The Church and the Jews*. Boston: Houghton Mifflin.

Fairweather, Eugene R. (1970) *A Scholastic Miscellany*. New York: Macmillan.

Leclerq, Jean (1961) *The Love of Learning and the Desire for God*. New York: Fordham University Press.

Morrison, Karl F. (1985) "The Gregorian Reform," in Bernard McGinn, John Meyendorff, and Jean LeClercq (eds.), *Christian Spirituality: Origins to the Twelfth Century*, New York: Crossroad.

Pelikan, Jaroslav (1978) *The Growth of Medieval Theology, 600–1300*. Chicago: University of Chicago Press.

Riley-Smith, Jonathan (1999) *The Oxford History of the Crusades*. Oxford: Oxford University Press.

Chapter 4: The Voice of the Pages: Incarnation and Hierarchy in the Medieval West

1 Twelfth-century Theology, Scholarship, and Piety

Abelard, Peter (1972) *The Story of My Misfortunes*. Trans. Henry Adams Bellows, New York: Macmillan.

Brooke, Rosalind and Brooke, Christopher (1984) *Popular Religion in the Middle Ages: Western Europe 1000–1300*. London: Thames & Hudson.

Carroll, James (2001) *Constantine's Sword: The Church and the Jews*. Boston: Houghton Mifflin.

Eidelberg, Schlomo (1977) *The Jews and the Crusaders: The Hebrew Chronicles of the First and Second Crusades*. Madison: University of Wisconsin Press.

Fairweather, Eugene R. (ed.) (1970) *A Scholastic Miscellany*. New York: Macmillan.

Hamilton, Bernard (1987) *Religion in the Medieval West*. London: Edward Arnold.

Hay, Denys (1964) *The Medieval Centuries*. New York: Harper and Row.

Hell, Helmut and Hell, Vera (1966) *The Great Pilgrimage of the Middle Ages: The Road to St. James of Compostela*. London: Barrie and Rockliff.

Herlihy, David (1985) *Medieval Households*. Cambridge, MA: Harvard University Press.

Hildegard of Bingen (1990) *Scivias*. Trans. Mother Columba Hart and Jane Bishop, New York: Paulist Press.

Holmes, George (1988) *The Oxford Illustrated History of Medieval Europe*. Oxford: Oxford University Press.

Janson, H. W. (1963) *History of Art*. Englewood Cliffs, NJ: Prentice-Hall.

Kienzle, Beverley Mayne (1998) "The Prostitute-Preacher: Patterns of Polemic against Medieval Waldensian Women Preachers," in Beverly Kienzle and Pamela J. Walker (eds.) *Women Preachers and Prophets*, Berkeley: University of California Press.

Leclercq, Jean (1961) *The Love of Learning and the Desire for God: A Study of Monastic Culture*. Trans. Catherine Misrahi, New York: Fordham University Press.

LeGoff, Jacques (1980) *Time, Work, and Culture in the Middle Ages*. Chicago: University of Chicago Press.

Lipton, Sara (1999) *Images of Intolerance: The Representation of Jews and Judaism in the Bible Moraliseé*. Berkeley: University of California Press.

Makdisi, George (1981) *The Rise of Colleges: Institutions of Learning in Islam and the West*. Edinburgh: Edinburgh University Press.

McManners, John (ed.) (1990) *The Oxford Illustrated History of Christianity*. Oxford: Oxford University Press.

Miles, Margaret R (1988) *Practicing Christianity: Critical Perspectives for an Embodied Spirituality*. New York: Crossroad.

Miles, Margaret R. (1989) *Carnal Knowing: Female Nakedness and Religious Meaning*. Boston: Beacon.

Morrison, Karl F. (1985) "The Gregorian Reform," in Bernard McGinn, John Meyendorff, and Jean Leclercq (eds.), *Christian Spirituality: Origins to the Twelfth Century*, New York: Crossroad.

Newman, Barbara (1987) *Sister of Wisdom: St. Hildegard's Theology of the Feminine*. Berkeley: University of California Press.

Newman, Barbara (1988) *Symphonia*. Ithaca: Cornell University Press.

Pelikan, Jaroslav (1978) *The Growth of Medieval Theology (600–1300)*. Chicago: University of Chicago Press.

Riley-Smith, Jonathan (1984) "The First Crusade and the Persecution of the Jews," in W. J. Shields (ed.), *Persecution and Toleration*, Oxford: Basil Blackwell.

Riley-Smith, Jonathan (1999) *The Oxford History of the Crusades*. Oxford: Oxford University Press.

Smalley, Beryl (1983) *The Study of the Bible in the Middle Ages*, 3rd edn. Oxford: Blackwell.

Stevens, John (1986) *Words and Music in the Middle Ages*. New York: Cambridge University Press.

Strayer, Joseph R. and Munro, Dana (1942) *The Middle Ages 395–1500*. New York: Appleton-Century-Crofts.

Sumption, Jonathan (1975) *Pilgrimage*. London: Faber and Faber.

2 Theology and the Natural World

Armstrong, R., Hellman, J., and Short, W. (eds.) (1999) *Francis of Assisi: The Saint*. New York: New City Press.

Francis and Clare: The Complete Works. (1982) Trans. R. Armstrong and I. Brady, New York: Paulist Press.

Hellmann, J. A. Wayne (1987) "The Spirituality of the Franciscans," in Jill Raitt (ed.), *Christian Spirituality, vol. II*, New York: Crossroad.

Knowles, David (1972) *The Evolution of Medieval Thought*. New York: Vintage Books.

Leff, Gordon (1958) *Medieval Thought: St. Augustine to Ockham*. Harmondsworth: Penguin.

Tavard, George H. (1987) "Apostolic Life and Church Reform," in Jill Raitt (ed.), *Christian Spirituality, vol. II*, New York: Crossroad.

Tugwell, Simon (1987) "The Spirituality of the Dominicans," in Jill Raitt (ed.), *Christian Spirituality, vol. II*, New York: Crossroad.

3 Thomas Aquinas

Fairweather, A. M. (ed.) (1954) *Aquinas on Nature and Grace*. Philadelphia: Westminster Press.
Saint Thomas Aquinas: Philosophical Texts (1960) Trans. Thomas Gilby, New York: Oxford University Press.
Shahan, Robert W. and Kovach, Francis J. (eds.) (1976) *Bonaventure and Aquinas*. Tuscon: University of Oklahoma Press.
Smalley, Beryl (1952) *The Study of the Bible in the Middle Ages*. Oxford: Oxford University Press.

4 Gothic Cathedrals

Adams, Henry (1933) *Mont-Saint-Michel and Chartres*. Garden City, NY: Doubleday.
Camille, Michael (1996) *Gothic Art: Glorious Visions*. New York: Harry N. Adams.
Calkins, Robert G. (1979) *Monuments of Medieval Art*. Ithaca: Cornell University Press.
Duby, Georges (1981) *The Age of the Cathedrals*. Trans. Eleanor Levieux and Barbara Thompson, Chicago: University of Chicago Press.
Gage, John (1993) *Color and Culture*. Boston: Little, Brown.
Mâle, Emile (1972) *The Gothic Image: Religious Art in France of the Thirteenth Century*. Trans. Dora Nussey, New York: Harper and Row.
Martindale, Andrew (1967) *Gothic Art*. New York: Oxford University Press.
Panofsky, Erwin (1979) *Abbot Suger on the Abbey Church of St.-Denis and its Art Treasures*, 2nd edn., Princeton: Princeton University Press.
Wright, Craig (2001) *The Maze and the Warrior: Symbols in Architecture, Theology, and Music*. Cambridge, MA: Harvard University Press.

Chapter 5: Death and the Body in the Fourteenth-century West

Aberth, John (2001) *From the Brink of the Apocalypse: Confronting Famine, War, Plague, and Death in the Later Middle Ages*. New York: Routledge.
Cohen, John (1982) "Death and the Danse Macabre," *History Today*, 32, August.
Hegeland, John (1984–5) "The Symbolism of Death in the Later Middle Ages," *Omega*, 15(2).
Horox, Rosemary (1994) *The Black Death*. New York: St. Martin's Press.
Huizinga, J. (1949) *The Waning of the Middle Ages*. New York: Doubleday Anchor.
Huppert, George (1986) *After the Black Death: A Social History of Early Modern Europe*. Bloomington: Indiana University Press.
Vrudny, Kimberly (2001) "Friars, Scribes and Corpses: Spiritual and Marian Resources for the Laity upon Arrival of the Black Death", unpublished doctoral dissertation.

1 Late Medieval Piety and Mysticism in England

The Book of Margery Kempe (1985) Trans. B. A. Windeatt, New York: Penguin Books.
Collis, Louise (1964) *Memoirs of a Medieval Woman: The Life and Times of Margery Kempe*. New York: Harper and Row.

Julian of Norwich (1978) *Showings*. Trans. Edmund Colledge, OSA and James Walsh, SJ, New York: Paulist Press.

Petry, Ray C. (1957) *Late Medieval Mysticism*. Philadelphia: Westminster Press.

2 German Mysticism: Meister Eckhart

Blakney, Raymond B. (1941) *Meister Eckhart: A Modern Translation*. New York: Harper and Row.

McGinn, Bernard (2001) *The Mystical Thought of Meister Eckhart: The Man from Whom God Hid Nothing*. New York: Crossroad.

3 Mysticism in Italy and Flanders

Bell, Rudolf, M. (1985) *Holy Anorexia*. Chicago: University of Chicago Press.

Bell, Rudolf M. and Weinstein, Donald (1987) *Saints and Society*. Chicago: University of Chicago Press.

Bordo, Susan (1993) *Unbearable Weight: Feminism, Western Culture, and the Body*. Berkeley: University of California Press.

Bynum, Caroline Walker (1982) *Jesus as Mother: Studies in the Spirituality of the High Middle Ages*. Berkeley: University of California Press.

Bynum, Caroline Walker (1987) *Holy Feast and Holy Fast*. Berkeley: University of California Press.

Catherine of Genoa (1979) *Purgation and Purgatory, The Spiritual Dialogue*. New York: Paulist Press.

Glucklich, Ariel (2001) *Sacred Pain: Hurting the Body for the Sake of the Soul*. Oxford: Oxford University Press.

Kieckhefer, Richard (1984) *Unquiet Souls: Fourteenth-Century Saints and their Religious Milieu*. Chicago: University of Chicago Press.

Thomas à Kempis (1902–18) *Opera Omnia*, 8 vols., M. Pohl (ed.). Freiburg.

4 Fourteenth-century Realism and Nonimalism

Fairweather, Eugene R. (ed.) (1970) *A Scholastic Miscellany: Anselm to Ockham*. New York: Macmillan.

Knowles, David (1962) *The Evolution of Medieval Thought*. New York: Vintage Books.

Leff, Gordon (1958) *Medieval Thought: St. Augustine to Ockham*. New York: Penguin.

Leff, Gordon (1976) *The Dissolution of the Medieval Outlook*. New York: Harper and Row.

5 Piety and Heresy

Baxandall, Michael (1972) *Painting and Experience in Fifteenth-century Italy*. Oxford: Oxford University Press.

Boureau, Alain (2001) *The Myth of Pope Joan*. Chicago: University of Chicago Press.

Brenon, Anne (1998) "The Voice of the Good Woman, An Essay on the Sacerdotal Role of Women in the Cathar Church," in Beverly Mayne Kienzle and Pamela J. Walker (eds.), *Women Preachers and Prophets through Two Millenia of Christianity*, Berkeley: University of California Press.

Elwood, Christopher (1999) *The Body Broken: The Calvinist Doctrine of the Eucharist and the Symbolization of Power in Sixteenth-century France*. New York: Oxford University Press.

Glucklich, Ariel (2001) *Sacred Pain: Hurting the Body for the Sake of the Soul*. New York: Oxford University Press.

Gottfried, Robert (1983) *The Great Pestilence*. London: Simpkin Marshall, Hamilton, Kent and Co.

Hills, Paul (1987) *The Light of Early Italian Painting*. New Haven: Yale University Press.

Hood, William (1993) *Fra Angelico at San Marco*. New Haven: Yale University Press.

Kamen, Henry (1998) *The Spanish Inquisition: A Historical Revision*. New Haven: Yale University Press.

Kieckhefer, Richard (1987) "Major Currents in Late Medieval Devotion," in *Christian Spirituality: High Middle Ages and Reformation*. New York: Crossroad.

Kienzle, Beverly (1998) "The Prostitute Preacher: Patterns of Polemic Against Medieval Waldensian Women Preachers," in Beverly Mayne Kienzle and Pamela J. Walker (eds.), *Women Preachers and Prophets through Two Millennia of Christianity*, Berkeley: University of California Press.

Ladis, Andrew (1986) "The Legend of Giotto's Wit and the Arena Chapel," *The Art Bulletin*, LXVIII(4), December.

Lambert, M. D. (1992) *Medieval Heresy: Popular Movements from the Gregorian Reform to the Reformation*. Oxford: Oxford University Press.

Merback, Mitchell B. (1998) *The Thief, the Cross, and the Wheel: Pain and the Spectacle of Punishment in Medieval and Renaissance Europe*. Chicago: University of Chicago Press.

Miles, Margaret R. (1985) *Image as Insight: Visual Understanding in Western Christianity and Secular Culture*. Boston: Beacon.

Miles, Margaret R. (1992) "The Virgin's One Bare Breast: Female Nudity and Religious Meaning in Renaissance Culture," in Norma Broude and Marry D. Garrard (eds.), *The Expanding Discourse: Feminism and Art History*, New York: Harper Collins.

Ocker, Christopher (1998) "Ritual Murder and the Subjectivity of Christ," *Harvard Theological Review*, 91(2).

Peters, Edward (1988) *The Inquisition*. New York: Free Press.

Marguerite Porete: The Mirror of Simple Souls (1993) Trans. Ellen L. Babinsky, New York: Paulist Press.

Ragusa, Isa and Green, Rosalie B. (eds.) (1961) *Meditations on the Life of Christ: An Illustrated Manuscript of the Fourteenth Century*. Princeton: Princeton University Press.

Rosconi, Robert (1998) "Women's Sermons at the end of the Middle Ages," in Beverly Mayne Kienzle and Pamela J. Walker (eds.), *Women Preachers and Prophets through Two Millennia of Christianity*, Berkeley: University of California Press.

Rubin, Miri (1991) *Corpus Christi: The Eucharist in Late Medieval Culture*. Cambridge: Cambridge University Press.

Thomas à Kempis (1975) *The Imitation of Christ*. Trans. Betty I. Knott, New York: Collins.

Vauchez, Andre (1993) *The Laity in the Middle Ages: Religious Beliefs and Devotional Practices*. Notre Dame: University of Notre Dame.

Vauchez, Andre (1997) *Sainthood in the Later Middle Ages*. Trans. Jean Birrell, Cambridge: Cambridge University Press.

Chapter 6: The Suffering Body of Christ: The Fifteenth Century

Eisenstein, Elizabeth L. (1980) *The Printing Press as an Agent of Change: Communications and Cultural Transformations in Early-Modern Europe*. New York: Cambridge University Press.

Kelly, Joan (1985) "Did Women Have a Renaissance?" in *Women, History, and Theory: The Essays of Joan Kelly*. Chicago: University of Chicago Press.

1 The Conciliar Movement

Gerson, Jean (1953) "On the Unity of the Church," in Matthew Spinka (ed.), *Advocates of Reform*, Philadelphia: Westminster Press.

Leff, Gordon (1976) *The Dissolution of the Medieval Outlook*. New York: Harper and Row.

Tierney, Brian (1998) *Foundations of the Conciliar Theory: The Contributions of Medieval Canonists from Gratian to the Great Schism*. Leiden: Brill.

Ullmann, W. (1967) *The Origins of the Great Schism: A Study in Fourteenth Century Ecclesiastical History*. Hamden, CT: Archon.

2 Italy: Fifteenth-century Preaching

Ames-Lewis, Francis (2000) *The Intellectual Life of the Early Renaissance Artist*. New Haven: Yale University Press.

Burckhardt, Jacob (1960) *The Civilization of the Renaissance in Italy*. New York: Mentor.

Chamberlin, E. R. (1982) *The World of the Italian Renaissance*. London: George Allen and Unwin.

Ficino, Marsilio (1985) *Commentary on Plato's Symposium on Love*. Trans. Jayne Sears, Dallas: Spring Publications.

Gabel, Leona C. (ed.) (1962) *Memoirs of a Renaissance Pope*. New York: Capricorn Books.

Hay, Denys (1977) *The Church in Italy in the Fifteenth Century*. New York: Cambridge University Press.

Leff, Gordon (1967) *Heresy in the Later Middle Ages, 1250–1450*. Manchester: Manchester University Press.

Murray, Peter and Murray, Linda (1963) *The Art of the Renaissance*. New York: Frederick A. Praeger.

Norman, Corrie E. (1998) *Humanist Taste and Franciscan Values: Cornelio Musso and Catholic Preaching in Sixteenth-Century Italy*. New York: Peter Lang.

Trinkhaus, Charles and Obermann, Heiko A. (1974) *The Pursuit of Holiness in Late Medieval and Renaissance Religion*. Leiden: E. J. Brill.

Verdon, T. and Henderson, J. (eds.) (1990) *Christianity and the Renaissance*. Syracuse: Syracuse University Press.

3 England: John Wyclif and the Lollards

Daly, L. J. (1962) *The Political Theory of John Wycliff*. Chicago: Jesuit Studies.

Duffy, Eamon (1992) *The Stripping of the Altars: Traditional Religion in England c. 1400–c. 1580*. New Haven: Yale University Press.

Pantin, W. A. (1955) *The English Church in the Fourteenth Century*. Cambridge: Cambridge University Press.

Spinka, Matthew (1953) *Advocates of Reform*. Philadelphia, Westminster Press.

4 Reform in Bohemia

Gregory, Brad (1999) *Salvation at Stake: Christian Martyrdom in Early Modern Europe*. Cambridge, MA: Harvard University Press.

5 The Isenheim Altarpiece

Hayum, Andre (1977) "The Meaning and Function of the Isenheim Altarpiece: The Hospital Context Revisited," *Art Bulletin*, LIX, December.

Hayum, Andre (1989) *The Isenheim Altarpiece: God's Medicine and the Painter's Vision*. Princeton: Princeton University Press.

Mellinkoff, Ruth (1989) *The Devil at Eisenheim*. Princeton: Princeton University Press.

6 Erasmus and Luther on the Human Condition

Bainton, Roland H. (1952) *The Reformation of the Sixteenth Century*. Boston: Beacon Press.

Dillenberger, John (1999) *Images and Relics: Theological Perceptions and Visual Images in Sixteenth-Century Europe*. New York: Oxford University Press.

Luther, Martin (1883ff.) *Weimarer Ausgabe*. J. C. Knaake *et al.* (eds.), Weimar.

Possett, Franz (2003) *The Front-runner of the Catholic Reformation: The Life and Works of Johann von Staupitz*. Burlington, VT: Ashgate.

Rupp, Gordon E. and Watson, Philip S. (eds.) (1966) *Luther and Erasmus on Free Will and Salvation*. Philadelphia: Westminster Press.

Schoeck, Richard J. (1990) *Erasmus of Europe: The Making of a Humanist, 1467–1500*. Savage, MD: Barnes and Noble Books.

Thulin, Oskar (ed.) (1966) *A Life of Luther: Told in Pictures and Narratives by the Reformer and his Contemporaries*. Trans. Martin O. Dietrich, Philadelphia: Fortress Press.

Tracy, James D. (1996) *Erasmus of the Low Countries*. Berkeley: University of California Press.

Chapter 7: Reforming the Body of Christ: The Sixteenth Century, Part I

Prologue

Blakney, Raymond B. (1941) *Meister Eckhart: A Modern Translation*. New York: Harper and Row.

1 The Lutheran Reformation

Christensen, Carl C. (1979) *Art and the Reformation in Germany*. Athens, OH: Ohio University Press.

Cook, John (1986) "Picturing Theology: Martin Luther and Lucas Cranach," in Osmund Overby (ed.), *Faith, Form, and Reform*. Columbia, MO: University of Missouri-Columbia Press.

Dillenberger, John (1999) *Images and Relics: Theological Perceptions and Visual Images in Sixteenth-Century Germany*. New York: Oxford University Press.

Edwards, Mark U. Jr. (1975) *Luther and the False Brethren*. Stanford: Stanford University Press.

Edwards, Mark U. Jr. (1983) *Luther's Last Battles: Politics and Polemics, 1531–46*. Ithaca: Cornell University Press.

Edwards, Mark U. Jr. (1994) *Printing, Propaganda, and Martin Luther*. Berkeley: University of California Press.

Haile, H. G. (1980) *Luther: An Experiment in Biography*. Princeton: Princeton University Press.

Kolb, Robert (1999) *Martin Luther as Prophet, Teacher, and Hero: Images of the Reformer, 1520–1620*. Grand Rapids: Baker.

Luther, Martin (1957–75) *Against the Heavenly Prophets in the Matter of Images and Sacraments*, *Luther's Works* (LW 40), Helmut T. Lehmann (ed.), Philadelphia: Fortress.

Luther, Martin (1957–75) *Commentary on Jonah* (LW 19), Philadelphia: Fortress.

Luther, Martin (1957–75) *Magnificat* (LW 32), Philadelphia: Fortress.

Luther, Martin (1957–75) *The Babylonian Captivity of the Church* (LW 36), Philadelphia: Fortress.

Luther, Martin (1961) *Lectures on Romans*, in Wilhelm Pauck (ed.), *Luther: Lectures on Romans*, Philadelphia: Westminster.

Lull, Timothy (ed.) (1989) *Martin Luther's Basic Theological Writings*. Minneapolis: Fortress.

Miles, Margaret R. (1984) "The Rope Breaks When It Is Tightest: Luther on the Body, Consciousness, and the Word," *Harvard Theological Review*, 77(3–4).

Ozment, Steven (1980) *The Age of Reform, 1250–1550*. New Haven: Yale University Press.

Ozment, Steven (ed.) (1989) *Religion and Culture in the Renaissance and Reformation*. Kirksville, MO: Sixteenth Century Journal Publishers.

Pelikan, Jaroslav (1959) *Luther the Expositor*. LW, Companion volume. St Louis.

Posset, Franz (2003) *The Front-runner of the Catholic Reformation: The Life and Works of Johann von Staupitz*. Burlington, VT: Ashgate.

Roper, Lyndal (1996) "Discipline and Respectability: Prostitution and the Reformation in Augsburg," in Joan Wallach Scott (ed.), *Feminism and History*. New York: Oxford University Press.

Scribner, Robert (1981) *For the Sake of Simple Folk: Popular Propaganda for the German Reformation*. New York: Cambridge University Press.

Strauss, Gerald (1978) *Luther's House of Learning: Indoctrination of the Young in the German Reformation*. Baltimore, Johns Hopkins University Press.

Tentler, T. N. (1977) *Sin and Confession on the Eve of the Reformation*. Princeton, Princeton University Press.

Trinkhaus, Charles and Obermann, Heiko A. (1974) *The Pursuit of Holiness in Late Medieval and Renaissance Religion*. Leiden: E. J. Brill.

2 The Radical Reformation

Bromiley, G. W. (1953) *Zwingli and Bullinger*. Philadelphia: Westminster Press.

Garside, C. (1966) *Zwingli and the Arts*. New Haven: Yale University Press.

George, Timothy (1987) "The Spirituality of the Radical Reformation," in Jill Raitt (ed.) *Christian Spirituality* vol. II, New York: Crossroad.

Gregory, Brad S. (1999) *Salvation at Stake: Christian Martyrdom in Early Modern Europe*. Cambridge, MA: Harvard University Press.

Phillips, Obbe (1957) "A Confession," in George Hunston Williams and Angel M. Mergal (eds.), *Spiritual and Anabaptist Writers*. Philadelphia: Westminster Press; Library of Christian Classics.

Williams, George Hunston and Angel Mergal (eds.) (1952) *Spiritual and Anabaptist Writers*. Philadelphia: Westminster Press.

3 Calvin

Benedict, Philip (2002) *Christ's Churches Purely Reformed: A Social History of Calvinism*. New Haven: Yale University Press.

Bouwsma, William J. (1988) *John Calvin: A Sixteenth Century Portrait*. New York: Oxford University Press.

Compier, Don H. (2001) *John Calvin's Rhetorical Doctrine of Sin*. Lewiston, NY: Edwin Mellen Press.

Cottret, Bernard (2000) *Calvin: A Biography*. Grand Rapids, MI: Eerdmans.

Douglas, Jane Dempsey (1985) *Women, Freedom, and Calvin*. Philadelphia: Westminster Press.

Duffy, Eamon (1992) *The Stripping of the Altars: Traditional Religion in England c. 1400–c. 1580*. New Haven: Yale University Press.

Eire, Carlos M. N. (1986) *War Against the Idols: The Reformation of Worship from Erasmus to Calvin*. Cambridge: Cambridge University Press.

Ellwood, Christopher (1999) *The Body Broken: The Calvinist Doctrine of the Eucharist and the Symbolization of Power in Sixteenth-Century France*. New York: Oxford University Press.

Gerrish, B. A. (1993) *Grace and Gratitude: The Eucharistic Theology of John Calvin*. Minneapolis: Fortress.

Kingdon, Robert M. (1967) *Geneva and the Consolidation of the French Protestant Movement, 1564–1572*. Madison: University of Wisconsin Press.

Kingdon, Robert M. (1971) "Social Welfare in Calvin's Geneva," *American Historical Review*, 76.

Kingdon, Robert M. (1995) *Adultery and Divorce in Calvin's Geneva*. Cambridge, MA: Harvard University Press.

Merback, Mitchell B. (1998) *The Thief, the Cross, and the Wheel: Pain and the Spectacle of Punishment in Medieval and Renaissance Europe*. Chicago: University of Chicago Press.

Miles, Margaret R. (1981) "Theology, Anthropology, and the Human Body in Calvin's 'Institutes of the Christian Religion,' " *Harvard Theological Review*, 74(3).

Monter, E. William (1976) "Women in Calvinist Geneva (1550–1800)," *Bibliothèque d'Humanisme et Renaissance*, 38, 467–84.

Muller, Richard (2000) *The Unaccommodated Calvin: Studies in the Foundation of a Theological Tradition*. New York: Oxford University Press.

Naphy, William G. (1994) *Calvin and the Consolidation of the Genevan Reform*. New York: Manchester University Press.

Otis, Leah L. (1985) *Prostitution in Medieval Society*. Chicago: University of Chicago Press.

Selinger, Suzanne (1984) *Calvin Against Himself: An Inquiry in Intellectual History*. Hamden, CT: Archon.

Terry, Richard (1932) *Calvin's First Psalter, 1539*. London: Ernest Benn Ltd.

4 Protestant Developments in the Later Sixteenth Century

Dillenberger, J. and Welch, C. (1954) *Protestant Christianity Interpreted Through Its Development*. New York: Macmillan.

Elton, G. R. (1963) *Reformation Europe 1517–1559*. San Francisco: Harper and Row.

Evans, G. R. (1992) *Problems of Authority in the Reformation Debates*. Cambridge: Cambridge University Press.

Harbison, E. Harris (1980) *The Christian Scholar in the Age of Reformation*. Philadephia: Porcupine Press.

Manshreck, Clyde L. (1958) *Melanchthon: The Quiet Reformer*. New York: Abingdon.

Midelfort, H. C. Eric (1984) "Sin, Melancholy, and Obsession: Insanity and Culture in Sixteenth-Century Germany," in Steven Kaplan (ed.), *Understanding Popular Culture: Europe from the Middle Ages to the Ninteenth Century*, Berlin: Mouton.

Parker, Geoffrey (1997) *The Thirty Years War*, 2nd edn. London: Routledge.

Pauck, W. (ed.) (1969) *Melanchthon and Bucer*. Philadelphia: Westminster Press.

Sabean, David Warren (1984) *Power in the Blood: Popular Culture and Village Discourse in Early Modern Germany*. Cambridge: Cambridge University Press.

Schaff, Philip (1877) *The Creeds of Christendom*. New York: Harper.

Chapter 8: Reforming the Body of Christ: The Sixteenth Century, Part II

1 Sixteenth-century Women

Bainton, Roland H. (1971) *Women of the Reformation in Germany and Italy*. Minneapolis: Augsburg.

Bainton, Roland H. (1973) *Women of the Reformation in France and England*. Minneapolis: Augsburg.

Bainton, Roland H. (1977) *Women of the Reformation from Spain to Scandanavia*. Minneapolis: Augsburg.

Barstow, Ann Llewellyn (1994) *Witchcraze: A New History of the European Witch Hunts*. San Francisco: Pandora.

Bilinkoff, Jodi (1989) *Teresa's Avila and Avila's Teresa: Religious Reform in a Sixteenth-Century City*. Ithica: Cornell University Press.

Bouwsma, William J. (1988) *John Calvin: A Sixteenth Century Portrait*. New York: Oxford University Press.

Brauner, Sigrid (1989) "Fearless Wives and Frightened Shrews: The Construction of the Witch in Early Modern Germany," in Jean R. Brink, Alison P. Coudert, and Maryanne Horowitz (eds.), *The Politics of Gender in Early Modern Europe*, Kirksville, MO: Sixteenth Century Journal Publishers.

Brink, Jean R., Alison P. Coudert, and Maryanne Horowitz (eds.) (1989) *The Politics of Gender in Early Modern Europe*. Kirksville, MO: Sixteenth Century Journal Publishers.

Clark, Stuart (ed.) (2001) *Languages of Witchcraft: Narrative, Ideology, and Meaning in Early Modern Culture*. London: Macmillan.

Couliano, Ioan P. (1987) *Eros and Magic in the Renaissance*. Chicago: University of Chicago Press.

Douglas, Jane Dempsey (1974) "Women and the Continental Reformation," in Rosemary Ruether (ed.), *Religion and Sexism: Images of Women in the Jewish and Christian Traditions*. New York: Simon and Schuster.

Douglas, Jane Dempsey (1985) *Women, Freedom, and Calvin*. Philadelphia: Westminster Press.

Frohlich, Mary (1993) *The Intersubjectivity of the Mystic: A Study of Teresa of Avila's Interior Castle*. Atlanta: Scholars Press.

Ginzburg, Carlo (1984) "The Witches' Sabbat: Popular Cult or Inquisitorial Stereotype?" in Steven Kaplan (ed.), *Understanding Popular Culture: Europe from the Middle Ages to the Nineteenth Century*, Berlin: Mouton.

Haile, H. G. (1980) *Luther: An Experiment in Biography*. Princeton: Princeton University Press.

Howell, Martha C. (1986) *Women and Patriarchy in Late Medieval Cities*. Chicago: University of Chicago Press.

Kelly, Joan (1982) "Early Feminist Theory and the *Querelle des Femmes*, 1400–1789," *Signs*, 8(11).

Midelfort, H. C. Eric (1972) *Witchhunting in Southwest Germany, 1562–1648*. Palo Alto: Stanford University Press.

Midelfort, H. C. Eric (1984) "Sin, Melancholy, Obsession: Insanity and Culture in Sixteenth-Century Germany," in Steven Kaplan (ed.), *Understanding Popular Culture: Europe from the Middle Ages to the Nineteenth Century*. Berlin: Mouton.

Scott, Joan Wallach (ed.) (1997) *Feminism and History*. Oxford: Oxford University Press.

Scribner, Robert (1989) "Popular Piety and Modes of Visual Perception in Late-Medieval Reformation Germany," *The Journal of Religious History*, 14(4), December.

Slade, Carole (1995) *St. Teresa of Avila: Author of a Heroic Life*. Berkeley: University of California Press.

Soman, Alfred (1986) "Witch Lynching at Juniville," *Natural History*, 10.

Stephens, Walter (2002) *Demon Lovers: Witchcraft, Sex, and the Crisis of Belief*. Chicago: University of Chicago Press.

Summers, Montague (ed.) (1971) *The Malleus Maleficarum of Heinrich Kramer and James Sprenger*. New York: Dover.

Trevor-Roper, H. R. (1956) *The European Witch-craze of the Sixteenth and Seventeenth Centuries*. San Francisco: Harper and Row.

2 Roman Catholic Reformations

Abraham, Gerald (1979) *The Concise Oxford History of Music*. New York: Oxford University Press.

Beny, Roloff and Gunn, Peter (1981) *The Churches of Rome*. New York: Simon and Schuster.

Bossy, John (1985) *Christianity in the West*. Oxford: Oxford University Press.

Certeau, Michel de (1992) *The Mystic Fable: The Sixteenth and Seventeenth Centuries*. Trans. Michael B. Smith, Chicago: University of Chicago Press.

Chastel, Andre (1983) *The Sack of Rome, 1527*. Trans. Beth Archer, Princeton: Princeton University Press.

Evenett, H. Outram (1968) *The Spirit of the Counter-Reformation*. Notre Dame, IN: University of Notre Dame Press.

Freedberg, David (1971) "Johannes Molinas on Provocative Paintings," *Journal of the Wartburg and Courtauld Institutes*, XXXIV.

Ganss, Geroge S. J. (ed.) (1991) *Ignatius of Loyola*. New York: Paulist Press.

Gerrish, B. A. (1993) *Grace and Gratitude: The Eucharistic Theology of John Calvin*. Minneapolis: Fortress.

Ginzburg, Carlo (1980) *The Cheese and the Worms: The Cosmos of a Sixteenth-Century Miller*, Trans. John and Anne Tedeschi, New York: Penguin.

Ginzburg, Carlo (1985) *Night Battles: Witchcraft and Agrarian Cults in the Sixteenth and Seventeenth Centuries*. New York: Penguin.

Goldscheider, Ludwig (1963) *Michelangelo*. Greenwich, CT: Phaedon.

Haliczer, Stephen (1993) *Inquisition and Society in Early Modern Europe*. Totowa, NJ: Barnes and Noble Books.

Harbison, Craig (1976) *The Last Judgment in Sixteenth-Century Northern Europe: A Study in the Relationship between Art and the Reformation*. New York: Garland.

Haskell, Francis (1963) *Patrons and Painters*. London: Chatto and Windus.

Hsia, R. Po-Chia (1998) *The World of Catholic Renewal 1540–1770*. Cambridge: Cambridge University Press.

Jedin, Hubert (1957–61) *A History of the Council of Trent*, 2 vols. Trans. Ernest Graf, London: Nelson.

Kamen, Henry (1998) *The Spanish Inquisition: A Historical Revision*. New Haven: Yale University Press.

Machlis, Joseph (1970) *The Enjoyment of Music*. New York: W. W. Norton.

Mâle, Emile (1932) *L'art religieux après le Councile de Trente*. Paris: Librarie Armand Colin.

Monssen, Leif H. (1981) "Rex Gloriose Martyrium: A Contribution to Jesuit Iconography," *Art Bulletin*, 8, March.

Murray, Linda (1977) *The High Renaissance and Mannerism*. New York: Oxford University Press.

Norman, Corrie E. (1998) *Humanist Taste and Franciscan Values: Cornelio Musso and Catholic Preaching in Sixteenth-Century Italy*. New York: Peter Lang.

O'Connell, Marvin R. (1974) *The Counter Reformation, 1560–1610*. San Francisco: Harper and Row.

Olin, John C. (1978) *The Catholic Reformation: Savanarola to Ignatius Loyola*. Philadelphia: Westminster Press, Christian Classics.

O'Malley, John W. (1993) *The First Jesuits*. Cambridge, MA: Harvard University Press.

O'Malley, John W. (2000) *Trent and All That: Renaming Catholicism in the Early Modern Era*. Cambridge, MA: Harvard University Press.

Peters, Edward (1998) *Inquisition*. New York: Free Press.

Russell, Jeffrey (1986) *Mephistopheles: The Devil in the Modern World*. Ithaca: Cornell University Press.

Vecchi, Periluigi (ed.) (1992) *The Sistine Chapel: A Glorious Restoration*. New York: Abrams.

Wittkower, R. and Jaffe, I. B. (eds.) (1972) *Baroque Art: The Jesuit Contribution*. New York: Fordham University Press.

3 English Reformations

Benedict, Philip (2002) *Christ's Churches Purely Reformed: A Social History of Calvinism*. New Haven: Yale University Press.

Collinson, Patrick (1997) "Hooker and the Elizabethan Establishment," in A. S. McGrade (ed.), *Richard Hooker and the Construction of Christian Community*. Tempe, AZ: Arizona State University Press.

Dickens, A. G. (1964) *The English Reformation*. New York: Schocken Books.

Duffy, Eamon (1992) *The Stripping of the Altars: Traditional Religion in England c. 1400–c. 1580*. New Haven: Yale University Press.

Elton, G. R. (1962) *The New Cambridge Modern History* II, *The Reformation*. Cambridge: Cambridge University Press.

Elton, G. R. (1984) "Persecution and Toleration in the English Reformation," in *Persecution and Toleration*, Oxford: Oxford University Press.

Gibbs, Lee W. (2002) "Richard Hooker: Prophet of Anglicanism or English Magisterial Reformer?" *Anglican Theological Review*, 84(4), Fall, 943–60.

Gregory, Brad S. (1999) *Salvation at Stake: Christian Martyrdom in Early Modern Europe*. Cambridge, MA: Harvard University Press.

Haigh, Christopher (1993) *English Reformations*. Oxford: Oxford University Press.

Hooker, Richard (1993) *The Folger Library Edition of the Works of Richard Hooker*. W. Speed Hill (ed.), 7 vols. (i–v, Cambridge, MA, 1977–90; vi, Binghamton, NY, 1993; vii, Tempe, AZ, 1998).

Lytle, Guy (1981) "Religion and Lay Patronage in Reformation England," in Guy Lytle and Stephen Orgel (eds.), *Patronage in the Renaissance*, Princeton: Princeton University Press.

Moorman, John R. H. (1953) *A History of the Church in England*. London: Adam and Charles Black.

O'Connell, Michael (2000) *The Idolatrous Eye: Iconoclasm and Theater in Early-Modern England*. New York: Oxford University Press.

Phillips, John (1973) *The Reformation of Images: Destruction of Art in England, 1535–1660*. Berkeley: University of California Press.

Voak, Nigel (2003) *Richard Hooker and Reformed Theology: A Study of Reason, Will, and Grace*. New York: Oxford University Press.

Watt, Tessa (1991) *Cheap Print and Popular Piety, 1550–1640*. Cambridge: Cambridge University Press.

Williamson, G. A. (ed.) (1965) *Foxe's Book of Martyrs*. Boston: Little, Brown.

Wittkower, R. and Jaffe, I. B. (eds.) (1972) *Baroque Art: The Jesuit Contribution*. New York: Fordham University Press.

Chapter 9: Rationalism and Religious Passion: The Seventeenth Century

1 Descartes and the Method of Doubt

Cragg, Gerald R. (1977) *The Church in the Age of Reason 1648–1789*. New York: Penguin.

Descartes, René (1960) *Discourse on Method and Meditations*. Trans Laurence Lafleur, Indianapolis: Bobbs-Merrill.

Manschreck, Clyde (1974) *A History of Christianity in the World*. Englewood Cliffs, NJ: Prentice-Hall.

McManners, John (ed.) (1993) *The Oxford History of Christianity*. New York: Oxford University Press.

Willey, Basil (1934) *The Seventeenth Century Background*. New York: Doubleday Anchor.

Williams, Bernard (1978) *Descartes: The Project of Pure Enquiry*. New York: Penguin.

Wilson, Margaret D. (ed.) (1969) *The Essential Descartes*. New York: Meridian.

2 Christianity in Seventeenth-century France

Lierheimer, Linda (1998) "Preaching or Teaching? Defining the Ursaline Mission in Seventeenth-Century France," in Beverly Mayne Kienzle and Pamela J. Walker (eds.), *Women Preachers and Prophets through Two Millennia of Christianity*. Berkeley: University of California Press.

Pascal, Blaise (1966) *Pensées*. Trans. A. J. Krailsheimer, Baltimore: Penguin.

Ramsey, Ann W. (1999) *Liturgy, Politics, and Salvation: The Catholic League in Paris and the Nature of Catholic Reform, 1540–1630*. Rochester, NY: University of Rochester Press.

Rapley, Elizabeth (1990) *The Devotees: Women and Church in Seventeenth-Century France*. Montreal: McGill-Queen's University Press.

Ward, W. R. (1999) *Christianity under the Ancien Regime, 1648–1789*. Cambridge: Cambridge University Press.

3 Italy: Baroque Art

The Age of Caravaggio, Metropolitan Museum of Art catalogue, 1985.

Bazin, Germain (1964) *Baroque and Rococo*. London: Thames & Hudson.

Beny, Roloff and Gunn, Peter (1981) *The Churches of Rome*. New York: Simon and Schuster.

Chadwick, Whitney (1990) *Women, Art, and Society*. London: Thames & Hudson.

Garrard, Mary (1989) *Artemesia Gentileschi: The Female Hero in Italian Baroque Art*. Princeton: Princeton University Press.

Freedberg, S. J. (1983) *Circa 1600: A Revolution of Style in Italian Painting*. Cambridge, MA: Harvard University Press.

Hollander, Anne (1975) *Seeing Through Clothes*. New York: Avon.

Manschreck, Clyde L. (1974) *A History of Christianity in the World*. Englewood Cliffs, NJ: Prentice-Hall.

Martin, John (1977) *Baroque*. New York: Harper and Row.

Miles, Margaret R. (1992) "The Virgin's One Bare Breast: Female Nudity and Religious Meaning in Renaissance Culture," in Norma Broude and Mary D. Garrard (eds.), *The Expanding Discourse: Feminism and Art History*. New York: Harper Collins.

Mosco, Marilena (ed.) (1986) *La Maddalena tra Sacro e Profano* (exhibit catalog) Milan: La Casa Usher.

Schama, Simon (1999) *Rembrandt's Eyes*. New York: Knopf.

4 Christianity in Seventeenth-century England

Benedict, Philip (2002) *Christ's Churches Purely Reformed: A Social History of Calvinism*. New Haven: Yale University Press.

Bunyan, John (1953) *The Pilgrim's Progress*. Glasgow: Collins.

Bunyan, John (1978) *Grace Abounding to the Chief of Sinners*. Grand Rapids: Baker Book House.

Carroll, Kenneth (1978) "Early Quakers and 'Going Naked as a Sign,'" *Quaker History*, 67, 69–87.

Hill, Christopher (1988) *A Turbulent, Seditious and Factious People: John Bunyan and His Church*. Oxford: Oxford University Press.

Hill, Christopher (1993) *The English Bible and the Seventeenth-Century Revolution*. London: Allen Lane.

Lamont, William (1975) *Politics, Religion, and Literature in the Seventeenth Century*. London: Dent.

McAdoo, H. R. (1965) *The Spirit of Anglicanism*. London: Adam and Charles Black.

Ricard, Robert (1966) *The Spiritual Conquest of Mexico*. Berkeley: University of California Press.

Whichcote, Benjamin (1901) Excerpts from *Select Sermons*; *Aphorisms* in E. T. Campagnac (ed.), *The Cambridge Platonists*, Oxford: Clarendon Press.

5 Germany: Pietism

Arndt, Johann (1979) *True Christianity*. New York: Paulist Press.

Boehme, Jacob (1978) *The Way to Christ*. New York: Paulist Press.

O'Regan, Cyril (2002) *Gnostic Apocalypse: Jacob Boehme's Haunted Narrative*. Albany: State University of New York Press.

Walsh, David (1983) *The Mysticism of Innerworldly Fulfillment: A Study of Jacob Boehme*. Gainsville, FL: University Presses of Florida.

Weeks, Andrew (1991) *Boehme: An Intellectual Biography of the Seventeenth-Century Philosopher and Mystic*. Albany: State University of New York Press.

6 Christianity in Canada and the Americas

Brown, Craig (ed.) (1997) *The Illustrated History of Canada*. Toronto: Key Porter Books.

Campeau, Lucien (1986) *Catastrophe Démographique Sur Les Grands Lacs: Les Premiers Habitants du Québec*. Montréal: Les Éditions Bellarmin.

Campeau, Lucien (1972) *La Premiere Mission Des Jesuites en Nouvelle-France*. Montréal: Les Éditions Bellarmin.

Gaskill, Malcolm (2001) "Witches and Witnesses in Old and New England," in Stuart Clark (ed.), *Languages of Witchcraft: Narrative, Ideology and Meaning in Early Modern Culture*, New York: St. Martin's Press.

Hall, David (1990) *Worlds of Wonder, Days of Judgment*. Cambridge, MA: Harvard University Press.

Hastings, Adrian (ed.) (1999) *A World History of Christianity*. Grand Rapids, MI: William B. Eerdmans.

Langer, Erick and Jackson, Robert H. (eds.) (1995) *The New Latin American Mission History*. Lincoln: University of Nebraska Press.

Miller, Perry (1939) *The New England Mind: The Seventeenth Century*. Cambridge, MA: Harvard University Press.

Noll, Mark (1992) *A History of Christianity in the United States and Canada*. Grand Rapids: Eerdmans.

Norton, Mary Beth (2002) *In the Devil's Snare: The Salem Witchcraft Crisis of 1692*. New York: Knopf.

Polzer, Charles, W., Naylor, Thomas H., Sheriden, Thomas E., and Hadley, Diane (eds.) (1991) *The Jesuit Missions of Northern Mexico*. New York: Garland.

Raphael, Ray (2001) *A People's History of the American Revolution: How Common People Shaped the Fight for Independence*. New York: Harper Collins.

Wilson, John F. and Drakeman, Donald L. (2003) *Church and State in American History*, 3rd edn., New York: Westview.

Chapter 10: Keeping Body and Soul Together: Eighteenth-century Christianity

Kee, Howard C., Hanawalt, Emily Albee, Lindberg, Carter, Seban, J.-L., and Noll, Mark (1991) *Christianity: A Social and Cultural History*. New York: Macmillan.

1 Pietism and Revivalism

Ahlstrom, Sydney (1972) *A Religious History of the American People*. New Haven: Yale University Press.

Dillenberger, John (1984) *The Visual Arts and Christianity in America: The Colonial Period through the Nineteeneth Century*. Chico, CA: Scholars Press.

Ernst, Eldon G. (2001) "The Emergence of California in American Religious Historiography," *Religion and American Culture: A Journal of Interpretation*, XI(1).

Hall, David D. (1990) *Worlds of Wonder, Days of Judgment: Popular Religious Belief in Early New England*. Cambridge, MA: Harvard University Press.

Hitchcock, Tim (2002) "Redefining Sex in Eighteenth-century England," in Kim M. Phillips and Barry Reay (eds.), *Sexualities in History*, New York: Routledge.

Jones, Colin and Wahrman, Dror (eds.) (2002) *The Age of Cultural Revolution: Britain and France, 1750–1820*. Berkeley: University of California Press.

Kelly, Veronica and Von Mucke, Dorothea E. (eds.) (1994) *Body and Text in the Eighteenth Century*. Stanford: Stanford University Press.

Machlis, Joseph (1955) *The Enjoyment of Music: An Introduction to Perceptive Listening*. New York: W. W. Norton.

Mack, Phyllis (1998) "In a Female Voice: Preaching and Politics in Eighteenth-century British Quakerism," in Beverly Mayne Kienzle and Pamela Walker (eds.), *Women Preachers and Prophets through Two Millennia of Christianity*. Berkeley: University of California Press.

Munck, Thomas (2000) *The Enlightenment: A Comparative Social History 1721–1794*. London: Arnold.

Pelikan, Jaroslav (1986) *Bach Among the Theologians*. Philadelphia: Fortress.

Raphael, Ray (2002) *A People's History of the American Revolution*. New York: Harper-Collins.

Spitta, Philipp (1951) *Johann Sebastian Bach: His Work and Influence on the Music of Germany, 1685–1750*. New York: Dover Publishing.

Van Kley, Dale K. (1996) *The Religious Origins of the French Revolution*. New Haven: Yale University Press.

Vogt, Peter (1998) "A Voice for Themselves: Woman as Participants in Congregational Discourse in the Eighteenth-century Moravian Movement," in Beverly Mayne Kienzle and Pamela Walker (eds.), *Women Preachers and Prophets through Two Millennia of Christianity*. Berkeley: University of California Press.

Ward, W. R. (1999) *Christianity Under the Ancien Regime, 1648–1789*. New York: Cambridge University Press.

Willey, Basil (1961) *The Eighteenth Century Background*. Boston: Beacon.

Wilson, John F. and Drakeman, Donald L. (2003) *Church and State in American History*, 3rd edn. New York: Westview.

Wesley, Susannah (1997) *The Complete Writings*. Charles, Wallace, Jr. (ed.), New York: Oxford University Press.

2 Deism and the Orthodox

Becker, Carl (1932) *The Heavenly City of the Eighteenth-century Philosophers*. New Haven: Yale University Press.

Chadwick, Henry (ed.) (1956) *Lessing's Theological Writings*. Stanford: Stanford University Press.

Cragg, Gerald (1960) *The Church in the Age of Reason*. New York: Penguin.

Edwards, Jonathan (1966) *Basic Writings*, Ola Elizabeth Winslow (ed.), New York: New American Library.

Maurer, Armand A. (1967) "Edwards, Jonathan," in Paul Edwards (ed.), *Encyclopedia of Philosophy*, New York: Macmillan.

Locke, John (1958) *The Reasonableness of Christianity*. I. T. Ramsey (ed.), Stanford: Stanford University Press.

Miller, Perry (1959) *Jonathan Edwards*. New York: Meridian Books.

Ramsey, Paul (1957) *The Works of Jonathan Edwards: Freedom of the Will*. New Haven: Yale University Press.

Stewart, M. A. (2000) *English Philosophy in the Age of Locke*. Oxford: Oxford University Press.

Willey, Basil (1940) *The Eighteenth Century Background*. Boston: Beacon Press.

3 Eighteenth-century Religion in France

Carroll, James (2001) *Constantine's Sword: The Church and the Jews*. Boston: Houghton Mifflin.

Munck, Thomas (2000) *The Enlightenment: A Comparative Social History, 1721–1794*. London: Arnold.

Rousseau, Jean-Jacques (1958) *The Creed of a Priest of Savoy*. Trans. Arthur H. Beattie, New York: Frederick Ungar.

Russell, Bertrand (1965) *A History of Western Philosophy*. New York: Simon and Schuster.

Van Kley, Dale K (1996) *The Religious Origins of the French Revolution*. New Haven: Yale University.

Ward, W. R. (1999) *Christianity Under the Ancien Regime, 1648–1789*. Cambridge: Cambridge University Press.

Postlude: The Word Made Flesh

Brown, David (2000) *Tradition and Imagination*. Oxford: Oxford University Press.

Brown, David (2000) *Discipleship and Imagination*. Oxford: Oxford University Press.

Index

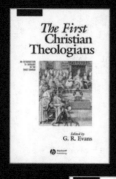
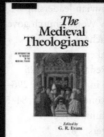

the Great theologians series

Written by world-renowned scholars, The Great Theologians series offers a comprehensive introduction to a range of key theological periods by focusing on the important writers of the time.

This comprehensive and lively series discusses the major strands of each of the periods under discussion, and explores the work of a range of influential figures. Each volume introduces the theological context, thought, and contributions of theologians of the time, offering students and scholars an essential resource and insight into the development of the history and theology of the Church.

The First Christian Theologians
An Introduction to Theology in the Early Church
EDITED BY G. R. EVANS
University of Cambridge

2004 ~ 246 x 171 mm ~ 296 pages ~ 0-631-23188-9 hb ~ 0-631-23187-0 pb

The Medieval Theologians
An Introduction to Theology in the Medieval Period
EDITED BY G. R. EVANS
University of Cambridge

2000 ~ 246 x 171 mm ~ 408 pages ~ 0-631-21202-7 hb ~ 0-631-21203-5 pb

The Pietist Theologians
EDITED BY CARTER LINDBERG
Boston University

2004 ~ 246 x 171 mm ~ 320 pages ~ 0-631-23517-5 hb ~ 0-631-23520-5 pb

The Reformation Theologians
An Introduction to Theology in the Early Modern Period
EDITED BY CARTER LINDBERG
Boston University

2001 ~ 246 x 171 mm ~ 400 pages ~ 0-631-21838-6 hb ~ 0-631-21839-4 pb

The Modern Theologians
An Introduction to Christian Theology in the Twentieth Century
Second Edition
EDITED BY DAVID F. FORD
University of Cambridge

1996 ~ 246 x 171 mm ~ 792 pages ~ 0-631-19592-0 pb

Blackwell
Publishing

For more information on this series, visit our website at **www.blackwellpublishing.com**